10 Projects You Can Do with Microsoft® SQL Server™ 7

Karen Watterson
Bill Shadish
Garth Wells

Wiley Computer Publishing

John Wiley & Sons, Inc.
NEW YORK • CHICHESTER • WEINHEIM • BRISBANE • SINGAPORE • TORONTO

Publisher: Robert Ipsen
Editor: Theresa Hudson
Associate Developmental Editor: Kathryn A. Malm
Managing Editor: Angela Smith
Text Design & Composition: Benchmark Productions, Inc.

This book is printed on acid-free paper. ♾

Published by John Wiley & Sons, Inc.

Published simultaneously in Canada.

Library of Congress Cataloging-in-Publication Data:

Watterson, Karen L.
10 projects you can do with Microsoft SQL Server 7 / Karen Watterson, Bill Shadish, Garth Wells.
p. cm.
"Wiley Computer Publishing."
ISBN 0-471-32751-4 (paper/CD-ROM : alk. paper)
1. Client/server computing. 2. SQL server. I. Shadish, Bill, 1959– . II. Wells, Garth, 1965– . III. Title. IV. Title: Ten projects you can do with Microsoft SQL Server 7.
QA76.9.C55W378 1999
005.75'85--dc21 99-26490
CIP

Printed in the United States of America.

10 9 8 7 6 5 4 3 2 1

To those individuals and forces that help each of us maintain our innate curiosity and love of exploration and discovery.

Karen Watterson

To my sons, Jason and Jared.

Bill Shadish

I would like to dedicate this book to my daughter, Sara Nicole.

Garth Wells

CONTENTS

FOREWORD

Karen Watterson is one of those people whom you can learn about by doing a Web search on her name. She has been around for awhile and worn a lot of hats over the years in the Computer Trade press. Be ready for a few hundred hits. The lady knows what she is doing.

Now, your question is why should you be buying a book with a title that sounds like the 1999 movie *Ten Things I Hate about You* (a comedy which was an updated version of Shakespeare's *Taming of the Shrew*).

The answer is simple. You probably just got a SQL Server database project. You don't know what you are doing, so you will have to learn from mistakes. There are two kinds of these "tutorial mistakes" in life: yours and someone else's. Learn from someone else's mistakes, not your own. It is much cheaper.

There is an attitude that once you have a database installed, you are pretty much finished with the project. All that other stuff—i.e., applications—will be written by a herd of low wage kids armed with the GUI front end tool de jour. It does not work that way in the real world.

What Karen and her co-authors do for each chapter that is so good and unique, as far as I know, is lay out the project like a cookbook. At the start of each project, you are given a short name for the project, the goal of the project and the supply list. Terms are defined immediately, and tools available for the SQL Server that you will need are listed and described.

The descriptions of the tools are heavy on the technology and the performance. The motivation for the tools is heavy on history, not on theory. That is, you might be told that Ted Codd invented the relational model, but you will not lapse into pages of the mathematics behind the relational model.

You get chunks of real code, with little notes like, "this will be useful in the such and such module later," so you don't waste anything. Obviously, the ten projects are not full software packages, but each project is a pretty good basic starter that will get you going.

So, how do you use this book? Find your project, read the chapters, then stick some Post-It notes on the parts you are going to code first. Hide the book in your desk drawer, so nobody will know that you are not the brilliant original thinker that you are pretending to be. Take credit for Karen's and her co-authors' work. Ask for a raise when you come in under budget and ahead of schedule.

Joe Celko
Independent Consultant
(71062.1056@compuserve.com)
www.celko.com

This book is about Microsoft's top-of-the-line database product called SQL Server 7.0. SQL Server is one of the key components of Microsoft's Windows NT BackOffice suite, but you don't *have* to have Windows NT or Windows 2000 to run SQL Server 7.0—SQL Server will even run on Windows 95 and Windows 98.

This isn't just another SQL Server book that presents an alternate view of Microsoft's own excellent SQL Server documentation and tutorial material—there are literally dozens of books that already do that. This is a hands-on "how to" book that was inspired by the vision of a science class experiment or lab manual—you know, something that provides a list of supplies, a bit of background, and then step-by-step instructions on how to proceed. But we wanted it to be more than an lab manual with recipes for a dozen projects—we wanted it to be conversational and fun to read—almost as though we were there looking over your shoulder "kibitzing."

In other words, this book isn't a formal, complete book on SQL Server 7.0. No, this book is supposed to help you get started doing what we think are going to be typical projects. It's also supposed to open your eyes to projects you might want to do down the road.

If you need a single reference book about SQL Server 7.0, we recommend Ron Soukup and Kalen Delaney's *Inside Microsoft SQL Server 7.0* from Microsoft Press. It's as close to an "official," Microsoft approved book as you can get. (Kalen also maintains a Web site at www.insidesqlserver.com. We also like Richard Waymire and Rick Sawtell's *Teach Yourself Microsoft SQL Server 7.0 in 21 Days*. Both Richard Waymire and Ron Soukup work for Microsoft, so both of these books seem to contain a rich assortment of "insider" tidbits.

If you need a single book about SQL (the data language), we recommend Joe Celko's *Instant SQL Programming*, but the more formal *Understanding the New SQL* by Jim Melton and Alan Simon is also good. You might also consider buying the SQL Server 7.0 documentation set in order to have the comprehensive Transact-SQL manual handy, too. (We also recommend Joe Celko's new, highly readable *Data and Databases* book for its conversational, non-academic coverage of basic database concepts.

If you're a Visual Basic programmer who wants to write VB programs that access SQL Server, we recommend both Bill Vaughn's *Hitchhiker's Guide to Visual Basic and SQL Server* and also Mike Otey and Phil Conte's book, *SQL Server Developer's Guide*.

Enough about *other* books. Our book is meant to be "done" as much as read and doesn't have to be read in sequential fashion. So if you've got an immediate need and want a solution right now, why not turn to the Table of Contents or index and see what it has to offer?

We expect many of you will have homegrown databases stored in Microsoft Access or Excel you want to upgrade to SQL Server now that it can run on Windows 9x. In Project One, we'll show you how! Probably all of you will want to use SQL Server over an

Intranet or the Internet. We've got several projects that range from simple Web publishing to setting up a full-blown e-commerce site. If you're interested in setting up a data mart or doing OLAP (online analytical processing), we've got projects to help you do that, too.

We view this book as a dynamic document that is the basis for a community. If you find errors, have suggestions, or just want to brag about your successes, please let us know. Send your comments, ideas, and/or questions; our addresses are at the end of this section.

Our goal is to make this a book that's both useful and, yes, even fun to read. Did you ever take a "lab class" in college? If you did, you probably had to buy both a traditional textbook and a lab manual. Well, think of this as your lab manual. So dive in. The water's great.

Karen Watterson
(karen_watterson@email.msn.com)
San Diego, California

Bill Shadish
(bills@fo.com)
Downington, Pennsylvania

Garth Wells
(garth@pdq.net)
Houston, Texas

ACKNOWLEDGMENTS

Many friends and colleagues have helped bring this book to print, but I'd especially like to acknowledge these: Judy DeMarsh, my best friend whose ongoing encouragement was crucial to the completion of the book; Mike Yocca, a Pittsburgh-based SQL Server guru who made several valuable suggestions to the stored procedures chapter; Joe Celko, ("Mr. SQL") who graciously agreed to write the foreword; and several individuals at ESRI, who helped with the mapping section in Chapter 14. Jon Kilburn deserves special thanks for his major contributions to Chapters 6 and 11.

In addition to those, I'd like to especially thank Judy's brother-in -law, Al Dodson, who generously shared his NWPlants database and Russell Sinclair, who worked with his firm, Teranet Land Information Services, to provide a "sanitized" version of the Work-Ord database we use in the book. I really wanted you to have examples of "real world" data—something beyond the familiar "pubs" database to work with—and I hope you appreciate the contributions of Al and Russell.

Finally, there are all the vendors who agreed to provide us with evaluation copies of their software. We've assembled what we think is a top-notch collection of software, but we know it will become dated, so be sure to download the latest versions from the vendors' sites.

ABOUT THE AUTHORS

Karen Watterson is an independent San Diego, California-based writer and consultant specializing in data warehouse and knowledge management issues. She's the editor of Pinnacle Publishing's monthly *SQL Server Professional* and *Visual Basic Developer* newsletters, co-author of *Windows 2000 Magazine's* "SQL Savvy" column, and author of four books. She's been using SQL Server since 1988 and can be reached at karen_watterson@email.msn.com.

Bill Shadish is a principal of Fundamental Objects, Inc. (www.fo.com) where he works with ActiveX controls, COM server, project management tools and handheld technology. Bill writes for a number of VB trade journals including *Visual Basic Developer* and *Inside Visual Basic*. He has co-authored three books, including this one. Contact Bill at bills@fo.com.

Garth Wells is an independent consultant who works out of Houston, Texas. He has worked in database design and development for more than six years and has worked with SQL Server since version 4.2. He has successfully implemented and/or managed database solutions in the following industries: Computer Design and Manufacturing, Automobile Finance, Software Development, and Commercial Real Estate Management and Financial Services. For more information on his projects and interest visit his company's Web site at www.DataDrivenWebSites.com.

PART ONE

Getting Started

CHAPTER 1

Introduction to SQL Server

Microsoft SQL Server 7 is an RDBMS (relational database management system). Relational databases are sometimes referred to as self-defining collections of tables. That's because, from the end-user's point of view, data appears to be stored in two-dimensional tables—similar to spreadsheets that contain, for example, data about customers, orders, products, and so on, organized into rows and columns. In addition to data tables, RDBMSs (sometimes abbreviated DBMSs) all have special tables called *catalogs* or *dictionaries* that contain information about particular databases—hence the "self-defining" part of the definition.

SQL Server, like most high-end enterprise RDBMSs, is designed to handle multiple users—thousands concurrently, and lots of data—gigabytes (1 billion bytes) or even terabytes (1 trillion bytes) of data (see Sidebar, *Specs: How Big Is Big?*). RDBMSs like SQL Server and Oracle are sometimes called OLTP (online transaction processing systems) because they're built to keep track of complex transactions. Banks, brokerages, airline reservation systems, grocery stores, and your own organization's accounting system, all use RDBMSs. The RDBMS software is responsible for keeping things in synch—not deleting customers with open invoices, for example—and for being able to perform "auto recovery" in case of system failure.

Specs: How Big Is Big?

Maximum database size: 1,048,516 terabytes*
Maximum files per database: 32,767
Maximum file size (data): 32 terabytes
Maximum file size (log): 4 terabytes
Maximum foreign key constraints per table: 63
Maximum nested subqueries: 64
Maximum filegroups per database: 256
Maximum tables per SELECT statement: 256
Maximum bytes of source text in a stored procedure: lesser of 250 megabytes or Maximum batch size (65,536* network packet size)
Maximum parameters per stored procedure: 256

*** That's over a million terabytes, folks—not just a single terabyte—mega, giga, tera—but a million. To get a feel for some terabyte databases (it's not uncommon for large organizations' data warehousing applications to be terabyte affairs), check out the TerraServer site that displays and sells satellite images (www.terraserver.com).**

Today, RDBMSs are also used to build data warehouses and data marts for so-called DSS (decision support systems) and BI (business intelligence) applications. These are usually "read-only" (as opposed to "read-write") databases that contain data that's been consolidated from multiple sources, both for fast access and to minimize the impact of "ad hoc" (unplanned and unscheduled interactive) queries on production OLTP systems. These data warehouses may contain copies of data from order entry, sales, help desk, and shipping databases, plus data from a variety of budget and forecast spreadsheets. For example, RDBMSs are also used to support OLTP in the form of e-commerce and real-time online customer support. They are asked to support mobile users, making it easier for road warriors to synchronize laptop and PDA (personal digital assistant such as a Palm Pilot or Windows CE device) data with the enterprise network.

In the past, organizations and their IT (information technology) staffs have been a lot better about getting data *into* databases than with giving users or customers access to the subsets of data they need in order to do their jobs or make decisions. In today's dynamic marketplace, that's changing. IT departments are expected to deliver data over intranets, support electronic commerce (e-commerce), and to better integrate their organizations' diverse data stores with what can be very complex supply chains.

In other words, users take it for granted that RDBMSs will safeguard their data. But they are no longer satisfied to have data disappear into what appears to them to be a series of black holes. They expect IT to make it easier for them to get data back *out* of their databases as well.

RDBMSs like Microsoft SQL Server (www.microsoft.com/sql) have moved into the limelight because they can help IT deliver cost-effective solutions in a timely manner.

How SQL Server Fits into Microsoft's Enterprise Architecture

Simply stated, SQL Server is Microsoft's main database product. There are others, notably Microsoft Access and Microsoft FoxPro (see Sidebar, *Microsoft's* Other *Databases*), but SQL Server is clearly Microsoft's database of choice for the future, and that's one reason it's part of Microsoft's Windows NT BackOffice. BackOffice is an integrated family of server products built on Windows NT, and it's the foundation for Microsoft's enterprise architecture. Members of the BackOffice family include:

Microsoft Windows NT Server. Windows NT Server is Microsoft's enterprise operating system. Other BackOffice products rely on Windows NT to provide services and generally only run under NT. A growing number of optional, no cost NT-based servers are available for free download. For example, in late 1998 these included Microsoft Internet Information Server (IIS)—which itself includes optional components like a newsgroup server, Microsoft Transaction Server (MTS), Microsoft Message Queue Server (MSMQ), Internet Connection Services for RAS, Microsoft Index Server, and the Microsoft NetShow server. Microsoft also ships a high-end Windows NT Enterprise Server that supports server *clustering* and automatic server failover. Clustering is a technique for grouping two or more computers together for high availability. In the Microsoft Cluster Server (MSCS), two-server clustering—originally known as *Wolfpack*—is supported through NT 4.0. With MSCS, if one server crashes, the other one can continue to process. Clustering in general is a relatively inexpensive way to increase both system availability and scalability with many "small" systems instead of one big system.

Microsoft SQL Server. SQL Server, the subject of this book, is a scalable high-performance RDBMS designed for enterprise-class, distributed client/server, and Web computing. Microsoft SQL Server is tightly integrated with Microsoft's Internet technologies like Active Server Pages (ASPs), ActiveX Data Objects (ADO), Advanced Database Connector (ADC), and Microsoft Transaction Server (MTS)—all of which are used in this book—but adheres to industry standards such as ANSI SQL. SQL Server only runs on Windows platforms. Oracle, which runs on many platforms including NT, is SQL Server's main competition.

Microsoft Exchange Server. Exchange is Microsoft's messaging, e-mail, and collaboration server. Messaging servers rely on databases, but curiously, not relational databases. That's because of the nature of message threads. It's easier to store messages in a pointer-based database system instead of a relational or table-based system. Exchange Server, which only runs on NT, competes neck and neck with Lotus Notes and cc:Mail.

Microsoft Site Server. Site Server is a comprehensive Web site environment for enhancing, deploying, and managing intranet sites that run Windows NT Server and Internet Information Server (IIS). IIS itself isn't officially part of BackOffice, but rather a free option in the NT 4.0 Option Pack. Microsoft's high-end, commercial version of Site Server is called Commerce Server.

Microsoft Proxy Server. Proxy Server is Microsoft's extensible firewall and Web cache server that provides secure Internet access, while improving network response time and efficiency.

Microsoft's *Other* Databases

SQL Server isn't Microsoft's only database, although it is certainly Microsoft's premier database. Microsoft has also been shipping Microsoft Access (www.microsoft.com/access) since December 1992, and, according to most estimates, there are probably over 20 million copies of Access "out there." You may think of Access as an entry-level relational database management product. It was really designed to be a single-user database management system, and it currently ships with the Professional and Developer Editions of Microsoft Office. Table 1.1 shows a brief history of Microsoft Access releases.

Jet refers to the underlying (and unadorned) database engine. Access is a superset of Jet and includes the Access GUI, report builder, programming language, and so on. Jet is also included with Visual Basic.

In May 1999, Microsoft released the first version of its new MSDE (Microsoft Data Engine), available free (msdn.microsoft.com/vstudio/msde) in Visual Studio 6.x Professional and Enterprise editions. MSDE is basically a desktop edition of SQL Server 7 without the SQL Server GUI, and Microsoft is positioning it as an alternative to Microsoft Access.

FoxPro and Visual FoxPro (//msdn.microsoft.com/vfoxpro/) are Microsoft's third major database product, although, curiously, Microsoft seems to view it

Table 1.1 Microsoft Access Release Dates

VERSION	RELEASE DATE	16/32 BIT	JET ENGINE VERSION
Access 1.0	12/92	16-bit	Jet 1.0
Access 1.1	05/93	16-bit	Jet 1.1
Access 2.0	04/94	16-bit	Jet 2.0
Access 2.0 SP1	10/94	16-bit	Jet 2.5
Access 95	11/95	32-bit	Jet 3.0
Access 97 Version7.0	01/97	32-bit	Jet 3.5
Access 2000	Q1/99	32-bit	Jet 4.0 (plus new Microsoft Database Engine, MSDE)
Pocket Access	Q1/99	32-bit (Win CE 2.x)	Jet 4.1

Microsoft SNA Server. SNA Server is Microsoft's server for providing connectivity with systems ranging from AS/400s to mainframes that use IBM System Network Architecture (SNA) networks. SNA Server evolves into the "Babylon" Integration Server in Windows 2000.

more as a programming language than as a database product. It's included as part of Visual Studio, for example, along with Visual Basic, Visual C++, and Visual J++. To be fair, FoxPro isn't a relational database product at all—it's a *file-based* data management system. Today, however, Visual FoxPro is a powerful database-programming environment, one that supports SQL and the development of sophisticated client/server applications.

FoxPro has roots that go way back to dBASE days when its predecessor, FoxBase, offered dBASE programmers a high performance, multi-platform alternative to Ashton-Tate's product line. You can still buy DOS, Macintosh, and even UNIX/Xenix versions of 16-bit FoxPro 2.6, but Microsoft's new 32-bit Visual FoxPro products are only available for Windows and the Macintosh.

Microsoft acquired Fox Software in 1992 and has continued to develop the FoxPro family, bringing it into the object-oriented world with successive releases of Visual FoxPro. There are still thousands of active FoxPro and Visual FoxPro developers, many of whom are using Visual FoxPro to develop new LAN-based client/server applications. Table 1.2 shows a brief history of FoxBase, FoxPro, and Visual FoxPro.

Table 1.2 Version History for FoxBase, FoxPro, and Visual FoxPro

VERSION	RELEASE DATE	16/32 BIT	COMMENTS
FoxBase+	07/86	16-bit	Compatible with dBASE III
FoxBase+ 2.0	07/87	16-bit	Compatible with dBASE III+
FoxPro 1.0	11/89	16-bit	
FoxPro 2.0	07/91	16-bit	
FoxPro Mac	Spring 94	16-bit	
FoxPro/Unix	08/94	16-bit	Xenix
Visual FoxPro	06/95	16/32-bit	
Visual FoxPro 5.0	04/97	32-bit	
Visual FoxPro 6.0	09/98	32-bit	

Microsoft Systems Management Server (SMS). SMS is Microsoft's integrated network management product for managing and troubleshooting networked PCs and for distributing software.

Microsoft sells more than one flavor of Microsoft BackOffice, and, given product rollout schedules, may sell standalone servers that may eventually be rolled into future versions of BackOffice. One example of a standalone server that isn't integrated into BackOffice is Microsoft Windows Terminal Server (WTS), which was launched in summer 1998.

In addition to the *Standard* Edition of BackOffice, Microsoft also sells BackOffice Small Business Server 4.5 (SBS) for organizations with a maximum of 50 concurrent users. There are other limitations as well: SBS must be installed as a Windows NT Primary Domain Controller, all SBS servers must be installed on the same machine, and SQL Server databases are limited to 10 gigabytes in size. The version of SQL Server 7 that ships with SBS does not include OLAP Services.

By the same token, Microsoft also sells *Enterprise* Editions of some of its BackOffice products. The Enterprise Editions for NT and SQL Server both support clustering and failover. As we mentioned previously, the key to clustering support is the Microsoft Cluster Server (MSCS, code name Wolfpack), which ships with Windows NT Server Enterprise Edition.

Microsoft Commercial Internet System (MCIS) is another example of BackOffice enterprise software. In addition to the Microsoft Site Server Commerce Edition, MCIS includes Membership System, MCIS Mail Server, MCIS News Server, Microsoft Exchange Chat Service, Microsoft Internet Connection Services for RAS, Commercial Edition, and Microsoft NetShow as well as MCIS Administration and Provisioning Service (MAPS) and various authoring and development tools.

By packaging so much core functionality into a single bundle, Microsoft has made Windows NT BackOffice a very cost-effective and productive product suite, one that provides the basic infrastructure that organizations need. Microsoft released BackOffice 4.5 in mid 1999 with a base price of about $3099.

Choices, Choices

Just as BackOffice isn't a single product, neither is SQL Server. First, there are several existing active releases. Some sites still use Microsoft SQL Server 4.21, typically running under Windows NT 3.51, and some still use SQL Server 6. Many more continue to use SQL Server 6.5 which, like SQL Server 7, originally shipped in several versions.

SQL SERVER 6.5

Now that SQL Server 7 has shipped, if you want a new copy of SQL Server 6.5, you really have to work at it. Microsoft's "Open" and "Select" customers who purchase SQL Server 7 can then contact Microsoft's Worldwide Fulfillment at 800-248-0655 to request the previous version. Retail customers may call Microsoft/Softbank at 800-426-9400 and follow the queue for "replacements." The latest Service Pack for SQL Server 6.5 was SP5a, corresponding to version 6.50.416.

SQL Server 7 Trial Copy
Cost: Free 120-day evaluation copy
There's a copy included with this book!

SQL Server 7 Standard Edition
Cost: $1399 with 5 CALs, $1999 with 10 CALs, $3999 with 25 CALs
Operating System: Windows NT 4.0 Server or Windows 2000 Server
RAM/Disk Space: 32M RAM/80M disk space
Support: Up to 4 processors
No Support for: OLAP Services partitoning
Miscellaneous: Also includes a copy of SQL Server 7 Desktop Edition—which also ships with Microsoft Visual Tools 6.0 Enterprise Editions and runs on Win9X, Windows NT 4.0 Workstation, or Windows 2000 Professional systems that support the Pentium instruction set. That is, not a 486.

SQL Server 7 Enterprise Edition
Cost: $7999 with 25 CALs, $10,999 with 50 CALs, $28,999 with 2500 CALs
Operating System: Windows NT 4.0 Server Enterprise Edition, Windows 2000 Advanced Server, or Windows 2000 Datacenter Server
RAM/Disk Space: 64M RAM/80M disk space
Support: Up to 8 processors—32 from some OEMs, OLAP Services partitioning, and VLM (Very Large Memory)—to 8GM under Intel EMA

SQL Server via MSDN Universal Subscription
Cost: $2499/year
This option (msdn.microsoft.com) gives developers quarterly updates of key Microsoft products including a limited license—for development and testing only—10-connection copy of Microsoft's BackOffice Test Platform, which includes SQL Server.

Microsoft SQL Internet Connector
Cost: $2999/processor for an unlimited-user access license for Internet use
You'll need this license if you want users to access SQL Server data over the Internet. If you purchase this unlimited-user access license for Internet use, you don't have to worry about tracking concurrent database connections or users from the Internet (you still need CALs for intranet use). Note that SQL Internet Connector isn't a physical product—it's just a piece of paper, a license.

Windows NT 4.5 Small Business Server
Cost: $1499
Includes: Windows NT Server 4.0 with SP4, Internet Information Server 4.0, Index Server 2.0, Exchange Server 5.5 SP2, SQL Server 7, Proxy Server 2.0, Fax Service 4.5, Modem Sharing Service 4.5, FrontPage 98, Internet Explorer 5.0, Outlook 2000, and 5 CALs.
Maximum Number of Concurrent Users: 50
Maximum SQL Server Database Size: 10 GB
Requirements: Must be installed as an NT Primary Domain Controller (PDC) with all servers installed on a single system.

In other words, anyone who buys BackOffice or BackOffice Small Business Server gets SQL Server "for free." In fact, Microsoft sees SBS as the entry point for small businesses that use SQL Server, where the BackOffice Standard Edition is appropriate for workgroups and large organizations. In fact, there's an even lower entry point: the SQL

Server Desktop Edition that runs on Win9x PCs or Windows NT 4.0 workstations in single-user mode. Although Visual Studio 6 Enterprise Edition originally shipped with SQL Server 6.5, Visual Studio owners can request the free Windows 2000 Developer's Readiness Kit from Microsoft and obtain a developer's edition of SQL Server 7.

MICROSOFT DATA ENGINE (MSDE)

Some people consider MSDE, the Microsoft Data Engine that ships with Office 2000 Enterprise, Access 2000, and Visual Studio as part of the SQL Server family, too. It was developed by the SQL Server team as an alternative to Access' traditional Jet engine and offers seamless upward compatibility with SQL Server 7. MSDE is basically a "stripped-down" version of SQL Server 7.

Data Warehousing and OLAP

One of the most exciting features in the NT-based versions of SQL Server 7 is the built-in OLAP Services. Note that OLAP Services does not come with SQL Server Desktop. You typically build a data warehouse or data mart before you do OLAP. You may also hear OLAP (online analytical processing) referred to as business intelligence—BI—or in conjunction with CRM (customer relationship management) and data mining applications. What's all the excitement about? OLAP focuses on data retrieval and analysis—using the data. By contrast, OLTP systems such as order entry systems are optimized for getting data *in*, not for generating reports or letting people do "slice-and-dice" operations on the data like OLAP and BI systems are. There are problems with letting end users "at" the production data. For example, end users may not know where the data is. It may be spread out over several tables, several servers, or even several databases. Or, end users may fire off runaway "SELECT *" queries that choke the network or keep data entry operators from doing their jobs. Worse yet, end users may accidentally delete or change production data.

Data warehousing and OLAP provide solutions to these problems. Data warehousing is an approach to storing data in which heterogeneous data sources (typically from multiple OLTP databases) are migrated to a separate homogenous data store that may contain pre-summarized data for easy retrieval. For a good discussion on the differences between OLTP and OLAP systems, read SQL Server's *Books Online* topic, *Transaction Processing vs. Decision Support*. Typical OLTP systems are order entry systems, airline reservation systems, ATM machines. They must be highly available, highly secure, and support lots of concurrent connections. The underlying database has to be optimized for getting data into the database (*writing* data to the database). OLAP and BI systems, however, are typically read-only systems. They must be optimized for flexibility since they are often asked complex "ad hoc" queries. OLAP systems are expected to help analysts do forecasts, prepare comparative analyses, and occasionally even assist with "data mining" and visualization. (*Books Online* is SQL Server's 13+ MB online help database. It's installed automatically when you install SQL Server.)

What are the differences between a data warehouse and a data mart? It really depends on whom you talk to. Some organizations refer to smaller, more topic-oriented data stores as data marts and data warehouses as consolidated *enterprise* data repositories. What's the difference between data warehousing and OLAP? It's really a question of semantics. Whereas a data warehouse or data mart are the data *stores* for analytical data, OLAP refers to the *technology* that enables client applications to efficiently access the data. OLAP provides the following benefits to analytical users:

- Pre-aggregation of frequently queried data, enabling a very fast response time to ad hoc queries. *Pre-aggregation* means having SQL Server perform time-consuming join operations in anticipation of queries that will want summarized (aggregated) data. With pre-aggregation, the join results are stored in the database itself.
- An intuitive multi-dimensional data model (made of data cubes) that make it easy to select, navigate, and explore the data—Excel-style.
- Tools and wizards to make it easy to define, populate, and administer the cubes.

We'll cover data marts, data warehousing, and OLAP applications in hands-on projects in Chapters 7, 8, and 9.

DNA

We realize that you're anxious to get started *doing* SQL Server projects, but we urge you to take a few minutes to read a bit about the big picture—circa late 1999—from Microsoft's perspective, because there's more to Microsoft's vision of enterprise architecture than BackOffice and SQL Server. For starters, there's Microsoft's DNA (Distributed interNet Applications) architecture. First described in late 1997, DNA (www.microsoft.com/dna) is Microsoft's vision—some would say buzzword—describing how today's distributed, component-based applications should be designed. DNA's main ideas are that most applications should be built to run over the Internet and that it makes sense to divide them up into three layers or tiers:

1. The client, user interface (UI), or presentation tier
2. The middleware tier where business logic resides
3. The data tier

The three-tier architecture contrasts with the two-tier architecture that was popular in the 1990s.

Components can be written for any of these layers and will often travel over the Internet between computers. The components are really just named chunks of code (written in virtually any language, but abiding by Microsoft's COM (Component Object Model) rules that accomplish some task or group of tasks. Components are often represented as rectangles with interfaces—sometimes referred to as *hooks* that stick out as shown in Figure 1.1. COM is in the process of evolving into COM+, which ships with Windows 2000. COM+ is usually described as a combination of COM and Microsoft Transaction Server (MTS). That means that transaction services are simply part of Windows 2000. COM+ also includes built-in event handling that makes it easier to implement so-called publish-and-subscribe applications.

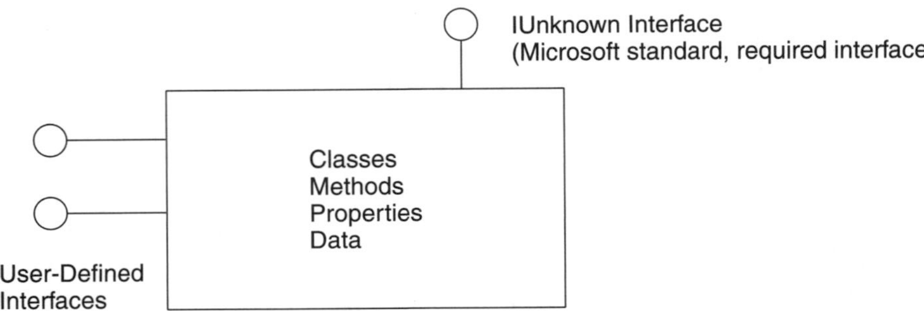

Figure 1.1 COM/COM+ components are usually represented as rectangles with programming interfaces like IUnknown sticking out.

COM plays a key role in the Windows DNA architecture. COM enables objects to talk to each other, and Distributed COM (DCOM) enables them to talk to each other over the network (and over HTTP via COM+). COM components are the middle-tier pieces that link the front ends (client tier) to the back ends (data tier) and provide business services that include data retrieval, manipulation, validation, and so on.

Windows DNA applications use a standard set of Windows-based services such as a Web browser, Web server, ActiveX components, dynamic HTML, scripting, transactions, message queuing, security, directory, database and data access, systems management, and user interface (see Table 1.3).

Table 1.3 Weaving It All Together with Microsoft's DNA

APPLICATION SERVICES	API OR STANDARD INTERFACE	MICROSOFT PRODUCT
Web server	HTML	Internet Information Server (IIS)
Web browser	HTML	Internet Explorer
Scripting	VBScript, Jscript	Host scripting language, Dynamic HTML
Transaction service	OLE Transactions	MTS
Message queuing service	Messaging API	MSMQ
Database	ODBC, OLE DB	Microsoft SQL Server
Mail and collaboration	MAPI, POP3	Outlook, Exchange Server
Java Virtual Machine (JVM)	Java SDK	Microsoft Java Virtual Machine
Universal data access	ADO, OLE DB, ODBC	Various: Microsoft SQL Server, Access, FoxPro, Visual Studio, etc.

Windows DNA 2000

On September 13, 1999, just prior to its annual DevDays event held simultaneously at scores of locations around the world, Microsoft updated DNA and announced Windows DNA 2000. New features include across-the-board support for XML (extended Markup Language—basically HTML for data) and its industry-specific extensions via BizTalk, and a new AppCenter Server. Simple Object Access Protocol (SOAP) is expected to replace DCOM as a way to handle remote procedure calls (RPC) across the Internet. The Windows DNA 2000 family of solutions includes the following, which are being rolled out incrementally beginning in late 1999.

Microsoft Windows 2000. The core Windows DNA services, including the COM+ component model and services, the high-performance IIS Web server, ASPs, transactions, messaging, data access, clustering and IP load balancing services, are now integrated into the operating system for greater consistency, easier management, and faster performance.

Microsoft Commerce Server 4.0. The next generation of the industry's leading packaged business-to-consumer commerce software provides deeper personalization, expanded site analysis and new product catalog features. Microsoft BizTalk Server. A business process integration solution that supports the BizTalk Framework, the BizTalk Server integrates applications within the enterprise and between businesses across the Internet through the exchange of XML-formatted business documents.

Microsoft "Babylon" Integration Server. This provides bidirectional network, data and application integration with a variety of legacy hosts.

Microsoft AppCenter. A new product that makes deployment and management of Windows DNA-based applications across high availability server "farms" as easy as managing a single server, AppCenter makes it easy to configure and manage arrays of servers.

Microsoft SQL Server "Shiloh." The next generation of the popular SQL Server 7.0 database adds native XML support and integrated data-mining capabilities, and takes full advantage of Windows 2000 for even greater scalability and availability.

Microsoft Visual Studio. The world's most popular set of development tools, spanning multiple languages, provides a common development environment for Windows DNA. It now includes the Windows 2000 Developer's Readiness Kit so developers can take full advantage of Windows 2000.

Digital Nervous System

In mid 1998, Microsoft began using the term *Digital Nervous System* to illustrate its vision for enterprise architecture (see Figure 1.2). According to the party line, a digital nervous system is built upon a commitment to six principles:

1. A PC-centric computing architecture
2. All information is available in digital form
3. Universal e-mail
4. Ubiquitous connectivity
5. Common end-user productivity tools
6. Integrated business-specific applications

Naturally, Microsoft hopes that its products will be the main ones that organizations use (see FYI: *We Eat Our Own Dog Food*), but even Microsoft realizes that most businesses need specialized applications to help perform specific functions. To function well as part of a Microsoft-centric digital nervous system, those business-specific applications will probably need to be BackOffice-compliant, and use Microsoft's COM and DCOM interfaces.

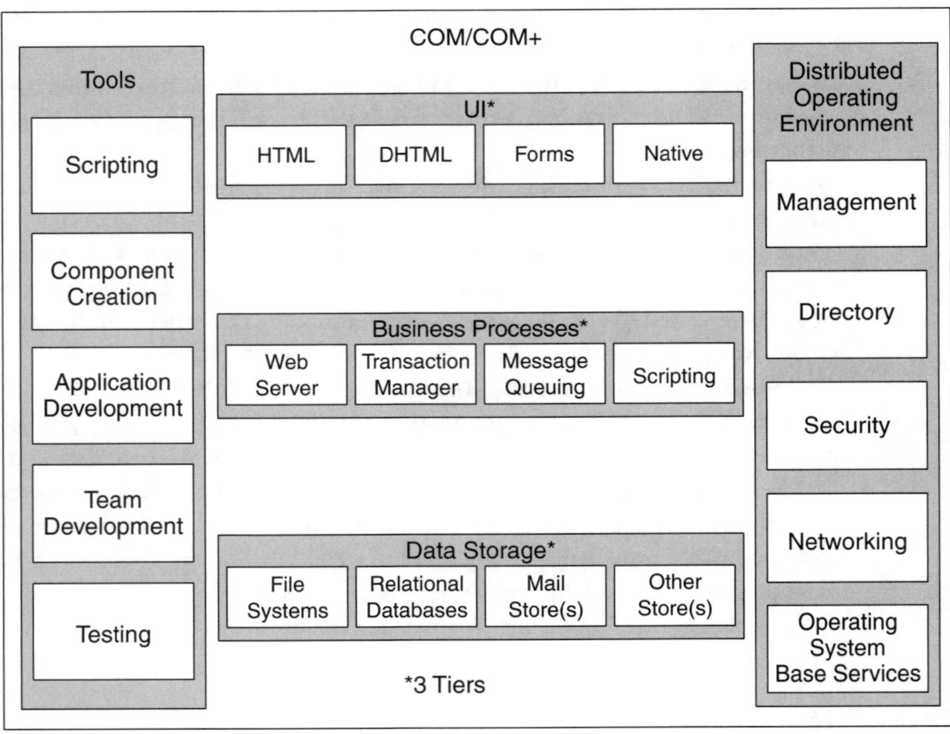

Figure 1.2 In Microsoft's vision of the future, Windows is the integrating platform that marries structured and unstructured data, data from mobile and enterprise computers, and internal with external data and applications.

WE EAT OUR OWN DOG FOOD

We're not sure if Bill Gates actually coined the phrase "we eat our own dog food," but he's used it on several occasions to describe how Microsoft tests and uses its own software. This includes SQL Server. For example, in a marketing case study, *Microsoft Moves Its Enterprise Business Operations* written in conjunction with the launch of SQL Server 7—Microsoft CIO, John Connors, described how Microsoft used SQL Server 7 for over 20 production systems, including key financial and customer service applications. "At that point," said Connors, "there were about 1700 people using Microsoft's SQL Server 7-based SAP R/3 system—doing about 600 thousand transactions a month." At that time, Microsoft also had an 80+ gigabyte MS-Sales data warehouse based on SQL Server.

Databases like SQL Server are used in all kinds of applications. Imagine a sales-force automation application, for example or a customer service or call center application. Call centers refer to people, locations, and/or software that handle incoming calls. The calls may be from people who want to place orders or make customer service inquiries. Think about how a human resources application might use e-mail to coordinate annual reviews, scheduled vacation, or handle expense reports. Visualize how an inventory system might link into your organization's extranet (which is a business-to-business intranet). Integrating your inventory system into your extranet could allow both you and your partners to do planning and financial analysis online and share data "instantaneously." In a similar fashion, your customer service or call center system might very well be integrated with the Internet to provide real time sales support and customer assistance.

Microsoft is encouraging developers who use tools like Microsoft's Visual Basic or Visual C++ to develop three-tier applications—separating the user interface portion that runs on a client PC or PDA from the middle tier that handles the business logic to the back end which supplies data services.

Microsoft Framework

Have you had enough of the party line and vision thing? Sorry, there's more, but this one is sort of interesting, because you don't hear that much about it unless you're an official Microsoft Certified Provider—it's the *Microsoft Framework (MSF).* MSF is basically Microsoft's methodology. You can also think of MSF as Microsoft's equivalent of a best-practices knowledge base. Microsoft encourages its large customers to consider adhering to the MSF and using it as a dynamic blueprint, one that provides both information (content) and a decision framework for IT. MSF assumes users will rely primarily on BackOffice for their infrastructure and provides a set of standards and guidelines that organizations are free to modify according to their own architectures and needs. As Microsoft says, the enterprise architecture should be designed to evolve with the organization.

Microsoft provides training on MSF. In 1999, you could take either of two, two-day classes for $1250 each: Solutions Development Discipline (SDD) or Designing Component

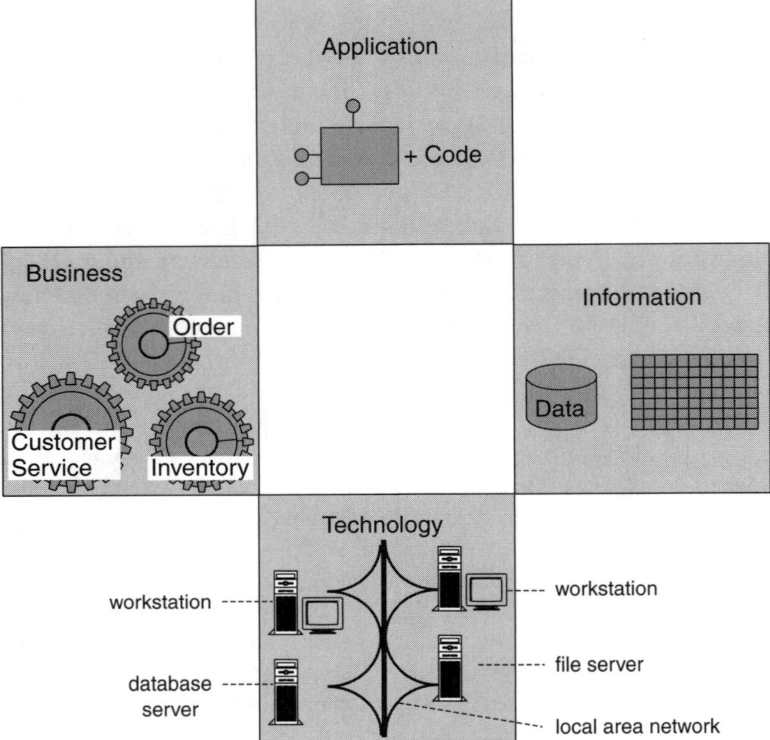

Figure 1.3 The Microsoft Framework is a methodology that can be viewed from different perspectives.

Solutions (DCS). SDD focuses on three models: Team Model, Process Model, and Application Model. DCS focuses on building components according to the three-tier model.

Figure 1.3 illustrates another way of thinking about enterprise architecture; depending on your perspective, you'll be looking at it from either a business (top management and planners), application (developers), information (IT staff), or technology (infrastructure implementers).

SQL Server Architecture

Okay folks, you've paid your dues toughing it through a couple of pages of big picture, architecture issues. Now it's time to hunker down into the book's topic—SQL Server. Today's relational database management systems are typically complex programs (65 MB worth) with many modules, but two of the most important components are the *query processor* and the *storage engine*. The query processor is the part of SQL Server that analyzes requests for data (typically in SQL) and works in conjunction with the data access engine (see Figure 1.4) to access the actual physical data. For now, let's focus on the storage engine.

In Microsoft SQL Server, data is stored in databases and organized so that it *appears* to be stored in tables. Physically, however, the data in a database is actually stored in two or more operating system files—typically one or two data files and a log file. Additionally, OLAP data cubes may be stored in CUB files.

Each SQL Server has multiple databases. As you can see in Figure 1.5, SQL Server has four *system* databases:

1. The *master* database is the main database for each SQL Server, and you should basically leave it alone. It stores crucial configuration information about the server.
2. The *model* database is a template, or starter, database that SQL Server uses each time it creates a new user database. The model database contains the system tables and standard user-defined stored procedures where everything from users to enterprise-wide triggers and business rules can be stored. Although it's possible to customize model for your organization, we recommend delaying doing that until you've had a few months' experience.
3. SQL Server uses the *tempdb* database to store temporary and intermediate results. Think of tempdb as SQL Server's own scratch pad.
4. The *msdb* database is a combination of the Microsoft Repository and the SQL Agent database. It contains information about scheduled tasks, including replication and backup, and various components, including COM objects and reports that may have been created with other Microsoft tools.

Northwind and pubs aren't really system databases, even though they ship with SQL Server. They're simply sample databases.

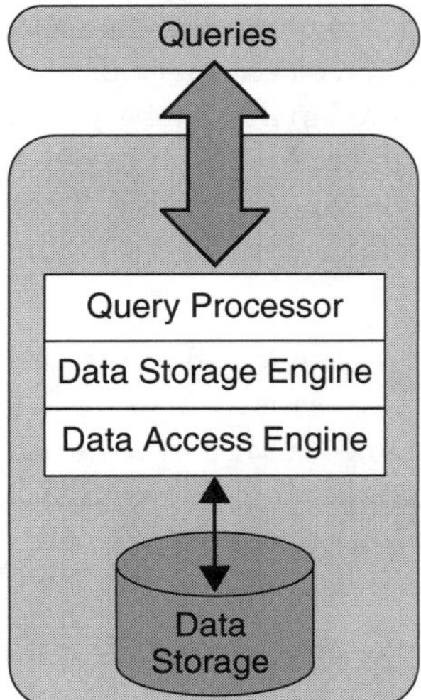

Figure 1.4 SQL Server's basic architecture. By convention, databases or data stores are usually represented as cylinders.

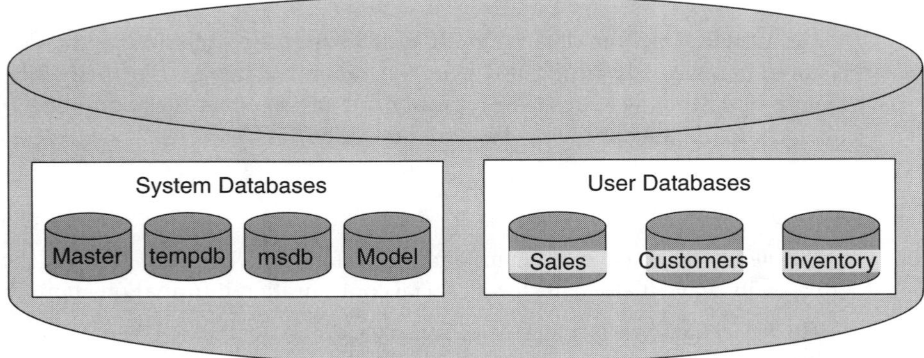

Figure 1.5 Each SQL Server has four system databases and one or more user databases.

THE DISTRIBUTION DATABASE

If you set up replication, you'll have an additional "system" database called *distribution.* The distribution database is used by the replication components of SQL Server, such as the Distribution Agent, to store data including transactions, snapshot jobs, synchronization status, and replication history information. Any server configured to participate as either a remote distribution server or as a combined Publisher/Distributor has a distribution database.

In addition to the system databases, each SQL Server will typically have one or more user databases. Microsoft recommends that you identify primary data files with an MDF filename extension. Some databases will also have secondary data files which contain data and information about data that's not stored in the database—often multimedia data such as images, maps, audio clips, and so on. Microsoft recommends that you give secondary files the NDF filename extensions. All databases have at least one log file (typically called an LDF file) which contains information required to recover a failed database

Some organizations have only one user database that contains all of the data for their organization. Some organizations have different databases for each group in their organization. Sometimes a database is created and maintained for use by a particular application such as a payroll or sales force automation application. Some applications just use one database; others may access several databases. Some databases are the active production databases; others are simply copies or replicas of the production database.

Unlike some RDBMSs, you don't have to run multiple server processes (copies of SQL Server) to allow multiple users to access the databases on a server. SQL Server is capable of handling thousands of users working in multiple databases on the same server at the same time, but each user will only have one current database.

SQL Server itself, though, actually consists of several Windows (NT) processes, or services:

MSSQLServer, the actual database engine

SQLServerAgent, the process which lets SQL Server perform scheduled activities and handle pre-defined alerts (available only on NT platforms)

DSDTC, the Microsoft Distributed Transaction Coordinator that SQL Server uses to handle multi-user transaction processing in an organized fashion (available only on NT platforms)

MSSearch, the full-text search engine that can be optionally installed to support full-text searches of text fields (available only on NT platforms)

MSOLAP, the optional OLAP server engine (available only on NT platforms)

SQLMail, the process which allows SQL Server to interact with POP3 mail servers including Microsoft Exchange

Both Windows 9x and Windows NT let you check which services are running via the Control Panel's Services icon. (MSSQL is the only service that absolutely has to be running in order for SQL Server to "be up.")

In the past, it's been a fairly complicated task to set up databases maintained by the storage engine. It entailed predicting how much storage was required, defining devices, pre-allocating storage to data and log files (see Figure 1.6), and deciding where the files were located. And all of that even before you started defining tables for your database. You pretty much had to be a trained DBA (database administrator) just to install SQL Server and fire it up.

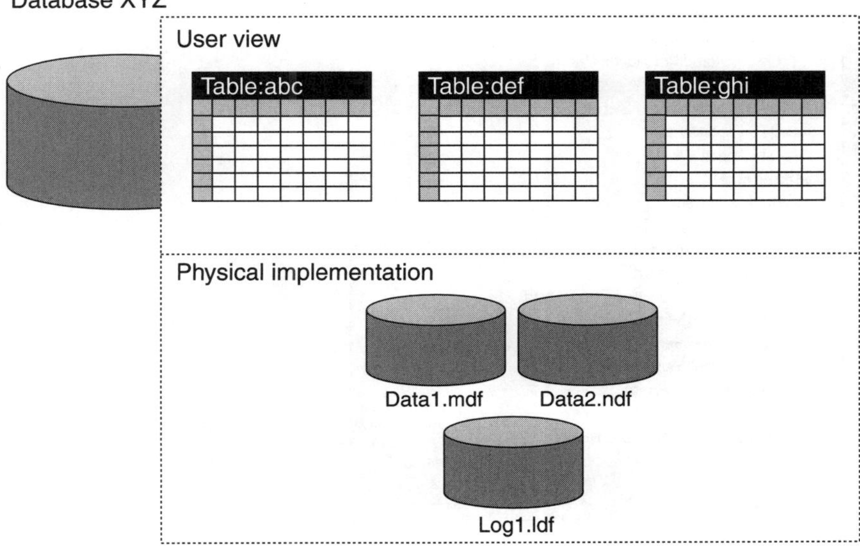

Figure 1.6 Databases are stored in normal operating system files called data and log files.

As you can see in Figure 1.6, a single SQL Server 7 database consists of two or more files. Microsoft recommends that you identify *primary data files* with an MDF filename extension. Some databases will also have secondary data files which contain data and information about data that's not stored in the database—often multimedia data such as images, maps, audio clips, and so on. As we mentioned previously, Microsoft recommends that you give secondary files the NDF filename extensions. All databases have at least one log file (typically called an LDF file) which contains information required to recover a failed database.

With SQL Server 7 Microsoft has focused on ease of use and introduced lots of wizards as shown in Table 1.4 that help both first-time and seasoned DBAs perform complex administrative tasks. For example, SQL Server 7 files autosize, so it's not necessary to make decisions about file size and pre-allocate space up front. Unless otherwise noted, the wizards can be accessed from the Tools menu in SQL Server Enterprise Manager as we did in Figure 1.7. The list in Table 1.2 isn't exhaustive—there are additional wizards for replication, cube building, and so on. Oh, and by the way, if the wizard comes with its own help, that probably is a clue that you're in for some heavy lifting.

Databases Consist of Tables

In Figure 1.5, you saw that every SQL Server server has four system databases and one or more user databases. The databases themselves consist of tables. Tables are simply

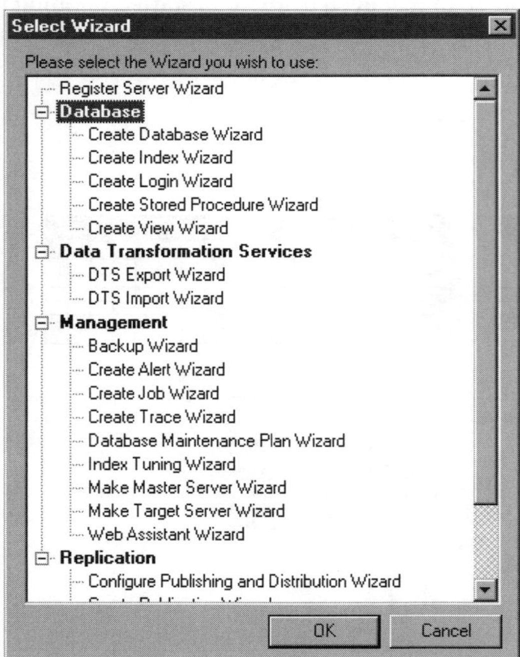

Figure 1.7 When you click on the Wizard icon (the wand with stars) on SQL Server's Enterprise Manager toolbar, you get a dropdown listbox of wizards, organized by category.

Table 1.4 The Wizards in Microsoft SQL Server 7

WIZARD	FUNCTION
Backup Wizard	Guides you through the process of backing up a database.
Failover Setup Wizard	Guides you through the process of setting up SQL Server Failover Support. This wizard is available only if you install SQL Server Enterprise Edition.
Configure Publishing and Distribution Wizard	Guides you through the process of configuring a publishing and a distribution server for replication. Help is included with this wizard.
Create Alert Wizard	Guides you through the process of creating an alert.
Create Database Wizard	Guides you through the process of creating a database.
Create Diagram Wizard	Guides you through the process of creating a database diagram.
Create Index Wizard	Guides you through the process of creating an index.
Create Job Wizard	Guides you through the process of creating a job.
Create New Data Source Wizard	Guides you through the installation of an ODBC data source and ODBC driver. Tests the validity of the connection. Help is included with this wizard. To access this wizard, in Control Panel, double-click ODBC Data Sources, and then click Add.
Create Login Wizard	Guides you through the process of granting SQL Server login access to users.
Create Publication Wizard	Guides you through the process of creating a publication for replication. Help is included with this wizard.
Create Stored Procedure Wizard	Guides you through the process of creating stored procedures for adding, deleting, and updating rows in a table.
Create Trace Wizard	Guides you through the process of creating a trace.
Create View Wizard	Guides you through the process of creating a view.
Database Maintenance Plan Wizard	Guides you through the process of creating a maintenance file that can be run on a regular basis. Works with the sqlmaint utility.
Disable Publishing and Distribution Wizard	Guides you through the process of disabling a publication and a distribution server for replication. Help is included with this wizard.
DTS Export Wizard	Guides you through the process of creating DTS packages to export data from a SQL Server database to heterogeneous data sources. Help is included with this wizard.
DTS Import Wizard	Guides you through the process of creating DTS packages to import heterogeneous data to a SQL Server database. Help is included with this wizard.

Continues

Table 1.4 The Wizards in Microsoft SQL Server 7 *(Continued)*

WIZARD	FUNCTION
Full-Text Indexing Wizard	Guides you through the process of defining full-text indexing on SQL Server character-based columns. Creates or modifies population schedules that determine when the information stored in the full-text catalog is updated.
Index Tuning Wizard	Guides you through the process of tuning an index.
Make Master Server Wizard	Guides you through the process of setting up a master server.
Make Target Server Wizard	Guides you through the process of setting up a target server and enlisting it into a master server.
Pull Subscription Wizard	Guides you through the process of enabling a subscription server to pull replicated data from a publication server. Help is included with this wizard.
Push Subscription Wizard	Guides you through the process of enabling a publication server to push replicated data to a subscription server. Help is included with this wizard.
Register Server Wizard	Guides you through the process of registering SQL Servers.
SQL Server Upgrade Wizard	Guides you through the process of upgrading SQL Server. The SQL Server Upgrade Wizard is not supported on the Win95/98 platform. To access this wizard, on the Start menu, point to Programs, point to Microsoft SQL Server - Switch, and then click SQL Server Upgrade Wizard.
Web Assistant Wizard	Guides you through the steps required to create a Web task that creates an HTML page, to import data from an HTML page, or to run an existing Web task.

two-dimensional structures like spreadsheets that are typically defined in terms of the columns (or attributes). The actual data is stored in the rows (or records). Tables often have "themes" and store specific data related to customers, invoices, or products.

SQL Server's *system* database called *master* stores information about the server configuration, setup, user login information, and so on. It contains these special tables:

sysaltfiles
syscacheobjects
syscharsets
sysconfigures
syscurconfigs
sysdatabases
sysdevices
syslanguages
syslockinfo
syslogins

sysmessages
sysoledbusers
sysperfinfo
sysprocesses
sysremotelogins
sysservers

User databases have a different set of special system tables in addition to the tables you set up:

sysallocations
syscolumns
syscomments
sysconstraints
sysdepends
sysfilegroups
sysfiles
sysforeignkeys
sysfulltextcatalogs
sysindexes
sysindexkeys
sysmembers
sysobjects
syspermissions
sysprotects
sysreferences
systypes
sysusers

All of these special system tables can be queried by authorized SQL Server users. However, although it's fun to query them like SELECT * FROM sysusers, the result sets are sometimes hard to decipher. Still, if you want to practice your SQL (see *The SQL SELECT Statement* later in this chapter), these tables give you something to start with. The sample Northwind and pubs databases, are likely to be a lot more interesting to query. These databases will be (were) automatically installed if you opt(ed) for the typical installation. Northwind, based on the database application that ships with Microsoft Access, contains the sales data for a fictitious company called Northwind Traders which imports and exports specialty foods from around the world. The Pubs database contains book information about a fictitious publishing company.

Remember, as long as you know the tablename, you can submit a SELECT * FROM <tablename> query.

The 10 user tables in the pubs database include authors, discount, employee, jobs, pub_info, roysched, sales, stores, titleauthor, and title. The 12 user tables in the Northwind database include employees, customers, orders, shippers, suppliers, categories, and others.

NORTHWIND

The Northwind database contains the table Northwind.dbo.dtproperties that stores a diagram of the database. To view the diagram in SQL Server Enterprise Manager, open the Diagrams folder in the Northwind folder and double-click Relationships. If you need to install/reinstall Northwind, navigate to the Mssql7\Install directory and use the osql utility to run the Instnwnd.sql script:

osql/Usa /Psapassword /Sservername /instnwnd.sql /oinstnwnd.rpt

Databases Contain Other Objects, Too

Tables alone don't make a SQL Server database. In fact, if you look at SQL Server's so-called *object-model hierarchy*, you'll see something like this:

SQL Server

Database

Objects

Tables

Columns

Indexes

Views

Constraints

Rules

Defaults

Triggers

Stored Procedures

Indexes

Indexes are the look-up mechanism that SQL Server uses to find records fast. If database products didn't have indexes, every time you submitted a query, the database engine would have to scan the entire table for matches. Such *full-table scans,* as they are known, can be efficient for small tables, but are a recipe for abysmal performance in databases with large tables. SQL Server uses two different kinds of indexes: *clustered* (where the records are automatically kept in a specific order rather than the order in which they were entered) and *non-clustered*. If you think about it, tables can only have one clustered index, so if you use one, be sure you think about the order in which records are most likely to be requested. Be sure to take advantage of SQL Server's index wizards both to create and tune your indexes. Lousy index selection is a major factor in poor performance.

Views

Views are another database object in the SQL Server hierarchy. Views are a lot like tables—or more accurately *virtual tables* that basically contain recipes for constructing a pre-defined selection of columns and/or rows from one or more tables. DBAs often create views to combine columns from one or more tables to make it easier for end users to retrieve data such as SELECT * FROM this month to retrieve current monthly data. See Chapter 4 for more on views.

Constraints

Constraints are a RDBMS's tool for helping ensure data integrity. Although it's virtually impossible to keep bad data from getting into a database, constraints can help ensure that customers get unique ids, that obviously out-of-range data isn't accepted, and that fields that require data don't get submitted with missing data (null entries). For more information on SQL Server's five different kinds of constraints, consult *Books Online* topics about primary keys, foreign keys, unique keys, check constraints, and "not null" constraints. Part of your Chapter 4 project deals with constraints.

Rules

Rules are related to constraints, but you can only have one rule per column. Rules, however, can use conditional expressions and reference lists of values for comparison purposes.

Defaults

Defaults are handy database objects that specify a value for fields in which no other data is explicitly entered.

Triggers

Triggers are stored procedures that are automatically executed with SQL Server modifies a record using INSERT, UPDATE, or DELETE operations. Triggers are often associated with *referential integrity*; a notion that reflects the need to keep related data in different tables in synch. See Chapter 12 for more on triggers.

Stored Procedures

Stored procedures are groups of T-SQL statements that are given a name, pre-compiled, and ready for easy re-use. See Chapter 12 for more on stored procedures.

The Roots of Relational Database Technology

Dr. E.F. Codd is the original "R-Man." He first proposed the relational model in his frequently cited—but rarely read—1969 IBM research report, *Derivability, Redundancy, and Consistency of Relations Stored in Large Data Banks*. He proposed the relational model as an alternative to the then popular hierarchical and network (or CODASYL) database models. Back then, databases were typically data files stored on tape and controlled by custom COBOL programs. The main difference between the older hierarchical and network database models and the relational model are that the relational model distinguishes between a database's physical file structure and its logical design. This means that application programs don't need to "know" details about physical file storage and pointers, for example.

Database pundits like to point out that the relational model is the only one with rigorous mathematical foundations. Part of the reason is that Dr. E.F. Codd is a mathematician. In fact, one of the reasons the relational model took so long to catch on may have been the mathematical language in which it was cast. Let's face it, not many of today's IT staffers read formal mathematical proofs in their spare time or converse about notions like the "existential quantifier" over lunch, and it wasn't any different twenty years ago. Dr. Codd's original paper, like today's relational model, was firmly steeped in predicate logic and couched in alien jargon which is one more reason to appreciate all the wizards and tutorials in Microsoft SQL Server 7.

If you really want to know, though, predicate logic differs from the more familiar two-valued propositional logic that is used as the basis for many computer operations. In two-valued Boolean logic, statements like "A = B" or "A > B" are evaluated as true or false. Period. Predicate logic, however, treats values as the *subjects* of its statements so more complex expressions can be constructed. "Is a number between," for example, is a predicate that requires three subject values in a statement like "A is a number between B and C." In other words, predicate logic lets you do more interesting things than simple two-valued logic does.

E.F. ("Ted") Codd invented the relational model in 1969. Later, in a classic two-part *Computerworld* article (10/14/85 and 10/25/85), he published 12 "basic rules" for "fully relational" databases. That list has subsequently grown to include 300 features organized into 18 classes, and you can read all about it in *The Relational Model for Database Management Version 2* (Addison-Wesley, 1990). Dr. Codd and an erstwhile partner, Chris Date, are considered the authorities on matters relational. Ted Codd worked for IBM off and on for over thirty years between 1948 and 1984.

Is SQL Server Really a Seventh Generation Product?

Keeping track of versions is always difficult—especially when there's more than one vendor involved. However, one thing is certain: relational database technology is solid as bedrock. It was invented two decades ago by a mathematician, and has clearly stood the test of time (see Sidebar, *The Roots of Relational Database Technology*).

Microsoft didn't invent SQL Server and, in fact, the first version of Microsoft's SQL Server was called Ashton-Tate/Microsoft SQL Server 1.0. No, Ashton-Tate (better known for the dBASE product family) didn't invent SQL Server either. Microsoft's involvement with SQL Server dates back to March 1987 when Microsoft and Sybase (www.sybase.com) signed an agreement granting Microsoft the right to port Sybase's SQL Server to the PC platform. Two years later (see Figure 1.8), in May 1989, the co-branded Ashton-Tate/Microsoft SQL Server 1.0 shipped with the 16-bit Microsoft OS/2 and LAN Manager. Almost a year later, in August 1990, Microsoft shipped SQL Server 1.1—again bundled with LANMan.

These 1.x PC versions of SQL Server were pretty much direct ports of the Sybase product, but in March 1992, Microsoft shipped the next version, SQL Server 4.2. By then Ashton-Tate was out of the picture, but Microsoft SQL Server 4.2 was still a 16-bit product. You could run it either under OS/2 1.3 or as a Netware NLM (Netware Loadable Module). It wasn't until the following year, in August 1993, that Microsoft shipped an NT version of SQL Server, SQL Server 4.21 for Windows NT 3.1. This version had the first GUI admin tools ever seen in the RDBMS world.

In April 1994, Sybase and Microsoft agreed to pursue independent development paths for SQL Server. Ironically, it was Sybase that ended up finding a new name for its product (Sybase Adaptive Server); Microsoft has maintained the original Sybase product name, SQL Server.

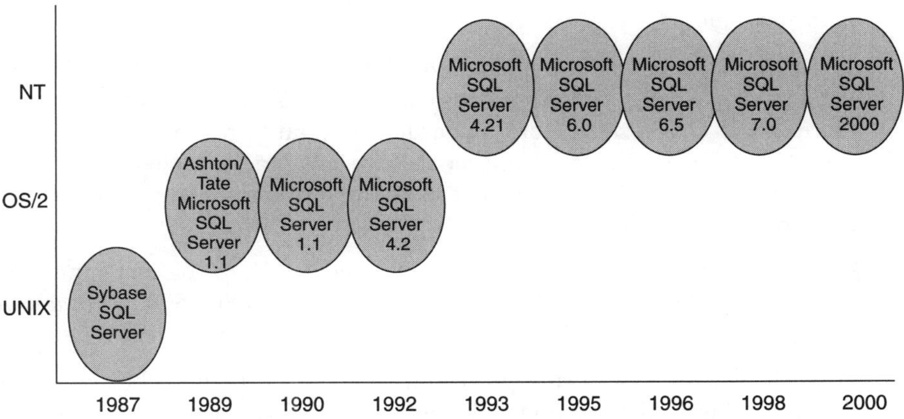

Figure 1.8 SQL Server timeline.

Did you notice that there never were versions 2 or 3 of SQL Server? Well, there wasn't a version 5 either. Microsoft shipped SQL Server 6.0 in June 1995 and SQL Server 6.5 in April 1996.

Which brings us (finally, you're probably thinking) to SQL Server 7 which shipped in late 1998.

Before proceeding—be patient, the rest of this book is almost all hands-on—there's one more topic we need to talk about briefly.

The "SQL" in SQL Server

"Mommy (Daddy), where did SQL come from?" How would *you* answer? What exactly *is* SQL? You probably know that it's an acronym that stands for *structured query language*. SQL (you can pronounce it either "sequel" or "ess cue ell") is a non-procedural, relational, data access language that lets you create, manipulate, and control relational databases. It's important because it's a common denominator—a sort of lingua franca—for communication both between applications and RDBMSs and between RDBMSs themselves. But SQL isn't a complete programming language because it doesn't have constructs for looping or branching, for example.

SQL has evolved since 1974 when it was first implemented as SEQUEL (Structured English QUEry Language, for you acronym chasers) on a prototype relational DBMS called System R at the IBM San Jose Research Laboratory. No, father Codd didn't invent SEQUEL; it was an IBM team led by Donald Chamberlin. System R eventually evolved into IBM SQL/DS and IBM DB2, and SEQUEL became SQL. The terms *SQL* and *relational* are related, but they're not synonymous.

SQL is a non-procedural English-like query language based on relational calculus. Relational calculus itself is a non-procedural, mathematical formalization, based on first order predicate logic, of the relational algebra operations. The gist of all that is that SQL queries should theoretically always return the right answer since SQL is based on math and logic.

Unfortunately, there isn't a single SQL. A host of standards organizations, notably ANSI (www.ansi.org, American National Standards Institute), the ISO (www.iso.ch, International Organization for Standardization), and The Open Group (www.opengroup.org, formerly X/Open), are constantly updating their versions of formal, *de jure* SQL standards. SQL-92 is the current standard, but a more object-oriented SQL:1999 is under development.

SQL-92, like the original SQL-86 and subsequent SQL-89, defines multiple levels of compliance, notably Entry SQL, Intermediate SQL, and Full SQL. With this version of SQL Server 7, Microsoft achieves full compliance with Entry Level SQL-92.

Nevertheless, work is already proceeding on SQL:1999, which borrows popular features from object-oriented models, but even pundits who have spent years working on the nascent SQL:1999 standard suspect that it will be far less relevant than previous versions of the SQL standard. Part of their discouraging prognosis is the emergence of appealing alternatives like Microsoft's *OLE DB* (Object Linking and Embedding, Database). OLE DB is a COM-based API that specifies the rules by which data providers and data consumers must play in order to share data. OLE DB is basically the logical successor to the widely used ODBC (Open Database Connectivity) API. Another reason for pessimism about SQL:1999 is that it's extremely complicated. Not only have each of the major RDBMS vendors developed their own proprietary, mainly procedural extensions to standard SQL (SQL Server's is called *T-SQL* for Transact-SQL), they've also developed their own techniques for supporting non-traditional database information such as maps, audio clips, and digital images.

The SQL SELECT Statement

Don't worry, you don't need to learn the SQL language in order to use SQL Server 7. There are, however, plenty of books that teach SQL, and you can always refer to James Hoffman's online tutorial at w3.one.net/~jhoffman/sqltut.htm if you're really interested. We've also provided an appendix (Appendix A) on what we consider to be SQL survival skills. Nevertheless, it *will* help if you have a basic understanding of the SQL SELECT statement. For starters, knowing how to write a simple SELECT statement will make it easy to find out if your SQL Server is working and which database is active.

One of the first things *we* do after installing a new SQL Server is to start the Microsoft SQL Server Enterprise Manager and see if everything's working as expected. Assuming you've registered the server (more on the details in Chapter 2), you simply navigate down the server tree to databases, click on the + symbol to expand the list, and click on pubs. Launch Query Analyzer from Enterprise Manager and simply type and execute the statements USE pubs. This is a non-SQL statement that just says "Make the pubs database the active one," where "pubs" is the sample database that ships with all versions of SQL Server and then SELECT * FROM authors. The SELECT statement tells SQL Server to return a list of all the data in the authors' table. The * symbol is a shorthand for "all." The data won't be sorted, but will simply be listed in the order in which it was first entered.

Usually, you won't want a list of *all* the data in a table—just *some* of it. You might not want all the rows (records). That's where the WHERE clause comes in. Here are some sample SELECT statements with WHERE clauses.

```
SELECT * FROM authors WHERE state = 'CA'
```

SELECT au_lname FROM authors WHERE state = 'UT' (note that we have replaced * with a specific column name, au_lname. We could have listed more columns, separated by columns. The order in which we list the columns determines the appearance of the returned data, and the returned data is often referred to as a "result set.")

```
SELECT * FROM authors WHERE contract <> 1
SELECT @@VERSION
```

These examples show that you typically use single quotes to designate 'text' data and to illustrate a fast way to make sure what version of SQL Server you're running.

Here's an abbreviated version of the syntax for the SELECT statement:

```
SELECT select_list
[INTO new_table_name]
FROM table_list
[WHERE search_conditions]
[GROUP BY group_by_list]
[HAVING search_conditions]
[ORDER BY order_list [ASC | DESC] ]
```

DOES CASE COUNT?

Unless your SQL Server has been installed to be case sensitive, it doesn't matter whether you type SQL statements in upper or lower case. SQL "keywords" are often shown in upper case to distinguish them from user data—your own database's table names, column names, and so on, but in the UNIX world, SQL commands are typically typed in all lower case.

Here are some additional details:

The select_list is a comma-separated list of expressions that describes the columns of the result set. Each expression defines both the format (data type and size) and the source of the data for the result set column. Each select list expression is usually a reference to a column in the source table or view the data is coming from, but can be any other expression, such as a constant or a T-SQL function. Using the * expression in a select list specifies that all columns in the source table are returned (in the order in which they have been defined). If you don't want to get *all* of the data, or if you want it in a different order, you can list the columns, separated by commas.

INTO new_table_name specifies that the result set is used to create a new table. The new_table_name specifies the name of the new table.

FROM table_list contains a list of the tables from which the result set data is retrieved. These sources can be: base tables or views in the local SQL Server or linked tables, which are tables in OLE DB data sources made accessible to SQL Server. As we mentioned previously, views are virtual tables that basically contain recipes for constructing a pre-defined selection of columns and/or rows from one or more tables. The FROM clause can also contain "join" specifications, which define the manner and order in which tables are combined.

WHERE search_conditions is the clause that restricts the data being returned. WHERE clauses act like filters. Only rows that meet the conditions contribute data to the result set.

GROUP BY group_by_list partitions the result set into groups based on the values in the columns of the group_by_list.

HAVING search_conditions provides an additional filter that can be applied to the result set. Logically, the HAVING clause filters rows from the *intermediate* result set built from the application of any FROM, WHERE, or GROUP BY clauses in the SELECT statement. HAVING clauses are most commonly used with a GROUP BY clause, although a GROUP BY clause is not required before a HAVING clause.

ORDER BY order_list [ASC | DESC] defines the order in which the rows in the result set are sorted. The order_list specifies the result set columns that make up the sort list, and ASC and DESC keywords specify if the rows are sorted in ascending or descending sequence. ORDER BY is important because relational theory specifies that the rows in a result set cannot be assumed to have any sequence unless ORDER BY is specified. ORDER BY must be used for any SELECT where the order of the result set is important.

Take a few minutes to continue to experiment with the pubs database. See if you can get an alphabetical list of authors, for example, or a list of authors whose either live in California or Utah. Even if you don't work at a computer where SQL Server is already installed, try to build the SELECT statements in your head. Again, even though point and click will often let you get away without knowing any SQL at all, it doesn't hurt to have a basic understanding of the SELECT statement and its main parts: FROM, WHERE, and ORDER BY.

We've included the complete syntax of the SELECT statement in SQL Server 7 here. Don't even try to memorize this; we simply want you to take a look at the complexity of the most powerful command in the SQL query language. (In case you're wondering, the SQL keywords are in upper case; data you provide is in lower case). Ultimately, when you or your applications need to retrieve data back from SQL Server, someone or some program will issue a SQL SELECT statement. Again, you don't have to know this command backwards and forwards. For one thing, you can always refer to it in SQL Server's *Books Online*. But, more important, GUIs (graphical user interfaces) shield you from having to type your own SELECT statements. By pointing and clicking, you'll be able to have some program create the SQL for you.

```
SELECT [ ALL | DISTINCT ]
    [ TOP n [PERCENT] [ WITH TIES] ] <select_list>
[ INTO new_table ]
[ FROM <table_sources> ]
[ WHERE <search_conditions> ]
[     [ GROUP BY [ALL] group_by_expression [,...n]]
        [HAVING <search_conditions> ]
        [ WITH { CUBE | ROLLUP } ]
]
[     ORDER BY {     column_name [ ASC | DESC ] }     [,...n]     ]
[ COMPUTE
    {     {     AVG | COUNT | MAX | MIN | SUM     } (expression) } [,...n]
    [ BY expression [,...n]
]
[ FOR BROWSE ]
[ OPTION (<query_hints>) ]
<select_list> :: =
    {     [ { <table_or_view> | table_alias }.]*
        |     { column_name | expression | IDENTITYCOL | ROWGUIDCOL }
```

```
              [ [AS] column_alias ]
          | new_column_name = IDENTITY(data_type, seed, increment)
          | GROUPING  (column_name)
          | { table_name | table_alias}.RANK
          | column_alias = expression
          | expression column_name
    }     [,...n]
<table_sources> :: =
    {     <table_or_view>
          | (select_statement) [AS] table_alias [ (column_alias [,...n]) ]
          | <table_or_view> CROSS JOIN <table_or_view>
          | <table_or_view>
              {    {     INNER
                         |     { FULL | LEFT | RIGHT }
                              [ OUTER ] [ <join_hints> ] [ JOIN ]
                  } <table_or_view> ON <join_condition>
              }
          | <rowset_function>
    }
[,...n]
<table_or_view> :: =
    {     table_name [ [AS] table_alias ] [ WITH (<table_hints> [,...n])
]
          | view_name [ [AS] table_alias ]
    }
<table_hints> ::=
    {     INDEX(index_name | index_id [,...n])
          | FASTFIRSTROW
          | HOLDLOCK
          | NOLOCK
          | PAGLOCK
          | READCOMMITTED
          | READPAST
          | READUNCOMMITTED
          | REPEATABLEREAD
          | ROWLOCK
          | SERIALIZABLE
          | TABLOCK
          | TABLOCKX
          | UPDLOCK
    }
<join_hints> ::=
    { HASH | LOOP | MERGE }
<query_hints> :: =
    {     { HASH | ORDER } GROUP
          | { CONCAT | HASH | MERGE } UNION
          | FAST number_rows
          | FORCE ORDER
          | MAXDOP number
          | ROBUST PLAN
```

```
    }
<join_condition> :: =
    { table_name | table_alias | view_name }.column_name
        <logical_operator>
        { table_name | table_alias | view_name }.column_name
<logical_operator>:: =
    { = | > | < | >= | <= | <> | != | !< | !> }
<rowset_function> :: =
    {     CONTAINSTABLE [ [ AS] table_alias]
            (     table, { column | *}, '<contains_search_condition>'
            )
        | FREETEXTTABLE  [ [ AS] table_alias]
            (     table, {column | * }, 'freetext_string'
            )
        | OPENQUERY (linked_server, 'query')
        | OPENROWSET
            ( 'provider_name',
                {
                    'datasource';'user_id';'password'
                    | 'provider_string'
                },
                {
                    [catalog.][schema.]object_name
                    | 'query'
                }
            )
<search_conditions> ::=
    {     [ NOT ] <predicate> [ { AND | OR } [ NOT ] <predicate> ]
        | CONTAINS
            (     {column | * }, '<contains_search_condition>'
            )
        | FREETEXT
            (
                {column | * }, 'freetext_string'
            )
        | fulltext_table.fulltext_key_column = fulltext_table.[KEY]
    } [,...n]
<predicate> ::=
    {
        expression { = | <> | != | > | >= | !> | < | <= | !< } expression
        | string_expression [NOT] LIKE string_expression
            [ESCAPE 'escape_character']
        | expression [NOT] BETWEEN expression AND expression
        | expression IS [NOT] NULL
        | expression [NOT] IN (subquery | expression [,...n])
        | expression { = | <> | != | > | >= | !> | < | <= | !< }
            {ALL | SOME | ANY} (subquery)
        | EXISTS (subquery)
    }
```

Summary

In this chapter, we've given you a brief introduction to RDBMSs, discussed the fundamental role SQL Server plays in the Microsoft vision of enterprise computing, and filled you in on some of the jargon Microsoft uses when describing its vision to corporate executives. We've provided some of the history for the other Microsoft databases, and introduced you to some of the basic concepts associated with relational databases and the SQL data access language.

Now it's time to roll up our sleeves and move on. In Chapter 2, we walk you through the installation process. Even if you or someone else has already installed SQL Server, please skim through Chapter 2 to make sure that you are aware of the different installation options.

CHAPTER 2

Installing SQL Server

Goal

The goal of this chapter is to show how to install SQL Server 7 Standard Edition along with an explanation for the different configuration options and their ramifications on server perfomance and operations.

YOU WILL NEED

- ✔ Pentium, Pentium II, Pentium Pro, or higher PC or DEC Alpha system with 183MB free disk space (or about 30MB for "compact" installation) and 32MB RAM (16MB RAM will suffice for bare-bones installations with no replication, but 128MB is recommended for standard production systems)
- ✔ Microsoft Windows 9x, Windows NT 4.0 (SP4 or higher) Workstation, Windows NT 4.0 (SP4 or higher) Server, Windows 2000 Professional, Windows 2000 Server, Advanced Server, or Datacenter Server
- ✔ Microsoft Internet Explorer 4.01, SP1 or higher
- ✔ Microsoft SQL Server 7.0

  Optional:

  - ✔ Microsoft SQL Server 7.0 SP1

In Chapter 1, you saw that there are two basic versions of SQL Server 7: Standard Edition and Enterprise Edition. Standard Edition, the "normal" one, includes both Desktop and Server versions and can be installed on Win9x and WinNT. Enterprise Edition runs on either Win NT 4.x Enterprise Edition or Win 2000 Datacenter Server. In addition to the two standard releases, Microsoft also sells other products such as Visual Studio Enterprise Edition and WinNT 4.5 Small Business Server (SBS) in which SQL Server is bundled. The bundled releases do, however, place limits on usage. The Visual Studio and SBS 4.5 versions limit simultaneous users to 15 and 50 respectively, and the SBS release limits the maximum database size to 10GB.

In this chapter, we're going to show you how to get the basic SQL Server 7 Standard Edition up and running. Many of you have probably already installed SQL Server 7, and, in this case, if you don't want to read the whole chapter, we recommend that you at least make sure you understand the ramifications for the configuration options you selected—by default or otherwise. Do you know, for example, whether you've opted for the Windows NT-only authentication model (or combined Windows NT and SQL Server authentication) which NT accounts you've assigned to SQL Server's various NT services? Do you know which server and database roles you've established and whether or not you've chosen a non-default character set, sort order, or Unicode collation? (The defaults are the 1250 ISO character set, the dictionary order/case insensitive sort order, and standard Unicode collation.) More importantly, do you understand how choosing the wrong option can affect your operations?

TEMPTED TO SKIP THIS CHAPTER?

Before you do, make sure you know not only the answers to these 10 questions, but also ponder the danger of *not* knowing the answers:

1. **What SQL Server version did you install—Desktop, Standard, or Enterprise?**
2. **How many client access licenses (CALs) do you have?**
3. **For NT installations, what user accounts have you assigned to MSSQLServer and SQLServerAgent services?**
4. **If you have installed OLAP Services, which user account did you assign to it?**
5. **Did you install the default 1250 ISO character set, the default dictionary order/case insensitive sort order, and standard Unicode collation, or did you override the defaults?**
6. **Have you migrated any databases onto the new server?**
7. **Did you migrate them for backward compatibility?**
8. **Have you set up any database roles?**
9. **Have you decided on a backup routine and performed the first one? What server roles have you assigned?**
10. **Have you documented your server installation configuration and database schema?**

FINDING OUT VERSION INFORMATION

There are several ways to find out if you have the first production version (as opposed to beta or SP versions) of SQL Server 7. If SQL Server is installed and running, and you see its icon on your taskbar, simply right mouse-click on the SQL Server icon. The popup should tell you which version of SQL Server is running. If it says 7.0.623, you're running the first release version of SQL Server 7. If you're using an end-user product or DBA utility that can send Transact-SQL (usually called simply T-SQL, SQL Server's version of SQL), execute the statement SELECT @@Version. (If you've installed SP1, it should say 7.0.699. To find out the bugs addressed in SP1, read Microsoft's Knowledge Base artlcle Q225019. To find out how to obtain SP1, read Q232570 available at http://support.microsoft.com/support/kb/articles/q232/5/70.asp.)

We're not going to talk formally about the migration process in this chapter simply because Microsoft has invested lots of time and money in creating top-notch migration wizards. You'll also find a lot of online help in SQL Server's *Books Online* topic, *Upgrading from an Earlier Version of SQL Server* that provides additional documentation if you need it.

Our assumption is that most of you are installing SQL Server for the first time, so we're going to focus on you. This isn't a networking book, so we assume that you already have your network up and running and that you understand the basics of Windows NT domains, security, accounts, and logins. (In Windows NT security, a domain is a collection of computers grouped for viewing and administrative purposes that share a common security database.)

Plan Ahead

The Boy Scouts sure got that one right. Take it from us—no matter how tempting it is, don't just pop your SQL Server CD into the drive and start installing the software. This is one product that deserves a little up-front planning. Refer to Table 2.1 for a summary of important considerations to think about before installing SQL Server.

First of all, make sure you've got enough horsepower for a minimum install. What you will eventually need to support your SQL Server applications is a lot harder to predict. That will depend on how big you expect your database(s) to be, what they'll be used for (online transaction processing or decision support), the maximum number of concurrent users, and so on. Some hardware vendors, including Dell, Compaq, and Hewlett-Packard, offer capacity planning and configuration help for SQL Server customers considering their hardware. In other words, you can get by installing SQL Server 7 on a 133 MHz Pentium class system that runs Windows 95, but don't expect to run your firm's main mission-critical application on this platform—or even most of the projects in this book. *For most of the projects, we assume that you'll have at least one Standard SQL Server that runs under Windows NT 4.0 Server or higher.*

Hardware

Yes, yes, we know that Microsoft is touting SQL Server as scalable, but, let's face it, any time you have to move software from one server to another, or add new storage, it's disruptive. If you can afford to buy a system that has room for growth—more CPUs, more disk storage, more RAM, do it now and install SQL Server on that system. Anyone who plans to use SQL Server for heavy-duty applications should consider investing in a multi-processor system with a fault-tolerant RAID-5 disk configuration.

WHAT'S WHERE

\Mssql is the default path, which you are free to change during installation. However, you should *not* delete or rename the \Binn or \Html directories or their contents.

SQL Server Security Basics

Basically, there are two parts to SQL Server security: authentication and user permission validation. *Authentication* occurs when users try to log into SQL Server, and *permission validation* occurs when they try to access or create database objects—add or retrieve data.

Before you install SQL Server, you need to decide if you're going to use Windows NT authentication mode or SQL Server authentication mode. If you're installing SQL Server on a Win9x platform, the choice is made for you—you have to use SQL Server authentication.

The advantages of NT authentication are that you can count on NT not only to provide secure validation, but also, optionally, for password encryption and/or expiration, account lockout after a fixed number of invalid attempts, and so on. You can set up auditing and even assign permissions on SQL Server objects to NT groups.

The other main advantage is that if you use NT authentication, users won't have to log into SQL Server separately. It's important to realize that regardless of the security mode you use, any user that accesses SQL Server must have an account (the SQL Server login) with SQL Server. In Windows NT authentication, the NT user account is the SQL Server login, but in SQL Server authentication, specific SQL Server logins must be created. *Guest* is a special login available to users who have access to SQL Server, but don't have explicit permissions to access databases. The Guest account can be deleted from all databases except the master and tempdb databases, for which it must exist.

The *sa* (for system administrator) is another special login that exists mainly for backward compatibility with all earlier versions of SQL Server. When you install SQL Server, you will always get a sa login—with no password—whether you want it or not. The sa is mapped to the all-powerful sysadmin fixed server role (see next paragraphs) and can't be changed or deleted, but you sure can—*and should*—set up a password for it because the sa login can do *anything* at the get

If you don't have an NT system yet, make sure you purchase one that's certified by Microsoft. Microsoft maintains a list of certified hardware at www.microsoft.com/ntserver/info/hwcompatibility.htm. Microsoft has a separate list for hardware that is certified for participation in clustering on Windows NT 4.0 Enterprise Server, a practice we expect to continue for Windows 2000 Advanced and Datacenter high-end servers.

BIGGER IS BETTER

Today you need 65MB minimum of disk space to install SQL Server. In 1992, Microsoft SQL Server 4.2 for OS/2 shipped on two 5.25-inch high-density floppies.

RAID (redundant array of independent disks) refers to disk systems that consist of multiple disk drives (an array) to provide higher performance, reliability, storage capacity, and

go. If you don't establish a password to replace the "empty" password, anyone who's ever used SQL Server may try to gain unauthorized access to your server by signing in as sa. The easiest way to manage logins is via the Enterprise Manager's Security folder (right-click on the Logins and then New Login or double-click on Logins to view and/or edit the current ones).

Just setting things up so users can log into a SQL Server doesn't mean they'll magically have access to the databases they need. You also have to take care of the permissions part, explicitly assigning users permissions to the database or databases you want them to be able to access. Each database maintains user accounts mapped to user logins. The easiest way to handle permissions is to take advantage of SQL Server built-in roles.

All users are automatically part of a database's Public role, so one common approach is to assign baseline permissions to Public that you want *all* users to have for each database. (Some DBAs prefer to revoke all permissions from Public and create their own user-defined "ourpublic" group.) In addition, all SQL Server databases automatically have so-called database-specific *database roles* and server-wide *fixed server roles*. You can also create additional user-defined, database-specific roles if you need to. Any user can be in more than one role, and, under NT authentication, you can assign entire NT groups to SQL Server roles if you so desire. The Microsoft SQL Server Introduction manual that ships with SQL Server provides a brief overview that starts on page 257, and, once you've read that, the *Books Online, Managing Security* topic is a good place to find out more about this admittedly complex topic.

There are three kinds of permissions in SQL Server:

1. ***Object permissions* control access to database objects such as tables and views.**
2. ***Statement permissions* specify which SQL statements such as SELECT and INSERT, a user can perform.**
3. ***Inherited or implied permissions* are automatically bestowed by virtue of membership in a role or to database object owners.**

lower cost. So-called *fault-tolerant arrays* (RAID 0 is not fault tolerant) arrays are categorized in RAID levels, 1 through 5 and 10. Each level uses a different algorithm to implement fault tolerance, with RAID levels 0, 1, and 5 being the most commonly used levels for SQL Server. RAID isn't a part of Microsoft SQL Server per se, but its implementation can directly affect SQL Server's performance. A hardware disk array almost always improves I/O performance.

At press time, you could download SQL7IOSTRESS.EXE, an I/O stress utility written by the SQL Server team, from http://support.microsoft.com/support/downloads/LNP220.asp. If it's not there when you try to get it, search Microsoft's MSDN site for sql70iostress.exe. Raid 0, which isn't "true" RAID since it isn't fault tolerant, requires a minimum of two drives to implement. RAID 0 has a very simple design—it implements a striped disk array where the data is broken down into blocks and each block is written to a separate disk drive. The advantage is that I/O perfomance is greatly improved because you're spreading the I/O load across many channels and drives. Best perfomance is achieved when data is striped across multiple controllers with only one drive per controller, but the downside of RAID 0 is that if one disk fails, all of the data on the strip set becomes inaccessible. One installation technique for RDBMSs is to configure the database on a RAID 0 drive and then place the transaction log on a mirrored drive (RAID1). This way you get the best disk I/O perfomance for database, but maintain data recoverability (assuming you perform regular database backups) through a mirrored transaction log.

RAID 5 improves read performance, but not write performance (parity) because I/O functions, such as striping and mirroring, are handled efficiently in firmware. Conversely, an operating system-based RAID offers lower cost but consumes processor cycles. When cost is a consideration and redundancy and high performance are required, Microsoft Windows NT stripe sets with parity are a good solution.

If data *must* be quickly recoverable, consider mirroring the transaction log and placing the database on a RAID 5 disk subsystem. RAID 5 provides redundancy for all of the data on the array, allowing a single disk to fail and be replaced in most cases without system downtime. RAID 5 offers lower write perfomance than RAID 0 or RAID 1 but higher reliability and faster recovery.

New generations of RAID are constantly being defined. RAID 10, for example, which requires a minimum of four drives to implement, is implemented as a striped array whose segments are RAID 1 arrays. In other words, RAID 10 has the same fault tolerance as RAID level 1, but also the same overhead for fault tolerance as mirroring alone. High I/O rates are achieved by striping RAID 1 segments, and RAID 10 is an excellent solution for sites who would have otherwise gone with RAID 1, but need some additional perfomance boost and are willing to pay for it. Depending on your controller, you may want to set stripe size at 16K or 64K. You can read more about hardware RAID at www.acnc.com/raid.html.

Hardware vendors such as Compaq and Dell have information on their Web sites that can help you with capacity-planning decisions. At press time, the URLs were www.compaq.com/activeanswers/about/lobby.html and www.dell.com/sql, but they may have moved. You can search for *capacity planning* or *Microsoft SQL Server* to find the relevant Web pages on their sites. Microsoft also provides some software that may help: SQLIO.EXE which continually reads and writes data in 8K pages to stress a hard disk's I/O capabilities for SQL Server 7 (which uses 8K pages) and SQLHDTST.EXE, a hard disk stress test utility originally written for SQL Server 6.5 and the updated version for SQL Server 7, the SQL70IOSTRESS.EXE utility mentioned above.

SYSTEM DRIVE

If your system drive (where the main Windows files are) is almost full, you may not be able to install SQL Server. Even if you choose to install SQL Server on a non-system drive or partition, you will need about 50MB free during the installation process.

JUKEBOX SUPPORT?

Because SQL Server can only access disks, the first thing you have to do is make the jukebox look just like a disk or set of disks, complete with drive letters. There are a variety of third-party products that let you do this. However, SQL Server simply wasn't designed to work well with jukeboxes that use a time-consuming technique of caching files to a real disk. Therefore, a smart alternative is to invest in a large RAID unit, create database(s) on it, and mark them read-only within SQL Server.

File Systems

You probably know that Windows supports several file systems, notably FAT-16, FAT-32, NTFS, and even an old version of the OS/2 file system. What you may not know is that server performance *in general* isn't affected by the file system used (FAT or NTFS), although most high-end SQL Server systems use NTFS. Basically, however, your choice of file system should be determined by factors other than performance—such as whether or not you need dual boot support. The File Allocation Table (FAT) file system allows dual booting with computers that run MS-DOS or Win9x, while the Windows NT file system (NTFS) has security and recovery advantages. If you don't need to dual boot Windows NT with MS-DOS or Win9x, NTFS is recommended.

NTFS

When running on Windows NT, SQL Server performance *can* be improved further if the databases are created on disks formatted with NTFS and, specifically, 64-KB extent sizes. For more information about formatting an NTFS disk, see your Windows NT documentation.

Aside from the potential performance improvements, there are several other compelling reasons to consider NTFS as your server file system. One is ease of upward migration to Windows 2000 which offers features like better encryption and disk-space quotas on a per-user basis. The more immediate payoff, however, is in the area of security. NTFS lets you set permissions for individual files and folders.

Software

Make sure you're willing to have IE 4.01 installed on the system where SQL Server will be installed. You'll need it to run SQL Enterprise Manager (the main management console that DBAs use to administer the server, its databases, and its users) and access the incredibly useful *Books Online*.

Understand that part of the installation routine installs the Microsoft Data Access Components (MDAC) and the latest (as of early 1999) version of ODBC. Whenever you install older versions of data access drivers with newer ones you can occasionally encounter unexpected side effects. For example, old applications may no longer run properly, so document any pre-installation ODBC-dependent applications that run on the server where you install SQL Server.

Make sure you know the requirements and limitations for the version of SQL Server you plan to install (see Table 2.1).

Table 2.1 SQL Server 7 Version Comparison

EDITIONS	DESKTOP	STANDARD	ENTERPRISE
Can be installed on	Windows 95, Windows 98, Windows NT 4.0 Workstation, Windows 2000 Professional	Windows NT 4.0 Server or Higher	Windows NT 4.0 Extended Edition (supports clustering) or Windows 2000 Datacenter
Requires Internet Explorer 4.01	Yes	Yes	Yes
Requires Windows NT 4.0 SP4	Not on Win9x systems	Yes	Yes, Windows NT 4.0 Enterprise Edition SP4
Provides extended (>2GB) memory support	No	No	Yes
Can provide failover support to a clustered server	No	No	Yes
Provides replication support	Full merge replication but only subscriber support for transaction replication.	Full	Full
Maximum CPUs	2	4	32
Database size limit	4GB per database	No limit	No limit

Table 2.1 *(Continued)*

EDITIONS	DESKTOP	STANDARD	ENTERPRISE
Can support multiple users	Yes, but not recommended for more than five users	Yes	Yes
Can run OLAP Services	No	Yes	Yes, including user-defined cube partitions
Can run Microsoft Search Service (MSSearch, SQL Server's full-text search)	No	Yes	Yes
Keeps a SQL Server Event Log	Not on Win9x platforms	Yes	Yes
Can run the SQL Server Performance Monitor (PerfMon)	Not on Win9x platforms	Yes	Yes
Can run the Version Upgrade Utility (to migrate SQL 6.x versions)	Not on Win9x platforms	Yes	Yes

WINDOWS 98

Windows 98 (unlike Windows 95) by default does not install Client for Microsoft Networks, which SQL Server needs. Before trying to install SQL Server 7 on a Windows 98 system, be sure you've installed the Client for Microsoft Networks. If you don't, you may see an error message about "Assertion failed" near what should be the end of the installation process, when setup actually tries to start SQL Server. You can install the Client for Microsoft Networks by selecting the Networking icon in the control panel and installing Client for Microsoft Networks. Reboot before you try to install (or re-install) SQL Server 7.

CONNECTIONS ≠ USERS

Connections aren't the same as users. Even if you have a license for 10 connections, you may not be able to have 10 users concurrently connected to SQL Server because some applications use more than one connection.

In addition to the limitations listed in Table 2.1, Win9x systems also lack support for the following capabilities: incoming Named Pipe connections, asynchronous I/O, transaction-based publishing, clustering, full-text search, and auto-detection of Unicode files.

Microsoft SQL Server Newsgroups

You can participate in any of several SQL Server Internet newsgroups by accessing Microsoft's public News server:

- **Clients (microsoft.public.sqlserver.clients)**
- **Connections (microsoft.public.sqlserver.connect)**
- **ODBC (microsoft.public.sqlserver.odbc)**
- **Programming (microsoft.public.sqlserver.programming)**
- **Replication (microsoft.public.sqlserver.replication)**
- **Server Engine (microsoft.public.sqlserver.server)**
- **Setup (microsoft.public.sqlserver.setup)**
- **Data Warehousing (microsoft.public.sqlserver.dwh)**
- **English Query (microsoft.public.sqlserver.eq)**
- **OLAP (microsoft.public.sqlserver.olap)**

If you use the newsgroups, you're sure to notice how certain individuals seem to contribute more than others. They provide helpful answers or suggestions, and you start to think of them as "gurus". Well, Microsoft rewards those kinds of people with MVP (most valued professional) status. As of early 1999, these were elite SQL Server MVPs, along with a brief biographical sketch. We don't list the MVPs to encourage you to contact these busy folks with your questions, but rather because when you see messages from them, they're generally worth reading. And we think just knowing the "big names" in the SQL user community gives you a sense of belonging to the growing community of SQL "Server-ites."

WTS SUPPORT: SP1 REQUIRED

Microsoft didn't support SQL Server 7 running on Windows NT Terminal Server (WTS), but included it in SQL Server's SP1 (service pack 1) release, so be sure to download it—and read its readme.txt and fixlist.htm files—before installing it.

Pre-Setup Checklist

In addition to thinking about the system that you plan to install SQL Server on, and making sure that you understand the implications of your version selection, there are also some other things that you should do before setup.

First of all, if you plan to install SQL Server 7 on to a system that already has SQL Server 6.x running on it, make sure you back up your entire SQL Server 6.x installation. That means the server as well as the individual databases. Then read the *Version*

- **Kalen Delaney (www.sqlserverinsider.com) is an independent SQL Server trainer and consultant based in the Seattle area and co-author of *Inside Microsoft SQL Server 7.0* (Microsoft Press, 1999).**
- **Trevor Dwyer is the Chief Database Consultant for The Group-Computacenter (UK) Ltd.**
- **Roy Harvey is a DBA for a well-known New England-based consumer products company.**
- **Gianluca Hotz, from Milan, Italy, is an independent consultant on Microsoft Technologies specializing in SQL Server.**
- **Tibor Karaszi is based in Stockholm and works as a SQL Server instructor and consultant for Cornerstone.**
- **Bruce margolin is another active MVP.**
- **Brian Moran is director of the Washington, D.C. area CIBER Solutions' SQL Quick Strike Team and a SQL columnist both for *Windows NT Magazine* and *SQL Server Magazine*.**
- **Bob Pfeiff is the Chief Technology Officer for Washington DC-based CrossTier.com.**
- **Neil Pike is an independent consultant on NT, SQL, and networking based in the UK. He maintains an excellent SQL FAQ at several sites including www.ntfaq.com.**
- **Steve Robinson is a consultant based in London.**
- **Tony Rogerson is an independent SQL Server troubleshooter and consultant based in London.**
- **Ron Talmage is an independent database consultant with Prospice, LLC, and author of *Microsoft SQL Server 7.0 Administrator's Guide* (Prima Publishing). He writes a monthly column for *SQL Server Professional,* serves as the *PASS* newsletter editor, and is the current president of the Pacific Northwest SQL Server Users Group.**

Upgrade information in *Books Online* and decide whether you're going to do a pipeline or tape upgrade. You might start with *Books Online, What to Read* topic that has links to an upgrading checklist and a section that describes how the Migration wizard works.

UPGRADE ADVICE

When upgrading an existing SQL Server version 6.x installation to SQL Server 7, choose the default Unicode collation. The master database in SQL Server 7 contains Unicode columns that were non-Unicode in the 6.x installation. If a non-default Unicode collation is chosen that sorts data differently than it was sorted in the 6.x installation, uniqueness constraints may be violated and conversion of SQL Server 6.x user objects to SQL Server 7 may fail. By the way, Unicode character/text data (which takes twice as much disk space to store as non-Unicode data) is stored using the nchar, nvarchar, and ntext data types in SQL Server.

INTEGRATED SECURITY

When installing SQL Server 7 on a computer with SQL Server 6.x already installed, make sure your SQL Server 6.5 is configured for integrated security. During the SQL Server 7 installation, SQL Server setup backs up the SQL Server 6.x Registry keys. If an error occurs later in the setup process, the Setup program tries to restore the SQL Server 6.x Registry keys. If you have revoked integrated security permissions in SQL Server 6.x, the setup program encounters another error trying to restore the SQL Server 6.x Registry keys and this can corrupt the Registry keys.

If you're installing on an NT system, make sure you do the following:

- Use a login that has NT administrator rights.
- Shut down all services that are related to SQL Server. This includes any programs that use ODBC, such as Microsoft Internet Information Services (IIS).
- Shut down Microsoft Windows NT Event Viewer and Regedt32.exe if they're running.
- Create a domain user account to assign to the MSSQLServer, SQLServerAgent, and MSDTC (Microsoft Distributed Transaction Coordinator) services if you're installing SQL Server on Windows NT and plan to perform any server-to-server activities. Win9x doesn't support Windows NT services; it only simulates them, so you don't have to worry about setting up user accounts when you're installing on Win9x.
- Assign a login account for each of the SQL Server services you plan to run. You can use a single login account for all of the services or specify different accounts for each user. The default account is the domain user account currently logged into the computer.

BE A SMART *BOOKS ONLINE* USER

SQL pros understand the idea of a nested SELECT—a SELECT within a SELECT. Well, you can harness the same idea to make efficient use of *Books Online*. Let's assume you've chosen the Search tab and entered "Unicode" as your search term. *Books Online* returns an overwhelming 207 hits. Check the Search Previous Results box at the bottom of the screen and enter a new search term such as "upgrade." The resulting 18 items will represent a search of the results from the previous search.

We liken *Books Online* to a multi-part WHERE clause—SELECT topics FROM BOL WHERE topictext LIKE ('xxx') and topictext LIKE ('yyy').

More on Assigning NT Accounts to SQL Server Services

Three types of accounts can be assigned to SQL Server services:

1. Local system. Microsoft Search service (MSSearch) SQL Server's "full-text" search engine, is always assigned the local system account. But remember the full-text search engine isn't installed by default during a normal SQL Server installation.

2. Local user. The local user account is associated with the local system and has no network access rights. This is useful for standalone installations and for some development environments.
3. Domain user. Both the local system and the local user accounts don't have network access rights so using a local account effectively restricts SQL Server from interacting with other servers. You need a domain user account to run remote procedure calls (RPCs), manage or execute replication, back up databases to network drives, and use the SQL Server Agent mail features with Microsoft Exchange. All domain user accounts must have permission to:

   - Access and change the SQL Server directory (\MSSQL7).
   - Access and change the MDF, NDF, and LDF database files.
   - Log in as a service.
   - Read and write registry keys at and under:
     * HKEY_LOCAL_MACHINE\Software\Microsoft\MSSQLServer
     * HKEY_LOCAL_MACHINE\System\CurrentControlset\Services\MSSQLServer
     *HKEY_LOCAL_MACHINE\Software\Microsoft\Windows NT\CurrentVersion\Perflib

Normally, you'll want to use a domain user account that is a member of the Administrators local group. Once you've installed SQL Server, you can change the user account assigned to any of the SQL Server services by using the Services application in Control Panel, and you can also change the MSSQLServer and SQLServerAgent services through SQL Server Enterprise Manager. Each service must be changed individually and the new user account doesn't take effect until the next time each service is (re)started.

DBCC (DATABASE CONSISTENCY CHECKER)

If you're migrating a SQL Server 6.x database into SQL Server 7, not only should you make sure you have a good backup before doing it, you should also plan to run the database consistency checker (DBCC) utility on your database(s) before upgrading. Depending on the extent of any logical inconsistencies that exist in the database, the upgrade process may not complete successfully. In a situation where there may not be sufficient time in a maintenance window to complete the upgrade and DBCC checks, consider running the DBCC checks on a backup or secondary server and using dumps of the databases to be upgraded. If you're not sure what DBCC is, read *Books Online* and search for DBCC. The *DBCC (T-SQL)* and *DBCC Help (T-SQL)* topics are particularly useful.

Although veteran DBAs tend to rely heavily on DBCC today, Microsoft's SQL Server development team has said that DBCC may go away in future versions of SQL Server as Microsoft automates more management functions.

Character Sets, Sort Order, and Unicode

A *character set*, also known as a code page, is a group of letters, digits, and symbols that make up the possible values for SQL Server's character-based data types char, varchar, and text. Each character set contains 256 values.

A sort order is a set of rules that determines how SQL Server collates and presents data in response to database queries. At various points in a query, SQL Server compares characters to see if they are equal. A *sort order* determines what characters are considered equal when compared. A case-insensitive sort order, for instance, considers an uppercase letter to be the same as its lower-case equivalent such as SELECT * FROM customers = SELECT * FROM CUSTOMERS. A case-sensitive sort order considers "C" different from "c". Another example is *accent sensitivity*—whether characters with accents are considered the same as their unaccented counterparts.

***Unicode* defines a set of letters, numbers, and symbols that SQL Server recognizes in the nchar, nvarchar, and ntext data types. It is related to but separate from character sets. Unicode has more than 65,000 possible values compared to 256 with a character set, and takes twice as much space to store each value. Unicode includes characters for most languages. A *Unicode collation* acts as a sort order for Unicode data. It is a set of rules that determines how SQL Server compares, collates, and presents Unicode data.**

If you aren't sure, or make some mistakes during installation, SQL Server's Create SQL Server Login wizard may be able to help you out of your fix. However, it can't make changes in character sets, sort orders, or Unicode collation orders. Changes in those orders require a complete reinstallation of SQL Server from scratch.

The Create SQL Server Login wizard allows you to do the following:

- Choose the authentication mode used to connect to SQL Server (Windows NT Authentication Mode or Mixed Mode) and add a Microsoft Windows NT or SQL Server login.
- Add a Windows NT or SQL Server user to a fixed server role. (*Roles* are a grouping of SQL Server, Windows NT users, or Windows NT roles with the same permissions. Roles allow you to apply or deny permissions to a group of users by only making a change to the role itself. Roles are owned and administered by SQL Server and can be nested. They can be assigned to Windows NT users, Windows NT groups, SQL Server users, or SQL Server roles.)
- Add a Windows NT or SQL Server user to one or more databases, thereby granting the user access to those databases.
- Grant SQL Server login access to a user.

Ready?

GET STANDARD

Remember that the decisions you make about character set, sort order, and Unicode collation are basically cast in concrete. If you need to change any of these later, you must rebuild the databases and reload the data. We recommend that you develop a standard within your organization for these options. Many server-to-server activities may fail if the character set, sort order, and Unicode collation are not consistent across all of the servers. SQL Server 2000 promises to both simplify character set/ sort order/collation troika into a single Windows 2000 collation, and to allow SQL Server to be far more flexible.

Autorun Installation

Once you've got your proverbial ducks in a line and are ready to install SQL Server, you'll be surprised by how easy it is to complete the installation process. Figure 2.1 provides an overview of the installation process.

Now you can insert your SQL Server 7 CD. If autorun doesn't kick in, browse the CD and double-click the AUTORUN.EXE file. You should see a menu like that shown in Figure 2.2 with options to read the release notes, browse *Books Online*, connect to the Microsoft SQL Server Web site, or install the product and prerequisites. Prerequisites for the appropriate platform should be installed prior to installing SQL Server 7.

At this point, double check to make sure that you've closed all applications that don't absolutely have to be running—especially any that use ODBC.

The Prerequisites

So what are the prerequisites?

Windows 98 and Windows 2000. There aren't any prerequisites for Windows 98 (aside from ensuring that Microsoft Client for Networking is installed, as we mentioned earlier) or for Windows 2000.

Windows 95. For Windows 95, you'll probably want to make sure that Internet Explorer 4.01 SP1 (service pack 1) is installed. All that you need is on the CD. Strictly speaking you don't have to install IE 4.01 if you only want to use SQL Server 7 without management tools or to perform a so-called "minimum" install—more about this in a minute. If you don't opt to install IE 4.01 SP1, you must install the updated DCOM 95 (also on your CD).

Windows NT Workstation, Server, or Enterprise Edition. You must apply NT's SP4. As with Windows 95 systems, you must also install IE 4.01 SP1 unless you only want to do a minimum install and don't plan to use the Enterprise Manager, other management tools, or *Books Online*.

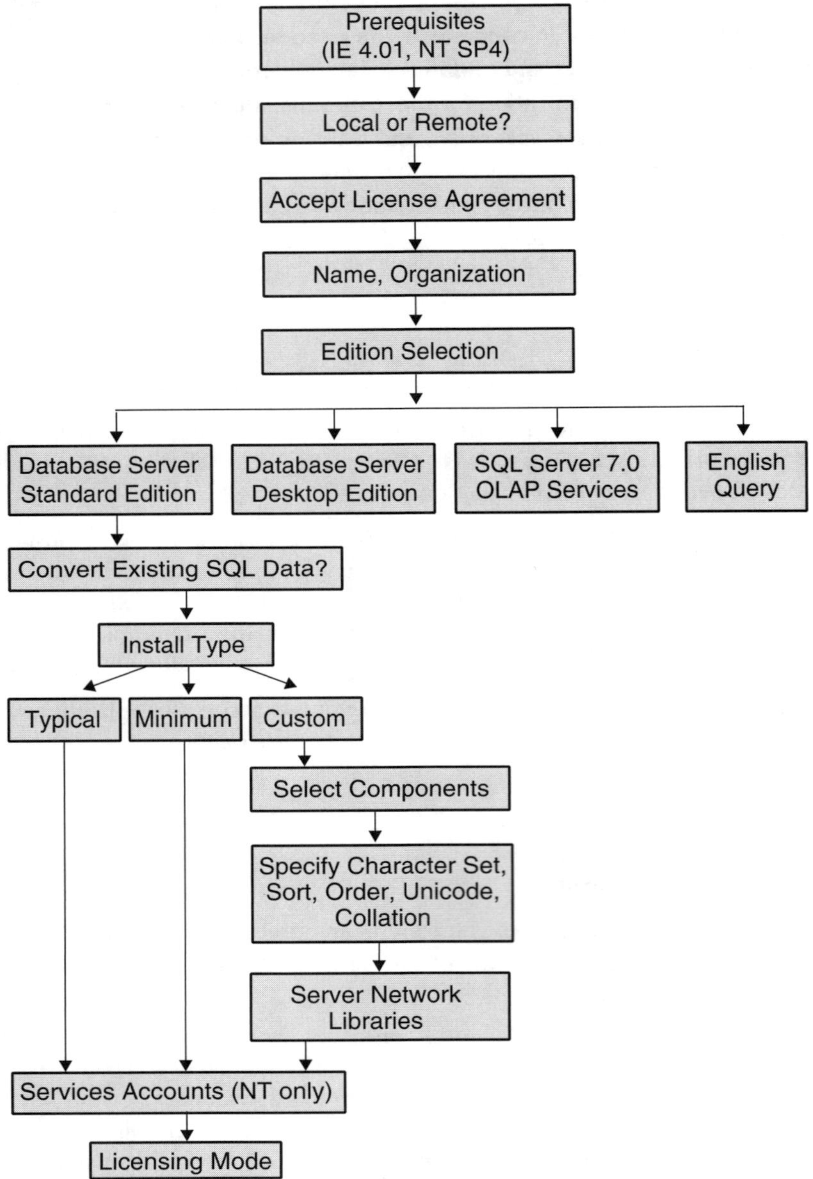

Figure 2.1 An overview of the initial installation process for SQL Server 7.

After all of the prerequisites are installed, you're ready to continue with the SQL Server 7 installation. As you can see from Figure 2.2, however, you're free to refer to *Books Online* or log onto the Microsoft SQL Server Web site for last-minute information.

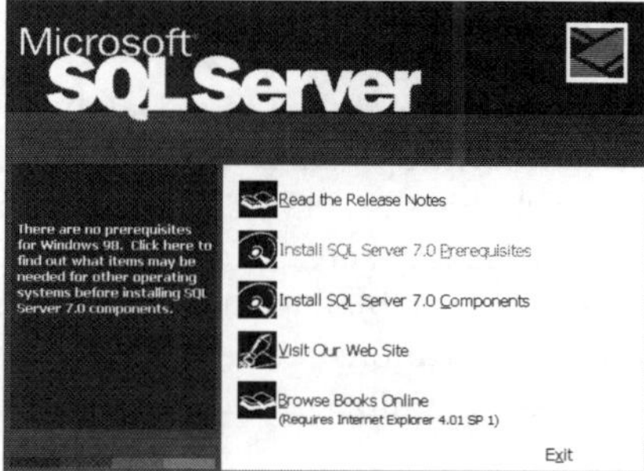

Figure 2.2 This should be the first screen you see when you start to install SQL Server 7 from the CD-ROM.

Assuming that you're ready to go, simply click on the Install SQL Server Components button (see Figure 2.3), and then click on the type of installation that you want to do—Local or Remote as appropriate. It's usually Local, which is for installing onto the PC that you're logged onto.

REMOTE SETUP

Remote Setup **is supported on Windows NT-to-Windows NT computers only and both computers must be of the same processor type. Remote Setup is not supported on a clustered Windows NT Server, so you can't use it to install Enterprise Edition. Remote Setup can only be used for a new installation. Remote Setup will only install the same version of SQL Server 7 on the remote computer as the one that is run on the source computer. For example, if you're running the SQL Server 7 Standard Edition on a Windows NT Server computer and attempt to remotely install SQL Server 7 Standard version to a Windows NT Workstation computer, the setup will fail. This is because Windows NT Workstation only supports the client installation for the SQL Server 7 Standard Edition or installation of the Desktop version of SQL Server 7. Use the same version of SQL Server on the local computer as the one you plan to install on the remote computers.**

Figure 2.3 This is where you tell Setup what you want to install.

Installation Options

After the SQL Server 7 Setup begins, it will check to see if the Open Database Connectivity (ODBC) files are available for updating. If any application or service is using the ODBC drivers, a dialog box is presented that shows the services or applications that must be stopped before Setup continues. If you see that screen, use the Windows Task Manager (Ctrl-Alt-Del is one way to invoke the Task Manager) to figure out what's running and to close the potentially offending applications. Once you do that, you can click on the Retry option to see if the ODBC files are unlocked.

READ-ONLY ODBC FILES

If your site has ODBC files with a read-only attribute, you'll have to change that using the ATTRIB command, attrib -r c:\windows\system\odbc*.* and/or attrib -r c:\windows\system\sqlsrv*.* or a file utility, such as the properties tab that can be accessed with a right-click in Windows Explorer. On computers that run Microsoft Windows NT, the ODBC files should be located in the \System32 directory. On computers that run Win 9x, they'll be in the system directory.

You'll be asked to read and agree to the license agreement, and then to provide your name and company name. The next big decision will be familiar to regular Microsoft software users. You will be asked to select one of three setup installation options: typical, minimum, or custom. A *typical* setup installs the main SQL Server binary (program) files to the MSSQL7 directory. A typical install (see Figure 2.4) requires 80–83MB for the program files, an additional 61–67MB on your (Windows) system drive, and about 31MB on your data drive, which can be a separate drive.

DON'T EVEN BOTHER TO TRY

Neither SQL Server data nor log files can be installed on a file system that uses compression.

Knowledge Base Articles

Not sure what the Knowledge Base "Q" articles are? Don't be shy! They're a veritable treasure trove of short articles categorized as information, bugs, fixes, and how to's. Online, you can access them at support.microsoft.com/support. The default two-part form expects you to select a product to narrow your search, but "all products" is also an option—and type in a question or keyword or request. If you select the advanced screen, you'll have more options, but the basic screen is fine for returning specific "Q" articles, for example. Typing Q220960 returns a link to the Knowledge Base article *INF: How to Include Other MMCs in SQL Enterprise Manager MMC.*

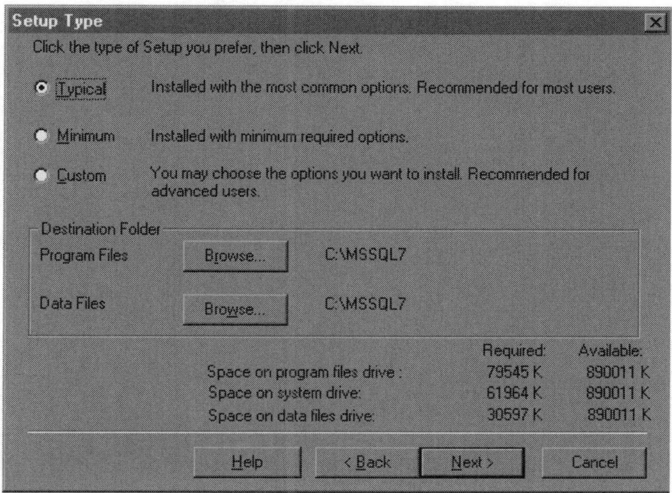

Figure 2.4 A typical install on a Windows 95 system requires about 170MB hard disk space.

Here's what you get when you choose the typical install:

- Named Pipes, TCP/IP, and Multi-Protocol network libraries
- ISO Character Set (1252)
- Dictionary order, case-insensitive sort order
- SQL Server *Books Online*, installs to the \mssql7 directory (which you can override using the Browse button)

If you don't want these default settings or the bare bones minimum install, you should opt for the *Custom* installation option.

If SQL Server Setup detects that SQL Server 6.x is installed on the computer, you'll be asked whether or not you want to convert existing SQL Server data. If you explicitly select the Yes, run SQL Server 7 Upgrade wizard that occurs at the end of the normal setup program. You don't have to make that decision right away. You can always run the Version Upgrade wizard later (from an NT system) by selecting Microsoft SQL Server then the Switch menu from the SQL Server 7 program group (see Figure 2.5).

The *minimum* install only requires about 16MB for program files, 38MB on your system drive, and about 21MB for data files. These are the items that will *not* be installed with a minimum install:

SQL Server Enterprise Manager. SQL Server Enterprise Manager is the main management console interface to the database, complete with wizards. Enterprise Manager is a graphical application that allows for easy, enterprise-wide configuration and management of SQL Server and SQL Server objects. You can use Enterprise Manager to manage logins, permissions, and users, create scripts, manage devices and databases,

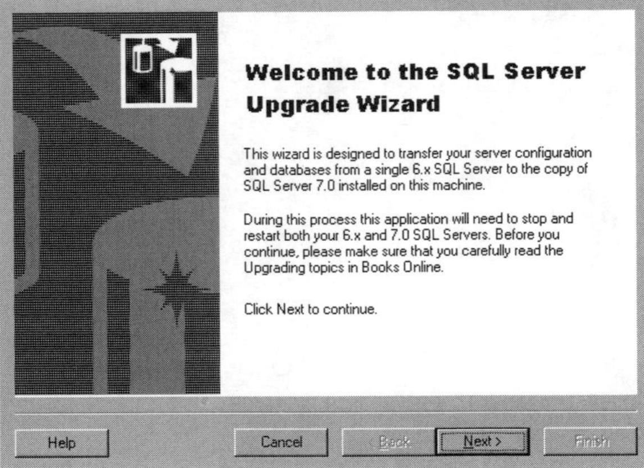

Figure 2.5 Once you've installed SQL Server, you can launch the Version Upgrade wizard at any time (from an NT system) by selecting the Microsoft SQL Server-Switch menu from the Programs menu.

back up databases and transaction logs, and manage tables, views, stored procedures, triggers, indexes, rules, defaults, and user-defined data types. You almost always will want this program and the associated standalone utilities (installed via the Client Utilities option) which include bcp, isql (command line utility for submitting SQL statements), osql (an alternate to isql that uses ODBC), ODBC, and DB-Library (SQL Server's original API).

SQL Server Profiler. A SQL Server tool that captures a continuous record of server activity in real-time. DBAs use SQL Server Profiler to monitor any number of server events and event categories, filter these events with user-specified criteria, and output a trace to the screen, a file, or another SQL Server. You'll probably want this tool in order to optimize performance once you've got your production system up and running.

SQL Server Query Analyzer. This is an extremely handy GUI (see Figure 2.6) that can be used to query the database and create and execute database objects like stored procedures and views. A stored procedure is a "precompiled" collection of T-SQL statements saved as an object within SQL Server and is processed as a single unit of statements sometimes called a job or a batch. SQL Server comes with several dozen system stored procedures that are already set up for performing routine chores and displaying information about databases and users, but you can also create your own. As the name implies, SQL Server Query Analyzer also provides capability for graphically analyzing queries.

Version Upgrade wizard. The Version Upgrade wizard helps to automate the migration of SQL Server 6.x data to 7. If you need to upgrade SQL Server 4.21 data, you must upgrade your database to SQL Server 6.5 first since you can only upgrade directly to SQL Server 7 from 6.x. Microsoft provides a copy of SQL Server 6.5 to 4.2x users that wish to upgrade to version 7. Wizards can be run at any time.

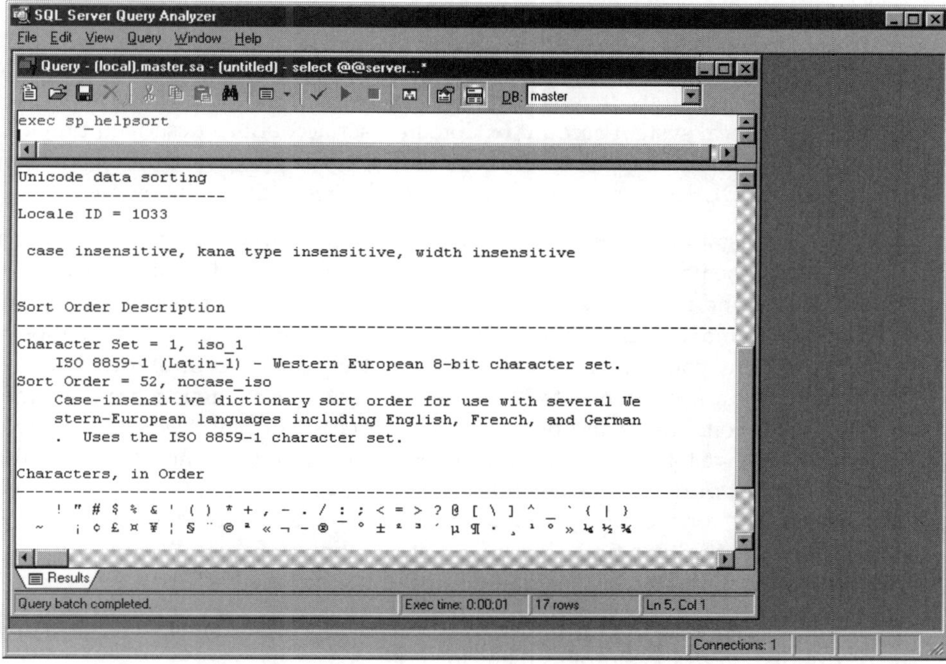

Figure 2.6 The Query Analyzer lets you submit queries and see the results. Here, we executed a system stored procedure to find out how the server was configured for sorting.

Client diagnostic utilities including *sqldiag* which gathers and stores information, along with the contents of the query history trace (if running), into \Mssql7\Log\Sqldiag.txt and Mssql7\Log\Sqldiag.trc. This output file includes error logs, output from sp_configure, and additional version information. If the query history trace was running when the utility was invoked, the trace file will contain the last 100 SQL events and exceptions. The sqldiag utility is intended to expedite and simplify information gathering by Microsoft Product Support Services (PSS, aka "tech support.")

SQL Server *Books Online*. This is Microsoft's gift to SQL Server DBAs and developers. It's the equivalent of an almost 12MB help file.

Replication objects. These are required if you want SQL Server to perform replication. *Replication* is duplication of table schema and data and usually involves two or more servers.

MS DTC Client Support. This is used to extend database transactions across multiple servers. The DTC refers to Microsoft *Distributed Transaction Coordinator* which—you guessed it—coordinates transactions across a network of systems that run Microsoft Windows.

Custom installation, as Microsoft veterans know, is extremely useful for experienced users who know exactly which components they do and do not want, but most of us use it when we want to reinstall or add selected features after the initial install.

Services Accounts and Licensing

The last major step—one that doesn't apply to Win9x installations—is the setup for the NT services accounts. If you choose the "same for each," you'll have to decide between using the local system account or domain user account as described previously. Normally, you'll use a domain user account. If you want to customize the assignments for the listed SQL Server services, you can do it either at this point or later.

If you're installing the Standard or Enterprise Editions of SQL Server, you'll also have to specify the licensing mode. There are basically two kinds of licenses for SQL Server: per server and per seat as shown in Figure 2.7. *Per server* refers to licensing SQL Server for a given maximum number of users at any time, irrespective of who those users are or how many you have. *Per seat* refers to licensing each user individually, assigning one CAL (client access license) to each user. Per server licensing is more economical if you have occasional users and not many SQL servers. Per seat licensing is more economical if you have lots of SQL servers and users that need to connect to each of them. Then you can just purchase one client license for each user's seat, no matter how many SQL servers they connect to. Figure 2.8 shows what the licensing screen looks like when you install SQL the first time. Figure 2.7 shows how you use Windows NT's licensing applet to adjust license information (usually by adding CALs).

To add CALs at a later time, you can use the License Manager in the Windows NT Administrative Tools program group.

That's it. The Setup program tells you it has enough information to continue and starts the file copy process. Next, Setup attempts to stop the MSSQL and the SQL Executive service if SQL Server 6.x is installed. The next step is to install the packages that are needed for additional support components. These components consist of: MDAC (Microsoft Data Access Components), MMC (Microsoft Management Console), MSDTC, HTML Help viewer, DLT Tape driver, and the (Monarch) full-text search engine. The selection of packages is based on the platform Setup is running on and the selections made by the user. Each package self-registers itself with the operating system and with SQL Server Setup. The appropriate entries for SQL Server, SQL Agent, and SQL Server-related components are also added.

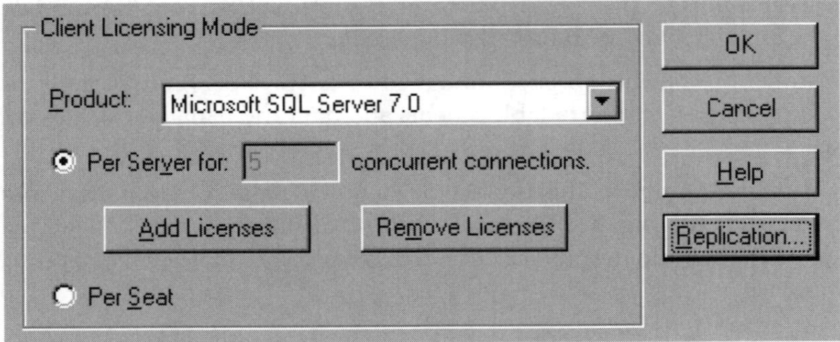

Figure 2.7 Setup of the Standard or Enterprise Editions of SQL Server 7 requires that you choose a licensing mode.

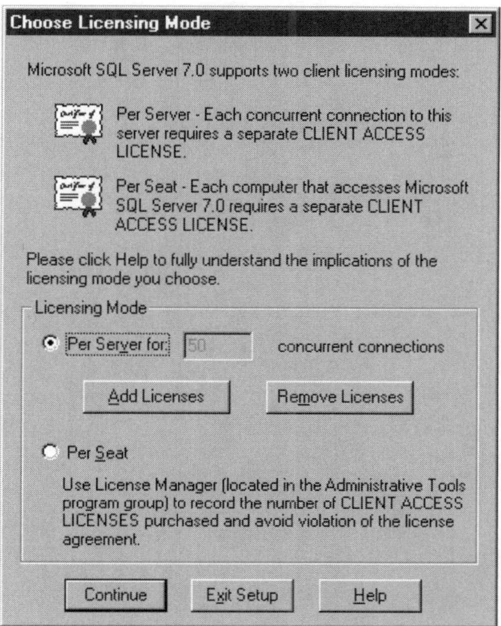

Figure 2.8 The licensing screen when you install SQL for the first time.

After the Registry values have been modified, the system path is updated to include the new Mssql7 entry and the SQL Server service is started. When the SQL Server service is running, Setup then runs CNFGSVR.EXE to set up the initial SQL Server configurations. Replication is installed, the program groups and icons are created, and a SETUP.ISS file in the Windows directory is updated. The following SETUP.ISS InstallShield text file is like a snapshot of what happened.

CONVERT THOSE OLD INI FILES

One of the most significant changes in moving to an InstallShield-based Setup has to do with unattended installations and un-installations. Unfortunately, conversion or support for existing INI files in the new Setup is not provided. For each existing INI file, you have to create a new ISS file yourself.

Example SETUP.ISS file

```
[InstallShield Silent]
Version=v5.00.000
File=Response File
[DlgOrder]
Dlg0=SetupMethod-0
Count=11
Dlg1=SdWelcome-0
Dlg2=SdLicense-0
```

```
Dlg3=SdRegisterUser-0
Dlg4=MessageBox-0
Dlg5=CDKEYDialog-0
Dlg6=SetupTypeSQL-0
Dlg7=DlgCpSortUnicode-0
Dlg8=DlgServerNetwork-0
Dlg9=DlgServices-0
Dlg10=SdStartCopy-0
[SetupMethod-0]
Component-type=string
Component-count=1
Component-0=Local
Result=1
[SdWelcome-0]
Result=1
[SdLicense-0]
Result=1
[SdRegisterUser-0]
szName=Bill Shadish
szCompany=Fundamental Objects, Inc.
Result=1
[MessageBox-0]
Result=1
[CDKEYDialog-0]
svCDKey=47346-111-1111111-26619
Result=1
[SetupTypeSQL-0]
szDir=C:\MSSQL7
Result=301
szDataDir=C:\MSSQL7
[DlgCpSortUnicode-0]
SortId=52
LCID=1033
CompStyle=196609
Result=45624544
[DlgServerNetwork-0]
NetworkLibs=4095
TCPPort=1433
TCPPrxy=Default
NMPPipeName=\\.\pipe\sql\query
Result=66268
[DlgServices-0]
Local-Domain=61680
AutoStart=61455
SQLDomain=FO
SQLDomainAcct=Administrator
SQLDomainPwd=0667b6f028feae
AgtDomain=FO
AgtDomainAcct=Administrator
AgtDomainPwd=0667b6f028feae
Result=1
```

```
[SdStartCopy-0]
Result=1
[License]
LicenseMode=PERSERVER
LicenseLimit=10
[Application]
Name=Microsoft SQL Server 7.0
Version=7.00.000
Company=Microsoft
```

Unattended Installation

If you want to do an *unattended installation*, you must first generate an InstallShield.ISS file. Start the SQL Server Setup program from the command line with the k=Rc switch and proceed through the dialog boxes to install SQL Server as normal. Doing this causes Setup to record your dialog box choices in a file named setup.iss, which is located in your Windows directory, but won't actually install SQL Server on the local computer. After this process is completed, you can move or copy the file to another location for use on other servers. To actually perform the unattended installation, you again start setup from the command line and reference the ISS file as follows: setupsql.exe -f1 <full path to iss file> -SMS –s.

If you don't specify the -SMS switch, the underlying InstallShield setup process, SQLSTP.EXE, starts a process to perform the Setup and will immediately return control back to the user. The -s switch causes Setup to run in a silent mode.

DON'T USE UNC WITH SETUP

When you run SQL Server's setup program, don't use a UNC (Universal Naming Convention) file path such as this:

\\Servername\Public\SS70\x86\Setup\Setupsql.exe. Instead, map a drive to the appropriate location and run the Setup program from the drive letter like this:

F:\SS70\x86\Setup\Setupsql.exe.

What if?

Let's face it, even when you plan ahead, even when you think you've got all of those ducks lined up, sometimes installations abort. Fortunately, there are log files that you can read to help you figure out where the problem lies. In addition to the SETUP .ISS file, several informational files are generated to help figure out why the problems occurred: Windows\Sqlstp.log, \Mssql7\Log\Errorlog, and \Mssql7\Install\Cnfgsvr.out. *Books Online* has a good section that describes how to decipher any SQLSTP.LOG file.

Another result of a successful installation is the generation of an uninstallation script file, called UNINST.ISU that is located in the directory that you installed the program files to. To start an unattended uninstallation, you must start the UnInstallShield executable file named ISUNINST.EXE, and direct it to your uninstallation script file. You might start with the *Books Online* topic, *Contents of the sqlstp.log file*.

INSTALLING MDAC/ODBC

To install (or re-install) the Microsoft Data Access Components (MDAC 2.1), try running mdac_201.exe off of the CD-ROM without any command line parameters, after first shutting down all non-essential applications and/or system services. Be patient—it can take a few minutes. To only install ODBC, run MDAC_TYP.EXE.

Uninstalling SQL Server

Sometimes you'll just want to uninstall the program. You have the following three options:

1. On the Start menu, point to Programs, and then point to Microsoft SQL Server 7 and click Uninstall SQL Server 7.
2. On the Start menu, point to Settings and click Control Panel. Double-click Add/Remove Programs. Select Microsoft SQL Server 7 from the list and then click Add/Remove.
3. Run a scripted uninstallation if you can. One of the results of a successful installation is the generation of an uninstallation script file called uninst.isu that is located in the directory you installed the program files to. Remember, to start an unattended uninstallation, you must start the UnInstallShield executable file named isuninst.exe, and direct it to your uninstallation script file.

We don't know about you, but we want positive proof that an installation has succeeded. Although you *can* simply continue to install other components such as OLAP Services and the English Query natural language development enviroment, we'd like to make sure that the basic SQL Server installation worked.

Proof Positive

If you exit the SQL Server installation routine at this point, SQL Server should be running. It may not be if you changed the default option to have SQL Server autostart.

You may also see a SQL Server Services Manager icon (a gray server with a green arrow) on your Taskbar that indicates that SQL Server is running. Hover your mouse over the icon to confirm that your server is running. (In case you're wondering about the server's name, the setup program under NT automatically gives SQL Server the same name as the server computer.) Right mouse click on the Server icon to see the Services Manager menu that contains options for pausing or stopping the server (see Figure 2.9). Why the "Pause" option? Occasionally DBAs want to pause the server just prior to a shutdown in order to warn users that the server will be shut down and to prevent additional users from logging on.

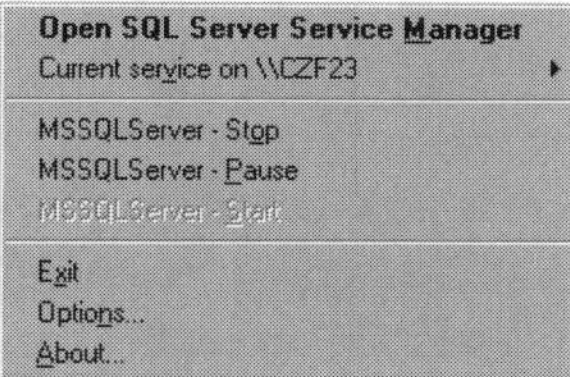

Figure 2.9 The SQL Server Services Manager icon should be on your Taskbar when SQL Server is running.

You don't need to leave the Services Manager dialog box open. SQL Server will keep running even if you close or minimize the SQL Server Services Manager. Unless you're running SQL Server on a Win9x system, you can also use the following command line utility to start the server:

```
net start mssqlserver
```

What Do DBAs Do, Anyway?

Not everyone appreciates the scope of the tasks performed by database administrators. To put things in perspective, it helps to realize that, in contrast to SQL Server DBAs who typically manage multiple SQL Servers and multiple databases, mainframe DBAs are typically assigned responsibility for a single database (see Chapter 12).

Unlike one-database mainframe DBAs, SQL Server DBAs often administer multiple databases and multiple servers at multiple sites. They create databases, including databases that are used as data warehouses or data marts, and may also create multi-dimensional, or "cube" databases for decision support and OLAP (online analytical processing) applications. They may work with a data architect, but, more often than not, they fill that role themselves.

DBAs are also responsible for making sure authorized users have appropriate access to organizational data. This often means coordinating with the network administrator in setting up user accounts and privileges and in monitoring database access and overall network security. It may also entail working with packaged application and supply chain administrators, because SQL Server is one of the most popular deployment platforms for applications from SAP, PeopleSoft, Baan, and so on.

One of the most important tasks DBAs perform is backing up the database(s). In addition to managing backups, DBAs are also typically responsible for establishing a disaster recovery plan. That means anticipating scenarios that could have a negative impact on database availability and practicing recovery procedures.

Continues

What Do DBAs Do, Anyway? *(Continued)*

DBAs also work with developers—making sure developers understand how to get the best performance out of their applications. And DBAs are increasingly involved in helping both individual users and remote sites set up replication to ensure efficient update and distribution of data.

Most of today's DBAs complain that they spend too much time in a "reactive" mode, responding to performance problems, data access questions, or even crises, so they want tools that will not only automate some of the tedious repetitive chores, but also help them quickly isolate problems. They also yearn for "smart" DBMSs (database management systems) which perform "auto-tuning" and allow the DBAs to play a more proactive role in their organization's database and knowledge management strategies.

In other words, DBAs have a lot of responsibility. In fact, the MOC (Microsoft Official Curriculum) for Microsoft's SQL Server System Administration for Microsoft SQL Server 7 course (see www.microsoft.com/mcp) describes an in-depth five-day course designed to prepare DBAs for deploying and managing SQL Server enterprise wide. But that's not to say that every DBA will need to take a week-long course. But both first-time DBAs who may simply be upsizing a Microsoft Access database to a Windows 9x version of SQL Server 7 and veteran SQL Server DBAs will surely appreciate the new scalability and ease-of-use features in SQL Server 7.

Running SQL Server Enterprise Manager

SQL Server Enterprise Manager is SQL Server's main console program. It provides a powerful scheduling engine, administrator-alert capability, and a built-in replication management interface. It also comes with Task Pads and wizards to make database chores easier to perform. DBAs can use SQL Server Enterprise Manager to perform the following tasks:

- Manage logins, permissions, and users
- Create scripts
- Manage backup devices and databases
- Back up databases and transaction logs
- Inspect error logs
- Manage tables, views, stored procedures, triggers, indexes, rules, defaults, and user-defined data types
- Create full-text indexes, database diagrams, and database maintenance plans
- Import and export data
- Run other SQL Server utilities like the Query Analyzer or Profiler

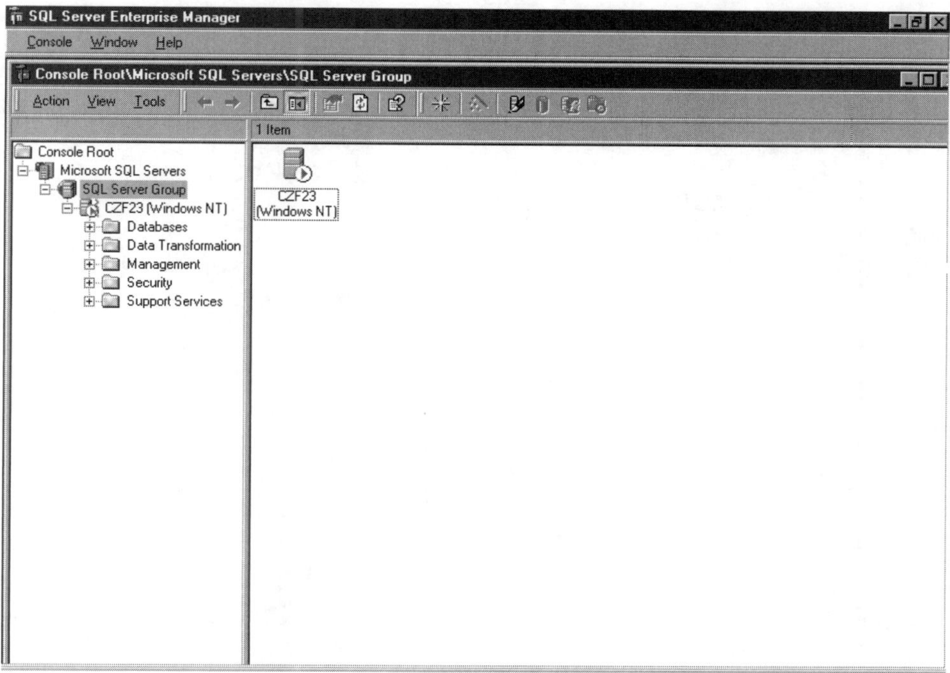

Figure 2.10 SQL Server Enterprise Manager.

To run SQL Server Enterprise Manager simply select the Start menu's Programs, and click on Microsoft SQL Server 7 and then Enterprise Manager as shown in Figure 2.10.

When you run SQL Server Enterprise Manager for the first time, it registers the local server that runs SQL Server automatically. Later, you can explicitly launch the Register Server wizard, e.g. from the menu or by clicking on the wizard (the magic wand) icon. You can also launch wizards from the Task Pad (see Figure 2.11) or use the Registered SQL Server Properties dialog box to register additional servers, to edit the settings for any registered servers, or to un-register servers.

To register a server, right-click a server or a server group and then click New SQL Server Registration.

REGISTER SERVER WIZARD

If you selected "From now on I want to perform this task without using a wizard" the last time you used the Register Server wizard, SQL Server Enterprise Manager displays the Registered SQL Server Properties dialog box. Otherwise, the Register Server wizard is started.

Then, in the Registered SQL Server Properties dialog box, enter the server name in the Server box. Assuming you're registering the local server, you should be able to simply type, Local. If you have difficulty connecting to a remote server, you may need to use the SQL Server Client Network Utility to configure access to the server.

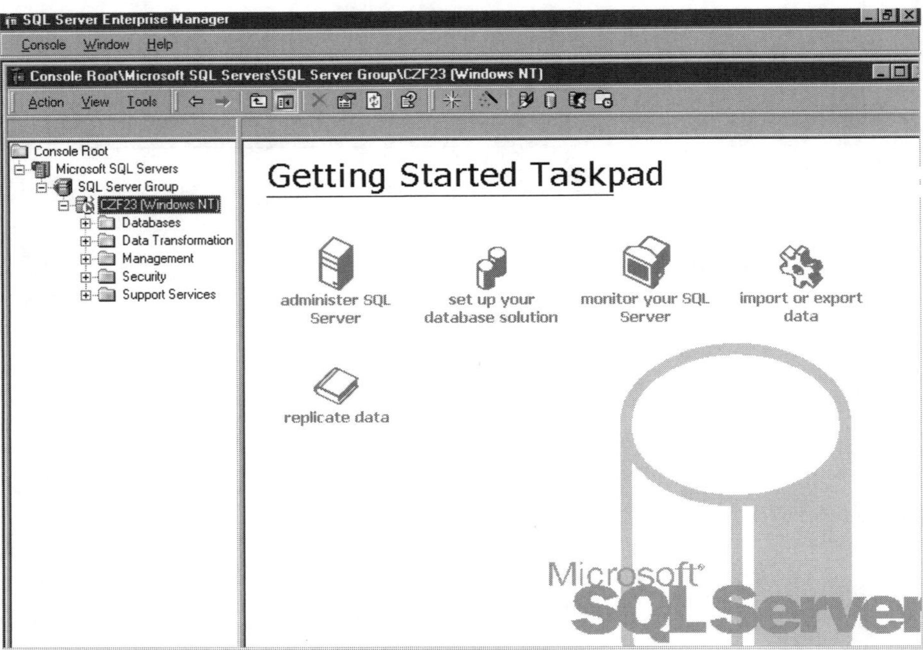

Figure 2.11 Drilling down through your server's hierarchy. Here you see the Enterprise Manager's Task Pad.

Select the security type for the connection between SQL Server Enterprise Manager (as a client) and the server running Microsoft SQL Server that is registered. You've got two choices: Windows NT authentication or SQL Server authentication. If you select SQL Server authentication, you must provide a login name and password. Select "Always prompt for login name and password" to always prompt the user for a login name and password, rather than storing your login id and password in your Registry.

You can also make decisions about turning service polling on or off by selecting or clearing "Display SQL Server state in console." Other options allow you to decide whether or not to display *system* databases and system objects such as master and model as opposed to only user databases, and whether or not to automatically start SQL Server when connecting.

Northwind

Microsoft Access users will be familiar with the Northwind application, and SQL Server 7 now includes it as a sample database, too. Expand the Databases hierarchy, and then drill into Northwind as shown in Figure 2.12.

When you highlight Northwind you'll see "general" information about the database (see Figure 2.13). The General tab displays basic information about each database including valuable information about its size and when it was last backed up.

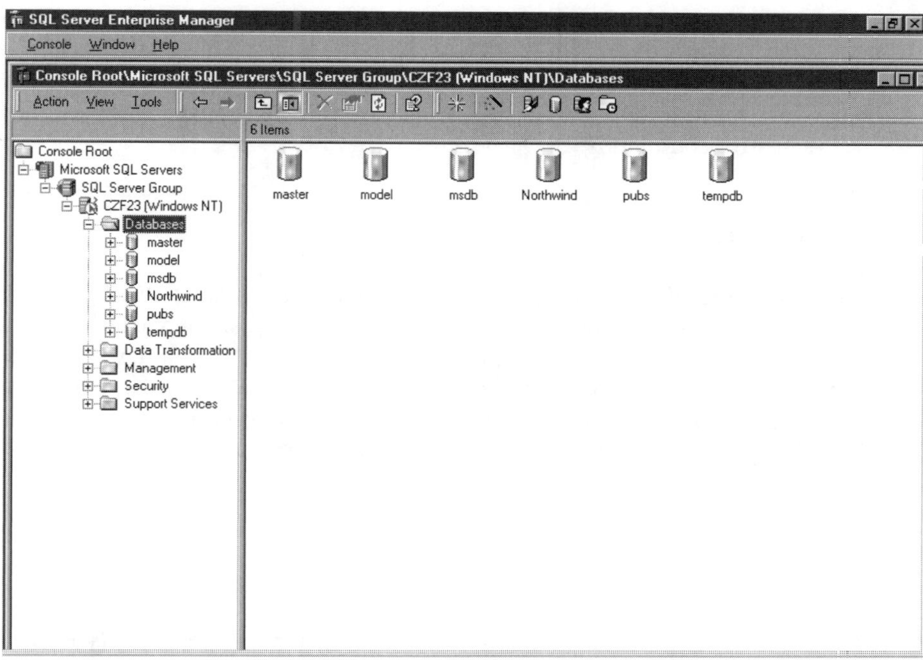

Figure 2.12 Your SQL Server should start with six databases: four system databases, and two sample databases—Pubs and Northwind.

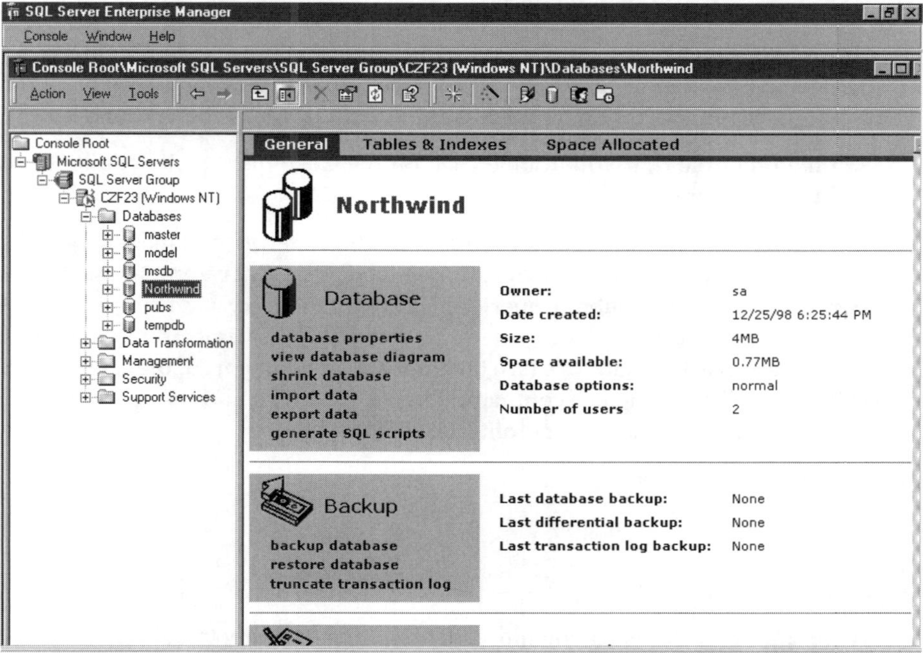

Figure 2.13 The General tab shown in the Northwind database.

If you're a command line person, you can log into your running copy of SQL Server by using the isql or osql utilities (both located in the \mssql\binn subdirectory) and submit T-SQL statements directly. To log in as "sa" with no password (the default, remember, which represents a security risk, so make sure you change it!), type either of these case-sensitive commands:

```
osql /U sa /P
isql /U sa /P
```

You'll see a DOS-like prompt (1>). Type these three statements (*these* aren't case sensitive), one per line. They make pubs the active database, ask for a list of authors, and tell SQL Server to execute the commands. When you see the 1> again, you can continue to experiment with SQL commands using the pubs database. Type in one or more commands, each on a separate line. When you want SQL Server to run the commands, type "go". To exit osql or isql, type "exit" when you see the 1>.

```
1 > use pubs
2 > SELECT * FROM authors
3 > go
```

As you can see, osql/isql don't offer much in the way of amenities (you can't save or edit your string of commands, for example), but they're fast and tend to be a favorite of old timers.

When you click on the Tables and Indexes tab you'll see information about the basic tables and indexes (see Figure 2.14). Indexes are used primarily to speed up data access.

Try highlighting Northwind's Tables in the left panel and then highlighting a single table such as Customers on the right panel. If you right mouse click on Customers, you'll be given the option of looking at the actual data as shown in Figure 2.15.

On the other hand, if you double click on the Customers table, you'll see a list of its fields (see Figure 2.16).

Isn't this fun? You can probably see how useful Enterprise Manager's graphical interface is. However, if you're anxious to see the Query Analyzer that many veteran SQL Server DBAs use to submit queries and commands, try launching it from the Tools menu. It's not very sexy, and when you run it the first time, it will default to putting you in the "master" database (see the upper right hand part of the screen with the drop down box). Try typing in a command like the following and then press F5 to execute it. Your results should look something like Figure 2.17.

```
SELECT @@VERSION
```

Start | SQL Server Enterprise Ma... 8:12 AM

Figure 2.14 SQL Server Enterprise Manager makes it easy to quickly review basic information about the tables and indexes in any database.

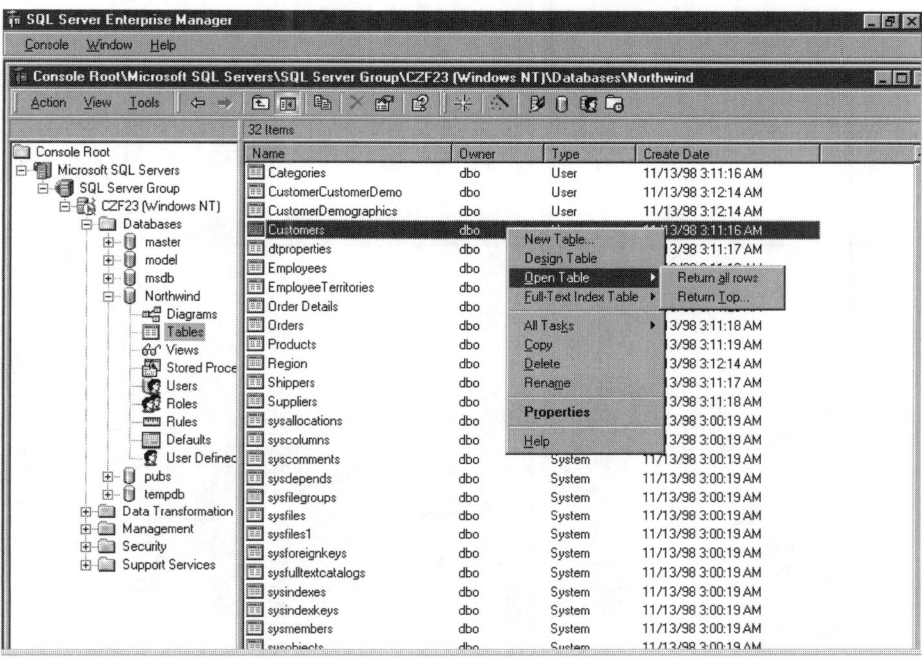

Figure 2.15 SQL Server Enterprise Manager makes it easy to quickly see what kind of data is contained in any table.

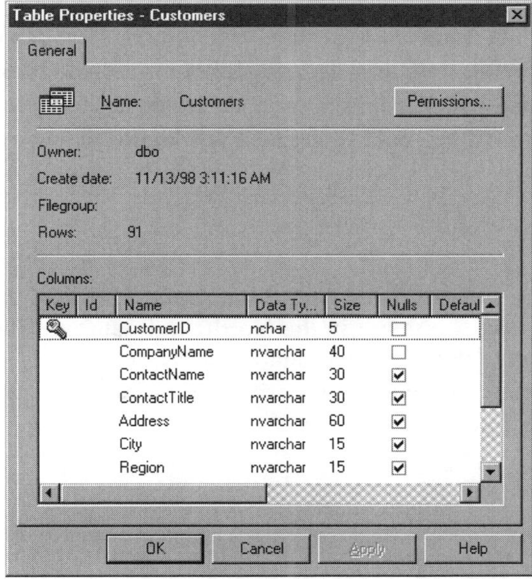

Figure 2.16 Double-clicking on individual tables displays their structure.

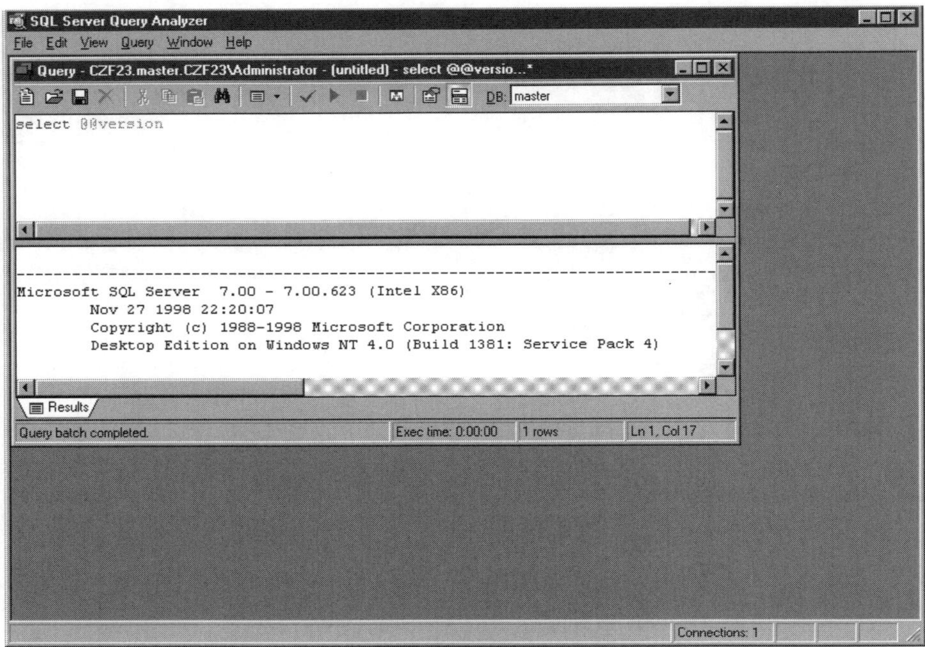

Figure 2.17 How to find out what version of SQL Server you're running.

DON'T MESS WITH THE "MASTER"

The master database is SQL Server's "super" database. Think of it as the database of databases, and don't mess with it. Don't use it to store user objects. Although veteran DBAs sometimes add special, well-tested, user-defined stored procedures to the master database (for reuse enterprise-wide), it's not a good idea to do *anything* to the master database—other than back it up—until you're sure you know what you're doing.

Then clear the query and type in a new query (to practice your SQL from Chapter 1):

```
SELECT * from customers
```

Bummer, an error message (see Figure 2.18). Why? Because we're in the Query Analyzer's default database, "master," we're not in the Northwind database. Remember you don't want to mess around with the master database anyway! Remedy the situation via the dropdown listbox in the upper right part of your screen and F5 it again. You should see something like Figure 2.19.

SQL Server Logs

Another component of SQL Server that pays to become familiar with is the *SQL Server Logs*. You can access them from Enterprise Manager (SQL Server Logs is in the hierarchy under management). If you click on the current one, you'll see an NT Event Viewer

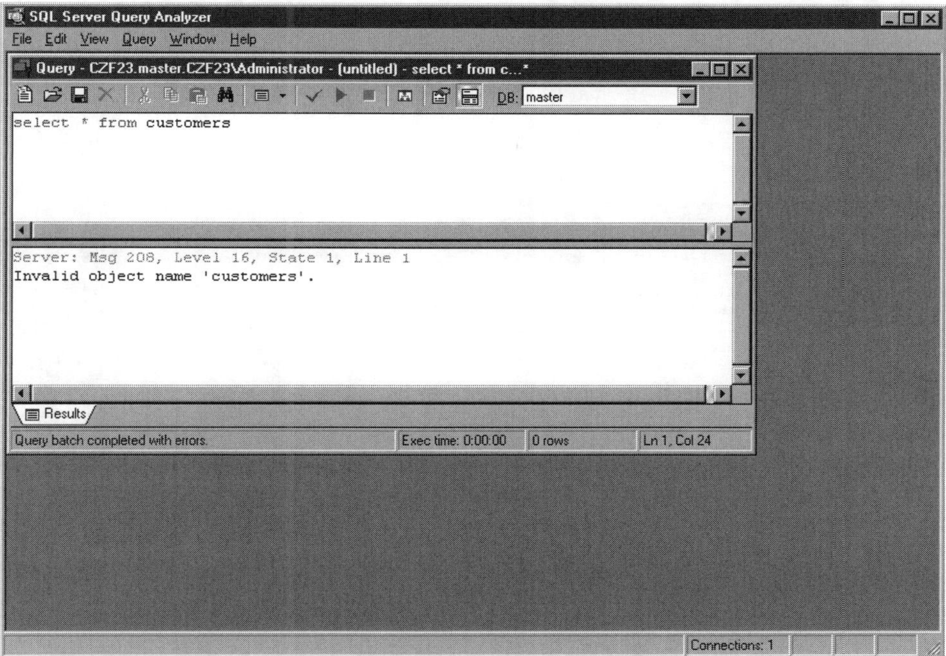

Figure 2.18 The SQL statement 'SELECT * from customers' generates an error message if 'master' is the active database.

type display full of details about what SQL Server has been doing. It's a good idea to monitor this log for error messages about server errors.

Windows NT offers a less detailed view of messages that pertain to SQL Server. You can read it by selecting the Event Viewer from the Administrative Tools group, and then filtering the events for applications via either the Log or View menu.

Experiment

Experiment some more with the Enterprise Manager and its tools. Take some time to see what wizards are available, and start thinking about a routine for backups. Use the Enterprise Manager's own Help (it's different from *Books Online*), but also plan to spend some time reading *Books Online* and probably a book dedicated to SQL Server administration. This one, remember, focuses on showing you how to create projects that solve typical problems. And we don't want to take much more time on all the ins and outs of installation.

If you have a clustering environment under Windows NT 4.0 Enterprise Edition or higher, refer to *Books Online*, notably the topic on *SQL Server 7.0 on Large Servers* and the SQL Server 7 installation notes for specific information about installation.

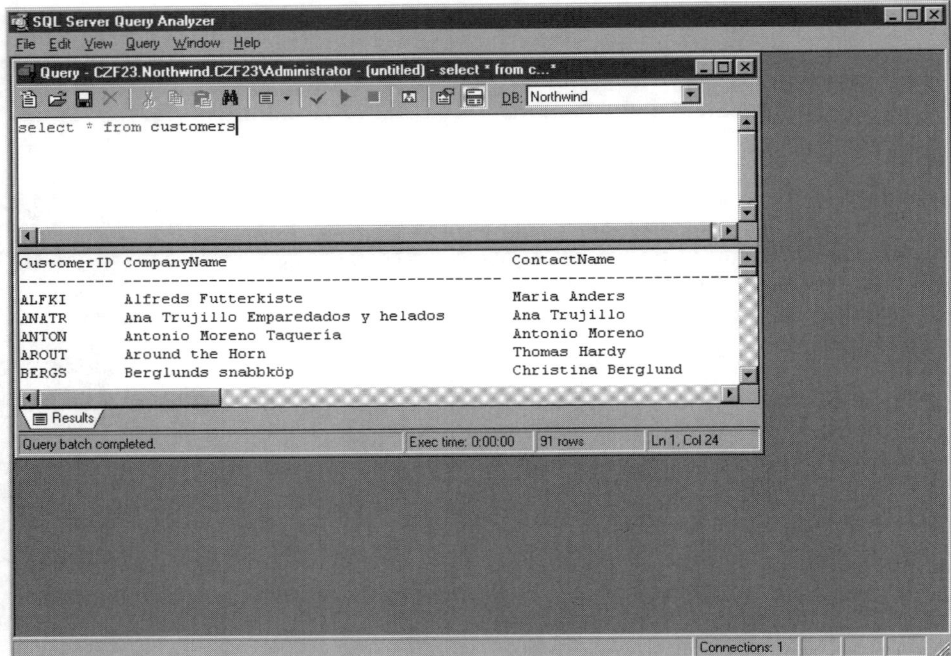

Figure 2.19 The same statement returns the expected data when Northwind is the active database.

Here are some more installation guidelines:

If you plan to install SQL Server's full-text search feature and have Microsoft Site Server 3.0 installed on the same computer, before installing SQL Server you must install Site Server 3.0 SP 1 (Service Pack 1). Without Site Server SP1 installed, uninstalling Site Server 3.0 may corrupt Full-Text Search in SQL Server.

BACKUPS AND FULL-TEXT INDEXING

Contrary to what you might expect, backing up a database doesn't back up full-text index data in full-text *catalogs*. However, if full-text indexes have been defined for *tables*, the metadata for the full-text index definitions are stored in the system tables in the database that contains the full-text index, so that metadata is backed up when a database backup is created. For more information, refer to *Books Online*.

If you try to start SQL Server 7 and receive the depressing error message "Your SQL Server installation is either corrupt or had been tampered with (unknown package id). Please rerun setup," it's probably because you've renamed the Windows NT Server computer that you installed SQL Server 7 on. SQL Server 7 uses the Windows NT Server computer name internally and if you change the Windows NT Server computer name, SQL Server detects a different name and generates the error message. The solution is to change the name back to what it was before or to drop SQL Server's servername and then rename it using T-SQL system stored procedures. Which procedures? Well, let's consider this a test. If you can use *Books Online* to figure out the answer, we figure you've earned your stripes and are ready to proceed with the fun stuff—the hands-on projects. But, before move on to doing projects, let's wrap up the installation.

Refining Your Installation

Once you're satisfied with proof positive that you successfully installed SQL Server, exit the Enterprise Manager and re-run setup. You can't run it from the Start menu's Microsoft SQL Server 7 menu, only from the Setup program on the CD. Once you select Local installation, you'll see the familiar installation menu. You can continue to install OLAP Services and/or English Query if you like. Or, you can click on the basic SQL Server version that you have. This time, however you won't be walked through the basic installation routine, you'll simply have the option of refining your installation options as shown in Figure 2.20.

At this point, it's probably a good idea to down the server and restart it and see what happens. Sometimes MS DTC (Microsoft Distributed Transaction Coordinator) will activate your dial-up service to the Internet when you start (or restart) your computer. To prevent MS DTC from automatically starting after restarting a Windows 98 computer, you may have to make a change to the system Registry.

REGISTRY EDITOR

Using Registry Editor incorrectly can cause serious problems that may require you to reinstall your entire operating system. Use Registry Editor at your own risk and never do it unless you've backed it up and updated your ERD (Emergency Repair Disk) or emergency boot disk.

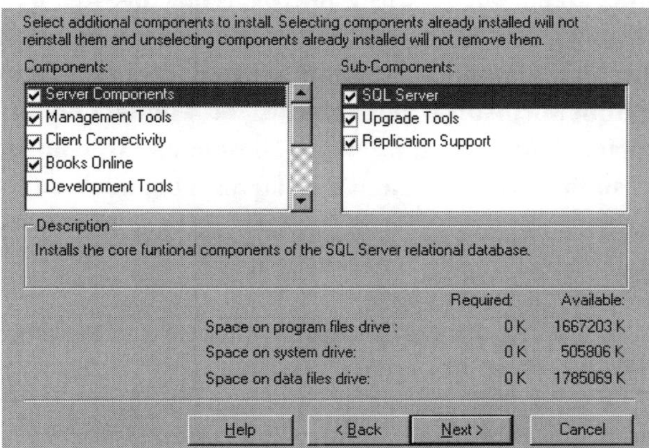

Figure 2.20 Installing SQL Server the second time around offers different options.

To prevent MS DTC from automatically starting, use Registry Editor to find the following key:

HKEY_LOCAL_MACHINE\Software\Microsoft\Windows\CurrentVersion\RunServices

When you find this key, you can delete the value entry named MSDTC. If you want to enable automatic startup of MS DTC again, use Registry Editor to create a value entry named MSDTC with the string value msdtcw –start under the registry key.

What's Where

The \Mssql directory is the default path, which you are free to change during installation. However, you should *not* delete or rename the \Binn or \Html directories or their contents. See Table 2.2 for a listing of the different directories and their contents.

Installing Client Utilities

Most of you will want to be able to administer SQL Server from a PC that isn't your main SQL Server. To do this, you'll need to install SQL Server's client utilities—a pretty straightforward task. Start Setup as you would for an ordinary server install, and select Custom for the setup type. On the Select Components window, clear the Server Components check box. Leaving the other Select Components, the check boxes selected installs the client utilities, *Books Online*, and client connectivity components. You need the client connectivity components in addition to the management tools for the tools to function properly when you connect to SQL Server.

GOOD DOCUMENTATION TAKES TIME

We've raved about *Books Online* so much that you probably wonder why you need *our* book (well, you do, of course!), but seriously, Microsoft has invested a lot in documentation for SQL Server. We asked Microsoft to estimate the number of person hours (note our politically correct terminology) spent creating documentation for SQL Server 7. The answer from Microsoft's Tom Kreyche, "I'd estimate about 156,000 hours. (Average of 25 people, at 40 hours a week, for 30 months.) Of course, that doesn't really account for all the overtime, but it's still a darn big number!"

SQL Mail

SQL Mail is a component of SQL Server that includes special extended stored procedures—system stored procedures that have names starting with xp_ instead of sp_—and allows SQL Server to send and receive mail messages through the built-in Windows NT MAPI (mail application programming interface). Using SQL Mail, for

Table 2.2 Directories and Their Contents

DIRECTORY	CONTENTS
\Mssql7\Backup	Default location for backup files
\Mssql7\Binn	Microsoft Windows NT client and server executable files, online Help files, and DLL files for extended stored procedures
\Mssql7\Books	Microsoft SQL Server Books Online files
\Mssql7\Data1	System and sample database files
\Mssql7\Ftdata1	Full-text catalog files
\Mssql7\DevTools\Include	OLE DB include (*.h) files used to create programs using ODBC, DB-Library, Open Data Services, SQL-DMO, Embedded SQL for C, and MS DTC
\Mssql7\DevTools\Lib	OLE DB library (*.lib) files used to create programs using ODBC, DB-Library, Open Data Services, SQL-DMO, Embedded SQL for C, and MS DTC
\Mssql7\DevTools\Samples	Files and examples used by ODBC, DB-Library, Open Data Services, SQL-DMO, Embedded SQL for C, and MS DTC
\Mssql7\Html	Microsoft Management Console (MMC) and SQL Server HTML files
\Mssql7\Install	Scripts run during Setup and the .out files that result from running the Setup scripts
\Mssql7\Jobs	Storage location for temporary job output files
\Mssql7\Log	Error log files
\Mssql7\Repldata	Working directory for replication tasks
\Mssql7\Upgrade	Files used for version upgrade from SQL Server version 6.x to SQL Server 7

example, you can set things up so that DBAs are alerted via e-mail when something bad happens to SQL Server.

Unlike SQL Server version 6.5, which only used the extended stored procedure approach—via xp_sendmail, to handle mail—SQL Server 7 can use either SQL Mail and its stored procedures or SQLServerAgent (formally SQLExecutive) which uses its own mail capabilities (SQLAgentMail) that are configured and operated separately from SQL Mail. Both SQL Mail and SQLAgentMail can connect with Microsoft Exchange Server, Windows NT Mail, or a Post Office Protocol 3 (POP3) server. For more information about using SQL Mail or SQLAgentMail, refer to *Books Online*.

Basically, to use either mail service, you need to have installed a mail client program on the SQL Server computer, and SQL Mail must run using a mail profile created in the same domain account that is used to start SQL Server 7. You can also opt to have the SQL Mail service start automatically. You'll also need to have an Exchange or other POP3 mailbox owned by the SQL Server service startup account. The easiest way to monitor and administer the SQL Mail service is in the Enterprise Manager, under the Support Services folder at the bottom of the hierarchy. Until you've configured things properly, including the option for autostart, however, you'll just see the red dot on the SQL Mail Service that indicates it isn't running.

SQL SERVER FAQS

The Microsoft "official" FAQ—don't get your hopes up, historically it's been pretty sparse—is at http://support.microsoft.com/support/sql/content/faq/default.asp, but several collections of what we think are superior "unofficial" FAQs can be found at:

- ✔ **www.swynk.com/faq/sql/sqlserverfaq.asp**
- ✔ **www.ntfaq.com/sql.html**
- ✔ **Compuserve MSSQL Forum lib 1**

Download the Latest SP

Although you're ready to proceed at this point, we recommend you download the latest SP. As of fall 1999, SP1 was available, and included updates both for SQL Server 7 and OLAP Services 7.0. We strongly recommend you go to the Microsoft Downloads page at http://microsoft.com/backoffice/downloads.htm#SQL, get it, read the README files, and then install it before proceeding. If there's an SP2 or later by the time you read this, you'll only have to apply the last service pack because they're cumulative.

Launching Projects

Ready for more hands-on? Let's *do it*! But before we do any "real" projects, let's invest some time in learning the backup thing. No, backup and restore isn't as fun as the other projects will be, but they're meat and potatoes, folks. Put yourself in a hey-this-will-be-fun mindset and turn the page. Your reward will be the confidence that *your* databases won't end up as toast.

CHAPTER 3

Backup and Recovery

Goal

The goal of this chapter is to explain the backup and recovery options available in SQL Server 7. We show how these options can be used to ensure minimal data loss and reduce recovery time to the bare minimum. In this chapter we walk through the complete process of assessing how much data you can afford to lose, explain the three backup options available in SQL Server 7, demonstrate how to recover a database to various points in time, and then show how to implement and test a backup and recovery plan.

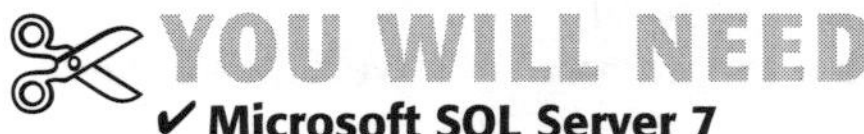

✔ **Microsoft SQL Server 7**

Optional:

✔ **Tape drive**

We would argue that this is the most important chapter in this book. Too many people overlook the importance of implementing a backup and recovery plan. If you read this chapter and then feel that this stuff isn't for you, that's fine, but do read it before making that decision.

Before We Get Started

Our goal for this book is to show how you can use SQL Server to add value to your company's operations. We have tried to accomplish this goal by showing you realistic projects that can be used in your business' daily operations. Explaining backup and recovery in a "project" format is almost impossible because of the background you need before you can actually complete a project. So, we've devoted a good number of pages that explain backup and recovery concepts and processes and have delayed the actual hands-on project to the final pages of this chapter. Yes, this format is a little different from our other chapters, but we feel it's the best way to ensure that you understand how to properly plan and implement a backup and recovery strategy.

Who Needs Backup and Recovery?

I (Garth) am one of the lucky ones. My first job as an IT Professional was under the direction of a gentleman who believed that losing data was simply unacceptable. I was taught to review the daily backup logs to ensure that they completed without errors, to rotate tapes on a frequent basis, to periodically test the validity of backups on another computer, and to store tapes off site so that in the case of a complete catastrophe, the most that we would ever lose was one week's worth of data. I thought that this was simply the way it was done—surely everyone took as much care of their data as we did of ours. Well, when I moved to my next position, I discovered that this wasn't the case. As a matter of fact, I've had several positions since then and only one of those subsequent companies matched the first company's rigorous approach to backup and recovery. A couple of the companies didn't even realize the danger they were in by having such poor backup and recovery processes.

Hopefully, by the end of this chapter, you'll not only be able to adequately assess the value of your data—even show your boss the numbers if you need to—but also prepare a planned and tested backup and recovery strategy that will ensure that your chances of data loss are minimized. As the saying goes, this stuff isn't rocket science. Yes, it's sort of boring (just as boring as insurance is until a tree falls on your house or you need major surgery), but it pays to be prepared. One of the first things you need to realize is that hardware failures aren't the only potential causes of data loss. Although most of us prepare for hardware failures, your backup and recovery strategy should also address each of these potential disasters:

- Hardware failure
- Natural catastrophe
- Malicious destruction of data
- Accidental destruction of data

The most common hardware failure to protect against is the loss of one or more of the hard drives on which your data is stored. Hard-drive failures can be the result of power surges, power spikes, or a design or manufacturing flaw in the drive. The most damaging event that you need to protect against is a natural catastrophe, which can include fire or flood and result in a complete loss of your facility. Malicious destruction of data can occur when a disgruntled employee decides to exact revenge by deleting data or setting a "trap" so that the database is rendered useless after they leave. Accidental destruction can occur when a developer or end user leaves the WHERE clause off an UPDATE or DELETE statement, has trouble understanding the finality of TRUNCATE TABLE, or other non-logged events. Understanding the back up and recovery capabilities of SQL Server 7 is key to ensuring that your data is recovered when you're faced with any of these events.

TRUNCATE TABLE

If you aren't familiar with TRUNCATE TABLE please read on. TRUNCATE TABLE removes all data from a table without recording the process in the transaction log. In other words, it deletes all of the data in the target table and the only way to recover it is to restore from the last good database backup.

The rest of this chapter focuses on:

- Placing a dollar value on your data
- The components of SQL Server 7's backup and recovery technology
- Creating a database backup
- Restoring a database from a backup

You Look Like You Need an Overview

SQL Server 7 provides several options for data backup and recovery. With so many options, it can be confusing to know which one to choose. Before the various system characteristics that dictate a particular backup and recovery strategy are discussed, a very general understanding of the backup options that are available is necessary. Each of these options are covered in great detail later in this chapter, so don't be concerned if you do not have a complete understanding of each option after completing this section. The immediate goal here is to give you a general idea about processing time, size requirements, and the ability to perform point-in-time recovery for each option.

The *database backup* is a complete backup of a database. It's the most time-consuming type of backup, requires the most space, and doesn't allow point-in-time recovery.

The *differential database backup* records all of the modifications that have occurred since the last database backup. This is less time-consuming and requires less space than the database backup, and also doesn't allow point-in-time recovery.

The *transaction log backup* records all modifications that have occurred since the last database or differential database backup. Used correctly, it's the fastest backup option, uses the least amount of space, and *does* allow point-in-time recovery.

How Much Can You Afford to Lose?

Have you ever asked a non-technical manager how much data they can afford to lose or how long they can afford to have their system down? If you've asked more than one, we'd be willing to bet you lunch that at least one of them answered with "none" or "zero time." Well, implementing a strategy that ensures no data loss and that system downtime is reduced to seconds is extremely expensive ($10,000+) and requires advanced skills to install and configure. These types of systems—referred to as highly available, hot standby, or failover systems—implement clustering supported only by SQL Server Enterprise Edition and are not addressed in this book. If you require this level of recovery, please see the *Books Online* topic, *Using SQL Server Failover Support*. In this chapter, we cover the strategies that apply to the majority of companies using SQL Server 7.

Implementing a sound backup and recovery strategy can be time-consuming and expensive. By placing a dollar value on the data that's stored in SQL Server and the business processes that the server supports, it becomes fairly easy to justify—either to yourself or your boss—the time and expense required to implement and test a backup and recovery strategy. When we say dollar value, we mean how much it costs to re-create the data and/or how much revenue or productivity would be lost by having to down the system while you recover lost data. Assess each backup and recovery option with the value of the data and business processes in mind. For example, there will be a huge difference in the dollar value of data that is downloaded from a mainframe into SQL Server, versus that which is generated by a mission-critical application. Why? Well, the mainframe data can be re-created at any time, but the mission-critical data is lost forever if the database in which it's stored is destroyed and without backup.

The first decision you need to make is how often you want your data backed up. The frequency of backup is determined by:

- Frequency of data change
- Database size
- Productivity or dollar loss that you'll incur if you lose data

Mission-critical transactional systems with hundreds or thousands of transactions per minute need much more attention than a decision-support system whose data is updated on a nightly basis. What would happen in a mission-critical environment if you only performed a database backup nightly at 9:00 P.M. and then experienced a hard disk failure at 4:00 P.M. the following day? All data modifications that occurred after 9:00 P.M. on the previous day would be lost. What if the database was 20 or 30 GB and took one hour to perform a database backup? Even if you can afford to lose the data modifications, can your operations afford to come to a halt for the hour or more it takes to restore the database? What about the time and money it would take to re-create the lost work? If you can't accept any of these results, database backup alone is not an acceptable option. This type of environment requires database backups on an infrequent basis, supplemented with both differential database backups and transaction log backups. A realistic approach might be to:

- Perform a database backup nightly at 10:00 P.M.
- Perform differential database backups every four hours during business operations. For an 8-to-5 operation, this would be Noon and 4:00 P.M.
- During business hours, perform transaction log backups every hour that a differential database backup isn't performed. For an 8-to-5 operation this would be 9:00, 10:00, and 11:00 A.M. and 1:00, 2:00, 3:00, and 5:00 P.M.

This strategy reduces the granularity of the backup and recovery process. Reducing the granularity of the backup and recovery process minimizes both data loss and recovery time.

So, how much can you afford to lose? You may not be able to pinpoint the exact figure at this precise second, but let's take an example that might help to get you to the right number. Let's say that you manage a Credit Application Processing System (CAPS) where there are at least 30 people who use the system during the normal business hours of 7:00 A.M. to 6:00 P.M. Just to make things simple, let's say that each of the users earn $10/hour and uses CAPS to perform all of their work. So, at a minimum you lose $300/hour in productivity for every hour's worth of data that is lost. Now, $300/hour may seem like nothing, but let's say the users process 20 credit applications/hour; your acceptance ratio is 1.5:10 and every accepted application yields the company $2000 in revenue. For every hour the system is down, you lose $6000 (1.5/10*20/hour*2000/contract) in revenue. We won't even talk about the intangible losses like employee frustration and reputation damage with your customers. As you can see, it's not hard to assign a dollar value on the benefits of implementing a sound backup and recovery strategy. The numbers you come up with should help to determine how much time and effort you need to spend on planning for backup and recovery.

Let's move on to describe the main component—the backup device—of backup operations and see how it's created.

GIVE ME TWO OPTIONS OR ELSE

You'll probably notice pretty quickly that in the next sections we show both the Enterprise Manager and T-SQL approaches to creating and executing backup components and processes. You may say to yourself, "These guys must have a lot of free time on their hands." Actually, it's not that we have so much free time, but we do recognize that some folks like GUIs and some folks like code. So, if you like GUIs, we've got you covered, and if you like code we've got you covered too.

Backup Devices

SQL Server uses a *backup device* to back up data. A backup device can be one of three types: disk, tape, or a named pipe. A *disk backup device* is an operating system file and can be stored on any disk media—hard drive, floppy, zip drive—like any other operating system file.

NETWORK BACKUP DEVICES

Previous versions of SQL Server couldn't use backup devices that weren't directly on the local server. SQL Server 7 adds this functionality for disk and named-pipe devices by allowing you to reference non-local disks with either the universal naming convention (UNC) or a local drive that has been mapped to a remote disk.

A *tape backup device* is used in the same manner as a disk backup device. A tape backup device, however, must be physically attached to the local server, so remote backups with tape backup devices aren't possible.

COMPATIBLE TAPE FORMATS

Unlike previous versions of SQL Server, version 7 uses the same tape format as NT. This allows you to use the same tape to backup both your NT files and SQL databases.

A *named pipe backup device* allows third-party software vendors to participate in database backup and recovery. Instead of referencing a specific backup device in the BACKUP or RESTORE statement, the named pipe that the third-party software uses is substituted. This allows vendors to extend the backup and recovery functionality in SQL Server and enables you to customize your backup and recovery strategy.

Regardless of the type of device you decide to use, you can reference a device either by its physical name or a user-friendly "logical" name that's an alias to the physical name. For example, when you create a device, you supply a physical name like C:\MSSQL7\Backup\pubs_backup.bak, but you can also associate a logical name like "pubs backup" for easy reference. The physical and logical names can be used interchangeably when backing up or restoring a database. The record for each device used by SQL Server is stored in the sysdevices system table, which is located in the master database.

SYSTEM DATABASES AND TABLES

The sysdevices table is called a system table because it's used by SQL Server to track server-level information. SQL Server uses four "system databases" and a lot of system tables to track both server-level and database-level information. If you want to be a SQL Server guru, you need to spend some time learning about system databases and tables. See the *Books Online* topics, *System Databases and Data* and *System Tables (T-SQL)* for detailed information.

PERMISSIONS

If you want to allow a user to create backup devices, you must make them a member of the fixed server role *diskadmin*. Of course, a member of the fixed server role *sysadmin* can perform any action within SQL Server, so they'll be able to create backup devices as well. If you aren't familiar with the concept of fixed server roles please see the *Books Online* topic, *Adding a Member to a Predefined Role*.

Creating a Backup Device

The backup device that we use throughout this chapter is a disk backup device created on the local hard drive. When you're in learning mode, a local disk device is fine. However, you should *not* use a local disk device on a production system. Why? Well, what would happen if the local drive failed? That's right, you not only lose your SQL Server databases, but the backups—and maybe your job—as well. There is a special case where a disk device can be used in a production environment, but it involves implementing RAID technology that allows you to mirror drives. We don't cover this scenario in this chapter.

Enterprise Manager

The following steps demonstrate how to create a disk backup device with SQL Server's Enterprise Manager (see Figure 3.1). This device is used with the pubs database examples found later in this chapter.

1. Expand the Server and then expand Management.
2. Select Backup, right-click and choose New Backup Device from the pop-up menu.
3. Type pubs_Disk_Device in the Name field and note how the File Name field changes as you type.
4. Press the OK button and you'll see the new device in the Details pane.

A record for the disk backup device was created in master..sysdevices, but the physical file (pubs_Disk_Device.Bak) will not exist in C:\MSSQL7\BACKUP until a backup is created using the device. Did you notice master..sysdevices in the previous sentence? The full reference to any database object is server.database.owner_name.object_name, but only the object_name is required. We use this notation (database..object_name) in order to avoid any confusion concerning where the object is located. For more information on Identifiers see the *Books Online* topic, *Using Identifiers as Object Names*.

Use Query Analyzer to examine the contents of this device's sysdevices record with the following code:

```
USE master
Go
SELECT * FROM sysdevices
WHERE name = 'pubs_Disk_Device'
```

Look at the phyname field and notice that it contains C:\MSSQL7\BACKUP\pubs_Disk_Device.BAK. Use NT Explorer to view the Backup sub-directory and notice that the physical file does not exist.

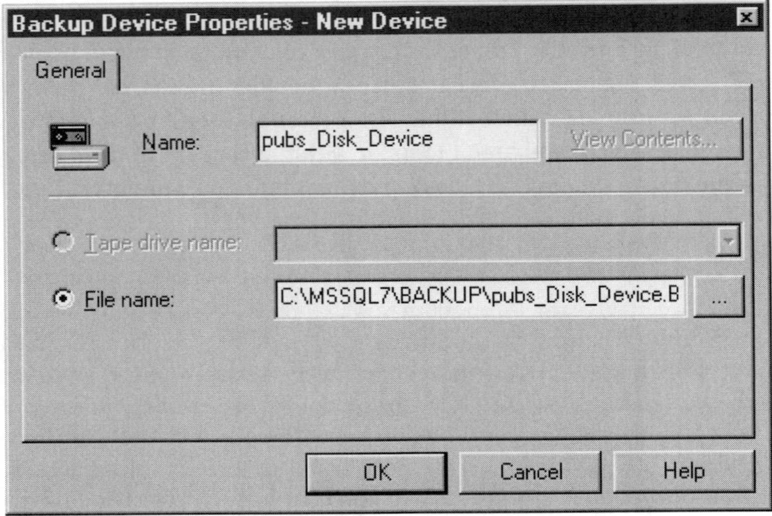

Figure 3.1 Creating a disk backup device.

WHAT ABOUT SIZE?

Did you notice that we did not specify a size during the device creation process? The size of a backup device is a function of the size of the backup(s) that reside on the device. There is no minimum size and the maximum size is the available space on the media on which the device resides.

Transact-SQL

Now we want to create the exact same disk backup device using Transact-SQL (T-SQL). When using T-SQL, a new backup device is added with the sp_addumpdevice system stored procedure. The following T-SQL code creates the same backup device as with the Enterprise Manager approach.

```
EXEC sp_addumpdevice 'disk','pubs_Disk_Device','C:\MSSQL7\BACKUP\pubs_
Disk_Device.bak'
```

The first parameter, disk, specifies the type of device created, and the second and third parameters specify the logical and physical names respectively. The complete syntax for sp_addumpdevice follows:

```
sp_addumpdevice {'device_type', 'logical_name', 'physical_name'}
[, {
{controller_type]}
|
'device_status'}
}
]
```

The available arguments are listed in Table 3.1.

Table 3.1 Sp_adddumpdevice Arguments

ARGUMENT	FUNCTION
device_type	Type of device created. The available choices are: disk→disk backup device, tape→tape backup device, and pipe→named pipe backup device.
logical_name	Logical name. 128 maximum characters.
physical_name	Location of device. 260 maximum characters. Physical_name must conform to the operating system file name or universal naming convention (UNC) rules and must include the full path. For tape backup devices this value is the name assigned to the device by NT.
controller_type	Maintained for backward compatibility but is ignored. You can optionally supply either controller_type or device_status but not both. The available options for controller_type are: Disk→2, Tape→5, and Pipe→6.
device_status	Indicates ANSI tape labels are read or ignored. You can optionally supply either controller_type or device_status, but not both. A value of skip causes the header to be ignored and noskip causes the header to read.

If you want to re-create the disk backup device using T-SQL you need to delete the existing device using the methods described in the next section.

DISK DEVICES AND PERMISSIONS

A disk backup device is just a file. Like any other file, the appropriate read/write permissions must be granted to the login under which SQL Server runs in order to avoid access-denied errors. Using a device located on a remote computer in another domain can be especially problematic, because you can forget to check permissions across domains.

Deleting a Backup Device

The following sections show how to delete a backup device with Enterprise Manager and T-SQL.

Enterprise Manager

You delete the pubs_Disk_Device backup device in Enterprise Manager with the following steps:

1. Expand the Server and then expand Management.
2. Select Backup and note that the device is shown in the Details pane. If the device is not visible, press the F5 key to refresh the Details pane.
3. Select pubs_Disk_Device in the Details pane, right-click, and select Delete from the pop-up menu. Click Yes to delete the device.

The Details pane automatically refreshes, and pubs_Disk_Device is no longer displayed—your actions deleted the backup device's record in sysdevices. If you use Enterprise Manager to delete a disk backup device, you'll need to use NT Explorer to delete the physical file. We didn't create a backup with pubs_Disk_Device, so no physical file was created.

AVOID BACKUPHISTORY BLOAT

Run sp_delete_backuphistory. SQL Server records information about every backup and restore operation performed on a server in several tables in msdb. To manage the size of msdb, schedule a SQL Server Agent job that executes sp_delete_backuphistory periodically to purge history information.

Transact-SQL

The T-SQL statement used to delete the pubs_Disk_Device disk backup device is listed here:

```
EXEC sp_dropdevice @logicalname = 'pubs_Disk_Device'
```

This statement calls the sp_dropdevice system stored procedure with the logical name of the backup device. The full syntax of sp_dropdevice is as follows:

```
sp_dropdevice [@logicalname =] 'device'
[, [@delfile =] 'delfile']
```

Where:

@logicalname is the logical name for the device name.

@delfile indicates that the physical file is deleted from the disk.

The second parameter allows you to delete the physical file at the same time the record is removed from sysdevices. The following code would, had a physical file existed, remove both the record in sysdevices and the physical file.

```
sp_dropdevice @logicalname = 'pubs_Disk_Device', @delfile = 'delfile'
```

If you decide to delete and re-create pubs_Disk_Device using T-SQL, review the subdirectory C:\MSSQL7\BACKUP and the table master..sysdevices to confirm that both methods have the same result. Also, make sure that the device is visible when you highlight Backup under the Management tree option. If it's not visible, simply right-click on Backup and select Refresh from the pop-up menu.

SYSTEM STORED PROCEDURES

System stored procedures are stored procedures provided by Microsoft that help you manage your server; there are a *ton* of them in SQL Server 7. If you want to be a SQL Server guru, familiarize yourself with as many system stored procedures as possible. Keep in mind that they are just like any other stored procedure, so if you want to see some advanced T-SQL, just open one up and take a peek. Please note that there is a special class of system stored procedures called *general extended procedures* (indicated by xp_...). The actual code for this type of system stored procedure is written in a programming language like C++, so you cannot view it using Query Analyzer. For

more information on system stored procedures see Chapter 12 and the *Books Online* topic, *System Stored Procedures (T-SQL).*

So far we've covered the three types of backup devices that are available and demonstrated how to create a disk backup. Now that you understand what a backup device is and how it's created, let's look at the different backup options available and see how we can use these options to place a backup on a device.

Backup Options

As we mentioned previously, SQL Server 7 offers three types of backups that can be performed on a database:

1. Database backup
2. Differential database backup
3. Transaction log backup

Generally speaking, the biggest difference between the three backup options is the frequency at which each should be used. As the number of transactions on a system increases, you want to use the database backup less often and rely more on the differential database and transaction log backup options. This is due to the system load that's required to perform a backup operation. If your high-volume system is running short of resources, you certainly want to minimize any operation that may affect its performance. After reading the following sections you'll understand why one option can tax the system more than another, and all of this will make perfect sense.

Database Backup

A database backup copies all of the data in a database to the backup device. The way *data* is used in the last sentence confuses more than a handful of people; they think that only the data in the tables is backed up. Actually, since SQL Server tracks *all* database objects such as tables, stored procedures, and user-defined types in special tables that make up the *database catalog* these objects are backed up as well. So, if you have a database backup and the database from which it was made is destroyed, you will *not* have to recreate all of the database objects and then restore the data. You simply restore the database backup, and all objects and data are recovered. Figure 3.2 shows that objects and data *are* the database.

The backup process has two steps:

1. Back up all of the data (yes, data = objects) for the pages allocated to the database.
2. Back up all of the transactions that occur during the backup process.

It's important that you understand the significance of this two-step process. The first step zooms through all of the pages and backs them up regardless of whether they are in use or static. Because the first step occasionally backs up a page that is in use (called a *dirty read*), the second step is required in order to capture the changes that occur on the *dirty* pages. An example may help to further explain the process.

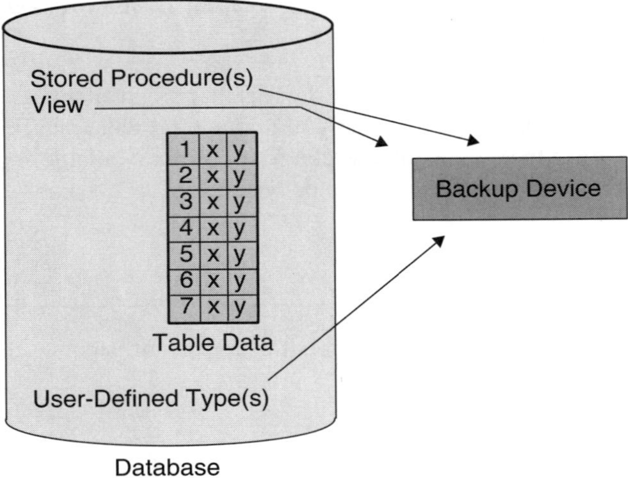

Figure 3.2 Objects and data.

Let's say that you start a database backup at 10:00 A.M. and it takes 45 minutes to complete. During those 45 minutes, a period of low activity, 100 transactions occurred. The first step backs up all of the pages allocated to the database, and the second step backs up the 100 transactions that occurred during the 45-minute period. This strategy, new to SQL Server 7, streamlines the backup process. In previous versions of SQL Server, the backup process was much less efficient because it skipped over an active page during backup. Once all of the non-active pages were copied, the backup process re-accessed the active pages and tried to copy them again. The version 7 strategy avoids the inefficient re-accessing of active pages by copying the transactions that occur during the backup process. The restore process, discussed in greater detail in its own section later in this chapter, restores all of the pages in the backup device and then applies the transactions that were stored with the backup. This ensures that the restored database is in the same state as the database when it was backed up. Figure 3.3 shows how the backup process retrieves the pages first, then the accumulated transactions.

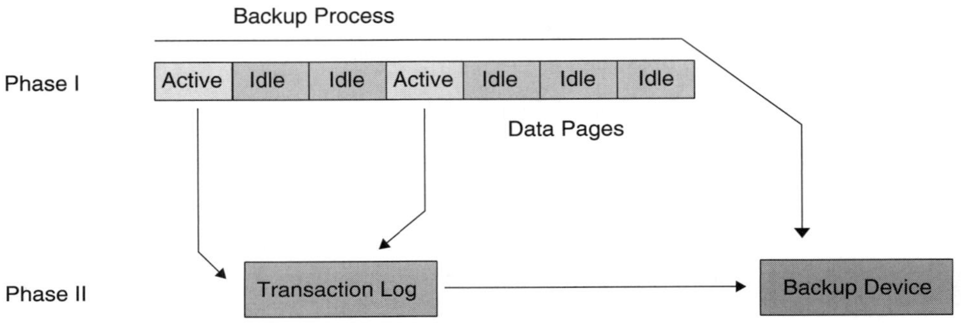

Figure 3.3 Data and transactions.

TRANSACTION LOG ACCUMULATES

The transaction log is not truncated when a database backup is created. If you plan to use database backups only, the truncate log on the CHECKPOINT option should be set to "true" so that the transaction log does not become full.

A database backup, when used without any other backup option, is usually used for fairly inactive databases—those databases that the business can afford to have unavailable for what might be a fairly extended period of time. A read-only data mart database, whose data source is a production database, is a good example of when to only use a database backup. If the mart is populated once a day and aggregations and calculations are performed after the data is loaded, performing a backup immediately after the loading and calculations are performed will suffice. If you experience a failure at any point before the next load (*refresh*, in data warehousing terminology) occurs, all you have to do is restore from the database backup.

The following examples cover the Enterprise Manager and T-SQL approaches to performing a database backup. Note the numerous options available using the T-SQL approach that aren't available to the "GUI guys" using Enterprise Manager.

REMOVING FILES INVALIDATES BACKUPS

Adding or removing a file from a database invalidates all backups created from the database when it was in its original state. Execute a database backup after a file is added or deleted from a database.

Enterprise Manager

The following example demonstrates how to use Enterprise Manager to backup the pubs database to the disk backup device created in the previous section.

In Enterprise Manager follow these steps:

1. Expand the Server and then expand Databases.
2. Select pubs and note that the Backup Information section in the Details pane displays None for all three backup options.
3. Right-click on pubs, highlight All Tasks and select Backup Database from the pop-up menu.
4. In the Name field type, pubs_Database_Backup.
5. Verify that the Database - Complete option is selected in the Backup section.
6. Select Overwrite Existing Media in the Overwrite section.
7. Click the Add button to select a backup device.
8. Select Backup Device and ensure that pubs_Disk_Device is listed in the text box. Click OK to continue.
9. Click the Options tab and select Verify Backup Upon Completion.

10. Select Initialize and Label Media, type in pubs_Backup_Set for the Media Set Name and click OK.

Figure 3.4 shows the Database Backup dialog.

Once the pubs database has been backed up, a message is displayed that indicates that both the backup and verification processes are successful. You can now use NT Explorer to examine the characteristics of the physical file that is used as the backup device. Open NT Explorer and select the C:\Mssql7\Backup sub-directory. Note that the filename is the name you supplied during the backup device creation process with a .BAK file extension. The .BAK extension is the default for disk devices and, even though it can be changed, should always be used. The options available with Enterprise Manager database backup are listed in Table 3.2.

Activate the initial Database Backup dialog (or look at Figure 3.4) for pubs and note that not *all* of the backup options are available. The transaction log is not available for pubs because the database option truncate log on CHECKPOINT (assuming the default configuration has not been changed) is enabled and this prohibits transactions from accumulating in the log. So, since no transactions can accumulate in the log, it makes no sense to have this option available.

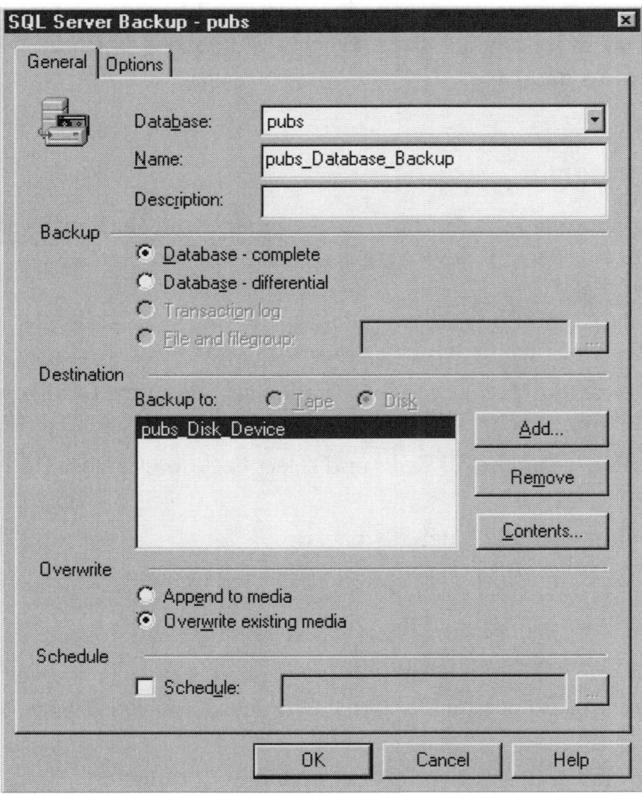

Figure 3.4 Database backup dialog.

Table 3.2 Enterprise Manager Backup Arguments

ARGUMENT	DESCRIPTION
Name	The name of the backup set; Can be up to 128 characters
Description	A description associated with backup
Database – Complete	Indicates that a database backup will be performed
Database – Differential	Indicates that a differential database backup will be performed
Transaction log	Indicates that a transaction log backup will be performed
File and File Group	Allows you to specify an individual file or file group
Backup to	Allows you to specify Disk or Tape for backup device type
Append to media	The backup will be appended to the device
Overwrite existing media	The backup will overwrite all backups on the device; This option destroys all existing backups on the device
Schedule	Allows you to schedule the backup
Verify backup upon completion	The device (file) will be checked to make sure it's complete and usable after the backup completes
Eject tape after backup	The tape will be ejected after the backup is complete
Check media set name and backup set expiration	The media set name and expiration date of the device will be checked against the supplied name and current date to make sure the names are the same and the expiration date is less than the current date
Backup set will expire	The date the backup can be overwritten
Initialize and label media	Overwrites any existing header information on the device and allows you to supply a label

DATABASE OPTIONS

If you are not familiar with the various database options that are available, please review the *Books Online* topic, *Setting Database Options*. The database options that affect backup procedures are discussed later in this chapter, but it's a good idea to understand how the other options impact operations.

One more thing before we move on. Did you happen to notice the file size of pubs_Disk_Device.Bak when you used Explorer to make sure it was in C:\MSSQL7\Backup? If you did, then you saw that it was a little more than 1.3 MB. If you go back to Enterprise Manager, highlight pubs and look in the Details pane you'll notice that the database size is listed as 2 MB. As we stated in the Backup Device section, the size of a backup device is completely dependent on the amount of data in the database (plus a little for file overhead). The pubs database has 2 MB allocated for data, but only about 75 percent of the allocated space is occupied.

Transact-SQL

To complete the same backup operation shown in the previous section with T-SQL, execute the following in Query Analyzer (only execute this statement if you did not create the backup in the previous section).

```
BACKUP DATABASE pubs TO pubs_Disk_Device
WITH INIT, NAME = 'pubs_Database_Backup', MEDIANAME = 'pubs_Backup_Set'
GO
RESTORE VERIFYONLY FROM pubs_disk_device
```

The BACKUP DATABASE statement accepts the database name and logical or physical name of the backup device, as well as the numerous arguments that follow WITH. In this example, INIT indicates that the contents of the backup device will be overwritten and MEDIANAME supplies a name for the media on which the backup device is located. Notice that RESTORE VERIFYONLY FROM must be used in order to confirm that the backup is valid.

The output generated by the statements are listed here:

```
Processed 152 pages for database 'pubs', file 'pubs' on file 1.
Processed 1 pages for database 'pubs', file 'pubs_log' on file 1.
Backup or restore operation successfully processed 153 pages in 1.671
seconds (0.745 MB/sec).
The backup set is valid.
```

The output shows that the backup process read 152 pages (your output may vary) for the database and 1 page for the transaction log. Although it may be easy to misinterpret, the message references pages read, not pages backed up. The number of pages that were actually backed up is recorded in the Errorlog (the active error log file) in the MSSQL7\Log sub-directory.

If you use disk devices and are concerned about available disk space, the following system stored procedure will provide a rough estimate for the size required to hold the backup.

```
sp_spaceused @updateusage = 'true'
```

Executing sp_spaceused with the updateusage argument set to 'true' displays, along with some other data, the database _size and unallocated space for the database. The actual size of the backup device will vary, but if you subtract unallocated from database_size and add a bit of overhead you will get an approximate file size for the device.

The full syntax for the backup database follows:

```
BACKUP DATABASE {database_name | @database_name_var}
TO <backup_device> [, ...n]
[WITH
[BLOCKSIZE = {blocksize | @blocksize_variable}]
[[,] DESCRIPTION = {text | @text_variable}]
```

```
[[,] DIFFERENTIAL]
[[,] EXPIREDATE = {date | @date_var}
| RETAINDAYS = {days | @days_var}]
[[,] FORMAT | NOFORMAT]
[[,] {INIT | NOINIT}]
[[,] MEDIADESCRIPTION = {text | @text_variable}]
[[,] MEDIANAME = {media_name | @media_name_variable}]
[[,] [NAME = {backup_set_name | @backup_set_name_var}]
[[,] {NOSKIP | SKIP}]
[[,] {NOUNLOAD | UNLOAD}]
[[,] [RESTART]
[[,] STATS [= percentage]]
]
```

The available arguments are listed in Table 3.3.

Table 3.3 BACKUP DATABASE Arguments

ARGUMENT	DESCRIPTION
database_name	This is the database name that's backed up.
backup_device [, ...n]	This is the device(s) that hold the backup. All devices must be in the same format. The maximum number of devices that can be referenced is 32.
BLOCKSIZE	This is the physical block size in bytes. This option is only valid for tape devices. The system determines the appropriate block size if one is not supplied.
DESCRIPTION	A description associated with backup.
DIFFERENTIAL	This backup includes only database changes since the last full backup is backed up. This option allows you to apply a single backup versus numerous individual log files.
EXPIREDATE	The date when the backup media set expires and can be overwritten. The SKIP option overrides checking for this option.
RETAINDAYS	The number of days that must elapse before this backup set can be overwritten. The SKIP option overrides checking for this option.
FORMAT	The media header information will be written on all volumes and all contents of the media will be invalidated. This option is only used with tape devices.
NOFORMAT	This option does not overwrite the media header information or invalidate the contents of the media.
INIT	The backup will be the initial item on the backup set and all contents of the device will be overwritten.

Continues

Table 3.3 BACKUP DATABASE Arguments *(Continued)*

ARGUMENT	DESCRIPTION
NOINIT	Default functionality that indicates the backup will be appended to the device.
MEDIADESCRIPTION	This is a description of the backup—maximum of 255 characters.
MEDIANAME	This is the name that will be written on all volumes of the backup set—maximum of 128 characters. If this value is supplied, but does not match the existing device's media name, the backup will fail.
NAME	This is the name of the backup set—up to 128 characters.
NOSKIP	This option verifies that the EXPIREDATE, RETAINDAYS, and media name are valid before they can be over-written.
SKIP	This option disables the verification of the items described in NOSKIP.
NOUNLOAD	This is a default functionality that indicates that a tape will not be ejected after the backup is complete.
UNLOAD	This function indicates that a tape device will be unwound and ejected after the backup is complete.
RESTART	This option indicates that a backup operation will be continued at the point it was interrupted. This option can only be used with tape devices and is only valid for backups that span more than one tape.
STATS	This option displays the percent complete of the backup.

FORMAT AND SKIP OVERWRITE DATA

It's important to note the ramifications of the FORMAT and SKIP options. FORMAT will completely overwrite an existing backup or volumes of which the current device is a member. SKIP will ignore any EXPIREDATE or RETAINDAYS specified when the backup was created. Use these options with extreme caution—there's no recovery if they're used by mistake.

DON'T USE DUMP DATABASE

In previous versions of SQL Server the DUMP DATABASE statement was used to perform the same function as BACKUP DATABASE. DUMP DATABASE is still supported in version 7, but it will *not* be supported in future versions of the product.

MULTI-TASKING TAPES

If you store a SQL Server backup on the same tape as an NT backup, you must supply a MEDIANAME.

The following code creates a backup of pubs that is appended (no initialization) to the existing device with an EXPIREDATE of 11/10/99. Modify the EXPIREDATE argument to some future date and execute the statement in Query Analyzer.

```
BACKUP DATABASE pubs TO pubs_Disk_Device
WITH NAME = 'pubs_Database_Expiredate', EXPIREDATE = '11/10/99'
```

Execute the following code and note the error messages generated.

```
BACKUP DATABASE pubs TO pubs_Disk_Device WITH INIT
```

The following error message is generated.

```
Server: Msg 4030, Level 16, State 1
The medium on device 'pubs_Disk_Device' expires on Nov 10 1999
12:00:00:000AM and cannot be overwritten.
Server: Msg 3013, Level 16, State 1
Backup or restore operation terminating abnormally.
```

Our existing backup is safe because we specified an EXPIREDATE during the original backup's creation and did not use the SKIP argument in the last example. The SKIP argument, coupled with INIT, would have caused the last example to overwrite the two previous backups and they would have been lost forever.

As mentioned earlier, the second step of the two-step backup process is to back up the transactions (accrued in the transaction log) that occur during step one (the processing of the database pages). Because of this reliance on the transaction log, non-logged operations cannot occur during the backup process. A non-logged operation does not get recorded in the transaction log. When the database option Select into/bulk copy is enabled the following actions will produce non-logged activity.

SELECT INTO

WRITETEXT

UPDATETEXT

In addition to non-logged operations, there are several file management actions that cause a backup to fail.

ALTER DATABASE...ADD FILE

ALTER DATABASE...REMOVE FILE

SHRINK DATABASE or SHRINK FILE

CREATE INDEX

If you attempt to execute a backup while one of these statements is in progress the backup will fail. If you attempt to execute any of the above statements while a backup is in progress the statement will fail.

Differential Database Backup

A differential database backup records all changes to the database since the last database backup. Before we create a differential database backup of pubs, let's make a change to pubs..authors so that these backups can be used in the *Restore Options* section later in the chapter.

MAKE SURE PUBS IS BACKED UP

The following UPDATE should only be completed if you followed the database backup steps in the preceding sections. Otherwise, the data in pubs..authors will be modified and might not correspond to other examples in this book or those found in the SQL Server 7 documentation.

Execute the following in Query Analyzer:

```
USE pubs
GO
UPDATE authors SET au_lname = 'McGwire'
```

This UPDATE will change all of the author's last names to McGwire.

Enterprise Manager

The following example demonstrates how to create a differential database backup of the pubs database to a disk backup device with Enterprise Manager.

In Enterprise Manager:

1. Expand the Server and then expand Databases.
2. Select pubs and notice (if you have been following along) that the Backup Information section in the Details pane displays today's date for the date of the last database backup that occurred.
3. Right-click on pubs, highlight All Tasks and select Backup Database from the pop-up menu.
4. In the Name field type, pubs_Database_Differential.
5. Select Database - Differential in the Backup section of the dialog.
6. Verify the pubs_Disk_Device is selected in the Destination section and that Append to media is selected in the Overwrite section.
7. Click OK.

Figure 3.5 shows the Differential dialog.

This backup operation allowed us to capture the McGwire update to the Authors table. If we restored either one of the database backups (pubs_Database_Backup or pubs_Database_Expiredate), the McGwire update would be removed. Although we've experimented with data changes, object (tables, stored procedures, views, and so on) changes can be recovered as well. If we accidentally drop a table or stored procedure

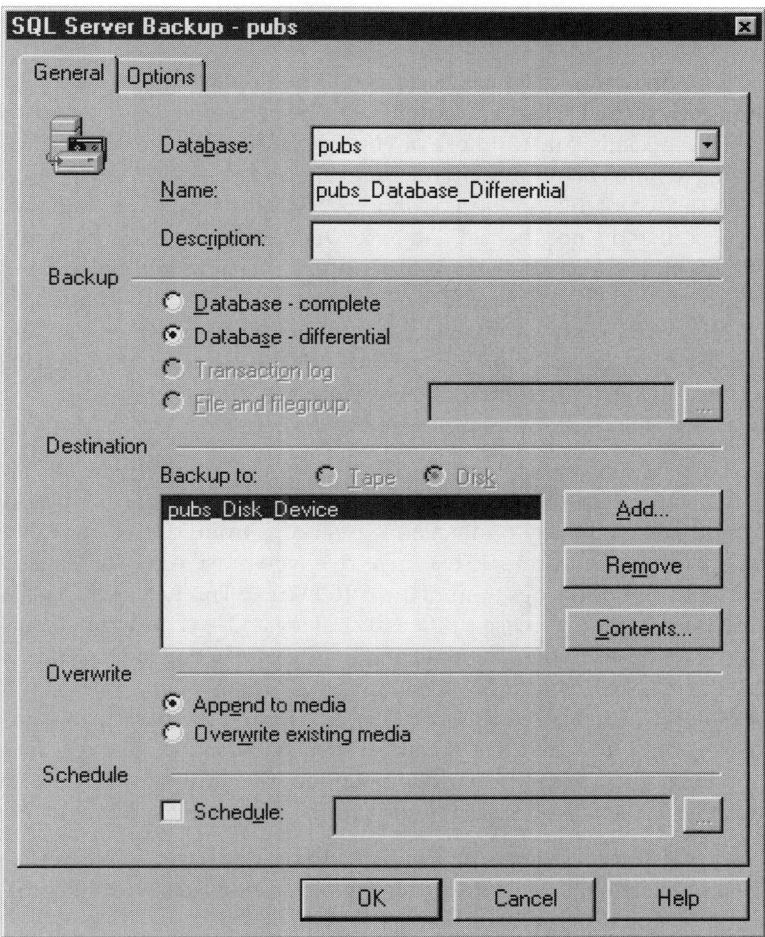

Figure 3.5 Differential database backup dialog.

after either of the database backups is created, we can recover the mistake by restoring from either one of the backups.

Transact-SQL

The T-SQL approach for differential database backups is almost identical to the database backup approach except that the DIFFERENTIAL argument is used. The following code produces the same result as the Enterprise Manager approach for differential backups (only execute this statement if you did not create the backup in the previous section).

```
BACKUP DATABASE pubs TO pubs_Disk_Device
WITH DIFFERENTIAL,NAME = 'pubs_Database_Differential'
```

For a detailed listing of the BACKUP DATABASE statement see the previous section *Database Backup: Transact-SQL.*

Transaction Log Backup

A database or differential database backup will not always give you the granularity necessary to ensure that your transactions can be recovered and restore time minimized. This is especially true for those of you who administer mission-critical transactional systems, where each transaction lost results in a loss of revenue and prolonged downtime is unacceptable. A transaction log backup records all of the database changes that occurred since the last database, differential database, or transaction log backup was executed. At first glance, it may appear that a differential database backup and a transaction log backup are similar, but there are important differences between the two. A differential database backup records all changes since the last database backup, while a transaction log backup records all of the changes recorded in the transaction log since the last differential database or transaction log backup. A differential database backup also records all non-logged operations.

A comparison of a differential database backup versus a transaction log backup will demonstrate an important difference. Let's say that you perform a database backup nightly at 9:00 P.M. and execute hourly transaction log backups from 8:00 A.M. to 7:00 P.M. If you experience a hardware failure at 1:15 P.M., to recover you must restore the nightly database backup and all of the hourly logs from 8:00 A.M. to 1:00 P.M. This will recover all but 15 minutes of database activity. If you use a different strategy and execute a differential database backup every four hours (Noon, 4:00 P.M.) and hourly transaction log backups every other hour (8,9,10,11,1,2,3,5,6,7), you'll only need to apply the nightly database backup, the Noon differential database backup, and the 1:00 P.M. transaction log backup. Again all but 15 minutes of activity is recovered. The second approach will reduce recovery time by minimizing the number of backups that need to be applied. Regardless of the strategy, you still lose 15 minutes worth of database activity. Figure 3.6 compares the two strategies.

To fully grasp transaction log backups, you need to have a basic understanding of what constitutes a transaction. The next section explains a transaction and how it relates to the transaction log and the database recovery process.

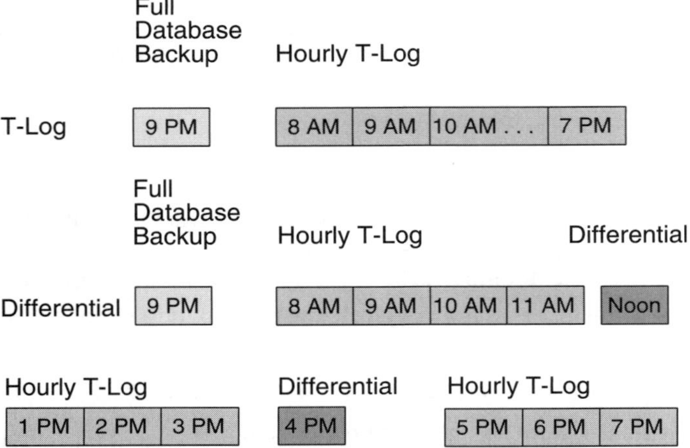

Figure 3.6 Differential database backup versus transaction log backup.

Transactions and the Transaction Log

A *transaction* is a logical unit of work that has an explicit start and finish. While a transaction is in progress the database is in a state of inconsistency. Once the transaction completes, and there are no other open transactions, the database is once again consistent. A classic example of this concept is an accounting system transaction that transfers funds between an individual's checking and savings accounts. There are two parts to this transaction: subtracting money from the checking account and adding money to the savings account. If the transaction fails after the first step, the individual will lose the money to be transferred to their savings account. Only when both steps are completed is the transaction complete. SQL Server 7 has the functionality to ensure that a transaction has either completed successfully, and was subsequently committed to the database, or fails and is rolled back to the original condition. SQL Server 7 uses a transaction log to record all changes that occur in a database. The transaction log is a separate file; that is it's created when a database is created. A quick review of the CREATE DATABASE statement shows how the transaction log is created:

```
Create Database database_name
[ ON [PRIMARY]
[ <filespec> [,...n] ]
[, <filegroup> [,...n] ]
]
[ LOG ON { <filespec> [,…n]} ]
[ FOR LOAD | FOR ATTACH ]

<filespec> ::=
( [ NAME = logical_file_name, ]
FILENAME = 'os_file_name'
[, SIZE = size]
[, MAXSIZE = { max_size | UNLIMITED } ]
[, FILEGROWTH = growth_increment] ) [,...n]

<filegroup> ::=
FILEGROUP filegroup_name <filespec> [,...n]
```

The [LOG ON { <filespec> } [,...*n*]] section specifies the file(s) to be used to store transaction information. If no filename is specified, the system creates a default file whose size is 25 percent of the data file(s) that is specified in the [ON { [PRIMARY] <filespec> [,...*n*]] section.

The transaction log is used to record all modifications that occur in a database. A modification does not become a permanent part of the database until the transaction log has verified that an entire logical unit of work is completed. For example, let's say that you have a batch of 10 INSERTS that comprise a transaction. Upon the start of this batch, an entry is placed in the transaction log that signifies the start of a transaction. Each INSERT modification is written to the log and an end transaction is written upon completion of the last INSERT. At this point, the log can verify whether a logical unit of work has been completed and it makes the changes permanent. If, at any point during the transaction, an error occurs or a ROLLBACK statement is executed, an end transaction is not written to the log and the changes are not applied to the database.

SQL Server also uses the transaction log to recover from unexpected shutdowns. Using the previous paragraph's example, let's assume that the server was unexpectedly shut down after INSERT number 7. Upon restarting the server, the transaction log is read and, since there was no end to the transaction, INSERTs number 1 through 7 are never made a permanent part of the database.

SQL Server's default configuration is to run in *AutoCommit mode*. In AutoCommit mode, SQL Server commits or rolls back every T-SQL statement. If the statement is successful, the modification is committed to the database, and if it fails the statement is rolled back. If you don't want to run SQL Server in AutoCommit mode, you can either issue an explicit transaction with BEGIN TRANSACTION or by setting the Implicit_Transaction option to on with SET IMPLICIT_TRANSACTION ON. The BEGIN TRANSACTION option allows the user to control the transaction's start and finish. The SET IMPLICIT_TRANSACTION option is connection-specific and continues to operate within a connection until SET IMPLICIT_TRANSACTION is turned off. When the IMPLICIT_TRANSACTION option is on, the user is only responsible for committing or rolling back transactions. After a transaction is either committed or rolled back, SQL Server starts a new transaction when it encounters any of the following statements:

ALTER TABLE

FETCH

REVOKECREATE

GRANT

SELECT

DELETE

INSERT

TRUNCATE TABLE

DROP

OPEN

UPDATE

Another important function that works in conjunction with a transaction log is the CHECKPOINT statement. A CHECKPOINT causes all of the pages that have been modified since the last CHECKPOINT to be written to disk. As we mentioned previously, pages that have been modified, but not written to disk are called dirty pages. CHECKPOINTs can be issued manually to force dirty pages to disk, but are primarily issued automatically by the system on an interval based on the maximum acceptable recoverable time and system activity. Maximum acceptable recoverable time is configured with the sp_configure system stored procedure option recovery interval. SQL Server monitors the number of transactions that have occurred since the last CHECKPOINT and continually calculates how much time it would take to roll back these transactions. Once the time to roll back the accumulated transactions exceeds the recovery interval value a CHECKPOINT is issued. A CHECKPOINT should be issued manually before shutting down a server if you do not use either the SHUTDOWN statement or SQL Server Service Manager to stop the server.

Once a CHECKPOINT has been issued, the transaction log has a start point for recovery. The recovery process will read the log to find the last CHECKPOINT and reverse or roll forward transactions accordingly.

Modifying Pubs for Transaction Log Examples

Before we proceed with the examples in the next two sections we need to modify pubs so that transactions can accumulate in its transaction log. When SQL Server 7 is installed the database option Truncate log on CHECKPOINT is enabled on the pubs database. As we discovered earlier in this chapter, the inactive part of the log is truncated when this option is enabled and a CHECKPOINT is issued. In addition to changing the database option we need to apply another update to pubs..authors so that the examples in the *Restore Options* section will have more meaning.

In order to change the database option complete the following steps:

1. Expand the Server and then expand Databases.
2. Select pubs, right-click and select Properties from the pop-up menu.
3. Click the Options tab and de-select Truncate Log on Checkpoint in the Settings section.
4. Click the Apply button and press OK.

Figure 3.7 shows the Database options dialog.

Since this option has been changed, a database backup must be performed in order to ensure that a transaction log backup can be applied to the database. Append another database backup to pubs_Disk_Device using pubs_Database_Post_Option as the backup Name.

Our next step is to apply another change to pubs..authors. Execute the following in Query Analyzer.

```
USE pubs
GO
UPDATE authors SET au_lname = 'Maris'
GO
```

Remember that the UPDATE applied in the previous section changed all of the authors' last names to McGwire. This time we simply change all of the authors' last names to Maris. After the transaction log backup is executed we will have the following to work with in the *Restore Options* section:

- Two database backups with the original copy of pubs
- A differential database backup with the McGwire update
- A database backup (post database option change) with the McGwire update
- A transaction log backup with the Maris update

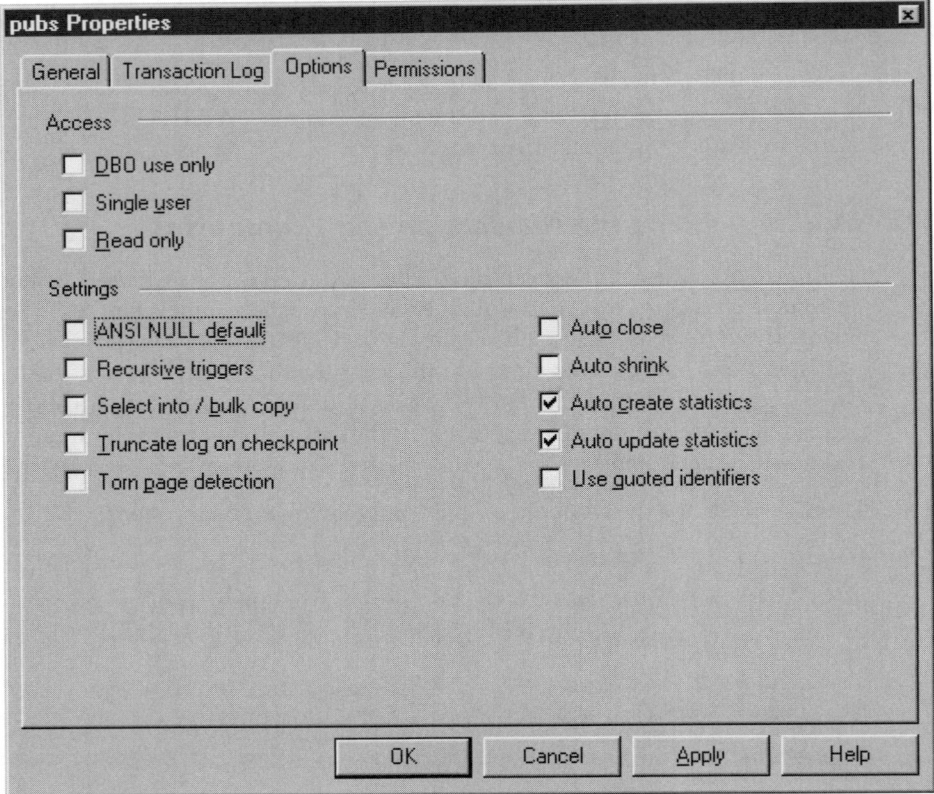

Figure 3.7 Database options dialog.

RE-INSTALLING PUBS

If you make a mistake during one of these exercises and find you can't recover the pubs database to its original state, don't worry, because there's a script on the SQL Server 7 CD that will recreate pubs for you. The script is called *instpubs.sql* and is located in the Install sub-directory. Simply open this script in Query Analyzer, click the Run button and all is well. If you do happen to use this script, take a look at some of the code used to create pubs. You may pick up a new trick or two by looking at the coding techniques from the "experts."

Enterprise Manager

Complete the following in order to create a transaction log backup of pubs with Enterprise Manager.

1. Expand the Server and then expand Databases.
2. Select pubs, right-click and highlight All Tasks then select Backup Database from the pop-up menu.

3. In the Name field type, pubs_Database_Transaction.
4. Select Database - Transaction log in the Backup section of the dialog.
5. Make sure that the pubs_Disk_Device is selected in the Destination section and Append to media is selected in the Overwrite section. Click OK.

Once the backup is complete, a message is displayed that informs you that the transaction log backup was successful.

Transact-SQL

In order to complete the same transaction log backup with T-SQL, execute the following (only execute this statement if you did not create the backup in the previous section).

```
BACKUP LOG pubs  TO pubs_Disk_Device WITH NAME =
'pubs_Database_Transaction'
```

The full syntax of for the backup log is shown here:

```
BACKUP LOG {database_name | @database_name_var}
{
[WITH
{ NO_LOG | TRUNCATE_ONLY }]
}
|
{
TO <backup_device> [, Ún]
[WITH
[BLOCKSIZE = {blocksize | @blocksize_variable}]
[[,] DESCRIPTION = {text | @text_variable}]
[[,] EXPIREDATE = {date | @date_var}
| RETAINDAYS = {days | @days_var}]
[[,] FORMAT | NOFORMAT]
[[,] {INIT | NOINIT}]
[[,] MEDIADESCRIPTION = {text | @text_variable}]
[[,] MEDIANAME = {media_name | @media_name_variable}]
[[,] [NAME = {backup_set_name | @backup_set_name_var}]
[[,] NO_TRUNCATE]
[[,] {NOSKIP | SKIP}]
[[,] {NOUNLOAD | UNLOAD}]
[[,] [RESTART]
[[,] STATS [= percentage]]
]
}
```

The three arguments shown in Table 3.4 are added to the others described in the *Database Backup* section.

Generally speaking, the only time you need to use the NO_LOG or TRUNCATE ONLY arguments is when the transaction log is full and you are prohibited from completing any more transactions until the log is cleared. Hmmm, that sounds a little funny, doesn't it? Well, here's the deal—performing a backup is an event that is recorded in the transaction log. So, if the log is full, the backup event cannot occur because the event cannot be recorded in the log. The only way to work around this is to specify that the backup event should not be recorded (NO_LOG) or to clear the log without backing it up (TRUNCATE_ONLY).

OUT OF LOG SPACE

If you run out of log space and are forced to clear the transaction log with NO_LOG or TRUNCATE_ONLY, you must execute a database backup or differential database backup immediately in order to recover the database to the point at which the log was cleared.

Virtual Log Files

A transaction log file is composed of more than one segment called a *virtual log file*. A virtual log file's minimum size is 256 KB and a transaction log file's minimum size is 512 KB. There's not a specific formula that can be used to calculate the number of virtual log files that compose a transaction log file, but a general concept can be used. If a log file grows in many small amounts, it will probably have many small, virtual log files. If it grows less frequently in large amounts, it will be composed of a few large, virtual log files. The important thing to remember is that just because you truncate the log, the entire size of the log will never be shown as available. The maximum unused value will always be the size of log *minus* the size of the virtual log file in use.

Database Options that Affect Backup Operations

There are two database options that affect backup operations:

1. Truncate Log on Checkpoint
2. Select Into/Bulk Copy

Table 3.4 Backup Log Arguments

ARGUMENT	DESCRIPTION
LOG	This option indicates that only the transaction log is backed up. By default SQL Server truncates the inactive portion of the log.
NO_LOG | TRUNCATE_ONLY	This argument indicates that the inactive part of the log will be removed and no backup executed. You don't need to specify a backup device because no portion of the log is saved; this argument is used to free space only.
NO_TRUNCATE	This argument indicates that the backup process will not clear the inactive portion of the log. This argument is used to backup the log if the database is damaged, marked suspect, or has not been recovered.

Truncate Log on Checkpoint causes the inactive part of the log to be truncated when a CHECKPOINT is issued. The inactive part of the log contains transactions that have completed and will not be used during recovery. *Select Into/Bulk Copy* allows non-logged operations to occur that affect transaction log backups. If a non-logged operation occurs you cannot make a transaction log backup. If SQL Server allowed you to create a transaction log backup after a non-logged operation and you tried to recover the database with the backup, the non-logged changes and all of the changes based on the non-logged changes would be invalid. After a non-logged operation is performed, you must make a database backup or differential database backup in order to recover the database or make subsequent transaction log backups. In order to see which options are checked complete the following in Enterprise Manager:

1. Expand the Server and then expand Databases.
2. Select pubs, right-click and select Properties from the pop-up menu.
3. Select the Options tab and view the available options.

NON-LOGGED OPERATIONS

Performing a non-logged operation prohibits you from creating a transaction log backup.

How to View and Verify the Contents of a Backup Device

In order to properly manage backup devices you must be able to review their contents. Backup devices can contain a mix of database, differential database, and transaction log backups. The ability to determine what type(s) reside on a device is critical. In addition, you must be able to verify that the contents of a backup device are still valid. You should note, when reading this section, that the Enterprise Manager method to view and verify device contents is more user-friendly than the T-SQL approach, but that the T-SQL approach provides access to advanced capabilities not available in Enterprise Manager.

Enterprise Manager

In order to see the contents of the backup device complete the following steps:

1. Expand a Server and then expand Management.
2. Select Backup and notice that the pubs_Disk_Device backup device is displayed in the Details pane.
3. Select the backup device, right-click and select Properties from the pop-up menu.
4. Click View Contents to see the backups contained on the device.

Note that all of the backups we performed are displayed in the View Backup Media Contents window as shown in Figure 3.8.

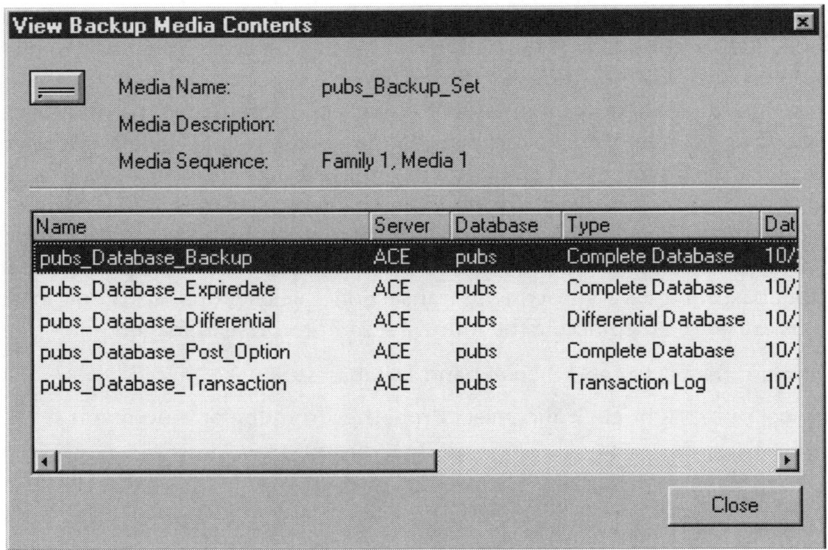

Figure 3.8 Viewing the contents of a backup device.

Transact-SQL

There are a number of T-SQL statements available to display information about the contents of a backup device. Although these statements can be used with both disk and tape backup devices, they are best used with tape backup devices. A quick review of how a tape is initialized and backups are recorded on tape will help you understand how the statements differ.

When a tape is formatted a media header is created on the tape that contains media name, description, software used to format the tape, and format date. This information can be accessed very quickly because it occurs once and is located at the beginning of the tape. Each time a backup is placed on the tape, backup header information is written. Backup header information includes information such as backup type—full or transaction—and start/stop time. In order to retrieve all of the backup header information on the tape, the entire tape must be read. On high-capacity tapes this process may prove very time-consuming.

RESTORE FILELISTONLY: Displays the database and log files on the device.

```
RESTORE FILELISTONLY
FROM <backup_device>
[WITH
[FILE = file_number]
[[, ] {NOUNLOAD | UNLOAD}]
]
```

RESTORE VERIFYONLY: Verifies that a backup or backup set is valid by confirming it is complete and that all volumes can be read.

```
RESTORE VERIFYONLY
FROM <backup_device> [,…n]
[WITH
[FILE = file_number]
[[,] {NOUNLOAD | UNLOAD}]
[[,] LOADHISTORY]
]
```

RESTORE LABELONLY: Displays the header information of the media.

```
RESTORE LABELONLY
FROM <backup_device>
```

RESTORE HEADERONLY: Displays backup header information about each backup on a device.

```
RESTORE HEADERONLY
FROM <backup_device>
[WITH {NOUNLOAD | UNLOAD}]
```

Restore Operations

Restore operations include the application of a database backup, which completely re-creates the database, or the use of either a differential database backup and/or transaction log backup(s) to reduce the granularity of recovery. Restoring a database backup completely re-creates the original database by creating all of the files on which the database was located, copying all of the information from the backup to the *new* database, and rolling back all incomplete transactions. To restore a differential database backup you must copy all of the changes that occurred since the last database backup and roll back all incomplete transactions. Restoring a transaction log backup applies all of the complete transactions contained in the log and rolls back any incomplete transactions. The process of rolling back incomplete transactions is called *recovery*.

Restoring a Database Backup

Restoring a database with a database backup completely re-creates the database as it existed when the backup was made. One of the ramifications of this process is that all but the following configurable database options are re-set to their value at the time the database backup was completed.

- Offline
- Merge Publish
- Published
- Subscribed Replication

You can override the "dbo use only" setting by including the WITH DBO_ONLY argument in the restore statement. Use this option if you don't want the database accessed until you've had time to review the contents to ensure that it contains the appropriate data.

RESTORING DATABASE OPTIONS

After restoring a database be sure to reset any database options that changed between the time the backup is created and the time the backup is applied.

Before the database backup is applied execute the following in Query Analyzer in order to verify the contents of pubs..authors.

```
SELECT au_lname FROM authors
```

Note that all of the authors' last names are Maris.

Enterprise Manager

The following steps demonstrate how to apply the original database backup to the pubs database.

1. Expand a Server and then expand Databases.
2. Select pubs, right-click and highlight All Tasks and select Restore Databases from the pop-up menu.
3. Click the down arrow next to First backup to restore and then select pubs_Database_Backup.
4. Select the Restore check box for the Backup set name, pubs_Database_Backup.
5. De-select the Restore check box for pubs_Database_Transaction and press the OK button.

Figure 3.9 shows the Restore Database dialog.

You'll receive the error message shown in Figure 3.10 if you did not close Query Analyzer or remove pubs as the database referenced in the query window.

In order to restore a database, the system administrator must have exclusive use of the database. You can go into Query Analyzer and either close the window or remove the pubs database as the focus to successfully apply the backup. Once you do this press the OK button in the Restore Database dialog. When the backup is complete you'll see a message that indicates that the database backup was successful. Execute the SELECT statement to verify that the authors' last names are the original values.

Before we move on to the T-SQL approach let's review the way that SQL Server attempts to help with restores by displaying the available backups on a device. Open the Restore Database dialog again with All Tasks - Restore Database, and notice that pubs_Database_Post_Option and pubs_Database_Transaction are displayed and checked (see Figure 3.11). These are the last two backups that we performed on the pubs database. SQL Server keeps track of the backups performed on a database and tries to help you by defaulting to the last one performed for each type of backup.

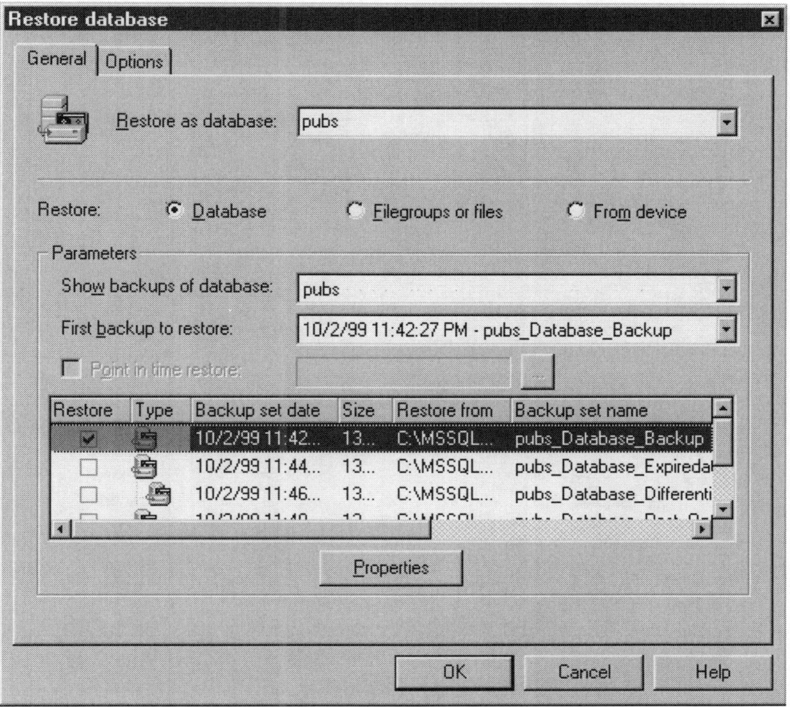

Figure 3.9 Restore database dialog.

Select pubs_Database_Backup and notice that all of the backup sets are displayed in the window as shown in Figure 3.9. By default, the latest database backup (pubs_Database_Post_Option) and the transaction log created after it are selected. Select the Restore option next to pubs_Database_Backup and notice that the pubs_Database_Post_Option is de-selected. SQL Server shows what backup sets are compatible. Select Restore for pubs_Database_Differential and notice that the pubs_Database_Expiredate is selected. In order to restore the differential, you must first apply the database backup created before the differential database backup. SQL Server uses seven tables (backupmediaset, backupmediafamily, backupset, backupfile, restorehistory, restorefilegroup, and restorefile) in the msdb database to track backup and restore operations. When using

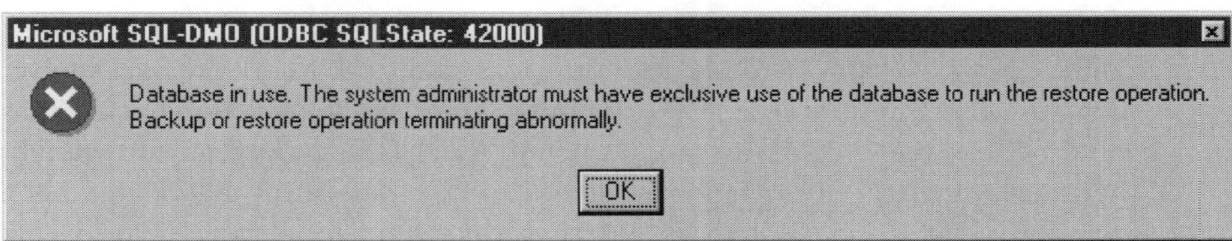

Figure 3.10 Restore error message.

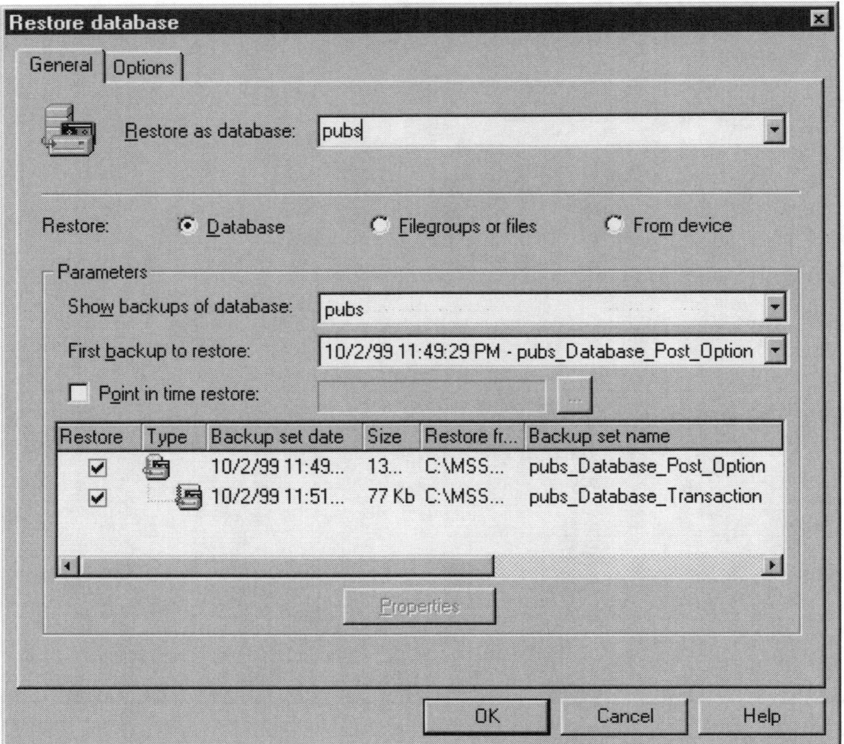

Figure 3.11 Most recent backups.

the Restore option in Enterprise Manager, these seven tables are used to determine the characteristics of the backup sets and to suggest the most efficient recovery strategy.

Transact-SQL

In order to complete the same database restore operation using T-SQL execute the following in Query Analyzer:

```
RESTORE DATABASE pubs FROM pubs_Disk_Device
```

To use any of the other database or differential database backups on the device, a *file number* is required. The original backup has a file number of 1 (because it was the first on the device) and this is the default for RESTORE DATABASE. As more backups are added to the device the associated file number is incremented by 1. The pubs_Database_Expiredate has a file number of 2 and ...the pubs_Database_Transaction has a value of 5. The Enterprise Manager approach allows you to choose the backup set you want by name or number, but with T-SQL it's not as easy. In order to determine the file number associated with a backup set on a pubs_Disk_Device, execute the following in Query Analyzer:

```
RESTORE HEADERONLY FROM pubs_Disk_Device
```

The resultset contains two fields, BackupName and Position, that allow you to choose the appropriate file number. The following T-SQL statement allows you to apply the pubs_Database_Differential—the third backup set on the device. (Do not execute this statement.)

```
RESTORE DATABASE pubs FROM pubs_Disk_Device WITH File = 3
```

The complete syntax for RESTORE DATABASE is listed here:

```
RESTORE DATABASE {database_name | @database_name_var}
[FROM <backup_device> [, ... n]]
[WITH
[DBO_ONLY]
[[,] FILE = file_number]
[[,] MEDIANAME = {media_name | @media_name_variable}]
[[,] MOVE 'logical_file_name' TO 'operating_system_file_name']
[,...n]
[[,] {NORECOVERY | RECOVERY | STANDBY = undo_file_name}]
[[,] {NOUNLOAD | UNLOAD}]
[[,] REPLACE]
[[,] RESTART]
[[,] STATS [= percentage]]
]
```

The arguments for RESTORE DATABASE are listed in Table 3.5.

Table 3.5 RESTORE DATABASE Arguments

ARGUMENT	DESCRIPTION
database_name	This is the database that will be restored.
<backup_device> [, ... n]]	This is the device that contains the backup.
DBO_ONLY	This argument indicates that the database will only be accessible to the dbo after the restore is complete.
FILE = file_number	This option indicates that the backup set will be restored.
MEDIANAME = {media_name | @media_name_variable}]	This is the name that will be written on all volumes of the backup set with a maximum of 128 characters. If this value is supplied, but does not match the existing media name of the devices the backup will fail.
MOVE 'logical_file_name' TO 'operating_system_file_name'	This argument indicates that the logical_file_name will be moved to the operating_system_file_name.
NORECOVERY	This argument indicates that uncommitted transactions will not be rolled back. This should not be used if you have more backups to apply to the database.
RECOVERY	This argument indicates that uncommitted transactions will be rolled back. This should not be used if you have more backups to apply to the database. *Continues*

Table 3.5 RESTORE DATABASE Arguments *(Continued)*

ARGUMENT	DESCRIPTION
STANDBY = undo_file_name	This argument indicates that the name of the file will contain information that is used to undo recovery.
NOUNLOAD	This is the default functionality that indicates that a tape will not be ejected after the backup is complete.
UNLOAD	This argument indicates that a tape backup device will be unwound and ejected after the backup is complete.
REPLACE	This argument indicates that any existing database with the same name should be overwritten.
RESTART	This argument indicates that a previously interrupted RESTORE operation should be restarted.
STATS [= percentage]	This indicates the percent of complete information that's displayed during the RESTORE process.

Restore to a Point of Failure

Restoring to a point of failure reduces the granularity of the amount of data you recover. You can recover all of the changes that have occurred since the last database backup with a differential database backup, all or part of the transactions that have occurred within a period with a transaction log backup, or a combination of both. The pubs database is currently in the same state as it was when you first installed SQL Server because the pubs_database_backup was applied in the previous section. Update changes were made to the authors' tables after the install, and we can use the differential database and transaction log backup to recover the database to the desired state.

Enterprise Manager

In this example, the pubs database is recovered to the McGwire change recorded in pubs_database_differential. To do this in Enterprise Manager, complete the following steps:

1. Expand the Server and then expand Databases.
2. Right-click on the pubs database, highlight All Tasks and select Restore Database from the pop-up menu.
3. Click the down arrow next to First backup to restore and select pubs_Database_Expiredate.
4. Select the Restore check box for the Backup set name pubs_Database_Expiredate and notice how pubs_Database_Differential is automatically selected.
5. De-select the Restore check box for pubs_Database_Transaction and press the OK button.

Once the two backup sets have been applied, a message that indicates that the restore was successful is displayed. Review the au_lname field to verify that all of the authors' last names are McGwire.

The next example will recover the database to its most current state when the Maris update is applied:

1. Expand the Server and then expand Databases.
2. Right-click on the pubs database, highlight All Tasks and select Restore Database from the pop-up menu.
3. Verify that the Restore check box for both pubs_Database_Post_Option and pubs_Database_Transaction are checked and press the OK button.

Review the au_lname field to verify that all of the authors' last names are Maris. The database can be recovered to any point in time as long as the rules for precedence are followed. This example is especially interesting because it demonstrates that the database backup performed after the database option was changed must be applied before the transaction log is applied.

Transact-SQL

Before we proceed, restore pubs to its original state with the following:

```
RESTORE DATABASE pubs FROM pubs_Disk_Device
```

The T-SQL approach is a little more detailed than Enterprise Manager because when you apply multiple backups all at once, Enterprise Manager takes care of the recovery process. The previous example in Enterprise Manager applied both a database backup and a transaction log backup sequentially in order to recover to the most current state. Because both backup sets were selected, the backup process did not recover (back out all open transactions) the database until the last backup was applied. The following T-SQL statements perform the same degree of recovery as the previous example, but notice how you must *explicitly* indicate when the database should not be recovered:

```
RESTORE DATABASE pubs FROM pubs_Disk_Device WITH FILE = 4, NORECOVERY
RESTORE LOG pubs FROM pubs_Disk_Device WITH FILE = 5
```

The first line applies pubs_database_post_option; the second line applies pubs_database_transaction with the RESTORE LOG statement. When the database backup is applied, you must explicitly tell the backup process not to recover the database. Recovery is default behavior, so the RESTORE LOG statement must indicate that the database should be recovered. The complete syntax for RESTORE LOG is listed here:

```
RESTORE LOG {database_name | @database_name_var}
[FROM <       _device> [, …n]]
[WITH
[DBO_ONLY]
[[,] FILE = file_number]
[[,] MEDIANAME = {media_name | @media_name_variable}]
[[,] {NORECOVERY | RECOVERY | STANDBY = undo_file_name}]
[[,] {NOUNLOAD | UNLOAD}]
[[,] RESTART]
[[,] STATS [= percentage]]
[[,] STOPAT = {date_time | @date_time_var}]
```

There's one additional argument not described in RESTORE BACKUP: STOPAT. The STOPAT argument indicates where the recovery process should stop when applying transactions from the backup. If the backup contains transactions that transpired from 10:00 to 11:00 A.M., and you need to recover to 10:30 A.M., this option is used.

Implementing a Plan

Now that you understand the basics of backup and recovery, let's implement a backup plan for the pubs database that you can use in your organization. Let's assume we work in an environment where the mission-critical application is only used Monday through Friday from the hours of 8:00 A.M. to 5:30 P.M. and implement the following:

- Daily database backup at 10:00 P.M.
- Two daily differential database backups at 1:00 P.M. and 6:00 P.M.
- Eight daily transaction log backups at 9, 10, 11, Noon, 2, 3, 4, and 5

Since we use hourly backups throughout the day, this reduces the maximum data loss to a little more than 59 minutes. Since we use differential database backups twice a day, this reduces the maximum number of backups needed to complete a restore to one database backup, one differential database backup, and four transaction log backups. Can you determine when the maximum number of backups is required? That's right—any time between 5:00 and 6:00P.M.

In this chapter we only cover the Enterprise Manager approach to implementing our plan. The GUI approach makes the scheduling aspect of this process much easier and we doubt that you will ever use T-SQL to schedule backups. The following example demonstrates how to implement the plan with Enterprise Manager.

Database Backup at 10:00PM

1. Expand the Server and then expand Databases.
2. Right-click on the pubs database, highlight All Tasks and select Backup Database from the pop-up menu.
3. Type in pubs_Daily_Backup_10PM in the Name field and select Overwrite existing media in the Overwrite section.
4. Select the Schedule option in the Schedule section and click the Ellipsis button to the right of the Schedule Description field.
5. Type in pubs_Daily_Backup_10PM in the schedule's Name field and click the Change button.
6. Verify that the Weekly option is selected in the Occurs section, select the Mon, Tue, Wed, Thur, and Fri options in the Weekly section and deselect the Sat and Sun options.
7. In the Daily Frequency section set Occurs once at to 10:00PM and press the OK button until the Backup dialog is cleared.

Figure 3.12 shows the Schedule dialog for the full database backup.

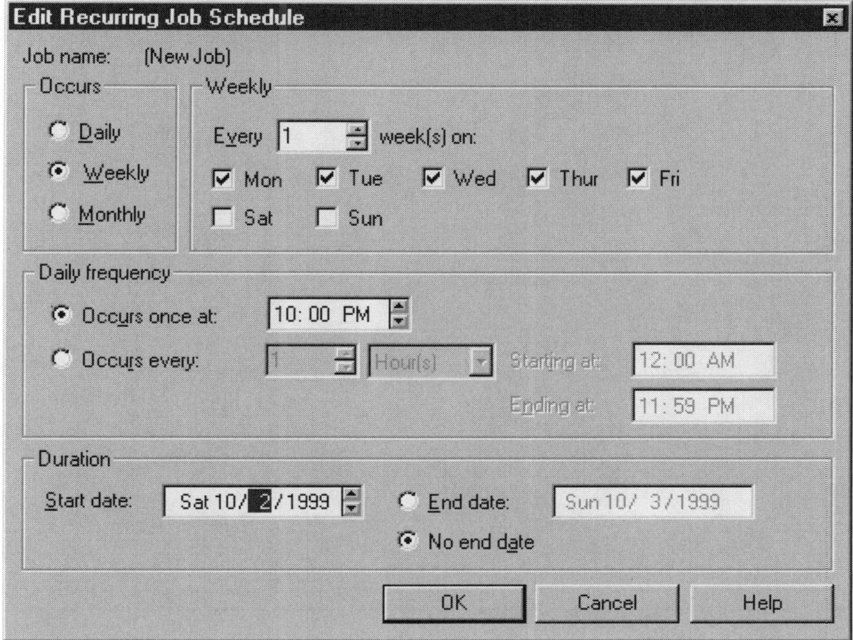

Figure 3.12 Schedule dialog for full database backup.

Differential Database Backup at 1:00PM and 6:00PM

1. Right-click on the pubs database, highlight All Tasks and select Backup Database from the pop-up menu. Type in pubs_Daily_DifferentialBackup_1_6PM in the Name field and verify Append to media is selected in the Overwrite section.
2. Select the Schedule option in the Schedule section and click the Ellipsis button to the right of the Schedule Description field.
3. Type in pubs_Daily_DifferentialBackup_1_6PM in the schedule's Name field and click the Change button.
4. Verify that the Weekly option is selected in the Occurs sections. In the Weekly section select the Mon, Tue, Wed, Thur, and Fri options and de-select the Sat and Sun options.
5. In the Daily Frequency section set the Occurs every to 5 hours Starting at 1:00PM and Ending at 6:00PM. Press the OK buttons until the Backup dialog is cleared.

Figure 3.13 shows the Schedule dialog for the differential database backup.

Transaction Log Backup at 9:00AM, 10:00AM, 11:00AM, and Noon

1. Right-click on the pubs database, highlight All Tasks and select Backup Database from the pop-up menu.

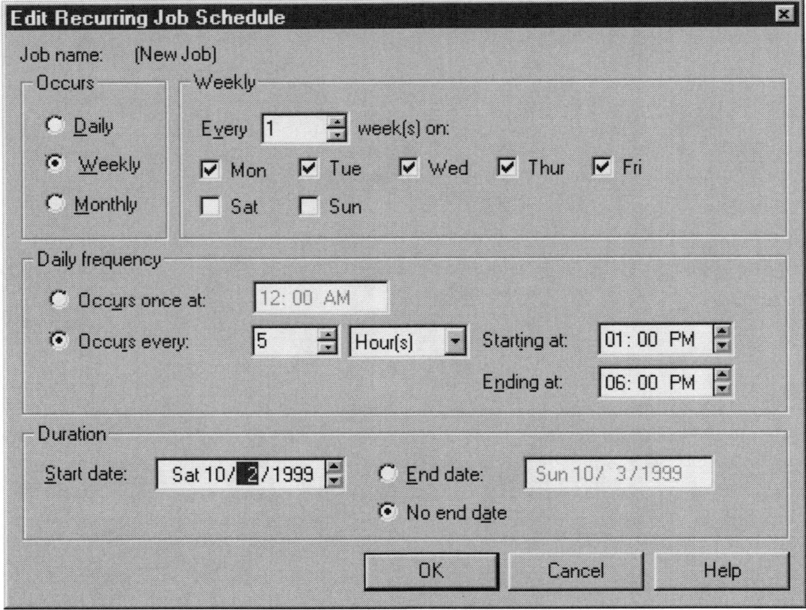

Figure 3.13 The Schedule dialog for the differential database backup.

2. Type in pubs_Daily_TransactionLogBackup_Morning in the Name field and verify that Append to media is selected in the Overwrite section.
3. Select the Schedule option in the Schedule section and click the Ellipsis button to the right of the Schedule Description field.
4. Type in pubs_Daily_TransactionLogBackup_Morning in the schedule's Name field and click the Change button.
5. Verify that the Weekly option is selected in the Occurs sections. In the Weekly section select the Mon, Tue, Wed, Thur, and Fri options and then de-select the Sat and Sun options.
6. In the Daily Frequency section set the Occurs every option to 1 hours, Starting at 9:00AM and Ending at 12:00PM. Press the OK buttons until the Restore dialog is cleared.

Figure 3.14 shows the Schedule dialog for the transaction log database backup.

Repeat the same steps for the afternoon series of transaction log backups, but be sure to modify the name. This was a little bit of work, but the good news is once you have your plan set correctly, all you have to do is monitor your log files to make sure that everything works properly.

Without knowing it, you just started using another feature of SQL Server 7 called *Jobs*. In order to see what we're talking about, do the following steps:

1. Expand the Server and then expand Management.
2. Expand SQL Server Agent and then select Jobs (see Figure 3.15).

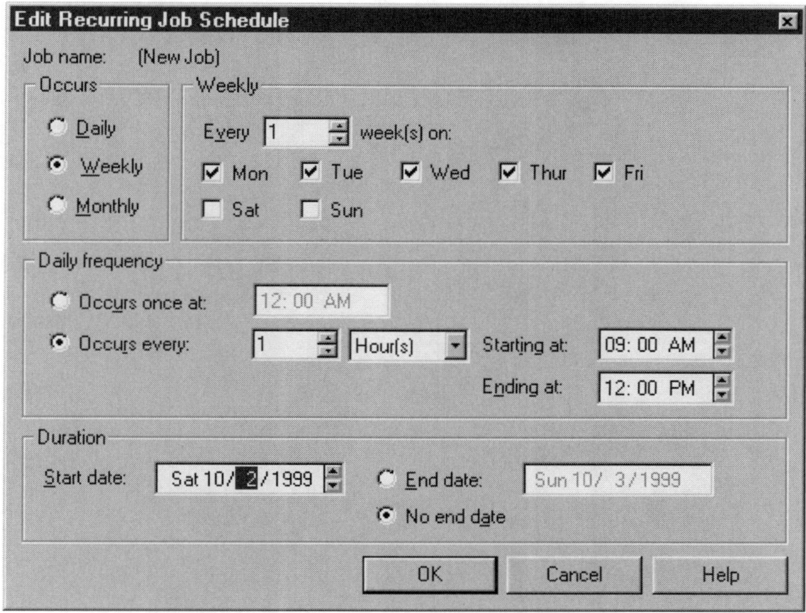

Figure 3.14 Schedule dialog for transaction log backup.

The values displayed in Figure 3.15 should look familiar. A Job is simply a scheduled task that SQL Server must perform. One of a Job's most important features is the ability to perform an action when it fails. Complete the following steps:

1. Double-click any of the Jobs listed in the Details pane.
2. Click the Notifications tab (see Figure 3.16).

Can you see all of the ways you can configure a Job to notify someone when it fails? We'll leave it to you to explore all the other neat things that you can do with Jobs, but the most important thing that you should know is that Jobs are executed by the SQL Server Agent service. If this service is not started/running, then no Jobs can be executed.

If the SQL Server Agent service is running, there will be a green arrow next to the SQL Server Agent option under the Management server tree. If you see a red dot, which means it's stopped, simply right-click on SQL Server Agent and select Start from the pop-up menu. If you want to configure the SQL Server Agent service to start automatically when SQL Server is started, you need to modify the service in Control Panel/ Services as follows:

1. Double-click on the Services icon in the Windows Control Panel.
2. Scroll down until you see the SQL Server Agent service and click Startup (see Figure 3.17).
3. Click the Automatic option in the Startup Type section and click OK.

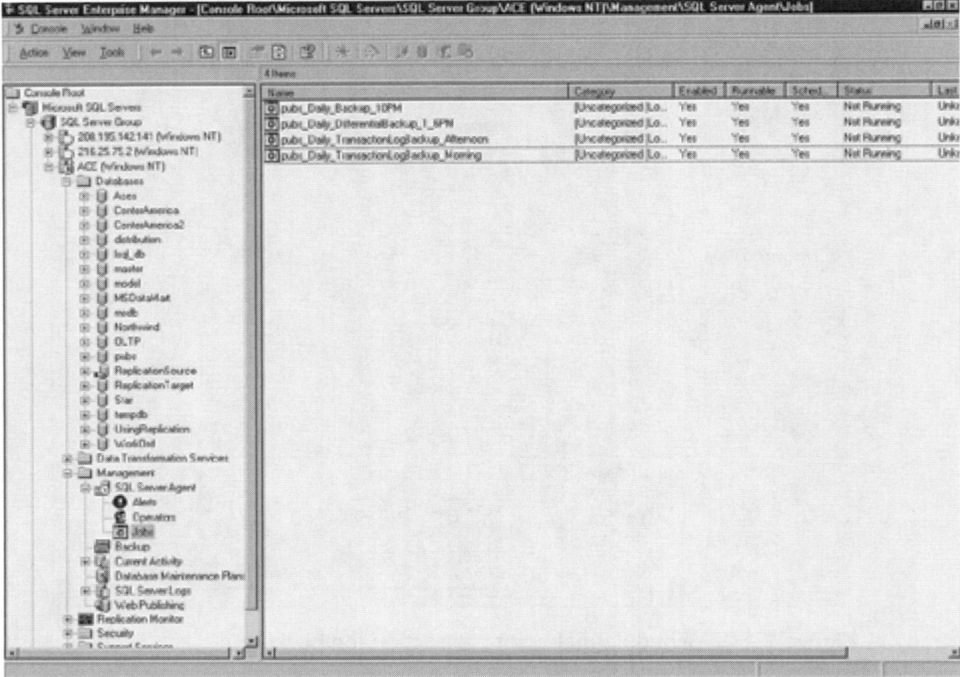

Figure 3.15 Jobs in the Details pane.

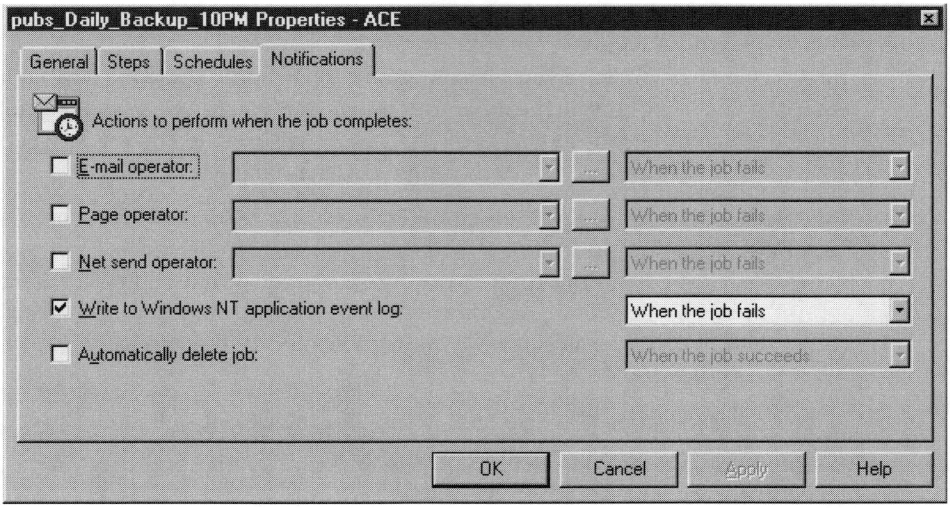

pubs_Daily_Backup_10PM Properties - ACE

General | Steps | Schedules | Notifications

Actions to perform when the job completes:

- [ ] E-mail operator: — When the job fails
- [ ] Page operator: — When the job fails
- [ ] Net send operator: — When the job fails
- [x] Write to Windows NT application event log: — When the job fails
- [ ] Automatically delete job: — When the job succeeds

OK | Cancel | Apply | Help

Figure 3.16 Job notifications.

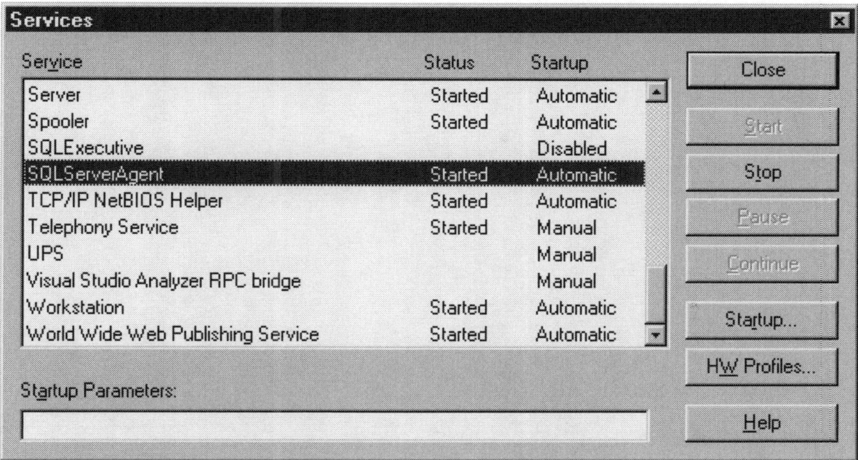

Figure 3.17 SQL Server Agent service.

Testing and Implementing Your Plan

If you've understood the material in this chapter and successfully completed the project, you should feel pretty comfortable with your knowledge of backup and recovery. But you're not done yet! We recommend that you create a copy of one of your production databases and implement a backup strategy that you feel will ensure minimal data loss. Wait a day or two until you have several backups and then use realistic scenarios to simulate recovering the database to various points in time. Do this until you are so comfortable with the process that you will not panic when this happens on a live database and you have several frantic co-workers asking about their data.

Once you're convinced that you have a firm grasp of backup and recovery, formulate and document an overall strategy for your company. Implement the strategy and then make sure you monitor the daily activities to ensure that all is working as expected. Periodically, simulate recovery scenarios to make sure that the data is being backed up properly. There may be times when all the effort seems like a waste of time, but then something unexpected will happen and all the effort will be justified.

PART TWO

Projects

CHAPTER 4

Project #1: Upsizing Your Desktop Database

Goal

The goal of this chapter is to show how to move data from Microsoft Access and Excel—and almost any other ODBC-comliant data source—into SQL Server 7.

- ✔ Microsoft SQL Server 7 installed
- ✔ TCP/IP-enabled network
- ✔ Microsoft Internet Explorer 4.0
- ✔ Microsoft Excel 2000 or Excel 97
- ✔ Microsoft Access 2000 or Access 97
- ✔ Access2000 work order database found on the CD-ROM under \Data\Access2000-WorkOrd.zip
- ✔ Access97 work order database found on the CD-ROM under \Data\Access97-WorkOrd.zip
- ✔ Sample Access NWPlants.MDB found on the CD-ROM under \Data\NWPlants.mdb and \Data\PlantPhotos.mdb
- ✔ Sample Excel Wineries.XLS spreadsheet found on the CD-ROM under \Data\Excel

We use the term *upsizing* in the generic sense to mean moving data from desktop databases, spreadsheets, documents, or text files into SQL Server 7. We think that there are literally millions of you out there who have purchased SQL Server 7 because you want to upsize.

In their simplest form, databases are basically lists, and most of us keep a variety of lists. You may have started a list in Microsoft Word or Excel—or even Notepad—and harnessed various sorting commands to alphabetize it (see the Tip: *Sorting in MS DOS, Word, and Excel* for a mini tutorial). However, if your list grows, or if you want to share it with others, chances are that you'll start to run into some problems like lists that are out of sync or difficult to search in a one-at-a-time fashion. Sound familiar? Perhaps you've created a Microsoft Access database—or used or inherited a vintage Xbase, Btrieve, or Paradox database. These desktop databases, designed primarily as so-called *file server* systems, can run out of steam with large data files or lots of concurrent users. (See FYI: *Visual FoxPro* for comments on Microsoft's Visual FoxPro.)

FYI EXCEL, ACCESS, OR SQL SERVER?

Before you decide whether or not to leave data in Excel or Access or to upsize to SQL Server, here are some things to consider:

- **Excel can store up to 65,535 records, the number of available rows. Because Excel uses RAM to store spreadsheets, your database may run into RAM limitations before it runs out of rows.**
- **Acesss can store more than 2 billion records and .mdb files of about 2 gigabytes but, for all effective purposes, your database is limited by the space on your hard disk. SQL Server is limited only by the available storage.**
- **Even though Access and SQL Server have a lot of built-in functions, Excel is generally a lot easier to use if you need to perform complex calculations or produce graphs or charts.**
- **Access isn't designed for transactions and doesn't let you "roll them back" like SQL Server does. With Access, transactions are applied directly to the database, complicating backups and increasing the risk of corruption, especially in a multiuser environment.**
- **SQL Server lets you assign permissions down to the field level, something that neither Excel nor Access do.**

FYI VISUAL FOXPRO

Curiously, Microsoft categorizes Visual FoxPro (VFP) as a programming language, not a database product—despite the fact that it's basically a descendant of dBase. Despite its file system origins, it scales quite well—far better than Access, for example—though not as well as SQL Server.

If you've got a VFP application, you can use the Upsizing Wizard that ships—complete with source code(!)—with Visual FoxPro versions 3.0 and higher, or you can use SQL Server's NT-based Data Transformation Services (DTS). The Visual FoxPro Upsizing Wizard is used to upsize Visual FoxPro tables to Microsoft SQL Server, including their rules, defaults, and referential interity (RI) when possible. At press time, the Upsizing Wizard only worked with SQL Server 4.21a, 6.0, and 6.5.

To use the Upsizing Wizard with Microsoft SQL Server 6.0, the SQL Server ODBC driver that ships with that version of SQL Server must be installed. To use Microsoft SQL Server 6.5, the SQL Server ODBC driver that ships with Visual FoxPro 5.0 or Visual Studio 97 must be installed. You need to make sure that the device, database, and log files on SQL Server are large enough for the tables to be upsized since VFP tables typically use more space on SQL Server than their local equivalents. For VFP 6.0, you can find the Upsizing Wizard source code at \<location of VFP in your system>\Tools \Xsource\xsource.zip. Knowledge base article Q136772, *INFO: General Information on the Visual FoxPro Upsizing Wizard* provides some useful information. A dozen other KB articles provide information about bugs and hints, especially about handling tricky issues associated with timestamps and nulls.

Microsoft Access 97, for example, won't let you create databases more than a gigabyte and Access 2000 is limited to two gigabytes, but we haven't heard of anyone who has successfully deployed an Access database anywhere near that large. (Gigabyte-plus databases in SQL Server 7 are commonplace, and there are a growing number of terabyte-plus databases.) Similarly, the Access spec says Access 97 will support up to 255 concurrent users. Yeah, right—5 or 10 seems to be more like it.

Performance and scalability aren't the only reasons people want to upsize from desktop databases or spreadsheet databases to real RDBMSs like SQL Server. Security and granular control of who-gets-to-see-what is another big incentive for upsizing. And some folks simply need to move from a non-Y2K program like Access 2.0.

SORTING IN MS DOS, WORD, AND EXCEL

If you've got a simple text file, you can harness Windows' SORT command by typing the following to alphabetize (case insensitive) a list, with the output going to the screen:

```
SORT filename
```

To send the output to a text file, you can modify the command as follows:

```
SORT filename1 > filename2
```

In Word, you can highlight the text you want to sort and use the Table|Sort command which lets you select your sort order as ascending or descending and specify the data to sort as text, numeric, or date. Like the MS DOS SORT command, Word's sort is case insensitive. Excel offers an even more sophisticated range of sorting options via the Data|Sort menu, and will let you sort in case-sensitive order.

Of course, not everyone purchased SQL Server because they want to upsize. Lots of you are undoubtedly considering moving data from more expensive UNIX, minicomputer, and even mainframe systems into SQL Server 7. In this chapter we're going to focus on upsizing, but the techniques that you learn in this chapter's projects will provide you with the skills to move data from just about any data source into SQL Server.

Some of you may want to download Microsoft's white papers on migration from http://www.microsoft.com/sql/interopmigrate/migrate.htm if you haven't done so already. As of early 1999, there were in-depth articles for migrating Oracle, Access, Sybase, and Btrieve databases. And there's nothing stopping you from checking other vendors' Web sites for *their* migration white papers. You'd be surprised how much you can learn about technical issues associated with migrating one database to another—even if the focus is on migrating from SQL Server to their RDBMS.

Upsizing to SQL Server—The Issues

As you prepare to tackle an upsizing (or downsizing) project, it doesn't hurt to remember that migrations like these are relatively common. In other words, lots of others have done what you're about to do and lived to talk about it.

The good news is that things are *much* easier today than they've ever been. For starters, most products ship with some sort of *file export* options that allow you to export data into any number of file formats that can subsequently be fed into SQL Server. Similarly, almost all products have a *file import* capability, and it's not uncommon to route a source file through more than one program in the process of preparing them for use in SQL Server. For example, you might export a mainframe file as text, load it into Excel and perform some simple data conversions, delete some unneeded columns, and then sort it before loading it into SQL Server. Access upsizers can use any of four or five Upsizing Wizards—you'll see how in this chapter—and Microsoft has also shipped an invaluable tool, DTS, with SQL Server 7. We'll use that, too.

Even with the wizards and DTS, database users and developers still face certain issues:

- How do I convert my data?
- What tools will be most helpful to me for my migration?
- Will the code, including macros, forms, and queries, associated with the old database still work?
- Are there any data-type changes in the two different systems? Will I lose any data?
- What's the best process for moving to the new platform?

If you're interested in the answers, this chapter's for you. We'll tackle an easy project first—migrating an Excel spreadsheet database into SQL Server. Then we'll show you two different techniques for migrating a large Access database into SQL Server—first with the Access 2000 Upsizing Wizard that ships with Office 2000 and then with DTS. Somewhere in the middle, we'll take a side trip and upsize a Northwest plants database.

	A	B	C	D	E	F	G
1	WINERY	MAIL ADDRESS	CITY	STATE	ZIP	PHONE	FAX
2	Alexia Sparkling Wines	18658-A -- 142nd Avenue N.E.	Woodinville	WA	98072	(425) 398-8392	
3	Ambrosia By Kristy	4921 -- 85th Avenue West	University Place	WA	98467	(206) 564-2065	
4	Andrew Will Cellars	12526 S.W. Bank Road	Vashon	WA	98070	(206) 463-3290	(360) 463-3524
5	Arbor Crest Wine Cellars	North 4705 Fruithill Road	Spokane	WA	99207	(509) 927-9894	(509) 927-0574
6	Badger Mountain Vineyards	1106 South Jurupa	Kennewick	WA	99337	(800) 643-9463	(509) 627-2071
7	Bainbridge Island Winery	682 State Highway 305 NE	Bainbridge Is.	WA	98110	(206) 842-9463	
8	Balcom & Moe Winery	2520 Commercial Avenue	Pasco	WA	99301	(509) 547-7307	(509) 547-7307
9	Barnard Griffin Winery	828 Tulip Lane	Richland	WA	99352	(509) 627-0266	(509) 627-7776
10	Baron Manfred von Vierthaler	17136 Highway 410 East	Sumner	WA	98390	(253) 863-1633	
11	Birchfield Winery	921-B Middle Fork Road	Onalaska	WA	98570	(360) 978-5224	(360) 978-5225
12	Bonair Winery	500 S. Bonair Rd.	Zillah	WA	98953	(509) 829-6027	(509) 829-6410

Figure 4.1 The Washington State Wine Commission's wineries database.

How Do I Convert My Data?

The different ways to convert and move the data range from manual to "almost" automatic. As we indicated previously, in our first project we'll start with a relatively simple example: an Excel spreadsheet. This is "real" data, given to us by the Washington State Wine Commission (www.washingtonwine.org) in early 1999.

One of the things that differentiates the various migration tools is whether or not they can create a new database for you as part of the migration. After all, if you're going to move data into a SQL Server database, there's got to be a database there to put it into. In our case, the Wineries spreadsheet is a single worksheet that contains just over 100 wineries (see Figure 4.1). The spreadsheet probably doesn't really need to be upsized into a SQL Server database, but it's easy for you to imagine that the Washington State Wine Commission might want to add lists of wines available from each of the vendors—or even offer them for sale. In that case, it would behoove them to use a database to keep track of everything, storing the additional data in separate database tables.

The Excel Project

To get our Excel spreadsheet database into SQL Server, we're going to need to do two major tasks:

1. Create a new database.
2. Import the data into a database table.

Step 1: Create a New Database (and Let the Wizard Do the Walking)

To create a WashWines database, we'll use the Enterprise Manager's Create Database Wizard.

Start Enterprise Manager by selecting the menu item or click on the icon (see the Tip: *Creating a Shortcut to Enterprise Manager*). Drill down from the Console Root until you find your active server.

CREATING A SHORTCUT TO ENTERPRISE MANAGER

Since the SQL Server install does not create a desktop shortcut to Enterprise Manager for you, you may want to create one yourself. Here are a couple of quick steps to create a desktop shortcut like this:

- **Open the My Computer icon, and continue to drill in through the drives and folders until you arrive at the one that holds the MSSQL tools (this will most likely be \MSSQL7\Binn).**
- **Right-click on the Enterprise Manager (SQL Server Enterprise Manager.MSC) icon and choose Create Shortcut. This will create a Shortcut to SQL Server Enterprise Manager.MSC in this folder—you'll probably want to rename this to something smaller, like EM.**
- **Now click and hold down on the new EM shortcut icon, and drag it onto the Taskbar's Start button at the bottom of the screen. This copies the shortcut to the startbar and gives you an EM choice when you click on start.**
- **Finally, click and hold down on the folders' EM shortcut again, and drag it onto your desktop. This removes the icon from the folder and puts it where you'll need it most—right under your nose.**

While you're at it, you may want to follow the same steps for the sqlmangr.exe - SQL Server Service Manager and the isqlw.exe - Query Analyzer.

The easiest way to start the Create Database wizard is to click on the Wizard icon on the Enterprise Manager's menu toolbar. The Wizard icon consists of stars and a wand and should be visible on the right side of the toolbar. However, the Wizard icon may be grayed out if you've just started Enterprise Manager. If so, simply drill down into Enterprise Manager's hierarchy until you've found your SQL Server and expanded its hierarchy.

WHICH RDBMS IS MORE ADVANCED?

Although some SQL Server DBAs dismiss Access as a "toy" RDBMS, many of those same DBAs have secretly coveted some of Access' advanced features such as TOP n (a quick way to find your best salespeople, for example) and AutoNumber fields, features which only recently became available in SQL Server.

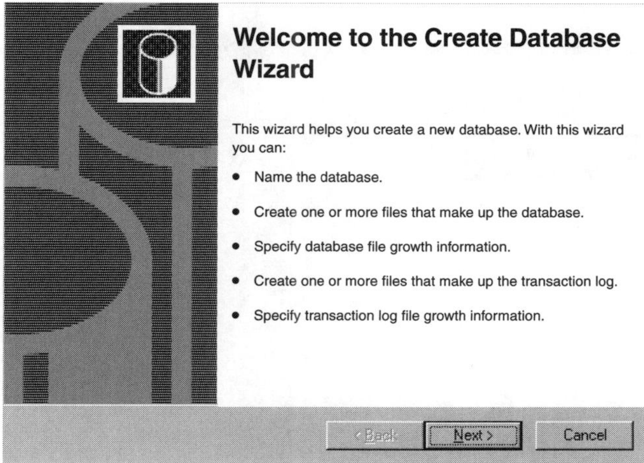

Figure 4.2 Running the Create Database Wizard.

You can also launch wizards via Enterprise Manager's Tools menu by clicking on Wizards and then expanding the appropriate category of wizards. In this case, the Create Database Wizard is in the first, Databases category. Double-click on Create Database Wizard to launch it. As you can see from Figure 4.2, you'll need to decide:

- What to name of the database
- The names and locations of the database's data and log files
- How the data and log files should grow

If you click on the Next button, you'll see that the default name of the new database is based on your login name, and that the default locations for the data and log files correspond to how you configured your SQL Server during installation. Change the database name to WashWines and adjust the data file and log file locations if you want to.

The next screen prompts you for the name (WashWines_data) and size (1 MB) for the database file. Because this is a simple, single-table project, go ahead and accept both the default name and size (see Figure 4.3).

The next screen asks you whether or not to let SQL Server handle growth, and, in most cases, we recommend that you "leave the driving" to SQL Server. Obviously, you might want to establish an upper limit, but let's just accept the defaults as shown in Figure 4.4.

The next two dialogs ask you similar questions about the log file and its growth. Again, just accept the defaults. The final screen displays a summary of your choices and gives you a chance to change your mind by clicking the Back button. Go ahead and click Finish. First, you should receive a message that indicates that the database was successfully created and then another message that asks whether or not you want to create a Maintenance Plan. Remember in Chapter 3 and our exhortations about the importance of backup plans? Well, on the off-chance that you skipped that chapter or didn't take

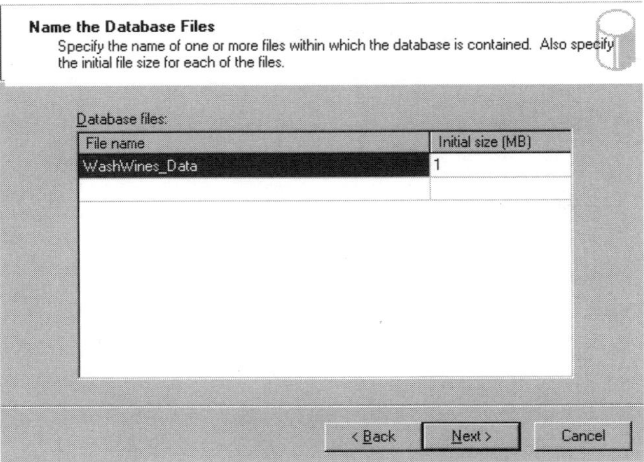

Figure 4.3 Deciding on database data file name(s) and size(s). Don't worry if your system shows something other than CZF23 at the top of the screen; that's simply the name of the server.

our advice and practice on your own data back then, here's another chance to practice those lessons (see Figure 4.5).

The Database Maintenance Plan Wizard makes it easy to run and/or schedule database integrity checks, update statistics, and perform database backups. Let's take a minute to explore.

Click on the Next button and you'll see that you're given the opportunity to select one or more databases to be maintained. Our new database, WashWines, is already

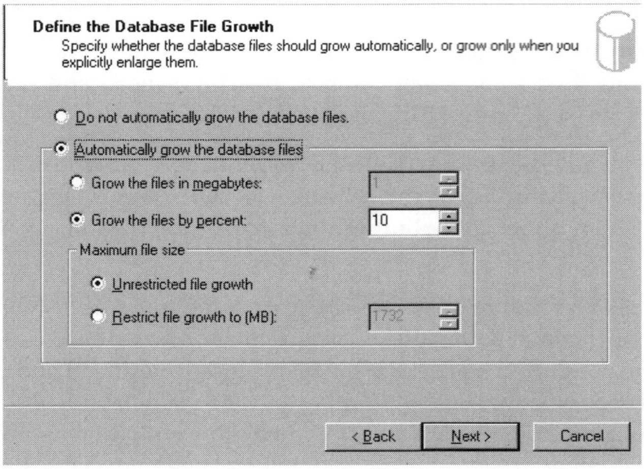

Figure 4.4 Making decisions about how the database should grow.

Figure 4.5 Running the Database Maintenance Plan Wizard.

selected by default, so just continue on to the next screen which deals with data optimization. Because we don't have any data in the database yet, leave all the boxes unchecked and continue to the Database Integrity Check screen. Again, continue past this screen where you can specify the database backup plan. We recommend that you test this on your system by specifying Media Available for your system and providing a date/time that's conveniently soon so you can see if it worked. Note that you must specify both your backup media and backup schedule. Subsequent screens ask additional questions about a backup disk directory, if you selected the backup to disk option, whether or not to back up the transaction log file, whether or not to generate a backup report, and where to store a backup history file. Pretty painless, isn't it?

Again, we recommend that you experiment with a backup plan with our simple database. Refer back to Chapter 3 where we suggest that you test your backup and restore strategy. Better now with a sample database than with the real thing. It's now time to create a table for the list of vintners and populate it with data. Well, guess what? There's a wizard to help us do this as well!

Step 2: Import the Data into SQL Server

Back to the Wizard menu, but this time expand the Data Transformation Services category and launch the DTS Import Wizard. Here's the Big Picture. The DTS Import Wizard wants to know our data source (the wineries.xls file that's on your CD-ROM) and our destination database (the new WashWines database in SQL Server). Ready?

As promised, the first input screen asks for the data source. Scroll through the data sources (probably up) and select the version of Excel that you're using as the Source. Then type in the path and filename of the wineries.xls file (see Figure 4.6). For our Excel spreadsheet, we don't have to worry about logins and passwords, but be advised that for most database files, we would.

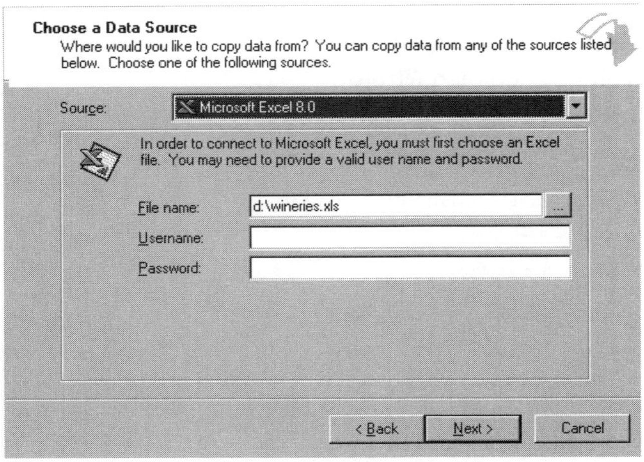

Figure 4.6 You need to tell the DTS Import Wizard what kind of data to import and where it's located.

The next screen asks for a destination server, the kind of authentication that we're using, and a target database. Probably the only thing you'll have to change is the bottom question about the target database. We've already set one up, so scroll down to WashWines.

The next screen confirms our selection so far: Excel8 to SQL Server, and basically asks if we want to copy entire source table(s)—our worksheet or workbook—or just part of it based on a query. Accept the default of copying table(s) from the source database. The next screen (see Figure 4.7) proposes a plan (importing a single table) and gives us the option of applying a Transform (see Figure 4.8) and even previewing the data. The DTS Import Wizard has provided the basic mappings for us—from Excel columns to

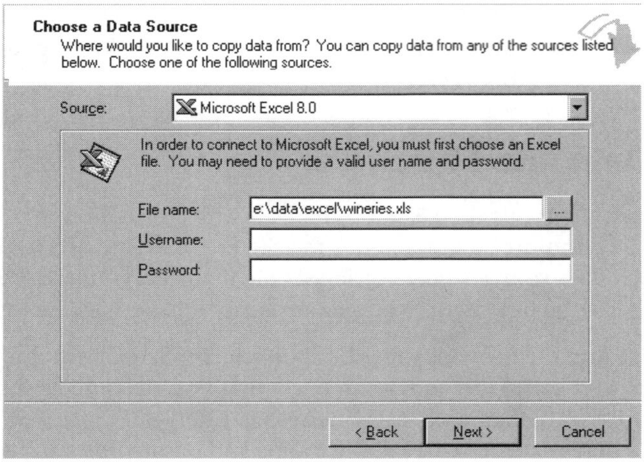

Figure 4.7 The wizard's plan.

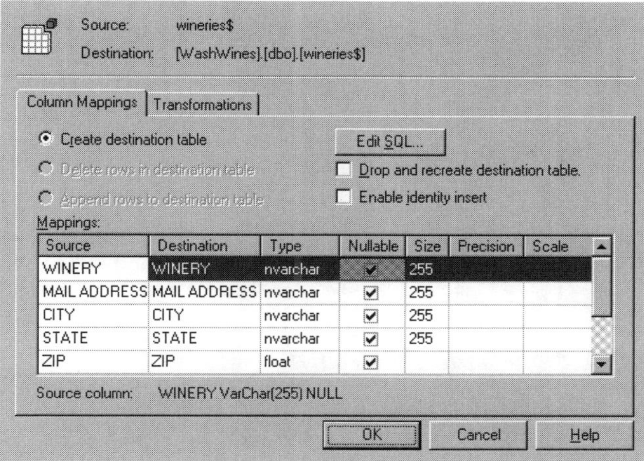

Figure 4.8 The DTS Import Wizard makes it easy to filter and even transform (modify) data on the way into SQL Server.

SQL Server table columns, and has assigned data types. Some of its guesses are correct but not all of them.

If you examine the proposed columns, you'll notice several things that don't seem right. The data types, for example, are mainly Unicode (we know that from the "n" at the beginning of nvarchar) varchar which can store up to 4000 characters. That's overkill for English language names and addresses of wineries. Similarly, the float data type, used for extremely high precision numbers, is unwarranted for ZIP codes. Read the *Books Online* topic, *Data Types (T-SQL)* for more information about SQL Server's data types (binary, bit, char, cursor, datetime, decimal, float, image, int, money, nchar, ntext, nvarchar, real, smalldatetime, smallint, smallmoney, text, timestamp, tinyint, varbinary, varchar, and uniqueidentifier). It also looks like we've ended up with a bogus column that the DTS Import Wizard has simply called F8 for field #8. You may as well highlight the F8 row and choose Ignore from the drop-down boxes associated with that field for both the source and destination.

It pays to take a bit of time to think about data types and field lengths up front. Although SQL Server is forgiving and lets you make changes in table designs at any time, changes are time consuming and can sometimes result in lost or truncated data. We'll make the following changes:

WINERY	**VARCHAR**	**50**	
Address	varchar	25	nullable
City	varchar	25	nullable
State	char	2	nullable
Zip	char	10	nullable
Phone	char	14	nullable
Fax	char	14	nullable
Ignore	0		

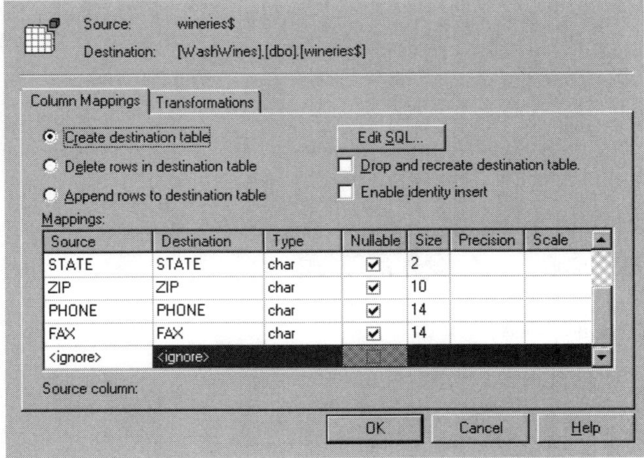

Figure 4.9 Using the DTS Import Wizard to define columns.

Note that we shortened the Mail Address field in the Excel worksheet to simply Address in SQL Server and require as little as a single entry in the Winery field (see Figure 4.9). Once that's done, click OK, preview your source data if desired, and continue. Have the wizard Run immediately and click Finish. Bingo! It's that easy (see Figure 4.10).

If Wizards Aren't Your Thing

Some folks don't like wizards, so here's one wizard-free method for creating a new database. You can also use the T-SQL CREATE DATABASE command if you're a code

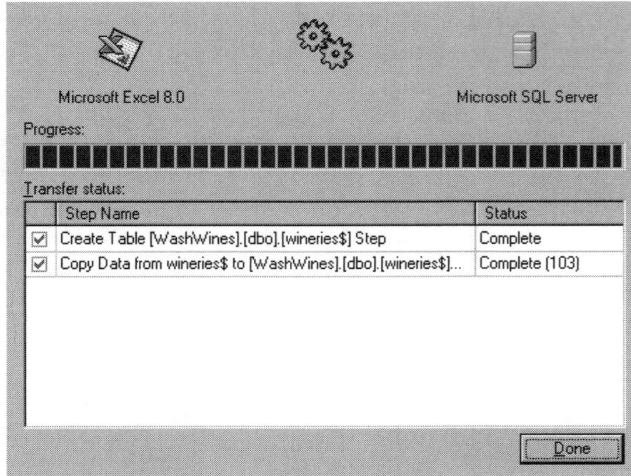

Figure 4.10 The DTS wizard confirms successful data transfer.

person. See the *Books Online* topic, *CREATE DATABASE (T-SQL)* if you're the roll-your-own-code type. You can *also* right-click on the word Database and choose the New Database menu choice as shown in Figure 4.11.

You'll be prompted for a database name, which we'll call Work. You'll also see places where you can choose your database's default size and the rate at which it will grow within SQL Server. Leave all of these set to the default values for now. If you click OK, Enterprise Manager will create an empty Work database on your server. Next, you can right-click on the new Work database icon or on its name in the list. Expand the server tree hierarchy and highlight the Tables section. Right click on Tables and choose New, Table. When prompted for a table name, enter Wineries. This displays the dialog shown in Figure 4.12.

The last step is to actually add the columns into the table. Figure 4.13 shows the "design" screen for your table. Here we've entered all of the fields from the Wineries spreadsheet and then some—an option that we didn't have in the DTS Import Wizard. Notice how we created columns for other items that we'd expect to want to store—Web site and an email address. Again, we still have to make data type decisions, but we can also establish default values.

When you finish the process, you're again left with a table, but just its skeleton—no data. To populate the table, you'd again have to use the DTS Import wizard or an older,

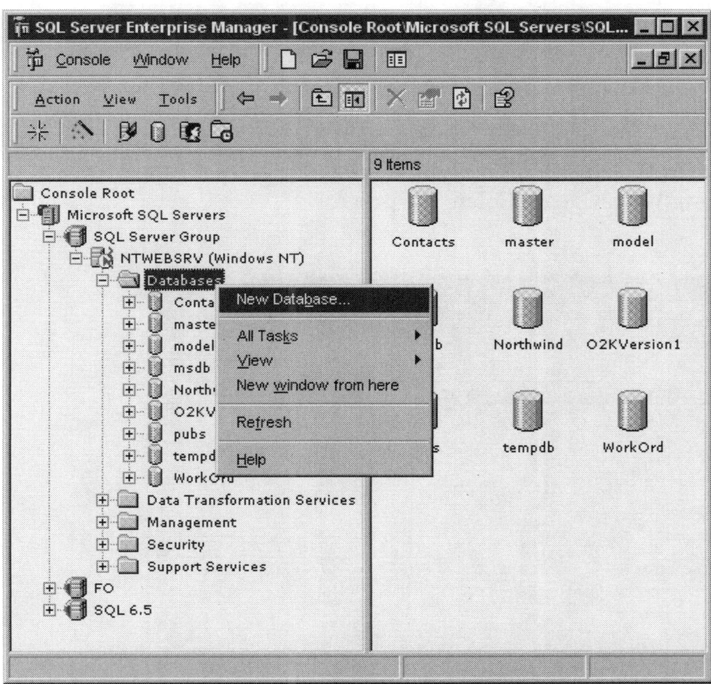

Figure 4.11 Creating a database within SQL Server on a system called NTWEBSRV.

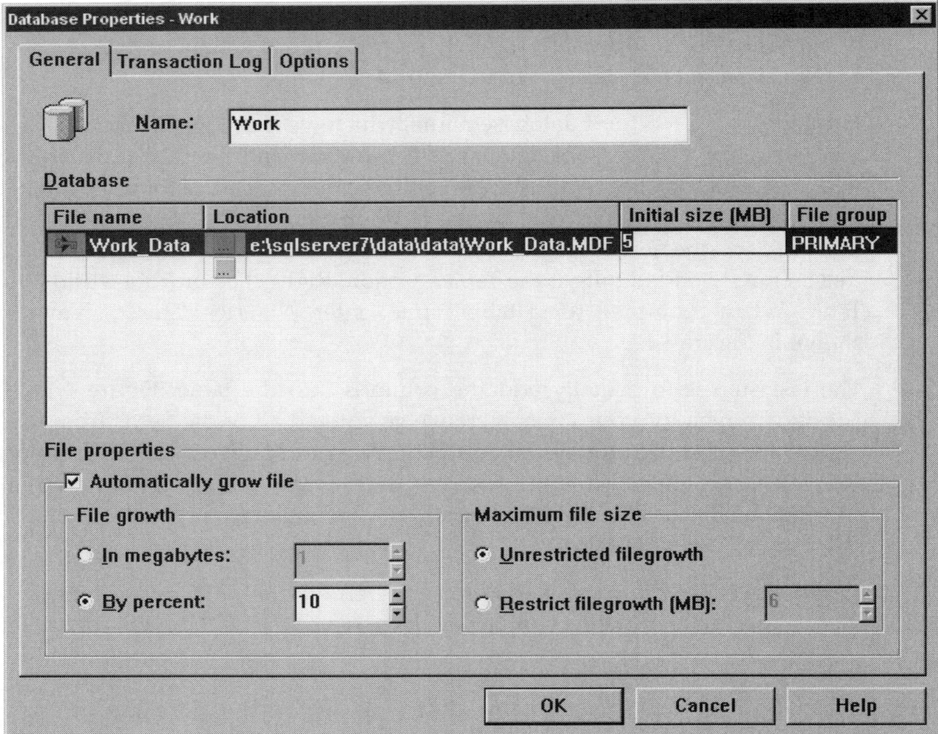

Figure 4.12 Table name and options.

generally unloved, command line utility called bcp, short for bulk copy program and discussed later in this chapter. Or, you could even move it into Access and then use Access' Upsizing Wizard to complete the process.

SQL Server Enterprise Manager - [2:New Table in 'Work' on 'NTWEBSRV']

Console Window Help

Column Name	Datatype	Length	Precision	Scale	Allow Nulls	Default Value
WineryName	varchar	50	0	0		
StreetAddress	varchar	25	0	0		
MailStop	varchar	25	0	0	✓	
City	varchar	25	0	0		
State	char	2	0	0		
Zip	char	10	0	0		
Phone	char	14	0	0	✓	('''')
Fax	char	14	0	0	✓	('''')
WebSiteUrl	varchar	75	0	0	✓	
ContactEmail	varchar	50	0	0	✓	

Figure 4.13 Defining the columns.

BRUTE FORCE VERSUS DTS

The good news is that you've got several options for getting desktop or other legacy data into SQL Server. You can export the contents of an Excel worksheet or Access table to an ASCII file. After that, you can then use SQL Server's bcp program to import the ASCII data. You can move data into Access 2000 in order to take advantage of the Access 2000 Upsizing Wizard. Another approach that might be useful for SQL Server 6.x users is to use the original Access 9x Upsizing Wizard to move Access 9x data into SQL Server 6.x and then into SQL Server 7. You can also use the new Access 97 Upsizing Wizard to move data directly into SQL Server 7.

Frankly, we think all of these suffer not only from indirection, but also from just plain making things more complicated than they need to be. We recommend learning DTS—using the DTS Import wizard barely scratched the surface—and trying it first. If, for some reason, DTS doesn't perform as desired, then try the other more brute-force approaches.

Non-DTS Upsizing Help

Each version of Access since Access 2.0 has its own Upsizing Wizard (Access 97 actually has two), and each version's wizard upsizes to only one version of SQL Server. Here are some resources where you can download the Access 95 and Access 97 Upsizing Wizards for free, download white papers, and find out about some third-party upsizing tools. (The Access 2.0 Upsizing Wizard is only available in the Access 2.0 Developer's Kit.)

Upsizing Wizards:

Microsoft Upsizing Wizard for Access 95 to SQL Server 6.0
www.microsoft.com/AccessDev/Articles/Exe/Upsize95.exe
Microsoft 1/97 Upsizing Wizard for Access 97 to SQL Server 6.5
www.microsoft.com/AccessDev/ProdInfo/Aut97dat.htm/support/mslfiles/AUT97.EXE
Microsoft 2/99 Upsizing Wizard for Access 97 to SQL Server 7
www.microsoft.com/products/developer/officedeveloper/Access/prodinfo/exe/wzos97.exe

Micrososft Upsizing Whitepapers:

support.microsoft.com/support/access/content/97downloads.asp#97Wiz
support.microsoft.com/support/access/content/97downloads.asp#97Whitepaper
www.asia.microsoft.com/accessdev/articles/autwp.htm

Jim Sturms' 5/96 Whitepapers Specifically for Upsizing Access 2.0:

technet.microsoft.com/cdonline/content/complete/Desk/Access/technote/ofc404.exe. Requires registration.

Continues

Non-DTS Upsizing Help ***(Continued)***

microsoft.com/library/techart/acc2sql_8.htm.support.microsoft.com/support/kb/articles/q237/9/80.asp, and support.microsoft.com/support/SQL/content/inprodhlp/_ole_db_provider_issues.asp. Good discussion of data type conversion issues.

Third-Party Upsizing Tools:

Aditi Updown
www.netsales.net/pk.wcgi/csica/prod/1120405-1
Aditi's Updown ($299.50) upsizes Access 2.0 databases to SQL Server.

Weir Performance Oracle/SQL Upsizer
www.weirperf.com/upsize.htm
As of late 1999, Weir Performance offered upsizers as add-ins to Access 2.0 and Access 95 ($349) and also a variety of Access2SQL translators for T-SQL, Oracle PL/SQL, and ANSI-92 SQL at a cost of $99.

USASoft's BCPump
www.usasoft.com/bcpump.htm (800-458-6010)
A $49 utililty that enhances SQL Server's native bcp. Downloadable evaluation copy available.

Embarcadero's DBArtisan
www.embarcadero.com
DBArtisan is one of several cross-platform DBA utilities that you can use to migrate data from one database to another.

Computer Associates (previously Platinum Technologies) Enterprise DBA
www.cai.com/products/roadmaps/enterprise_perfomance
Enterprise DBA is another cross-platform DBA package that you can use to migrate data.

Upsizing Access Databases

One of the first questions most Access owners ask is, "Will my code still work if I upsize to SQL Server?" The answer isn't easy.

If you're a serious Access user or developer, you realize that Access databases store data and application code (forms, queries, and so on), in a single MDB. Yes, we realize some of you may have seen the light and created Access applications where you actually store the data and application objects in separate MDBs, but most folks just have a single MDB.

Each version of the Access Upsizing Wizard migrates a little bit more of the application logic such as constraints into SQL Server. However, if you have a lot of Access module-based code, you're pretty much out of luck, especially if the code is in the original Access Basic (as opposed to more recent versions of Visual Basic for Applications, or

VBA). You may as well steel yourself for the necessity of writing new code or implementing non-Access features in SQL Server.

For example, triggers and stored procedures that run from within the SQL Server database will provide a higher degree of centralization and control, than is possible by writing VBA code within Access to accomplish the same things. However, when we discuss the SQL Server conversion process in Method 2 later in this chapter, you'll see that you have a wizard-assisted choice to make when upsizing with DTS. You can choose to simply copy your data tables into SQL Server, copy the tables and link the Access database to the SQL Server database, or create a new Access application to interact with SQL Server in a client/server application format. If you choose the latter option, SQL Server creates an Access application that is client/server in nature and starts you off with a template for a SQL Server-oriented application.

Another issue to keep in mind is that if you have any VBA code that uses Data Access Object (DAO), you may want to migrate to ADO. ADO is the current data access method of choice for Microsoft, and will soon be the only method that you can garner any real support for when you get into trouble.

BEFORE YOU START

1. **Test the database in Access and make any repairs to the source code. After all, why upsize something that doesn't work right in the first place. This is especially relevant to inherited databases.**
2. **Back up your database. No matter which technique you choose for upsizing (and there's nothing prohibiting you from trying more than one and then proceeding with the one that requires the least clean-up), make sure you have a complete backup of your Access database before proceeding.**
3. **Then, you may want to make a special copy of the Access database for the upsizing process where you make adjustments for SQL Server's naming conventions, such as no embedded spaces in object names.**
4. **Plan file location for SQL Server data and log files. Expect that your upsized database will occupy two to three times the space it did as an Access database and expect to have to perform some amount of manual post-upsizing work, no matter which technique you use. DbOpenTable and the Seek method used with DAO Recordsets, for example, are Jet-specific code. DAO Container, Document, Index, QueryDef, and Relation objects all have some methods that are not supported in SQL Server.**

What about Data Types?

As you saw with our Excel example when we used the DTS Import Wizard to migrate Excel data into SQL Server, each column in a table has to be assigned a data type. Excel has certain data types (text, number, currency, date, time, percentage, and so on) as does Access.

SQL Server and Access are both databases built by the same company, so don't they at least have the same data types? Unfortunately not. There are data-type changes between Access and SQL Server and the wizard will automatically map these for you as follows:

- Microsoft Access memo fields to SQL Server text fields
- Access OLE fields to SQL Server image fields
- Access text fields to SQL Server varchar fields

You'll find that the wizards and tools do a pretty fair job of handling the conversions and that if there are any real data portability problems, it's that SQL Server is a little less lenient than Access regarding bad data within fields. Our project deals with how Access allows you to store incorrect values within date fields, while SQL Server does not (prompting a data conversion issue during an import).

You'll also see that SQL Server provides a lot of internal features to validate the data it holds, such as triggers. Again, SQL Server may be a little unwilling to accept faulty data and require that you spend some time on converting the data properly, but in the long run, you (and your clients) are better off with correct data values stored within the database.

Object and Method Changes

The following Access objects and methods are not supported in SQL Server 7:

Container
Index
Relation
Document
QueryDef (you'll probably want to change these into views and/or stored procedures)
Dynaset object (exclusive)

The following Access methods are not supported in SQL Server 7:

CompactDatabase
CreateField
DeleteQueryDef
ListTables
RepairDatabase
SetDefaultWorkspace
CreateDatabase
CreateQueryDef
ListParameters
OpenQueryDef
Seek

Also note that Access' validation rules are transformed into triggers in SQL Server, and that its relationships are mapped into a combination of SQL Server triggers and foreign keys.

Conclusion

If you contemplate upsizing an Access application to SQL Server, remember that you may need to redesign your applications. SQL Server, for example, unlike Access, supports transaction processing complete with "commits" and "rollbacks."

The Access Projects: Upsizing the WorkOrd Database

In our first project in this chapter, you saw how there were several different ways to move your data from Excel into SQL Server 7. In this project, we take a fairly substantial Access database and port it to SQL Server and, as with the Excel project, show you several alternative methods for doing this.

This section should convince you that there is more than one way to skin a cat today. We take our WorkOrd database (\Data\WorkOrd\Access2000\WorkOrd.mdb on your CD-ROM) and upsize it into SQL Server using two different methods: first via the Office 2000 Upsizing Wizards and then using DTS. As part of this process, we also "sideways-size" our database, this time from Access into an Excel workbook. You'll see that it's relatively easy to take data from many different types of sources (Excel, FoxPro, Access, ODBC sources, text files, and relational databases) and move them into one or more of the same types of data collections.

The Source Data

Our database is an Access 97 database that contains word order data. Although it's based on a real firm's data model, the data has been modified and isn't proprietary or real. Nevertheless, we wanted to give you the opportunity to experiment with what we consider to be a lot more real world data than the pubs or Northwind sample databases.

WorkOrd contains only tables—no Forms, Reports, or Modules. The tables, along with their field and row counts, are shown in Table 4.1.

Table 4.1 The WorkOrd Database's Tables

TABLE NAME	FIELDS	ROWS
tblItemAssignment	3	170,350
tblRequest	6	26,117
tblRequestItem	9	216,829
tblWorkOrder	6	24,017
tblWorkOrderTask	5	81,668
tlkpDocumentSource	2	3
tlkpItemStatus	2	3
tlkpRequestReason	2	4

Continues

Table 4.1 The WorkOrd Database's Tables *(Continued)*

TABLE NAME	FIELDS	ROWS
tlkpSite	2	13
tlkpTaskType	2	7
tlkpUrgency	3	6
zstblDefaultTasks	3	7

Figure 4.14 illustrates the relationships among the WorkOrd tables.

Method 1: Use the Upsizing Wizard

In Method 1, we use the Upsizing Wizard that's included with Office 2000, and we assume that you have both Office 2000 and SQL Server 7 installed. First we upgrade the Access 97 database into Access 2000 format, and then use the Access 2000 Upsizing Wizard to move the data into SQL Server 7. (If you download the new Access 97 Upsizing Wizard, you don't have to do this step.)

THE ACCESS 97 UPSIZING WIZARD

The Access 97 Upsizing Wizard (www.microsoft.com/AccessDev/ProdInfo/exe/wzcs97.exe) allows you to easily move Access 97 data directly into SQL Server 7 without first converting your database into Access 2000 format. Otherwise, it looks and works virtually the same as the Access 2000 Upsizing Wizard. As with the previous Access Upsizing Wizards, you can preserve the values of any of the AutoNumber data type fields (automatically incrementing values, usually used to provide a unique index to your table rows) that are in your MDB tables. You can also choose whether or not to have your Access MDB tables linked to the newly created SQL Server tables. This allows you to easily create a traditional client/server application which can then be performance tuned by moving some of the client-side Access code into server-side stored procedures (See Chapter 12 for more on stored procedures).

Once you start Access 2000 and load the Access 97 version of WorkOrd (see Figure 4.15) choose the Tools, Database Utilities, Convert Database, To Current Access Database Version... menu item as shown in Figure 4.16. Note that you need to have a printer driver installed on your system in order to run this utility. From here you can convert your database from Access 97 to Access 2000. Allow some time for this conversion to occur; in our case, using a Pentium II, P300 with 98 MB of RAM and 1 GB of free disk space, our conversion from Access 97 to Access 2000 took about 12 minutes.

CONVERSIONS REQUIRE LOTS OF ROOM

Make sure that you provide plenty—and we mean plenty—of disk space for these conversions. The conversion tools generally require 1.5 times as much disk space as the database itself to perform the upgrades—and more if you're low on RAM since Windows uses your disk space to supplement RAM.

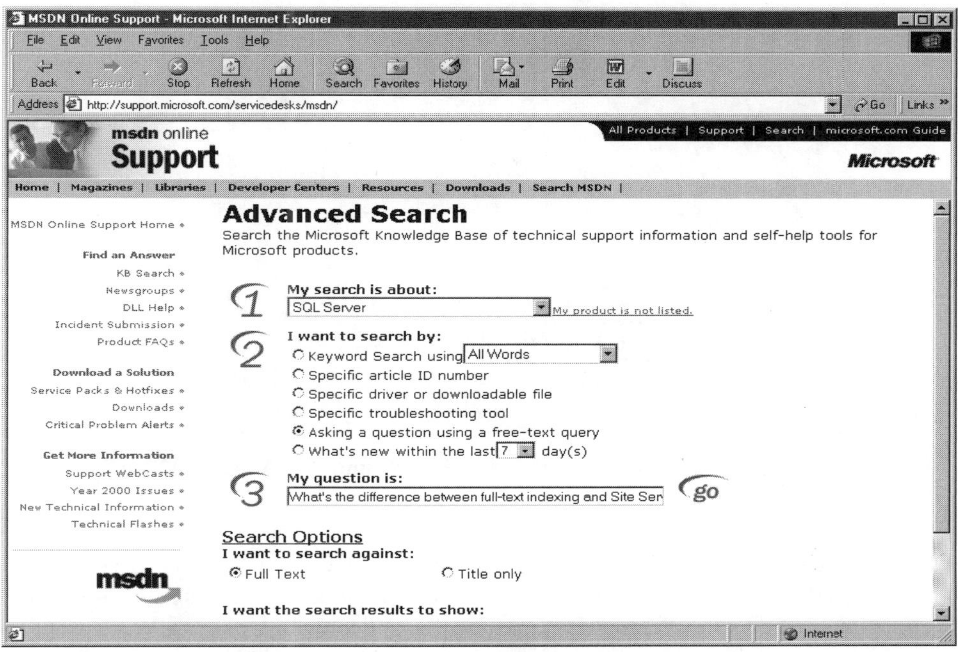

Figure 4.14 How the WorkOrd database is designed.

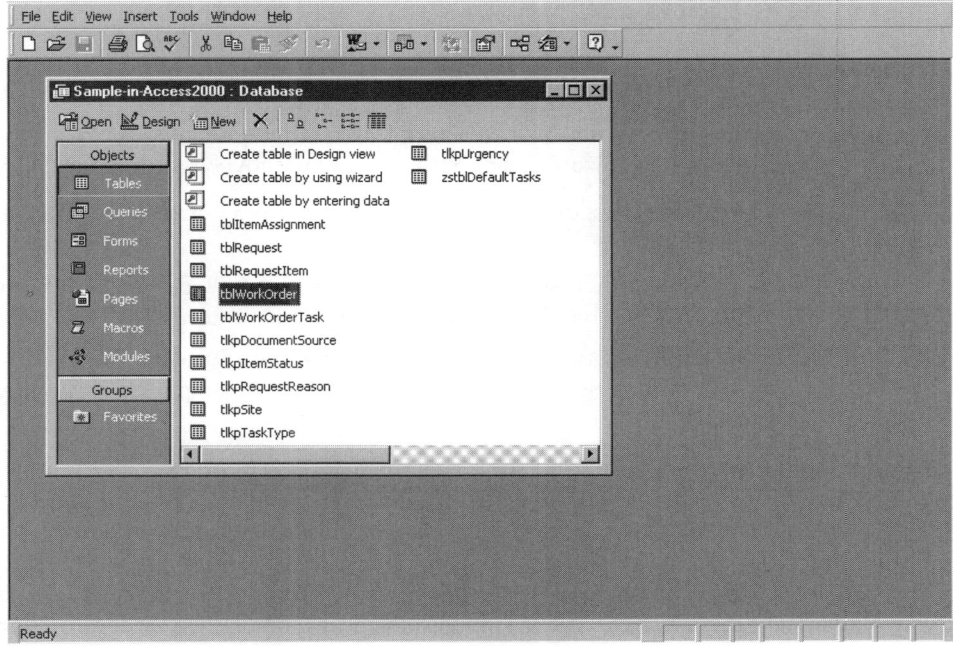

Figure 4.15 WorkOrd in its Access 2000 MDB format.

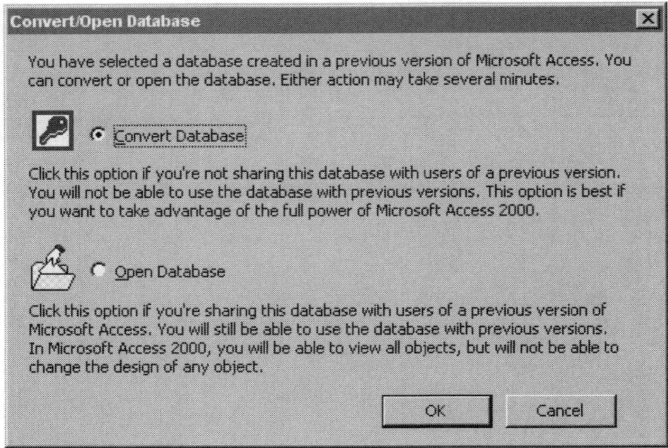

Figure 4.16 Converting an Access 97 MDB into and Access 2000 MDB.

Once the database is converted to Access 2000, we're ready to proceed with the Access 2000 Upsizing Wizard. (If you prefer, you can load the Access 2000 version of WorkOrd from the CD-ROM.) Unfortunately, the Office 2000 Upsizing Wizard isn't automatically installed along with Access—so don't be surprised if you're prompted to insert your Office 2000 CD-ROM when you first attempt to run the wizard from the Tools, Database Utilities menu. Another slight annoyance is that you *must* have a printer driver installed on the system from which you're running the Access 2000 to SQL Server Upsizing Wizard.

Upsizing Wizard Operations

Before starting the Access 2000 Upsizing Wizard, it pays to know what your options will be. Basically, the wizard supplies three ways to move your data to SQL Server.

1. Upsize only the data, data types, and data sizes from your Access database into a SQL Server database.
2. Create a front-end Access database that is linked to SQL Server, and then create the application that handles the data processing by your users.
3. Create a new Access application (an .ADP, or Access Database Project file) that contains all of the original Access database objects—generating a true client/server application.

It may also be beneficial to do some preliminary work in Access. For example, because embedded spaces aren't supported in SQL Server, you may want to make changes in Access rather than accept the underscores that the wizard uses in lieu of spaces. SQL Server also has more stringent naming rules (see the *Books Online* topic, *Indentifier Names*). Tables and other objects can have names up to 128 characters long, including letters, digits, and these special symbols: the @ at symbol, the _ underscore symbol, the # number symbol, and the $ dollar symbol. The first character must be a letter or the @

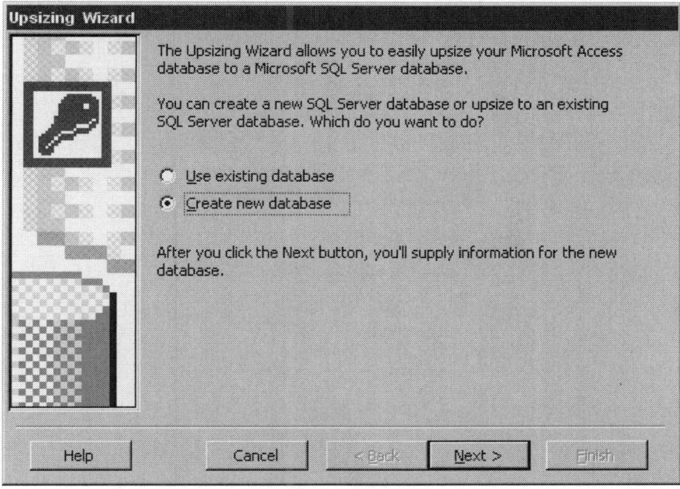

Figure 4.17 Use an existing or new database.

sign. SQL Server also has a fairly long list of "reserved" words or keywords. You should not use any of these words as table, column, or other object names. Examples of words that you should not use include SELECT, CREATE, TABLE, and, ORDER—words that are used in T-SQL. See the *Books Online* topic, *Reserved Keywords (T-SQL)* for a long list. Other potential problem areas include Access tables that include GUIDs or defaults like Date$ and Now$.

Once the wizard gets underway, the first thing that it does is to ask what SQL Server database you want the upsized data deposited in. Figure 4.17 shows that you can choose to either use an existing SQL Server database or create a new database in SQL Server for your data. In most cases, you'll want to create a new database. If you decide to use an existing SQL Server database, you'll need to choose one in the next screen. If you're creating a new database, then you'll need to name it. We called ours WordOrd.

Figures 4.18 and 4.19 show the screens that guide you through the process for deciding which tables to move from Access into SQL Server. As you probably know, clicking on the >> button shown in Figure 4.18 moves *all* of the tables into the selected window.

Figure 4.19 shows the different table attributes that you can have upsized to SQL Server including indexes, validation rules, default data settings, and table relationships. You can have the wizard automatically add timestamps to your tables and select between declarative referential integrity (DRI) or trigger-enforced referential integrity. Notice that the wizard gives you the option to only create the table structure in SQL Server or to create the table structure and migrate the data.

SKELETON ONLY, PLEASE

Creating only the table structure—and not loading any data into the tables—can be handy. First, it's a quick way to create SQL for the database schema. That SQL, of course, can also be edited and serve as part of the new database's documentation.

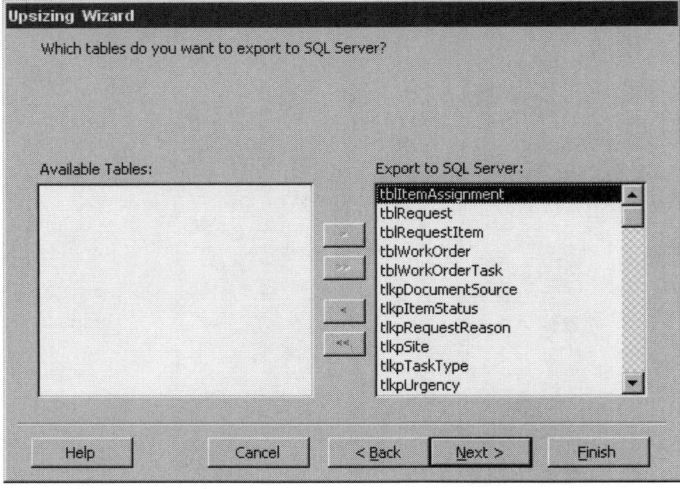

Figure 4.18 Selecting the tables to copy to SQL Server 7.

Second, it's a great way to create a database when you've got lots of data to migrate. Having the structure allows you to examine it in SQL Server—and perhaps make some changes—before committing to what could be a long loading process.

Once you've made decisions about validation rules, default settings, and so on, you get to make the big decision about any Access application that may be attached to the data. Figure 4.20 shows the key wizard screen that lets you decide whether or not to simply

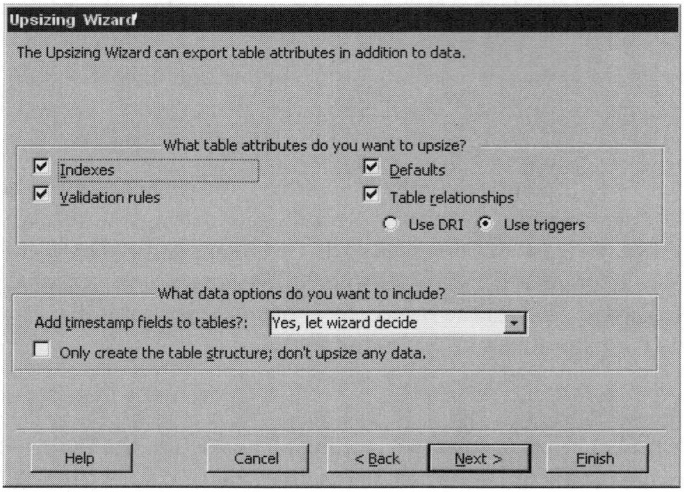

Figure 4.19 Selecting the table attributes.

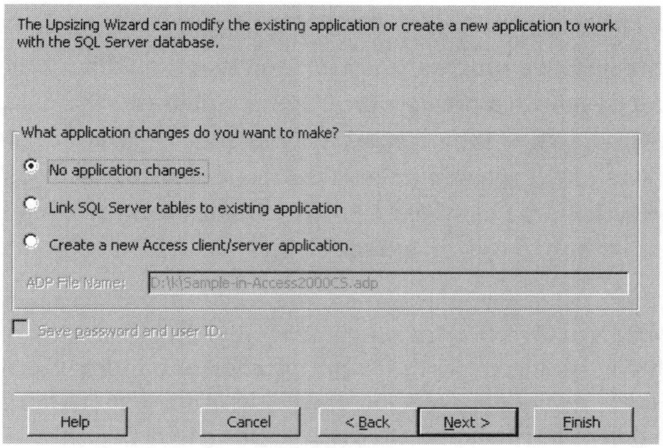

Figure 4.20 Another important choice—to link or not to link.

move the data into SQL Server, link the tables to the original Access applications, or create a client/server version of the application instead.

If you're using the Access 97 Upsizing Wizard, the screen will look a bit different as shown in Figure 4.21.

After the wizard has enough information to complete its work, you can press the Finish button to send it on its way. If you're lucky, you'll be rewarded with an empty (no problems) Upsizing Report.

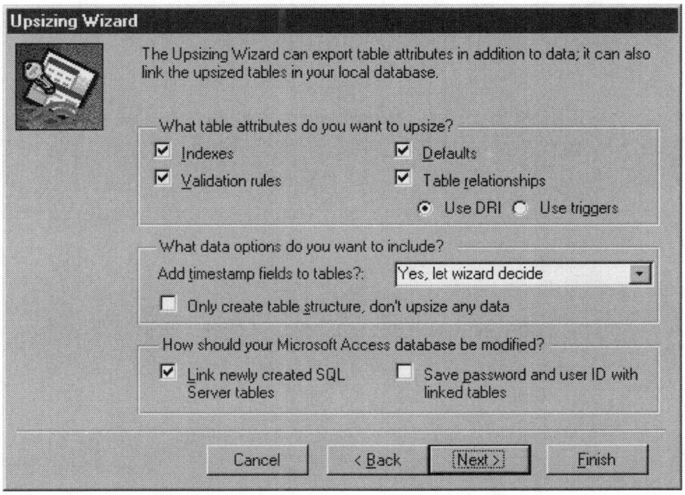

Figure 4.21 The Access 97 Upsizing Wizard's final screens differ slightly from those of Access 2000.

RE-RUNNING THE UPSIZING WIZARD

If you need to re-run the upsizing process, keep in mind that the Office 2000 Upsizing Wizard will *not* overwrite a previous SQL Server database. The wizard adds an index to the file name and then creates a completely separate version. In this case, WordOrd Version1 is created on a subsequent upsizing re-run. Keep this in mind if you work with large databases. You'll probably want to drop previous versions before trying to upsize again.

If, on the other hand, the Upsizing Wizard runs into problems, you may see the message shown in Figure 4.22. An Overflow message generally refers to a data conversion error. Unfortunately, the Upsizing Report may not provide any more information, in which case you'll need to check data types on each side of the equation manually—using Access and the Enterprise Manager—to discover the problem.

In our case, some of the date fields contained invalid data—enough to confuse the Upsizing Wizard. After we isolated the problem and changed the data value to a valid date in the original Access database, we re-ran the wizard with success.

WANTED: COMMON SENSE

None of the various versions of the Access Upsizing Wizard does a good job at providing visual clues to errors that occur during the upsizing process. In fact, it may look like everything went well when it in fact did not. To make sure that you've copied everything that you expect to, make sure to check the box to generate a report, which is located on the final dialog of the Upsizing Wizard screen. Review this report before continuing on to the old "tried-and-true" common sense method of checking by hand, such as comparing number of rows, before and after versions of a variety of random records, and so on. Wizards are great, but they don't come with a lot of common sense. . . .

Prove It

As you know by now, we like "proof positive" that things have worked, so as soon as the Upsizing Wizard lets us know that it's done its thing, we fired up the Enterprise Manager to see the fruits of our—well, maybe the wizard's—labor (see Figure 4.23). Obviously, you'll want to spend some time confirming that the data was migrated as expected. You might want to check for the following:

- The number of user tables

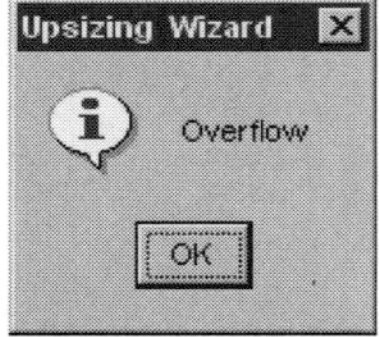

Figure 4.22 An Overflow message indicates data conversion problems.

- The number of rows in the Access tables versus the number of rows in the SQL Server tables
- The data types located in the tables
- What default values were assigned
- What the new stored procedures do

Pretty neat, isn't it? Just a few minutes' work migrating a real-world database. Now about that database Maintenance Plan. . . .

Upsizing a Northwest Plants Database

Before we use DTS to upsize the WorkOrd database, let's use the Access Upsizing Wizard on a more complex database, NWPlants. This is another real-world database of Northwest plants used by two Seattle-area nurseries to print signs with plant photos on them. Unlike the WorkOrd database, NWPlants includes forms, reports, and queries, none of which would be effectively upsized. This is an example where we probably want to just upsize the data, linking to it from the existing Access front-end application. Figure 4.24 shows the Access tables in NWPlants (notice that the plant photos are contained in a link table). Figure 4.25 displays the database structure.

Copy the two MDB files off your CD onto your own hard disk and start Access 2000. Delete the tblPhotos link (you won't be deleting the actual Photos database) and re-create

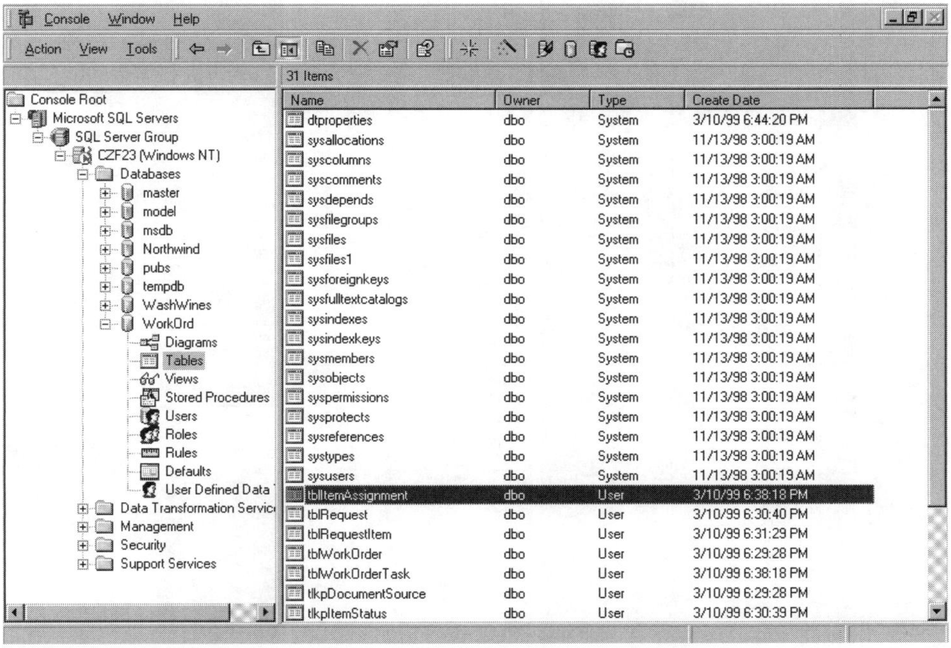

Figure 4.23 Notice the user tables created by the Upsizing Wizard.

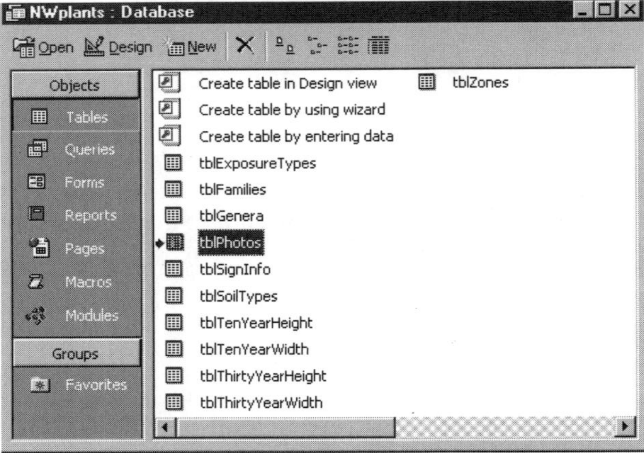

Figure 4.24 The tables in NWPlants.

based on wherever you placed the PlantPhotos.MDB file on your system. You can do that by highlighting the tblPhotos table in the NWPlants tables view and select Delete. Then right-click on the Object item called Tables and select Add a link. Provide the File name that corresponds to the location of the 64+ MB PlantPhotos.MDB file on your system. Click on Link, highlight the tblPhotos selection, and press OK.

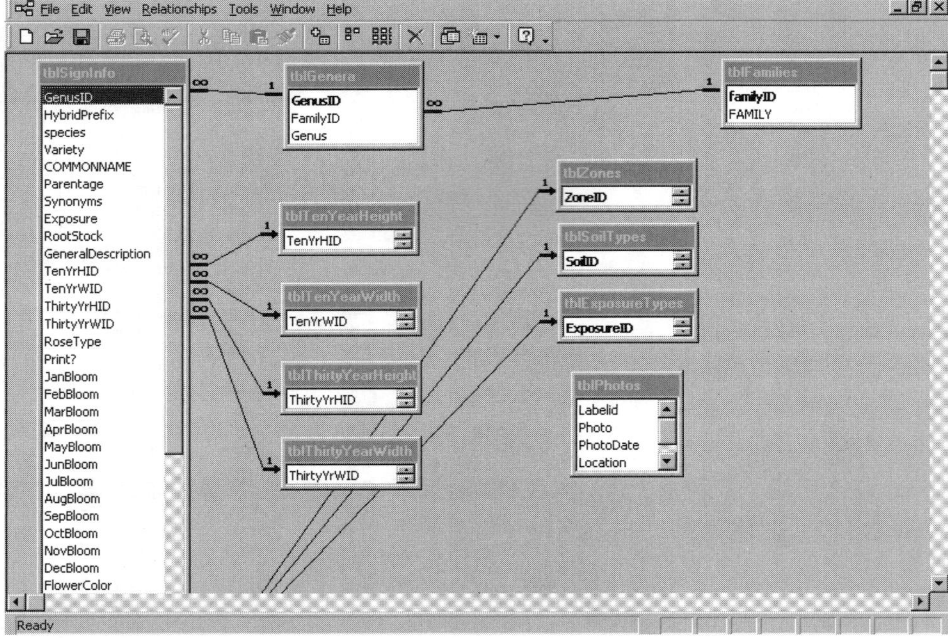

Figure 4.25 The relationships in NWPlants.

You can now proceed on your own for the rest of this project. Here's what you'll want to do:

1. Launch the Upsizing Wizard from the Access 2000 Tools, Database Utilities menu.
2. Accept the option to Create New Database.
3. Select the SQL Server on which to locate the new database and provide password and login information.
4. Accept the recommended database name of NWplantsSQL and tell the wizard to migrate all tables. Then de-select the tblPhotos (it will probably be better to keep the large image files on the local PC).
5. Accept the wizard's defaults for table attributes.
6. This time, however, tell the wizard that you want to link the SQL Server tables to the existing application.

Solving a Problem

Using the Access 2000 Upsizing Wizard, we encountered problems with the fairly large (4410 rows) tblSignInfo table (it didn't upsize) and received a strange error message that the "expression you entered refers to an object that is closed or does not exist." Despite examining the table in Access' design mode, we couldn't find anything "weird" about it, so we decided to try to use DTS to migrate that single table and then manually link it from our original Access database. That worked fine as you can see in Figure 4.26. Notice that the linked table is prefixed with dbo (database owner), indicating that the "live" data is now under SQL Server's control.

Figure 4.27 shows that DTS has done its job importing data from the Access tblSignInfo table into the new SQL Server NWplantsSQL database.

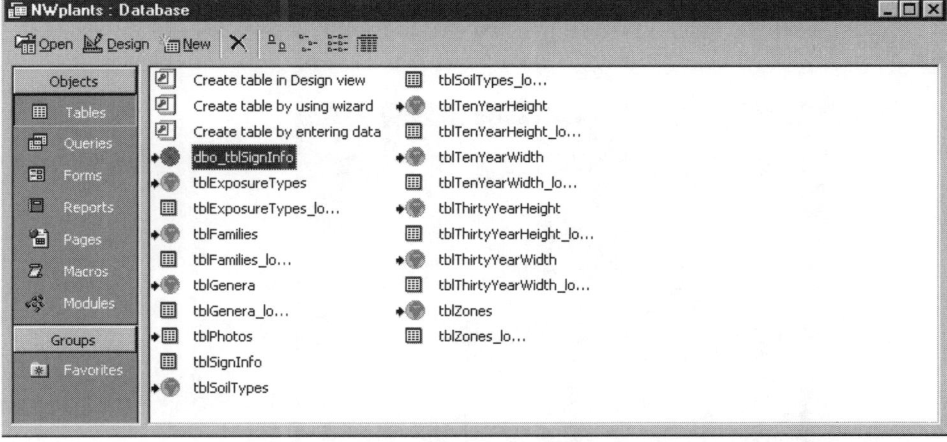

Figure 4.26 All of the tables in NWPlants except the table with plant photos are now "linked" to SQL Server that serves as the "main" database.

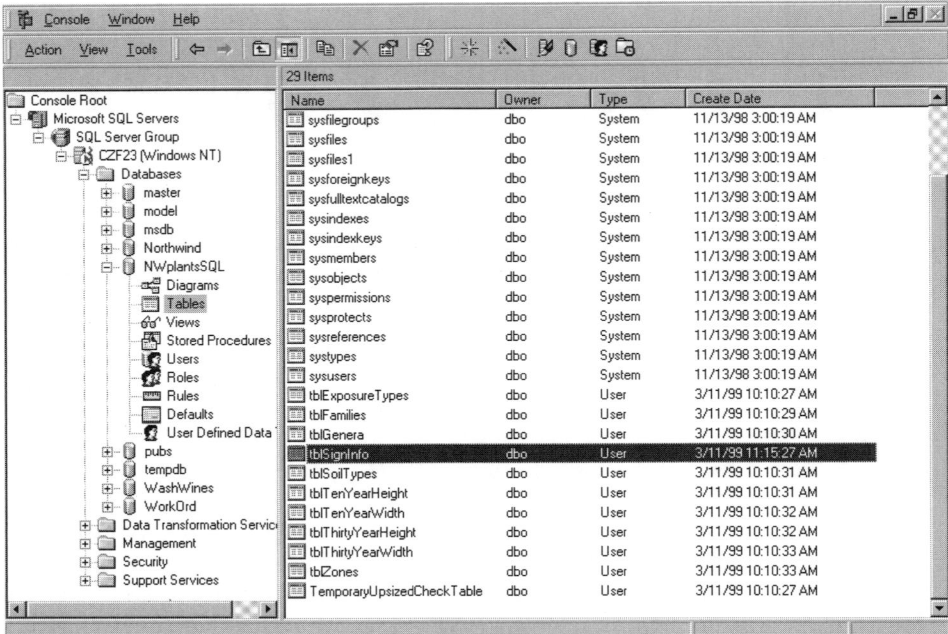

Figure 4.27 Enterprise Manager shows the new NWplantsSQL database.

We encountered the same problem with the tblSignInfo table when using the Access 97 Upsizing Wizard on a different system, but also encountered a new Warning message as you can see in Figure 4.28. Fortunately, this new message was explicit enough that we didn't have any problems figuring out what to do.

The Lesson: there's nothing to say that you can't mix and match upsizing tools and techniques. NWPlants, like many Access databases was created as a labor of love

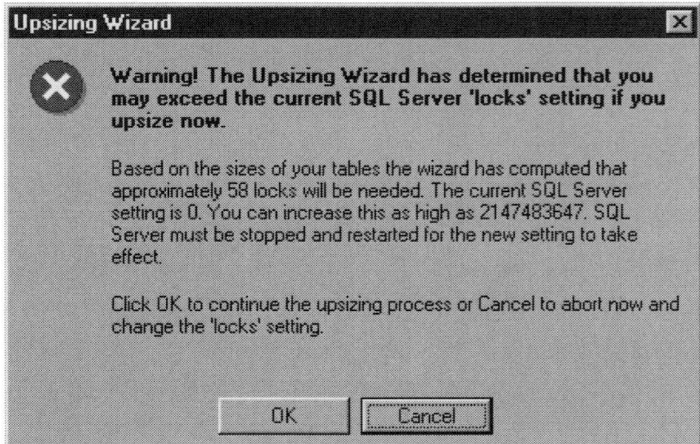

Figure 4.28 Some Upsizing Wizard error messages are pretty easy to understand.

by a nursery employee who wanted to print signs that were both educational and colorful—adding scanned photos as he took them. But it's not hard to imagine what you could do with such a database under SQL Server's control. You could put it online and let potential customers search by desired plant characteristics or soil types. The database could also serve as the basis for online nursery sales and so on. Have fun experimenting!

MSDE

In late spring 1999, Microsoft began to ship the Microsoft Data Engine (MSDE) with the professional, enterprise, small business, and developer versions of Office 2000 and similar versions of Visual Studio and its tools. MSDE is essentially a stripped down desktop version of SQL Server, and, as you can imagine, it offers Access users and ISVs a truly simple migration path to SQL Server. It also offers ISVs the opportunity to distribute "desktop" evaluation versions of software that's meant to run on SQL Server on MSDE first. For more information about MSDE, go to msdn.microsoft.com/vstudio/msde.

Remember that Access 2000 users can create new Access applications in either the Access 2000 MDB format (the default) or in the newer ADP format.

Now we'll return to the WorkOrd sample database in Access, but use DTS rather than the Upsizing Wizard to upsize it. This time we'll spend a bit more time drilling down into the DTS feature set to take advantage of some of its advanced features.

Method 2: Use DTS

As you saw earlier in the Excel and NWPlant projects, DTS is a very powerful utility. What's more, it's not even limited to SQL Server migrations. You can use DTS to move Access data into Oracle, Oracle data into Excel, or DB2 data into Sybase. Here are some of the previously painful data-porting tasks that can be simplified using DTS:

- Mapping names with embedded spaces into your target database. (SQL Server doesn't accept them, but many Access databases have them.)
- Performing table lookups—on the fly while in the process of importing your data—for field values in the source database.
- Cleansing data—something that's often crucial when building data marts or data warehouses.
- Copying tables or use queries and joins to create the result set that you want to use to populate a target data source.

DTS also lets you create special programs called *packages* that contain the migration or conversion instructions—packages that can be re-used, packages that can be stored as standalone files within the special msdb database or in the Microsoft Repository. The package can be executed immediately or scheduled for execution at a later date and time. DTS packages are used extensively in replication and in updating data warehouse data.

THE MICROSOFT REPOSITORY

The Microsoft Repository (MSR) is a developer-oriented SQL Server database designed to store just about any programming objects, including documents. It's installed by default by SQL Server and a version of it is included in the Microsoft Database (msdb) as a set of tables.

The actual application that kicks off DTS is called *dtswiz.exe*—found in the MSSQL7\Binn directory. You can launch DTS by selecting the SQL Server program group's Import and Export Data menu item, from the Enterprise Manager's Tools, Data, Transformation Services menu, or from Enterprise Manager's wizard menu as we did in the Washington Wines Excel project.

You may recall that DTS asks you to identify both Source and Target databases (see Figure 4.29), and that SQL Server ships with a good number of OLE DB drivers. OLE DB is DTS' preferred method of data access. However, you can also choose to connect via any ODBC connection that you have. Here's the basic list of choices:

Text files
Visual FoxPro
dBase III, IV, and 5
Microsoft OLE DB provider for Microsoft SQL Server
Microsoft OLE DB provider for OLAP Services
Microsoft OLE DB provider for Oracle
Microsoft ODBC driver for SQL Server

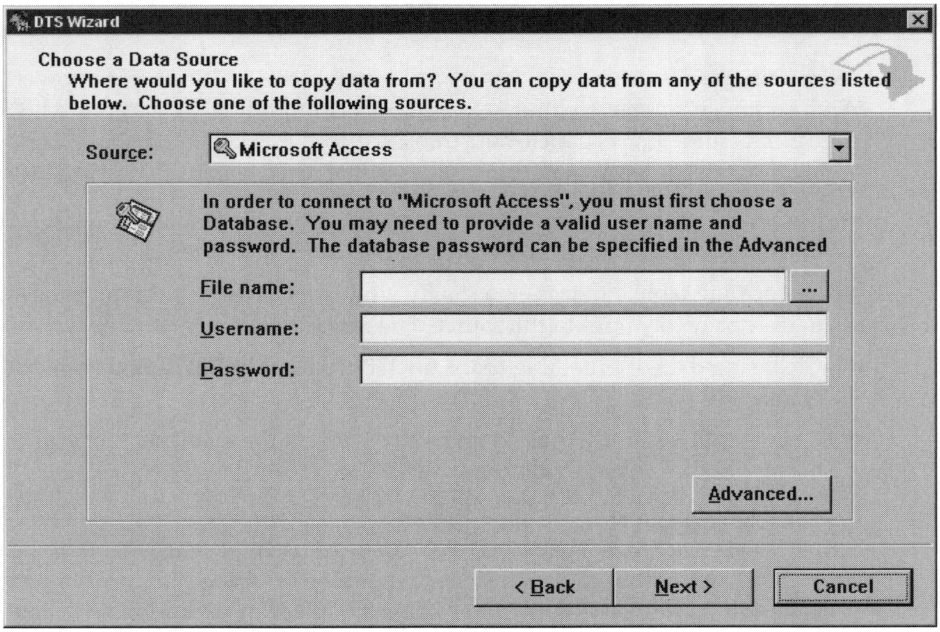

Figure 4.29 Choosing an input data source.

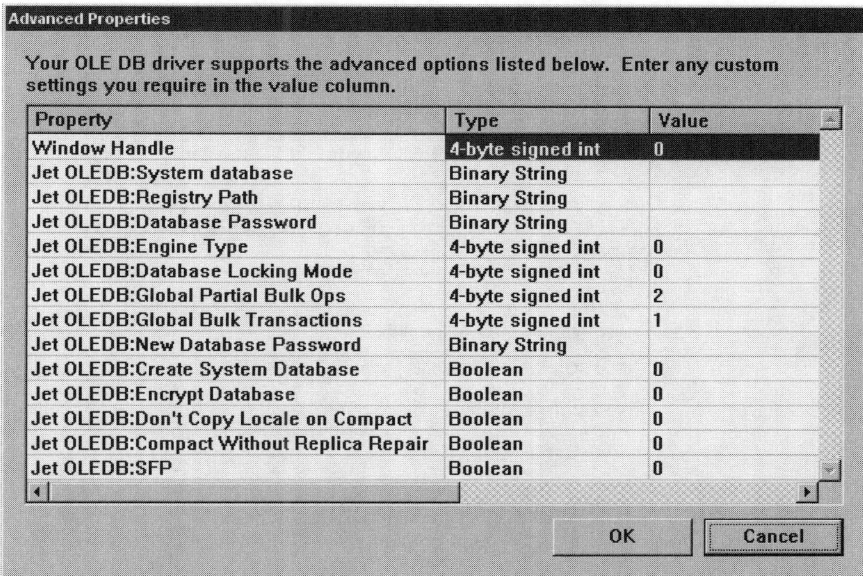

Figure 4.30 Database configuration options.

Microsoft ODBC driver for Oracle
ODBC data sources
Access (versions 2 and up)
Paradox (versions 3 and up)
Microsoft Jet 3.51 OLE DB provider
Excel (versions 3 and up)

Notice that DTS makes it easy to upsize "old" desktop databases including Access 2.0 and Access 95.

The DTS Wizard selection screen has an Advanced button that, when chosen, allows you to drill into the actual core options of your source database as shown in Figure 4.30. For example, you can change the database's password and choose whether to encrypt it or not. You can then continue on to choose a destination for your data (see Figure 4.31).

As we said previously, the really cool thing is that you don't have to specify just a SQL Server 7 database as your output target. The target can be everything that was found on the source list—from an ODBC or OLE DB host, to SQL Server, to an Excel spreadsheet or text file.

Also remember that you have the option to choose <default> or <new> as the actual database to store the tables that you want to copy into. If you choose <default>, your copied tables are placed into SQL Server's Master database—something that we *strongly* recommend you avoid.

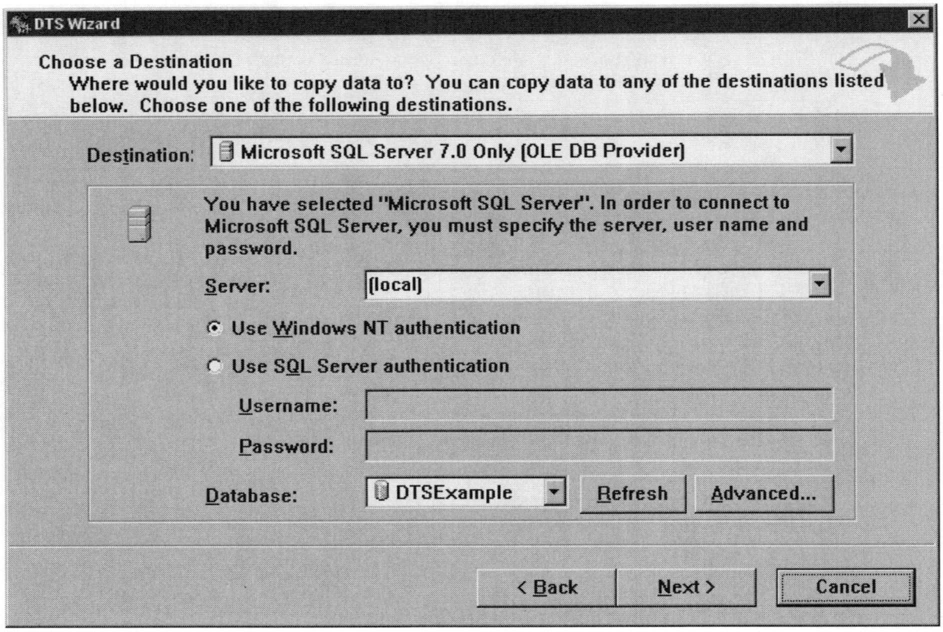

Figure 4.31 Choosing a destination for your data.

If you select <new>, then you have to decide how large you want the newly created database data and log files to be. Remember how the Upsizing Wizard shielded us from sizing decisions? When we do the port into SQL Server, we'll use a database name of DTSExample. The next screen gives you the opportunity to "filter" the data that you import by supplying a SQL query. If you choose a Query Builder button, you can construct a SQL query graphically and on the fly as in Figure 4.32.

This dialog contains a nice drill down and selection process for you to construct a query visually. In a further beautiful display of ergonomic smarts, this dialog continues on to ask you for the sort order that you want the data drawn out in and whether you have any selection criteria (WHERE clause) to add to the query. See Figure 4.32. When you finish stepping through the query builder, the resulting SQL syntax is deposited back into an editable text box like that shown in Figure 4.33.

You can also choose to launch a Later Execution dialog if you want the DTS transformation to occur at a later date and time. The resulting SQL Syntax looks like this:

```
SELECT 'tblItemAssignment'.'ItemID', 'tblItemAssignment'.'StatusID',
'tblItemAssignment'.'WorkOrderID'
FROM 'tblItemAssignment'
WHERE 'tblItemAssignment'.'WorkOrderID'>140
ORDER BY 'tblItemAssignment'.'ItemID'
```

The DTS wizard will automatically create a table in SQL Server 7 if you don't already have one by that name in the target database. Remember that the wizard always gives

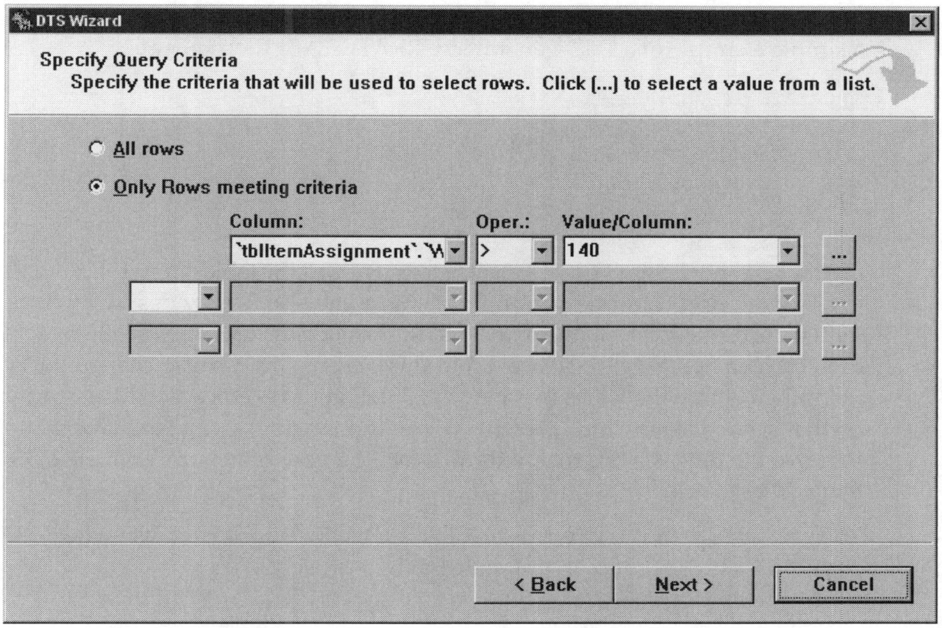

DTS Wizard

Specify Query Criteria
Specify the criteria that will be used to select rows. Click [...] to select a value from a list.

All rows
Only Rows meeting criteria

Column: `tblItemAssignment`.`W
Oper.: >
Value/Column: 140

< Back | Next > | Cancel

Figure 4.32 Using DTS' SQL query builder.

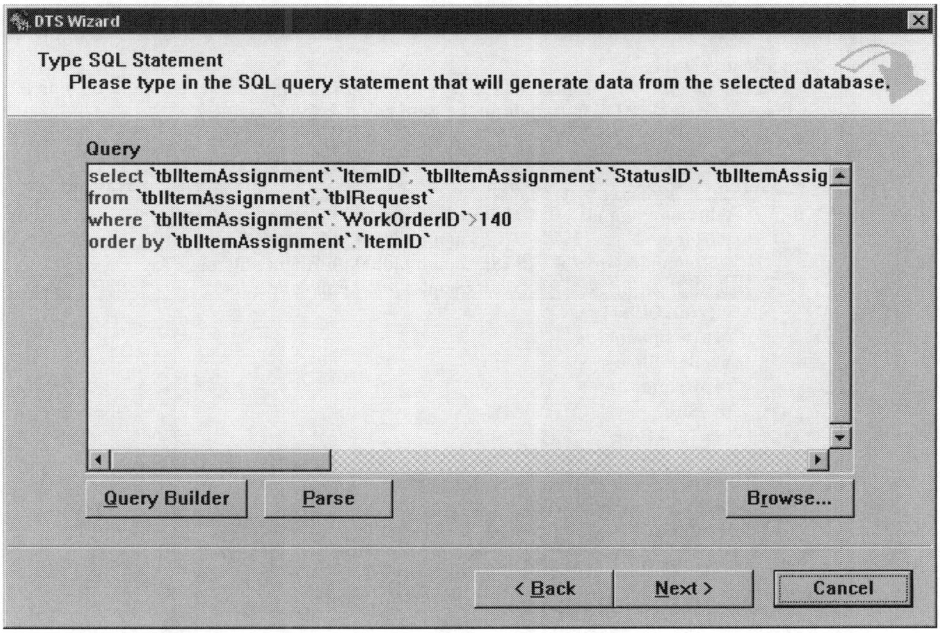

DTS Wizard

Type SQL Statement
Please type in the SQL query statement that will generate data from the selected database.

Query

```
select `tblItemAssignment`.`ItemID`, `tblItemAssignment`.`StatusID`, `tblItemAssig
from `tblItemAssignment`,`tblRequest`
where `tblItemAssignment`.`WorkOrderID`>140
order by `tblItemAssignment`.`ItemID`
```

Query Builder | Parse | Browse...

< Back | Next > | Cancel

Figure 4.33 The resulting SQL text.

you a chance to see the SQL *before* it actually attempts to manipulate a database. Here's a simple example of a DTS-generated CREATE TABLE statement:

```
CREATE TABLE [Results] (
[ItemID] int NULL
, [StatusID] int NULL
, [WorkOrderID] int NULL
)
```

Figure 4.34 shows that you can choose to move specific tables from the source to the target. Notice the apostrophes around the table names—this provides a way to move tables with embedded blanks in the name into the target database. You can change the name of each table in the target database. From this screen, you can also change the actual field mappings within the tables (see Figure 4.35). Figure 4.36 shows the Transformations tab on that same dialog, which presents you with the actual script language that's executed to move the data. Notice that, with this tab, the very brave can alter the VBScript code that will be executed.

You can select either JavaScript or VBScript as the language to use when adding your own code to this section. In this code listing we use VBScript.

```
Function Main()
      DTSDestination("ItemID") = DTSSource("ItemID")
      DTSDestination("WorkOrderID") = DTSSource("WorkOrderID")
      DTSDestination("StatusID") = DTSSource("StatusID")
      Main = DTSTransformStat_OK
```

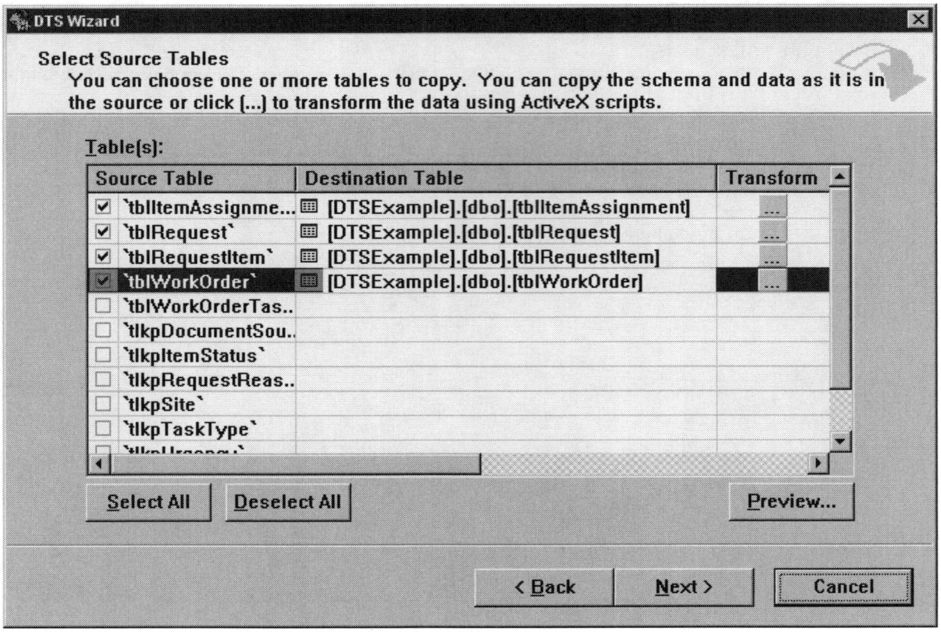

Figure 4.34 Naming and describing the tables.

```
End Function
```

Here we use JavaScript:

```
//*****************************************************************
//  Java Transformation Script
//  Copy each source column to the
//  destination column
//*****************************************************************

function Main()
{
     DTSDestination("ItemID") = DTSSource("ItemID");
     DTSDestination("WorkOrderID") = DTSSource("WorkOrderID");
     DTSDestination("StatusID") = DTSSource("StatusID");
     return(DTSTransformStat_OK);
}
```

The Preview button on the Transformation tab allows you to see (up to the first 100 lines) what the result of your code will look like (see Figure 4.37). The Advanced Transformation Properties dialog (found by clicking the Advanced button on the Transformations tab) allows DTS to handle the promotion or demotion of data values (which involves moving 16-bit values to 32-bit values, where appropriate and cutting 32-bit values to 16 bits, where necessary). You can also allow Null conversions (NOT NULL to Null data type translations) and similar data manipulations, all by setting option buttons.

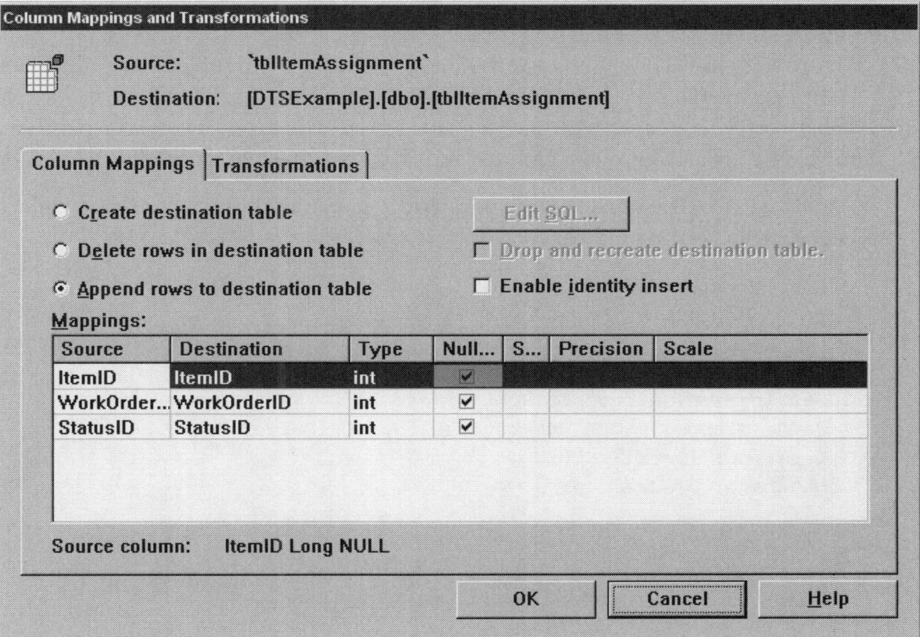

Figure 4.35 Column mappings and transformations.

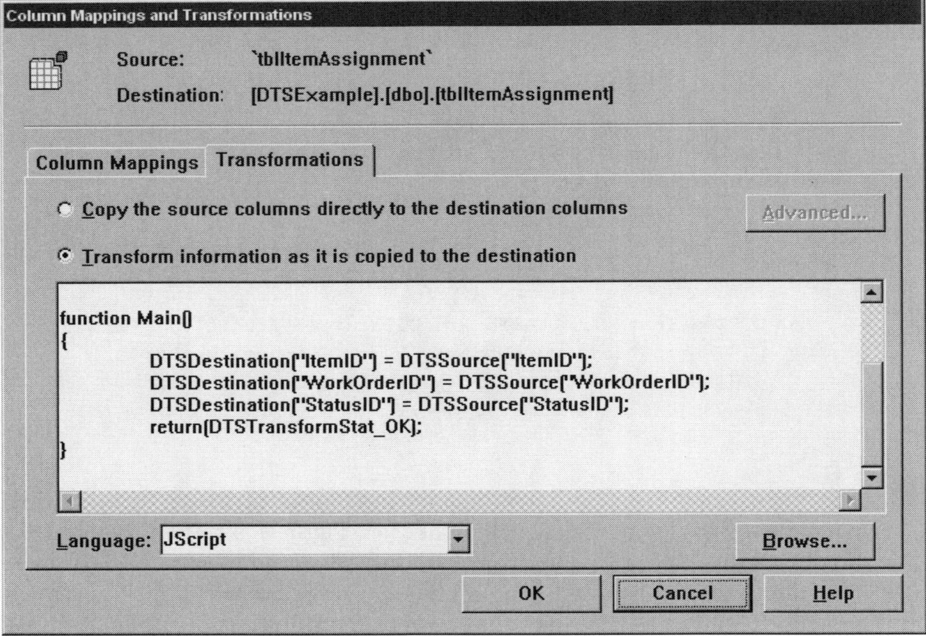

Figure 4.36 Transformations tab.

Figure 4.38 shows how you can schedule the "package" to run at a later time. You can also choose (conveniently) to store the package into the repository, SQL Server, or a stand-alone file. If you choose to store the package, the wizard will prompt you for a name, a password to access the package, and a file path and name (if you store it to a binary, unreadable file).

As a final step, the wizard will show you a screen that describes the specific actions to be taken, as is shown in the next code listing.

```
Source: Microsoft Access
Using Microsoft Jet 4.0 OLE DB Provider
Location: E:\SQLServer7\Russell\Copy (2) of Sample.mdb

Destination: Microsoft SQL Server
Using Microsoft OLE DB Provider for SQL Server
Location: (local)
Database: DTSExample

Tables
`tblItemAssignment` -> [DTSExample].[dbo].[tblItemAssignment]
`tblRequest` -> [DTSExample].[dbo].[tblRequest]
`tblRequestItem` -> [DTSExample].[dbo].[tblRequestItem]
`tblWorkOrder` -> [DTSExample].[dbo].[tblWorkOrder]
```

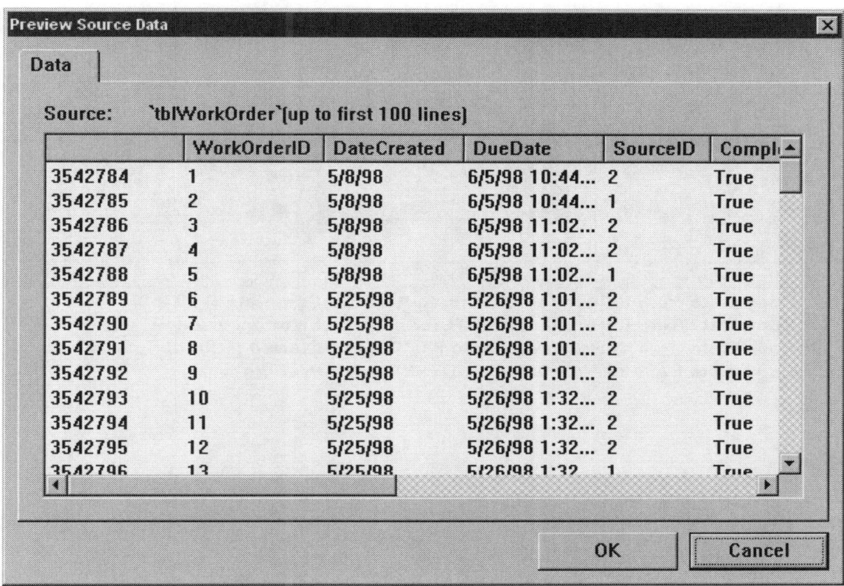

Figure 4.37 Previewing the Access to SQL Server import.

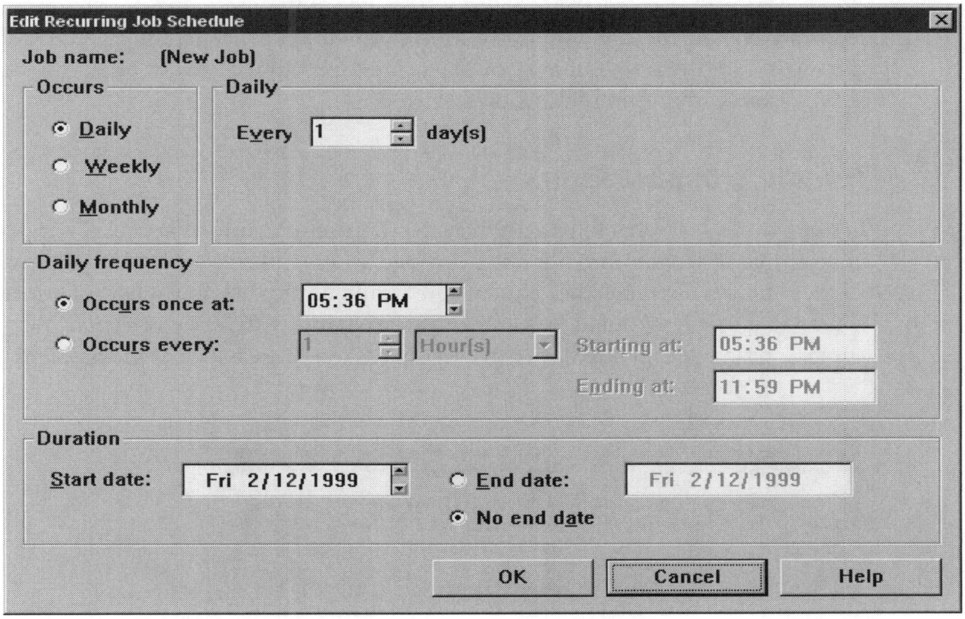

Edit Recurring Job Schedule
Job name: (New Job)
Occurs
Daily
Weekly
Monthly
Daily
Every 1 day(s)
Daily frequency
Occurs once at: 05:36 PM
Occurs every: 1 Hour(s) Starting at: 05:36 PM
Ending at: 11:59 PM
Duration
Start date: Fri 2/12/1999
End date: Fri 2/12/1999
No end date
OK Cancel Help

Figure 4.38 Scheduling the package for later execution.

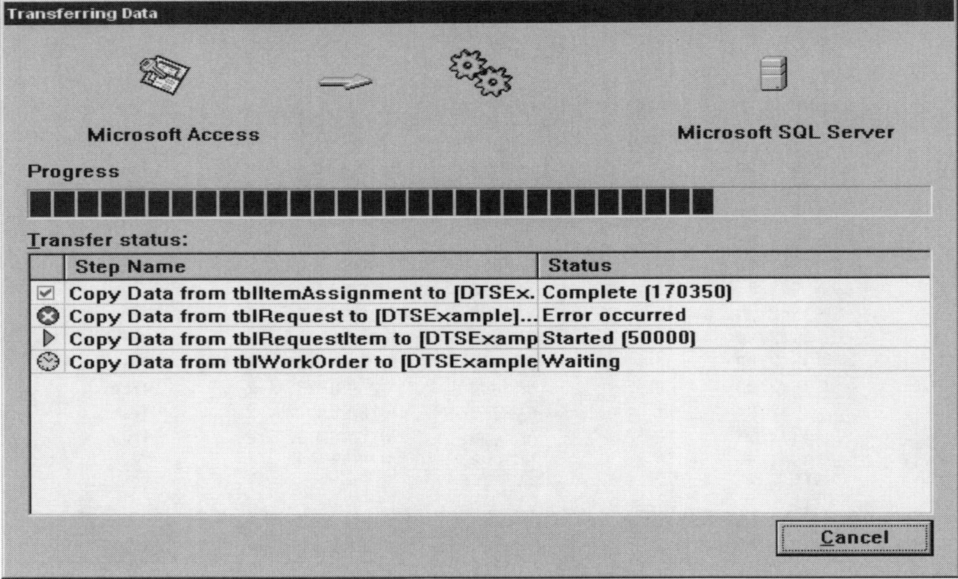

Figure 4.39 Information displayed during the copy.

Figure 4.39 shows the wizard's output screen, as it moves through the data to convert. You'll notice that there are the all-too-familiar stop sign icons on this screen. These icons are shown for any data translation errors that occur. Actually, DTS does a pretty fair job of handling a number of translation issues but that doesn't help the target data source from coming up with its own errors.

Handling Import Errors

Let's take a look at what happens when an error occurs during the copy. Figure 4.40 shows an example of what information is displayed when you click on an import error. As you can see, there is not much there, and it sure would be nice to know what column in row 771 is having a problem, but at least we know in what row the error occurred. With the DTS copying process suspended, we can open Access and take a look at the problem.

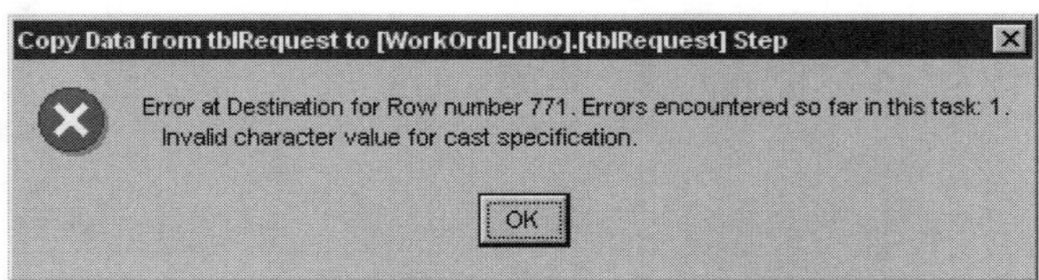

Figure 4.40 Example pop-up error information from clicking an error within the Copying dialog.

Microsoft Access - [tblRequest : Table]

Request ID	Site Log	Requester	Site	Request Date	Receive Date/Tim
768	M1041	R. Leman	Montreal	26-Oct-1998	26-Oct-1998 11:31
769	M1034	R. Leman	Montreal	26-Oct-1998	26-Oct-1998 11:44
770	M1036	R. Leman	Montreal	26-Oct-1998	26-Oct-1998 11:45
771	M1037	R. Leman	Montreal	01-Oct-226	26-Oct-1998 11:46
772	M1038	R. Leman	Montreal	26-Oct-1998	26-Oct-1998 11:52
773	M1040	R. Leman	Montreal	26-Oct-1998	26-Oct-1998 11:53
774	M1045	R. Leman	Montreal	26-Oct-1998	26-Oct-1998 11:54
775	A42	I. French	Quebec City	26-Oct-1998	26-Oct-1998 11:54
776	A43	I. French	Quebec City	26-Oct-1998	26-Oct-1998 11:56
777	A44	I. French	Quebec City	26-Oct-1998	26-Oct-1998 11:57
778	M1052	R. Leman	Montreal	27-Oct-1998	26-Oct-1998 12:01
779	M1046	R. Leman	Montreal	27-Oct-1998	27-Oct-1998 9:54
780	M1050	R. Leman	Montreal	27-Oct-1998	27-Oct-1998 10:02

Record: 771 of 26117

Document Request ID

Figure 4.41 Peeking into the Access data to figure out the problem.

In Figure 4.41, you can easily see that the Request Date column contains an invalid date of 01-Oct-226. Changing this to a valid date and then re-running the DTS copy corrects the problem. You can also trap for "bad" dates and replace them with "good" ones (e.g., '01/01/90') that allows the package to execute.

Figure 4.42 shows the representation of the newly created DTSExample database in the Enterprise Manager.

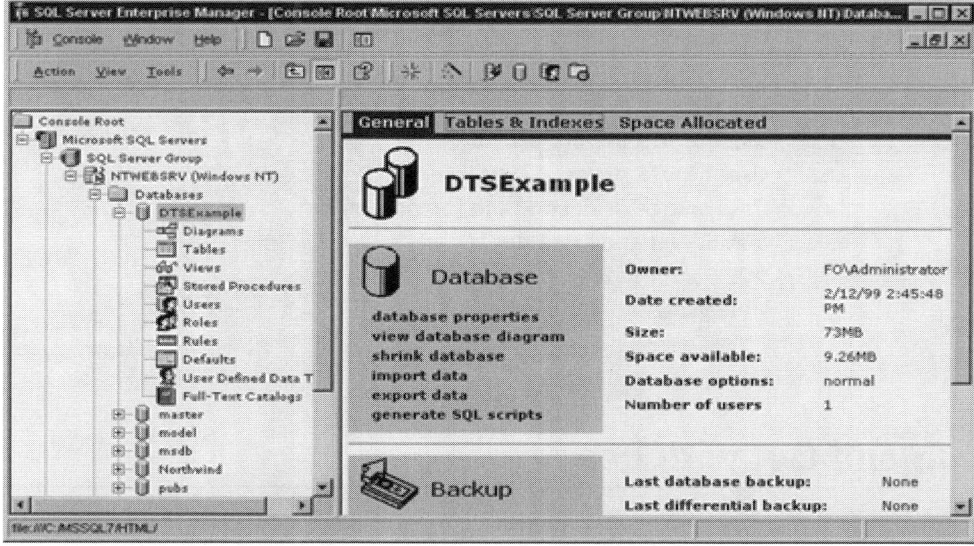

Figure 4.42 Viewing the new database in Enterprise Manager.

USING DTS TO HELP WITH DATA CLEANSING

If you have external data that's "infected" with a few small, but hard-to-find data scrubbing errors then you can use DTS to find and correct them. Let's assume that you have your input data in Access and want to move the tables from there into SQL Server. If you run DTS it will fail on every data error that it encounters—stopping after the first error. However, you can set the Drop & Create Destination table flag in the Data Transformations tab (found on the table selection screen under the […] button). Then, allow DTS to fail on a bad row. Edit the row with Access and use the DTS [Back] button to move back just one step in the DTS chain to retry the table import. Stepping back and forth like this makes for an easy way to handle locating and correcting a few data errors in a large input data set.

As a final note on DTS, there are help files for DTS and the DTS Wizard that can be found under \WINNT\Help (see the compiled help files dtspkg.chm and dtswiz70.chm). Check here for more information on this killer utility.

The dtswiz Utility - Command Line Options

The dtswiz command line utility is used to kick off DTS. It allows you to set up .BAT batch or .CMD files to run DTS packages, if you want to. The dtswiz utility provides command-line access to the DTS import and export wizards.

Syntax

dtswiz [{/? | {/n | [/u *login_id*] [/p *password*]} [/f *filename*] {/i | /x}
{/r *provider_name* | [/s *server_name*][/d *database_name*] [/y]}}]

?	**Displays help**
n	**Uses NT authentication**
u	**User name**
p	**Password**
f	**Filename**
i	**Use the DTS import wizard**
x	**Use the DTS export wizard**
r	**Data source or destination provider name**
s	**SQL Server server name**
d	**SQL Server database name**
y	**Hide system databases**

In and Out with bcp

As mentioned earlier, prior to DTS, bcp (bulk copy program) was the tool for moving data into or out of SQL Server. If we tell you that it has remained virtually unchanged since it was first introduced by Sybase, will that give you an idea of how old it is? Although you can actually run bcp interactively (see Table 4.2), you'd be crazy to try—and even constructing its format files is a giant pain that's extremely error-prone. We don't recommend that you use bcp unless you have a compelling reason to do so. DTS and its packages are the way to go. The following listings represent the pseudo user interface as provided by a typical bcp session. This is the actual result of copying the WordOrd database table to disk with bcp. Here we dump the contents of the tblRequests table into a disk file, called c:\trequests.txt. The first time that we run this, we let bcp drive us through the fields to export from this table manually, supplying the parameters for how to separate the individual data fields, as well as the actual data type to store the field to.

Table 4.2 Simulated Interactive Session Using bcp

C:\>**mssql7\binn\bcp workord..tblrequest out c:\trequests.txt**
Password:
Enter the file storage type of field RequestID [int]:
Enter prefix-length of field RequestID [0]:
Enter field terminator [none]: ,
Enter the file storage type of field SiteLog [nvarchar]:
Enter prefix-length of field SiteLog [1]:
Enter field terminator [none]: ,
Enter the file storage type of field Requester [nvarchar]:
Enter prefix-length of field Requester [1]:
Enter field terminator [none]: ,
Enter the file storage type of field SiteID [int]:
Enter prefix-length of field SiteID [0]:
Enter field terminator [none]: ,
Enter the file storage type of field RequestDate [smalldatetime]:
Enter prefix-length of field RequestDate [0]:
Enter field terminator [none]: ,
Enter the file storage type of field RequestDate [smalldatetime]:
Enter prefix-length of field RequestDate [0]:
Enter field terminator [none]: ,
Enter the file storage type of field ReceiveDate [datetime-null]:
Enter prefix-length of field ReceiveDate [1]:
Enter field terminator [none]: ,
Do you want to save this format information in a file? [Y/n] y

Continues

Table 4.2 Simulated Interactive Session Using bcp *(Continued)*

Host filename [bcp.fmt]: c:\trequest.fmt
1000 rows successfully bulk-copied to host-file. Total received: 1000
1000 rows successfully bulk-copied to host-file. Total received: 2000
1000 rows successfully bulk-copied to host-file. Total received: 3000
1000 rows successfully bulk-copied to host-file. Total received: 4000
1000 rows successfully bulk-copied to host-file. Total received: 5000
1000 rows successfully bulk-copied to host-file. Total received: 6000
1000 rows successfully bulk-copied to host-file. Total received: 7000
1000 rows successfully bulk-copied to host-file. Total received: 8000
1000 rows successfully bulk-copied to host-file. Total received: 9000
1000 rows successfully bulk-copied to host-file. Total received: 10000
1000 rows successfully bulk-copied to host-file. Total received: 11000
1000 rows successfully bulk-copied to host-file. Total received: 12000
1000 rows successfully bulk-copied to host-file. Total received: 13000
1000 rows successfully bulk-copied to host-file. Total received: 14000
1000 rows successfully bulk-copied to host-file. Total received: 15000
1000 rows successfully bulk-copied to host-file. Total received: 16000
1000 rows successfully bulk-copied to host-file. Total received: 17000
1000 rows successfully bulk-copied to host-file. Total received: 18000
1000 rows successfully bulk-copied to host-file. Total received: 19000
1000 rows successfully bulk-copied to host-file. Total received: 20000
1000 rows successfully bulk-copied to host-file. Total received: 21000
1000 rows successfully bulk-copied to host-file. Total received: 22000
1000 rows successfully bulk-copied to host-file. Total received: 23000
1000 rows successfully bulk-copied to host-file. Total received: 24000
1000 rows successfully bulk-copied to host-file. Total received: 25000
1000 rows successfully bulk-copied to host-file. Total received: 26000
26117 rows copied.
Network packet size (bytes): 4096
Clock Time (ms.): total 1442 Avg 0 (18111.65 rows per sec.)

Most DBAs create format files to use with bcp rather than try to run bcp interactively. Here's a summary of bcp's syntax.

bcp {[[*database_name*.][*owner*].]{*table_name* | *view_name*} | "*query*"}
{**in** | **out** | **queryout** | **format**} *data_file*
[**-m** *max_errors*] [**-f** *format_file*] [**-e** *err_file*]
[**-F** *first_row*] [**-L** *last_row*] [**-b** *batch_size*]
[**-n**] [**-c**] [**-w**] [**-N**] [**-6**] [**-q**] [**-C** *code_page*]
[**-t** *field_term*] [**-r** *row_term*]
[**-i** *input_file*] [**-o** *output_file*] [**-a** *packet_size*]
[**-S** *server_name*] [**-U** *login_id*] [**-P** *password*]
[**-T**] [**-v**] [**-R**] [**-k**] [**-E**] [**-h** "*hint* [,...*n*]"]

The arguments for the bcp utility are shown in Table 4.3.

Table 4.3 Arguments for the bcp Utility

BCP ARGUMENTS	WHAT THEY MEAN
database_name	This is the database to work with. Defaults to the user's default database.
Owner	This argument allows you to specify an owner for the table or view, other than the user.
table_name	This is either the destination table when copying into SQL Server or the source table when copying out.
view_name	This is either the destination view when copying into SQL Server or the source view when copying out.
query	A Transact-SQL query.
in | out | queryout | format	Selects the direction of the copy. The queryout command is used only when you pull directly from a query. The format command is used when creating a format file.
data_file	The data file to copy or create.
-m *max_errors*	The number of errors that can occur before bcp is terminated.
-f *format_file*	Location of the format file.
-e *err_file*	Create an error file to store rows that bcp cannot copy.
-F *first_row*	Allows you to choose which row to start with.
-L *last_row*	Allows you to choose less than the total number of rows to copy.
-b *batch_size*	Allows you to choose the number of rows to batch together into one transaction.
-n	Use the native database types.
-c	Use char as the storage type.
-w	Use Unicode characters as the storage type.

Continues

Table 4.3 Arguments for the bcp Utility *(Continued)*

BCP ARGUMENTS	WHAT THEY MEAN
-N	Use native (database) data types for non-character data and Unicode characters for character data.
-6	Use SQL Server 6.x data types.
-q	Use quoted identifiers when names include non-ANSI characters.
-C *code_page*	Specifies the code page of the data in the data file.
-t *field_term*	Choose the terminator between fields. The default is \t (tab character).
-r *row_term*	Choose the row terminator. The default is \n (new-line character).
-i *input_file*	The path of a response file that can hold all of your answers to the questions that bcp will ask when run.
-o *output_file*	The bcp command prompt output file.
-a *packet_size*	Bytes, per packet, sent to or from the server. The default is 4096.
-S *server_name*	The SQL Server to connect to.
-U *login_id*	The SQL Server login ID.
-P *password*	The SQL Server login password.
-T	Use a trusted connection rather than a login id and password.
-v	The bcp version number.
-R	Use regional formats for currency, date, and time data.
-k	Place null values into empty columns rather than the column defaults.
-E	Identity column values are in the input data file.
-h *"hint [,...n]"*	Allows you to set up hints for the data copied using SQL Server 7+.

An example of the format file that our bcp session generated is shown here. The format of this file is further defined in the *Books Online* topic, *Using the bcp Format File*. Once you've become familiar with format files, you can start to code these by hand *before* starting into bcp, saving you that step at runtime.

```
7.0
6
1       SQLINT       0     4     ","                     1     RequestID
2       SQLNCHAR     1     200   ","                     2     SiteLog
3       SQLNCHAR     1     200   ","                     3     Requester
4       SQLINT       0     4     ","                     4     SiteID
5       SQLDATETIM4        4     ",           "          5     RequestDate
6       SQLDATETIM4 1      4     ","                     6     ReceiveDate
```

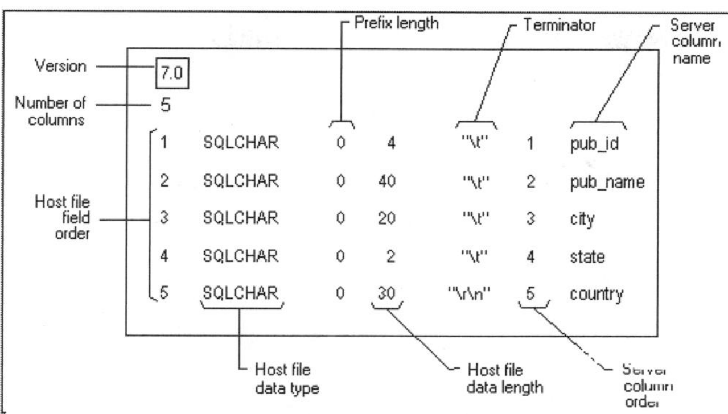

Figure 4.43 Breakdown of a bcp format file's contents.
Source: Microsoft Corporation, *Books Online*, © 1999

Figure 4.43 is from *Books Online* and does a fairly good job of describing the contents of a format file.

WHAT'S NEW IN THE SQL SERVER 7 BCP

There are some relatively minor changes to the bcp utility with SQL Server 7. Most notably, bcp now uses the ODBC API to perform bulk operations, rather than DB-Library calls. This impacts the way that bcp handles how Money and Date/Time fields are processed. For example, the default ODBC format for dates is (yyyy-mm-dd hh:mm:ss), while the default DB-Library version, used by the previous versions of bcp is (mmm dd yyy hh:mm). The bcp utility handles most of these, but you need to make sure that you use the same version of bcp for both the import and the export pieces of the process. You can check your bcp version using the -v parameter, that is bcp -v. Running the same version on both the export and import sides ensures that the data changes between the 6.x and 7.x versions of bcp are correctly handled.

Summary

By now, we hope you're comfortable using both the Access 2000 Upsizing Wizard and the invaluable DTS. We think that SQL Server 7 breaks new ground in providing easy-to-use upsizing and migration tools and hope that you are ready to tackle upsizing your own databases.

CHAPTER 5

Project #2: Publishing SQL Server Data to HTML

Goal

The goal of this chapter is to show you how to publish SQL Server data on your intranet as static Web pages using the Web Assistant Wizard and Excel.

- ✔ **Microsoft SQL Server 7**
- ✔ **Microsoft SQL Server 7**
- ✔ **TCP/IP-enabled network**
- ✔ **Internet Explorer 4.0 or higher**
- ✔ **Microsoft Excel 2000**

Optional:

- ✔ **Microsoft Front Page 9x**
- ✔ **Personal Web Server 1.0/1.0a/4.0, and/or Internet Information Server 4.0, and/or a third-party Web Application Server**

Well, now that you've installed SQL Server and perhaps upsized or migrated some data into it—don't worry if you haven't, you can "play" with Northwind, pubs, or other sample data such as the WorkOrd or plants databases—you're probably anxious to make the data available on your network and/or the Internet. Maybe you even want to do e-business, using your database for inventory and customer data and order tracking. We do supply projects that get you started on building Internet and e-commerce sites, but in this chapter, we're just going to take the first step: publishing database data on an intranet. Let's walk before we run.

To follow along with this chapter, we assume that you've installed SQL Server 7 along with the pubs and Northwind sample databases included on the CD-ROM. Aside from that, the only other real requirement is that you've got a network with the TCP/IP protocol installed and are using Microsoft Internet Explorer 4.0 (IE4) or higher. We use a variety of popular Microsoft Office and Windows NT products in this project to show you what you can do with SQL Server data once you've put it on your intranet. Don't worry, though, you don't need all of them to participate in this chapter and get the gist of how to publish and access HTML pages that contain SQL Server data. Are you ready?

First we'll use the Web Assistant Wizard that's built into SQL Server. We'll build a project that implements a "push" mode of information distribution. Then we'll shift gears and put on an end-user hat and see how easy it is to use Excel to access SQL Server data—and then save the result in HTML format.

HTML

Hypertext Markup Language, or HTML, is a system of marking up, or tagging, a document so that it can be published on networks such as intranets and the Web. Documents prepared in HTML include reference graphics and formatting tags. You use a Web browser (such as Microsoft Internet Explorer) to view these documents.

Intranet Basics

An *intranet* is basically a network designed for information processing and sharing *within* an organization. It's often contrasted to the *Internet*, which is a global network, and *extranets*, which are somewhere in between. Think of extranets as intranets that extend out to business partners and special customers.

You don't need another lecture on the security risks associated with linking your company's computers to the Internet or the special business and legal liabilities you may incur when conducting business via extranets. However, you do need to think again about security before you put SQL Server data up on your firm's intranet. We spend an entire chapter drilling down into the details of creating intranets in the next chapter.

Who should have access to the data? Depending on where you post the HTML pages, you may be able to control access at the file or sub-directory level. How often do you plan to update the HTML pages? Like document files, they're "static" unless you update them. The SQL Server Web Wizard can't help you make security decisions, but it sure can make generating simple static HTML pages a whiz.

The Dirty Dozen

In the February 8, 1999, issue of *Infoworld*, their "Test Center" section focused on network security tools and listed 12 problems found most frequently by leading security assessment providers:

1. **Hosts that run unnecessary services such as denial of service and anonymous FTP**
2. **Unpatched, outdated, vulnerable, or default-configured software and firmware—you have replaced the default passwords for NT Administrator and SQL Server sa accounts, haven't you?**
3. **Information leakage through services such as SNMP, SMTP, finger rusers, systat, netstat, Telnet banners, Windows NT TCP 139 SMB (server message block), and zone transfers to non-name server hosts**
4. **Misappropriated trust relationships like rlogin, rsh, and rexec**
5. **Misconfigured firewall or router access-control lists**
6. **Weak passwords**
7. **Misconfigured Web servers such as CGI scripts, anonymous FTP, and SMTP**
8. **Improperly exported file sharing services like NetWare File Services or Net BIOS**
9. **Misconfigured or unpatched Windows NT servers**
10. **Inadequate logging, monitoring, and detecting capabilities**
11. **Unsecured remote-access points**
12. **Lack of comprehensive policies, procedures, standards, and guidelines**

Start Thinking Ahead

Although this chapter focuses on creating static Web pages that contain information from your SQL database, many of you will want to use SQL Server data on your Internet site. Here are some reasons for using a database on your Web site:

- To let potential customers see a "virtual" catalog.
- To gather information from visitors (via a form) that you can add to your company's mailing list.
- To test different products and marketing ideas and then store the information in a survey database.
- To allow feedback from customers that you can then store in a customer-service database.

Easiest First

SQL Server 7 includes the *Web Assistant Wizard*, a tool that you can use to generate standard HTML files from SQL Server data. HTML files, also known as Web pages, can be viewed by using an HTML browser such as Internet Explorer or Navigator. You can use the Web Assistant Wizard to generate a one-time query that generates Web pages. You can also use the Web Assistant Wizard to run a stored procedure, a series of T-SQL statements that are run as a group. You might, for example, update an HTML file whenever certain data changes, using a trigger. You can also use the Web Assistant Wizard to run queries or stored procedures at scheduled intervals.

As *Books Online* says in the topic *Using the Web Assistant Wizard*, you can use the Web Assistant Wizard to:

- Schedule a task to update a Web page automatically. For example, update a price list whenever a new item is added or a price is changed, thereby maintaining a dynamic inventory and price list for customers and sales staff.
- Publish and distribute management reports including the latest sales statistics, resource allocations, or other SQL Server data.
- Publish server reports that are of particular interest to DBAs with information about the users who currently access the server and any locks that are held. SQL Server can lock entire databases, entire tables, 8K "pages" (SQL Server's unit of storage), or individual rows.
- Publish information outside of SQL Server using extended stored procedures.
- Publish server "jump" lists (hyperlinks) using a table of favorite Web sites.

The Web Assistant Wizard runs from SQL Server Enterprise Manager, so anyone running it needs to have permission to run Enterprise Manager. Enterprise Manager, you remember, is the administrative tool for SQL Server that allows you to:

- Define groups of servers that run SQL Server. Register individual servers in a group.
- Configure all SQL Server options for each registered server.
- Create and administer all SQL Server databases, objects, logins, users, and permissions in each registered server.
- Define and execute all SQL Server administrative tasks on each registered server.
- Design and test SQL statements, batches, and scripts interactively by invoking SQL Server Query Analyzer.
- Invoke SQL Server's wizards.

DON'T CONFUSE SQL SERVER'S WEB ASSISTANT WIZARD WITH WINDOWS' WEB PUBLISHING WIZARD

Microsoft ships two different "personal" Web servers: FrontPage Personal Web Server (FP PWS) and Microsoft Personal Web Server (MSPWS, generally found in c:\program Files\Web Publish\WPWIZ.EXE). At press time, there are three versions of MSPWS: 1.0, 1.0a, and 4.0. The 1.x versions work with Windows 95. The 4.0 version is available both in the Windows 4.0 NT Option Pack (microsoft.com/ntserver/all/downloads.asp) and as part of Windows 98. There are many Microsoft Knowledge Base, or "Q" articles about both FP PWS and MSPWS. Microsoft goes to great length to position these

products as "personal" Web servers for development and testing: "Microsoft Personal Web Server (PWS) 4.0 is a desktop Web server. If you are connected to an intranet, or a corporate network, you can share documents with your coworkers from your own computer. Use PWS to develop and publish your personal home page. You can also test your Web site before you upload it to an Internet service provider."

Running the Web Assistant Wizard

The easiest way to start the Web Assistant Wizard is to click on the Wizard icon on the Enterprise Manager's menu toolbar. The Wizard icon consists of stars and a wand and will be on the right side of the toolbar. However, the Wizard icon may be grayed out if you've just started Enterprise Manager and don't have a database selected. If so, simply drill down into Enterprise Manager's hierarchy and select a database, such as Northwind.

You can also launch the Web Assistant Wizard via Enterprise Manager's Tools menu and by clicking on Wizards, and then expanding Management until you see the Web Publishing option. Right-click on Web Publishing and select New Web Assistant Job. This will launch Web Assistant Wizard.

Let's say that you want to create some Web pages based on Northwind data. Rather than just launch the Web Assistant Wizard right off the bat, let's take a minute to browse the Northwind database to see how it's organized. If you highlight Northwind, click on the + button to expand the hierarchy, and then click on Tables. You'll see a pretty long list that contains 32 items as shown in Figure 5.1.

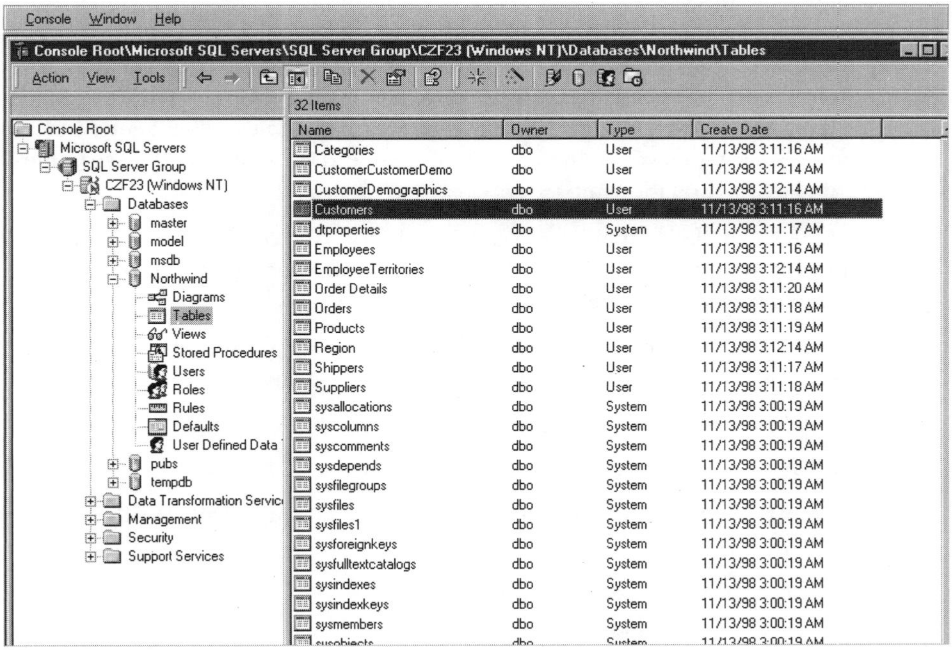
Console Window Help
Console Root\Microsoft SQL Servers\SQL Server Group\CZF23 (Windows NT)\Databases\Northwind\Tables
Action View Tools
32 Items
Console Root
Microsoft SQL Servers
SQL Server Group
CZF23 (Windows NT)
Databases
master
model
msdb
Northwind
Diagrams
Tables
Views
Stored Procedures
Users
Roles
Rules
Defaults
User Defined Data
pubs
tempdb
Data Transformation Servic
Management
Security
Support Services
Name Owner Type Create Date
Categories dbo User 11/13/98 3:11:16 AM
CustomerCustomerDemo dbo User 11/13/98 3:12:14 AM
CustomerDemographics dbo User 11/13/98 3:12:14 AM
Customers dbo User 11/13/98 3:11:16 AM
dtproperties dbo System 11/13/98 3:11:17 AM
Employees dbo User 11/13/98 3:11:16 AM
EmployeeTerritories dbo User 11/13/98 3:12:14 AM
Order Details dbo User 11/13/98 3:11:20 AM
Orders dbo User 11/13/98 3:11:18 AM
Products dbo User 11/13/98 3:11:19 AM
Region dbo User 11/13/98 3:12:14 AM
Shippers dbo User 11/13/98 3:11:17 AM
Suppliers dbo User 11/13/98 3:11:18 AM
sysallocations dbo System 11/13/98 3:00:19 AM
syscolumns dbo System 11/13/98 3:00:19 AM
syscomments dbo System 11/13/98 3:00:19 AM
sysdepends dbo System 11/13/98 3:00:19 AM
sysfilegroups dbo System 11/13/98 3:00:19 AM
sysfiles dbo System 11/13/98 3:00:19 AM
sysfiles1 dbo System 11/13/98 3:00:19 AM
sysforeignkeys dbo System 11/13/98 3:00:19 AM
sysfulltextcatalogs dbo System 11/13/98 3:00:19 AM
sysindexes dbo System 11/13/98 3:00:19 AM
sysindexkeys dbo System 11/13/98 3:00:19 AM
sysmembers dbo System 11/13/98 3:00:19 AM

Figure 5.1 Listing the tables in the Northwind database from Enterprise Manager.

"Whoa!" yelled the Access users, in reference to all of those "sys" tables that were never part of the "original" Northwind database. *It* only had eight tables:

1. Categories
2. Customers
3. Employees
4. Order Details
5. Orders
6. Products
7. Shippers
8. Suppliers

Now, however, there are not only all those system tables such as sysallocations, syscolumns, and so on included, but also four more "user" tables—Territories, CustomerCustomerDemo, CustomerDemographics, and Region have been added. Well, we suspect that Microsoft included the four new user tables to make Northwind more representative of an enterprise database.

A Brief Side Trip

Curious how all of the tables relate to each other and what the deal is with the CustomerCustomerDemo table? Is that a typo or what? Actually, it's not. The CustomerCustomerDemo table is a "link" table that relates—SQL Server is a relational database management system, remember—the Customer and CustomerDemographics tables.

To get a visual appreciation for Northwind's user tables, click on the Diagrams icon in the Enterprise Manager's left panel, and then double-click on Relationships. You should see what's called an entity-relationship (ER) diagram of the original Northwind database as shown in Figure 5.2 (without the new tables—shame on Microsoft!). If you hover your mouse over any of the lines that join the tables, you'll see names of the foreign key (FK) relationships.

Yes, yes, we realize that you're eager to do the Web publishing thing, but bear with us for a bit more opportunistic exploration. We think the side trip is both useful and interesting, and we guarantee it's no primrose path.

We suspect some of you will want to "fix" the diagram and add the new tables. It's easy, and, as you might expect, you have two choices:

1. Add the tables to the existing diagram.
2. Create a new diagram.

Rather than change the original ER diagram that ships with Northwind, let's create a new one.

1. Close the Relationships diagram and right-click on the Diagrams item in the Enterprise Manager's hierarchy.

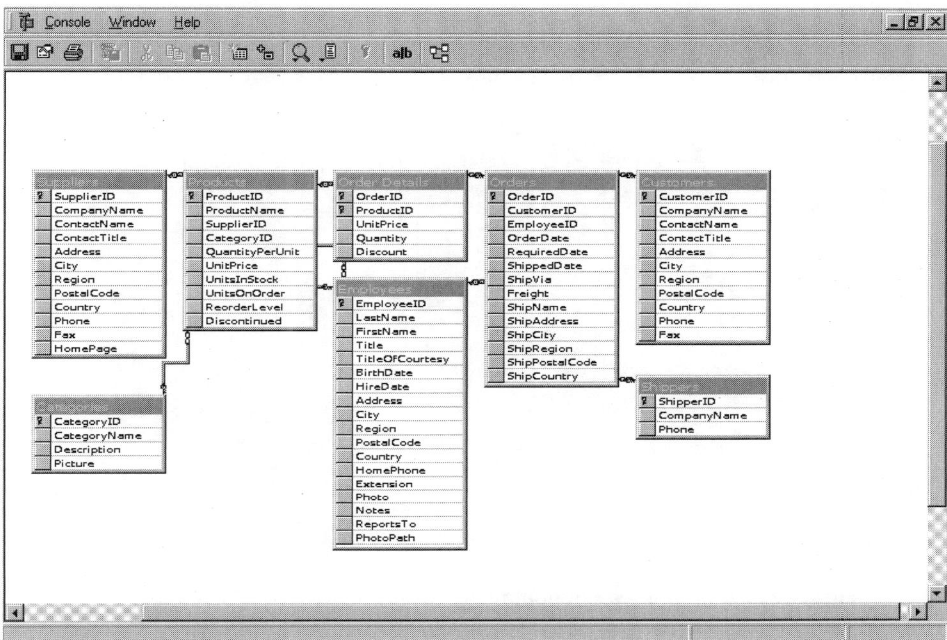

Figure 5.2 Entity-relationship (ER) diagram for the original Northwind database.

2. Select New Database Diagram. This should launch the Create Database Diagram Wizard.
3. Click Next and then check the Add Related Tables Automatically checkbox shown in Figure 5.3 to add related tables. You can leave the default level of related tables alone, since we only need one level in this simple database.
4. Add all of the tables (some will be automatically added thanks to your entry in the checkbox, so you'll only have to do seven clicks to add them all). Proceed to the next screen where you can look at the list of tables that you've selected.
5. Press the Finish button and you'll see a basic ER diagram!

None of the relationships have names, and the tables may not be arranged in the way you want. Experiment with right-clicking to your heart's desire. It won't take long to "gussy up" that wizard-generated ER diagram if you're interested. Pretty it up, print it out, and impress your boss!

Okay, back to work. Click on the Disk icon on the menu bar and save your work as Northwind2 or something equally creative, and close the diagram. You should see your new diagram represented along with the original Relationships diagram in the Enterprise Manager's right-hand panel as shown in Figure 5.4.

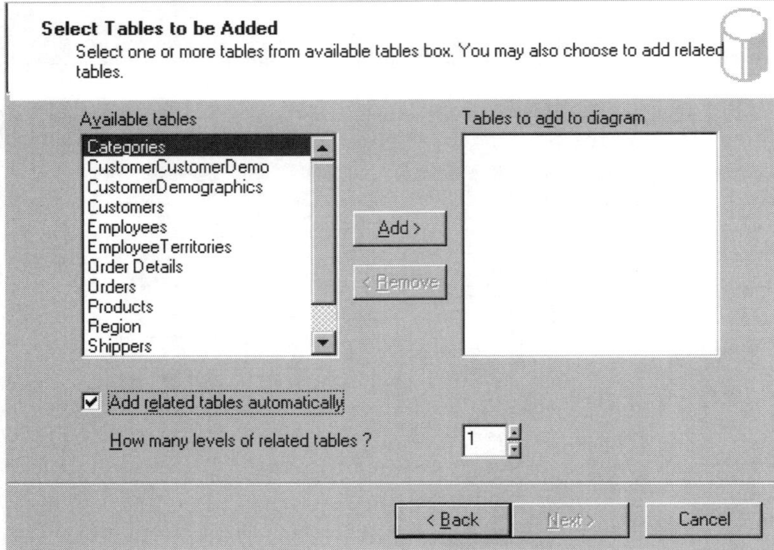

Figure 5.3 Creating a new database diagram.

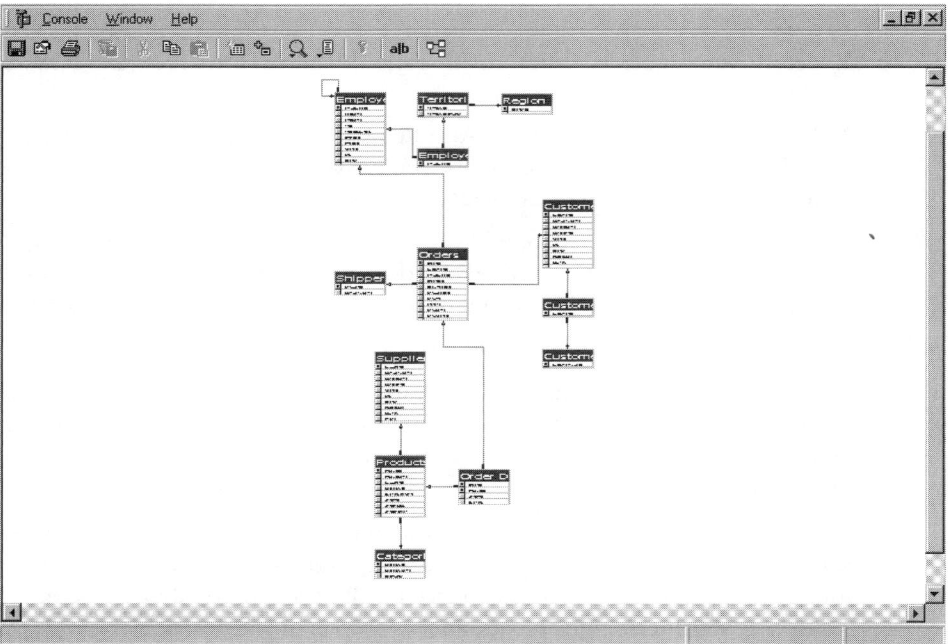

Figure 5.4 A new Northwind ER diagram that shows *all* the user tables.

Back to the Main Road

Let's return to the job at hand which is to prepare some Northwind data for publication on our intranet. In the Enterprise Manager, with Northwind expanded, select the Tables icon again. You should see the list of 32 tables. Let's say that we want to publish something about Customers and their Orders. Chances are that you're not exactly sure what data is contained in those tables, so it makes sense to find out before you get started with the Web Assistant Wizard.

Double-click on Customers to see what fields are available. Note that Northwind has 91 customers as shown in Figure 5.5.

Chances are you'd want to include both the customer (CompanyName) and contact person (ContactName) fields. Do you want to include the customer ID (CustomerID) field too? Well, maybe, maybe not—it depends on your company. In this case, we'll assume not.

Okay, what kind of information is in the Orders table? Double-click on Orders to find out. As you can see, it has lots of information and you have to use the scrollbar to see all of the fields. Probably the most interesting fields, however, are the order ID and date fields. Make a mental note of what you'd like to include in your HTML page and note that Orders has 830 rows.

Do you need any data from OrderDetails? Probably not.

Once you've got an idea about what you want to publish, click on the Wizard icon on the Enterprise Manager's menu or select Wizards from the Tools menu. If you use the icon approach, you'll have to expand the Management Wizard's hierarchy as shown in Figure 5.6.

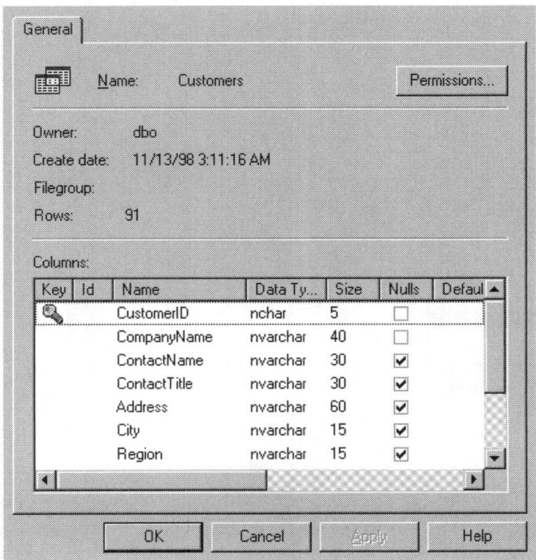

Figure 5.5 Northwind's Customer table.

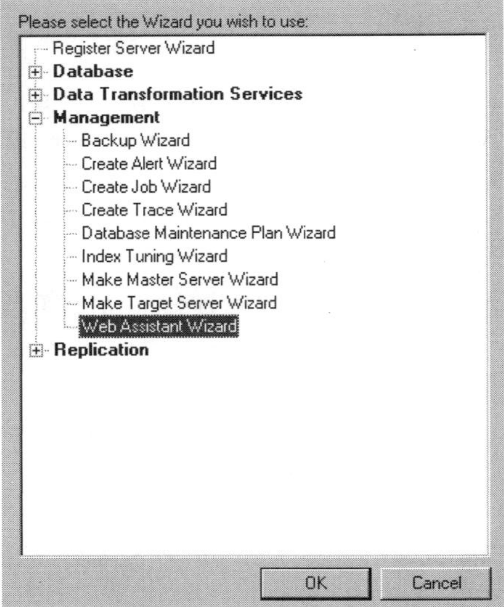

Figure 5.6 One way to run a wizard is by clicking on the Enterprise Manager's Wizard icon (wand and stardust).

Double-click on the Web Assistant Wizard to launch the wizard and then click Next to continue. You should see a dialog box with a drop-down listbox that lists the available databases. Select Northwind as we've done in Figure 5.7.

Next, you'll be asked to name your Web Assistant job. Accept the default title and first option which simply involves selecting tables and columns. Later we'll explore more complex options that use stored procedures and SQL.

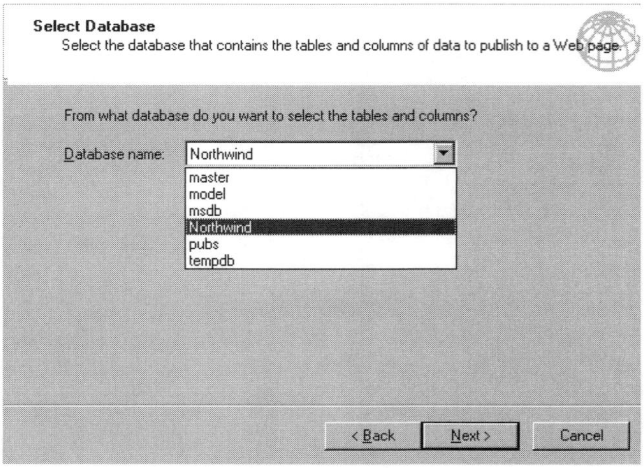

Select Database
Select the database that contains the tables and columns of data to publish to a Web page.
From what database do you want to select the tables and columns?
Database name: Northwind
master
model
msdb
Northwind
pubs
tempdb
< Back
Next >
Cancel

Figure 5.7 Selecting the Northwind database.

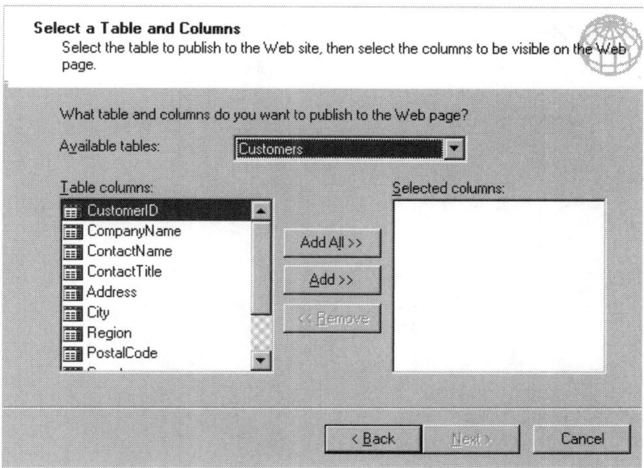

Figure 5.8 Preparing to select the columns we want from the Customers table.

The next screen asks you to specify tables and columns. The Categories table and its columns are the default simply because Categories is the first user table if you list them in alphabetical order. Select the Customers table (see Figure 5.8). We'll add the columns we want from the Orders table after we've taken care of Customers.

Add the CompanyName and ContactName fields from the Customer table and click Next. You'll see a more complex screen that gives you options for setting up some selection criteria if you don't want to list all of the customers (see Figure 5.9). Let's skip this for now.

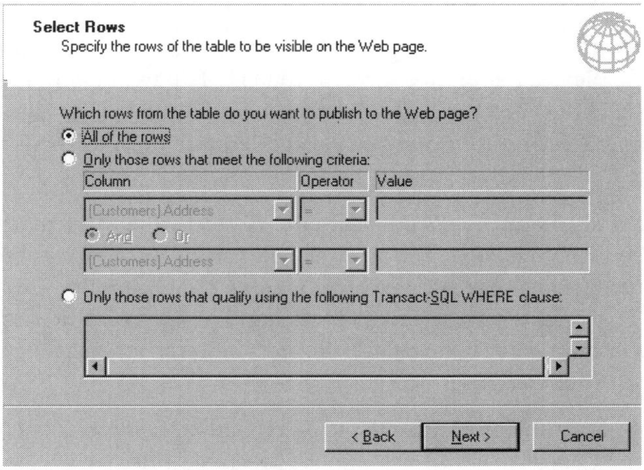

Figure 5.9 The Web Assistant Wizard even gives you the option of publishing a subset of the rows. The Address field appears in the dimmed-out column in the middle of the screen because if you list Customer fields in alphabetical order, it's the first.

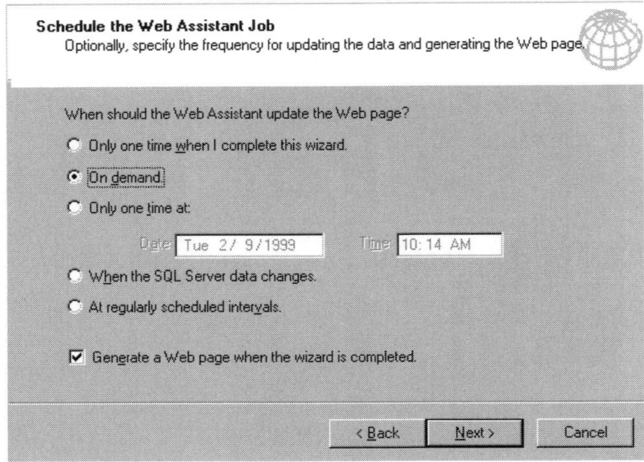

Figure 5.10 You can also specify whether or not to have the HTML pages updated.

Figure 5.10 shows a screen that provides important options for specifying how you want the HTML pages updated—if you do.

Our options for updating the HTML pages are:

- Just publish the HTML now.
- Publish it later on demand.
- Publish it at one specified future time.
- Publish it whenever SQL Server data changes.
- Publish it at regularly scheduled intervals.

Let's go with SQL Server's default—publishing it as soon as we're done with the wizard. The next screen displays a default location for the HTML page that for most of you will be c:\MSSQL7\HTML\WebPage1.htm as shown in Figure 5.11. Make a mental note of the location and accept it for now. You need adequate privileges to create files in the default directory.

The next screen asks if you want the Web Assistant Wizard to help format the page. Hey, why not? Let's see what it will do for us. The Character Set option is useful, especially for international publishing, because it converts data from the current SQL Server setting to the character set specified. A meta tag that specifies the chosen character set is inserted automatically if you select the "Yes, help me format the Web page" option. Click the Next button to continue.

We can probably come up with better titles than "Microsoft SQL Server Web Assistant" for our title page and "Query Results" for our HTML table title, so let's replace the default entries with "Order Status" and "Customer Orders." On the next page, click on the second radio button to suppress column names and accept the other defaults. On the following page, decline the offer to provide any hyperlinks.

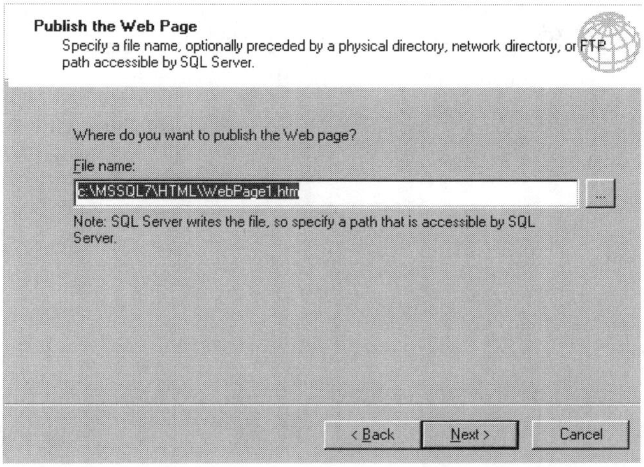

Publish the Web Page
Specify a file name, optionally preceded by a physical directory, network directory, or FTP path accessible by SQL Server.

Where do you want to publish the Web page?

File name:

c:\MSSQL7\HTML\WebPage1.htm

Note: SQL Server writes the file, so specify a path that is accessible by SQL Server.

< Back | Next > | Cancel

Figure 5.11 Deciding where the Web Assistant Wizard's output should be stored.

The wizard will then ask a *really important* question about treating potentially large numbers of rows. Northwind, as you may know, doesn't contain a lot of data—just 91 customers and 830 orders—but most real-world databases do. Here, we're given the option for limiting the number of rows outright, as well as deciding whether to simply list them on a single scrolling page or as a linear sequence of pages. Let's accept the default for now.

What's up with the Completing the Web Assistant Wizard screen shown in Figure 5.12? Don't we get the opportunity to add columns from the Orders table?

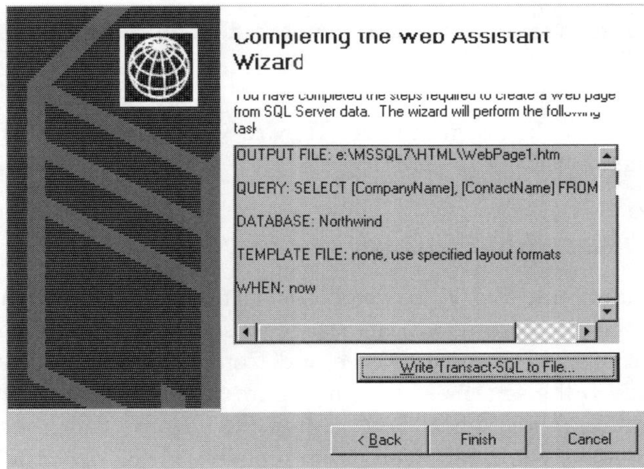

Figure 5.12 Completing the Web Assistant Wizard.

Nope, sorry Charlie (Primrose Path #1). Web Assistant Wizard is great for quick, single-table publishing, but only works for multi-table publishing if you provide the SQL—either by typing it in or by providing a stored procedure to do it.

Go ahead and have the wizard Write Transact-SQL to File so that you can examine it. Then cancel the operation. Here's the T-SQL output from our Web Assistant Wizard job:

```
EXECUTE sp_makewebtask @outputfile = N'c:\MSSQL7\HTML\WebPage1.htm',
@query=N'SELECT [CompanyName], [ContactName] FROM [Customers]',
@fixedfont=1, @HTMLheader=3, @webpagetitle=N'Customer Orders',
@resultstitle=N'Order Status', @dbname=N'Northwind',
@whentype=1,@procname=N'Northwind Web
Page',@codepage=65001,@charset=N'utf-8'
```

This is an example of T-SQL. The EXECUTE statement tells SQL Server to run a stored procedure, in this case sp_makewebtask. The parameters—identified by the @ symbol—tell SQL Server:

- Where to save the output
- What the query is
- What font and font size to use
- What to call the Web page and HTML table
- The source database
- How often the Web task we just created should run
- What the procedure name is
- What code pages and character sets to use

For more information on stored procedures—or on calling this particular one—consult *Books Online* and Chapter 12.

DID YOU KNOW...

The Web Assistant Wizard is really just a fancy input routine for the sp_makewebtask stored procedure.

Curious about those "Ns" in the previous code? They're SQL Server's way of flagging Unicode data as we mentioned in Chapter 4.

Running the Web Assistant Wizard, Take Two

Well, that didn't work out quite like we expected, so let's try again. Re-launch the Web Assistant Wizard, select the Northwind database, choose the Customers table, and then select the two columns—CompanyName and ContactName—as before. That should bring you back to the screen—shown in Figure 5.9—where you can specify rows. You may think that this is where you can tell the wizard to also include the Orders table. Unfortunately, you can't. Even if you type in your own WHERE clause, you're still limited to the single Customers table.

We need to figure out another approach. We could modify the code generated by the wizard, but we'd probably have to experiment which might result in mistakes with syntax and punctuation. Let's back up two screens (or simply exit and re-launch Web Assistant Wizard one more time) and stop at the Start a New Web Assistant Job screen, the first screen after we select the database. Notice that we have two alternatives for publishing data from the tables and columns that we select:

1. Publish the results of a "user" stored procedure—in other words, one we write ourselves.
2. Provide our own T-SQL.

These options, if you think about it, really amount to the same thing: we need to provide some T-SQL either on-the-fly or from something that we've already written, tested, and saved as a stored procedure. Unfortunately, there's no Query Wizard like you find in Microsoft Query or Access. And, if you examine the Northwind database, the object hierarchy in the Enterprise Manager doesn't have any "queries" like Access databases.

ACCESS QUERIES AND FORMS

SQL Server doesn't store queries or forms the way Access does. The easiest way to emulate Access' stored queries in SQL Server is with stored procedures, but you need to use third-party tools like Visual Basic or Visual InterDev to mimic Access' forms for SQL Server.

Well, let's see what we can come up with. Refer to *Books Online*, *SELECT (T-SQL)*, "The SQL SELECT Statement" section in Chapter 1, or Appendix A on SQL for help writing a SELECT statement. We're probably going to need something like this:

```
SELECT <select_list>
FROM <table_source>
```

Okay, how about this?

```
SELECT CustomerID, CompanyName, ContactName, OrderDate, RequiredDate,
ShippedDate FROM Customers, Orders
```

To test a query like this from Enterprise Manager, run the SQL Server Query Analyzer from the Tools menu. You should see a pretty blah screen that may have one or two horizontal windows. On the toolbar's right side, you'll see the active database that is probably master. Change that to Northwind. Then, click on the icon just to the left of DB. This icon (or Ctrl-R) controls whether or not you see the Results pane. You want to, so make sure you have two horizontal windows.

Now type in our SELECT statement. Don't worry about case unless you installed your SQL Server with a case-sensitive sort order. We display the SQL keywords in upper case simply by convention.

Once you've typed in the command, select Query/Execute from the menu or simply press F5. You should see an error message as shown in Figure 5.13.

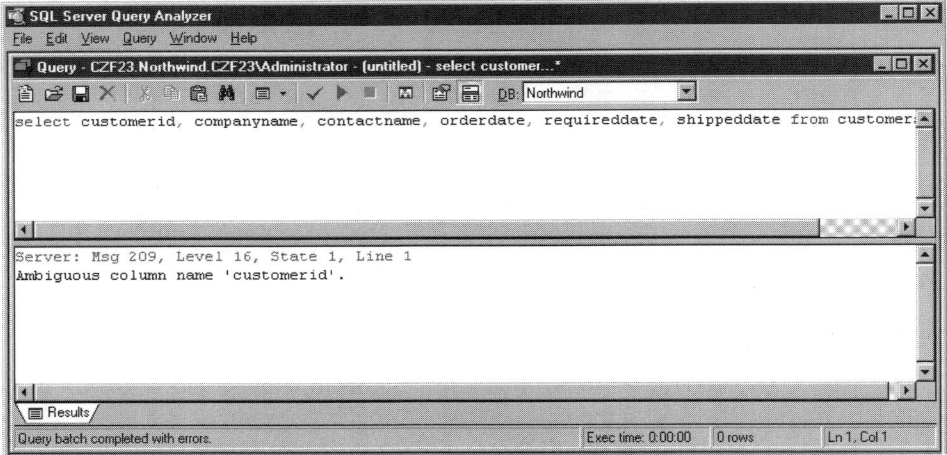

Figure 5.13 Our multi-table SELECT statement didn't work since we didn't "qualify" the column names with their table names.

Our multi-table SELECT statement didn't work since we didn't "qualify" the column names with their table names. When you have more than one table, you have to "qualify" the otherwise ambiguous column names that exist in more than one table by specifying the source table—hence the Customers.CompanyName, and so on.

If you re-use what you typed into Query Analyzer earlier, but add "Customers." and "Orders." in front of the column names, like the following, you'll see a globe icon on the toolbar just to the right of Northwind that indicates that the query is executing.

```
SELECT Customers.CustomerID, Customers.CompanyName, Customers.ContactName,
    Orders.OrderDate, Orders.RequiredDate, Orders.ShippedDate,
FROM Customers, Orders
```

Eventually you'll see a screen similar to that in Figure 5.14. Take a minute to study the output window, especially the lower, right-hand side where the status bar displays 75530 rows. Whoa! No *wonder* it took so long to finish the query. What happened?

NO CONTINUATION CHARACTERS NEEDED

T-SQL doesn't use continuation characters like some programming languages do. You can use hard carriage returns to break up lines as we did in Figure 5.14 without affecting the command.

What happened was that we didn't ask for a *join*. We assumed that SQL Server was smart enough to read our minds and only return "matches"—that is, combinations of Customers and Orders that matched on the basis of Customer and Order Numbers. Wrong. It interpreted our call as a request to combine every row in the Customers table with every row in the Orders table. The result? A Cartesian product—product because it consists of 91 customers times 830 orders, and 91*830 = 75,530 rows.

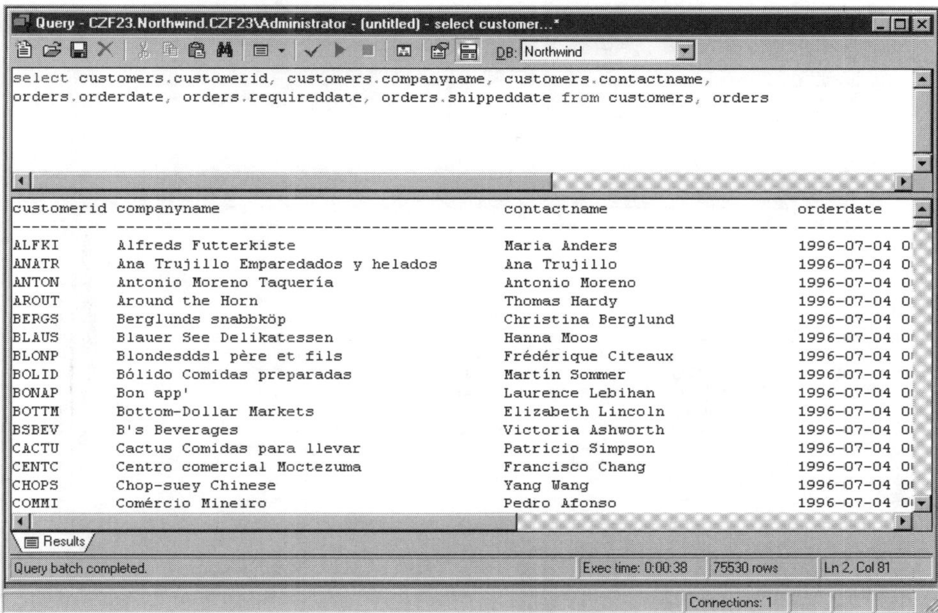

Figure 5.14 It's easy to ask for a Cartesian product if you're not careful.

Okay, back to the drawing board. It turns out that we need to use a join. Now, there are several kinds of joins, but the most common one is an *inner join*. You use inner joins to display information when matching rows are found in both tables. You use *outer joins* primarily to search for orphan records, since outer joins allow you to restrict rows from one table while still allowing all rows from another table. We want an inner join, so add the WHERE clause as we've done here:

```
SELECT Customers.CustomerID, Customers.CompanyName, Customers.ContactName,
    Orders.OrderDate, Orders.RequiredDate, Orders.ShippedDate
FROM Customers, Orders
WHERE Customers.CustomerID = Orders.CustomerID
```

That's better—only 830 rows. That looks about right. The output isn't pretty, especially with all those repeated entries, but at least we're headed in the right direction (see Figure 5.15). Note that you can't join tables on text or image Columns. Do you see now why end users like query tools and report writers that shield them from writing SQL? Go ahead and save your SQL by selecting File, then click on Save, and call your query something like custord1.sql.

Using Our Own Code

Now let's see how we can use this code in the Web Assistant Wizard. Re-launch the wizard, select the Northwind database, and accept the default job name. This time, however, select the third radio button, Data from the Transact-SQL statement I specify.

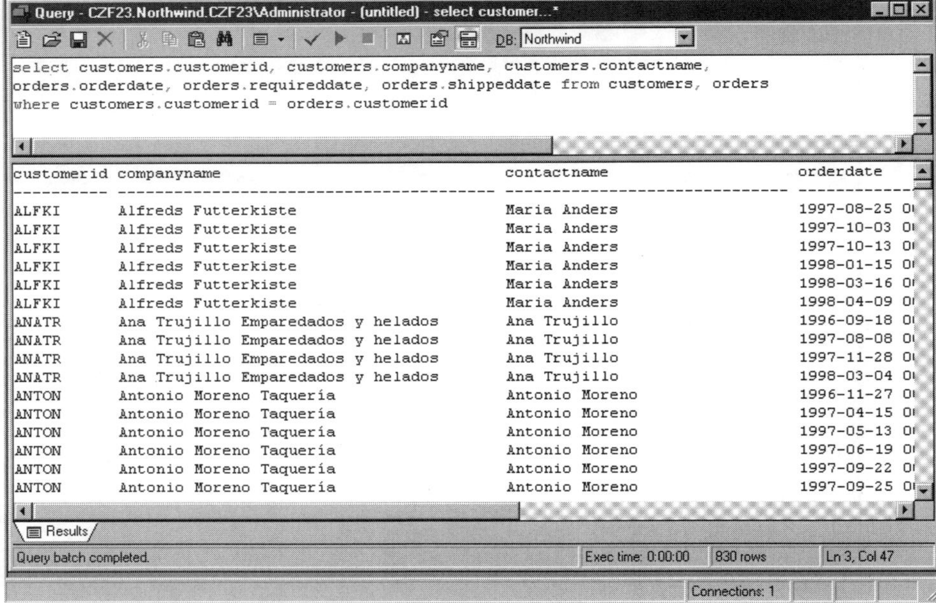

Figure 5.15 We modified our erroneous Cartesian product query by adding a WHERE clause to create an inner join.

Open the custords.sql code in Notepad and then copy and paste it into the Write a SQL Query window as we did in Figure 5.16 or simply re-enter it.

At the end of the wizard, accept the default for only generating the pages once, and simply accept the rest of the defaults for Web page location, help with formatting,

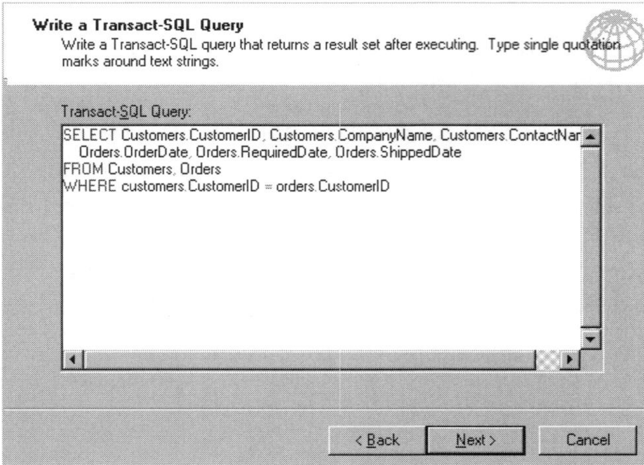

Figure 5.16 One of the Web Assistant Wizard's options is to let you type in your own SQL on the fly.

default titles, page formatting, lack of hyperlinks, and all rows. Opt to save your code again, but this time in ANSI format as custord2.sql. Select Finish.

You can explore the fruits of your labor using your favorite browser as in Figure 5.17. Assuming that you chose all of the defaults, it will probably be in c:\mssql7\html\webpage1.html.

Although the grid format is nice, the output leaves a lot to be desired. Also, frankly, who wants to scroll through over 800 rows of data?

Even though this kind of HTML page may be useful—colleagues can save it on to their local system and perform local manipulations, searches, and so on, it's more likely that you'd want to post exceptional items, such as customers with unfilled (pending) orders. To do that, you can use the IS NULL clause. NULLs are strange beasts in SQL. They're not the same as zeros, nor the same as the null string or a space character. You can't compare them (one NULL doesn't equal another NULL) nor can you even use them in a clause such as WHERE ShippedDate = NULL. You *can*, however, use IS NULL and IS NOT NULL to find columns with missing data as in this statement:

```
SELECT ContactName, Phone, OrderDate FROM Customers, Orders
WHERE Customers.CustomerID = Orders.CustomerID AND ShippedDate IS NULL
```

If you try this in Query Analyzer, you'll see that 21 orders have not been shipped (see Figure 5.18).

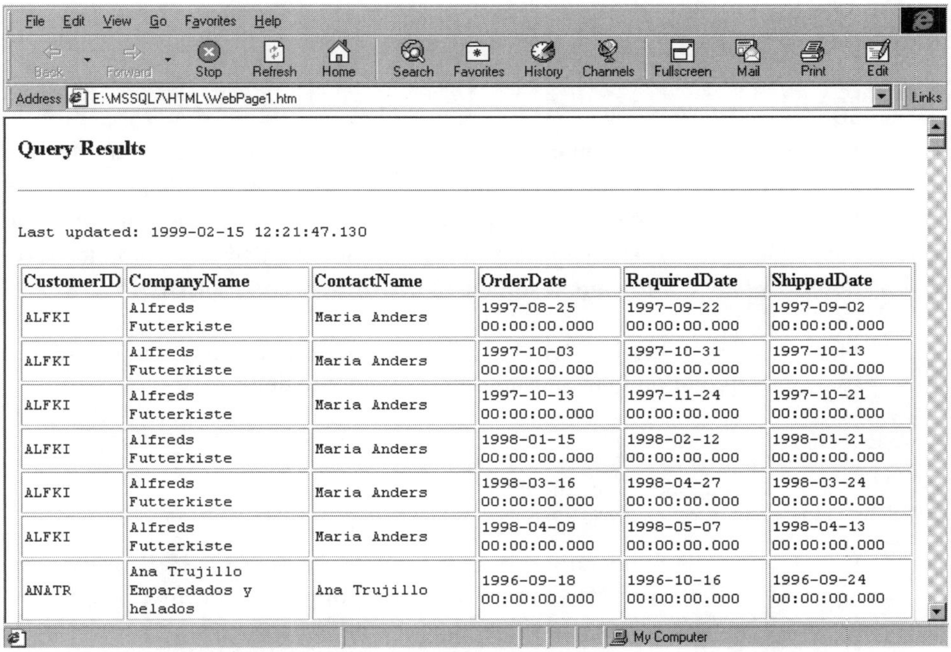

Address E:\MSSQL7\HTML\WebPage1.htm

Query Results

Last updated: 1999-02-15 12:21:47.130

CustomerID	CompanyName	ContactName	OrderDate	RequiredDate	ShippedDate
ALFKI	Alfreds Futterkiste	Maria Anders	1997-08-25 00:00:00.000	1997-09-22 00:00:00.000	1997-09-02 00:00:00.000
ALFKI	Alfreds Futterkiste	Maria Anders	1997-10-03 00:00:00.000	1997-10-31 00:00:00.000	1997-10-13 00:00:00.000
ALFKI	Alfreds Futterkiste	Maria Anders	1997-10-13 00:00:00.000	1997-11-24 00:00:00.000	1997-10-21 00:00:00.000
ALFKI	Alfreds Futterkiste	Maria Anders	1998-01-15 00:00:00.000	1998-02-12 00:00:00.000	1998-01-21 00:00:00.000
ALFKI	Alfreds Futterkiste	Maria Anders	1998-03-16 00:00:00.000	1998-04-27 00:00:00.000	1998-03-24 00:00:00.000
ALFKI	Alfreds Futterkiste	Maria Anders	1998-04-09 00:00:00.000	1998-05-07 00:00:00.000	1998-04-13 00:00:00.000
ANATR	Ana Trujillo Emparedados y helados	Ana Trujillo	1996-09-18 00:00:00.000	1996-10-16 00:00:00.000	1996-09-24 00:00:00.000

Figure 5.17 Our inner-join combination of customers and orders.

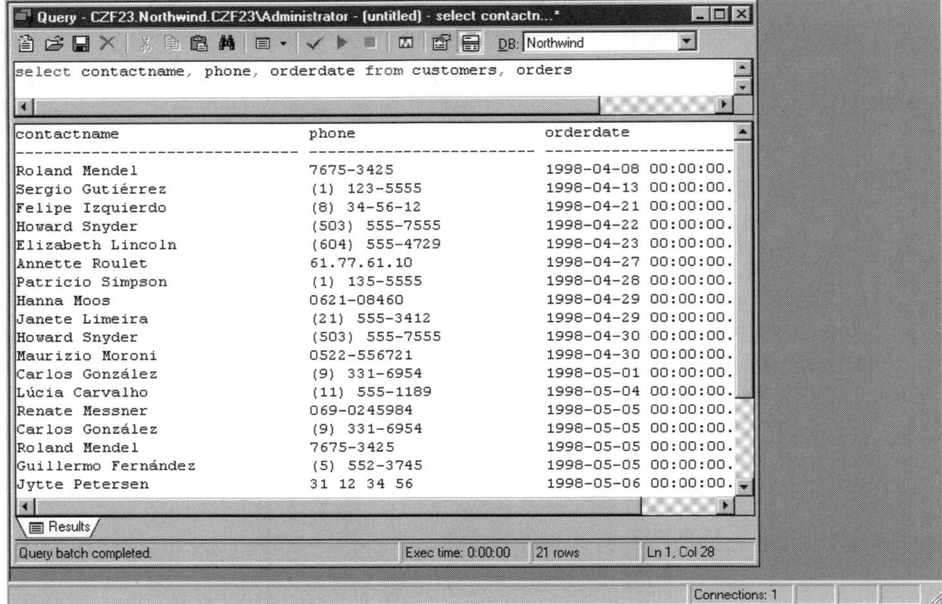

Figure 5.18 Creative use of IS NULL and IS NOT NULL in SELECT statements can return rows with missing data.

REMOVING DUPLICATES

SQL Server doesn't have a single command to "get rid of" duplicates that are in your database. Ideally, you will have established unique key fields for all of your tables to prevent duplicates from "getting in," but, as you saw in the Chapter 4, it's tempting to disable constraint checking if you use a utility like bcp to import your data. The best technique for removing duplicates is to use the UNION command. Refer to *Books Online, Combining Results with UNION* for a brief discussion.

Many useful queries involve dates, and the main thing to remember with them is to use single quotation marks around them as shown here:

```
SELECT ContactName, Phone, OrderDate FROM Customers, Orders
WHERE Customers.CustomerID = Orders.CustomerID
AND and ShippedDate is NULL
AND OrderDate > '5/1/98'
```

If you don't like the default datetime format, use the CONVERT (*data_type*[(*length*)], *expression* [, *style*]) function—notably the style option—for controlling appearance and format. The *Books Online, CAST and CONVERT (T-SQL)* topic describes the style codes. You may also want to explore the DATEPART(), DAY(), MONTH(), YEAR(), and GET-DATE () functions.

Missing Data and NULLs

As we said, NULLs are strange beasts in SQL. You can start to learn more about them by reading *Null Values* and *NULL Comparison Search Conditions* in *Books Online*, but the main rules about NULLs are:

- NULLs are neither equal to each other nor to any value. To test for a NULL, you need to use the IS NULL or IS NOT NULL predicate. The one exception is that NULLs *are* treated as equal to one another when forming groups.
- NULLs propagate in operations and functions. Add or multiply two values, one of which is a NULL, and you'll get a NULL.

Joe Celko does an excellent job describing how NULLs can emerge in his *Data and Databases* book. He cites the ANSI X3 Interim Report 75-02-08 and the SPARC Study Group 1975 as listing 14 different kinds of incomplete data. He describes the most common reasons that values may be missing using a hospital scenario:

1. Unknown. A patient arrives in a coma and we don't know the patient's name.
2. Not applicable. The patient is a man, so data about number of pregnancies is irrelevant.
3. Missing. A "cash-on-hand" field shouldn't necessarily be filled out as "zero" if the patient arrives without a wallet.
4. Not classified. If the diagnosis or ethnic background is unknown, there may be a special code to reflect that unknown status.
5. Erroneous data. What if a faulty instrument provides a value that's out of range based on database constraints?
6. Illegal results. This would reflect an illegal calculation (divide by zero) or some other absurd result such as a negative age, but you would know that some effort had been made to obtain it.
7. Error in representation. Here the calculation is valid, but the database can't represent the results for one reason or another such as numeric overflow or invalid dates.
8. Limited values. When all of a certain set of values must appear in a database, you can run into a variety of problems like if a desired value has already been used.

SQL'S BUILT-IN FUNCTIONS

Most people don't take enough time to find out all of the built-in functions that are part of SQL. In addition to the useful COUNT (*), AVG, and SUM expressions, there are also the normal assortment of string, mathematical, and date functions. Do yourself a favor and spend a few minutes reading about them (especially the *Functions (T-SQL)* and *Using Functions* topics) in your SQL Server manuals, *Books Online*, or introductory SQL Server book. It's also not hard to add column headers to your output in order to replace the default column names or to strip off the ugly time portion that is a part of the datetime data type's default display. How's that for piquing your curiosity?

One More Brief Side Trip

As long as we're in the "roll-our-own-SQL" mind set, we may as well spend a few minutes exploring another easy-to-use, but often overlooked feature of SQL—the *view*. Views, as you may recall from Chapter 1, are virtual tables. Aside from their definition, they don't take up space in the same sense as tables filled with raw data do, because views are really pre-defined joins. Once they're set up, you can treat them just like tables. Do you see where we're headed? Instead of having complex SQL statements with qualified column names, wouldn't it be nice to have one or more "pseudo" tables (views) that you could query?

Let's go back to the Enterprise Manager and look at the Northwind database hierarchy. Bingo! Just below the Tables category, there's one for Views. Northwind has a pretty overwhelming list of views, but notice that a lot of them are system views— automatically created for SQL Server for one reason or another. If you double-click on the first view, "Alphabetical list of products," you'll see its SQL definition (see Figure 5.19).

Now, the Web Assistant Wizard doesn't treat views like tables (it should) in its easiest-to-use first option—only tables and columns. However, you can probably see how much nicer it would be to type:

```
SELECT * FROM Invoices
```

instead of

```
SELECT Orders.ShipName, Orders.ShipAddress, Orders.ShipCity,
Orders.ShipRegion, Orders.ShipPostalCode,
      Orders.ShipCountry, Orders.CustomerID, Customers.CompanyName AS
CustomerName, Customers.Address, Customers.City,
      Customers.Region, Customers.PostalCode, Customers.Country,
      (FirstName + ' ' + LastName) AS Salesperson,
      Orders.OrderID, Orders.OrderDate, Orders.RequiredDate,
Orders.ShippedDate, Shippers.CompanyName As ShipperName,
      "Order Details".ProductID, Products.ProductName, "Order
Details".UnitPrice, "Order Details".Quantity,
      "Order Details".Discount,
      (CONVERT(money,("Order Details".UnitPrice*Quantity*(1-
Discount)/100))*100) AS ExtendedPrice, Orders.Freight
FROM Shippers INNER JOIN
             (Products INNER JOIN
                     (
                             (Employees INNER JOIN
                                     (Customers INNER JOIN Orders ON
Customers.CustomerID = Orders.CustomerID)
                             ON Employees.EmployeeID = Orders.EmployeeID)
                     INNER JOIN "Order Details" ON Orders.OrderID =
"Order Details".OrderID)
             ON Products.ProductID = "Order Details".ProductID)
      ON Shippers.ShipperID = Orders.ShipVia
```

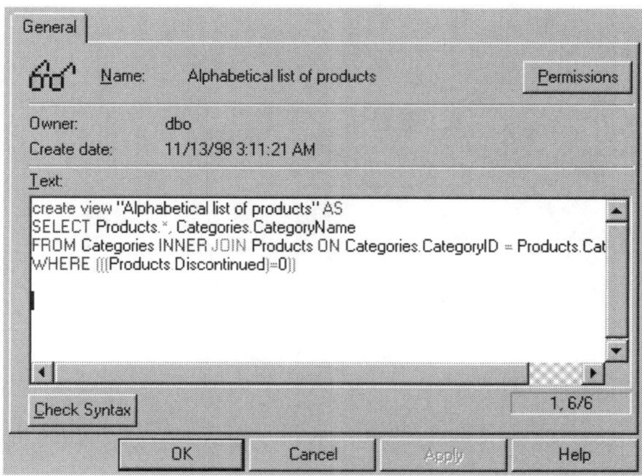

Figure 5.19 Examining the code behind a view definition.

The easiest way to create your own views is to use Enterprise Manager's View Wizard. To find it, expand the Database node in the Wizard dialog box and click on Create View Wizard.

Follow the prompts and try to create a view for Customer Orders that hasn't been shipped yet (hint: the Orders table's DateShipped field is NULL). Once you've established Northwind as the database and selected the Customers and Orders tables (see Figure 5.20), you'll need to select the columns that you want to include in the view—probably the CustomerID, CompanyName, ContactName, OrderID, OrderDate, and RequiredDate.

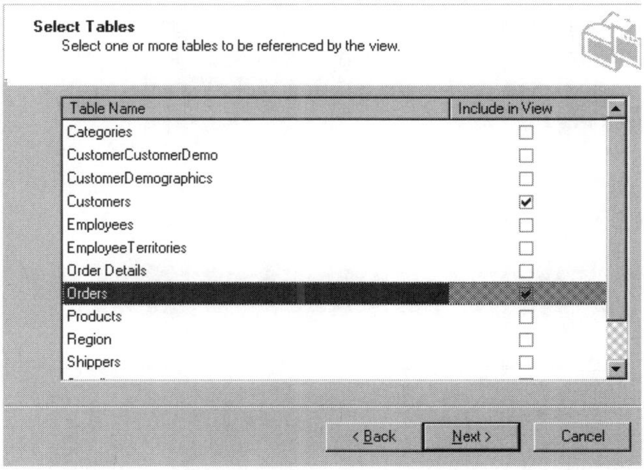

Figure 5.20 Using Enterprise Manager's Create a View Wizard.

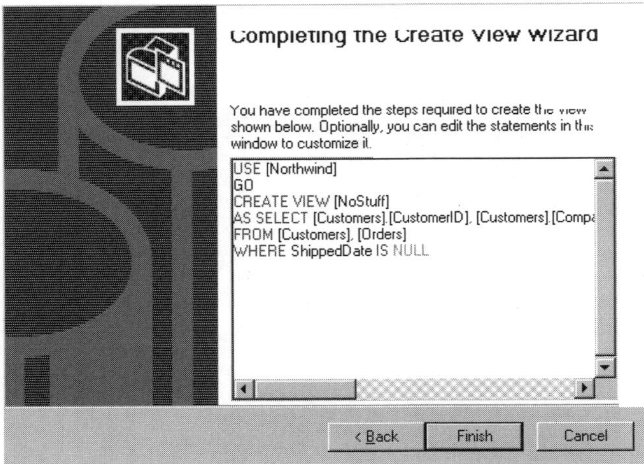

Figure 5.21 Completing our view definition for Customers with Outstanding Orders.

You'll need to enter, WHERE ShippedDate IS NULL as your SQL qualifying clause. We called our view NoStuff. The wizard's final screen allows you to view and edit the code as shown in Figure 5.21.

Back in the Enterprise Manager, you should see your new view in the Views hierarchy. We've now completed our side trip.

Running the Web Assistant Wizard Using Stored Procedures

Before we re-launch the Web Assistant Wizard, let's find out if Northwind has any stored procedures. Click on Stored Procedures in the Northwind hierarchy and note the 25 stored procedures in the right-hand pane. Double-click on those stored procedures that you're interested in to see the underlying SQL. We selected the CustOrderHist stored procedure in Figure 5.22.

It looks like this:

```
CREATE PROCEDURE CustOrderHist @CustomerID nchar(5)
AS
SELECT ProductName, Total=SUM(Quantity)
FROM Products P, [Order Details] OD, Orders O, Customers C
WHERE C.CustomerID = @CustomerID
AND C.CustomerID = O.CustomerID AND O.OrderID = OD.OrderID AND
OD.ProductID = P.ProductID
GROUP BY ProductName
```

As we mentioned earlier in this chapter, the @ symbol is associated with a parameter that the stored procedure expects the user to enter—here, a CustomerID.

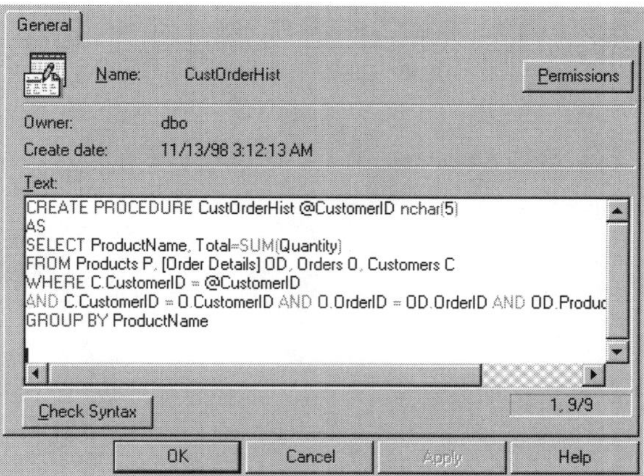

Figure 5.22 Examining Northwind's CustOrderHist stored procedure.

For now, let's return to the Web Assistant Wizard and see what we have to do to schedule an HTML report to run on demand when the CustOrderHist stored procedure is executed.

If you re-launch the Web Assistant Wizard, choose Northwind as your database, and select the wizard's stored procedure option, you'll see a list of Northwind stored procedures. Select the CustOrderHist stored procedure. As you might expect, given the previous code listing, the screen asks for a Customer ID. Use the Query Analyzer (SELECT CustomerID FROM Customers) to find some valid data (see Figure 5.23), or just type in ANTON which *is* a valid Customer ID. After you navigate through the remainder of the wizard's now-familiar screens, and opt to publish the results at the conclusion of your Web Assistant Wizard session, you'll be rewarded with the results you see in Figure 5.24.

STORED PROCS

Most SQL Server veterans refer to stored procedures as *stored procs,* not *stored procedures.*

Well, we've come up against another limitation to Web Assistant Wizard—the need to provide parameters up front, even for delayed or periodic publishing in those stored procedures that require parameters. Of course, not all stored procedures require parameters, and there's nothing to prevent you from periodically posting something like an HTML page with unfilled orders using our NoStuff view.

WEB ASSISTANT WIZARD'S DEFAULT WEB PAGE

Accepting Web Assistant Wizard's default Web page is dangerous since it will overwrite existing pages without telling you.

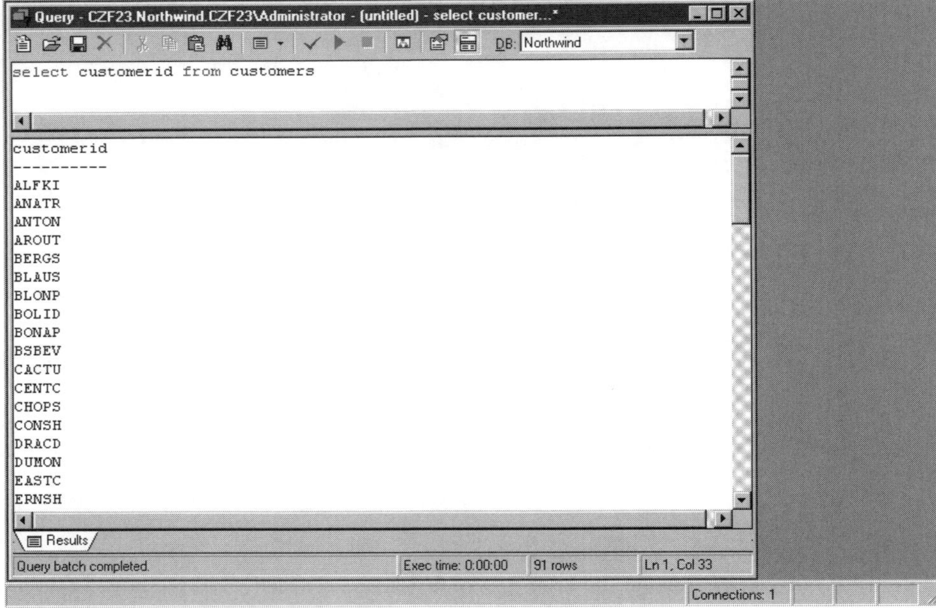

Figure 5.23 Obtaining some valid Customer IDs from the Customers table.

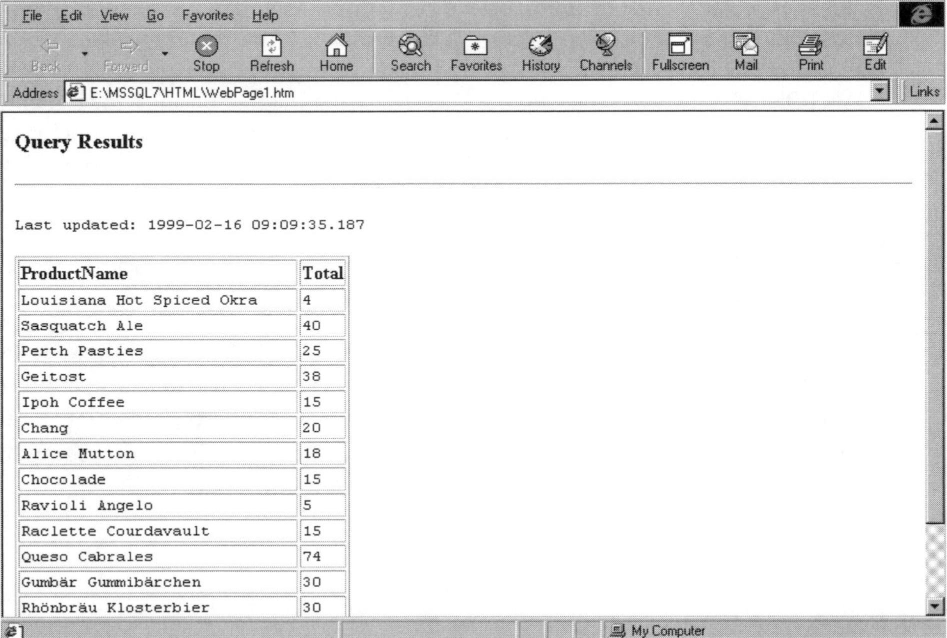

ProductName	Total
Louisiana Hot Spiced Okra	4
Sasquatch Ale	40
Perth Pasties	25
Geitost	38
Ipoh Coffee	15
Chang	20
Alice Mutton	18
Chocolade	15
Ravioli Angelo	5
Raclette Courdavault	15
Queso Cabrales	74
Gumbär Gummibärchen	30
Rhönbräu Klosterbier	30

Figure 5.24 Web Assistant Wizard's default HTML page from CustOrderHist for Customer Anton.

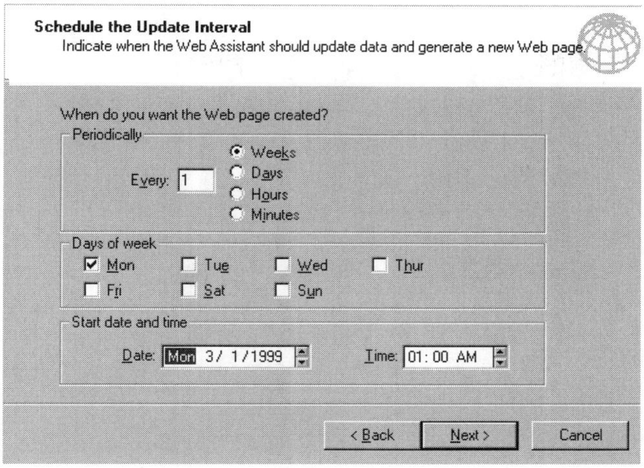

Figure 5.25 Using Web Assistant Wizard to set up scheduled generation of HTML pages.

In order to do this, re-launch the Web Assistant Wizard, select the third option for providing the SQL, and enter:

```
SELECT * FROM NoStuff
```

Request scheduled page generation, for every Monday at 1:00A.M. as shown in Figure 5.25. Now *that* could be useful.

Earlier in the chapter we mentioned how you can use a trigger to update an HTML page whenever certain data changes. We're going to delay providing you with the answer until Chapter 12 when you learn how to do some T-SQL programming using stored procedures.

Taking Stock

By now, you should be darned familiar with the Web Assistant Wizard, and you may decide it's too limited for your needs. Nevertheless, it can be useful for quick-and-dirty HTML-page generation.

In the process of experimenting with Web Assistant Wizard, you've learned a fair amount about the SELECT statement, joins, views, and stored procedures. Not bad, reader! Let's move on to explore how you can use Excel to generate HTML pages with SQL data.

Using Excel to Publish SQL Server Data

Microsoft Office has supported HTML format since Office 95, and integration keeps getting better and easier. At press time, Office 2000 was the latest version of the package, so

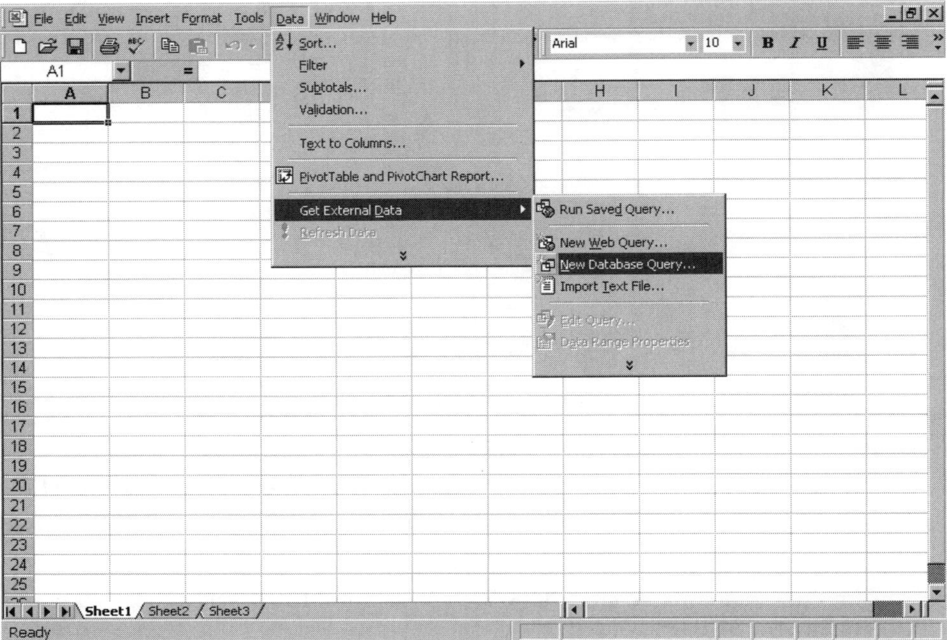

Figure 5.26 Using Excel 2000 to access SQL Server data.

we're using it. Please understand if screens or functionality varies a bit from what you may have in earlier versions of Office.

Let's fire up Excel and select Get External Data from the Data menu. Then, if you select New Database Query, you'll be prompted to select a data source as shown in Figure 5.26. Note that the dialog window's three tabs (we're actually running Microsoft Query) are for databases, saved queries, and OLAP sources. Also note that the option for using the Query Wizard is selected by default. Depending on how you've used Excel before, you may or may not have a SQL Server data source set up, and you may or may not already have saved queries or OLAP connections.

Once you've set up the query, you have the option of saving it for reuse or having the results of the query fed directly back into Excel, with you specifying a row and column for them to land in. We're going to use the latter option to start with.

Rather than choose an existing data source, let's create a new one called SQL7 using the SQL Server driver (see Figure 5.27). Give your connection a name and click on the Connect button. Assuming that your system can connect to a SQL Server, you'll be asked to provide login information. What you need to type in will depend on the type of security (NT or SQL) that you're using. Click on the Help button if you run into problems.

Click on the Options button and select Northwind as your default database (see Figure 5.28).

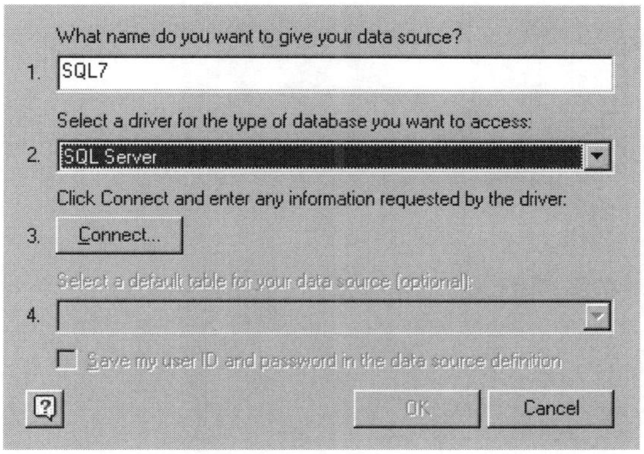

Figure 5.27 Defining a new data source.

The next screen lets you choose a default table and decide whether or not to save your user ID and password in the un-encrypted data source definition. The choice is yours.

Go ahead and connect using the Query Wizard. The first screen you see should list Northwind's tables, and probably also its views and synonyms (configurable via the Options button where you can also specify whether you want to display the items in alphabetical order or not).

Select the same columns from Customers and Orders as we did earlier when we used SQL to create our join statement (see Figure 5.29).

See how easy it is to preview data from the highlighted column by pressing the Preview button.

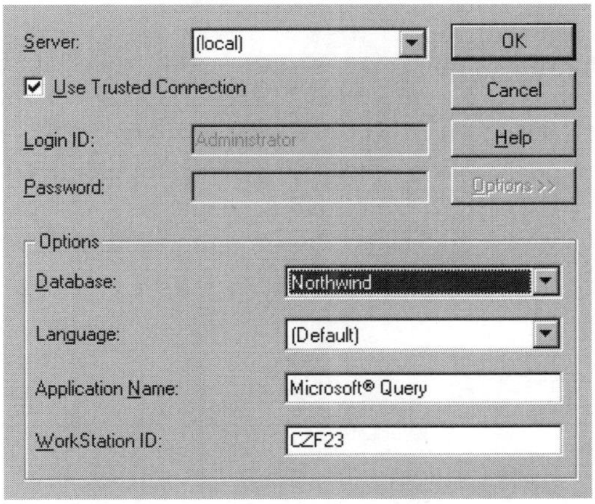

Figure 5.28 Establishing a default database for the Excel data source.

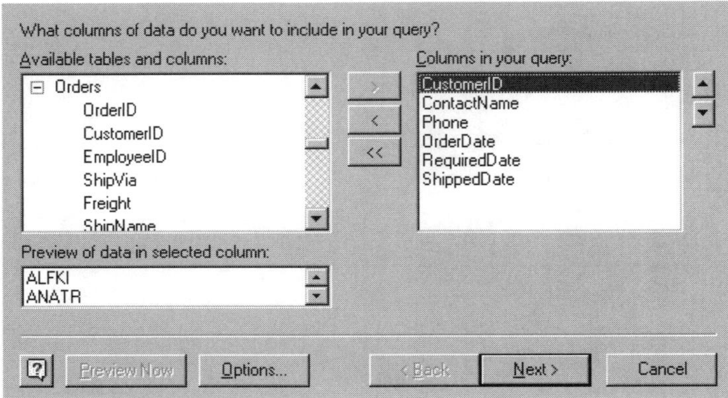

Figure 5.29 Selecting columns from multiple tables—even views—is a snap with Excel's Microsoft Query.

The next screen allows you to filter the data. Highlight the ShippedDate field and select "Is null" from the drop-down listbox. If you remember our woes with the Cartesian product, you may try to enter something for the CustomerID field, but none of the options let you set up a WHERE clause that equates to:

```
WHERE Customers.CustomerID = Orders.CustomerID
```

There's only one way to figure out why. Go ahead and execute the query and accept the defaults for location. Save the query if you so desire. The result, as shown in Figure 5.30, indicates that Microsoft Query was smart enough to do the inner join for us.

Boy, this is pretty cool! Excel's File menu gives you the option of saving the output as an HTML page, even previewing it first. But, before you do, you're free to "pretty-it-up" using any of Excel's features.

Try it again, this time experiment on your own and notice that the Data Source is already set up for you. Try to run a query without the Microsoft Query Wizard. You'll discover that your interface is reminiscent of the Access query screen. If you saved your query, try the Run Saved Query option. Find out what happens if you opt for querying a URL. Remember that Excel lets you e-mail spreadsheets, create graphics, and so on. Excel is an extremely popular end-user tool for manipulating database data and creating reports.

Summary

Creating static HTML pages isn't right for everyone, but it can satisfy some needs by providing shared access to data stored in SQL Server. You've seen how easy it is to do using either the Web Assistant Wizard or Excel.

	CustomerID	ContactName	Phone	OrderDate	RequiredDate	ShippedDate
2	ERNSH	Roland Mendel	7675-3425	4/8/98 0:00	5/6/98 0:00	
3	RANCH	Sergio Gutiérrez	(1) 123-5555	4/13/98 0:00	5/11/98 0:00	
4	LINOD	Felipe Izquierdo	(8) 34-56-12	4/21/98 0:00	5/19/98 0:00	
5	GREAL	Howard Snyder	(503) 555-7555	4/22/98 0:00	5/20/98 0:00	
6	BOTTM	Elizabeth Lincoln	(604) 555-4729	4/23/98 0:00	5/21/98 0:00	
7	LAMAI	Annette Roulet	61.77.61.10	4/27/98 0:00	5/25/98 0:00	
8	CACTU	Patricio Simpson	(1) 135-5555	4/28/98 0:00	5/26/98 0:00	
9	BLAUS	Hanna Moos	0621-08460	4/29/98 0:00	5/27/98 0:00	
10	RICAR	Janete Limeira	(21) 555-3412	4/29/98 0:00	6/10/98 0:00	
11	GREAL	Howard Snyder	(503) 555-7555	4/30/98 0:00	6/11/98 0:00	
12	REGGC	Maurizio Moroni	0522-556721	4/30/98 0:00	5/28/98 0:00	
13	LILAS	Carlos González	(9) 331-6954	5/1/98 0:00	5/29/98 0:00	
14	QUEEN	Lúcia Carvalho	(11) 555-1189	5/4/98 0:00	6/1/98 0:00	
15	LEHMS	Renate Messner	069-0245984	5/5/98 0:00	6/2/98 0:00	
16	LILAS	Carlos González	(9) 331-6954	5/5/98 0:00	6/2/98 0:00	
17	ERNSH	Roland Mendel	7675-3425	5/5/98 0:00	6/2/98 0:00	
18	PERIC	Guillermo Fernández	(5) 552-3745	5/5/98 0:00	6/2/98 0:00	
19	SIMOB	Jytte Petersen	31 12 34 56	5/6/98 0:00	6/3/98 0:00	
20	RICSU	Michael Holz	0897-034214	5/6/98 0:00	6/3/98 0:00	
21	BONAP	Laurence Lebihan	91.24.45.40	5/6/98 0:00	6/3/98 0:00	
22	RATTC	Paula Wilson	(505) 555-5939	5/6/98 0:00	6/3/98 0:00	

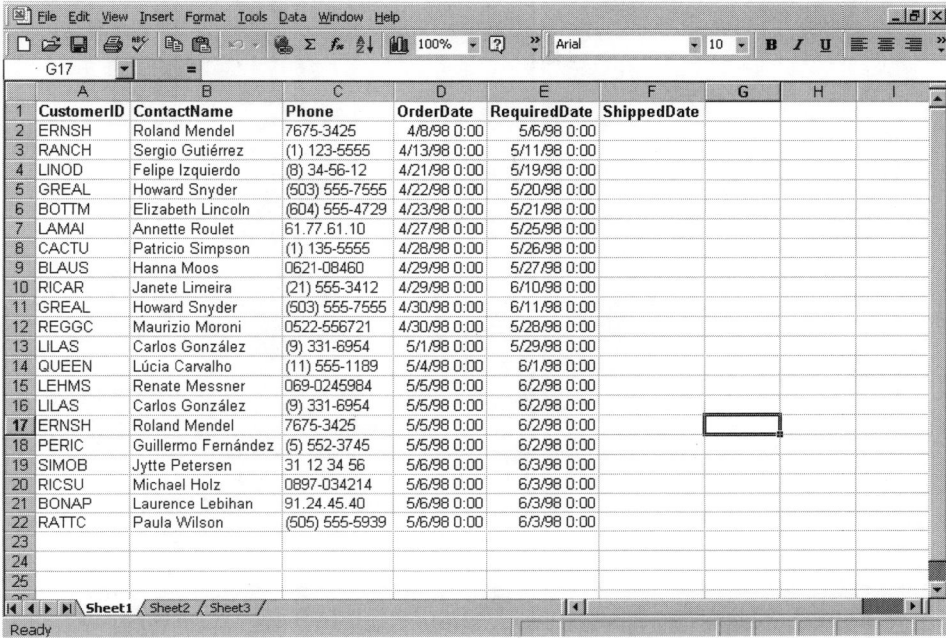

Figure 5.30 Microsoft Query has populated our Excel spreadsheet.

Today, virtually all Web tools have ODBC access built in and provide interfaces similar to what you've used in this chapter to set up queries that retrieve data. Most also provide more sophisticated features that make it easy to build forms that collect data—data that can either be entered into the database or simply used to enter query parameters, or filters. We'll see how to use Microsoft's own tools to build more sophisticated, interactive Web sites starting with the next chapter.

If you'd rather continue on your own in experimental mode, consider dusting off a copy of FrontPage, Visual InterDev, Personal Web Server, and/or IIS and see what magic you can do. For a more guided approach, though, just turn the page.

CHAPTER 6

Project # 3: Building a Corporate Intranet with Internet Information Server

Goal

In this chapter, which is really a long project, you'll set up Microsoft's Internet Information Server (IIS) and create a simple, human resources (HR) intranet. Along the way, you'll learn basic Windows and IIS security, intro HTML, and how to use Active Server Pages (ASPs) to interact with SQL Server.

- ✔ **Prerequisites: Windows NT 4, SP4, with TCP/IP networking installed**
- ✔ **Microsoft Internet Information Server 4 (IIS) or higher**
- ✔ **Microsoft Internet Explorer 4 or higher**
- ✔ **Microsoft SQL Server 7**
- ✔ **Source code files on CD**

If you need to set up an intranet for your organization, need to establish a simple Internet Web site, and don't really have any idea how to start, then this chapter's for you. As you might expect, we're going to assume that you'll want to let users have access to some data that's stored in a SQL Server 7 database.

Imagine that your boss has finally "Seen The Light" and wants a Web site and *fast*. Who knows where he got the wild hair, but anyway, you've received your marching orders. We've asked an industry colleague, Jon Kilburn, to write the chapter for us, based on his memory of how it was the first time. Ah, yes. . .

Setting Up Internet Information Server (IIS)

Manuals? What manuals? Microsoft doesn't seem to print manuals anymore. You're supposed to read them from the CD—in the convenience of your office where you're *never* interrupted. Well, a word of advice: at least read the CD's README files before you let Setup do its thing. You'll also do yourself a giant favor if you check out the MSDN site or ASP sites such as www.15seconds.com. for any files that summarize the current advice about the installation order of components.

Microsoft's Internet Information Server (IIS) gives you everything you need to publish your documents (your site) over the Internet. IIS 4 is provided on the Windows Option Pack CD, which ships with NT 4.0 Server or higher, but which is also available from the Microsoft download site. IIS includes support for the Web, ftp (file transfer protocol), and Gopher services. In order to use IIS, the TCP/IP networking protocol must be installed in your NT network. There are dozens of books out there vying for your eyeballs—and dollars—that will be glad to tell you more than you want to know about networking and TCP/IP.

Basically there are two particular types of networks that we plan to discuss: intranets and the Internet. What's the difference? Well, for starters, an intranet only allows access to a server for a specific group of users, whereas the Internet is simply a huge global network that allows *anyone* access—well, virtually anyone—obviously some sites will restrict you based on a user name, password, and authorization level. You can use IIS to support both intranets and the Internet.

SETTING UP IIS PERMISSIONS

When you configure IIS, you can apply permissions to the default directories that only allow certain members of a group access. This lets you test and debug the site before taking it online.

So what does IIS let you do? During the evolution of the Internet, several methods for publishing and retrieving data were developed and these methods were broken down into two parts: the client and the server. The client component initiates the contact (or conversation, if you will) with the server and can be written in any language that conforms to the specifications of the communication method or protocol. On the server side, the server component "listens" for the incoming request from the client and then determines how to best respond to the request. IIS is a server-side component.

Installing IIS

Fortunately for us, installing and configuring IIS is pretty easy. All you really need is the NT 4.0 Option Pack. If you use IE4, as opposed to IE5, and haven't already installed IE 4 SP2 (Internet Explorer 4.0 Service Pack 2), you should probably do that before you install IIS. I, for one, encountered a number of difficulties that didn't seem to manifest themselves when I installed IE4 before setting up IIS. However, IIS and IE5 seem to be a stable combination, irrespective of the order installed. Nevertheless, I strongly recommend (again) that you check the Microsoft Web site for any updates or bug postings regarding the use of IE 4, IE 5, and/or IIS.

GIVE IIS ITS OWN SERVER

Although it's certainly possible to install IIS and SQL Server on a single, Windows NT server, we strongly recommend against it for anything other than development.

After you install IE 4/5, including the latest SPs, patches, and hot fixes, open the NT control panel and double-click on the Network icon. The Networking dialog box should appear. In the Network dialog box click on the Services tab to bring it to the foreground as shown in Figure 6.1.

Next, choose the Add button. This opens the Select Network Services dialog as shown in Figure 6.2.

In the Select Network Services dialog find and double-click on Internet Information Server. You will be prompted for the path to the installation files, just place the NT CD in the CD drive and type in the drive letter.

Next you will be presented with the Internet Information Setup dialog box. Simply select the options to install. Following the Setup dialog box will be the Directory Publishing dialog box. This dialog allows you to configure what the root directory for each service will be. Finally, the installation program copies the files.

HOTMAIL AND MSN ON APACHE?

According to a 1999 story by *Wired* magazine, www.wired.com/news/news/email/member/technology/story/20768.html, parts of Microsoft's MSN run on the free Apache Web server on top of Unix. Similar rumors persist that Microsoft's HotMail also will run on an Apache Unix server. Does Microsoft know something we don't about IIS or NT?

Configuring IIS

While there are a number of little tricks to configuring IIS, we don't feel that it's something we need to discuss at length. Not only do situations vary from server to

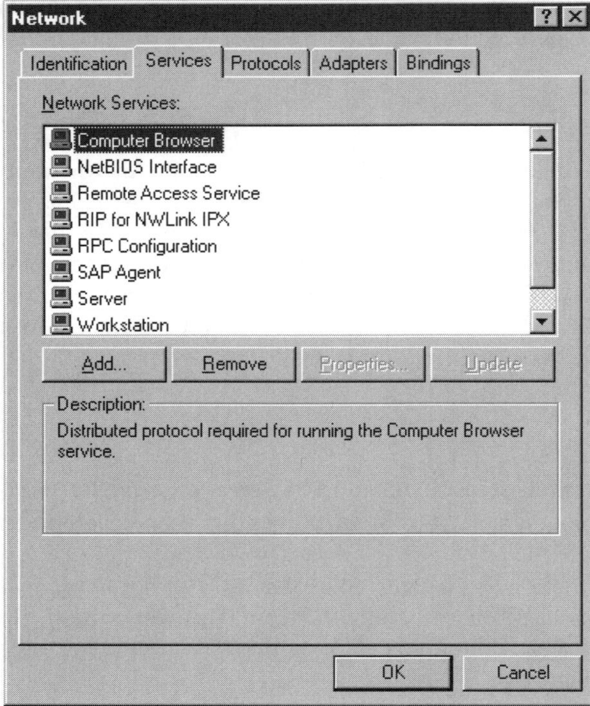

Figure 6.1 Windows NT's network dialog.

server, but any observations we may make now are likely to age quickly. Instead we recommend that you check out one of the many books available on Microsoft Internet

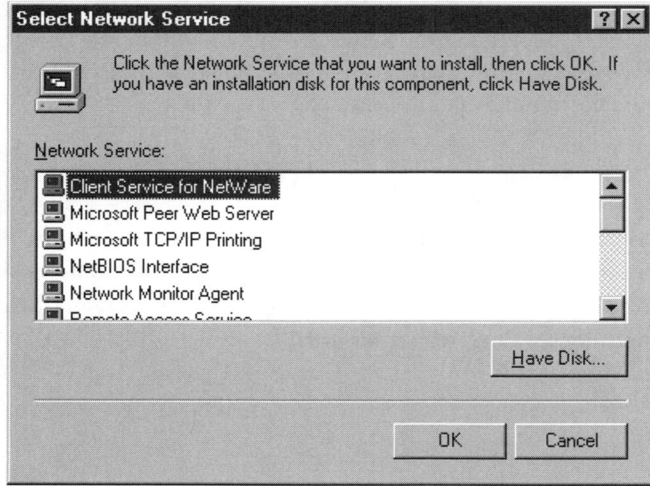

Figure 6.2 Select Network Services dialog.

IIS Utilities

Microsoft Press sells a book called the *Microsoft Internet Information Server Resource Kit* (ISBN: 1-572-31638-1) that was published in early 1998, but its two CD-ROMs contain some useful utilities, most of which you can't find anywhere else unless your subscribe to *MSDN* (the IIS Resource Kit shipped in the June 1999 batch, for example). For more information about the book, or another online subscription service, Reslink, offered by Microsoft, go to mspress.microsoft .com/reslink/IISResKit/book/.

The Microsoft Web Capacity Analysis Tool (WCAT) is one of the utilities that's also available for download from msdn.microsoft.com/workshop/server/toolbox/ wcat.asp as a 1.1MB .ZIP file. WCAT runs simulated workloads, so, by using WCAT, you can test how your IIS and network configuration respond to a variety of different client requests for content, data, or HTML. WCAT is also included on the Windows 2000 Resource Kit Companion CD-ROM. Another utility you can download for free from msdn.microsoft.com/workshop/server/iis/ixcptmon.exe. is the IIS Exception Monitor, which was created by Microsoft Product Support Services (PSS) to troubleshoot server instability issues similar to the following:

- IIS exits and a Dr. Watson error log is generated.
- The Web service exits abnormally.
- The browser returns an "ASP 0115" error.
- The browser returns a "Server Application Error" message.
- The browser returns a "Server Too Busy" error.

Related URLs:

support.microsoft.com/support/kb/articles/Q160/3/60.ASP

msdn.microsoft.com/workshop/server/iis/ixcptmon.asp

msdn.microsoft.com/workshop/server/iis/readlogs.asp

A *KB* article you may want to read, especially to learn about MetaEdit in the IIS Resource Kit, is "Description of Adsutil and MetaEdit Utilities Used to Modify the Metabase" (support.microsoft.com/support/kb/articles/Q240/2/25.ASP).

Adsutil is a command-line utility written in VBScript that uses the Cscript.exe command line scripting utility that comes with the Windows NT Option Pack. The Metabase Editor (MetaEdit) is a tool that provides similar functionality to the Windows NT Registry Editor. Using MetaEdit, you can browse and modify attributes in the Metabase. Note that in using MetaEdit, you can make changes that may damage your IIS configuration.

Information Server—whatever the current version is, and, that you learn about current snafus by monitoring the Microsoft IIS newsgroups and discussion list maintained by www.15seconds.com. We'll limit our comments to IIS' directory structure and the Service Manager.

First, an overview of how the directory structure works. During the installation you were prompted to enter a default directory for the World Wide Web, File Transfer Protocol, and Gopher publishing directories. When IIS is installed, it will create WWWROOT, FTPROOT, and GOPHROOT directories, respectively. Each of these specified directories acts as the "root" directory for its service. This means that for information to be visible to each service, it must be contained within the directory specified for that service. For example, if you want to access a Web page using the WWW protocol, the HTML file should be placed in the wwwroot directory. To have an initial Web page come up, it should be placed in the wwwroot directory. By default, IIS looks for a file named default.htm in this directory. A sample Web site is placed in the wwwroot directory when you install IIS.

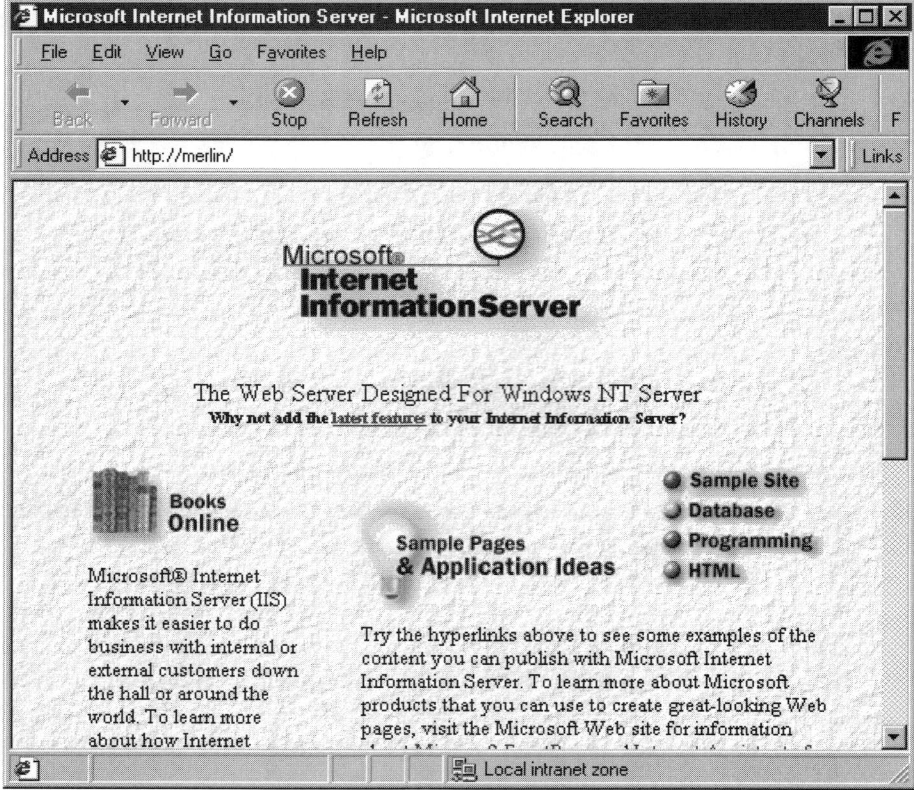

Figure 6.3 IIS default Web site.

To access the default Web site all you need to do is type http:// followed by the name of your NT server. For example, if the name of my NT server is Merlin, to jump to my default Web site, I simply type http://merlin. This activates the default Web site installed by IIS that looks similar to Figure 6.3.

The IIS Service Manager

The *IIS Service Manager* is the central control panel for configuring the operation for all of the services provided by IIS. You can find it in the Microsoft Internet Information Server folder under Programs | Windows NT 4.0 Option Pack. Select the Internet Information Services Manager option, which brings up the Internet Information Services Manager as shown in Figure 6.4.

Managing Security

Under Windows NT, a system administrator—or program—can grant users and groups varying levels of access to system resources. Depending on how you configure your server, you can have lax security, "Big Brother" tight security, or anything in between. If you install IIS or any other Internet Web Server for that matter, bear in mind that the "world" now has access to your machine, and consequently, your company.

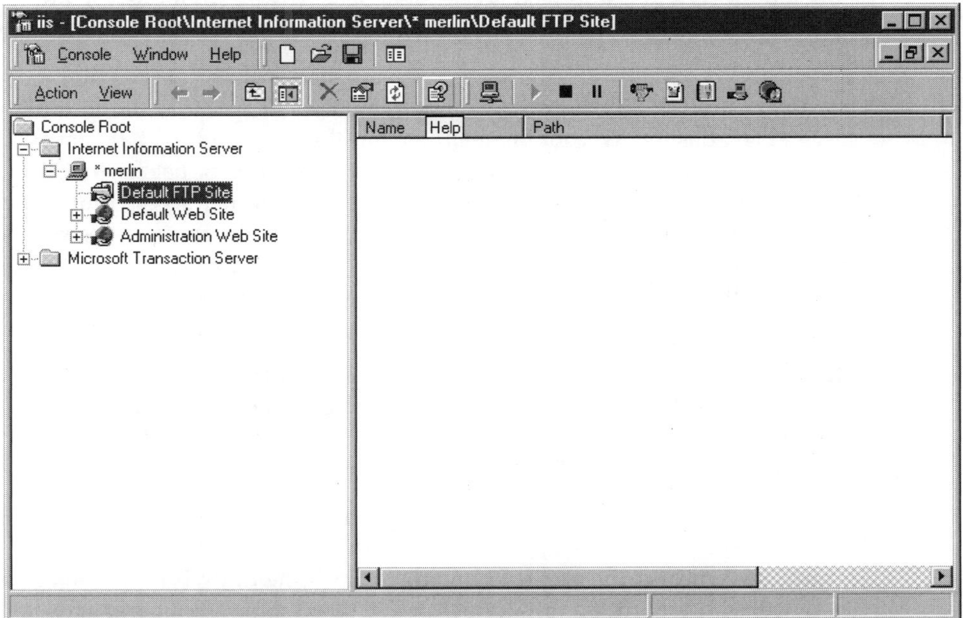

Figure 6.4 Internet Information Services Manager.

So before we start writing code for our HR application, it behooves us to review just a bit about Windows NT security. There are two security types that we plan to discuss: physical and network security.

Physical Security

Step one is to make sure that your server is physically secure. To prevent unauthorized access when the system administrator isn't sitting in front of it, your server should be locked up. If someone can get to your server, that same someone can get to your network. Exactly how you lock up your server is up to you. You can lock the server in a climate-controlled room or you can have the server placed in a housing with a locking front plate. You should really have a document with security policies and guidelines such as how keys are tracked and secured. And, as your organization grows, your physical security policy will probably need to change. It should be audited at least quarterly in most organizations.

Network Security

You also need to take certain precautions to ensure that an assault on your server can't be made either through your network or from the Internet.

Remember that once you've connected your server to the Internet, you've basically opened the door to your server. Although physical barriers such as hardware firewalls can help prevent unauthorized access, cheaper software solutions, including the security features built into Windows NT, can potentially provide a reasonably high degree of security.

Hardware firewalls are computer devices that stand between the Internet and your server. Each has its own unique features, but the end result is that firewalls filter out unauthorized users. Another benefit to some firewall products is that they can help enforce policies, such as, limiting the duration of Internet access time for users, and opening and closing ports at scheduled times. Firewalls can also restrict the type of sites accessed and the types of files transferred. Software based firewalls are available, and while they provide much of the same features, they often use up valuable system resources and cannot fully isolate the server as a hardware firewall can.

The bottom line is that you need to set up the security policies on your NT server. Make sure guest accounts are disabled, rename the administrator account, and most importantly, make sure that you understand the security implications for installing software such as FTP, WWW, or e-mail servers.

Windows NT provides a variety of security features—far too many for us to fully cover in this chapter. The primary means of applying these features is through the access control system and the New Technology File System, or NTFS. Windows NT was designed with security in mind, notably C2, since some US federal agencies can only purchase software that's C2 certified.

C2

So what's C2, anyway? In a nutshell, C2 security is the National Computer Security Center's (NCSC) designation for a level of security called Controlled Access Protection. It holds users accountable for their actions and requires that the operating system have a way of tracking which processes a user initiates and with what files those processes interact. When a user has finished with an object, it must not be available for reuse by another user who does not have the proper authority. Users may individually grant others access to their data, but not to a level higher than delegated to them by the administrator. Although Windows NT server can be configured to C2-level security, you don't get C2 "out of the box" as the default. It takes some doing.

Windows NT runs special applications called *services*. Services are programs that start along with the operating system and run in the background (WWW Publishing Service for example). Services, along with all applications that run on Windows NT, must be run within the context of a user's or system account.

Which brings us to the subject of *Access Control*. The Access Control List (ACL) is a list of entries associated with a file or folder that specifies which users and groups have access to that folder or file. Each entry in an ACL assigns a user or group one or more of the following access levels to a file:

None. No access is granted.

Read. A user may view or execute this file, but not change the contents in any way.

Write. A user may change the contents of this file.

Execute. A user can run a program

Delete. A user may delete this file.

Change Permissions. This attribute is different in that it allows a user to change the access rights to this file for a single user or an entire group.

Take Ownership. Allows a user to take the ownership of this file.

Folders have a similar set of privileges:

None. A user cannot access this folder.

Read. A user may view the file names and sub-folder names

Write. A user can add files and subfolders

Execute. A user can change folders.

Delete. A user may delete a folder or subfolders.

Change Permissions. A user can change the permissions on a folder or subfolder.

Take Ownership. A user can take the ownership of this folder.

Please note that Windows NT supports two types of file systems: FAT32 and NTFS. The use of ACLs is only supported by NTFS, and it's generally considered good practice to use NTFS on a system that hosts WWW services and runs IIS.

Understanding User Accounts and User Groups

Everyone who has access to an NT system is identified by a user account, which is comprised of a user name, password, and number of logon parameters applied to that user. Each user who has been identified by the NT system is then made a member of at least one user group.

User Groups are a collection of user accounts that have been granted a common set of privileges. Placing users in a group makes applying changes to permissions much simpler. Users and user groups are created through the User Manager. The User Manager Utility is found by selecting the Start | Programs | Administrative Tools menus (see Figure 6.5).

When a user is highlighted, you'll notice the groups assigned to that user are displayed. You can edit a user by either double-clicking on the user or selecting the user and choosing the menu options User | Properties. From the User Properties dialog, you can assign a user to a group, set password expirations, modify their profile, and even determine when a user may access the network (see Figure 6.6).

When an application runs, it must draw its permissions from somewhere. Which means, in essence, that when a program runs it *impersonates* the user who has been authenticated through the login process. Then when the application attempts to access resources the access to those resources must also be granted or denied based on the permissions of the impersonated user.

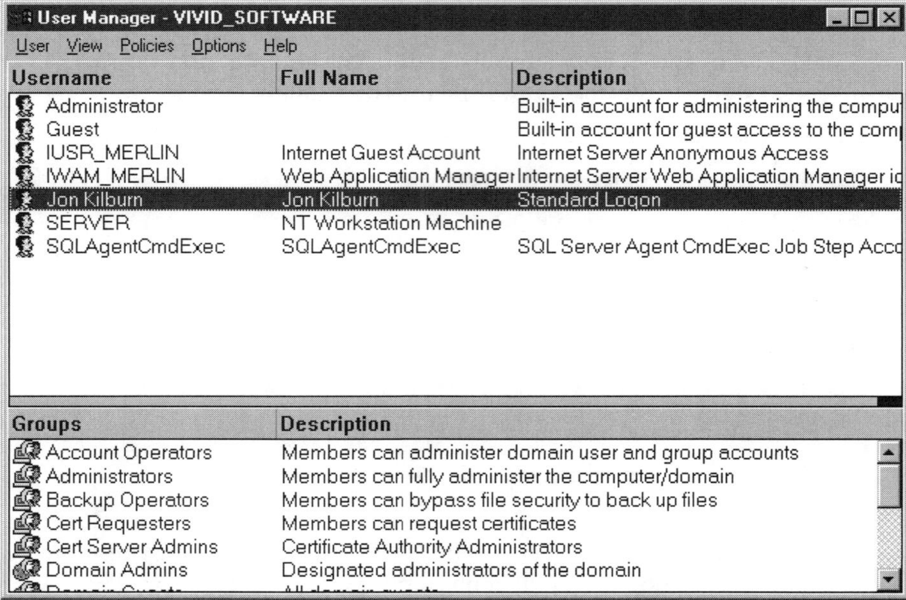

Figure 6.5 User Manager.

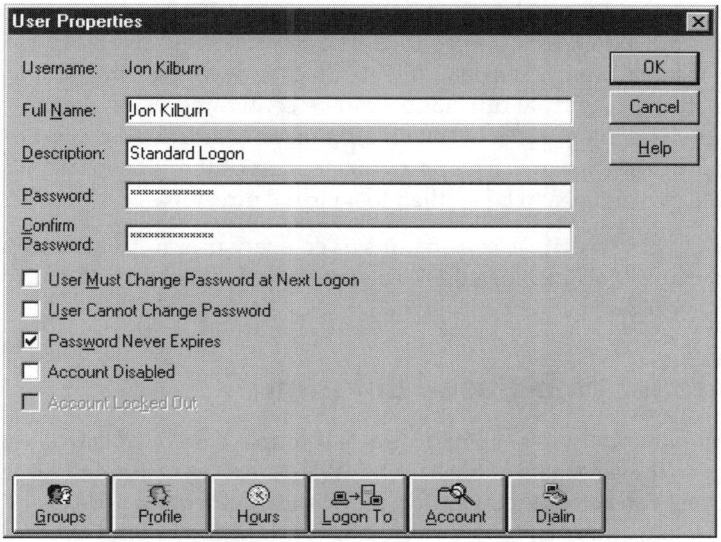

Figure 6.6 User Properties dialog.

Understanding Domains (NT4)

A Windows NT 4.x domain is a logical group of computers which share a set of common users accounts and security information which is stored in the NT Domain Services database. You use a version of the User Manager called the User Manger for Domains to maintain the information in the NTDS database. (Note that the domain model used in NT3.51/4 is replaced by Active Directory Services in Windows 2000.)

A domain includes an NT server designated the Primary Domain Controller (PDC) that is responsible for storing the master NTDS database. In addition, you may have one or more Backup Domain Controllers (BDCs) which maintain copies of the NTDS database. A user may log on to a domain and use any connected computer as long as he can be validated by either the PDC or a BDC. The BDC can share the workload in a heavily used network as well as provide redundancy in case the PDC becomes unavailable. PDC and BDCs can also function as application servers. In our case, for simplicity's sake, we run IIS on a PDC. This is not something we recommend except for development.

Once a user has successfully logged onto the domain, the NT security system dictates what resources that user may access. Different resources have different levels of access (as outlined the earlier Network Security section).

Aliased or Virtual Directories

The IIS and ASP services are basically built on top of the NTDS model. As a result, all files and directories are protected via the ACL permissions. All users who access your IIS server must therefore be given authenticated access.

The WWW service of IIS restricts the files on the server that can be accessed to those that are under the WWWROOT directory. The WWWROOT directory was created when IIS was installed, and is the default Web directory. Access to any additional directories, which are called virtual directories, can be configured using the IIS console. A virtual directory is a mapping between an alias name that is used as part of the URL and a physical directory name. The properties dialog of the IIS console allows Read and Executable permissions to be applied to a virtual directory.

In order to apply NT security access to our server, every user must be associated with an NT user account. This includes the Web server itself that is treated much the same way as any other user.

Creating an Intranet Web-Based Solution

Now comes the fun part. We're going to create a simple employee database and some tables which we'll eventually publish to the Web, creating a simple HR application where employees can access their medical plans, the number of sick days and vacation days they have left, and even their performance review. Tables 6.1, 6.2, and 6.3 depict the basic tables. Nothing fancy—after all, this is just an example.

Creating user-defined data types and tables interactively can be a time-consuming process. However, there's another way to do it using a *script*. So what's a script? A script is a series of T-SQL commands (reminiscent in some ways to stored procedures) that can be executed from the SQL Server Query Analyzer. Listing 6.1 shows a simple database script that creates the UDT and tables for our exercise.

Table 6.1 Table Name: Employees

COLUMN NAME	DATA TYPE	SIZE	DESCRIPTION
Emp_ID	Integer		Primary Key – Generated
First_Name	T_Name		First Name
Last_Name	T_Name		Last Name
Address	T_Name		Employee Address
City	T_Name		City
State	Varchar	2	State
Zip_Code	Varchar	5	Zip Code
Date_of_Birth	Datetime		Date of Birth
SSN	Varchar	11	Employee SS Number
Start_Date	Datetime		Date this employee started
End_Date	Datetime		Date this employee left the company
Marital_Status	Varchar	1	Married, Single (M or S) (Bit is an alternate data type)

Table 6.1 *(Continued)*

COLUMN NAME	DATA TYPE	SIZE	DESCRIPTION
Num_Depend	Smallint		Number of Dependents (Tinyint is an alternate)
Sick_Days	Smallint		Number of Sick Days Left
Vacation_Days	Smallint		Number of Vacation Days Left
Contact	T_Name		Emergency Contact
Contact_Phone	Varchar	12	Contact Phone Number

Table 6.2 Table Name: Medical_Plans

COLUMN NAME	DATA TYPE	DESCRIPTION
Plan_ID	Integer	Primary Key
Description	T_Name	Description of this Medical Plan

Table 6.3 Table Name: EmpMedical_Plans

COLUMN NAME	DATA TYPE	DESCRIPTION
Emp_ID	Integer	Employee ID
Plan_ID	Integer	Link to Medical Plans Table

This script has several parts. The first part is the user-defined data type creation section. Obviously, we have to create a UDT before we can create database tables that uses it. The next section is the Table Creation section. Here we simply use the CREATE TABLE command and define each of the table (field) elements along with any restrictions. Notice that

```
/* ============================================================ */
/*   Database name:  HR Sample                                  */
/*   DBMS name:      Microsoft SQL Server 7x                    */
/*   Created on:     8/2/99  11:45 AM                           */
/* ============================================================ */
if exists(select 1 from dbo.systypes where name ='T_NAME')
  execute sp_droptype T_NAME
go
execute sp_addtype T_NAME, 'varchar(30)', 'null'
go
/* ============================================================ */
/*   Table: EMPLOYEE                                            */
/* ============================================================ */
create table EMPLOYEE
(
```

Continues

```
    EMP_ID                      int                   not null,
    FIRST_NAME                  T_NAME                not null,
    LAST_NAME                   T_NAME                not null,
    ADDRESS                     T_NAME                null    ,
    CITY                        T_NAME                null    ,
    STATE                       varchar(2)            null    ,
    ZIP_CODE                    varchar(5)            null    ,
    DATE_OF_BIRTH               datetime              null    ,
    SSN                         varchar(11)           not null,
    START_DATE                  datetime              not null,
    END_DATE                    datetime              null    ,
    MARITAL_STATUS              varchar(1)            not null,
       constraint CHK_STATUS check(MARITAL_STATUS IN('M', 'S')),
    NUM_DEPEND                  smallint              null    ,
    SICK_DAYS                   smallint              null    ,
    VACATION_DAYS               smallint              null    ,
    CONTACT                     T_NAME                null    ,
    CONTACT_PHONE               varchar(12)           null    ,
       constraint PK_EMP primary key (EMP_ID)
)
go
/* ============================================================ */
/*   Table: MEDICAL_PLANS                                       */
/* ============================================================ */
create table MEDICAL_PLANS
(
    PLAN_ID                     int                   not null,
    DESCRIPTION                 varchar(30)           null    ,
       constraint PK_PLAN primary key (PLAN_ID)
)
go
/* ============================================================ */
/*   Table: EMPMEDICAL_PLANS                                    */
/* ============================================================ */
create table EMPMEDICAL_PLANS
(
    EMP_ID                      int              not null,
    PLAN_ID                     int              not null,
       constraint PK_PLAN primary key (PLAN_ID)
)
go
```

Listing 6.1 The CreHR.SQL script for generating the HR sample database, UDT, and database tables.

we have also created column constraints. There are actually several types of constraints that you can define here: primary keys, foreign keys, and column-level validation.

In our example we have created a primary key on EMP_ID and defined a column-level constraint (to prevent invalid data entry into the database) on the MARITAL_STATUS column. To run the script we simply choose Tools, SQL Server Query Analyzer. When the Query Analyzer first opens, you *must* change the database from the default (which is master) to the database you wish to work with, in this case, Employee (see Figure 6.7 and the ReadMe.txt file in the Chapter 6 zip file on your CD).

FYI

INTRANET STARTER SUITES

Don't forget about the BackOffice 4.5 Intranet Starter Suites that are basically turnkey publishing and collaboration server sites. Common templates include a team directory where users fill out a profile upon their first visit, a news engine, and an events calendar. The publishing site uses Site Server, and the expense-reports template requires MTS, Exchange, and Excel. Another starter suite component provides a help-desk template and application. And guess what runs under the hood in each of the "instant" intranet sites? You got it—SQL Server.

To run the script, simply choose the File/Format/Open menu option. A T-SQL script file is generally saved with a .sql extension. When the script is loaded you can either select the green arrow (Run) or you can use the menu options, Query/Execute. After the script is finished you can exit the Query Analyzer. We're now finally ready to create the Web site that will interact with the HR database.

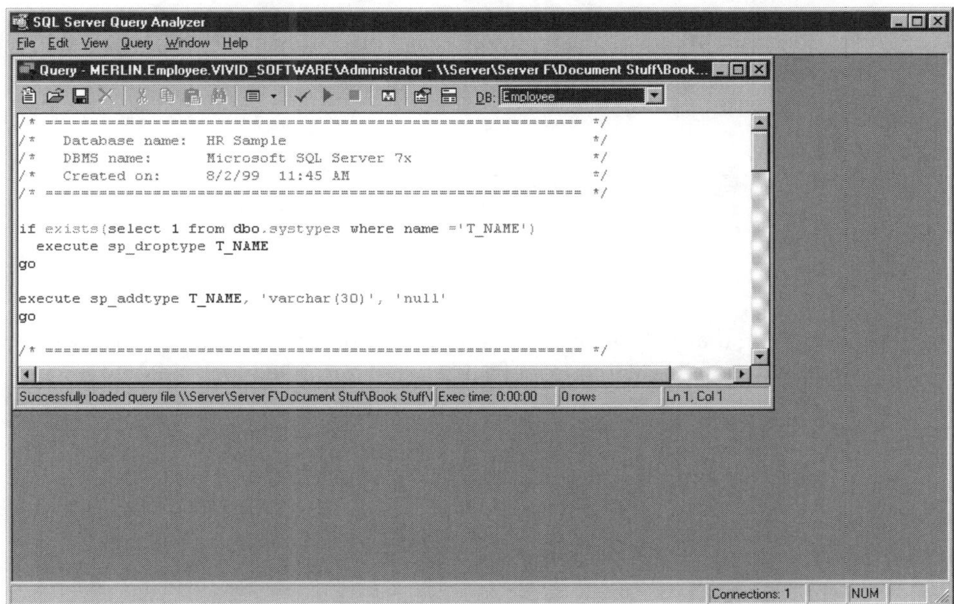

Figure 6.7 The SQL Query Analyzer.

Creating the Human Resources Web Site

Well, you've made it this far, so now we move on to the fun stuff—creating and accessing our HR site. For those of you new to HTML, here's a brief lesson in HTML and submission methods. If you're already familiar with HTML, you can skip on to the section on ASP.

HTML

HTML is the generally accepted language for creating Web pages. HTML "documents" are really just a series of begin and end tags. So what's a tag? A *tag* is similar to the begin/end relationship in a programming language. Each tag has a specific and defined function as well as a number of parameters. HTML tags are enclosed within bracket <> symbols and each end tag sequence is prefaced with a forward slash, /. Here's an example:

```
Begin Tag: <html>
End Tag: </html>
```

Web browsers such as Internet Explorer and Netscape make use of HTML tags to render Web pages. HTML is designed primarily for *static* representation. This means that it doesn't support looping, branching, or event trapping. A scripting language such as VBScript or JavaScript generally provides these features. We'll discuss both in a moment. Tags are used for a variety of functions such as headings, colors, tables, and much more.

While the HTML language is simple, it can be confusing at first, because so much code between the begin/end tags is left justified like this:

```
<html>
<head>
<META HTTP-EQUIV="Pragma" CONTENT="no-cache">
<title>VividSoftware.com</title>
</head>
<body>
</body>
```

Everything that falls between <html> and </html> is executed as HTML code. Here's what that same HTML code looks like when formatted for readability:

```
<html>
   <head>
<META HTTP-EQUIV="Pragma" CONTENT="no-cache">
<title>VividSoftware.com</title>
   </head>
   <body>
   </body>
</html>
```

You have to admit that the latter is a lot easier to decipher. Here's a brief rundown for each of the sections within the HTML code:

Web Page Heading (<head>...</head>). This is the heading used to have a formal structure that holds the formatting information about a page. Now it's become much more abbreviated and usually only holds the Web page title.

Web Page Title (<title>...</title>). A Web page's title is quite important, even though many Web programmers don't realize it, and omit it, because the title is the text that appears in the title bar of the Web browser when your page is displayed. It's also the text that appears in your Web page directories like Yahoo, Lycos, and Alta Vista.

Web Page Body (<body>...</body>). This is the section where most of the action really takes place. The body can make use of several keywords, known as *attributes*, to control such things as the Web page's background color, the default color of the text, or the color of a hyperlink. This is the section where we create controls, display graphics, and even accept user input. Keep in mind, though, that the controls that are used within the body section are somewhat limited in that they're static and aren't validated until such time as a submission occurs. Table 6.4 shows a list of control names.

Some of the HTML controls share similar properties such as the <input> tag. The *<input> tag* identifies the type of control. For example:

```
<input type="text" size=10 name=FIRST_NAME>
```

This line of code within a body section creates a simple text edit named FIRST_NAME whose contents can be examined at a later time. Some quick notes on each of the controls.

Text Controls (Text and TextArea)

There are actually three types of HTML text controls: password, single line, and multi line. The password control is referenced as Password, the single-line text control is known as Text, and the multi-line text control is a TextArea control.

The major difference between a Text control and a TextArea control is that a TextArea control is its own tag and accepts two more parameters (rows and columns):

```
<TextArea name="sample" rows=5 cols=6 value="This is just a sample
multi line text control">
</TextArea>
```

Table 6.4 Control Types

CONTROL NAME	DESCRIPTION
Text Box	A Standard Text Input
Text Area	Multi-Line Text Input
Radio Button	Radio Button
Check Box	Check Box
Push Button	Push Button

To create a Text or Password control, use an <input> tag and specify the input type.

```
<input type="Text" size=8 value="Jon">
```

Radio Button

Just like radio buttons used in VB or VBA, radio buttons used in HTML must also be placed within a group. To group a radio button you simply create each button with the same name.

Check Boxes

An HTML check box works like check boxes in VB or VBA. Default values are assigned to the checked property.

Push Buttons

The real oddity about a push button in HTML is that the Value property actually represents the button's caption and there aren't any height or width properties. A push button's size depends on the width of the value (or caption). Push buttons can respond to a number of events such as OnClick, OnFocus, and OnSubmit.

Frames

Before we move ahead and create our first site we should examine another key piece of HTML—*frames*. What's a frame? It's how we divide an HTML page into a series of panels—each containing its own distinct URL. This allows for split-screen navigation. Often we open a Web site to discover navigation on the left and content on the right as shown in Figure 6.8.

Submission Methods

Submission methods are the means through which data is passed from the browser to the server. There are basically two types of submission methods: GET and POST. When you create a Web page, you define the method through which data is passed in the FORM section.

Get

When a user is ready to interact with a Web page, either through a push button or hyperlink, the way a form passes information (or submits it) is determined by the form method attribute. The first method is referred to as the GET method. Suppose you had a form with a couple of fields, say first name, last name, and date of birth, and that when the user selects a submit button, you want to pass the information to the server.

```
<form name="SampleGet" action="Respond.asp" method=GET>
     First Name : <input type="text" name=FIRST_NAME >
```

```
        Last Name : <input type="text" name=LAST_NAME>
      Date of Birth : <input type="text" name=DOB>
      <input type=submit value="Submit">
</form>
```

When the page is submitted via the Submit button, this information is passed to the Respond.asp page via the query string, appended to the URL, after a question mark. The complete URL is visible in the browser Address field and looks like this:

```
http://merlin/respond.asp?first_name=Bob&last_name=Jones &dob=9/11/68
Limitations of Get
```

A query string isn't always the best way to send information. For starters the values of the variables are clearly visible in the browser's address box and can be intercepted. If you need a password, you certainly don't want the password to appear in the query string. There are other limitations as well—the amount of data that can be sent to the URL is limited to 1000 characters.

Post

Don't despair. There's another way to pass data from the form section between pages. Instead of using the GET method attribute we can use the POST method. Post puts the information inside the HTTP header, instead of adding it to the query string.

In the case of our previous page, the first name, last name, and date of birth fields are encoded into the request header, leaving no sign of them in the browser's Address box. In order to retrieve information passed through post we must use the Request Object.

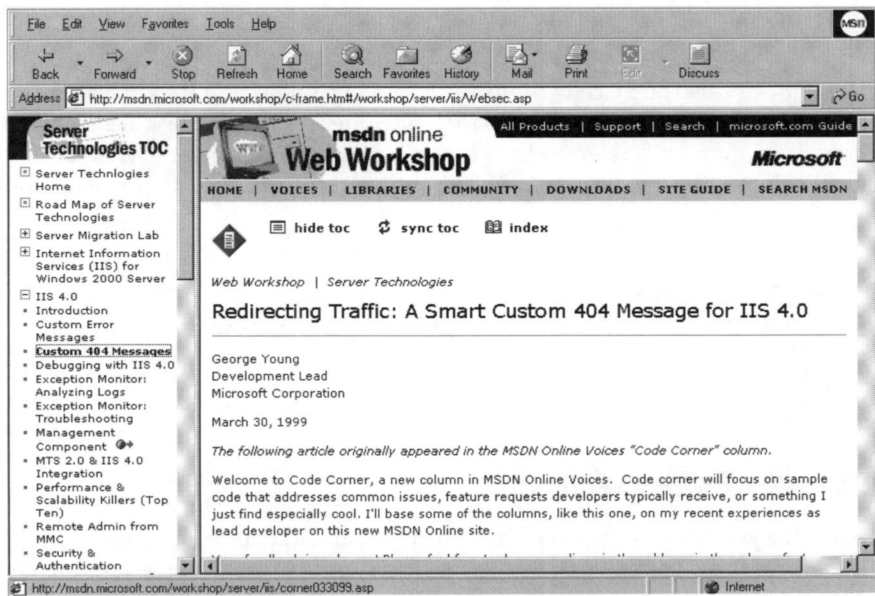

Figure 6.8 Part of the MSDN Web site.

The Request Object captures all the information from each individual request made by the client. Scripts can then use the methods and properties of the Request Object to extract information from these objects. Through the Form Method of the Request Object we can interrogate the value of any control:

```
Request.Form("First_Name")
```

Scripts

Earlier, I said I'd talk a bit more about scripting languages. A scripting language is often a subset of a full programming language such as Visual Basic. Some scripting languages such as JavaScript are actually interpreted by the browser. Other languages such as VBScript and PERL require a server-side interpreter. Some scripting languages are identified by a <script language> tag. JavaScript is one such language. For example:

```
<head>
<script language="JavaScript">
function rusure()
{
   var question;
   question = confirm ("Are you sure you want to cancel your order?")
   if (question !="0") {
      return true;}
   else {
    return false;
  }
}
</script>
</head>
```

VBScript can also be placed within a <script> tag, but as you'll soon learn, it can also be placed in the body section of an HTML document between the <% and %> tags. Only now the document is referred to as an Active Server Page. Here's what an example Sub routine looks like if we need to present a user with a message about an invalid entry:

```
<head>
<script language="VBScript">
Sub InvalidResponse
   MsgBox "You have entered an invalid response."
End Sub
</script>
</head>
```

Active Server Pages (ASPs)

Now that you have a grasp of what both HTML and a scripting language is, we will move ahead and focus on Active Server Pages (ASPs). An HTML document is referenced by its .htm extension. An Active Server Page document is referenced by its .asp extension.

ASP is a Microsoft server-based technology that you can use to build dynamic and interactive Web sites. As with most new technologies, we're sure you have a few questions. What can it do? How does it work? Can I use it to turn on the TV?

While we can't swear that you can use ASP to turn on your TV—not yet anyway—we can answer a few of the simpler questions. ASP can do many things. It is, in fact, a useful (although not as robust as we'd like) technology that supports a variety of scripting languages and allows developers to build dynamic and interactive Web pages using server-based technology.

Since it's a *server-side* technology, it lets you create reasonably stable, secure applications—and ultimately better Web sites.

MTS PACKAGES AND ASP APPLICATIONS

Programmers who develop transaction-oriented Web sites for e-commerce often use the Microsoft Transaction Server (MTS) as part of their solution. MTS uses a concept called packages to define a process within the MTS system. When you want to use a component (an in-process COM object) within MTS, you install it in an MTS package that MTS registers. MTS uses the MTS executive (mtx.exe) to run the components in a package, and you can even let a package run inside the process that calls an object in an MTS package. For example, if an ASP application calls a component in an MTS package, the package executes in the IIS process, inetinfo.exe. Although this can yield great performance, it's risky, because if an object within a component dies the intetinfo process also dies and brings down the server and every Web application that it runs.

Dynamic Web Pages

So now that you've heard the hubbub, how about some practical examples? ASP is most useful in generating dynamic Web pages, and responding (or interacting) with those pages. Great, you say, but what's a *dynamic Web page*? It's a Web page that's *generated* by the server. Meaning, that an initial *template* page (in this case an ASP document) is run by the server, and, based on runtime input, generates a final *static* page that is sent to your browser.

Here's an example of what an ASP page can be used for. Consider the standard Web site's Login page. You provide information such as a user name and a password. You then submit the information by pressing the Login button (or whatever the button is named). A welcome screen appears with your full name and welcomes you to the site. If you right-click in your browser and from the popup menu select View Source, you'll only see the final (or static) HTML.

Let's unravel the mystery of how the welcome screen was built. We'll start by examining the simple login page (see Figure 6.9 and Listing 6.2). Notice that the form method is POST and the action is to launch the file LoginValidation.asp. The LoginValidation.asp file attaches to a SQL Server database, validates the user name and password, and generates a welcome screen using the user's First and Last names combined.

Figure 6.9 A sample login page.

```
<html>
<head>
<title>MySite.Com Member Log In</title>
<meta HTTP-EQUIV="expires" CONTENT="Fri, March 26, 1999 GMT">
<meta HTTP-EQUIV="Pragma" CONTENT="no-cache">
</head>
<body bgcolor="#FFFFFF">
<div align="center"><center>
<table border="0" cellpadding="0" cellspacing="0" width="600">
  <tr>
    <td align="center" bgcolor="#FFFFCC"><font face="Arial, Helvetica"
    size="4"><b>MySite.com
    Member Login</b><p>Please Type Your Username and Password, Then
    Click 'Log In':<br>
    <br>
    </font></td>
  </tr>
  <tr>
    <td align="center" bgcolor="#FFFFFF"><form method="POST"
    action="LoginValidation.asp">
       <div align="center"><center><table border="0" cellpadding="0"
       cellspacing="0" width="600"
      height="99">
```

```
        <tr>
          <td width="268" bgcolor="#FFFFCC" valign="top" align="right"
          height="25"><font
          face="Arial, Helvetica"><strong>Username:
          </strong></font></td>
          <td width="332" bgcolor="#FFFFCC" valign="top" align="left"
          height="25"><font
          face="Arial, Helvetica"><input type="text" name="USERNAME"
          size="20"> </font></td>
        </tr>
        <tr>
          <td width="268" bgcolor="#FFFFCC" valign="top" align="right"
          height="25"><font
          face="Arial, Helvetica"><strong>Password:</strong></font></td>
          <td width="332" bgcolor="#FFFFCC" valign="top" align="left"
          height="25"><input
          type="password" name="PASSWORD" size="20"> </td>
        </tr>
        <tr>
          <td width="600" bgcolor="#FFFFCC" valign="top"
          align="center" colspan="2" height="49"><br>
          <font face="Arial, Helvetica"><input type="submit"
          value="Log In"></font></td>
        </tr>
      </table>
      </center></div>
    </form>
    </td>
  </tr>
</table>
</center></div>
</body>
</html>
```

Listing 6.2 Login.html.

When the user clicks the Submit button the browser launches the file LoginValidation.asp. Let's look at the LoginValidation.asp page shown in Listing 6.3.

```
<!-- #include file="adovbs.inc" -->
<%
       Option Explicit
       Dim cSQL             ' SQL statement
       Dim oConn            ' Connection Object
       Dim oRs               ' Recordset
```

Continues

```
        Dim cUserName                     ' UserName From Form
        Dim cPwd                          ' Password From Form
        Dim cFullName                     ' Users Full Name

        ' Using the Request object get the user name
        cUserName = Request.Form("USERNAME")
        ' Using the Request object get the password
        cPwd = Request.Form("PASSWORD")
        ' Build the SQL Statement
        cSQL = "SELECT * FROM auth_users WHERE Ucase(username) = '" &
                Ucase(cUserName) & "'"
        ' Open the Connection
    Set oConn = Server.CreateObject("ADODB.Connection")

    ' Make Native Connection Through ADO to SQL Server 7.0
    oConn.Open "Driver={SQL Server};Server=Merlin;UID=sa;" & _
                "WSID=;Language=us_english;DATABASE=Sample;" & _
                "PASSWORD=;"
        ' Open Recordset
        Set oRs = oConn.Execute(cSQL)
        ' No Records?
        If oRs.EOF then
                ' Not found!
                Response.Redirect "NotFound.Html"
        Else
                ' Validate Password
                If Trim(Ucase(oRs("password"))) <> Trim(Ucase(cPwd))
                        ' Not valid
                        Response.Redirect "NotValid.Html"
                Else
                        cFullName = Trim(oRs("firstname")) & " " &
                                    Trim(oRs("lastname"))
                End If
        End If
        ' Close Recordset
        oRs.Close
        Set oRs = Nothing
        ' Close Connection
        oConn.Close
        Set oConn = Nothing
        ' The part that follows is the HTML for welcoming the user
%>
<html>
<head>
<title>New Page 1</title>
<meta name="GENERATOR" content="Microsoft FrontPage 3.0">
</head>
```

```
<body>
<form name="welcome" action="nextpage.html" method="post">
  <div align="center"><center><p><big><big>Welcome
<% Response.Write(cFullName) %> </big></big></p>
  </center></div><div align="center"><center><p><input type="submit"
value="Continue"
  name="Continue"></p>
  </center></div>
</form>
</body>
</html>
```

Listing 6.3 LoginValidation.Asp

Notice that the top half of the page looks almost exactly like a Visual Basic application, with a few exceptions:

- It includes support for #include files.
- Variables cannot be typed.
- It contains HTML.

Combine the concepts and behold (!): a dynamic Web site. The interaction between the site and the user is now complete. Now let's go back and see what we can do with our sample HR database. In maintaining this employee database there will be a number of forms:

A Home Page or Site Map

A browse of all employees

Add/Edit of an employee

A browse of all benefits

Add/Edit of benefits

Employee Sick day/Vacation day

Consider that we want to build the HR home page. The page must interact with the user in the following ways.

- Display a menu of actions.
- Accept a choice.
- Guide the user to the correct area.

The HR home page should have only a few basic items as shown in Figure 6.10.

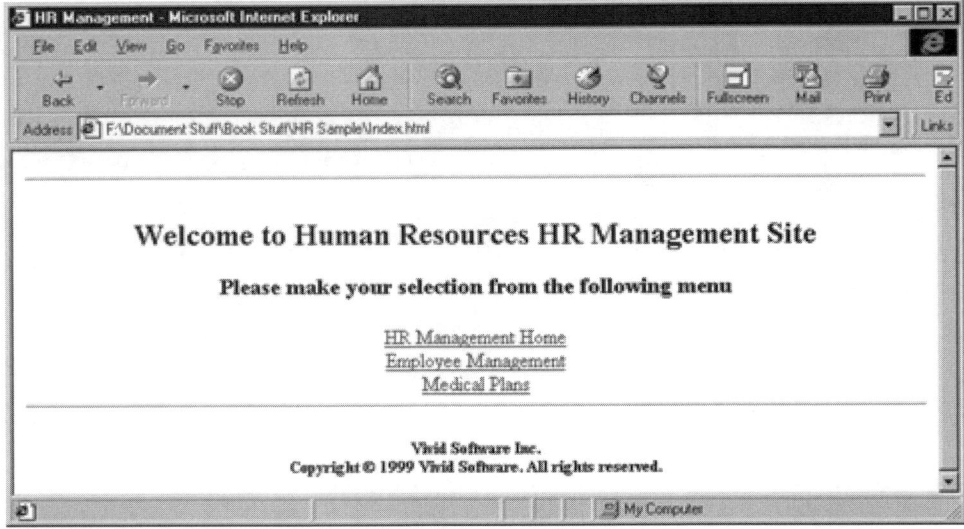

Figure 6.10 The HR Management menu.

The key to making the menu work is to declare the hyperlinks. Hyperlinks can be declared inside the <A> tag using the HREF identifier.

```
<A HREF="index.htm">HR Management Home</A>
<BR>
<A HREF="EmpSearch.html">Employee Management</A>
<BR>
<A HREF="MedSearch.html">Medical Plans</A>
```

Notice that the HREF identifier points to the next Web page to open. By clicking on the link users are guided to one of the three pages: the current index page, an employee search page, or the medical plans search page. Clicking on a menu option will now jump the user to the requested page.

GO TO THE TOP

You've probably seen those Return to Top buttons at the bottom of a long Web page. To implement them, you need to put an internal anchor at the top of your page—something like the following code:

```
<BODY>
<a name = "top"></a>
<h1> Here's the top heading</h>
<p>
```

Your first paragraph content goes here:

```
</P
```

Then, for your "top" buttons, the code will be something like this:

```
<a href="#top"><IMG
SRC="images/top.gif"></a>
```

Now that the menu is under our belt, let's tackle the task of administration. By definition, in order for there to be employees and medical plans to search for, we must also provide the capacity to add an employee or medical plan. There are really two phases to the administration: adding an employee or plan and editing an employee or plan.

First we begin by creating the employee search screen (Listing 6.4).

```
<html>
<html>
<head>
<title>HR Management</title>
<script language="JavaScript">
function goHome()
{
        /* Simple Jump to home index page */
        location.href="Index.html"
}
function goNew()
{
        /* Simple Jump to home medical plan maintenence page */
        location.href="EmpMaint.asp?mode=0"
}
</script>
</head>
<body>
<hr>
<div align="center"><center>
<table WIDTH="100%" BORDER="0">
  <tr>
        <h1><FONT color=#800000 face="Times New Roman"
    size=6> </FONT></h1>
    </td>
  </tr>
  <tr>
    <td COLSPAN="2" ALIGN="middle"><br>
    <h2>Employee Search</h2>
    </td>
  </tr>
</table>
<table border="0" cellpadding="5" cellspacing="0" width="675">
  <tr>
    <td colspan=7 align="center" width="675" bgcolor="#800000"><font
face="Arial, Helvetica" size="-1" color="#FFFF00">
        <b>Enter an employee number to search for or leave blank for
all</b></font>
    </td>

  </tr>
  <tr>
        <form method="POST" action="EmpBrowse.asp">
      <div align="center"><center>
```

Continues

```
        <td align="left" height=70 valign="middle" bgcolor="#FFFFCC"
colspan=5>
                        <br>
                <font face="Arial, Helvetica" size="-1">Employee
Number :</font>
                        <input type="text" name="EmpNo" size="10">
                <br><br>
                </td>
        </tr>
        <tr>
                <td align="center" height=40 valign="middle" colspan=5>
                        <input type="button" value="Add New"
OnClick="javascript:goNew()">
                        <input type="Submit" value="Search">
                        <input type="reset" value="Reset">
                        <input type="button" value="Home"
OnClick="javascript:goHome()">
         </td>
        </tr>
        </form>
</table>
</div>
<hr>
<h5>Vivid Software Inc.<br>
Copyright © 1999 Vivid Software. All rights reserved.<br></h5>
</body>
</html>
```

Listing 6.4 The EmpSearch.html.

From the employee search screen we can now choose to enter a new employee (via the Add New button) or we can search for an existing employee. The Add new button opens up an edit form, while the search button will call the EmpBrowse.asp Page.

Notice that at this point the Web pages aren't dynamic. EmpSearch uses the POST form method to call the page EmpBrowse.Asp. If you run the page, EmpBrowse.asp, you'll notice that a table that contains all the current employees is displayed. How did we do this?

ADO/OLE DB Database Access

First we must establish a connection to the SQL Server database, and we do this with Active Data Objects (ADO). ADO is the current Microsoft technology for allowing programmers to establish a native connection between the server and the ASP document. How is this new? Previously, we used Open Database Connectivity (ODBC) to establish a connection between a database and a document. ODBC added an interface layer, which communicated with the application, translated the commands, and then sent the commands to the server. This approach, while effective, is slower and more cumbersome than ADO.

ADO, like its predecessors, (DAO and RDO) relies on an underlying layer of software to actually perform the interaction with the data source. The underlying software layer is referred to as OLE DB. OLE DB is the interface that provides the application with a standard means of accessing data stored in various formats such as SQL Server, Access, or Oracle. If you're confused by all of this, don't worry for now since you'll get a more in-depth discussion in our e-commerce and VB SQL projects. You can also "read all about it" up on the www.microsoft.com/data site. And we mean *all* about it. Most people don't bother with the details and simply use the newest Microsoft data access technologies, ADO and OLE DB.

OLE DB takes the ODBC concept a step further, moving towards a standard means of accessing data from dissimilar sources. The primary difference is that ODBC focused on using SQL as the means to access data; OLE DB focuses on accessing any type of data, anywhere, anyhow.

There are, of course, a few problems. Well, for starters ADO doesn't support all of the same features as DAO. ADO mostly includes the RDO style functionality and some DHTML technology.

To create and work with an ADO connection, we need to do two things:

1. Connect to the Server (SQL Server 7 in this case) and the database within the Server (HR Sample).
2. Select the operations to perform (SELECT, INSERT, DELETE, and so on) on a table.

You should, by now, be at least partially well versed in SQL Server's SELECT, INSERT, UPDATE, and DELETE statements. If not, see Appendix A for our SQL Survival Guide. So, first let's break down the parts of the ADO connection:

Driver. This is the portion that defines the data source type.

Server. This is the actual name of the Server—in our case, MERLIN.

User ID (UID). This is defined at the Server level.

Language. What language?

Database. This is the database to open.

Password. This is the user's password.

The following code shows what the actual connection code looks like when attempting to connect to the SQL Server Merlin server and to open the HR Database using ADO.

```
Dim oConn    ' Connection Object
' Open the Connection
Set oConn = Server.CreateObject("ADODB.Connection")

' Make Native Connection Through ADO to SQL Server 7.0
oConn.Open "Driver={SQL Server};Server=Merlin;UID=sa;" & _
           "Language=us_english;DATABASE=Employee;" & _
           "PASSWORD=;"
```

"Just like that," you have a connection that you can work with. We mentioned earlier that ASP supports the use of an Include file. *Include files* are files that contain any valid

ASP definitions. Since ASP doesn't support VB-style "Global" or module variables—it *does* support Application variables as in global.ASA—you should place all shared code in a central file (or set of files) that can then be "included" in your ASP pages.

In this case, we've created a file that contains all of our connection information and named it HRConn.Inc. In this file, we have both the functions to open and close a connection. While this code can reside in an ASP file, by centralizing the functions in a single file and then including the HRConn file (Listing 6.5) in all subsequent ASP pages, we only need to make a change in one place and all the ASP pages are instantly updated.

In order to let ASP open the Employee database, we need to copy the two Include files: one that contains all of the defined constants for ADO (adovbs.inc) and another that contains our two functions to open and close connections. We simply place the following two lines of

```
'
' File --- HRConn.Inc ---
'
'
' Open a Connection to The Server
'
Public Function OpenConnection()
'
' Function :  OpenConnection
' Params   :  None
'
' Author   :  Jon Kilburn
'             http://www.VividSoftware.Com
' Date     :  8/3/99
'
' Purpose  :  Consolidates the code to open a new database
'             Connection. This is essential since it will
'             allow for changes to be issolated to this file.
'
    Dim oConn    ' Connection Object
    ' Open the Connection
    Set oConn = Server.CreateObject("ADODB.Connection")

    ' Make Native Connection Through ADO to SQL Server 7.0
    oConn.Open "Driver={SQL Server};Server=Merlin;UID=sa;" & _
               "Language=us_english;DATABASE=Employee;" & _
               "PASSWORD=;"
    ' Return Connection
    Set OpenConnection = oConn
End Function
Public Sub CloseConnection(oConn)
'
' Function :  CloseConnection
' Params   :  None
'
' Author   :  Jon Kilburn
```

```
'               http://www.VividSoftware.Com
' Date      :   8/3/99
'
' Purpose   :   Consolidates the code to close an open database
'               Connection.
'
   oConn.Close
End Sub
```

Listing 6.5 HRConn.Inc Include file.

code at the top of the EmpBrowse.asp page, and now we have database accessibility:

```
<!-- #include file="adovbs.inc" -->
<!-- #include file="HRConn.inc" -->
```

Next, we need to create the connection, then build a cursor for all of the employees, and then load the table. We simply repeat the process for each employee. Note that Listing 6.6 is actually broken into two sections. The top section should appear at the very top of the EmpBrowse.asp document. The second section appears right after the

```
Section 1
<%
     Option Explicit
     Dim cSQL                  ' SQL statement
     Dim oConn                 ' Connection Object
     Dim oRs                   ' Recordset

     ' Create Connection
     Set     oConn = OpenConnection()
     ' Build SQL Statement
     If Request.Form("EmpNo") = "" Then
            ' No Employee number, select all
            cSQL = "SELECT * FROM employee"
     Else
            ' Only the employee with this number
            cSQL = "SELECT * FROM employee WHERE emp_id=" &
                   Request.Form("EmpNo")

     End If

     ' Retrive Cursor

     Set oRs = oConn.Execute(SQL)
```

Continues

```
%>
Section 2
<%
        ' Walk the Cursor Loading the Table
        Do While Not oRs.EOF
%>
                <td align="left" height=30 valign="middle"
bgcolor="#FFFFCC" colspan=3>
                        <font face="Arial, Helvetica" size="-1">
<%
        Response.Write(oRs("First_Name")) & " " & _
                Response.Write(oRs("Last_Name"))
%>
                        </font>
                </td>
<%
                oRs.MoveNext
        Loop
        ' Close Cursor
        oRs.Close
        Set oRs = Nothing
        ' Close Connection
        Call CloseConnection(oConn)
%>
```

Listing 6.6 Sections of ASP code to display employees.

form method declaration portion. They're broken out here so that you can see them more clearly than when they're actually embedded in the ASP document.

Manipulating the Table Contents

Now that we have displayed an Employee table, we have two things we can do with each employee: modify the employee data or delete the employee. The Delete button simply calls a VBScript function that launches a delete of the current row id. The Edit button on the other hand has to be more sophisticated. The form that we use to modify an employee is the same form that we use to add an employee. However, by passing a mode identifier in the Query string, we can make the EmpMaint.asp page behave differently.

Employee maintenance is handled through one form (see Figure 6.11). This form (EmpMaint.Asp) will interrogate the contents of the Query string to determine if a mode has been passed. Zero (0) represents the default mode of Add, while one (1) represents a modification to an existing employee. If we modify an existing employee there will be

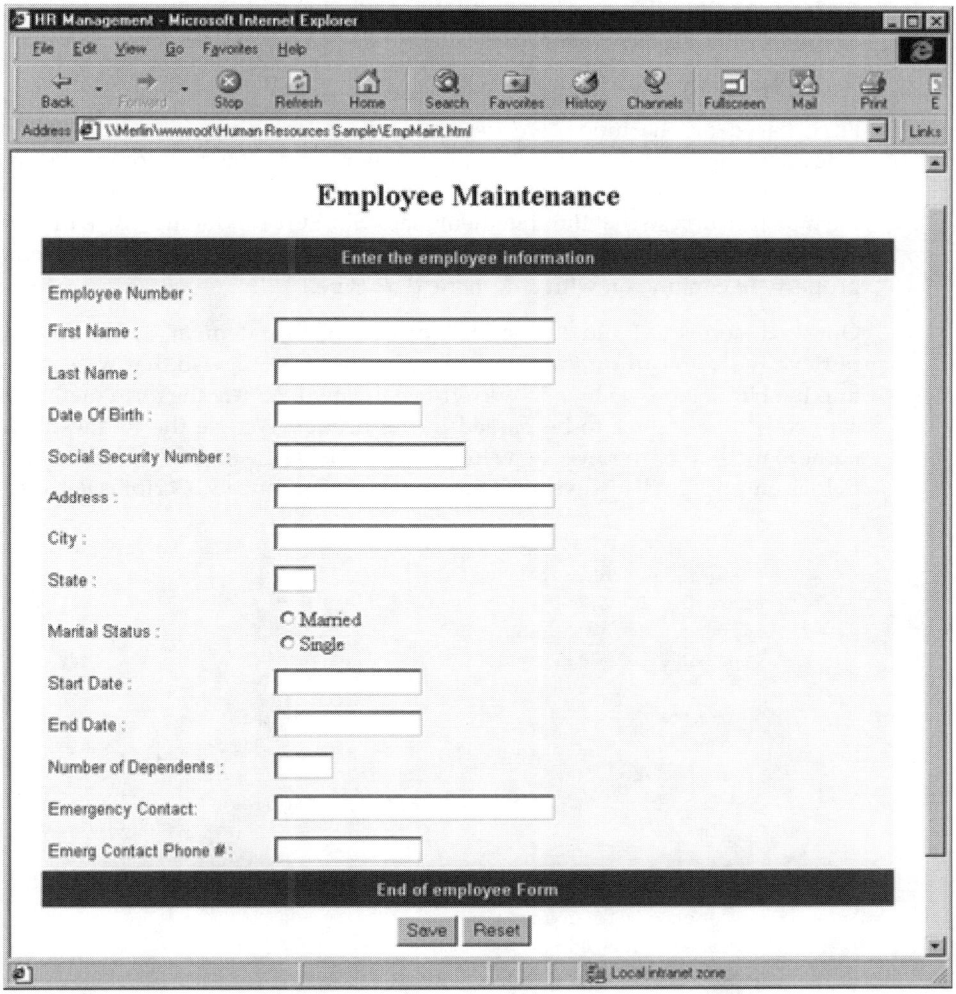

Figure 6.11 The Employee Maintenance screen.

a third parameter buried in the Query string, which is the internal row id. This allows us to open a recordset and apply the values to the fields.

Notice that the form method defines SaveEmp.asp as the file that's executed by the Post action. When the user presses the Submit button the browser opens the SaveEmp.asp page and processes the contents. There are several actions that we must do in order to make the update occur properly.

1. Determine (based on mode) if we are using UPDATE or INSERT.
2. If we perform an INSERT we must create a new row identifier for this employee.

3. If we use INSERT we must build the INSERT statement, otherwise build an UPDATE statement.
4. Display user feedback.

First, based on the mode, we determine if we're editing or adding an employee. Adding means that we need to create a new row id. This is accomplished by using a special type of select statement known as SELECT MAX. We pass the column name to the max function so that the statement reads SELECT MAX(emp_id) + 1 FROM survey. This generates a new column id. (An alternate technique would be to use the Identity property in conjuncton with a numeric data type.)

Our next step is to build an INSERT (or UPDATE) statement. To do this, we need to retrieve the values from the Employee Maintenance page so that we can insert them into the HR database. How do we retrieve the fields? Since the form method is Post we can expect the values to be passed in the header. We use the Request.Form (<field name>) method to retrieve the value of the field (see Listing 6.7). Please note that if the field is empty, it will always return an empty string, since VBScript is *not* strong typed.

```
<%@ language = "VBScript" %>
<% Option Explicit %>
<!-- #include file="Adovbs.inc" -->
<!-- #include file="HRConn.inc" -->
<%                              7
       Dim cSQL                 ' Insert Statement
       Dim iNext                ' Next ID for Survey
       Dim oConn                ' Connection Object
       Dim oRs                  ' Recordset Object
       Dim Mode                 ' What Mode are we in?
       Dim HaveErr              ' Did we encounter an Error?

       Const Field_Count = 0
       Const Mode_Add = 0
       Const Mode_Mod = 1

       Mode = Request.QueryString("mode")
       If Mode = "" Then
              Mode = Mode_Add
       Else
              Mode = CInt(Mode)
       End If

       ' Create a New Connection
       Set oConn = OpenConnection
       On Error Resume Next

       If Err.Number <> 0 Then
              Response.Write "The Following Error Occurred while
              Opening the File <br>"
```

```
            Response.Write Err.Description & "<br>"
            Response.Write Err.Number & "<br>"
            HaveErr = True
        Else
            If Mode = Mode_Add Then
                ' Get Next Id
                cSQL = "SELECT MAX(emp_id) + 1 FROM employee"
                Set oRs = oConn.Execute(cSQL)

                ' Store Next Id
                iNext = oRs(Field_Count)

                ' Check for first time entry
                If IsNull(iNext) Then
                    iNext = 1
                End If

                ' Build the SQL Statement
                cSQL = "INSERT INTO Employee " & _
                   "(emp_id, first_name, last_name, address,
                   city, state, zip_code," & _
                   "date_of_birth, ssn, start_date,
                   marital_status, " & _
                   "num_depend, contact, contact_phone,
                   sick_days, vacation_days"

                    If Request.Form("END_DATE") <> "" Then
                        cSQL = cSQL & "end_date "
                    End If
                    cSQL = cSQL & _
                    ") VALUES (" & _
                    iNext & ", '" & _
                    Request.Form("FIRST_NAME") & "', '" & _
                    Request.Form("LAST_NAME") & "', '" & _
                    Request.Form("ADDRESS") & "','" & _
                    Request.Form("CITY") & "', '" & _
                    Request.Form("STATE") & "', '" & _
                    Request.Form("ZIP") & "', '" & _
                    Request.Form("DOB") & "', '" & _
                    Request.Form("SSN") & "', '" & _
                    Request.Form("START_DATE") & "', '" & _
                    Request.Form("MSTATUS") & "', " & _
                    Request.Form("NUM_DEPEND") & ", '" & _
                    Request.Form("CONTACT") & "', '" & _
                    Request.Form("CONTACT_PHONE") & "', " & _
                    Request.Form("SICK_DAYS") & ", " & _
                    Request.Form("VACATION_DAYS")

                    ' Check for an Ending Date
```

Continues

```
                If Request.Form("END_DATE") <> "" Then
                cSQL = cSQL & ", " & Request.Form
                ("END_DATE") & "'"
                End If
                ' Add the finishing touches
                cSQL = cSQL & ")"
Else
        ' Retrieve Current Employee Id
        iNext = Request.Form("emp_id")
        cSQL = "UPDATE Employee SET first_name = '" & _
                Request.Form("FIRST_NAME") & "', " & _
                "last_name = '" & _
                Request.Form("LAST_NAME") & "', " & _
                "address = '" & _
                Request.Form("ADDRESS") & "'," & _
                "city = '" & _
                Request.Form("CITY") & "', " & _
                "state ='" & _
                Request.Form("STATE") & "', " & _
                "zip_code = '" & _
                Request.Form("ZIP") & "', " & _
                "date_of_birth = '" & _
                Request.Form("DOB") & "', " & _
                "ssn = '" & _
                Request.Form("SSN") & "', " & _
                "start_date = '" & _
                Request.Form("START_DATE") & "', " & _
                "end_date = '" & _
                Request.Form("END_DATE") & "', " & _
                "marital_status = '" & _
                Request.Form("MSTATUS") & "', " & _
                "num_depend = " & _
                Request.Form("NUM_DEPEND") & ", " & _
                "contact = '" & _
                Request.Form("CONTACT") & "', " & _
                "contact_phone = '" & _
                Request.Form("CONTACT_PHONE") & "', " & _
                "sick_days = " & _
                Request.Form("SICK_DAYS") & ", " & _
                "vacation_days = " & _
                Request.Form("VACATION_DAYS") & " " & _
                "WHERE emp_id = " & iNext
End If

' Execute this Insert
oConn.Execute(cSQL)
' Handle any Errors
If Err.Number <> 0 Then
```

```
                Response.Write "The Following Error Occurred while
                Opening the File <br>"
                        Response.Write Err.Description & "<br>"
                        Response.Write Err.Number & "<br>"

                        HaveErr = True
                End If

                ' Done
                Call CloseConnection(oConn)
                Set oConn = Nothing
        End If
%>
<html>
<head>
<title>HR Management</title>
<script language="JavaScript">
function goHome()
{
        /* Simple Jump to home index page */
        location.href="Index.html"
}
</script>
</head>
<body>
<hr>
<div align="center"><center>
<table WIDTH="100%" BORDER="0">
  <tr>
        <h1><FONT color=#800000 face="Times New Roman"
    size=6> </FONT></h1>
    </td>
  </tr>
  <tr>
    <td COLSPAN="2" ALIGN="middle"><br>
    <h2>Employee Maintenance</h2>
    </td>
  </tr>
</table>
<table border="0" cellpadding="5" cellspacing="0" width="675">
  <tr>
    <td colspan=7 align="center" width="675" bgcolor="#800000"><font
face="Arial, Helvetica" size="-1" color="#FFFF00">
        <b>Employee Information Updated</b></font>
    </td>

  </tr>
  <tr>
```

Continues

```
    <%
        If Not HaveErr Then
        %>
        <td align="center" bgcolor="#FFFFCC"><font face="Arial,
        Helvetica">Employee Information
            has been properly updated.</font></td>
            </td>
        <%
        Else
        %>
        <td align="center" bgcolor="#FFFFCC"><font face="Arial,
        Helvetica">Employee Information
            has not been updated.</font></td>
            </td>
        <%
        End If
        %>
    </tr>
</table>
</div>
<table>
    <tr>
                <td align="center" height=40 valign="middle" colspan=5>
                <input type="button" value="< Back"
                OnClick="javascript:
                history.go(-1)">
                <input type="button" value="Home"
OnClick="javascript:goHome()">
        </td>
        </tr>
</table>
</div>
<hr>
<h5>Vivid Software Inc.<br>
Copyright © 1999 Vivid Software. All rights reserved.<br></h5>
</body>
</html>
```

Listing 6.7 SaveEmp.asp code to save employees.

STRONG TYPING

Strong typing is a characteristic of programming languages that prevents programs from changing the data type of a variable during program execution.

We must now place all of the files in a directory on the server so that we can access them using Internet Explorer. IIS creates a directory named InetPub on the server, and under InetPub, you'll find the root directory for all www activity. It's called wwwroot. In order to keep the files in their own sub-directory, we should create a Survey directory underneath wwwroot. So the fully qualified path is InetPub\wwwroot\Human Resources on the server Merlin.

To access the Human Resources site, bring up Internet Explorer, and type the http:// server name (since my server name is Merlin, if you type Merlin, it maps to the InetPub\wwwroot directories) followed by the Human Resources directory and Survey page.

```
http://merlin/Human Resources/Index.Html
```

The main index page should now pop up in your browser leaving you free to move about the Web site as you please. The full source code for the site can be found on the accompanying CD.

Summary

As we said at the beginning of this chapter, this entire chapter has been a project. You've set up IIS, created a simple HR database (or used the script from the book's CD to create it), have seen how to write some HTML code, and how to use ASP pages to create a rudimentary HR site that would be perfect for an organization's intranet. With any luck, we've touched a nerve and you're ready to implement your own intranet.

This chapter didn't really focus on SQL Server directly, but in a sense that will be true for many of the applications you build with SQL Server. To borrow an analogy from the film industry, SQL Server tends to have supporting roles rather than "star" roles.

In the next chapter, we shift gears and focus more on SQL Server, showing you how you can use it to build a simple data mart.

CHAPTER 7

Project #4: Create a Single-Source Data Mart

Goal

The goal of this chapter is to show how to set up a simple data mart from one data source.

YOU WILL NEED

- ✔ **Microsoft SQL Server 7**
- ✔ **WorkOrd database in SQL Server 7**

Optional:

- ✔ **WordOrdDM.ZIP**

In Chapter 1, we mentioned online analytical processing (OLAP) as being one of the Really Neat Things in SQL Server 7, and briefly described how it was different from online transaction processing (OLTP). OLAP is more for decision support and business intelligence (BI), and typically worked with *cubes* of data so that end users can "slice and dice" their data, while OLTP is geared towards supporting large numbers of discrete transactions. Table 7.1 provides a useful summary of the differences between OLTP and OLAP systems.

We also spoke about data marts and data warehouses as approaches to storing data from heterogeneous data sources (typically from multiple OLTP databases) in a centralized read-only data store—often with pre-summarized data for easy retrieval. Data marts and data warehouses basically differ in scope. A data mart differs from a data warehouse in that its contents do *not* cross-functional or organizational boundaries. Data marts offer rapid, low cost, responsive solutions to local decision-support requirements.

Terminology can be an emotional issue. "Don't call it a data mart," Karen remembers an IT staffer pleading, "it's a data *warehouse*." What's the difference? Does it matter? See Table 7.2 for a general comparison.

The "Classic" Definition for Data Warehousing

Bill Inmon, the prolific author and co-founder of Prism Solutions (later acquired by Ardent Software) and more recently founder and CEO of Pine Cone Systems—sometimes referred to as the "father of data warehousing"—first defined a data warehouse in 1992 as a "subject-oriented, integrated, non-volatile, and time-variant collection of data in support of management's decisions." (See *Building the Data Warehouse, Second Edition*, Wiley 1996, for the latest edition of his classic book on data warehousing).

Table 7.1 Comparing OLTP and OLAP Systems

OLTP	OLAP
Optimized for getting data *in.*	Optimized for getting data *out.*
Associated with operational data.	Associated with copies or subsets of operational data.
Access is read/write.	Access is read only.
Many concurrent users.	Few concurrent users.
Characterized by short transactions of a predictable nature such as INSERT, UPDATE, and DELETE.	Characterized by long transactions of an *ad hoc* nature.
Contains very granular, atomic data.	Often contains summarized or pre-aggregated data.

Table 7.2 Data Warehouses and Data Marts Basically Differ in Scope

DATA WAREHOUSE	DATA MART
Constructed to meet the information needs of the entire enterprise.	Constructed to meet the needs of a specific business unit or function.
Large initial investment often authorized by the board.	Much smaller initial investment (typically less than $100,000) authorized at the line of business level.
Focus on long-term ROI.	Focus on short-term ROI.
Can take years to build.	Typically deployed in 30-90 days.
Manages extensive amounts of atomic-level history.	Primarily focused at manipulating summary and/or sample data.
Owned and managed by IT, generally based on standardized terms and calculations.	Often owned by department, region, or line-of-business (LOB) division. Not necessarily implemented in accordance with any enterprise standards.
Generally requires team of experts (network, database, and business) to implement.	Often can be implemented by small team headed by a DBA.
Typically provides a consistent view of data	Independent data marts may provide different answers to the same question.
No risk of multiple extract requests to OLTP sources.	Multiple, redundant extracts are typically needed to support multiple data marts.

Even though Inmon has refined his ideas about data warehouses, it's useful to examine the original definition. So let's consider the four components:

Subject-oriented. Inmon realized that, thanks to independent operational OLTP systems such as general ledger, order entry, order processing, inventory, and accounts payable, it was often nearly impossible to get an overall view of sales, or customers. Hence his notion was that warehouses should be organized by subject, or business activity. He didn't mean that data warehouses should be limited to one subject (that's more what data marts are). He meant that the information in them should be organized by subject.

Integrated. This was—and remains—the fundamental incentive for building data warehouses or data marts: to combine information that resides in different systems. That may sound easy, but providing consolidated and internally consistent data is extremely challenging. Coping with different naming conventions for customers and products is easy compared with handling "dirty" —inaccurate or incomplete—information, not to speak of the challenge of reconciling different currencies over time.

Non-volatile. Non-changing. In other words, read-only.

Time-variant. Not just a snapshot of an organization's data at a given instant in time, but containing temporal data. One of the greatest appeals of data warehouses and data marts is that they contain historical data that allows you to perform trend analysis.

Today's more process-oriented definition focuses on warehous*ing* rather than warehouses. It's a set of processes (some say an architecture) by which related data from many operational systems is merged to provide an integrated, read-only view of data that may span multiple business divisions. In fact, Inmon, in his book, *Corporate Information Factory* (Wiley, 1998), offers a refined view of a corporate information factory that consists of the following components:

Applications. The family of systems from which the corporate information factory (CIF) gathers raw, detailed data.

An integration or transformation layer. Where the data gathered by the applications is refined into a corporate structure.

Data warehouse. A subject-oriented, integrated, time-variant (temporal), and non-volatile collection of summary and detailed data used to support the strategic decision-making process for the enterprise.

Data mart. Customized, summarized data from the data warehouse tailored to support the specific analytical requirements of a given business unit.

Operational data store. A subject-oriented, integrated, current-valued, volatile collection of detailed data used to support the up-to-the-second collective tactical decision-making process for the enterprise.

Metadata. The information catalog infrastructure to the corporate information factory.

The Internet and intranet. The lines of communication along which data flows and different components interact with each other.

It's interesting that Inmon doesn't explicitly mention OLAP, but it's probably because he views OLAP as primarily from the client, rather than the server point of view. We'll talk about that more in Chapter 9.

ANCIENT HISTORY

Sometimes it seems that data warehousing came "out of nowhere" in the 90s, but it really has emerged from a long history that stretches back to the 60s. Databases themselves—at least once direct access storage device (DASD) began to replace tape—were originally envisioned as being able to provide "a single source of data for all processing," according to Inmon. Data processing departments developed batch processing and exception reports (the infamous "green bar" reports) to help management obtain a consolidated view or the organization. Later, they developed fancy executive information systems (EIS) which were usually personalized "briefing books" written for executives. Finally, when spreadsheet programs exploded onto the scene, more complex proprietary data and financial analysis programs emerged as the true forebears of today's data warehouses and OLAP tools.

Data Warehousing FAQs

What's the relationship between data marts and data warehouses? Are data marts just little data warehouses or what?

Generally, it's a question of scope. Data warehouses tend to be more enterprise-wide, while data marts are more subject- or business-unit specific. Both are almost always "read only" and need to be periodically updated.

Some people say you should do the enterprise data warehouse first and then spawn off workgroup data marts. Others say you should start small with data marts. Who's right?

There's no easy answer, but current wisdom seems to be to start small.

Can you do data warehousing over the Internet? Can you use a browser to get data from a data warehouse?

It's easy to deliver HTML reports based on data in data warehouses or marts, and although it's a little more challenging to provide interactive access, virtually all vendors provide you with tools to do it.

Where do OLAP and ROLAP fit in?

Online analytical processing is a term coined by Codd and Date in a paper commissioned by Arbor Software (now Hyperion Software) that observed that OLTP relational databases weren't well suited for interactive, analytical processing of the sort popularized by spreadsheets. (You can read the classic paper online at warehouse.chimenet.org/software/datastore/dataware/coddc0.html). Relational on-line analytical processing (ROLAP) refers to engines and tools that add multi-dimensionality to data that resides in the RDBMSs, using techniques like star schema.

What exactly is star schema?

Star schema refers to special database designs that make relational databases suitable for ad hoc, slice-and-dice queries. They consist of fact and dimension tables, the idea being to mimic a multi-dimensional database with views of data, such as sales by region or time, that are likely to be explored. *Snowflaking* refers to splitting up the dimensions (decomposing them).

Do data warehouses need bit-mapped indexes to offer good performance?

Bit-mapped indexes are compressed indexes where each bit relates to a column value in a single row of a table. They're especially useful for indexing large amounts of non-volatile data on fields that have low cardinality (not a lot of unique values, such as gender fields) and when involved in joins with other bit-mapped indexes because binary operations are extremely fast. Indexes (bit-mapped or otherwise) have a significant downside, however. Not only do they tend to take up lots of space (they're often larger than the warehouse/mart

Data Warehousing FAQs *(Continued)*

itself), they also have to be kept up to date (potential performance hit), and generally need programmer/developer skills to set up and/or maintain. SQL Server doesn't have bit-mapped indexes in Version 7, but they're expected in a future version.

What's business intelligence (BI)?

Business intelligence (BI) is an amorphous term that refers to any number of techniques and/or tools that help people analyze their data—and that of their competitors—perform trend analysis, make forecasts, and devise and calculate metrics of interest to them.

What's data mining? Is it related to data warehouses or BI?

When you query a data warehouse or mart, you generally have a hypothesis and want to obtain specific data to validate your hypothesis. Multi-dimensional or OLAP tools usually let you drill down and roll up to help figure out *why* the answer was what it was. Data mining and knowledge discovery, on the other hand, generally refer to techniques and algorithms for finding unexpected relationships in your data—for performing knowledge discovery, or KD. See Chapter 13 for more on data mining.

Why does everyone get so excited about *data cleansing*?

The sad truth is that most corporate data contains both erroneous data, and, more often, data fraught with internal inconsistencies. One of the hardest decisions is *where* to do the data cleansing—in the original source data, in some intermediate staged database store, in the transformation process itself, or in the final data warehouse or mart. Sadly, even if you do it at each of these stages, you'll still probably end up with some bad data.

What's metadata?

Metadata is data about data. In other words, it's information about the structure of a data source and is often stored in what's called a database catalog or system repository. Metadata will contain information about table and field names, for example, along with data types, rules, and so on.

Sometimes I hear the term *federated data marts*. What does this term refer to?

We think of federated data marts as a compromise between multiple, standalone data marts and a single enterprise database. The term was not chosen lightly. Federations of states such as the United States represent a balance of power between the central federal government and the state governments. Similarly, federated data marts are built along some shared design guidelines—often via a common staging area—but aren't as tightly linked to a single, central data warehouse as a collection of dependent data marts are.

(S)MART ANALOGY

It may be useful to use a Wal*Mart, PETsMART, and Kmart analogy. We usually think of those stores as local "marts" or stores, but they rely on distribution warehouses for their contents. However, neither the local marts nor the regional warehouses actually create any of the products. Warehouses usually get their products from the manufacturers that produce them. In other words, there's a parallel between the retail production supply chain (manufacturer‡distributor‡local retail stores) and the information supply chain (operational systems‡data warehouse‡data mart).

Data Marts

As if the information "ecosystem" weren't complicated enough, what with data warehouses, data marts, and operational data stores, you'll often read about *independent* and *dependent data marts*. Actually, the distinction is useful and not that hard to grasp. Independent data marts are simply ones that are created more or less "out of the blue" by a department or line of business unit. They're often created "Rambo-style" without the help—or even the knowledge—of IT to solve a particular need. Somehow, they'll need to be updated (load-and-go operations aren't likely to be successful since they'll rapidly result in stale data.) Independent data marts are sometimes unflatteringly called *stovepipe* systems to indicate that they're not integrated with anything else. Their appeal is that they're quick and usually cheap to build.

Dependent data marts, on the other hand, are subsets of the big mother data warehouse and are theoretically consistent with that, and with any other dependent data marts. Why are we harping on consistency? Because it's not uncommon for upper management to be faced with conflicting sets of numbers from different departments or business units. Perhaps one manager based his numbers on more up-to-date data. Perhaps the underlying sets of data simply weren't similarly cleansed. Dependent data marts exist in a hierarchy and often represent delayed gratification. After all, you can't have a dependent data mart until you have a data warehouse. And building a data warehouse can be incredibly complex and expensive for large organizations with a long history.

Buy or Build?

Irrespective of whether you choose to build a data warehouse or a data mart, you'll invariably face the buy versus build decision. Some software vendors have "soup-to-nuts" data mart bundles, often with a few days of quick-start consulting. Others offer packages that target specific vertical markets. Some offer tools that handle only a portion of the data warehousing process such as the extraction or data cleansing phases. ERP vendors including SAP and Baan have their own data warehouses that are built to work with their own ERP software. And there are probably thousands of consulting firms and systems integrators who will be happy to help you build a data mart or data warehouse.

MAJOR INCENTIVES FOR DOING DATA WAREHOUSING

- **Reduction in time to locate, access, and analyze information**
- **Faster time-to-market for products and services**
- **Replacement of older, less flexible or less responsive decision support systems**
- **Better customer service performance, often by integrating with CRM systems**
- **Integrate with ERP to support an information supply chain**
- **Obtain strategic advantage over competitors**
- **Consolidation of disparate information sources**

Populating a Data Warehouse or Data Mart

Whether you're building a data mart or a data warehouse, and whether you're using a store-bought package or rolling your own, the steps are basically the same:

1. Understand your source data and decide what parts you want to use.
2. Design the new database.
3. Extract the data.
4. Do transformations (cleansing, data type conversions, and any aggregations or calculations).
5. Load the target database.

Inventory Your Data

Inventorying your data may sound easy and straightforward, but it isn't if you're dealing with "old" systems (often programmed by programmers who aren't even alive any more) for which any documentation (if it ever existed) has been lost. Expect cryptic codes, and fields whose meanings have evolved over time. It doesn't hurt to do some preliminary inspection of the raw data to get an idea of how "clean" it is. Expect data ownership issues and turf wars, especially if it looks like the data is a mess. This is also a good time to consider how you might integrate external data feeds into the end product.

It should go without saying that this is the time to find out what the end users want to do with the data. Given the current wisdom of building data marts and warehouses incrementally, it doesn't pay to just dump everything into a giant new structure, especially since it will have to be refreshed with new data. When your users' eyes are bigger than your refresh window's stomach, you're in for some problems. What end users want to do with the data should dictate what you extract. Generally your data mart or data warehouse will consist of both current and older detail data along with some lightly-summarized data and some-highly summarized data.

Design the New Database

You need to decide whether to stick to a relational approach—ROLAP—or to take a different tack and build the data warehouse based on a dimensional model. The appeal of Microsoft's OLAP Services and DTS is that you can use them to create either type of model—or indeed a so-called *hybrid* or HOLAP model. We discuss Microsoft's OLAP Services in greater detail in Chapter 9, but here's a quick summary:

Multi-dimensional online analytical processing (MOLAP) database. SQL Server's OLAP Service's can create multi-dimensional cubes by retrieving data from SQL Server 7 (or any RDBMS that supports OLE DB or ODBC interfaces) and then place those detailed data and the desired aggregations in a specialized OLAP store (distinct from standard SQL Server files).

Relational online analytical processing (ROLAP) engine. OLAP Services can also be used to create ROLAP warehouses or marts where aggregations and tables that support star schema are actually stored in non-normalized tables in a SQL Server database.

Hybrid online analytical processing (HOLAP). Aggregated summary data is stored in the multi-dimensional database, while the detailed transaction-level data remains in the relational database.

Extract the Data

Extracting data is the first of three steps that are often abbreviated with *ETL* for *extract, transform*, and *load*. There are three basic approaches to the extraction process.

1. Write code to do the extraction. This can be a combination of JCL and COBOL for mainframe data or simply SQL.
2. Use a commercial product that generates code for you.
3. Use an extraction and transformation engine such as Microsoft's DTS.

Data Cleansing and Transformation

Data cleansing and transformation is often the killer step that takes a lot longer than anyone expects. This is the step where the data is integrated and made consistent. Product ID from one production system is almost always stored in a different format than product ID from another production system. Consolidating them isn't always easy.

Many data type, mathematical calculations, and date-and-string conversions can be done using SQL functions and operations, but, as you can imagine, this is bound to be tricky. Data quality and missing values loom as common challenges. When you've got more than a handful of data sources, it will often pay to use a commercial extraction and transformation tool.

Load

DTS is undoubtedly the easiest choice for anyone who wants to populate a SQL Server database. DTS has the added advantage of being able to do some data scrubbing. Bulk copy is another option, as is data staging via some intermediate steps. For large projects, it's often useful to do trial runs with subsets of the *real* data.

That's a brief overview of the differences between data marts and data warehouses and the features they share in common. There are literally scores of books on the topic of data warehousing, and you may want to look at some of them. Some are database specific. Others have an obvious platform (Windows/COM or Unix) bias. Many focus on life cycle and project management issues. A few give starter "templates" or "models" for starter databases that can be very useful. We can recommend two:

Chris Adamson and Michael Venerable's *Data Warehouse Design Solutions* (Wiley, 1998)

Len Silverston, Bill Inmon, and Kent Graziano's *Data Model Resource Book* (Wiley, 1997)

Other Methodologies

In the interest of simplicity, we have probably erred in limiting our data warehouse/mart "recipe" to five steps, though Cognos' "Technical Requirements" (see Figure 7.1) are similar. For an even more granular approach, we recommend you look at Shaku Atre's

TECHNICAL REQUIREMENTS

DATA ACQUISITION

This step involves identifying, capturing, and transforming data from legacy systems, operational systems, ERP systems, and other corporate data sources and then loading them into the data warehouse. It can be challenging: often companies discover that the data they want for the warehouse doesn't exist or suffers from inaccuracies or inconsistencies or both.

Data Cleansing

Data administrators explore the structure and quality of source data, often in collaboration with business users. After determining the condition of the data, administrators must then reconcile irregularities and integrate overlapping data. This is called "scrubbing" or "cleaning" the data.

Extraction, Transformation, and Loading

These three steps are often handled by toolsets that support a metadata repository and scheduling engine that coordinates the various processes while maintaining data integrity.

Extraction tools or processes retrieve source data from operational and other corporate systems. Transformation tools let administrators apply business rules to integrate data from multiple tables and source systems. Transport and load tools move operational data from the source system to the transformation server, usually through file transfers.

DATA ACQUISITION CONSIDERATIONS

- Identify and map best possible sources
- Understand data structures
- Determine degree of data quality
- Apply business rules for integrating data
- Extract, transform, and transport data

METADATA MANAGEMENT

Metadata, or "data about data," is the foundation of a data warehouse. For administrators, common metadata makes it easier to troubleshoot, maintain, and tune a data warehouse with minimal manual intervention. For end users, it ensures that warehouse data is consistent and meaningful.

Creating common warehouse metadata can be difficult, however, because many systems store their metadata in proprietary formats or storage mechanisms. Data warehouse vendors are vying to offer a metadata repository, or to partner with other vendors to establish common metadata standards.

METADATA CONSIDERATIONS

- Identify metadata requirements
- Determine needs for shared versus local metadata
- Determine requirements for managing and accessing metadata
- Establish metadata management procedures
- Determine technical architecture (centralized versus distributed)

DATABASES AND INFORMATION SERVERS

The databases and servers optimal for a data warehouse depend on many factors, including the business needs, the warehouse addresses, the nature and extent of source data, the ways that users will access and use warehouse data, and the characteristics of the organization's computing and network environment.

Relational Databases

The ubiquity of SQL and ODBC have made relational databases the most popular platform for data warehouses and data marts. Companies with terabyte-capacity warehouses typically require a database capable of leveraging the parallel processing capabilities of highly scalable, multiprocessing Unix platforms. Companies that need to rapidly deploy less extensive, high-performance data warehouses built on distributed client/server computing might choose a database running on Microsoft Windows NT.

Multidimensional Databases

Multidimensional databases store data in a matrix-like structure to provide rapid responses to multidimensional queries—for example, sales by region by product by channel. Multidimensional databases contain high-quality, summarized data, allowing users to look at business data from any angle, in any combination. Most OLAP tools automatically create multidimensional databases (MDBS).

DATABASE AND INFORMATION SERVER CONSIDERATIONS

- Define a logical structure for source data
- Develop detailed models and specifications
- Create and document databases, indexes, backup procedures, etc.
- Define security requirements
- Select databases and information servers
- Implement database schemas

HARDWARE PLATFORM

As with databases and information servers, the optimal hardware platform for a data warehouse or data mart depends on the nature and scale of the warehouse, and on the organization's computing and network environment. Data warehouse platforms range from single to complex parallel processing systems. In Web environments, a Web server, an application server, or both will be the front end of the data warehouse platform. The Web server sends HTTP requests to the database, while the application server typically handles back-end processing and HTML translation for clients.

HARDWARE PLATFORM CONSIDERATIONS

- Service-level agreement for response time at various levels
- Number of users accessing the environment
- Number and sizes of tables at various levels
- Complexity of load algorithms
- Amount and timing of data being loaded

ADMINISTRATION AND MANAGEMENT

Without thorough planning and product selection, companies may need to hire additional staff to administer and manage their data warehouse—undermining the bottom-line impact of the warehouse. So administration and management requirements should be first-level warehouse design considerations. In general, administrators want centralized, open systems that address the needs of all users; for example, central management of metadata. Monitoring usage is essential for capacity planning and for eliminating response time bottlenecks. It also helps IT optimize database indexes and decide which standard reports should be built or discarded.

ADMINISTRATION AND MANAGEMENT CONSIDERATIONS

- Move applications and databases into production
- Identify and archive dormant data
- Deploy administrative functions: acquisition management, data management, service management, change management, and systems management

DEPLOYMENT, CONSULTING, AND TRAINING

Maximizing data warehouse return on investment with BI requires more than best-of-breed tools and an optimal architecture—it also requires an effective implementation strategy. As they deploy BI across the enterprise, innovative, industry-leading companies exhibit common patterns. By distilling these patterns into detailed guidelines, BI best practices like Cognos' 24 Ways™ help organizations get real value to every warehouse user as quickly as possible.

Because building a data warehouse is a complex process with many potential problem areas, hiring consultants is almost always a prerequisite to success. The range of consulting expertise available is wide: from analysts who evaluate vendors and products, to strategic consultants who help develop or refine strategies, to systems integrators who design and implement a complete solution. Many consulting organizations also offer onsite education and training for both IT and end users.

DEPLOYMENT, CONSULTING, AND TRAINING CONSIDERATIONS

- Evaluate need for consultants
- Hire experienced, highly qualified consultants
- Perform post-implementation evaluations
- Develop training documentation and courses
- Conduct training and measure results

Figure 7.1 Cognos' technical requirements.

Reprinted with permission from Cognos, Inc. 1999.

12-step Data Warehouse/Data Mart Navigator at www.atre.com/navigator. You may still be able to order a free poster! Here are her twelve steps; the site has much more detail:

1. Determine users' needs
2. Determine DBMS server platform
3. Determine hardware platform
4. Information and data modeling
5. Construction of metadata repository
6. Data acquisition and cleansing
7. Transformation, transportation, and population
8. Determine middleware connectivity
9. Prototype querying and reporting
10. Data mining
11. OLAP
12. Deployment and systems management

Note that there are other data warehousing methodologies out there, but they're generally not as publicly available as Shaku's.

Now let's look at data warehousing from Microsoft's point of view.

Microsoft Enters the Fray

To its credit, starting at least as early as 1996, Microsoft realized it couldn't offer all of the components required in a comprehensive data warehousing environment by itself. So it formed an alliance of industry players including Business Objects, ExecuSoft Systems, Informatica, NCR, Pilot Software, Platinum Technology (now owned by Computer Associates), Praxis International, and SAR AG and announced its Framework for Data Warehousing in September 1996 (see Figure 7.2).

As you can see, Microsoft's framework illustrates both the general nature of the process for building, using, and managing data marts and warehouses in an admittedly COM-centric world and shows how various components fit together.

Two enabling technologies comprise the core Data Warehousing Framework: the integrated metadata repository and the data transport layer (OLE DB). These technologies make possible the interoperability of many products and components involved in data warehousing:

- OLE DB provides for standardized, high-performance access to a wide variety of data, and allows for integration of multiple data types. As we know, Microsoft has been successful in promoting "extensions" to OLE DB for OLAP, data mining, and a dozen industry-specific extensions.
- Microsoft Repository (MR) provides an integrated metadata repository that is shared by the various components used in the data warehousing process. Shared metadata allows for the transparent integration of multiple products from a variety of vendors

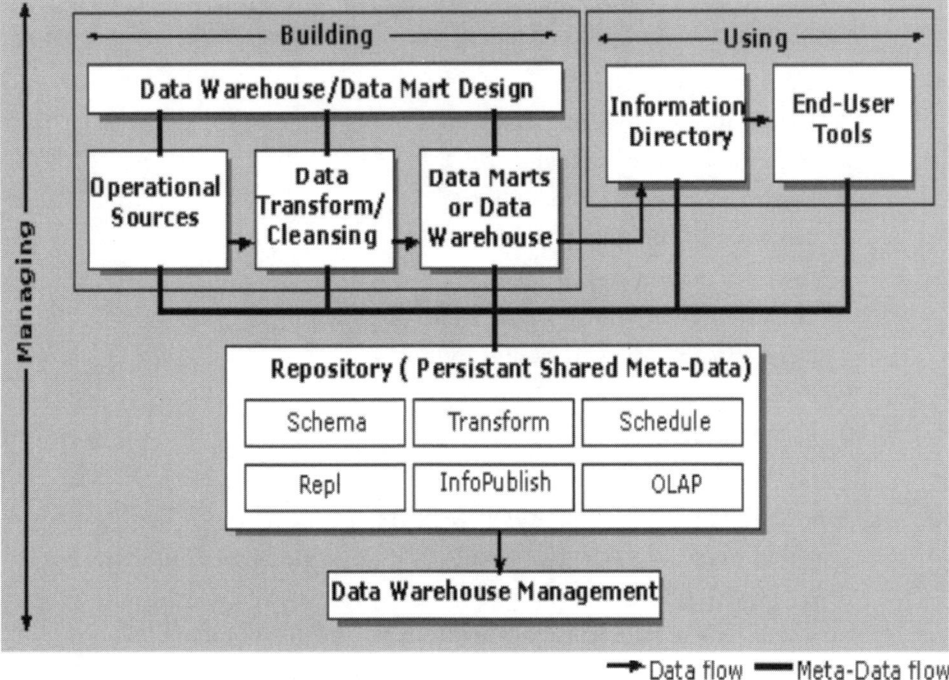

Figure 7.2 Microsoft's framework for data warehousing.

including mainframe ISAM/VSAM (indexed sequential access method/virtual storage access method) files, data in hierarchical databases and e-mail and file system stores, graphical, geographical, and multimedia data, and so on. Now in release 2.1, Microsoft Repository is slowly gaining support. Basically, the Microsoft Repository, which is a component of SQL Server in the MSDB database, is a database that stores descriptive information about software components and their relationships. It consists of an open information model (OIM) and a set of published COM interfaces. See Table 7.3 for a list of MR's information models. The Meta Data Coalition has given MR its blessing.

For more information on repositories, check out the following resources:

Proceedings from the Second IEEE Metadata Conference, held September 16 to 17, 1997, in Silver Spring, Maryland (www.llnl.gov/liv_comp/metadata/md97.html)

Association for Information and Image Management (AIIM), which provides repository specifications (www.aiim.org)

The Stanford Digital Libraries Project (walrus.stanford.edu/diglib/pub)

Reference site for D-Lib Magazine (www.dlib.org/reference.html)

Data Management Association (DAMA) International; sponsors an annual metadata conference (www.dama.org)

The Data Administration Newsletter (www.tdan.com)

Table 7.3 Summary of Information Models in Microsoft Repository 2.x

MODEL PREFIX	DESCRIPTION
RTIM	Repository Type Information model; the meta-meta model
UML	UML model; a representation of the conceptual UML 1.0 model, an industry standard for analyzing, specifying, designing, constructing, and visualizing the artifacts of a software system
UMX	UML Extension model; a set of generic extensions to UML that realizes the potential of some of UML 1.0's pre-defined stereotypes
DTM	Data Type model; a set of UML extensions that supply numerous common data types
CDE	Component Description model; a set of generic component-related UML extensions that describe runtime (executable) components and those components' specifications
COM	COM model; a set of COM-specific extensions to the CDE and the DTM
GEN	Generic model; a set of general-purpose interfaces that are relevant across diverse information models
DBM	Database model; a set of extensions to UML that cover generic database concepts
SQL	SQL Server model; a set of Microsoft SQL Server-specific extensions to the DBM
OCL	Oracle model; a set of Oracle-specific extensions to the DBM
DB2	DB2 model; a set of DB2-specific extensions to the DBM
IFX	Informix model; a set of Informix-specific extensions to the DBM
TFM	Database Transformation model; a description of movement of data between databases
OLP	OLAP model; an extension of the DBM that describes multi-dimensional databases
SIM	Semantic Information model; an extension of the DBM that lets users interact with database data without learning query languages

Source: Microsoft Corporation (msdn.microsoft.com/repository/oim)

TEXAS INSTRUMENTS HELPED TO DEFINE THE MICROSOFT REPOSITORY

The first time we heard about a Microsoft Repository was at an Enterprise Days briefing about OLE strategy back in 1995. At that briefing, Texas Instruments (TI) and Microsoft shared the stage to describe a strategy for a component repository that would help developers with application development. Our notes refer to the repository as an answer to component anarchy and part of Microsoft's strategy for moving toward *cooperating components*. The fact that TI was involved shouldn't be

too surprising. TI was a big CASE player. Remember how CASE was popular in the 80s and early 90s as a methodology and/or basket of diagramming notations for describing computer aided software engineering. Texas Instruments' Information Engineering Facility (IEF), which TI later renamed Composer by IEF, and which Sterling Software acquired in 1997 and renamed COOL:Gen, like other CASE tools, was built around a central repository.

THE POLITICS OF METADATA

In December 1998, Microsoft announced that it was joining the Meta Data Coalition (MDC), an industry group that attempts to bridge the gaps between proprietary metadata stores. The MDC has produced Meta Data Interface Standard (MDIS) 1.1, which promises to be a valuable basis for interoperability. For information about MDIS, see www.mdcinfo.com. Ironically, IBM, which was a charter member of the MDC and instrumental in developing the MDIS spec, pulled out of that group (coincidentally also in late 1998, when Microsoft joined) in order to focus its efforts on a single metadata exchange mechanism. IBM thinks that, "OMG and XMI is positively the way to go," according to Jeff Jones, Program Manager, Data Management Marketing, IBM Software Solutions. Muddying the very political waters of all this is the fact that Oracle unilaterally announced its "industry standard" Common Warehouse Metadata (CWM) that the OMG is supposedly working on as part of its XMI initiative. Needless to say, we think the SQL Server-hosted Microsoft Repository will prevail.

According to Microsoft's view of the data warehouse world, these are the key components:

- Operational data sources
- Design/development tools
- Data extraction and transformation tools
- DBMS capable of supporting MOLAP, ROLAP, and HOLAP multi-dimensional structures
- Data access and analysis tools
- System management tools

Practice Makes Perfect

Well, you're probably anxious to try your hand at creating your own data mart, and we propose to give you some practice. In the rest of this chapter, we'll lead you through creating an extremely simple, single-source data mart. In the next chapter, we'll up the ante a bit and show you how it isn't that much harder to create a data mart from multiple sources. We avoid calling it a data warehouse, because it seems to us that term should be reserved for something a bit grander than the "starter" projects we supply in the book.

Ready?

Creating a Data Mart

In this section, we look at how to create an actual data mart that we'll abbreviate as DM. We will use the tools within SQL Server 7, along with the ideas that go into creating a DM, to develop a business unit view of the WorkOrd database. Our goal is to provide "information" to the Canadian business unit of the firm using WorkOrd, using the data within the WorkOrd database itself.

As a background goal of our DM setup, we don't want to do anything to conflict with setting up a full-blown data warehouse in the future. In fact, we may wish to make our efforts the model that is used by other business units in the company to gain access to decision-making information. So we want to work as closely as possible with corporate to not do anything too unique.

Analysis

For the purposes of our project, let's assume that a company already maintains operational data in the form of our WorkOrd database. Internal applications, possibly with external data feeds, populate the tables within WorkOrd, on a per-request basis. Let's further assume that there is no corporate data warehouse in place to help with the summarization of our data, and further, that there are no plans to create such a DWH in the immediate future. For this example we have chosen to talk to someone at the corporate level to see what sort of data and naming standards they want to have in place, before our business units create decentralized data marts.

For our example, we will stick with the data-naming schemes adopted at the corporate level and use the same column names for our local DM as exist in the corporate WorkOrd database. This will also make it easier to share information with other business units.

Other things to consider during the Analysis phase are any security concerns related to the data within WorkOrd. For our example, the DM will be read-only so corporate isn't concerned with changes made to the data. It is also assumed that the business units have full access to the data within WorkOrd.

Overview of WorkOrd Contents

Once we get beyond the big picture topics, then we need to look into WorkOrd to see what type of *information* we can glean out of it.

WorkOrd contains work order detail information, for work orders originating from the offices shown in Table 7.4.

What we'll begin with as our DM goal, is to try and look for things that pop out as areas of data that (while we collect data), isn't used directly today. We want to pull out the data that corresponds to one business unit. For the purposes of our example we'll pretend (don't you love that word?) to include only Montreal and Edmonton.

Table 7.4 The tlkpSites WorkOrd Table

SITEID	SITE
1	Toronto
2	London
3	Hamilton
4	Ottawa
5	Montreal
6	Vancouver
7	Calgary
8	Edmonton
9	Regina
10	St. Johns
11	Quebec City
12	Kingston
13	Boston

Business Needs First

Before you build, or think about building anything at all, the first thing that you'll want to do is to capture the essence of the business needs that prompted your data mart project.

- Why do they (your customers) want to do this?
- What is missing in the currently available data (if any) that they need?
- What can be added around the process and into the captured data to enhance your final answer?

It is good practice to check occasionally with other business units, who may have the same needs as you to ensure that they have already started a similar DM project. If nothing else, you can present a "unified front" of end-user requirements to the overall corporate entity at the point in time when they *are* ready to consider an enterprise DWH.

"Seeing" What You Have

As you may remember from Chapter 3, our WorkOrd database contains work order request information, keyed by salesman and city. You should use the steps in Chapter 3 to create a SQL Server version of WorkOrd if you haven't done so already.

Even if you plan to create a completely standalone data mart, and there are no corporate DWH or other rules in place, as a responsible corporate citizen you should try to provide some infrastructure around your work. You can do this by coming up with reasonable naming schemes, data update schedules that don't conflict with production

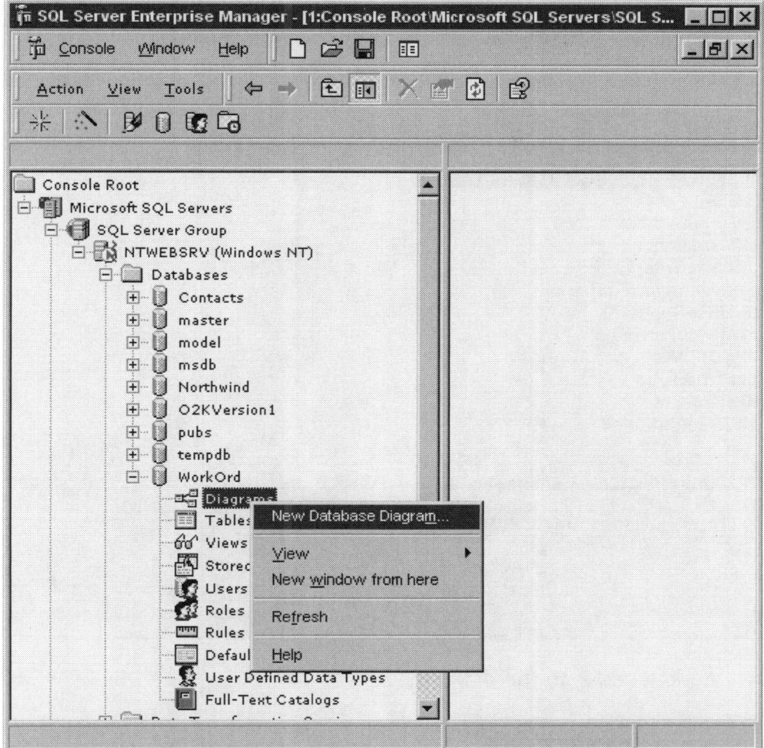

Figure 7.3 Finding the diagramming tool.

data requirements and, perhaps even diagramming the look of the tables that will go into making up your data mart.

As part of our project, we'll go into the steps to diagram the WorkOrd database tables. Fortunately, SQL Server's Enterprise Manager has a Database Diagramming tool to make this all a bit easier than in the past. The first step is to run EM. Right-click on the WorkOrd database. Then right-click on Diagrams, within the options available under WorkOrd (see Figure 7.3). From there, right-click on the New Database Diagram pop-up menu selection. This starts up the diagramming tool.

Then, using the subsequent screen shown in Figure 7.3 you can choose which of the WorkOrd database tables you want to include in your diagram.

If you're in the Database Diagram tool (see Figure 7.4) and trying to move tables from one (obscured) portion of the display to another, remember that you can select multiple tables with a click-drag mouse operation and move them all at once. You can *also* click-drag from the visible portion of the screen out to hidden areas in the same movement—the diagram tool will move the screen for you in the direction you're attempting to select.

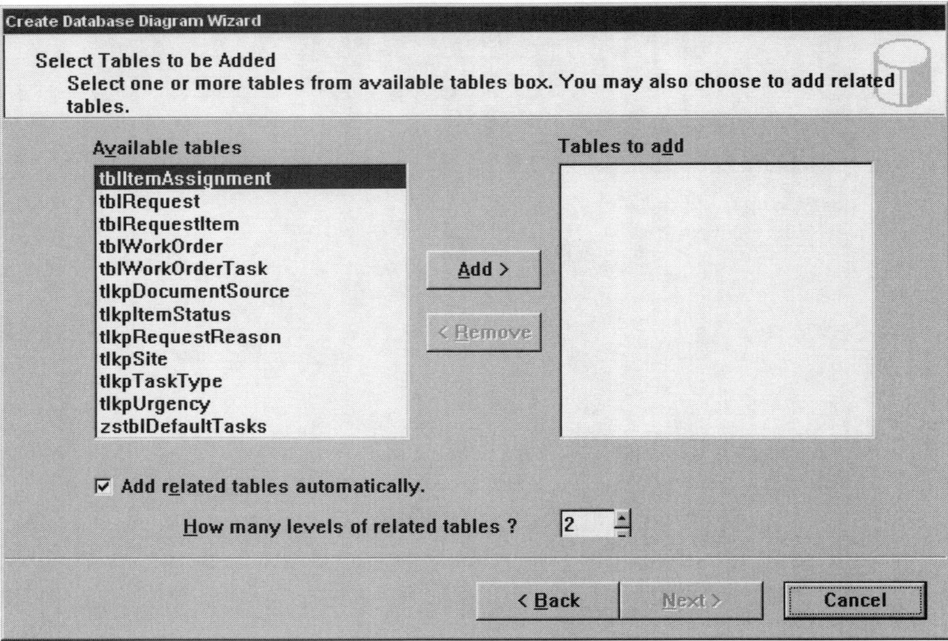

Figure 7.4 Adding tables to the diagram.

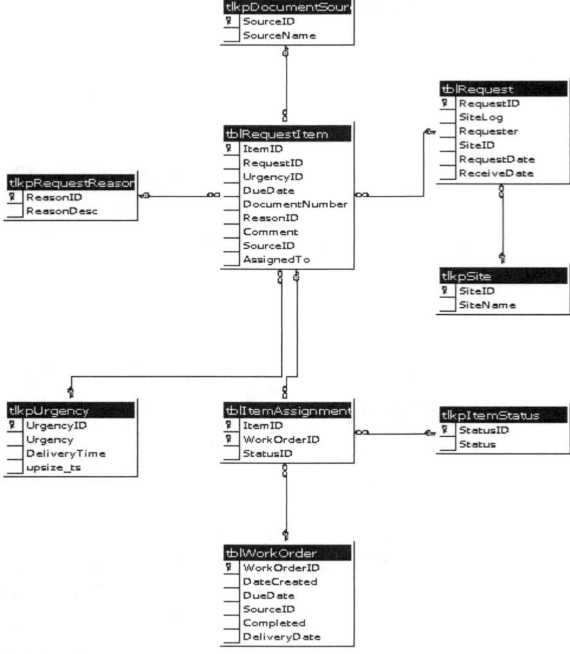

Figure 7.5 The end result—an annotated ER diagram.

Note that we supply a complete WorkOrd database diagram that depicts the inter-table relationships on the CD.

Creating the SQL to Load the DM

Next, we're going to pull from the overall operational data source (WorkOrd), a data set specifically for the Montreal (siteID=5) and Edmonton (siteid=8) offices. We're also going to summarize this data by Document Source, within that office. While we provide a few other data fields within this summarized, read-only view of the data, our goal is to answer one specific question initially—how to demonstrate the power that a regional data mart can provide.

To do this, we want to show our regional product manager which source (CD, Paper, or Server) is the most requested in each of these offices. In order to keep track of this, we need to understand things such as whether or not our customer base moves from one medium to another over time. This allows us to set up more favorable long-term supplier contracts, negotiate more favorable transportation deals, and help to ensure that we keep an adequate supply of future materials, just by analyzing the current flow of data into the data mart today. Notice that each of these goals also has a hidden agenda—*we are better placed against our regional competitors by using today's data to assess our future needs*. Presenting this sort of example to our regional management team should make it relatively easy to interest them in doing this for other areas within the organization. Some other immediate questions might be in what cities are sales growing the fastest (implying that this is where we might want to consider new hires next year).

So, logically, we want to present information to the regional managers that resemble something like that shown in Figure 7.5. Using this information, they can then determine the relative quantities of paper versus CDs used within each office in this Canadian Business Unit. From this they can be better prepared to deal with firms that sell them paper and printing supplies, CD-creation materials, services (such as label making), and the other things that go into the production of these items. The business unit can also determine if their is a shift in customer demand from paper to CDs, which also allows the business unit to adjust paper and CD supplier contracts as time goes on.

Just so that you can play along at home, the SQL query in the following code is used to derive the totals found in Figure 7.6. The number 5 represents the SiteID for Montreal and 8 is the SiteID for Edmonton. We were able to easily generate this SQL statement by creating a view in EM as shown in Figure 7.7. Using the View tool, you can model the information around until you get it to return the results that you want.

Site	DocumentSource	CountOfSourceID
Montreal	CD	2004
Montreal	Paper	2139
Edmonton	CD	44517
Edmonton	Paper	23931

Figure 7.6 Seeing how much of each source our sites use.

```
SELECT tlkpSite.SiteName, tlkpDocumentSource.SourceName,
  COUNT(tblRequestItem.SourceID) AS CountOfSourceID
        FROM tblRequest INNER JOIN
  tblRequestItem ON
  tblRequest.RequestID = tblRequestItem.RequestID INNER JOIN
  tlkpDocumentSource ON
  tblRequestItem.SourceID = tlkpDocumentSource.SourceID INNER
   JOIN tlkpSite ON tblRequest.SiteID = tlkpSite.SiteID
WHERE (tblRequest.SiteID = 5) OR
    (tblRequest.SiteID = 8)
GROUP BY tlkpSite.SiteName, tlkpDocumentSource.SourceName
```

The view creation tool in Figure 7.7 works very much like the way queries are designed in Microsoft Access. You choose the tables to add to the view, then select the actual fields (columns) to display and relate the tables to build the desired result—just as you would in Access. The SQL Server designer version is a bit nicer than the one in Access, in that you can see the SQL directly within a separate panel, instead of having to open a separate window with the Access View SQL option. In the same way, the view's resulting data can be displayed directly within a separate panel beneath the view's design, instead of having to go to a separate window.

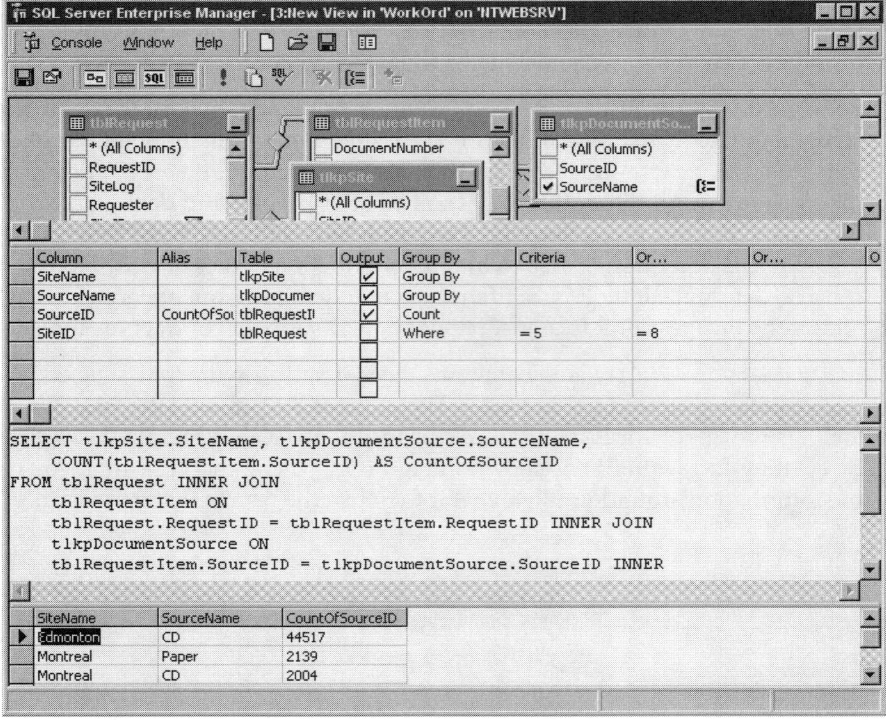

Figure 7.7 Using the View options to build our result set.

Following up the Sale

Once we've convinced the local management team that a data mart can be used to help with current and future business decisions, we need to be ready to support ongoing DM usage. The very next thing that management will probably want is a guarantee that the data is up to date. In other words, they're going to want assurances that the information within the data mart refreshed on a periodic (as in nightly, weekly, monthly, and so on) basis. We can use SQL Server's DTS to update our data mart information and create a DTS *package* to do this. A DTS package can hold, among other things, the instructions to create or refresh a data mart database. This includes where to pull the data mart's data from and exactly where to place the data once retrieved.

To set up a DTS package within Enterprise Manager, navigate the WorkOrd hierarchy down to the Data Transformation Services option. Click on Local Packages and then right-click New Package. From here, we will create a new database, called WorkOrdDM, a simple data mart that will hold just the information relevant to our local business unit—remember from Chapter 3 that there are several ways to run the DTS wizards and to create packages. You can also use the scripting languages to enhance transformation services within DTS to add values from lookup tables to your result set as part of the local data mart load.

From the DTS window, choose Data. Here's where we select the actual operational data set that will be included in our data mart; this is in our example in the WorkOrd database. So select option 1, MS OLE DB Provider for SQL Server. On the resulting General tab, choose our local SQL Server as our existing connection and pick WorkOrd for our Database. Notice that this places a SQL Server icon into the client area of our DTS workspace.

Next, let's create our Data Mart database, our DTS Target. This is the database that we'll call WorkOrdDM.This database can, and probably should be, on a different data server in a production application, but you can create it on your local SQL Server machine just to see how it works. You'll need to do this before proceeding. Figure 7.8 shows the connection screen that you use to establish a connection to our new DM database.

There are several ways to go about using DTS to load the data into our data mart. We can create a task, which would run on a user-specified basis. To create a task, from the DTS window, choose Task. Selecting this option presents you with the menu choices shown in Figure 7.9. But just to show you what the task screens look like, go on to create a SQL Task (option 3. Execute SQL Task). You can see that you have a number of options for exactly how to transfer this information using either process or data-driven methods.

As your client's interest in this project increases, they may then desire to see more detail or higher levels of summarization. To allow for this you simply need to alter the local database (WorkOrdDM) to encompass the newly-desired fields and change the DTS package to pull the new detail from the central site to load these new fields.

However, we don't need to create a special task to create our WorkOrdDM database, since we can handle the translation ourselves using straight SQL, so cancel out of the task screen.

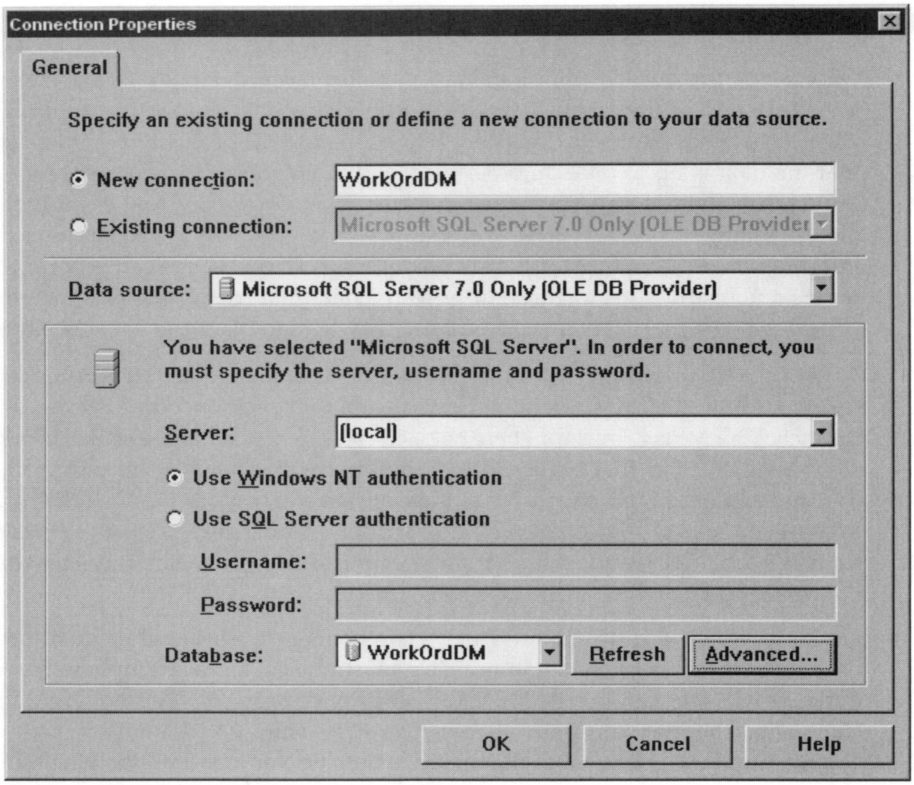

Figure 7.8 Using DTS to create a connection for our data mart.

Figure 7.9 Task creation options.

Visually Connecting

Now—and you're going to like this—all we need to do to move our data from our operational data to a DM is a few clicks with a mouse. Using the Control key and your mouse, first select the origination connection (WorkOrd), then our destination connection (WorkOrdDM). Click on the Workflow menu and then Add Transform. This generates an on-screen image like the one shown in Figure 7.10. The gray line that is drawn shows the direction that the data flows in. Keep this handy for explaining to IT that you really are performing Read-Only operating for the corporate operational data. Click on the gray line to verify or change any of the parameters that are used to move the data from the source to the target database.

To test your package, go to the Package menu and choose Execute. This refreshes the data in the WorkOrdDM database. Note that we only move the four summary level rows into the WorkOrdDM database each time. You will want to apply a TimeDate column to WorkOrdDM so that we can begin to build a time series of the results each time the transformation occurs.

Figures 7.11 through 7.13 show you the different tabs that are available in the DTS transformation dialogs. Here you can review the actual DDL code that is executed to create the DM tables, the properties of the columns that are created, and look to see exactly what source data columns are used to populate the target DM data columns.

Figure 7.12 shows exactly what the resulting data columns within the DM will look like including their name, data type, size, whether the field can contain nulls, and so on. If you want to, you can adjust these at this point.

Figure 7.13 shows how the data columns from the source database are mapped into columns within our data mart. You can choose to do a direct 1:1 column copy or,

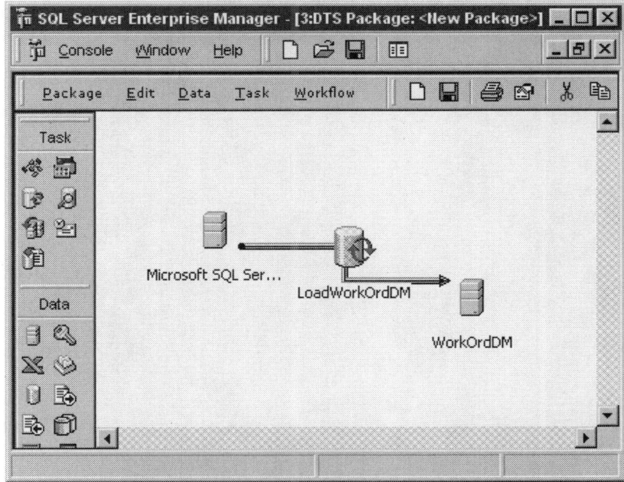

Figure 7.10 Graphical view of a Data Transformation Package.

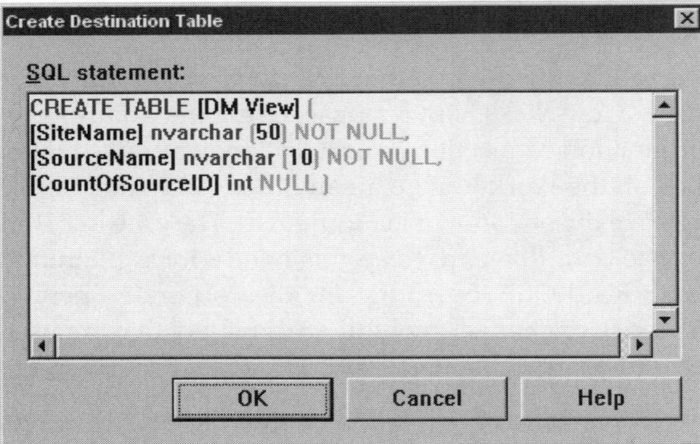

Figure 7.11 Reviewing the Transformation DDL syntax.

change the option at the bottom of this screen to apply an ActiveX script against the column when processed.

If you select to use an ActiveX script, the screen shown in Figure 7.14 is presented. Here you can work with combinations of source and target table columns, scripting code,

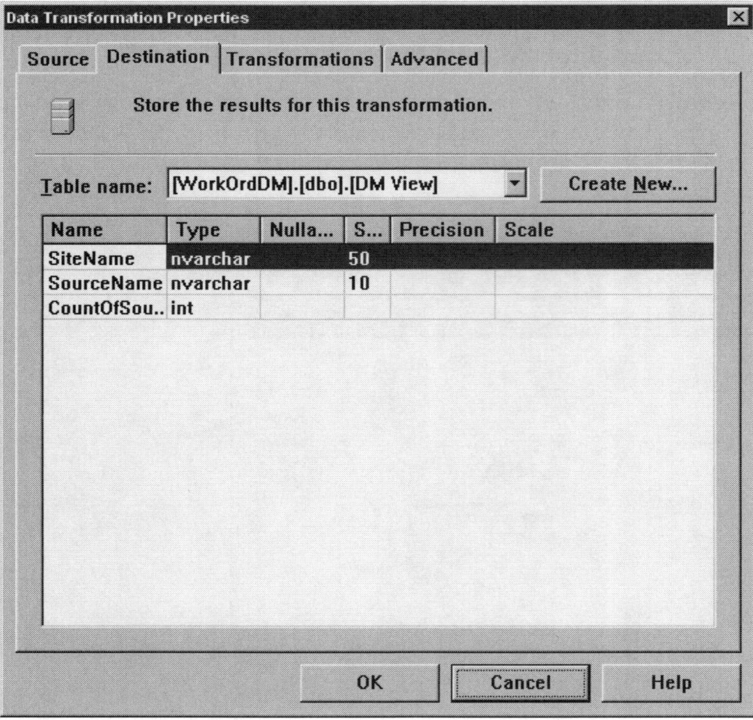

Figure 7.12 Graphically seeing what columns will be created.

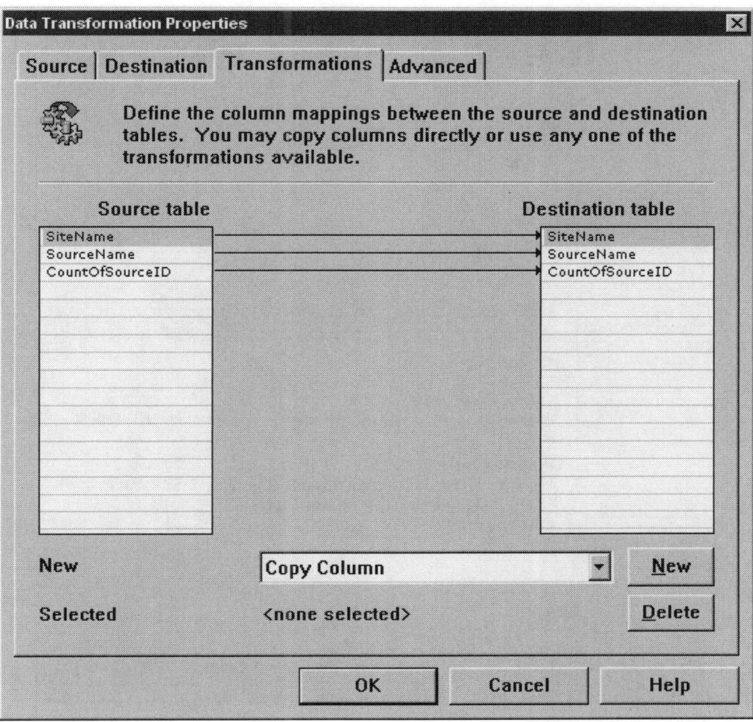

Figure 7.13 Viewing the Transformation Column Map.

and selection boxes of Boolean, and other functional operators to set up script to be applied against a column when the package is run. This is a very powerful feature—one which complete, third-party packages exist for today.

The last step in our process is to actually execute the transformation. If any errors occur, they are graphically represented with the system error icon shown in Figure 7.15. To see exactly what the problem is and then correct it, click on the row with the error icon. One immediate issue that frequently occurs on big data loads is a SQL time-out problem, which is the problem shown in Figure 7.15. To allow yourself a bit more time for a large SQL query to execute, you can click on the gray line that connects the two data connections and adjust the time that the query is allowed to run in from there.

Once we have worked through setting up this package, we can save it to reuse later (see Figure 7.16). You can save the package into SQL Server, the Repository, or as a separate file. You can also give it a password so that you can control who actually gets to use it. We saved our DTS package with the name MonthyDMLoad.

After saving your DTS package you can now apply additional DTS features against it. For example, you can set up an automated schedule for when this package is used to refresh the DM data as shown in Figure 7.17. This screen shows that you can cause the package to run on any date, at any time, and even schedule a start and stop date for it

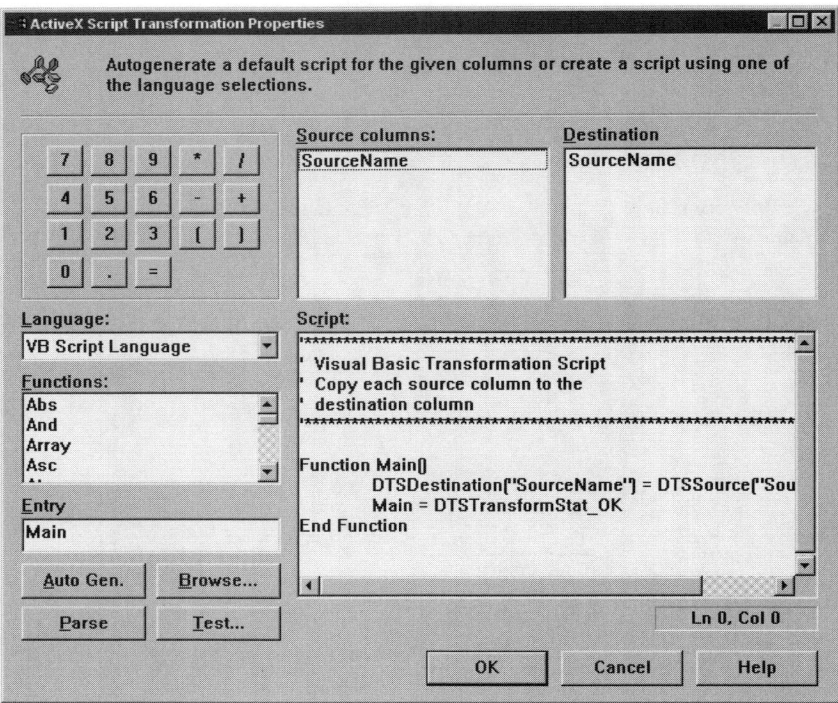

Figure 7.14 Data Transformation Script Editor.

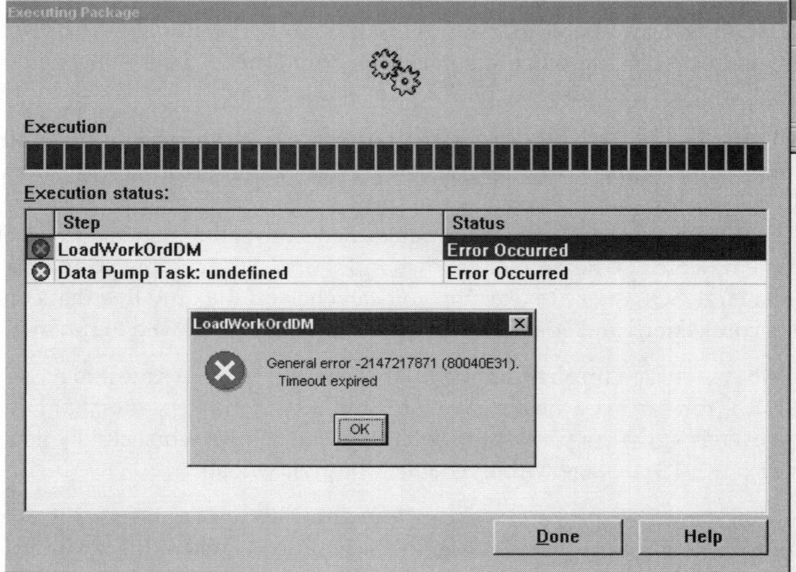

Figure 7.15 Handling transformation errors.

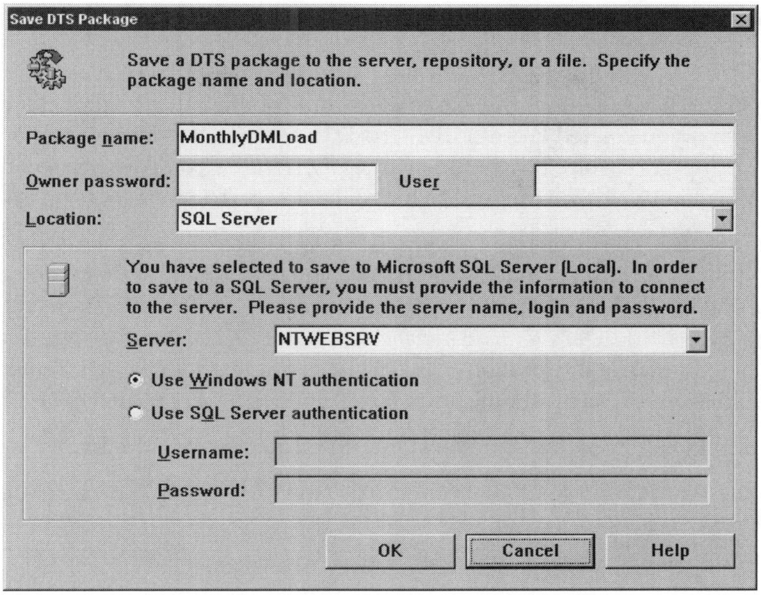

Figure 7.16 Saving the monthly DM load package.

to run a specified number of times. By now you should start to see the amazing power that SQL Server 7 provides, along with DTS, to set up data marts regardless of whether they are local to the SQL Server machine or in a wholly different environment.

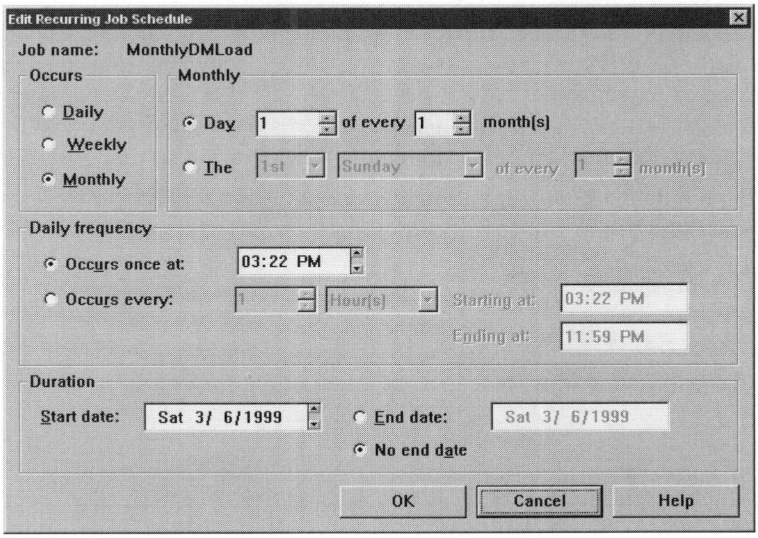

Figure 7.17 Scheduling refresh dates.

Loading the WorkOrdDM from the CD

On the book's CD, you'll see a ZIP file called WorkOrdDM.ZIP which contains the data (.MDF) and log files (.LDF) for the extremely simple one-table data mart created in this chapter. Even if you created WordOrdDM via DTS as described in this chapter, we urge you to try to "open" it from the ZIP files on the CD, because you'll learn a technique that comes in very handy when you need to move databases from one location to another.

The trick is to use the system stored procedure sp_attach_db. sp_attach_db is a fairly complex stored procedure, and it's often used in conjunction with sp_detach_db, so you'll want to study its syntax in *Books Online* (*sp_attach_db (T-SQL)*). There's also a great Knowledge Base article, Q224071 *INF: Moving SQL Server 7.0 Databases to a New Location* that describes how to change the location of the data and log files for any SQL Server 7.0 database. (You must have system administrator (sa) privileges to use sp_attach_db.)

To try your hand at "moving" the WorkOrdDM created by Bill, do this:

1. Copy the WordOrdDM.ZIP file from the CD to your \mssql7\data directory and unzip the two files.
2. Start Enterprise Manager and run the Query Analyzer.
3. Enter these commands:

```
Use master
Go
sp_attach_db 'TestDM1' 'c:\mssql7\data\WorkOrdDM.MDF'
```

4. Press the F5 key or otherwise execute the script. (The log file will automatically be attached.) Assuming the script completed successfully, exit Query Analyzer and then exit Enterprise Manager. Then run Enterprise Manager again in order to "see" the new database.
5. Expand the hierarchy tree in EM and navigate down to TestDM1 and then to Tables. You should notice one user table called DM View. Because this table has an embedded space in its name, you should rename it DMView. The easiest way to do that is to right-click on the table name in EM's right-hand pane that lists all the tables, choose Rename, and enter the new name without the embedded space.
6. Now fire up Query Analyzer and make sure you can use the new database that you created via the sp_attach_db command:

```
use TestDM1
Go
select * from DMView
```

You should see the same four rows that are listed in Figure 7.6.

Closing the Loop

This chapter focuses on the read-only type of DM/DWH solution since that is how they are generally deployed in the corporate world. However, there may be cases where local and the central management groups will eventually want to create new data elements to store new bits of information that they come up with by studying the data within the marts.

As an example of this, the Montreal office in our examples may want to share with their sister Edmonton office any evolving trend information that they can derive by studying the document usage statistics. The regional office that Montreal and Edmonton report to may also be interested in having these offices share their findings. The same may apply to the overall corporate entity that the regions report to. Corporate may decide that it wants to gather this information on a monthly basis, so that they can more closely monitor ongoing vendor agreements and contracts.

Once new data elements are desired they will need to be created in the central operational data area and updated. The cycle is completed by pulling the new operational data back out to the corporate DWH or the data marts in the field.

Making this entire cycle of information flow easily is difficult, since corporate entities tend to only allow read-only operational data access for their field offices, branches, and regions.

Summary

Again, the DTS facilities in SQL Server 7 show their strength and usefulness in the DM/DWH application area. DTS makes it easy to create simple data marts, with automated refreshes, and perform data transformations. As always, some of your biggest problems in this area will be addressing company policies and politics in order to move forward. And it will be at least a little while before you are allowed to update the corporate operational data with the results of your data mart exploratory experiences.

Congratulations! You've just built your first data mart. That experience, combined with the concepts presented at the beginning of the chapter, should have you rarin' to go to build you own data mart or warehouse. But before you do, you may want to read the next two chapters to how to build a data mart from multiple data sources and how to build OLAP cubes.

CHAPTER 8

Project #5: Creating a Multi-Source Data Mart with Data Transformation Services

Goal

The goal of this chapter is to show you how to use Data Transformation Services (DTS) to create a data mart from multiple, disparate data sources. In other words, how to take data stored in different formats such as text, Access, and Excel and, using DTS, combine them into a single format in SQL Server.

YOU WILL NEED

- ✔ Microsoft SQL Server 7 with Service Pack 1 (SP1) Installed. SP1 fixed quite a few problems with Data Transformation Services (DTS). For details on the DTS-related problems resolved by SP1, please see section 5.8 of the readme.txt file that accompanies the SP.
- ✔ If you plan on using a WIN95 or WIN98 computer with Internet Explorer 5, you need to apply the fix discussed in Knowledge Base Article: Q225084.
- ✔ MSDataMart script and data files on CD-ROM

Overview

To fully understand this chapter you must have a fundamental understanding of both data marts and the star schema database design technique. We'll provide a brief overview of star schema database design, but if you aren't familiar with basic data mart and data warehouse principles, please take a few minutes to at least skim the concepts at the beginning of Chapter 7 before continuing.

In the Goal Section we mentioned that we plan to work with disparate data sources. When we use the term *disparate* we are referring to sources whose data isn't generated by a single system and most likely isn't stored in the same format. For example, there are thousands of companies who still use systems that store data in a proprietary format as well as other systems that are *open*—ODBC or OLE DB compliant.

WHO'S OPEN AND WHO'S CLOSED

Systems that store data in a proprietary format are referred to as *closed*, while those that store their data in ODBC or OLE DB-compliant formats are referred to as *open*.

When you're dealing with systems whose data format is proprietary, the ability to report on and analyze data captured by the system is often restricted to the utilities provided by the software vendor. Most have report generators, but very few have utilities that allow you to perform any meaningful analysis. So, when you want to perform any interesting analysis on the data you must get it into a format that can be manipulated by your data analysis software. This limitation is one of the reasons there are virtually no new systems developed that utilize a proprietary format and that the existing systems that suffer from this limitation are being redesigned to use database backends like SQL Server 7 that allow data analysis and sharing to be accomplished very easily. The fact that these systems are dying out, however, doesn't mean we can ignore them. We think that most of you, at one time or another will have to move data from one of these legacy systems into SQL Server. Chances are that a text file will be your main vehicle for migrating proprietary data into SQL Server. Why? Well, all of the proprietary systems that we've worked with have a reporting tool that allows you to create custom reports and output (spool) the data generated by the report to a text file. This allows you to consolidate and sort data from the closed system and get it into a format that can be imported into one that is open. This is certainly crude, but you will most likely run into a business situation where this approach is necessary and this chapter will detail how it should be handled. This chapter will also show you how to transfer/transform data from Excel and Access into a SQL Server data mart.

As we said, virtually all new systems developed within the past several years have been open and thus are either ODBC compliant, OLE DB compliant, or both. The manufacturers of these systems (and/or third-party vendors) provide ODBC or OLE DB drivers that allow you to access their data and transfer it to any other ODBC- or OLE DB-compliant system. The ability to share data in this manner has had a tremendous affect on the ease of implementing data warehousing and data mart solutions. A simple data transfer between two open systems is shown in Figure 8.1.

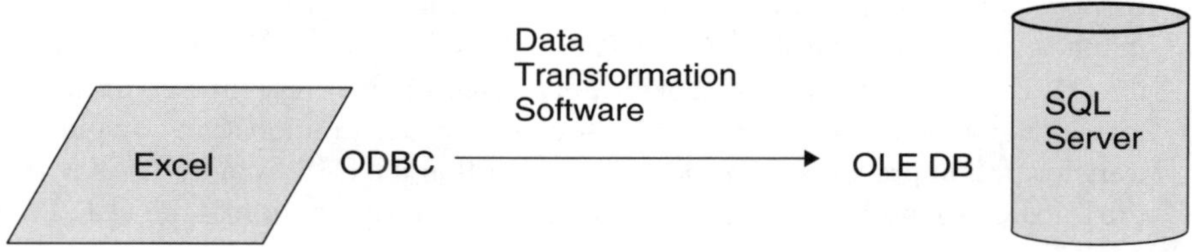

Figure 8.1 Transferring data with open systems.

Microsoft has been a big proponent of data sharing and has made a concerted effort to give all their products the ability to *talk* to one another. In addition to this effort, they have gone a step further with SQL Server 7 and provided technology that was specifically designed to help transfer data from one format to another. This technology is referred to as Data Transformation Services (DTS) and is one of the most useful new features found in SQL Server 7. You've probably already used DTS (either in the last chapter or earlier in this book), but we still want to have a quick review of what we plan to use in *this* chapter so that you don't have to go to another chapter to brush up on the concepts required for this project.

The main tool that we work with in this chapter is the DTS Package Designer (DTSPD). The DTSPD allows you to graphically define the steps involved in moving data from a source to a destination. Among other things, it allows you to specify the:

- Data source
- Data destination
- Data transformations
- Events that need to occur before and after the transfer

A key component that we use in the packages is the DTS Data Pump. The Data Pump is the software that (bet you couldn't guess) facilitates the transfer of data. It uses the available software drivers to connect to, read, and transfer data from the same or different storage formats. The processes that the Data Pump uses are shown in Figure 8.2.

DTS DATA PUMP DOESN'T LIMIT YOU TO SQL SERVER

The DTS Data Pump doesn't restrict you to transferring data between a SQL Server source and destination. Your source and destination can be any data store as long as it has an ODBC or OLE DB driver or is a text file. You can, for example, transfer data directly from an Excel spreadsheet to an Access DB, because both have drivers that allow the Data Pump to connect to and transfer data.

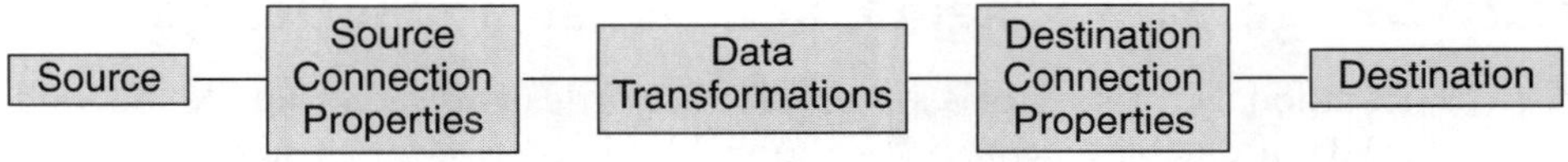

Figure 8.2 DTS Data Pump.

By now, you've probably used either the Import/Export Wizard (a component of DTS) or maybe even designed a simple DTS Package. In this chapter we go to the next level with the DTSPD and show you some of its more powerful features—notably its ability to transform data while it's in transit from the source to the destination. Can you guess where this transformation process will occur? Remember that the DTS Data Pump is what facilitates the transfer, so the ability to change the data must be a function of the Data Pump.

The Data Pump allows you to change the data with either scripting languages or a custom transformation created with a COM object or an .EXE file. We'll cover scripting language transformations in this chapter, but *Books Online* has a few topics such as *Extending DTS with Custom Applications* that you can read that cover COM/.EXE-based transformations. The Data Pump allows you to transform data in transit using VBScript, JScript, or PerlScript. Since the bulk of you will already be comfortable with VBScript, this makes it the logical choice and so all of our transformations will be completed with it. Don't worry, if you're not a VBScript guru, the transformations created in this chapter are fairly straightforward and are explained in detail.

Before plunging into the project, we need to cover some basic data transformation concepts. We will transform data in one of two ways:

1. During the transfer process
2. After the transfer process

A simple example will help show the difference. Let's say that the source data uses a cryptic code to designate geographical location, but you want the destination to contain a value that's easily recognized. When the first method is used, the transformation of the cryptic code occurs while it's in transit from the source to the destination. With the second approach, we store the data in a temporary table at the destination and convert the value ("scrub" the data) inside the database. The reasons to use one over the other depend on, among other things, the amount of data involved and the skill level of the person doing the transfer. If the amount of data to be transformed is significant and complex transformations need to be performed, then you might realize some performance gains by implementing the scrubbing inside the database. If complex transformations need to be performed and your scripting abilities are limited, then your only choice will be to implement post-transfer scrubbing using T-SQL. The two different processes are shown in Figure 8.3.

There is one more topic that we need to cover before we start the project: *star schema database design technique*. We provide a pretty dense mini-tutorial of what's a pretty complex topic, so if you don't "get" it the first time you read it, don't worry. Just "bookmark" this section as a handy set of recipes for both normalized and de-normalized star schema databases.

OLTP Design, Star Schema, and Dimensional Design

Traditional OLTP systems are almost always designed according to the tried-and-true tenets of database *normalization* to yield related two-dimensional tables. OLAP systems (which we'll talk about in more detail in Chapter 9) are designed for multidimensional manipulation and according to the dimensional model. A star schema

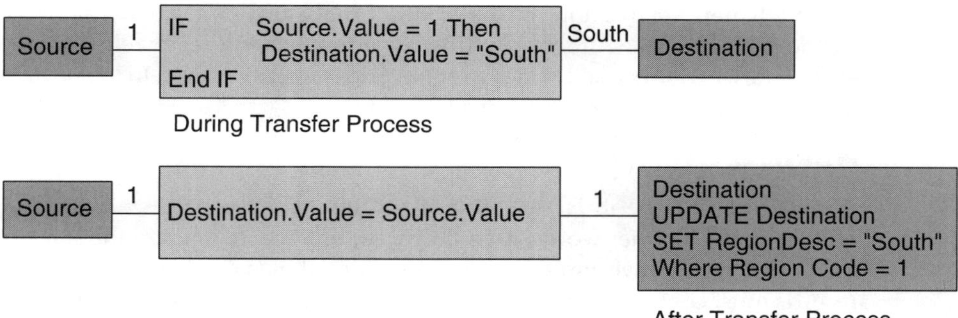

Figure 8.3 Transformation processes.

design is basically a relational approximation of the OLAP data model. To appreciate star schemas, you really have to understand traditional design of normalized systems. What follows is a cram course.

Designing a Normalized Database

OLTP systems that use relational databases are typically designed as *normalized* databases. You create tables for entities, make sure each table has a primary key, identify relationships between tables, and "link" them, typically by placing a copy of the primary key from the "one" side of a one-to-many relationship in the "many" table. The reason you go to all of this trouble is to avoid what are called *update anomalies* (where you have more than one copy of data in the database, but updates are only done to one) and to ensure data consistency during transactions. A well-designed database should also be easier to maintain. The downsides of normalized databases is that you generally end up with a lot of little tables that:

1. May need to be indexed
2. Often require performance-sapping JOINs to recombine the tables into a meaningful form in response to end-user queries
3. Have two-dimensional table structures that don't allow users to have a multidimensional view on their data

Is Normalization Just for Eggheads?

The first time I (Karen) ran across this term in a database context, it conjured up memories from physics and vectors. "Normal," I remembered, was another way of saying perpendicular or orthogonal. One tried to *normalize* things to get them in terms of a unit vector.

Think of normalization as an analytic process that produces a stable set of data items and results in semantic integrity. E.F. Codd refers to normalization as "a very simple elimination procedure;" others use the term *decomposition*. The point is that normalization works from an original starter design.

Although there are five normal forms, most professionals view *third Normal Form (3NF)* as "normal enough." Although additional normalization may yield a more pure and elegant design, it invariably does so at the price of performance. In the next sections we provide descriptions for the normal forms.

First Normal Form (1NF)

A table is said to be in First Normal Form (1NF) if it contains no repeating groups of data items. In other words, all occurrences of a record contain the same number of fields and don't have multiple occurrences of the "same" field within one record; records must contain atomic values (no multi-value fields) for all attributes. Additionally, one or more columns should have been assigned primary key status in tables that meet the criteria for 1NF. Here are some examples of tables that *aren't* in 1NF because of repeating groups:

PATIENT
Patient (key)
Address
HomePhone
1stVisitDate
1stVisitDiagnosis
1stVisitCharge
2ndVisitDate
2ndVisitDiagnosis
2ndVisitCharge
...

EMPLOYEE
EmployeeName (key)
Address
HomePhone
WorkExt
School1
Degree1
School2
Degree2
School3
Degree3
...

INVOICE
Invoice (key)
InvoiceDate
CustomerName
Account#
Item1
Quantity1
Unitprice1
Item2
Quantity2
UnitPrice2
...

We imagine that most of you intuitively see the problems with the previous tables. What is the maximum number of patient visits—or degrees, or invoice items—that we should plan for? If we overestimate, we'll end up with a lot of space-consuming blank fields filled with nulls. Nulls, by the way, are a problem in themselves, since not all DBMSs treat nulls quite the same way. On the other hand, if we underestimate, we'll run into problems when we need more fields than we've provided.

Solution? Create a new table for the repeating fields, where each group of repeating fields has its own row. This second table becomes the detail or child table and is related to its master or parent table in a many-to-one type relationship. The detail tables in our examples might be called PatientVisits, EmployeeDegrees, and InvoiceItems.

Second Normal Form (2NF)

A table is in Second Normal Form (2NF) if, in addition to meeting the criteria of 1NF, all non-key attributes are functionally dependent on the entire key. *Primary keys* are fields or combination of fields that provide unambiguous reference to individual records. 2NF only pertains to tables with *composite keys*—keys that consist of more than one attribute. If your table doesn't have any composite keys and is in 1NF, it's automatically in 2NF as well.

To understand functional dependencies, consider a formal definition: For any relation R, attribute A if functionally dependent on attribute B if, for every valid instance, the value of B determines the value of A.

One way to think of second normal form is that it precludes multi-thematic tables. Look at the following examples of tables that aren't in 2NF because of partial key functional dependencies. In the first table, you have a combination of both invoice and product data. In the second table, you store both product and supplier data. Both cases are almost guaranteed to result in data redundancy and all the headaches that redundancy implies, like modification and deletion anomalies. Anomaly, as you know, is a euphemism for problem. Look at the second table and assume you order a dozen products from the same supplier. What if the supplier moves? You'll have to update his address data in the Product table for all of the products you order from him. If you don't, you've lost your data integrity, since the supplier's address will no longer be an unambiguous value.

INVOICE	**PRODUCT**
Invoice# (key)	ProductCode (key)
InvoiceDate	ProductName
ProductCode (key)	ProductDescription
ProductName	SupplierName (key)
ProductDescription	SupplierAddress
ProductSize	SupplierPhone
ProductWeight	SupplierContact
InvoiceQuantity	QOH
InvoicePrice	Cost
UnitPrice	

So far, so good, but what about 3NF?

Third Normal Form (3NF)

A table that, in addition to meeting the criteria for 2NF, contains no transitive dependencies is said to be in Third Normal Form (3NF). A data item or attribute is transitively dependent on another data item (the key) if the attribute data item is functionally dependent on a second attribute data item, which in turn is functionally dependent on the key data item.

Does that definition leave you cold? Try this: transitive dependencies occur when a data item in a record is not a key, but identifies other data items as though it were a key. Don't be surprised if normalizing to 2NF also achieves 3NF. Real-world examples with multi-thematic tables like the INVOICE and PRODUCT tables shown previously will generally have transitive dependencies. And those transitive dependencies will tend to disappear when you split the tables to gain 2NF.

It's important to recognize when a table is in third normal form, since 3NF has become the de facto standard in the industry as "normalized enough." Here's an easy way to remember 3NF: non-key fields that are "determined by the key, the whole key, and nothing but the key."

Beyond 3NF

If "normalized enough" offends your sense of purity, bear in mind that most tables that meet the requirements for 3NF also satisfy the criteria for 4NF and 5NF. Fourth and fifth normal forms both deal with rarely-encountered multi-valued dependencies. Somewhere between 3NF and 4NF, however, is another widely-recognized normal form, *Boyce-Codd Normal Form (BCNF)*. You may want to know the subtle distinction.

BCNF will differ from 3NF only for tables that have more than one candidate composite key. *Candidate keys* aren't simply mega-keys that contain all the attributes in a table, for example. Candidate keys are those keys that contain the same number of attributes as the chosen key which itself is usually referred to as the primary key or superkey. Clear as mud, right? Consider an Employee table that contains both social security numbers and employee IDs, with the social security number as the primary key. The employee ID field represents a candidate key.

Since BCNF only affects tables with composite keys, it's really just another manifestation of the multi-theme table problem, so often you'll intuitively achieve BCNF when you decompose tables to attain 2NF. Consider, for example, a project management database where employees can be either project team members or advisors. Assume further that employees can be assigned to several projects concurrently, and that projects are assigned one or more project advisors, but that any individual advises no more than one project. A ProjectEmployee table (ProjectNumber, ProjectMember, ProjectAdvisor) might be established with ProjectNumber and ProjectMember as the primary key. The combination of these two data items uniquely identifies the ProjectAdvisor. But ProjectMember and ProjectAdvisor also uniquely identify the ProjectNumber. This table is not in BCNF. To satisfy BCNF, the table must be split into two, two-column tables. Perhaps you begin to see the problems of going beyond 3NF. To achieve BCNF in this example, you would have to decompose the ProjectEmployee table into two, two-column tables, and this entails the overhead of an extra column. What do you gain? Elimination of the redundancies associated with repeating ProjectAdvisor names and ProjectMember. If a project advisor quits, the change has to be made to all records for which the advisor was associated.

Fourth and fifth normal forms are often dismissed with a "beyond the scope of this discussion..." largely because they deal with independently-valued attributes that make up a composite primary key. Like BCNF, 4NF and 5NF address design problems that you have probably solved intuitively by the time you achieve 3NF. Another employee table example illustrates problems associated with having a table that isn't in 4NF. Visualize records in a table that consists of EmployeeName, EmployeeJobSkill, and ForeignLanguage, where knowledge of foreign language is not associated with EmployeeJobSkill. For talented employees who know several languages, we have a real problem that is based on having independently multi-valued attributes as our primary key. What's the solution? You guessed it—break up the table into two, two-column tables: EmployeeSkills (EmployeeName, EmployeeJobSkill) and EmployeeLanguages (EmployeeName, ForeignLanguage).

Fifth normal form only applies to tables that contain cyclic dependencies and results in a single table decomposed into three or more tables. A table that does not meet 5NF will consist of a composite key, and probably nothing but a composite key. We think of 5NF as an extension of 4NF, one that requires simultaneous, rather than iterative, decomposition of the initial table.

Denormalization

You're probably wondering about the performance hit associated with fully normalized designs that consist mainly of three- or four-column tables. If one of the columns is the primary key, and another one is the foreign key, that's a lot of overhead. Furthermore, in order to recombine the data in response to user queries, the DBMS has to perform time-consuming joins. End users could care less about normal forms—they want accurate answers fast.

Any database design can be fully normalized, but the question is whether it *should*—especially in an OLTP system. The reality is that sometimes we compromise our "correct" database design to achieve better performance. We combine one or more tables into a one that does not adhere to the rules of normalization through a process called denormalization. Unfortunately, there aren't any easy rules of thumb to guide you in denormalization decisions. Here's a tactical checklist to help you approach the problem:

- Narrow down the database processes that cause poor performance.
- Gather some metrics by measuring the response times for the various database processes at different times of the day.
- Does the situation occur often or is it a rare, but time-killing occurrence?
- Does the situation involve adding new records, changing existing data during queries, or some combination of those?
- Consider potential alternatives to denormalization:
    - Can you minimize the problem by adding a faster CPU, more RAM, or a larger, faster hard disk?
    - What about an alternate architecture such as a reporting server where the queries are made on replicated data that has been staged locally? Unfortunately, this means trial and measurement.

DOCUMENT YOUR DESIGN GRAPHICALLY

Use the Database Diagram Wizard that comes with SQL Server to document the underlying designs of any SQL Server databases. See the *Books Online* topic, *Database Diagrams*, for more information on using this tool to graphically manipulate your database structure.

Designing Star Schema Databases

As we stated earlier, even in OLTP systems, denormalization is sometimes used to increase database performance. But in decision-support and OLAP systems, denormalization is a fact of life because it allows you to mimic multi-dimensional analysis that lets users slice-and-dice their data, even though its underlying structure remains two-dimensional. Star schema design evolved as a technique to let users ask questions that involve more than two dimensions such as, "What was the sales volume for Rio MP3 players in our Midwest region during the third quarter?" In that example, the three dimensions are product, location, and period.

Star schema designs are usually represented by central *fact* tables (often sales, but potentially with any key performance indicators—KPIs) surrounded by so-called *dimensional* tables. In a relational database, fact and dimension tables are joined through the multi-part primary key in the fact table. Figure 8.4 illustrates a star schema design for a marketing campaign (central fact table = sales, dimensional tables: store, product, promotion, time_by_day, and customer), a retail grocery store (central fact table = sales, dimensional tables: product, store, organization, time), and another sales model (central fact table = sales_facts, dimensional table: customer, product, sales_unit, and time_period). Oh, and when you hear people talk about *snowflaked* schema, they're talking about star schema that have been further denormalized, such as with sub-categories of products.

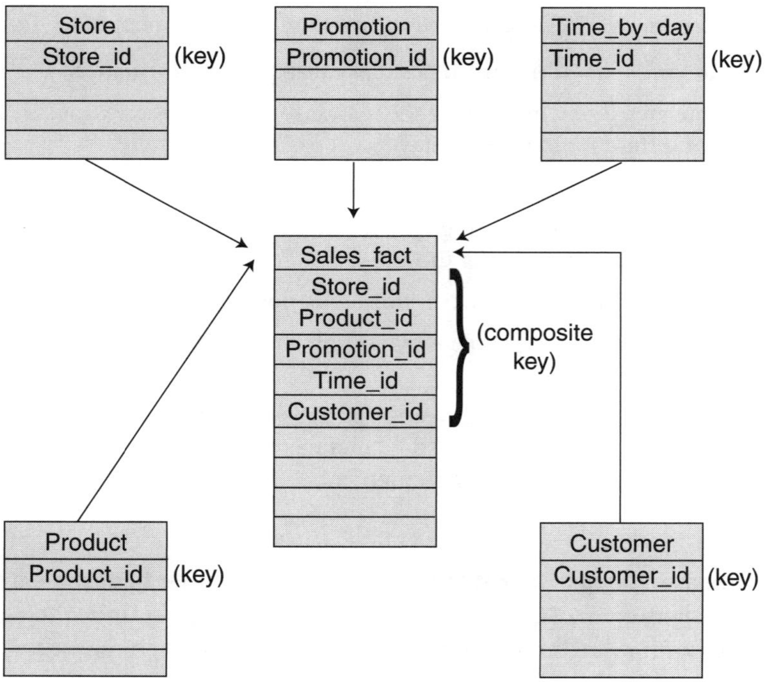

Figure 8.4a Star schema design.

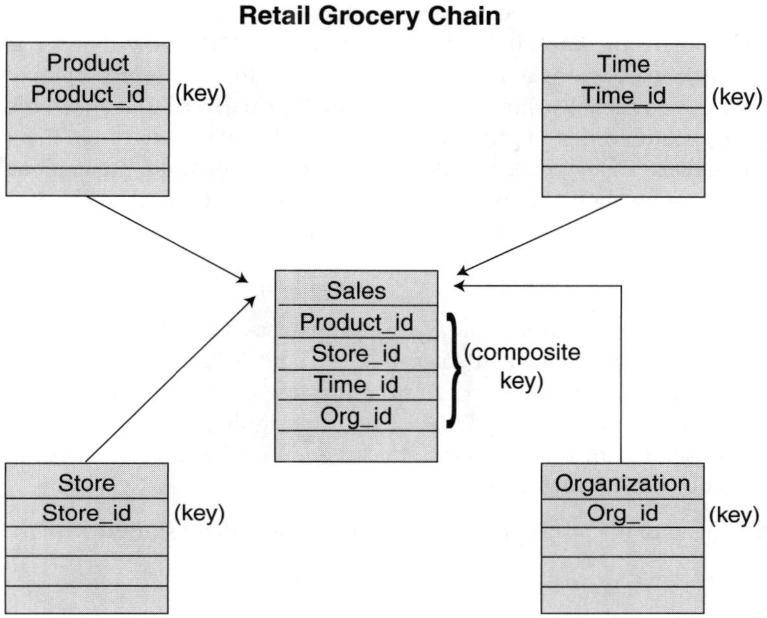

Retail Grocery Chain
Product
Product_id
(key)
Time
Time_id
(key)
Sales
Product_id
Store_id
Time_id
Org_id
(composite key)
Store
Store_id
(key)
Organization
Org_id
(key)

Figure 8.4b Star schema design.

Generic Sales Model
Customer
Customer_id
(key)
Product
Product_id
(key)
Sales
Customer_id
Time_period
Time_id
(key)
Sales_unit
Sales_untit__id
(key)

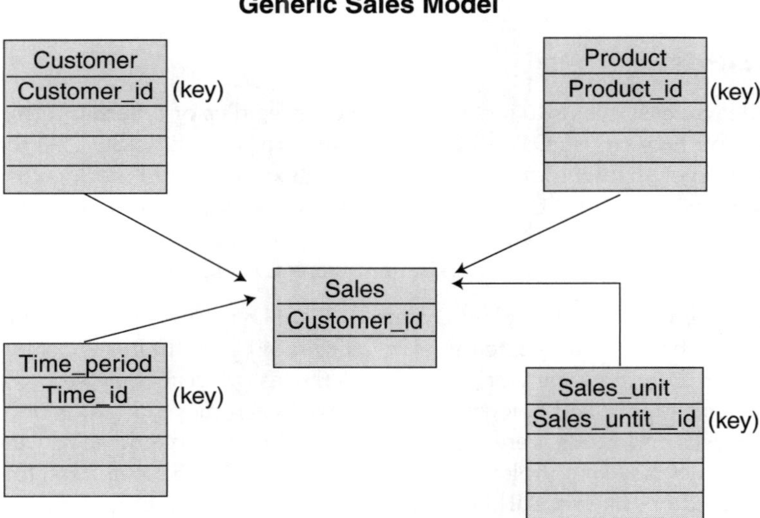

Figure 8.4c Star schema design.

Okay, the star schema design technique isn't that hard to get. Once you've done a few of them, the dimensions literally jump out at you, and you know that the fact table's primary key is just a composite key based on the keys in the dimension tables. But the question is, can you see why they're considered denormalized? The answer is that they represent duplicate copies of the "real" data. And that means there's a chance of update anomalies. *Dimensional modeling* lets you create multi-dimensional models from scratch, first by choosing the facts, then the dimensions, and by designing aggregations. We'll talk more about that in the next chapter.

Parting Thoughts

It's funny. You'd think relational database design—say to 3NF—would be rather cut and dried, but the truth is, most DBAs feel there's a bit of "magic"—or at least an art—associated with it. And, as with programming, some people are just plain better at it than others. Another funny thing, DBAs used to designing OLTP systems may have a hard time "loosening up" and creating star schema database designs. But one thing's for sure: practice makes perfect.

Well, with that said, it's time to put theory to practice and get started with the projects.

Project

First of all, we want to start off by saying that this project is going to be one of the more fun ones found in this book. Why? Well, it has several moving parts and we get to use some really cool technology (introduced in SQL Server 7) to accomplish our goal. "Enough hype," you might be thinking, "tell me what we're going to do." We're going to take data stored in three different formats (Excel, Text, and Access) and transfer/transform it into a SQL Server 7 database that utilizes the star schema database design.

Business Scenario

It would be real easy for us to just throw two or three files of different formats at you and show you how to use DTS to transfer/transform them into SQL Server and say "done." However, that wouldn't give you any context for the real-world situations that you're going to encounter. So, instead of taking the easy way out, we create a business scenario that adds context to the data we plan to use. This should allow you to better understand how to use DTS to solve similar business problems.

Our fictional company is called Plant Dynamics. Plant Dynamics has been in business for nine years and has recently started to experience rapid growth. In the beginning, they simply sold an assorted variety of plants, but in the last six years they've expanded into the commercial supply and landscaping business. When they started, there were only three employees and funds were very limited, so all inventory and sales were kept by hand. Today, they have 50 employees and use a small LAN (15 computers) to handle all computer-based operations. All the accounting is done with a proprietary accounting package and they have several other "pieces" of useful information that are maintained with either Access or Excel.

The owner of Plant Dynamics has contacted you, a database consultant, and has expressed concern about the ability of the current systems to keep up with expected growth. He feels the current accounting package does not allow him to adequately analyze sales data and the instances of "stand-alone" data maintained in Access and Excel is getting out of hand. He wants to move toward a corporate database environment where the bulk of the operational data is consolidated and analyzed from a single source. He does not, however, want to commit the funds to accomplish this without seeing how this type of environment can benefit his operations.

You tell him that this isn't the first time you've seen this type of environment and think that a "proof-of-concept" project will convince him that the benefits of changing the environment will certainly outweigh the pains and money required to make the change. You both agree that he will pick the three most important data stores that need to be analyzed and that you'll come up with an estimate for creating a data mart that will allow him to review and analyze the data from a single source.

KEEPING DOWN THE COSTS WITH EVALUATION SOFTWARE

If you ever encounter a situation where the client is very concerned about initial costs, suggest that the 120-day evaluation copy of SQL Server be used instead of spending the money to buy a product they may not need. It's the smart thing to do and will impress the prospective client by showing them you're interested in saving them money.

After several specification meetings you agree that the data mart will consist of sales, shipment quality, and customer satisfaction data. The origin of the data is listed here:

- The sales data will come from the proprietary accounting package in the form of five text files.
- The shipment quality data is stored in an Access database and is accessed directly.
- The customer satisfaction data is stored in an Excel spreadsheet and is accessed directly.

As mentioned earlier, when you need to get data extracts from a proprietary or closed system, you usually use the report writer that comes with the system to create a report that contains the desired data and then print the report to a text file. In order to adequately analyze the sales data, you need five reports and thus five extract files. The structure of each extract file is shown in Figure 8.5.

The other two pieces of data that we need to transfer to the mart are held in an Excel spreadsheet and an Access database. The customer satisfaction data, which is gathered by calling the customers two times a quarter, is stored in an Excel spreadsheet. The shipment quality data is gathered by the Shipping and Receiving Manager and is based upon a visual inspection of all shipments. Both data sources have simple structures that are shown in Figure 8.6.

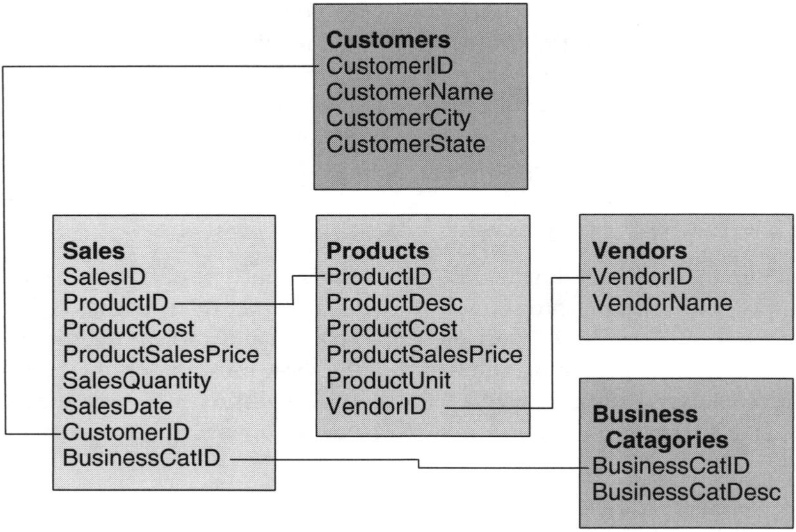

Figure 8.5 Sales, Products, Customers, Vendors, and BusinessCategories files.

Our goal is to transfer and transform the data so that it "fits" the star schema design model shown in Figure 8.7.

Transferring and Transforming the Data

We now know the format and structure of all the data sources we want to consolidate and the desired format for the consolidated data, so we are just about ready to start creating the DTS packages needed to transfer the data. Before we start creating the packages, let's go ahead and copy the data and script files from the CD and create a database that contains the structure of our star schema design. In order to facilitate this process, create a sub-directory on your local hard drive called MSDataMart and copy all the *.txt,

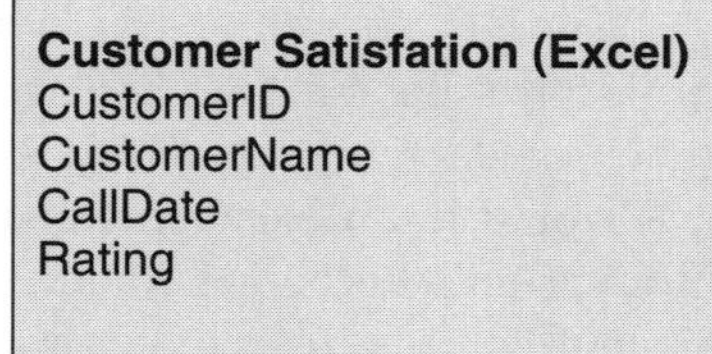

Figure 8.6 Customer Satisfaction and Shipment Quality data sources.

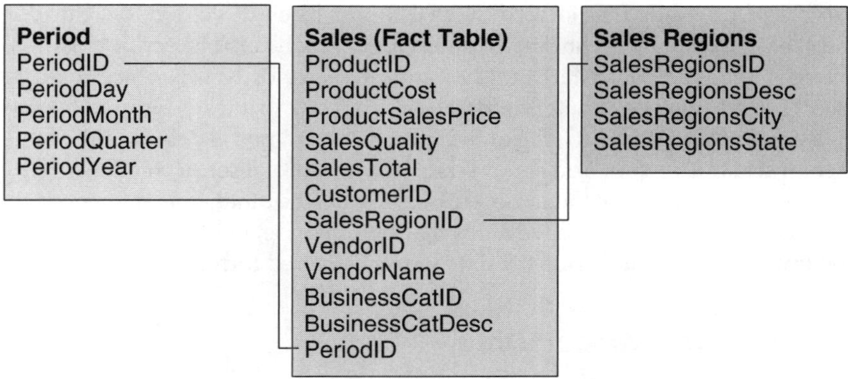

Figure 8.7a Data Mart database model.

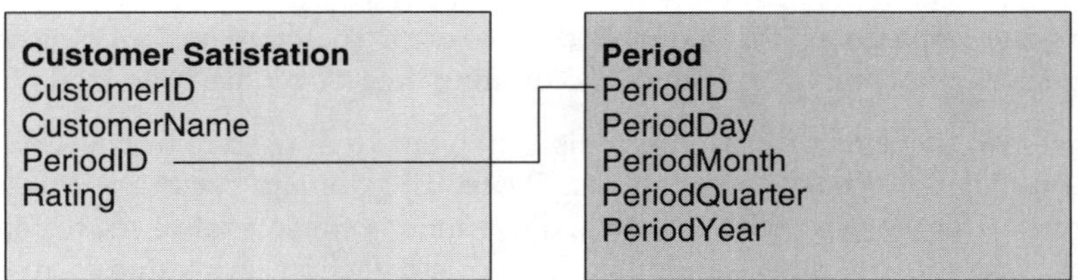

Figure 8.7b Data Mart database model.

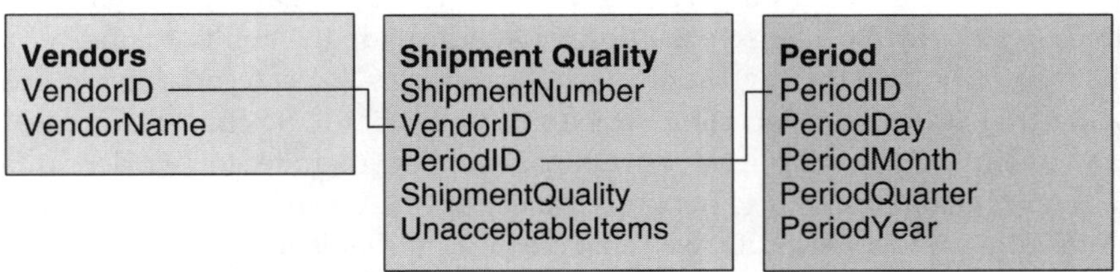

Figure 8.7c Data Mart database model.

Transition Tables

Business Catagories
BusinessCatID
BusinessCatDesc

Customers
CustomerID
CustomerName
CustomerCity
CustomerState

Products
ProductID
ProductDesc
ProductUnit
VendorID

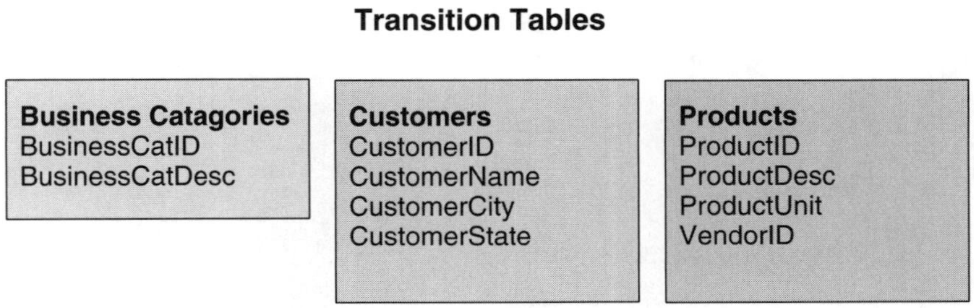

Figure 8.7d Data Mart database model.

*.xls, *.sql and *.mdb files located in the Chapter_8 sub-directory. To create the database and tables, execute the ch8.sql script in Query Analyzer. The script creates a database whose name is MSDataMart that has an initial size of 10 MB. Once the database has been created, the script sets the database options "Truncate log on checkpoint" and "Select into/Bulk copy" to true and then creates and populates all of the tables needed to complete this project. You should note that the ch8.sql script contains more code than that needed to create the database. It also contains the other code referenced throughout the chapter. Now that we have a destination database, we can create the DTS package that transfers and transforms the data into the desired format.

Customer Satisfaction Data

As you can see from Figure 8.6, the customer satisfaction data consists of four fields. If we could ensure that there were no typos (remember this is an Excel spreadsheet so the CustomerID values are not validated) in the CustomerID values, then we wouldn't need to transfer the CustomerName. However, we can't determine whether they're valid until they can be compared against a qualified set of data. Therefore, we're going to transfer all of the data and compare it with the accounting data *after* it has been loaded.

There are two fields in the customer satisfaction data that need to be transformed during the transfer process: Rating and CallDate. The domain for the Rating field is 1 through 4. After working with this data, day after day for several years, the employees of Plant Dynamics all understand what level of satisfaction each value corresponds to. However, you decide it would be better to store a verbal descriptor in the mart and ask them to supply the descriptors (see Table 8.1).

The second field that needs to be converted is CallDate. One of the things we want to accomplish with the star schema design is to provide the ability to analyze all events that contain a date by Day, Month, Quarter, or Year. You can certainly do this without using the Time dimension table Period shown in Figure 8.7, but the queries that contain the time analysis wouldn't be optimal—and the main reason we denormalize with the star schema design is to maximize query speed. So, in order to transform the CallDate values into a PeriodID, we must create a mechanism by which the CallDate values can be correlated to their corresponding PeriodIDs. The code used to populate the Period table is shown here and is contained in the ch8.sql file:

```
DECLARE @CurrentDate datetime,
        @CurrentMonth char(3),
        @CurrentQuarter varchar(6),
        @CurrentYear smallint

SELECT @CurrentDate = '1/1/1990'

WHILE @CurrentDate < "1/1/2005"
 BEGIN
  SELECT @CurrentQuarter = CASE
                             WHEN DATEPART(Month,@CurrentDate)_
                                  BETWEEN 1 AND 3 THEN 'Fourth'
```

```
                                    WHEN DATEPART(Month,@CurrentDate)_
                                         BETWEEN 4 AND 6 THEN 'First'
                                    WHEN DATEPART(Month,@CurrentDate)_
                                         BETWEEN 7 AND 9 THEN 'Second'
                                    ELSE 'Third'
                                    END

   SELECT @CurrentYear = CASE
                                    WHEN DATEPART(Month,@CurrentDate)_
                                         BETWEEN 1 AND 3 THEN_
                                         DATEPART(Year,@CurrentDate)-1
                                    ELSE DATEPART(Year,@CurrentDate)
                                    END

 SELECT @CurrentMonth = SUBSTRING(DATENAME(Month,@CurrentDate),1,3)

   INSERT Period
   (
    PeriodDay,
    PeriodMonth,
    PeriodQuarter,
    PeriodYear
   )
   VALUES
   (
    @CurrentDate,
    @CurrentMonth
    @CurrentQuarter,
    @CurrentYear
   )
   SELECT @CurrentDate = DATEADD(day,1,@CurrentDate)
  END
```

At first glance, this may appear to be a complex piece of code, but when you break it down into pieces it gets pretty simple. The first thing you should notice is that the range of values in the Period table is limited to 1/1/1990 through 1/1/2005, as indicated by the initial *@CurrentDate* value and the upper limit for *@CurrentDate* used in the WHILE loop. The next thing you should pick up on is that we've used what may appear to be convoluted logic to determine the quarter to which *@CurrentDate* belongs. Well, one thing we haven't told you is that Plant Dynamics operates on a fiscal year

Table 8.1 Rating Transformation Values

RATING VALUE	DESCRIPTOR
1	Never do business with us again
2	Unsatisfied
3	Satisfied
4	Very satisfied

that doesn't correlate one-to-one with the calendar year (lots of firms use fiscal years that do not correspond to the calendar year). The first quarter of their fiscal year correlates to the second quarter of the calendar year, so 4/1/YYYY is the first day of first quarter for year YYYY. The CASE statement helps us figure out which quarter *@CurrentDate* belongs to by determining the month-range in which it falls. We use the DATEPART function with the Month parameter to return the integer value associated with the month for *@CurrentDate* and BETWEEN to determine where the value falls. The same type of logic is used to determine the fiscal year, but it's even easier since we're only concerned with the first three months of each year. Once the quarter and year have been determined, the SUBSTRING and DATENAME functions are used to return the first three characters of the month's name. At this point all of the data values needed to create a record have been determined, so they're inserted into the Period table. Now that you understand what the code does, go ahead and review the contents of the table to make sure that the statement performed as expected. Now that the Period table is populated, we have to create a mechanism that will allow us to determine what date value goes with each PeriodID. This functionality is implemented in the DTS Data Pump via a DTS Lookup. In short, it allows you to specify a query that executes for each value from the source that needs to be "looked up" in a table that resides in the destination. So, as the data is transferred, the following query is executed for each CallDate value from the source.

```
SELECT PeriodID
FROM Period
WHERE PeriodDay = ?.
```

The process is shown in Figure 8.8.

We now have all of the requirements necessary to create the package components that will facilitate this transfer. In order to create the package complete the following:

1. Right-Click on Data Transformation Services off the server tree and select New Package.
2. Click the Data option on the main menu and select Microsoft Excel 8.0.
3. Click the ellipsis button next to the File Name field and specify the location for CustomerSatisfaction.XLS. The file should be located in the MSDataMart subdirectory that you created at the beginning of this section. Your screen should look like Figure 8.9. Click the OK button to close the Connection Properties dialog.

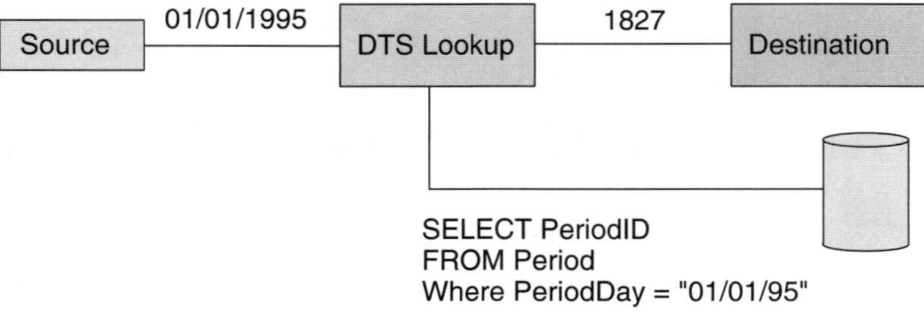

Figure 8.8 DTS Lookup.

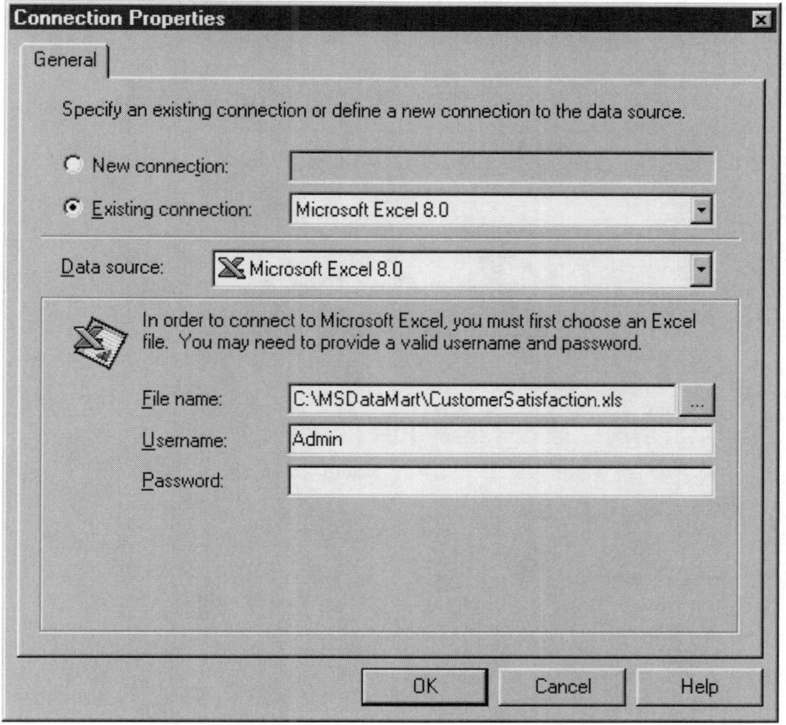

Figure 8.9 Excel data connection.

4. Click the Data option on the main menu and select Microsoft OLE DB Provider for SQL Server.
5. Provide the required login information so that you can specify MSDataMart as the destination database. Your dialog should look like Figure 8.10. Click the OK button to close the Connection Properties dialog.

So far all we've done is place connection parameters for the source and destination data on the Design Sheet. In order for us to actually *transfer* the data, we need to add a transformation workflow event:

1. Click on the Microsoft Excel 8.0 icon on the Design Sheet.
2. Hold down the Shift key and click on the Microsoft OLE DB icon—both icons should be highlighted.
3. Release the Shift key, Click on the Workflow option on the main menu and select Add Transform. Your Design Sheet should now look like Figure 8.11.
4. Go ahead and save the package with Package/Save off the main menu and use the name PlantDynamics.

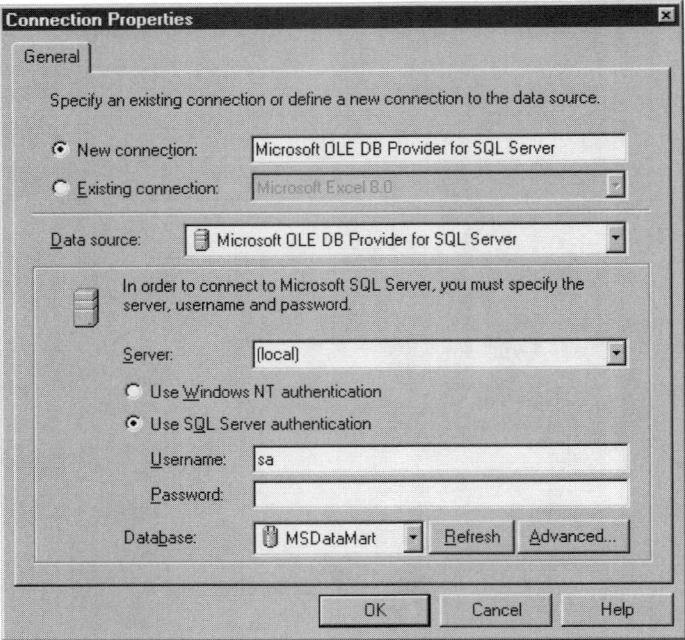

Figure 8.10 SQL Server data connection.

Hopefully all of this has been a review for you, but we did want to cover the initial package creation process in detail for those of you who may not have used it before. With the existing configuration, we're ready to copy the values in the source *directly* into the destination fields. Double-click on the Workflow arrow and click the Destination tab. Select CustomerSatisfaction from the Table Name drop-down box and click the Transformations tab. Figure 8.12 shows how the default transformations are configured.

DATA TRANSFORMATION SERVICES WIZARD

The Data Transformation Services Wizard—which can be accessed via the Import and Export Data selection inside the Microsoft SQL Server 7 menu group—can be used to automatically create a DTS Package. The Wizard walks you through the steps of selecting a source and destination, specifying transformations, and then gives you the option of saving the parameters to a package. The wizard is ideal for non-recurring data import/export processes, but can also be handy for creating packages. Once you get familiar with creating packages using the method shown in the previous sections, give the wizard a try and then decide which method you prefer.

Notice that both of the Rating fields are selected (see the gray background) and that Selected Transformation at the bottom of the dialog says Copy Column. If you highlight each column mapping (select the arrow between the source and destination), the Selected Transformation for each will be Copy Column.

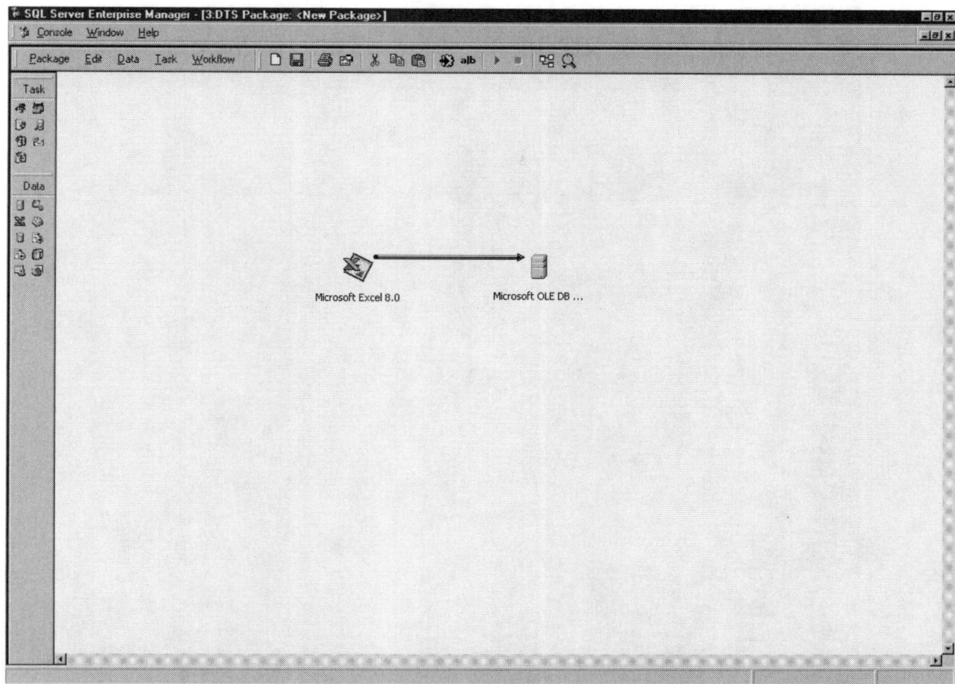

Figure 8.11 Data Sources with Workflow.

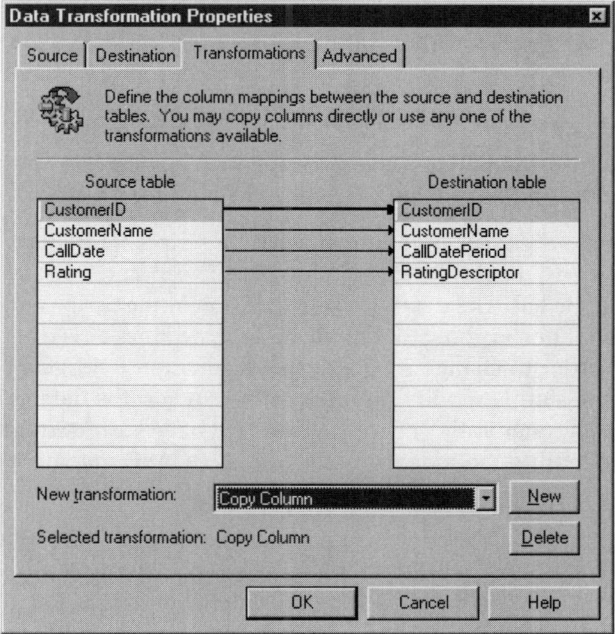

Figure 8.12 Default transformation configuration.

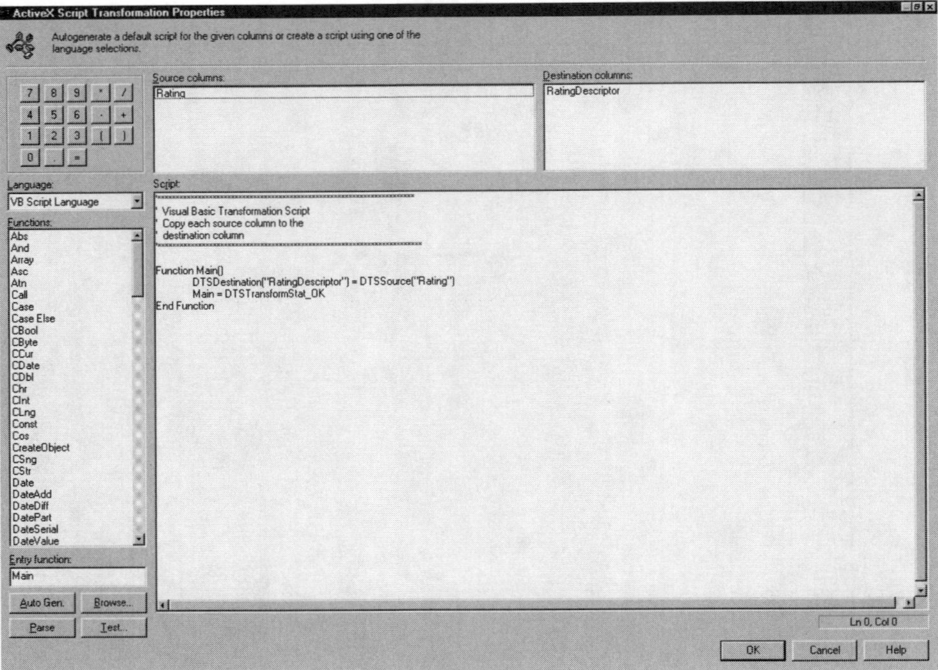

Figure 8.13 ActiveX Script transformation properties.

This, of course, is *not* what we want for all of the columns. The next series of steps allows us to use VBScript to transform the Rating values from the source to Descriptor values in the destination.

1. Select the arrow that goes between the Rating fields and click the Delete button.
2. Change the New Transformation to ActiveX Script and click the New button. You should get a screen that, when maximized, looks like Figure 8.13.

This screen is very useful when designing transformation scripts. The source and destination columns are clearly displayed at the top of the screen and a list of VBScript functions are shown on the left. The default transformation in the Script window simply tells us that the destination is going to receive the source values as is—again, this is not what we want. In order to change it so that the destination field gets populated with the desired data, we simply modify the VBScript to convert the data as it's transferred. For those of you familiar with VBScript, you might have surmised that the best way to handle this is to modify the code using the SELECT CASE statement as shown in Figure 8.14.

Even if you aren't familiar with VBScript, you'll notice that SELECT CASE works just like the CASE statement (T-SQL CASE) that you're used to working with, but uses a slightly different syntax. Once you have typed in the statement, use the Parse button at the bottom-left of the screen to check for typos. After you have parsed the statement, use the Test button to create a temporary text file that contains the transformed values.

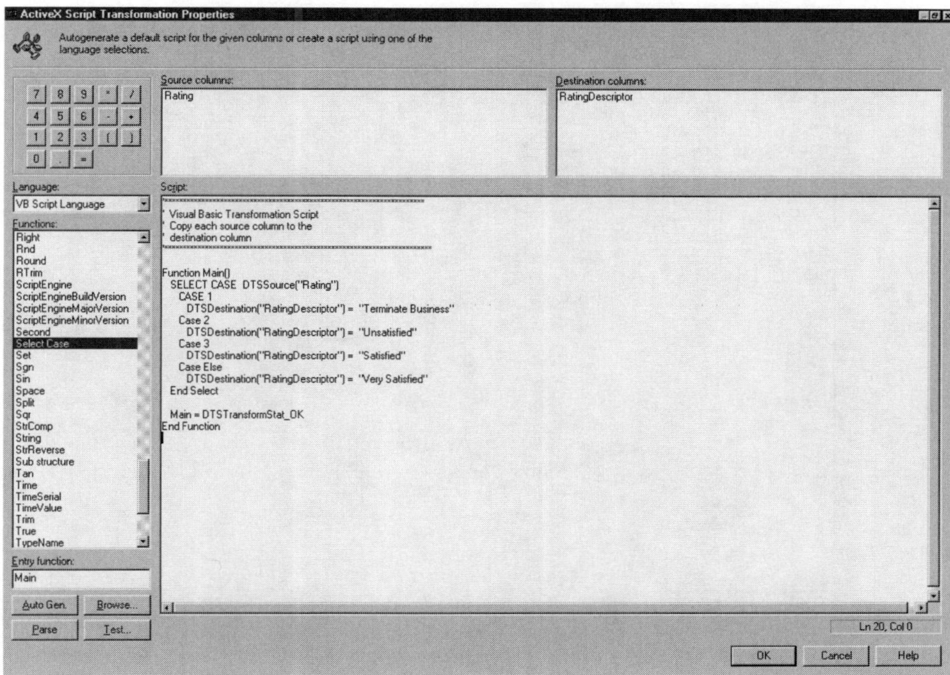

Figure 8.14 VBScript transformation.

We highly recommend using the Test button and examining the results with great scrutiny. Save the modified transformation by exiting to the Design Sheet, right-clicking, and selecting Save.

We've created the transformation for the Ratings, now it's time to create the transformation that allows the Data Pump to determine what PeriodID corresponds to each CallDate. We'll do this via a DTS Lookup by completing the following steps:

1. Double-click on the Workflow arrow and select the Advanced tab.
2. Click the Lookups button and click Add.
3. Type PeriodIDLookup for the Name, and then press the Tab key.
4. Select Microsoft OLE DB Provider for SQL Server in the Connection drop-down box.
5. Click the Ellipsis button under Query.
6. Select and drag the Period table into the query workspace (the gray area).
7. Click the checkbox next to PeriodID.
8. Modify the SELECT statement as follows:

```
SELECT PeriodID
FROM Period
WHERE PeriodDay = ?
```

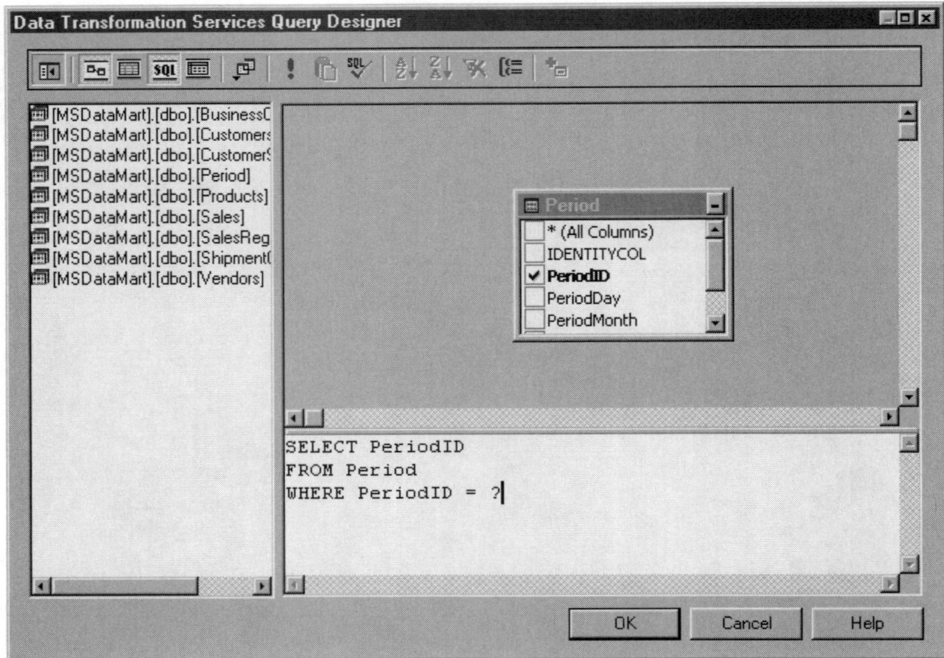

Figure 8.15 DTS Lookup for PeriodID.

Figure 8.15 shows the final result of these actions.

1. Click the OK button until you return to the Data Transformation Properties dialog.
2. Click the Transformations tab, select the arrow between CallDate and PeriodID and click the Delete button.
3. Select ActiveX Script in the New Transformation field and click the New button.
4. Modify the transformation code as follows:

```
DTSDestination("PeriodID") =
DTSLookups("PeriodIDLookup").Execute(DTSSource("CallDate").Value)
```

5. Click the Parse button to verify the syntax.
6. Click the Test button to verify that the results of transformation are as expected.

TEST BUTTON FAILS WITH DTS LOOKUPS

If you have typed the code in the Script window as it appears here it is valid and produces the desired results. The Test button, however, will indicate that it is not valid in both the RTM and SP1 versions of SQL Server 7. Simply double-check your typing and proceed as if the Test button processed the code without errors.

7. Click OK until you return to the Design Sheet and then save the package.

Well, there you have it. We've created a DTS Package that transfers and transforms the data from CustomerSatisfaction.xls to MSDataMart..CustomerSatisfaction. In order to execute the package simply right-click in the Design Sheet and select Execute. Once the package has completed the transfer—this is important—review the data carefully to make sure the results are as expected.

Shipment Quality Data

The shipment quality data is stored in an Access database. Take a second or two to review Figures 8.6 and 8.7 so you can re-familiarize yourself with the source and destination table structures. After you've become comfortable with the table structures take a look at the source data in the Access database. As you can see this is pretty straightforward. A graphic of the transfer/transformation is shown in Figure 8.16.

We're now going to add this transfer component to the package in which the Customer Satisfaction component is located. Grouping all of the related transfer components in the same package allows them to be executed as a single unit of work and managed in one location. The steps for creating this component follow. If you closed the package after completing the last section, simply double-click PlantDynamics in Local Packages. Local Packages is under the Data Transformation Services server tree option.

1. Click the Data option on the main menu and select Microsoft Access.
2. Supply the path and file name in the File Name field. If you've been following along, your value will be C:\MSDataMart\ShipmentQuality.mdb.
3. Click the Data option on the main menu and select Microsoft OLE DB Provider for SQL Server.
4. Specify the required login information so that you can specify MSDataMart as the destination database.
5. Click on the Microsoft Access icon on the Design Sheet.
6. Hold down the Shift key and click on the Microsoft OLE DB icon—both icons should be highlighted.
7. Release the Shift key, click on the Workflow option on the main menu and select Add Transform.
8. Add a description to both components by clicking Package and then select Add Text Annotation. Label the last component we created Customer Satisfaction and this one Shipment Quality.

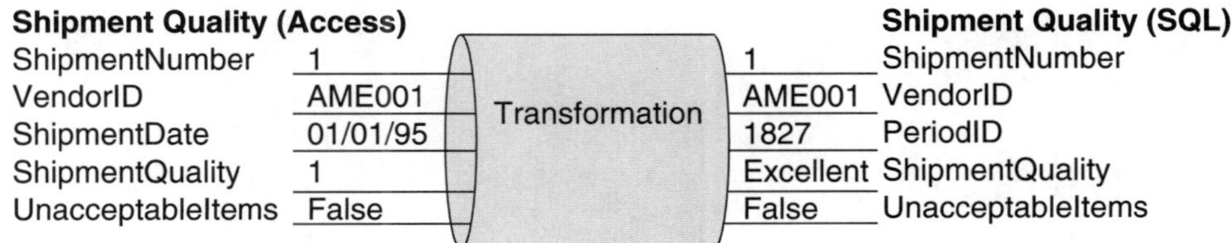

Figure 8.16 Shipment Quality transfer.

9. Go ahead and save the package by right-clicking in the Design Sheet and select Save. When you're finished, your Design Sheet should look like Figure 8.17.

We've added the data source and destination, but as we saw during the Customer Satisfaction component creation process, the default configuration is a one-to-one column mapping from the source to the destination and this is *not* what we want. The following steps allow us to create the needed transformations:

1. Double-click the Workflow arrow and click the Destination tab. Select ShipmentQuality from the Table Name drop-down box and then click the Transformations tab followed by the Advanced tab.
2. Click Lookups and then click the Add button.
3. Create the lookup in the exact same manner as the previous section, but note that the connection to SQL Server has a suffix of 2 (expand the Connection Field to see the full name):
   - Name: PeriodIDLookup
   - Connection: Microsoft OLE DB Provider for SQL Server 2
   - Query: `SELECT PeriodID FROM Period WHERE PeriodDay = ?`
4. Click OK until you return to the Data Transformation Properties dialog and select the Transformations tab.
5. Select the ShipDate and PeriodID and click Delete.

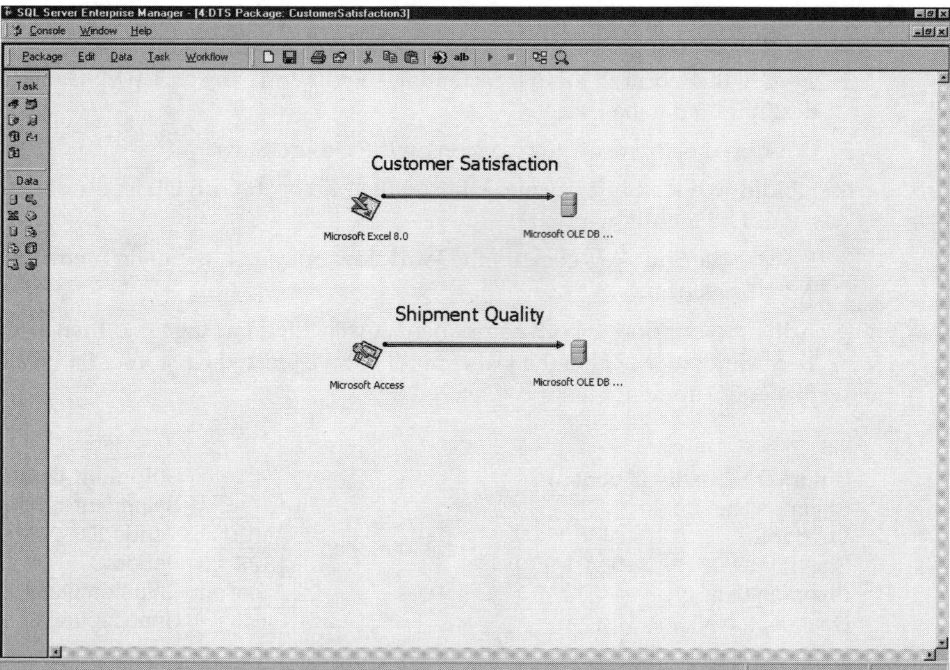

Figure 8.17 Design Sheet with two components.

6. Change the New Transformation field to ActiveX Script and click New.
7. Modify the transformation code to look like the following:

```
DTSDestination("PeriodID") =
DTSLookups("PeriodIDLookup").Execute(DTSSource("ShipmentDate").Value)
```

8. Press OK to return to the Design Sheet and save the package by right-clicking and selecting Save.

This should all look very familiar, but in case you're a little confused, we'll tell you that we simply used a DTS Lookup to transform ShipDate (stored in the source) to PeriodID (stored in the destination).

The next step is to transform the numerical values in the source to text descriptions within the destination. The following steps show how to complete these transformations.

1. Double-click the Workflow arrow and select the Transformations tab.
2. Select the ShipmentQuality fields in both the source and destination and click Delete.
3. Change the New Transformation field to ActiveX Script and click New.
4. Modify the transformation code to look like the following:

```
Select Case  DTSSource("ShipmentQuality")
      Case 1
         DTSDestination("ShipmentQuality") = "Excellent"
      Case 2
         DTSDestination("ShipmentQuality") = "Good"
      Case 3
         DTSDestination("ShipmentQuality") = "Acceptable"
      Case 4
         DTSDestination("ShipmentQuality") = "Poor"
      Case 5
         DTSDestination("ShipmentQuality") = "Rejected"
      Case Else
         DTSDestination("ShipmentQuality") = "BadData"
   End Select
```

5. Press OK until you return to the Design Sheet and save the package by right-clicking and select Save.

All we've done here is to assign a text description to the numerical values in the source. You should notice that the Case Else part of the statement allows us to trap for values that are not within the domain for this field. Once the transformation is complete, we can check for this value ("BadData") to determine which source records need to be fixed.

We need to create a similar transformation for the UnacceptableItems field and this can be accomplished with the following steps:

1. Double-click on the Workflow arrow and select the Transformations tab.
2. Select the UnacceptableItems fields in both the source and destination and click Delete.

3. Change the New Transformation field to ActiveX Script and click New.
4. Modify the transformation code to look like the following:

```
If DTSSource("UnacceptableItems") = "False" Then
      DTSDestination("UnacceptableItems") = "No"
   Else
      DTSDestination("UnacceptableItems") = "Yes"
   End If
```

5. Press OK until you return to the Design Sheet and then save the package by right-clicking and selecting Save.

The source field in Access is a Yes/No data type, so this transformation simply converts the True or False to a Yes or No. Well, there you have it—we've completed all of the transformations needed for the ShipmentQuality component. This stuff gets pretty simple once you create a couple of transformations. Don't you think? Go ahead and execute the package by right-clicking and selecting Execute. Verify the data was transferred correctly by reviewing the contents of ShipmentQuality.

Sales Data

The next component we need to create is for the sales data. It is slightly more complicated than the previous components, but since it follows the same general logic we're sure that you'll get through without any problems.

Take a minute to review the sales-related tables in Figures 8.6 and 8.7. Assume that we used the accounting's package report generating program (remember our business scenario) to generate the following data files (located in the MSDataMart sub-directory):

- Sales.txt—Data specific to an individual sale
- Products.txt—Description for items sold
- Customers.txt—Customer information
- Vendors.txt—Vendor information
- BusinessCategories.txt—Product line descriptions

The following general overview of the processes required to transform the data to its desired state should give you a good idea of the task at hand. Don't worry if you have a little trouble "seeing" all that's needed, just keep in mind that as we go through the detailed steps it will eventually make perfect sense. The first series of processes that we need to create are simple column-to-column transfers for the Customers, Vendors, Products, and BusinessCategories data. After that is complete we create a post-transformation process that populates the SalesRegions table using the City and State information in the Customers table. The next step is a transfer/transformation process for the Sales data. The last step is a post-transformation process that updates Sales with SalesTotal, CustomerName, SalesRegionID, VendorID, VendorName, and BusinessCatDesc. The sales data transformation process is shown in Figure 8.18.

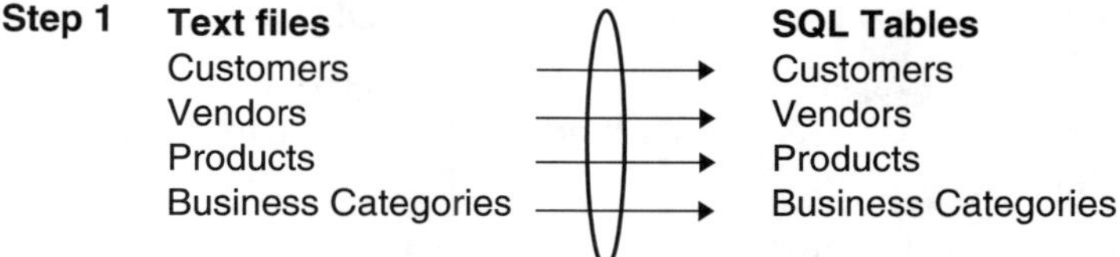

Column-to-column transfers with no transformations

Step 2 **Post Transformation SQL Task for Creating Sales Region Table**

```
INSERT Sales Region
SELECT . . .
FROM Customers
```

Step 3 **Post Transformation SQL Task for Populating Sales**

```
UPDATE Sales
FROM Sales, BusinessCategories
SET Sales.BusinessCatDesc =  BusinessCategories.BusinessCatDesc
Where Sales.BusinessCatID =  BusinessCategories.BusinessCatID
```

. . . One UPDATE for each field where Description resides in another table

Figure 8.18 Sales data transfer/transformation processes.

Let's get started with the simple column-to-column transfers for the Customers, Vendors, Products, and BusinessCategories data. The following steps show how to create the transfer for this data.

If you closed the package after completing the last section, simply double-click PlantDynamics in Local Packages. Local Packages is under the Data Transformation Services server tree option.

1. Click the Data option on the main menu and select Text File (Source).
2. Supply that path and file name in the File Name field and click OK. If you have been following along your value will be C:\MSDataMart\Customers.txt.
3. Ensure Fixed Field is selected on the Select File Format dialog and click Next.
4. Ensure that the column breaks (indicated by the black lines) occur at positions 5, 20, and 35 and that the end-of-file marker (indicated by the red line) occurs at position 37. Click Finish and then OK.
5. Click the Data option on the main menu and select Microsoft OLE DB Provider for SQL Server.
6. Provide the required login information so that you can specify MSDataMart as the destination database and click OK.
7. Click on the Text File (Source) icon on the Design Sheet.

8. Hold down the Shift key and click on the Microsoft OLE DB icon—both icons should be highlighted.
9. Release the Shift key, Click on the Workflow option on the main menu and select Add Transform.
10. Add a description to the process by clicking Package and then select Add Text Annotation.
11. Double-click the Workflow arrow and select the Destination tab. Select Customers from the Table Name drop-down box.
12. Click the Transformations tab and notice that the source columns are labeled Col001-Col004, and that the transformations are applied in sequential order. This means that the columns in the destination table must be in the same order as the text file fields in order for the default mapping to work. When you encounter a situation where the destination is not in the same order as the source, simply delete the default mappings and adjust accordingly.
13. Click OK to return to the Design Sheet and then save the package by right-clicking and selecting Save. Your Design Sheet should look like Figure 8.19.

Repeat this same process for the Vendors, Products, and BusinessCategories text files. Make sure the column breaks and the end-of-file mark corresponds to the following:

Vendors.txt: column break at 6 and end-of-file mark at 21.

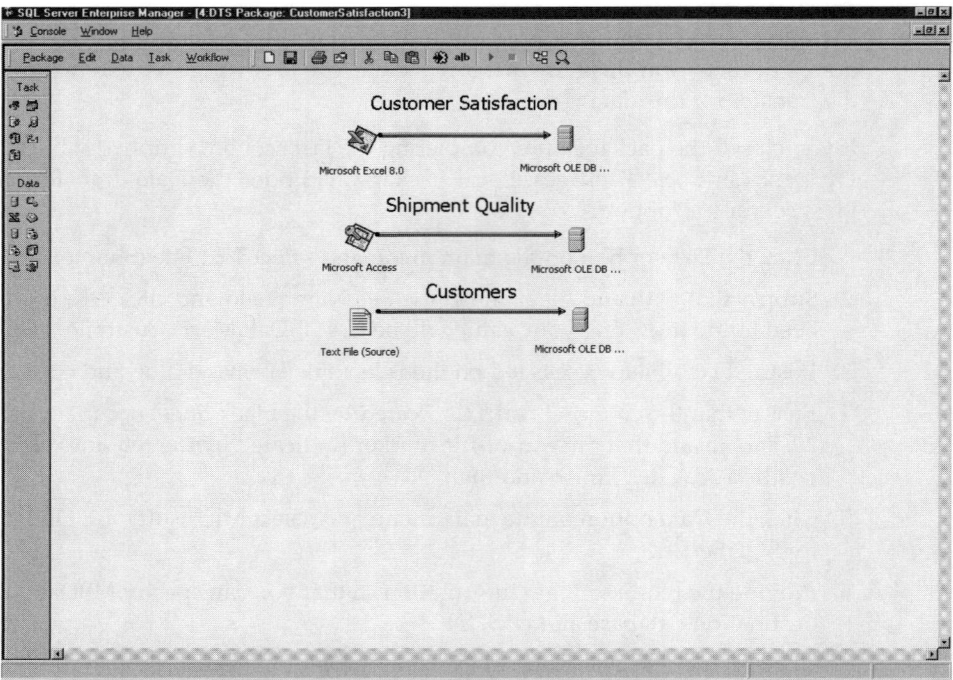

Figure 8.19 Design Sheet with three processes.

Products.txt: column break at 5, 25, 30, 35, and 40 and end-of-file mark at 46. Note that the default mappings are not correct. The mappings for Col001 and Col002 are correct, but Col005 should be mapped to ProductUnit and Col006 should be mapped to VendorID. In order to correct these mappings simply delete the existing ones, select the correct source and destination (e.g. Col005/Product Unit) and click the New button.

BusinessCategories.txt: column break at 5 and end-of-file mark at 25

When you finish, your Design Sheet should look like Figure 8.20.

The next step is to create a post-transformation process that populates the SalesRegion table. We haven't talked about this type of process yet, so don't worry if you have no idea how to implement it. It is really quite simple though. The logic of the process is such that if Customer data is successfully transferred, populate the SalesRegion table with CustomerCity and CustomerState. The SQL that will truncate and then populate the table is listed in the next code segment. You should note that the SalesRegion table uses an Identity value for the primary key, so this value doesn't need to be supplied in the INSERT. Also notice that we use an over-simplified CASE Statement to associate a Sales Region with the state in which a customer resides.

```
TRUNCATE TABLE SalesRegions

INSERT SalesRegions
(
 SalesRegionDesc,
```

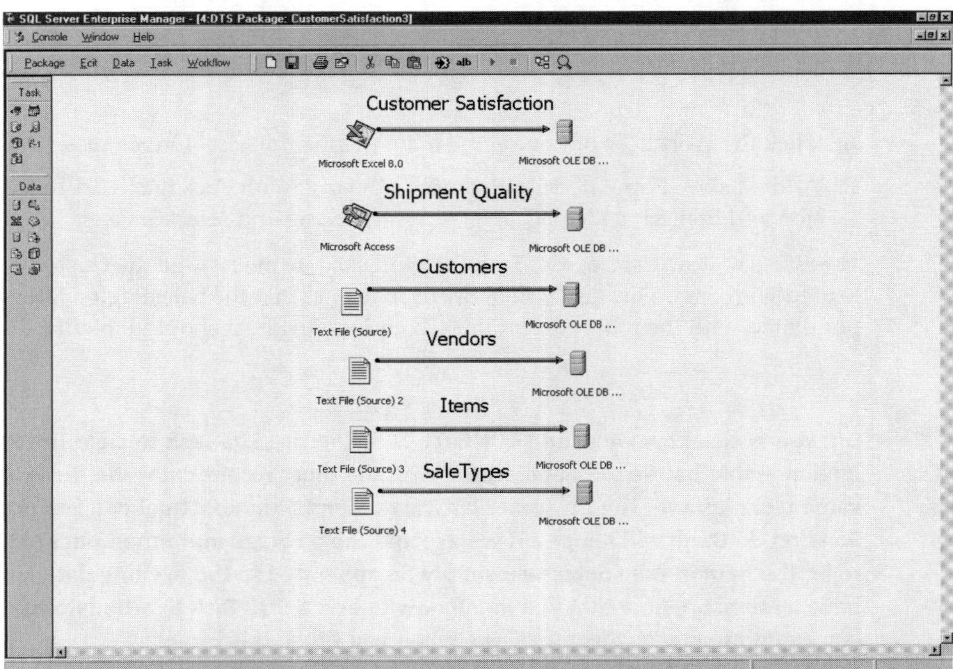

Figure 8.20 Design Sheet with six processes.

```
  SalesRegionCity,
  SalesRegionState
 )
  SELECT DISTINCT
    CASE WHEN CustomerState IN ('TX','GA') THEN
              'South'
         WHEN CustomerState IN ('NY','IL') THEN
              'North'
         ELSE
              'Other'
    END,
    CustomerCity,
    CustomerState
  FROM Customers
```

Complete the following to create this process.

1. Click Task on the main menu and select Execute SQL Task.
2. Select Microsoft OLE DB Provider for SQL Server 3—this connection is for the customer transfer process.
3. Type the code listed above (or copy it from ch8.sql) in the SQL Statement window and click Parse Query to ensure that there are no syntax errors. Make sure you use single quotes, because double quotes cause the parser to error out. Click OK to return to the Design Sheet.
4. Select the Server icon associated with the Customers process (Microsoft OLE DB Provider for SQL Server 3).
5. Hold down the Shift key and select the SQL Task icon—both icons should be highlighted.
6. Click the Workflow option on the main menu and select On Success.
7. Add a Label (Populate SalesRegion) to the task with Package/Add Text Annotation and then save the package by right-clicking and select Save.

That's it. We now have a SQL Task that will execute every time the Customers table is loaded with data. This task will allow us to ensure that the SalesRegion table is always populated with the most current data. Your Design Sheet should look like Figure 8.21.

CLEANING DESTINATION TABLES

Did you notice how we used TRUNCATE TABLE in the SQL Task to clear the SalesRegions table before we populated it with the most recent data? We did not use this same technique for the CustomerSatisfaction and ShipmentQuality transformations. So what do think will happen if we execute the package more than once? That's right, the data in the source will simply be appended to the existing data and we will have a mess. So, now that you know how to add a SQL Task to a transformation you can experiment with this technique when you finish this project.

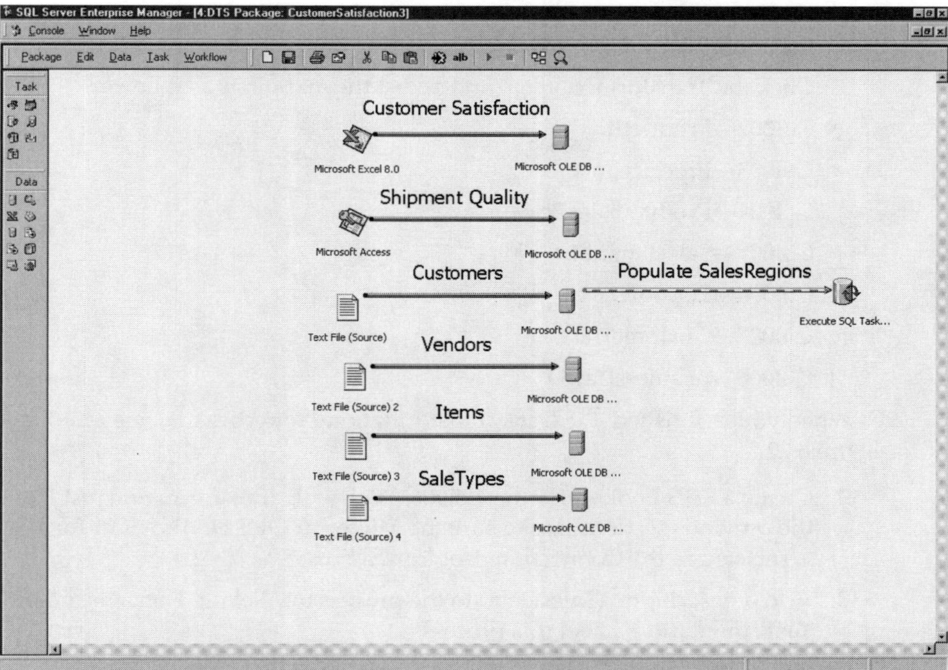

Figure 8.21 Design Sheet with six processes and a task.

The next step is to create a transfer/transformation process for Sales.txt. This is similar to the processes created in the previous sections in that we use a DTS Lookup to transform the SalesDate to a PeriodID. The following steps create the process.

1. Click the Data option on the main menu and select Text File (Source).
2. Supply that path and file name in the File Name field and click OK. If you have been following along your value will be C:\MSDataMart\Sales.txt.
3. Ensure Fixed Field is selected on the Select File Format dialog and click Next.
4. Ensure the column breaks occur at positions 5, 10, 15, 20, 25 , 35, and 40 and that the end-of-file marker is at 45. Click Finish, and then OK.
5. Click Data option on the main menu and select Microsoft OLE DB Provider for SQL Server.
6. Specify the required login information so that you can specify MSDataMart as the destination database and click OK.
7. Click on the Text File (Source) icon on the Design Sheet.
8. Hold down the Shift key and click on the Microsoft OLE DB icon—both icons should be highlighted.
9. Release the Shift key, click on the Workflow option on the main menu, and select Add Transform.

10. Double–click the workflow arrow and select the Destination tab. Select Sales from the Table Name drop-down box.
11. Click the Transformation tab and adjust the mappings as follows:

    Col002→ProductID

    Col003→ProductCost

    Col004→ProductSalesPrice

    Col005→SalesQuantity

    Col006→PeriodID

    Col007→CustomerID

    Col008→BusinessCatID

When you're finished, the Data Transformation Properties dialog should look like Figure 8.22.

12. Create a DTS Lookup for the Col006→PeriodID transformation just like we did in the previous sections. Make sure the Microsoft OLE DB Provider for SQL Server 7 is selected in the Connection drop-down box.
13. Add a description (SalesData) to the process by clicking Package and select Add Text Annotation. Label this process.

Did you notice that the SalesTotal, SalesRegionID, VendorID, VendorName, and BusinessCatDesc do not have mappings in Figure 8.22? We use an Execute SQL Task to populate these fields *after* the data is transferred. The code that the task executes is listed here:

```
UPDATE Sales
SET SalesTotal = ProductSalesPrice*SalesQuantity

UPDATE Sales
SET Sales.SalesRegionID = SalesRegions.SalesRegionID
FROM Sales, SalesRegions, Customers
WHERE Customers.CustomerID = Sales.CustomerID AND
      Customers.CustomerCity = SalesRegions.City AND
      Customers.CustomerState = SalesRegions.State

UPDATE Sales
SET Sales.VendorID = Products.VendorID
FROM Sales, Products
WHERE Sales.ProductID = Products.ProductID

UPDATE Sales
SET Sales.VendorName = Vendors.VendorName
FROM Sales, Vendors
WHERE Sales.VendorID = Vendors.VendorID


UPDATE Sales
```

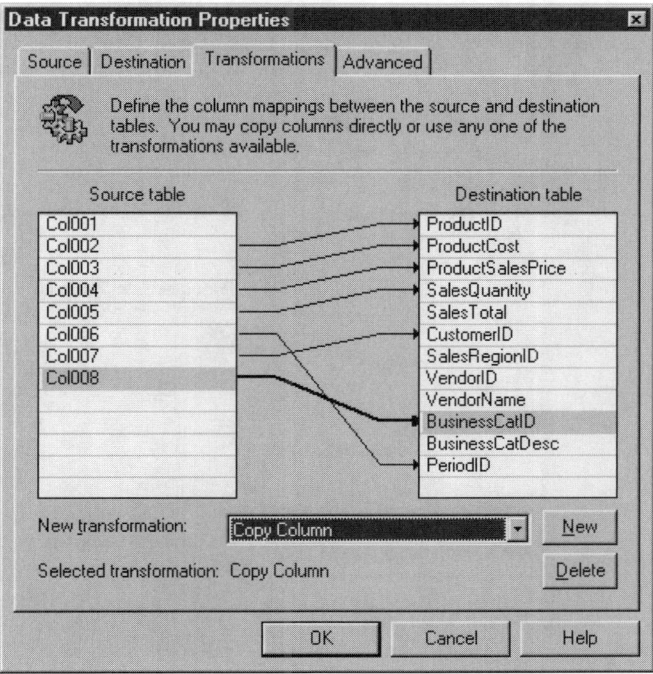

Figure 8.22 Data Transformation Properties dialog.

```
SET Sales.BusinessCatDesc = BusinessCategories.BusinessCatDesc
FROM Sales, BusinessCategories
WHERE Sales.BusinessCatID = BusinessCategories.BusinessCatID
```

To create the task simply follow the same instructions as you did to create the SQL Task (make sure you specify the Microsoft OLE DB Provider for SQL Server 7 in the Existing Connection drop-down box) that creates the SalesRegion table, but substitute the previous code listing. The previous code is contained in the ch8.sql file if you want to expedite the process. When you're through, label the task (Complete SalesData) and your Design Sheet should look like Figure 8.23.

That's it folks. We have created all of the necessary components, so now it's time to execute the package and analyze the results. To execute the package simply right-click the Design Sheet and select Execute.

USE DTS LOOKUPS WITH CAUTION

Are you wondering why we put so much of the data population code for the Sales table in a post-transfer SQL Task instead of a DTS Lookup? The main reason is because you can experience significant performance degradation when using DTS Lookups. The only reason we decided to use one for this project at all is that we thought you might run across them in *Books Online* and wonder how they are created. The syntax can be

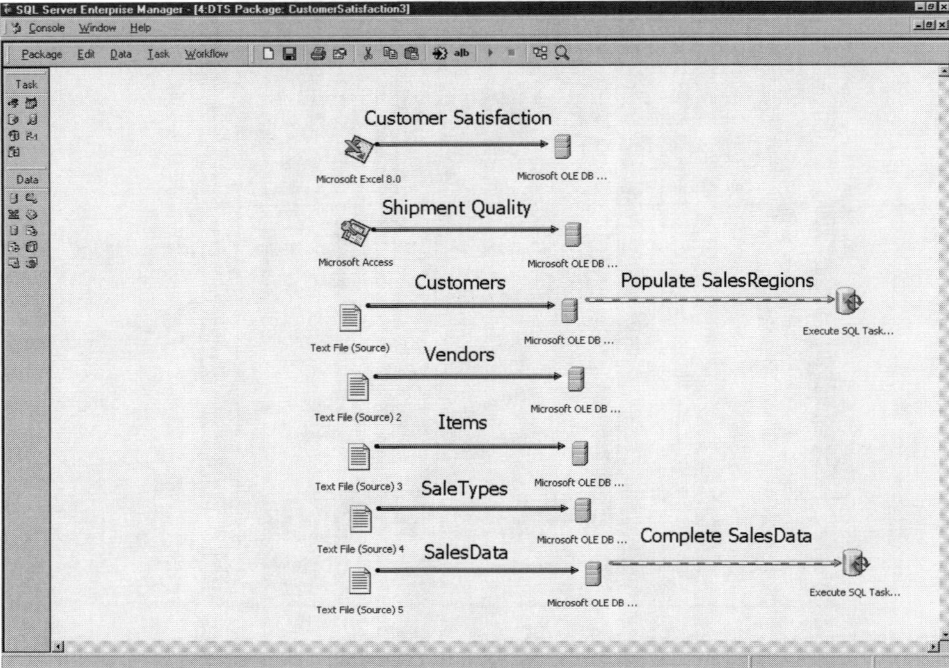

Figure 8.23 Completed Design Sheet.

a little tricky, so we thought we might reduce your learning time if we used one in this project. The reason they are so slow is that they execute for each record transferred from the source. So, if you have 100,000 records transferred from the source table, the stored procedure has to execute 100,000 times. The T-SQL we used in the SQL Task, on the other hand, executes only once and is much more efficient.

Verifying the Data

One of the most important aspects of transferring data from one format to another is to make sure that the destination data is congruent with the source data. We know what you're thinking, "we thought the process through and it was fairly straightforward, so there's no way that we could have made any mistakes." Well, we're here to tell you regardless of how thoroughly you think through the process, you can *still* make a mistake. So, the prudent thing to do is to implement some checks and balances that verify that nothing "bad" happened during the transfer/transformation process. No, it's not nearly as fun as implementing a cool transformation, but it's probably more important. After all, people will make crucial decisions off of "your"data.

The easiest way to validate the destination data is to compare it against known values from the source. For example, if the proprietary accounting package used by Plant

Dynamics can create a report that summarizes sales data, then run the report and compare it to the data in the data mart. Suppose the accounting package has a report that will count the number of items sold by ProductID. All you need to do to ensure that the data mart's sales data is correct is to execute a query that counts sales by ProductID. The following query will do just that.

```
SELECT ProductID COUNT(ProductID)
FROM SalesData
GROUP BY ProductID
```

All you really need to do is use common sense to make sure the data is correct. Pick a random statistical sampling of data and compare before and after. If you have five different classifications for Shipment Quality in the source, then you need five different classifications for Shipment Quality in the data mart.

Summary

As you can see, creating a data mart from multiple, disparate data sources can be a little tedious, but it's certainly not a task that should overwhelm you. We started out with source data in three different formats (Excel, Access, and Text) and ended with a star schema database that contained all of the data necessary to analyze three separate business processes. Of course, we've really only scratched the surface of the functionality available in DTS, so take what you've learned here and experiment with your own data. It won't be long before you're able to combine the disparate data your organization generates into a single source that will allow the decision makers of the company to make better, more informed decisions.

CHAPTER 9

Project #6: Working with OLAP Services

Goal

The goal of this chapter is to give you a firm grounding in the concepts behind OLAP Services, OLAP clients, and the MDX language and then to experiment with some ready-made cubes.

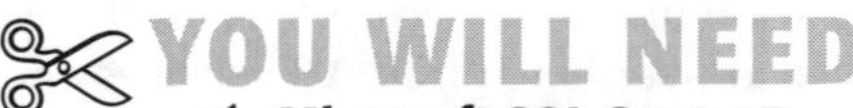

- ✔ Microsoft SQL Server 7
- ✔ Microsoft SQL Server OLAP Services installed on a Windows NT system
- ✔ FLIGHTS.CUB data file from accompanying CD

Recommended:

- ✔ OLAP Services SP1, OLAP Add-ins, Excel 2000

In Chapters 1 and 7, we discussed concepts such as the differences between online transaction processing (OLTP), online analytical processing (OLAP), data warehouses, and data marts. Remember that OLTP systems are systems whose main goal is to capture transactional data—data from order processing, manufacturing, or customer service operations. Canned end-of-month reports are often printed and distributed to everyone on a distribution list (whether the recipients want them or not), with mid-cycle *exception* reports printed and distributed as needed. These reports are *static* and present a rear-view mirror perspective on an organization's performance. They're often resource-intensive, and, because they're based on transaction-level detail, are often hard to interpret from a big picture point of view.

OLAP technology, on the other hand, is designed more with business analytics in mind. Because OLAP systems store and access data as *dimensions* that represent business factors like time, products, customers, and geographical regions, users can explore their data interactively—and along any combination of dimensions. They can slice and dice, drill down, roll up, and apply statistical functions to any set of numbers they select. Note we said *numbers.* OLAP, which is something like a cross between RDBMSs and spreadsheets, is used to analyze numerical data by category. It's not used to analyze text, objects, or any other non-numerical data. As you can imagine, OLAP isn't limited to working with operational systems' sales data. OLAP is increasingly harnessed to analyze customer relationship management (CRM), enterprise resource planning (ERP), and e-commerce data.

OLAP technology basically comes in two flavors: OLAP servers and OLAP clients. Microsoft SQL Server OLAP Services (henceforth Microsoft OLAP Services or simply OLAP Services) is server technology and only runs on Windows NT systems (as the NT service called MSSQLServerOLAPServer). Microsoft also ships a client-side component called the PivotTable Service, but PivotTable Service isn't a full-blown program like Cognos' NovaView or Knosys' ProClarity. PivotTable Service simply provides an OLE DB for OLAP interface that client tools and custom programs can use. In the first release of OLAP Services, OLAP Manager, which we'll use in this project, is the closest thing you'll find to a client tool. Figure 9.1 depicts an overview of OLAP Services and how it relates to RDBMS data and OLE DB for OLAP.

PIVOTTABLE SERVICE VERSUS EXCEL'S PIVOTTABLE FEATURE

Don't be confused by the similarity of the names. They're really totally different entities. OLAP Services' PivotTable Service component is really an in-process COM server. To a client, such as Visual Basic or a third-party OLAP client, the PivotTable Service exposes an OLE DB for OLAP interface that the client uses to obtain metadata and issue queries.

In this chapter, we're going to drill down into OLAP Services. Fair warning: OLAP isn't a slam dunk. Just because you "get" relational databases doesn't guarantee that you'll "get" OLAP "just like that." OLAP, after all, is multi-dimensional—spatial, if you will—while tables, the fundamental work unit of relational databases, are two-dimensional. It's been my experience (Karen's) that, just as some people find algebra easier than geometry, some people "get" RDBMSs a lot easier than they do OLAP. You might think

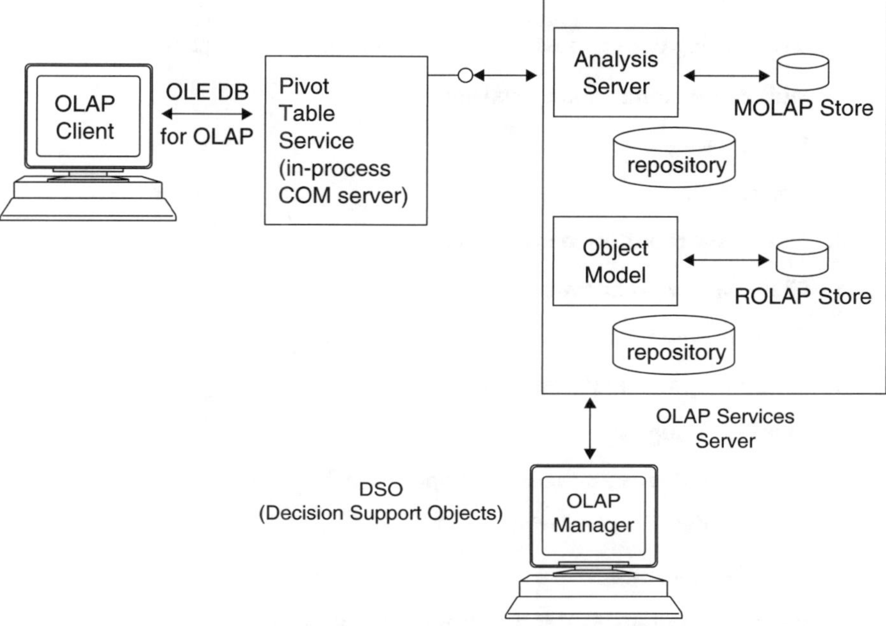

Figure 9.1 An overview of the OLAP system that ships with SQL Server.

of it as a left brain/right brain thing. The dichotomy isn't quite as stark as the differences between traditional programming and object-oriented programming, but almost.

We assume you've already installed OLAP Services. Remember, it can only be installed on an NT system, but that it can't be installed on a Windows NT 4.x domain controller (DC). That's because the OLAP Administrators must be a local group and a DC doesn't have a local group. Strangely enough, you won't necessarily get an error message that says the installation failed if you try to install it on a DC. You just won't be able to run OLAP Manager. Another bug: if, by chance, you're running Windows NT Server Enterprise Edition version 4.0 with the /3GB switch enabled on a computer that has 4GB RAM installed, the setup fails during OLAP Services installation with the following error message: Error 111 - Not enough Memory. KB article Q238304 describes the workaround.

Where Did OLAP Come From?

In case you're wondering, Microsoft didn't invent OLAP. No, its roots go *way* back to at least 1993 when Dr. Ted Codd, the "father" of relational database technology, published a white paper, *Providing OLAP to User Analysts: An IT Mandate*, whose message was that OLAP tools and their related *cubes* are better suited to tasks that require complex data analysis than relational databases. In that seminal white paper—which was partially funded by Arbor Software (now Hyperion Software)—Codd listed 12 rules for OLAP (subsequently expanded to 18 in 1995), that parallel his earlier 1985 article that appeared in *Computerworld* that had listed 12 rules for relational databases.

FYI CODD'S 12 RULES FOR OLAP

If you're burning with curiosity to know what those 12 rules were, here you go:

1. **Multidimensional conceptual view**
2. **Transparency**
3. **Accessibility**
4. **Consistent reporting performance**
5. **Client/server architecture**
6. **Generic dimensionality**
7. **Dynamic sparse matrix handling**
8. **Multi-user support**
9. **Unrestricted cross-dimensional operations**
10. **Intuitive data manipulation**
11. **Flexible reporting**
12. **Unlimited dimensions and aggregation levels**

Nigel Pendse and Richard Creeth of the *OLAP Report* (www.olapreport.com) later refined Dr. Codd's definition with what they called the FASMI test which states that OLAP applications should deliver Fast Analysis of Shared Multi-dimensional Information.

The idea is to load up an OLAP server with data that's likely to be combined. For example, think about all the possible ways to analyze clothing sales by brand name, size, color, store type, display location, season, promotional campaigns, advertising, and so on. Now imagine such a multi-dimensional hypercube filled with all of that data along with Excel-type tools that let you explore, for example, how various colors in a new line of underwear did as a result of a special Mother's Day sale, or how your department's advertising budget should be revised based on current year-to-date figures. OLAP products are particularly useful for time series analyses and for recursive calculations like allocating overhead as a percent of revenue contribution by product line.

Now, however, rather than fantasize about the types of calculations you'd like to do if you had a multi-dimensional cube full of figures, focus on the image of the giant multi-dimensional hypercube itself. You can probably see how quickly cubes can *explode*, not only because of a tremendous amount of raw and/or aggregated data, but also due to the need for building and maintaining specialized indexes that provide the required quick access.

For example, consider the OLAP Council's (www.olapcouncil.org) APB-1 sales and marketing benchmark application. It consists of six dimensions: Product (10,000 products and seven levels of products), Customer (1000 customers with three levels of customers), Scenario (16 scenarios), Time (86 time periods that consist of two years of monthly data), Measures (15 measures that represent financial calculations like margins), and Channel

(10 channels). In all, there are over 2 trillion possible combinations for all members and all dimensions. As you can imagine, most of the intersections would be empty—something that's referred to as data sparsity. One of the major challenges faced by OLAP vendors is how to deal with sparsity and the closely-related database explosion.

DATABASE EXPLOSION

At his OLAP Report site (www.olapreport.com), Nigel Pendse does a first-rate job of explaining the database explosion in OLAP. As sparse dimensions are added, there are higher order compounding effects, so that the compounding effect will be more than exponential. Pendse explains, "The effect is painfully simple: if you load, say, 50MB of external data into a six-dimensional structure, it is likely to shrink to perhaps 20MB if stored in an efficient multi-dimensional database (or to grow somewhat if stored in a star schema). But if you then pre-calculate every possible result, the database size will probably grow to at least 1GB, and possibly several times larger, particularly if the data is not stored with maximum efficiency. If, however, you started with 100MB of 8 dimensional data that shrank to 40MB when stored efficiently in an MDB, you might find that your fully-calculated database had exploded to more than 30GB (assuming, of course, that the software did not break or you did not run out of disk capacity first). Vendors may show off about their ability to work with databases of this size, but that is ducking the issue: they are using 30GB to store much less than 100MB of data, which is hardly something to boast about." He goes on to note that even if your software and hardware can handle GB+ cubes, the time to create (and update) the result may also be a prohibiting factor. Most organizations can't afford a multi-day data load window.

One approach is to only store cells (intersections) that contain data. But this ultimately relies on indexes which can quickly overwhelm the server since the index and keys tend to take up more space than the data itself. Other MOLAP products take a *multi-cube* approach and break the hypercube into a series of small, dense, pre-calculated cubes. Others rely on sophisticated compression algorithms.

ROLAP, MOLAP, HOLAP, (SCHMOLAP)

If you're not sure how multi-dimensionality, OLAP, and star schema are related, don't feel alone. OLAP products—which have their roots in decision support systems (DSS) and executive information systems (EIS)—originally stored their data in proprietary multi-dimensional form. *Star schema*, on the other hand, refer to a technique for adapting traditional relational databases to do OLAP where a central fact table containing values that can be aggregated is connected to a set of dimension tables. Informix's MetaCube and Microstrategy's DSS Server are well-known relational OLAP products that use star schema.

In the early days of OLAP technology, most vendors assumed that the only possible solution for OLAP applications was a specialized, proprietary, non-relational storage model that ultimately became known as MOLAP for multi-dimensional OLAP. Later, other vendors discovered that they could adapt RDBMSs for OLAP by introducing new database structures such as star and snowflake schemas, using bitmap indexes, and storing aggregates in a de-normalized version of traditional RDBMSs. These vendors called their technology Relational OLAP (ROLAP). MOLAP implementations usually outperform ROLAP technology, but generally aren't as scalable. On the other hand, ROLAP implementations are more scalable and are often attractive to customers because they leverage investments in existing relational database technology.

OLAP Services, however, lets you do it all: ROLAP, MOLAP, or HOLAP (hybrid OLAP, which combines MOLAP and ROLAP by creating multi-dimensional models and uses relational database storage systems). Under the HOLAP model, detail records (the largest volumes) are typically stored in the relational database, with aggregations stored in cube structures. Here's a quick summary:

Multi-dimensional OLAP (MOLAP) database. SQL Server's OLAP Services can create multi-dimensional cubes by retrieving data from SQL Server 7 (or any RDBMS that supports OLE DB or ODBC interfaces) and then places those detailed data and the desired aggregations in a specialized OLAP store, distinct from standard SQL Server files, that contain both the lowest level cell data held in the fact table and all pre-calculated aggregations. Aggregations are usually pre-calculated sums or averages that improve query response time by having the answers ready before the questions are asked.

MOLAP, then, is a high-performance, multi-dimensional, data-storage format that stores data on the OLAP server. MOLAP storage is appropriate for small to medium-sized data sets where copying all of the data to the multi-dimensional format would not require significant loading time or utilize large amounts of disk space.

ACCORDING TO AMIR NETZ

Amir Netz, one of the prime architects of OLAP Services (see FYI: *Where Did OLAP Services Come From?*) thinks MOLAP's reputation for not scaling well is undeserved in the case of OLAP Services. When a user posted a question on the microsoft.public .sqlserver.olap newsgroup in summer 1999, Amir replied, "What is a good size for MOLAP? I have not seen yet the database that our MOLAP did not handle. The reasons for using ROLAP/HOLAP aren't usually related to scalability. They are more related to the level of comfort you have with relational technologies and some of the infrastructure that it has (replication, back-up). You can also reuse the relational tables in a relational application."

Relational OLAP (ROLAP) engine. OLAP Services can also create ROLAP warehouses or marts where aggregations and tables that support star schema are actually stored in non-normalized tables in a SQL Server database. With ROLAP, data remains in the original relational database tables, but a separate set of relational tables is used to store and reference aggregation data. ROLAP is ideal for large databases or legacy data that is infrequently queried.

Hybrid OLAP (HOLAP). Aggregated summary data is stored in the multi-dimensional database, while the detailed transaction-level data remains in the relational database.

Unfortunately, there aren't any simple rules to help you decide which storage model to opt for. You'll need to balance these items:

- Volume of data to be stored
- Size of the largest dimension
- How often the data needs to be updated
- How often you expect to change the database dimensions
- Number of concurrent users and whether they require read only or read/write access
- Whether the data will be shared by other applications
- Your server's hardware

In general, however, ROLAP will tend to result in slower processing and querying, so you will probably want to avoid it unless you have compelling reasons to maintain the tight integration with the underlying relational system. In deciding between MOLAP and HOLAP, consider how frequently users are likely to require access to the fact table data and how long they're willing to wait for a query at this most granular level. If query time is a deciding factor, use MOLAP. Otherwise, use HOLAP. Where Is OLAP Data Stored?

Each OLAP Services server stores databases in a single directory tree, with each database having its own sub-directory. Within a database's directory, there are separate .DIM files for each dimension that contain all the detailed information about the dimension such as the member keys, values for member properties, and parent-child relationships. Under Windows NT 4.x, the device and directory used for the OLAP Services' root directory needs to be large enough to contain all databases (and their files), since they will need to be on a single logical device. This constraint will probably be eliminated under Windows 2000, allowing you to mount logical disk devices with a directory tree.

Each cube—cubes are the logical storage medium for OLAP—associated with the database has its own sub-directory that contains a basic descriptive .MDL file plus files that contain MOLAP-format data for one or more partitions. OLAP Services also maintains its own internal representations of cubes—along with other metadata associated with the databases, dimensions, and their components in a Jet/.MDB repository called MSMDREP .MDB located in the \bin directory that contains the server executables. See Figure 9.2.

WHERE DID OLAP SERVICES COME FROM?

When Microsoft launched the Plato project in 1996, Rony Ross and her firm, Panorama Software Systems Ltd., had already been shipping the EIS product whose server portion was to become OLAP Services for over a year. According to Ross, who has a BSc. in Mathematics/Statistics from Tel Aviv University, an MSc. in Computer Science from Weissman Institute of Science, an MBA in Marketing form Tel Aviv University Business School, and who has done graduate work in AI at UCLA, Amir Netz, now with Microsoft, was the "most prominent developer" behind Plato. When I asked Rony what feature of Panorama's Plato she was proudest of, she said "the way the product handles the issue of database explosions...Most older systems would either put a limit on the number of dimensions to be used or would create

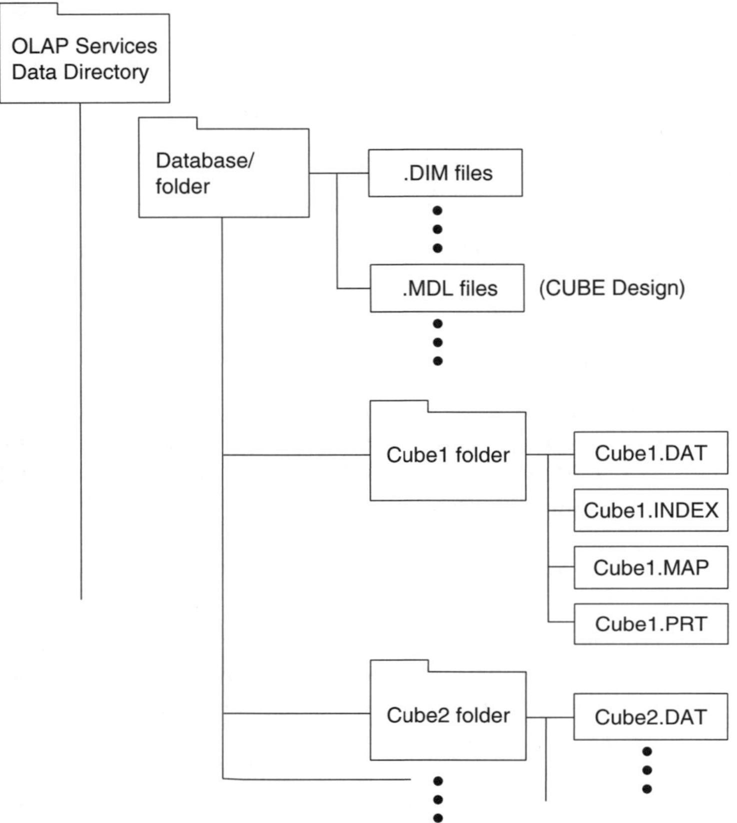

Figure 9.2 An overview of the directory structure associated with OLAP Services.

huge multi-dimensional databases. Panorama has a very smart mechanism to figure out how to intelligently create the multi-dimensional database in a way that takes into account various factors such as actual user requirements—based on a learning mechanism, desired multi-dimensional size, etc."

In early 1997, Microsoft acquired Panorama's server technology, and each of the six-man development team accepted jobs with Microsoft. Panorama continues to develop a client product to access OLAP Services, and Cognos has the exclusive worldwide rights to sell Panorama's OLAP client as NovaView.

OLAP-Speak

Before you start using an OLAP product, it helps to have a basic understanding of dimensions, measures, hierarchies, members, cubes, cells, and the basic types of actions you're likely to perform on multi-dimensional data.

Measures are the quantitative values in the database that you want to analyze. Typical measures are sales, cost, and budget data. Measures are analyzed against the different dimension categories of a cube. For example, you may want to analyze sales and budget data (your measures) for a particular product (a dimension) across various countries (specific levels of a geography dimension) during two particular years (levels of a time dimension).

Dimensions represent the facts, factors, entities, or perspectives you want to analyze. A dimension is a collection of members of the same type, and each data point in a multidimensional data set is associated with one member from each of the multiple dimensions. The simplest way to create dimension information is to use the value from a single column. Dimensions will have names like [Time] or [Products].

Dimensions are typically organized into hierarchies of information that map to columns in a relational database. Dimension hierarchies are grouped into levels that consist of dimension members. Each level in a dimension can be rolled together to form the values for the next highest level. For example, in a time dimension, days roll into weeks or months, and months roll into quarters.

Dimensions can be either *shared* or *private*. Shared means that the dimensions are visible to the entire database and may be used by one or multiple cubes that automatically join along shared dimensions in queries and virtual cubes. A private dimension is cube- (or virtual cube-) specific and is defined within the context of its cube. Because private dimensions are always "processed" with their cube, there's no chance that a private dimension will ever be processed—either fully or incrementally—separately from the cube. (More about cube processing below.) The main limitation of private dimensions is that you can't define virtual dimensions from the properties of private dimensions.

Dimension *tables* such as location or product associated with star schema describe the grouping data by which data values such as sales from the central fact table can be aggregated. Dimension tables contain member names, hierarchy information, and sometimes other data pertaining to attributes/member properties.

The most important characteristic of a dimension is the number of levels and members contained within it. Basically, the more members per dimension level, the more memory and disk space will be used, the longer the processing will take, and the larger the indexes.

Hierarchies are attributes of dimensions and refer to the organization of members into a logical tree structure. They basically define the drill-up and drill-down paths for query navigation. A time dimension, for example, may consist of a hierarchy of hours, days, weeks, months, quarters, and so on. The geography region might consist of neighborhood, city, district, state, region, and country. Most members will have connections both up (to a parent) and down (to a child) in a hierarchy. A member with no parent is a root member, and one with no children is a leaf member.

Most hierarchies are designed either via *consolidation* or via *snowflaking*. With the consolidation approach, you embed an entire hierarchy into a dimension table, effectively de-normalizing entities like products or customers. Snowflaking, which gets its name from the appearance that results from adding hierarchical table extensions to arms of a star in a star schema, maintains some level of normalization and results in a lower overall row count, but requires complex joins to access actual values.

By the way, you aren't limited to a single hierarchy for each dimension. OLAP Services lets you define multiple hierarchies using a dot notation within the dimension's name, such as [Sales].[ByCategory] and [Sales].[ByDepartment].

A *member* is a single element or unit within a dimension that represents one or more data occurrences. A member can be either unique or non-unique. For example, 1997 and 1998 represent unique members in the year level of a time dimension, whereas January represents a non-unique member in the month level because there can be more than one January in the time dimension if it contains data for more than one year. Members have names that can be used to identify them in queries, and OLAP Services uses a *member key* to identify members and access related data values in storage. Generally speaking, you should keep the member key value as small as possible, because the server does a lot of comparing of member keys. Use integer rather than text/string data types for member keys whenever possible.

In addition to member keys, members also have properties. A good strategy is to store minimum properties for the dimension at the highest level possible, such as on state rather than city or neighborhood. Members have rather complex, unique names that start with the name of the dimension and move down the hierarchy, with dots (.s) that separate the elements.

SOME THINGS *ARE* CAST IN CONCRETE

In the first version of OLAP Services—the one that ships with SQL Server 7—if you want to change any of the items shown here, you'll have to blow away your cube or dimension and rebuild it from scratch with the desired name.

- **Database names**
- **Dimension names**
- **Cube names**
- **Cube or dimension data sources**

A *cube* is a subset of data from the data warehouse or data mart that's organized and summarized into multidimensional structures. Each cube dimension can contain a hierarchy of levels which contain increasingly detailed information. Cubes, by the way, aren't limited to three dimensions and can, in fact, contain up to 64 dimensions. The OLAP Manager ships with ten wizards, one of which is the Cube wizard which helps you define your cubes.

When you "process" a cube, the aggregations designed for the cube are calculated and the cube is loaded with the calculated aggregations and data. Processing a cube involves reading the dimension tables to populate the levels with members from the actual data, reading the fact table, calculating specified aggregations, and storing the results in the cube. (Physically, you should see a .PRT, a .MAP, an .INDEX, and a .DATA file associate with each cube. These files contain, respectively, minimal information about a partition, a "map" of the data and internal indexing structures, the actual index, and the actual data including any aggregations.) Only after a cube has been *processed* is it available for querying by users. OLAP Services provides you with the option of doing incremental updates and of refreshing cube data.

If you have SQL Server Enterprise Edition installed (the "high-end" version that requires the top or the line version of Windows NT that supports clustering), the OLAP Manager allows you to store, manage, and distribute cube data using partitions. Partitions, which are physically segregated storage regions, can be optimized individually, but queried together as a whole. Partitions allow you to separate cube data across a cluster of servers. For example, you may choose to store older, less-often-queried data on a slow server with more recent, frequently-queried data stored on a high-speed server. Data slices, which represent a subset of the data in a partition, allow you, for example, to create separate slices for certain products across all years.

PARTITION CONFUSION

Confused why your non-Enterprise Edition version of SQL Server's OLAP Services sample Warehouse cube has two partitions even though "standard edition" isn't supposed to support them? Well, join the club. Although they may have been created with a "real" Enterprise Edition, it's far more likely that they were created with a beta version that supported partitions before Microsoft made the marketing decision to only allow user-defined partitions in the EE. At least it shows that even a non-EE version of OLAP Services can *use* a partitioned cube. You can see the value of partitions when you think about the partitionless Sales cube. You need to run incremental process and change the name of the fact table to sales_fact_1998 and sales_fact_dec_1998 in order to see the full data of sales for both years and also for the international operations in Canada and Mexico. Some innovative users have created a three-partition version of Sales using EE, archived the database (using the Add-ins feature) and restored it on a server with a Standard version of OLAP Services. This will work fine but you won't be able to add any more partitions.

Partitions are really a "must" for any serious OLAP project because, among other things, they solve the problem of identifying the new data that was inserted to the data-mart since the last process. By reprocessing the partition that holds the last month data every day, you can be quite sure that you don't process anything twice—or miss anything.

You can also define virtual cubes—which are similar to views in relational databases—and local cubes. When you create a virtual cube, you include measures and dimensions from multiple cubes to create a larger view of the data. Virtual cubes, like RDBMS views, can be effectively used to restrict access to data. Also, by using the CREATE CUBE and INSERT INTO statements, end users can define local cubes can be stored either in MOLAP or ROLAP formats for offline analysis (analysis while not connected to OLAP Services.) The PivotTable Service, which creates the local cubes, assigns them a default file extension of .CUB.

Local cubes can be saved either as ROLAP or MOLAP cubes. MOLAP cubes generally offer better performance, but take up more space than ROLAP cubes. (When you define a ROLAP local cube, only the local cube structure definition and dimension members are stored locally, not the actual data, so users must have access to the ROLAP provider—not the OLAP server—in order to access their local cube.) Any third-party OLAP client products worth its salt will make it easy for users to save local .CUB files.

As you can see, OLAP cubes are very different from the tables in relational databases. Cubes are created via dimensional modeling, not entity-relationship modeling; the relationship (no pun intended) between RDBMSs and OLAP is like that of algebra to geometry, one being more analytical, one more spatial.

Creating a Multi-Dimensional Database

There are several ways you can create a multidimensional database. You can do it programmatically using DSO (Decision Support Objects). You can do it more or less in two steps, first using DTS (Data Transformation Services) to create a data warehouse or mart, and then create a dimensional model based on the data warehouse. Or you can just use the Cube Wizard.

WHAT'S DSO?

Decision Support Objects is a set of objects whose methods, properties, and collections allow a programmer to control OLAP servers. DSO is specific to OLAP Services and isn't part of OLE DB for OLAP or ADOMD (ADO MultiDimensional). DSO is to OLAP as SQL-DMO is to SQL Server.

Whichever approach you use, the first step is to make sure you know your raw data including its data types and overall integrity. You may want to do some preliminary "cleanup" or preparation before using DTS to populate your first cube.

The second step is to figure out the measures and dimensions of the cube. This will probably be hard at first, but once you've got a few dimensional models under your belt, it will become easier.

If you use the OLAP Manager, the next step is to create the OLAP Services database, and then to create the dimensions based on tables in the data source.

Finally, you'll get to construct the cube or cubes that connect fact tables to dimensions and define the aggregations.

Well, I think we deserve a break. Let's experiment.

Investigating an Existing Multi-Dimensional Database

Before we jump into OLAP Services, use your Explorer to examine the files associated with OLAP Services. The default installation is ..\Program Files\OLAPServices. Drill down into the data\Food Mart sub-directory (see Figure 9.3); Notice how most of the

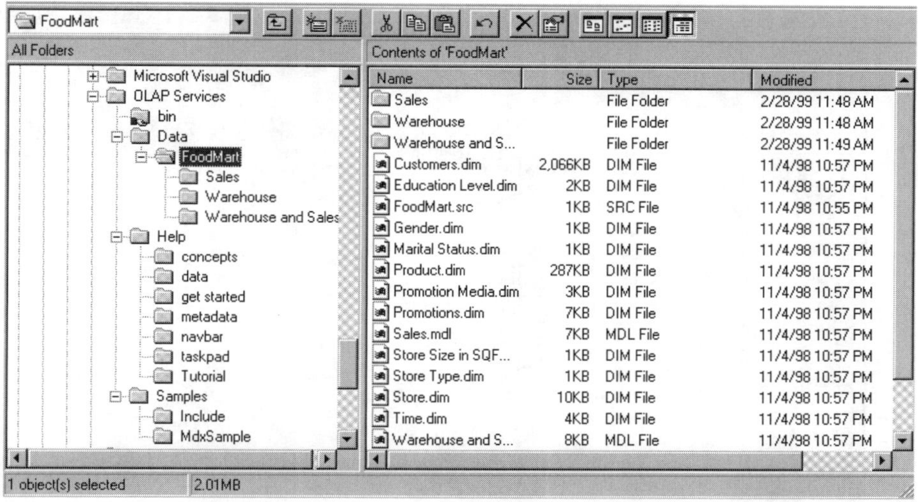

Figure 9.3 Using Explorer to see what files are associated with OLAP Services.

files are .DIM and .MDL files. If you try to inspect any of them with a word processor, you'll discover that they aren't "plain" text files, but that they're binary. According to the documentation, they're also compressed according to a proprietary algorithm.

EMPTY WAREHOUSE AND SALES FOLDER

Don't be surprised to see an empty sub-directory under Food Mart called Warehouse and Sales. That refers to a FoodMart "virtual cube", so it's like a placeholder.

Notice that the Customers' .DIM file, for example, is a bit over 2 MB. If you open the ...\OLAP Services\Samples sub-directory, you'll see that the underlying .MDB file is just over 23 MB. If you have Microsoft Access and open the FoodMart.MDB file, you'll see that it contains 15 tables. The Customer table, for example, whose table structure is displayed in Figure 9.4, contains a fair amount of data about 10,281 customers. If you examine each of the tables, you'll discover that the sales fact table for 1998 is the largest table (see Table 9.1).

Examining the underlying data, as mentioned previously, is the first step in figuring out how to build your multi-dimensional database. In the case of FoodMart, Microsoft has already built it for us. Let's see how they've organized it. To do that, we'll need to use OLAP Manager.

Okay, enough of Microsoft Access, let's see how OLAP Manager works.

We're going to assume that you've successfully installed OLAP on your NT workstation or server (remember, OLAP Services won't run under Win9x).

Start the OLAP Manager from the Start Menu | Programs | Microsoft SQL Server 7.0 | OLAP Services | OLAP Manager and expand the console root until you find your server. Double-click on it or select Connect from the Action menu. If you aren't successful,

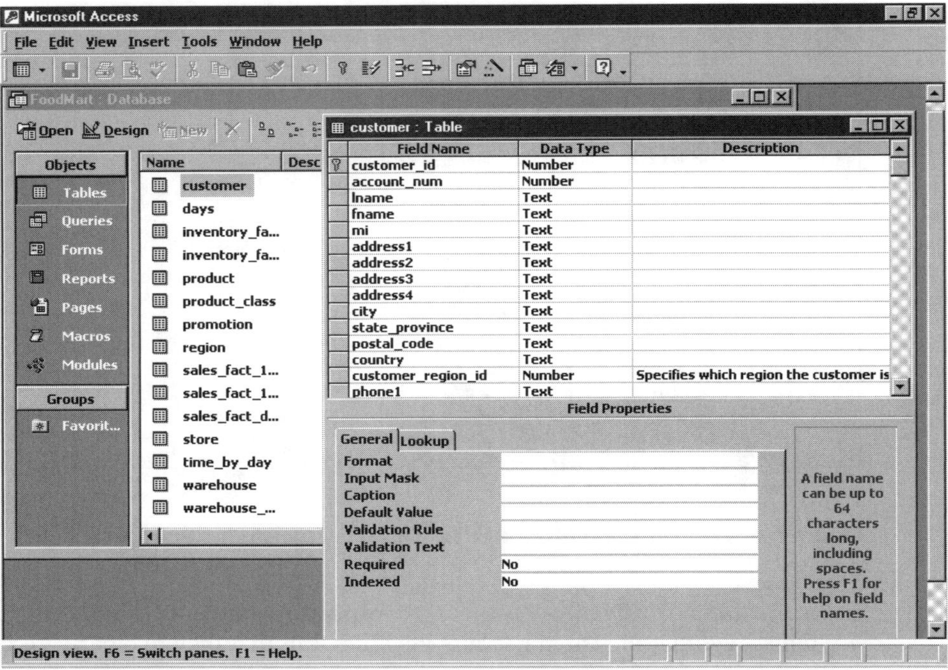

Figure 9.4 Looking at FoodMart's source database, FoodMart.MDB.

Table 9.1 If You Have Microsoft Access, You Can Double-Check Our Work

TABLE IN FOODMART.MDB	NUMBER OF ROWS
Days	7
Inventory_fact_1997	4070
Inventory_fact_1998	7282
Product	1560
Product_class	110
Promotion	1864
Region	110
Sales_fact_1997	86837
Sales_fact_1998	164558
Sales_fact_dec_1998	8325
Store	24
Time_by_day	730
Warehouse	24
Warehouse_class	6

click on the menu bar's Help icon (the question mark—it should be on the far right) and read through the sections on *Installing OLAP Services* and *Troubleshooting*. If that doesn't work, consider Uninstalling and re-installing OLAP Services and try again.

CANNOT CONNECT ERROR

If you try to connect to an OLAP server from the OLAP Manager on a remote client computer, you will receive the message "Cannot connect to the <DataSourceName> data source " if the ODBC data source name (DSN) for the OLAP database isn't defined on the remote client computer. The solution is to define a DSN on the client computer. The DSN must have the same name as the one that has been defined for the cube that you want to browse in your OLAP server. Refer to KB article Q238034 for more information.

In fact, there's another situation where you may run into problems connecting, but this one's a bug. If a user is a Windows NT administrator for the OLAP server computer but is *not* a member of the OLAP Administrators group, cube access is always denied. This occurs even if the user is mapped to a role that has read or read/write access to the cube. This behavior is seen from clients such as the MDX sample application, Excel 2000, and so forth, and can result in errors such as "Unable to open cellset. Access to (<cube name>) was denied", "Unable to expand node. Access to (<cube name>) was denied", or "Microsoft Excel was unable to get necessary information about this cube. The cube might have been reorganized or changed on the server. Contact the OLAP cube administrator and, if necessary, setup a new data source to connect to the cube". The solution is to remove the user from the Administrators group on the server computer. See KB article Q236315 for more information.

Assuming that you were successful, you should see the OLAP Manager's main screen with the console hierarchy on the left and the Taskpad on the right as shown in Figure 9.5. It looks a lot like SQL Server's Enterprise Manager.

It's worth spending a few minutes reading through the three main topics in the Understanding OLAP Concepts task. It provides a good review of the basics on cubes, virtual cubes, and data storage that you read about earlier in this chapter.

The *OLAP Manager Tutorial* is also very good, but it will take you a good hour to do, so keep that in mind when you do run through it. We recommend that you delay doing the tutorial until you've explored the Sales and Warehouse cubes discussed in the next section. The OLAP Services on the Web task works pretty much as advertised and tries to log you on to www.microsoft.com/sql/70/gen/olap.htm. You may, for example, want to install the latest service pack (remember, they're cumulative, so you generally won't have to install an SP1 if there's an SP2). As of summer 1999, there was an optional OLAP Manager Add-In kit that you can download for added functionality in these areas:

Archiving and restoring databases. The kit archives and restores OLAP Services databases from within the OLAP Manager. This utility also enables databases to be archived from one server and restored to another.

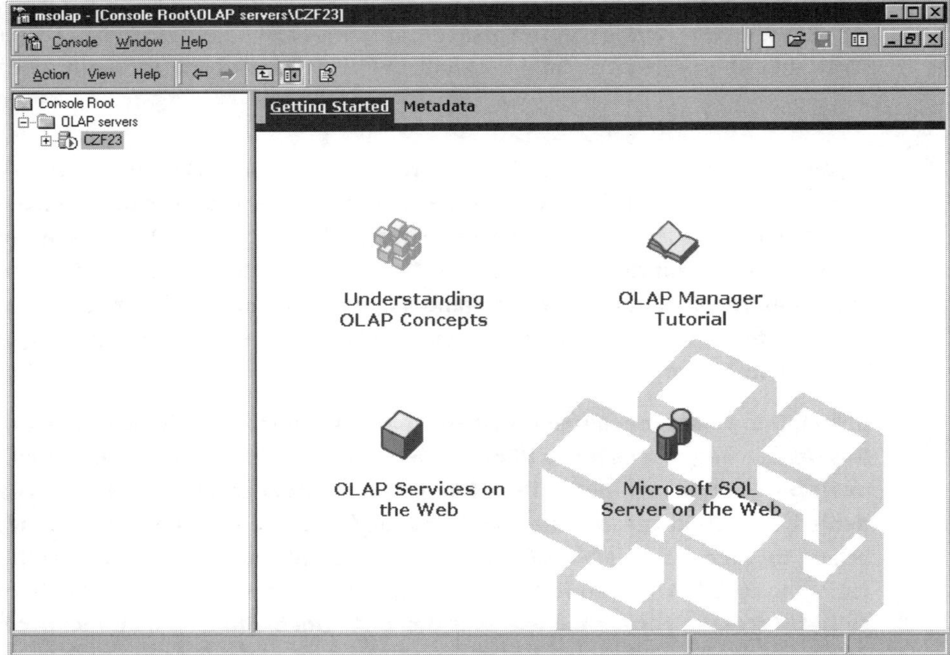

Figure 9.5 The OLAP Manager.

Calculated members manager. This utility manages calculated members in virtual cubes.

Copying and pasting objects. This utility uses the copying and pasting functionalities to more easily manage objects within the OLAP Manager tree view (metadata movement).

Obviously archiving and restoring OLAP Services databases is an important function, so we strongly recommend that you download and install (see Figure 9.6) the add-ins which are available on the right-click menus of the appropriate objects in the OLAP Manager:

- To access the Calculated Member Manager, in the OLAP Manager, right-click a virtual cube, and then click Manage Calculated Members. To access the FoodMart sample virtual cube, expand OLAP Servers, (the server), FoodMart, Cubes, and Virtual Cubes.
- To access the Copy and Paste Objects add-in, select the object you want to copy in the OLAP Manager tree view, and then click Copy.
- To access the Archive and Restore Databases add-in, select a database in the OLAP Manager tree view, and then click Archive.

You can get more details by reading the AddinsReadMe.txt installed in the Help subfolder of the OLAP Services folder.

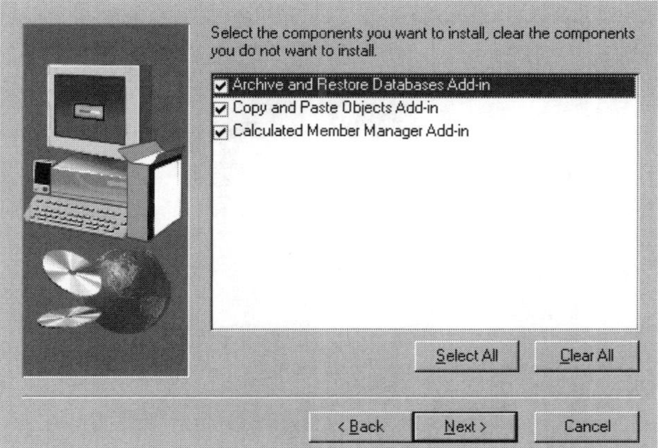

Figure 9.6 Installing ADDINS.EXE—available from the Microsoft downloads site.

BUILD YOUR OWN OLAP SERVICES ADD-INS

You can build you own Add-In for OLAP Services. For more information, read OLAP Services' own *Books Online* article, *Building Add-in Programs*.

Exploring the Sales Cube

Now let's go over to the Console tree and drill down to see what we've got. If you did a standard installation (including the sample database), you should see the FoodMart database. When you expand it, you'll see its three main folders: Cubes, Virtual Cubes, and Libraries. Expand the Cube folder to see the cubes that make up the FoodMart database. There are two: Sales and Warehouse. Expand each of the cubes, and then focus on the Sales cube. Expand the Sales cube's Dimensions and Measures (feel free to expand the Partitions, too, but there's only one since the example wasn't set up for an Enterprise Server with clusters and all that.) On the left, highlight the Sales cube's Dimensions level. Then, over on the right, click on the Metadata tab. You should see something like Figure 9.7.

The dimensions overview provides a snapshot of the available dimensions and the number of their levels. There are a dozen dimensions in Sales:

- Customers
- Education level
- Gender
- Marital Status
- Product
- Promotion Media
- Promotions

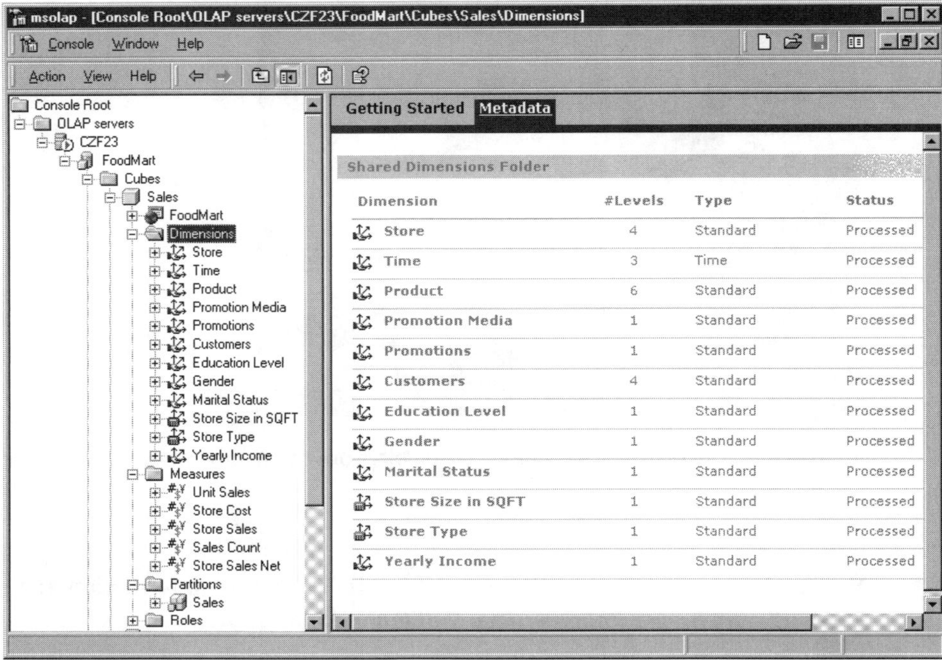

Figure 9.7 Beginning to explore the FoodMart Sales cube.

- Store
- Store Size in SQFT
- Store type
- Time
- Yearly income

The depth of the hierarchies, remember, reflect how much you can drill up and down once you start to examine the data. Notice that, aside from Product, Store, and Customers, our hierarchies are pretty flat. The Metadata tab also indicates that all the dimensions have been *processed*. Remember that dimensions have to be processed before they're available, since that's when the cube gets populated.

If you click on Store, you'll see there are 24 stores. If you click on Product (see Figure 9.8), you'll see how that hierarchy is designed and how many members are associated with each level.

Notice also that the Product dimension is used in three cubes: Sales, Warehouse, and the virtual cube called Sales and Warehouse.

Take a minute to explore the other dimensions—and the Warehouse cube.

Now return to the Sales cube and highlight the Sales cube and right-click to see the menu as shown in Figure 9.9.

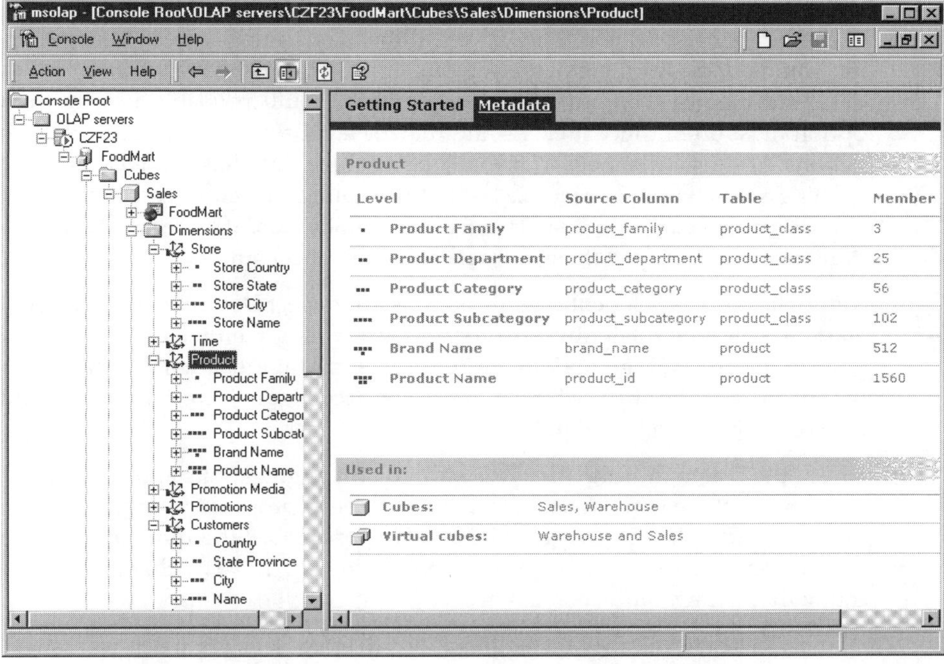

Figure 9.8 Not unexpectedly, FoodMart has more products than customers or stores.

Let's explore the menu's options. We don't want to create a new cube or edit the current one, so let's start with the third choice, Process.

If you select Process, you'll see there are three options: incremental update, refresh data, or process. Populating a *really* large cube can take hours or even days, and that's why the incremental and refresh options are useful. An incremental update adds new

Figure 9.9 OLAP Manager's cube level menu.

data to a partition in the cube and updates aggregations but does not process changes to a cube's structure such as measures, dimensions, and so on, or changes to its existing source data. An incremental update creates a temporary partition from the new data and merges it into an existing partition. You'll probably use the refresh data option most often, since it clears and reloads a cube's data and recalculates its aggregations. You use this method if the cube's source data has changed but its structure hasn't. As you would expect, the last option rebuilds the cube from scratch, completely restructuring a cube based on its current definitions and then recalculating its data. We don't need to do any of them, so just escape or cancel out.

Right-click on the Sales cube again and this time select Design Storage. OLAP Manager starts the Storage Design wizard for you. The first screen tells you that this is where you design the storage options for your data and aggregations. Click Next and read that the Sales cube already has aggregations (see Figure 9.10), 53 of them, and that the Sales cube is set up for MOLAP storage.

Check the box to indicate that you want to add aggregations and click Next. This is a key screen where you have to select one of three approaches to aggregations. Press the Help key. The Storage Design wizard's Help describes the three options. Remember how we said that when wizards had their own help, it was a clue that you were dealing with a "heavy" topic?

1. Services determine which aggregations to store. This approach works well when you have limited storage space.
2. Set the percentage of performance gain and let the necessary aggregation tables take as much storage space as they need.
3. Manually determine the best balance by watching the progress of the Performance vs. Size graph.

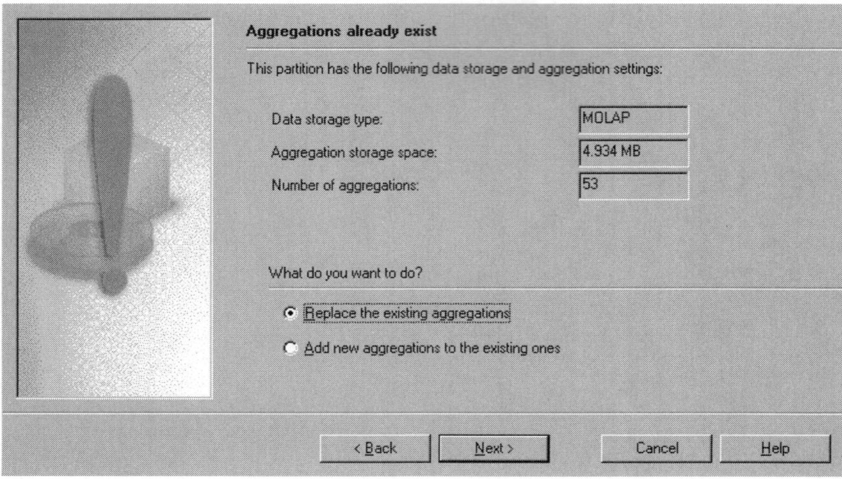

Figure 9.10 The Sales cube's storage.

We don't really want to change anything now, so simply close the help window and press Escape or Cancel to exit the Storage Design wizard.

Back to the Sales cube's right-click menu. The next of the right-click Sales cube's options are to run the usage-based optimization wizard. You should do this after a few days of a new cube's usage, and thereafter every week or so until things seem to run pretty well. We don't need to run this one now, either, so escape out.

Now comes the one you've been waiting for—Browse Data (see Figure 9.11).

You'll see the Cube Browser appears when you right-click a processed cube and then click Browse Data, or when you click Browse Sample Data in the last step of the Cube wizard. (The Browse Sample Data feature is a really neat feature that does just what it says—check out the data in table form if you're not sure which table contains what data.)

The top part of the Cube Browser is called the Slicer pane; the bottom half is the Data grid. Note that the default layout has Customers along one axis of the Data grid and all the Measures (compare with Measures listed in the console hierarchy on the left).

VERSION INFORMATION

The "1.0" release of OLAP Services that shipped with SQL Server 7 was 7.0.1073. You'll know you installed SP1 if OLAP Manager's Help About screen says 7.0.1295.

Okay, let's see how this cube stuff works.

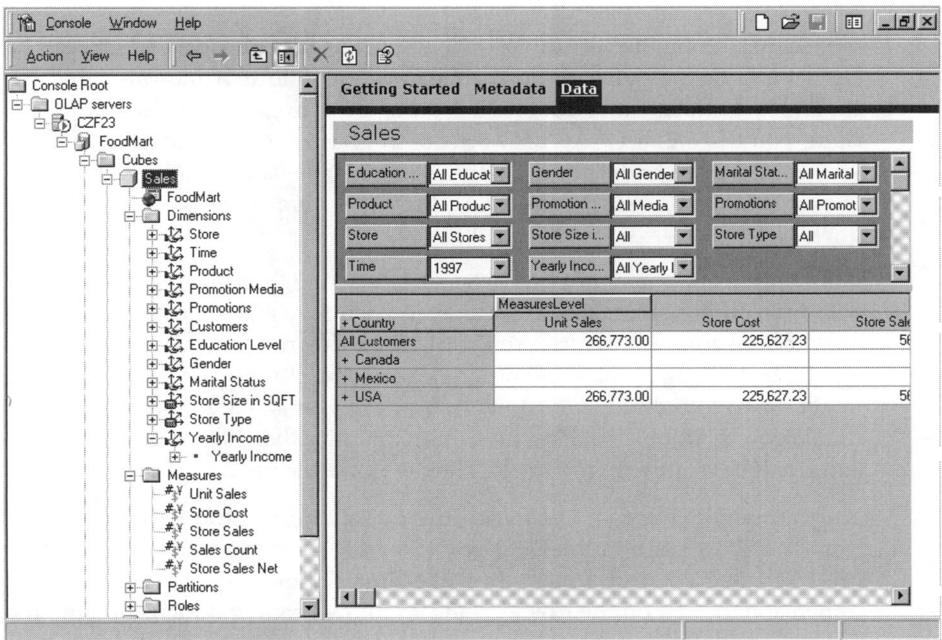

Figure 9.11 OLAP Manager's Cube browser allows you to quickly browse multi-dimensional data in a flattened, two-dimensional grid format.

Figure 9.12 Exploring data in the Cube Browser.

Notice that, along the vertical axis, Country, Canada, Mexico, and USA all have a plus (+) symbol on the left side of their names—a code that indicates that they can be expanded. Go ahead and double click on Country to expand it. As you attempt to scroll right, you'll see that OLAP Browser doesn't have the best interface in the world and why third-party vendors of OLAP client tools have value to add in this arena. You can improve things by sizing the Cube Browser window or simply choose View and uncheck Console Tree (see Figure 9.12).

Well, that display may not be particularly exciting, but it should provide you with a better feeling for what OLAP folks mean when they talk about sparse data. Now double-click on State/Province. You're drilling down the Customers dimension. You should be looking at sales and other measures by city. You've got one more level to go to get down to individual customers. You can jump back to the top of the Customers dimension by double-clicking on Country. Notice that Measures along the horizontal axis don't have any plus symbols. They're not drillable.

You can easily change a Data grid row or column by simply dragging a dimension from the Slicer pane to the Data grid. To view sales totals by store location for each product category, you would drop the Stores dimension onto the Measures Level dimension located on the row axis and drop the Product dimension onto the Country dimension located on the column axis. In Figure 9.13, we drilled down into the Non-Consumable Products category into Periodicals and Magazines until we saw subtotals of magazine sales by subcategory.

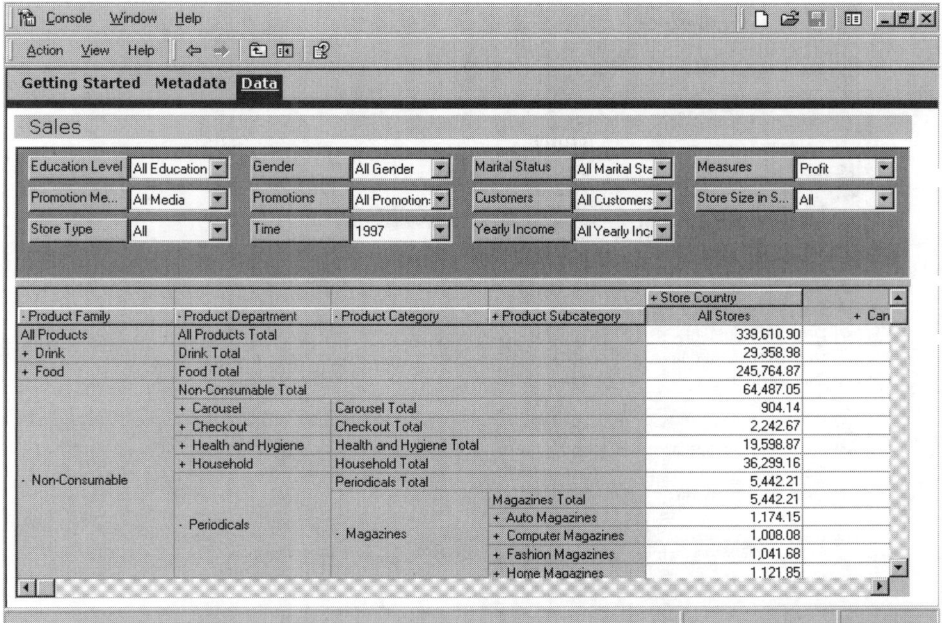

Figure 9.13 Drilling down through products to see sales totals by store.

The Cube browser has an internal memory limit that you may reach if you attempt to browse too much data or drill down too deeply. When you reach the limit, the following (depressing) message is displayed:

Unable to display current view of cube.

Unable to Allocate Memory for Flexgrid.

Surprisingly, this is one place you can't solve things simply by throwing more memory at it. If you reach the limit, says Microsoft helpfully, "reduce the amount or depth of data you are attempting to browse or use another browser."

USE CUBE BROWSER WITH VB

You can use the Cube Browser with VB by adding it to your project from the Project|References menu. Note that Cube Browser (msmdcb.ocx) isn't data aware, so you'll have to write code using the Connect or ConnectWStr methods (see Figure 9.14). Note: the first version of this OCX doesn't have a print method.

What would you do to investigate Product sales by Time? Right! Just drag Time onto the horizontal axis where Country is. Now put Customers back along the horizontal axis, and drag Time so that it's *next* to Country, not on top of it. The result should be similar to Figure 9.15.

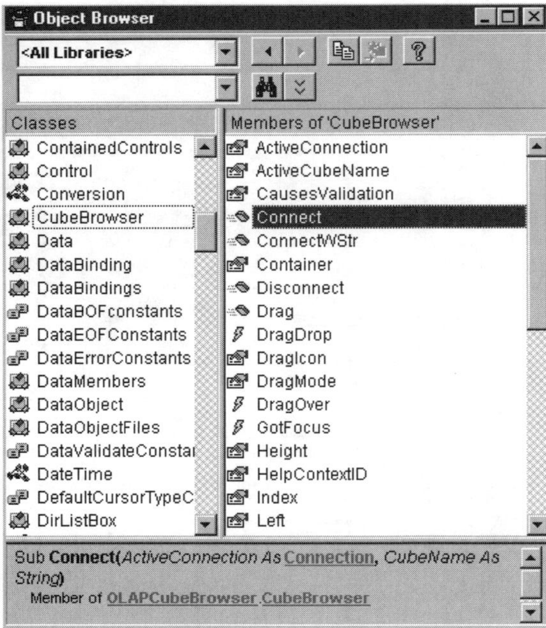

Figure 9.14 You can call the Cube Browser from within a VB or other COM-compatible program.

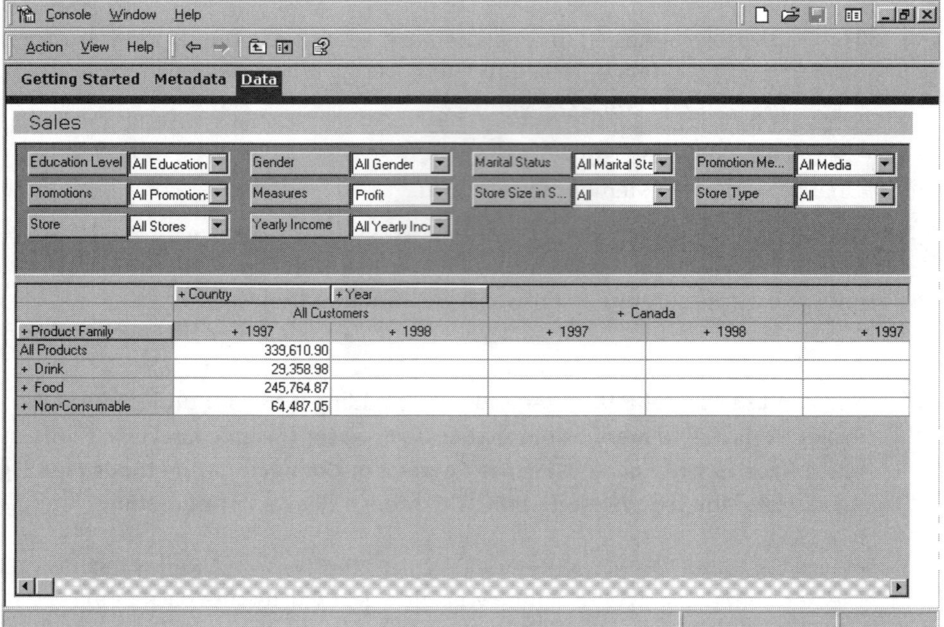

Figure 9.15 Adding complexity to our two-dimensional view.

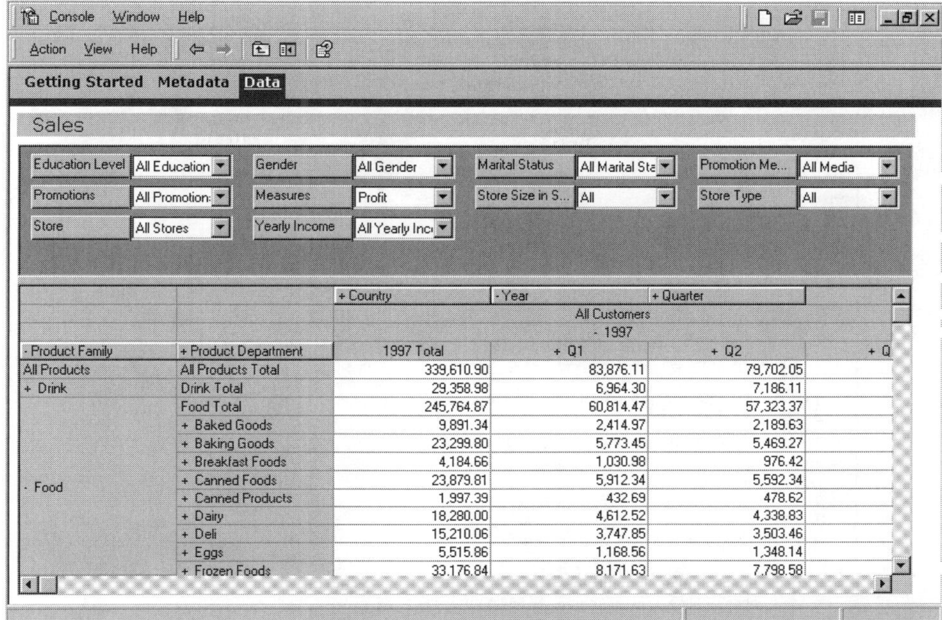

Figure 9.16 Examining sales by location and time.

As you can see, this cube stuff is pretty nifty once you get the hang of it. Double-clicking on Year starts you down the Time hierarchy, which is how most people use OLAP. Spend some time drilling down through Time and Products as we did in Figure 9.16.

Okay, back to work. We were *supposed* to be exploring the Sales cube's right-click context menu, remember? Use the View menu to make the Console tree visible again, highlight the Sales cube, and right-click on it. The item below Browse Data is Usage Analysis. If you select that, OLAP Manager launches the Usage Analysis wizard. Well, we don't need to generate any reports now, but now you know what's available to you. The reason Usage Analysis is important is to help you (and OLAP Services) figure out which data should be kept in cache and which dimensions just plain aren't being used.

The next choice, Manage Roles, sounds reminiscent of SQL Server roles. If you click on help, you'll get some, as seen in Figure 9.17. Remember, though, that you're *not* dealing with SQL Server roles here. SQL Server doesn't even need to be running since we're using a MOLAP database.

The Sales cube doesn't have any roles defined. The default cube settings are in force: all users get Read-Only access to the cube. It's easy to add roles, though, as you can see in the Help window. Escape out of that and look at the Sales right-click menu again.

The last main menu item is Write-Enable, which does just what it says. (If you've installed the Add-ins, you'll also have a Copy option (for the Copy and Paste Objects Add-in.)

By now, you should have a pretty good feeling of what's in the Sales cube. Let's see what the Warehouse cube contains.

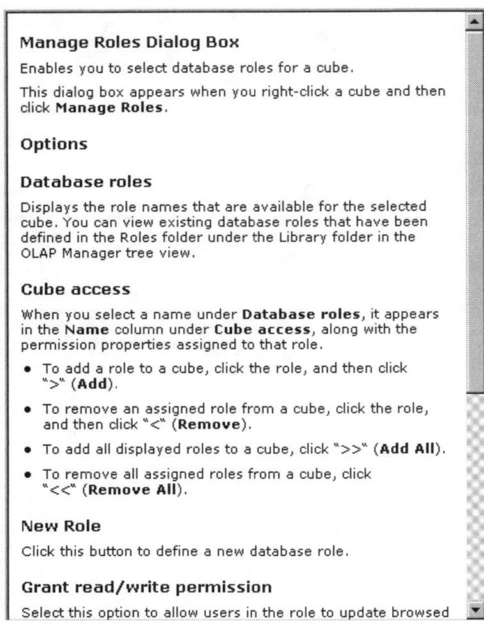

Figure 9.17 Getting help on OLAP Services' roles.

The Warehouse Cube

In the console tree, move your cursor down to the Warehouse cube and click on the plus symbol to make it the active cube. Before drilling down and expanding the dimensions and measures, put Highlight the Cube icon and right-click on it. This time, select Edit. When you do, you'll see the Cube Editor—along with one of those infamous star schemas! You may want to click on the Properties bar as we have in Figure 9.18.

Well, we don't want to change the cube's design (you can also create a new cube using the Cube Editor), so let's close this window and return to the OLAP Manager. Go ahead and expand the Warehouse cube's dimensions and measures as you did with the Sales cube.

Warehouse isn't quite as complicated as the Sales cube was. Warehouse only contains six dimensions (Store, Time, Product, Store Size in SQFT, Store Type, and Warehouse) and seven measures (Store Invoice, Supply Time, Invoice Cost, Warehouse Sales, Units Shipped, Units Ordered, and Warehouse Profit.) Highlight the Warehouse cube icon, click on it, and right-click to display the Context menu as we did with Sales. Select Browse Data to open the Cube Browser. The default display is Products by Measures. Let's replace Products with Country by dragging Warehouses from the Slicer on top of products. When you explore Country, you'll see that FoodMart only has warehouses in the USA. Expand the State/Province dimension to display warehouse locations by city. If you scroll over to Warehouse Profit along the Measures axis, you'll see that the San Francisco warehouse is neither very profitable nor very active (see Figure 9.19). It might be a candidate for downsizing.

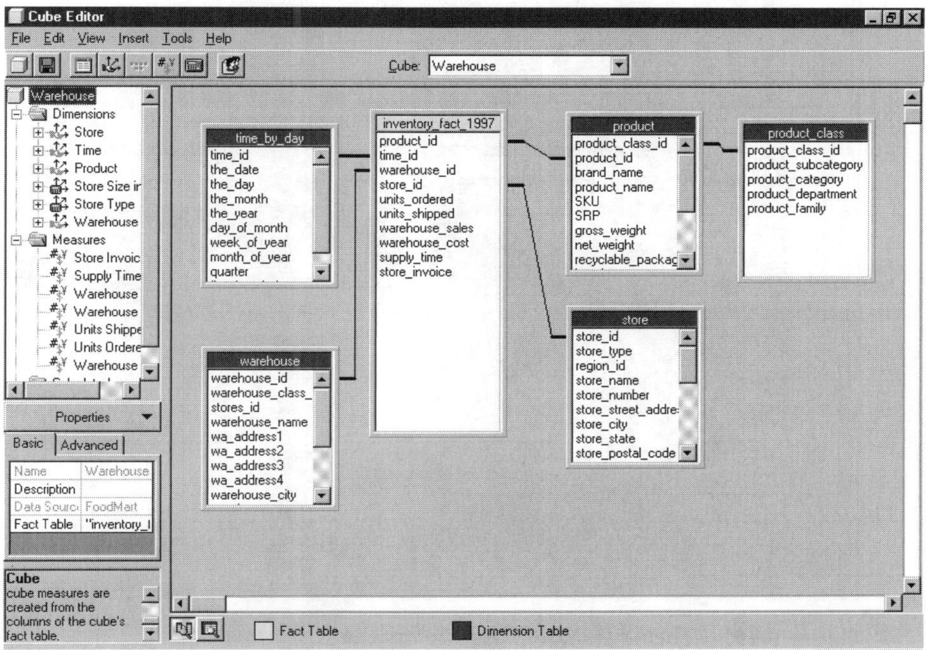

Figure 9.18 Examining the Warehouse Cube in the Cube Editor.

By now you should know enough to explore this cube on your own, and by now you're probably wondering how to build cubes.

Run the OLAP Manager Tutorial

We could walk you through the process of building a cube, or of creating a star schema database based on Northwind, for example, but, frankly, that would take too much space and would duplicate good work that's already available to you from the OLAP Manager's Taskpad. Earlier in the chapter, we said that building a cube consisted of four basic steps:

1. Figure out where your raw data is.
2. Figure out the measures and dimensions of the cube.
3. If you use the OLAP Manager, the next step is to create the OLAP Services database, and then to create the dimensions based on tables in the data source.
4. Finally, you'll get to construct the cube or cubes that connect fact tables to dimensions and define the aggregations.

If you run the OLAP Manager Tutorial (see Figure 9.20), Microsoft will walk you through the steps for creating a Sales-like cube with a central fact table based on 1997 sales, several measures, and four dimensions. Don't worry, you'll have a wizard to help! We highly recommend that you do that *now*. Once you're done, we'll continue together, exploring the client side of OLAP.

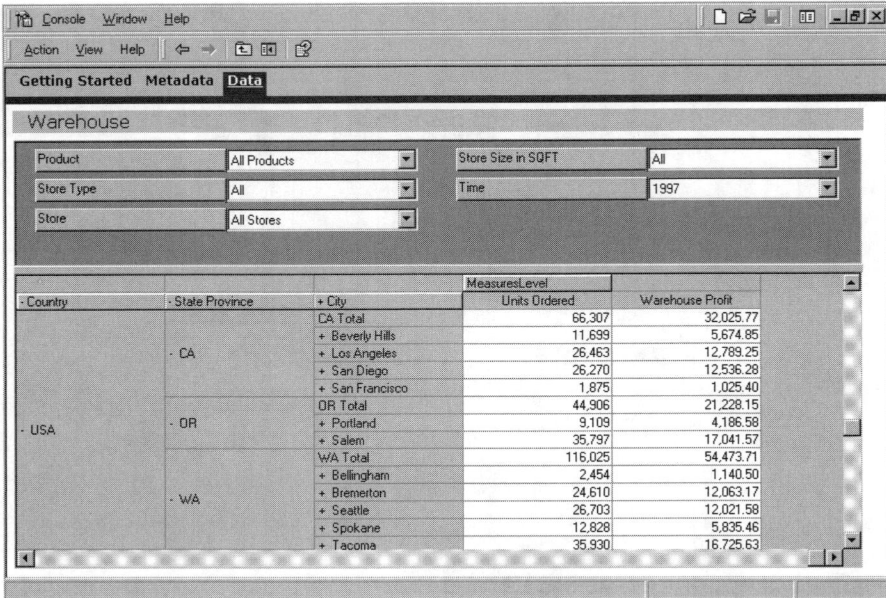

Figure 9.19 Looking at Warehouses by measures.

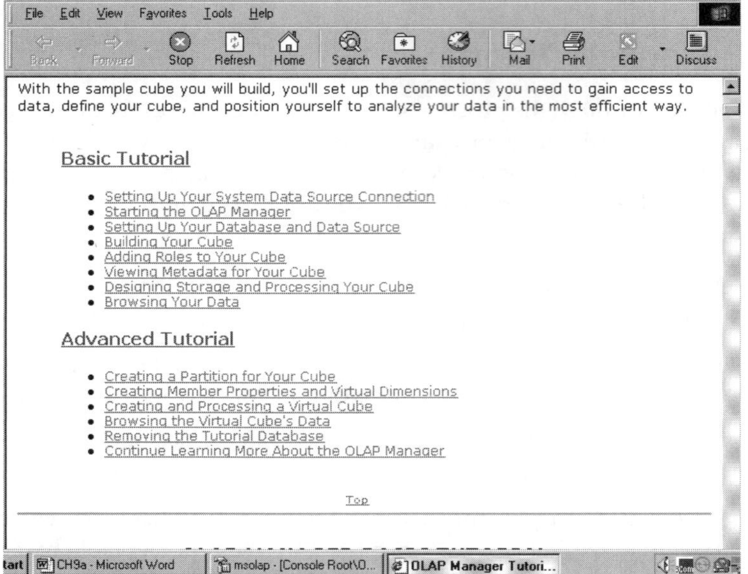

Figure 9.20 The topics covered in the OLAP Manager tutorial.

OLAP: The Client Side

Our goals in this section are to:

1. Show you how to use Excel 2000's pivot table feature to look at the Sales cube data.
2. Run the sample MDX sample application from the OLAP Services' start menu and give you a crash course on MDX.

Sounds deceptively easy...

Excel's Pivot Table

Okay, if you've got Office 2000 (specifically Excel 2000) installed, fire it up and select Data | Pivot Table from the menu. (You may be prompted to supply your Office 2000 CD so that Office can install MS Query.)

The Pivot Table and Pivot Chart wizard (1 of 3) should start up. Select External Data Source and click Next. On the second screen, click on the Get Data when prompted to Choose Data Source, click on the OLAP Cubes tab and select <new data source>. Create an imaginative name for the cube, such as FoodMartSales and accept the default "Microsoft OLE DB Provider for OLAP Services" provider in the second blank space (see Figure 9.21).

When you click on Connect, another wizard will prompt you through the process of selecting a cube. We don't have a local cube, so leave the OLAP Server button checked and type in the name of your OLAP Server. (If OLAP Manager is still running, it will be the name at the top of the console tree just below OLAP Servers.)

You'll be asked to choose a (MOLAP) database to work with. FoodMart will probably be the only one you have, if this is the first time you've worked with OLAP Services. When you click on Finish, you'll be returned to the Create New Data Source dialog where you can select Sales as your cube (see Figure 9.22).

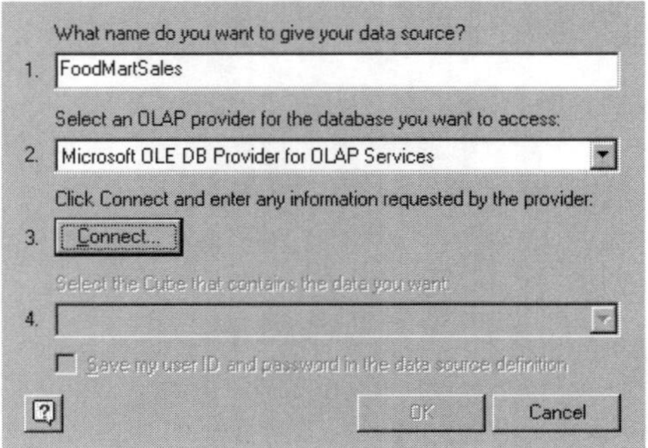

Figure 9.21 Configuring MS Query to load an OLAP cube into Excel 2000's pivot table.

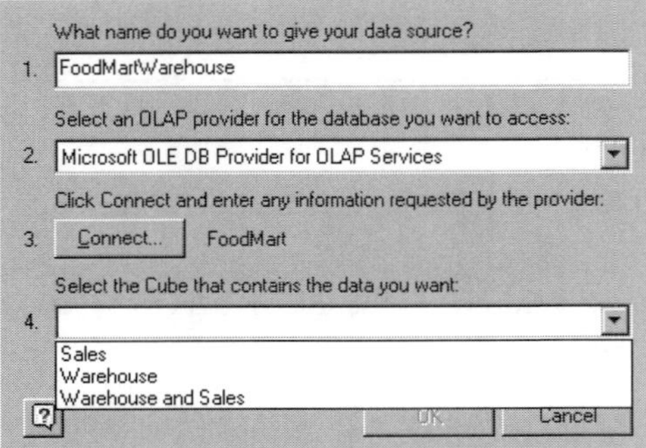

Figure 9.22 Finishing MS Query's OLAP Cubes Data Source wizard.

MS Query's wizard should hand you off (back) to the Pivot Table and Pivot Chart wizard (Step 2 of 3) (still!) where you can safely click Next. You probably have an empty worksheet in front of you and can safely accept the default, but you may want to look at the Layout… option (see Figure 9.23).

Whether you select the axes here or not, you'll see that you can use the same drag-and-drop approach you used in the OLAP Manager's OLAP Browser. In the Pivot Table, however, you need to select at least three items (time is optional): the axes and the data field. You might, for example, want to track Promotions by Store, and then use Sales and Cost as the data fields as in Figure 9.24. (Don't forget to click on the down and up arrows to see all the dimensions.)

Again, I'm going to let you experiment some more on your own. This rather primitive interface may be enough for some of your Excel users.

Once you've examined the familiar FoodMart data from Excel, copy the FLIGHTS.CUB file from the book CD onto your hard disk. This contains sample data from a fictitious airline. Use the Data | Data PivotTable and PivotChart wizard as before

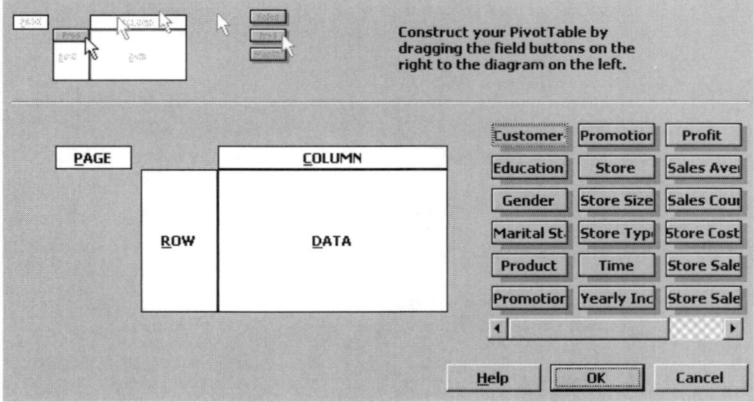

Figure 9.23 Selecting dimensions with Excel's Pivot Chart wizard.

Media Type	Data	USA	Grand Total
Bulk Mail	Store Sales	9349.07	9349.07
	Store Cost	3740.9516	3740.9516
Cash Register Handout	Store Sales	14321.33	14321.33
	Store Cost	5715.668	5715.668
Daily Paper	Store Sales	16479.81	16479.81
	Store Cost	6559.2281	6559.2281
Daily Paper, Radio	Store Sales	14169.42	14169.42
	Store Cost	5668.7721	5668.7721
Daily Paper, Radio, TV	Store Sales	20173.97	20173.97
	Store Cost	8055.216	8055.216
In-Store Coupon	Store Sales	8162.46	8162.46
	Store Cost	3263.1107	3263.1107
No Media	Store Sales	414026.92	414026.92
	Store Cost	165214.8545	165214.8545
Product Attachment	Store Sales	15898.25	15898.25
	Store Cost	6306.2437	6306.2437
Radio	Store Sales	5213.61	5213.61

Figure 9.24 Investigating promotions from the FoodMart's Sales cube in Excel's Pivot Table.

and specify an external data source by clicking on the Get data bar in Wizard Step 2, and then select OLAP Cubes for your data source. Select New Data Source and call your data Airline. Select Microsoft OLE DB for OLAP Services as the OLAP provider, and click on the Connect button. When you see the Multidimensional Connection wizard dialog, override the default radio button (OLAP Server) and select Cube File. Click on the ... button to locate FLIGHTS.CUB on your hard disk, and click Finish (finally!). Go ahead and let your ID and password be saved with the definition file if you're comfortable with that.

You'll probably have to go through the beginning (get data) procedure again in order to *use* the Airline data connection you just defined. Instead of having to define a new data source, however, you should be able to select Airline. Do that, and let Excel put the data in the default location. Drag Destinations into the vertical axis where it says Drop Row Fields Here. Drag Time onto the section where it says Drop Column Fields Here. Next drag Gross Profit into the Data Items section.

Now expand the West Europe destination. Notice that certain destinations such as Dusseldorf and Leipzig don't seem to be doing too well (see Figure 9.25).

Isn't it fun to have something other than FoodMart to play with? I'll let you slice and dice on your own now. If you enjoy this, and can see how useful data like this would be in the "real world", we'd say you've graduated and deserve a gold star.

	Year			
Destination	1996	1997	1998	Grand To
	40660	55138	72718.35	16851
	3677.6	4936	6173.8	147
	4970.5	6773	7686.85	194
	2081.2	2914	3348.95	834
	9087.2	12019	15956.95	3706
Amsterdam	2165.4	2951	3549.85	866
Antwerp	695.4	902	1078.4375	2675.
Barcelona	390.25	524	696.6	161
Bonn	15.75	22	32.2	[illegible]
Brussels	1983.9	2620	3409.75	801
Copenhagen	521.85	734	990.85	22
Dusseldorf	-176.25	-256	-232.6375	-664
Frankfurt	3801.9	4825	5673.7375	14300.
Geneva	1742.85	2359	2582.8875	6684
Helsinki	562.8	739	975.2	
Leipzig	-30.45	-39	-44.85	-1
Lisbon	82.5	139	156.4	3
London	7985	11467	12056.2	315
Madrid	1254.75	1719	2207.6	518
Manchester	755.6	974	1257.5625	2987.
Marseilles	689.8	950	1263.6	29

Sheet2 / Sheet3

Figure 9.25 Exploring the Flights data, a local .CUB file.

SAVING YOUR OWN LOCAL CUBE

In Excel 2000, once you have a cube you like, select "Create local data file" from PivotTable-Client/Server Settings menu. Then choose File|Save As Web Page option. Select "Add Interactivity" to the checkbox and viewing option.

Local cube files can be navigated "offline" when you don't have a connection to the server. Obviously, they are static and only allow as much drill-down detail as they had when they were set up.

Excel uses OLAP Service's Pivot Table Service (PTS)—the client part of OLAP Services—and, as you've seen, PTS really doesn't provide any user interface to view data. As the Help file in OLAP Services says, "Custom applications and products offered by Microsoft and other vendors can use Pivot Table Service to retrieve and manipulate multi-dimensional data, but must provide their own end-user interface." Common presentation formats include custom grid controls, cross-tabs, graphs, HTML tables, or other custom interfaces or controls. Table 9.2 lists a representative sample.

You can also create ASPs that enable users to query cubes and view returned datasets with Web browsers. For more information, see the *Books Online* help topic *Sample Web Programs*.

However, Microsoft SQL Server OLAP Services *does* include the MDX Sample Application, which provides a user interface for querying cubes with multi-dimensional expressions (MDX) and viewing the returned datasets.

Table 9.2 Representative OLAP Clients for OLAP Services

VENDOR	URL	COMMENT
Appsource Wired for OLAP	www.appsource.com or www.hyperion.com	Licenses technology from OLAP@Work. Multiplatform.
Brio Technology Brio Query	www.brio.com	Multiplatform
Business Objects WebIntelligence	www.businessobjects.com	Multiplatform
Cognos NovaView, PowerPlay, and Impromptu	www.cognos.com	Download the free Multidimensional Manager
Comshare DecisionWeb	www.comshare.com	
Data Dynamics DynamiCube/ActiveCube OCX	www.datadynamics.com	Requires programming
Hummingbird Software BI/Analyze (formerly Andyne Computing's PaBLO)	www.hummingbird.com	Acquisition of LeoLogic's Genio may make integrated high-end data mining available sooner than other vendors do
Internetivity DbProbe	www.internetivity.com	Java-based, multiplatform
KNOSYS ProClarity	www.knosysinc.com	Can serve as "hub" for other vendors' add-ins
Maximal Innovative Intelligence Max	www.maxsw.com	End user product strong on visualization
mb Cizer	www.cizer.com	
OLAP@Work OLAP @Work(Excel add-in)	www.olapatwork.com	Can be used both with Excel 97 and Excel 2000
Portola Systems' Coronado	www.portolasystems.com	Another product targeting end users
Seagate Software Seagate Analysis (free)	www.seagatesoftware.com	Does not support calculated members

The MDX Sample Application

On your desktop click Start, point to Programs, point to Microsoft SQL Server 7, point to OLAP Services, and then click MDX Sample Application. You should see a Connect dialog box with your server's name in the top box. Make sure MSOLAP is the entry in the Provider box. When you press OK, you should be rewarded with a pretty blah-

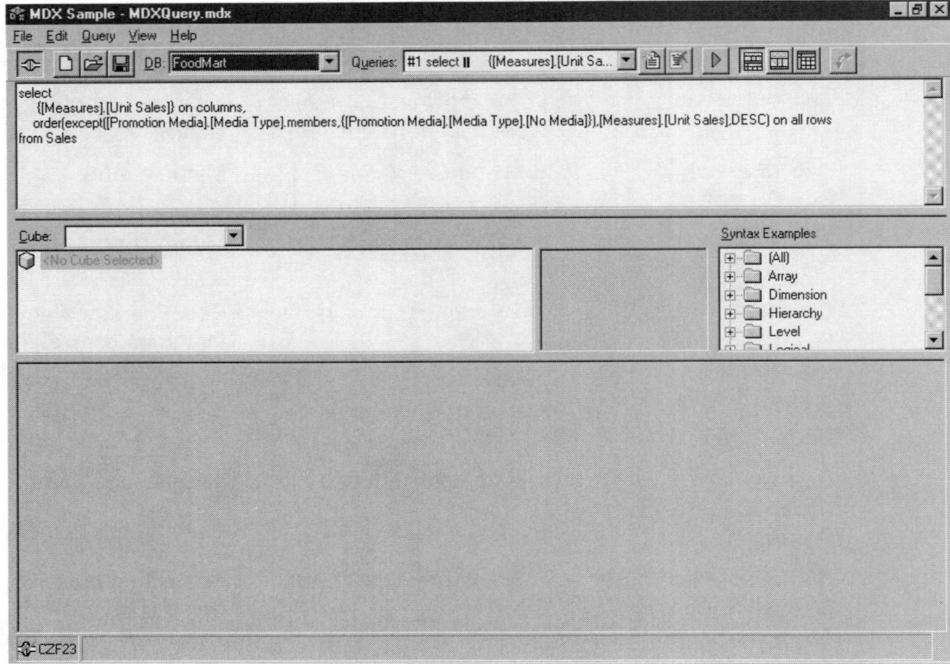

Figure 9.26 The MDX Sample Application's client window.

looking screen—Figure 9.26—that's suspiciously reminiscent of SQL Server's Query Analyzer. (If you have trouble connecting, make sure that the server name supplied is the computer on which the OLAP Server is installed *and running*.)

You'll probably see that FoodMart is the default database, but that no cube is selected yet. Before we try to execute any queries, let's look at the example in the top box. Arghhh, it's written in some obviously foreign language that isn't even SQL.

```
select
    {[Measures].[Unit Sales]} on columns,
    order(except([Promotion Media].[Media Type].members,{[Promotion
Media].[Media Type].[No Media]}),[Measures].[Unit Sales],DESC) on rows
from Sales
```

Well, if we calm down a minute, we can probably see what it's asking for. If you execute the query (press F5 or the green, right-arrow icon on the Title Bar, or select the Query | Run menu items) you'll get a sorted list of unit sales by promotion type at the media type level. We've excluded sales associated with promotions that didn't use media, and we've asked for the results to be diplayed in descending order.

Notice that this "starter" sample query only specifies two of the Sales cube's 13 dimensions: [Unit Sales] and [Promotion Media]. To uniquely identify a measure value in the cube, you need to specify a member from each dimension. This combination of members, one from each dimension, is called a *tuple*. Dimensions that aren't specifically referenced are assigned a default value.

Clear as mud, right? Well, time to regroup and figure out the basics of MDX, don't you think?

The MDX Language

As we stated earlier, MDX stands for multi-dimensional expressions, and it's a syntax for modeling and querying OLAP databases and cubes. Traditional SQL statements alone can be used to query cubes, but they'll only return 2-D rowsets. To return a multi-dimensional dataset, you have to use MDX, which Microsoft refers to as a *dialect* and documents in the 250-page OLE for DB specification. OLE DB for OLAP is a set of objects and interfaces for developing and accessing multi-dimensional data providers. When we wrote this book, the most current version of the specification (available for download at www.microsoft.com/data) was the December 1998 *OLE DB for OLAP Programmer's Reference* (12/98). The manual consisted of seven chapters and three appendices:

Chapter 1 OLE DB for OLAP Overview

Chapter 2 OLE DB for OLAP Concepts

Chapter 3 Advanced MDX

Chapter 4 OLE DB for OLAP Objects and Schema Rowsets

Chapter 5 OLE DB for OLAP Code Samples

Chapter 6 Mapping MDX to SQL Statements

Chapter 7 OLE DB for OLAP Reference

Appendix A Cotypes

Appendix B Multi-dimensional Expressions (MDX) Grammar

Appendix C OLE DB for OLAP Changes for OLE DB 2.1

MDX, although primarily developed by Microsoft's Amir Netz—the "father" of MDX who acknowledges contributions from Cristain Petculesco, Mosha Pasumansky, Sasha Berger, Murali Vanketrau—has enough industry backing that it's already the *de facto* OLAP query language. SQL just isn't enough, especially when it comes to doing calculations. You can build complex queries that return the result of some calculations in a single row dataset. You can do cursor programming to walk through a series of rows, one row at a time. You can use SQL to create new tables or views that contain calculations or aggregates. But there's nothing quite like the spreadsheet equivalent of embedding calculations themselves into a cell. MDX addresses these limitations, and if you're going to do any OLAP programming, you'll have to learn it. OLAP client tools, of course, will try to shield end users from the underlying syntax, just as database query and report generators shield end users from the underlying SQL.

MDX Built-in Functions

OLAP Services provides over 100 built-in MDX functions for defining sophisticated, calculated members in the Cube editor's Calculated Member Builder—which is where the real action is as far as OLAP goes. Functions are provided in the following categories:

Array functions. Example: SetToArray(«Set»[, «Set»]…[, «Numeric Expression»]) converts one or more sets to an array.

Dimension functions. Example: «Hierarchy».Dimension returns the dimension that contains a specified hierarchy.

Hierarchy functions. Example: «Level».Hierarchy or «Member».Hierarchy returns a level's or member's hierarchy.

Level functions. Example: «Member».Level returns a member's level.

Logical functions. Example: IsEmpty(«Value Expression») determines if an expression evaluates to the empty cell value.

Member functions. Example: «Dimension».Current Member or «Dimension».Default Member returns the current or default member of a dimension. Study functions in this category—you'll want to master them to get full benefit from MDX.

Numeric functions. Example: Avg(«Set»[, «Numeric Expression»]) returns the average value of a numeric expression evaluated over a set. There are all kinds of statistical functions, such as linear regression, correlation, variance, covariance, and standard deviation, as well as more familiar ones such as count, sum, average, here that reflect OLAP's original primary function as a tool for doing financial analysis.

AVERAGE OF A SET ≠ AVERAGE OF A MEASURE

It's easy to get confused between AVG of a Set and AVG of a measure. Avg({Products},Sales) will give the average sales per product (total sales divided by the number of products). However, AVG of the measures sales is the average sales amount in a transaction (total sales divided by the number of transactions). You can see that the results aren't the same.

Since there's no "set of transactions" in MDX, you can't use the MDX AVG function for the latter type of average. To do that, however, you can create a SUM measure of the column you want to average like [Total Salary], and then create a COUNT measure of the same column, such as[Number of Payments]. Then, you can create a calculated member on the measures dimension [Average Salary] as [Measures].[Total Salary]/[Measures].[Number of Payments].

Set functions. Examples: <<Dimension>>.Members or <<Hierarchy>>.Members or <<Level>>.Members—Filter(«Set», «Search Condition»), Order(«Set», {«String Expression» | «Numeric Expression»}[, ASC | DESC | BASC | BDESC]), and Distinct(«Set») which eliminates duplicate tuples from a set. You'll also find drill-down, drill-up, and crossjoin functions in this category.

String functions. Example: IIf(«Logical Expression», «String Expression1», «String Expression2»)

Tuple functions. Example: «Set».Current

Unfortunately, MDX syntax seems to use a combination of traditional function syntax—function (arguments), and a more object-oriented format—Object.Function (arguments). If there's some intuitive way to "know" ahead of time which style to use for which function, it eludes us.

GENERAL TIPS FOR PROGRAMMERS USING OLE DB FOR OLAP

1. **Always quote your table names and column names. Example:**

```
"SELECT " strSource = strSource & "{[Measures].members} ON COLUMNS,"
strSource = strSource & "NON EMPTY [Store].[Store City].members ON ROWS"
strSource = strSource & " FROM Sales"
```

2. **Always fully qualify the column names with the table names.**
3. **Try to build the cube with the dimension/cube editor in the OLAP Manager to see how the properties were set by the OLAP Manager. Use OLAP Manager as a model for setting properties.**
4. **Look especially at the properties of FromClause, JoinClause, SourceTable, SourceColumn, MemberKeyColumn, and MemberNameColumn.**

Learning MDX

To specify a dataset, the MDX statement must contain information about the following:

- The cube or cubes that set the scope of the query
- The number of axes
- The dimensions projected on each axis and the level of nesting at which each dimension appears on the axis
- The members or member tuples to include from each dimension
- The sort order
- When filtering is involved, the members from a non-projected dimension on which the data will be filtered for members from projected dimensions

An example of a sales cube *member* might be Smith, [2000].[Q1].Jan. An example of a tuple (which is basically a multi-dimensional member) might be (Smith, USA, (Computers, [2000]), while a set, which will be surrounded by curly braces if it consists of members from more than one dimension, might be {Smith, [Product].[Doc Martens]}, {[Time].January 2000] : [Time].April 2000]} or [2000].Children or TopCount(SalesReps .Members,10,Sales). Note the Excel-like use of the colon to specify a range of members in a set.

Unfortunately, MDX doesn't force you to use unique names. We think of unique names as the cube equivalent of fully-qualified names and generally equate unique names with lots of notation symbols, especially brackets. Every cell has a unique name. We strongly recommend getting in the practice of fully qualifying your measures and dimensions and members. Once you start using named sets, saved MDX queries, or external functions, for example, it's unlikely that you can know for sure that a name like Store is unique.

A typical MDX statement takes the following form:

SELECT <axis_specification> [, <axis_specification>...]

FROM <cube_specification>

WHERE <slicer_specification>

The dimensions of the dataset are called *axes*. Each axis consists of one or more dimensions projected on it. Data is retrieved for multiple members along an <axis_specification>. Along Slicer dimensions, however, data is only retrieved for a single member.

COLUMNS BEFORE ROWS

The MDX language forces you to specify the column axes first followed by the row axes.

For example, imagine that you have four dimensions: Geography, Products, Measures, and Quarters and two measures: Sales and Cost. The application wants to see Sales for USA for each product category and each quarter. The output looks like this:

	FOOD, 000S	DRINK, 000S	HEALTH/BEAUTY, 000S
Quarter 1	480.1	54.2	5.08
Quarter 2	521.2	48.4	5.32
Quarter 3	521.8	59.7	5.28
Quarter 4	538.4	58.3	5.33

In this example, the Quarters and Products dimensions are the axis dimensions and Measures and Geography are the Slicer dimensions. If you want to formulate what we're doing in geometrical terms, start by visualizing a 4-D hypercube. Each dimension is an edge of this hypercube. Now move along the Measures edge and select the point Sales. This selects a three-dimensional cube associated with this coordinate. In this cube, move along the Geography edge and select the point USA. This selects a two-dimensional slice in the cube. Then display the appropriate sub-slice of the two-dimensional slice. As the OLE DB for OLAP documentation says, "Essentially, slicer dimensions serve to extract a p-dimensional shadow of the n-dimensional cube ($p <= n$). The axis dimensions slice this shadow cube along one or more axes and display the result in tabular form."

Visualizing multi-dimensional datasets can be difficult. One method is to limit the presentation to a flattened, two-axis medium, nesting multiple dimensions on a single axis. This is how the OLAP Manager's Cube Browser and Excel's Pivot Table work. As you saw previously, nesting produces subheadings and the members of a nested dimension are displayed as subheadings beneath (or beside) the members of the nesting dimension.

Calculated Members

Most people agree that *calculated members* are the real power behind OLAP since they're what lets you model complex business logic. So what are they? A calculated member is a dimension member whose value is calculated at runtime using an expression that you specify when you define the calculated member (interactively or in code). Calculated members can also be defined as measures. The beauty is that you only store the *definitions* for calculated members; Values are calculated in memory when needed to answer a query.

This means that calculated members are basically "free." They let you add members and measures to a cube without increasing its size. Although calculated members must be based on a cube's existing data (such as members), you can create complex expressions by combining this data with arithmetic operators, numbers, and any of those 100+ built-in functions.

Microsoft Visual Basic for Applications (VBA) Expression Services is also included with OLAP Services and is automatically registered, but the Microsoft Excel worksheet library must be installed separately from OLAP Services. It, too, is automatically registered. If you're a programmer, you can create your own user-defined functions (UDFs) in a COM-compatible language, register them manually by clicking Register in the Calculated Member Builder.

ALIEN LIBRARIES

OLAP Services supports only some functions in libraries other than the OLAP Services function library. It basically comes down to this: Functions are supported only if they accept as arguments only string or numeric data types, or array or variant data types that contain string or numeric values. In addition, functions are supported only if they return only string or numeric data types or variant data types that contain numeric values. It is recommended that you test each function separately from these libraries before you expose the resulting data to users.

So what's an example of a calculated member? Well, here's an easy one: you can create a calculated member called Euro that converts dollars to euros by multiplying an existing dollar measure by a conversion rate. Euros can then be displayed to cube users in a separate row or column.

By the way, you're likely to encounter *solve order*, the order in which the calculated member is solved in case of an intersection with other calculated members. Solve order is the OLAP equivalent of precedence. You can create members, for example, either interactively with the WITH clause in your SELECT statement or for use in multiple queries in a session with the CREATE MEMBER statement.

```
WITH MEMBER [Measures].[Avg Ytd Sales]
AS 'Avg(Ytd(),[Unit Sales])'
SELECT {[Unit Sales],[Avg Ytd Sales]} ON COLUMNS,
Descendants{[1997],[Month[KM2]]) ON ROWS FROM Sales

CREATE MEMBER [warehouse].[measures].[warehouseprofit]
```

```
AS '[measures].[warehouse sales] - [measures].[warehouse cost]',
SOLVEORDER=3
```

The main difference between the WITH and CREATE MEMBER statements is that calculated members defined with the WITH clause only persist the lifetime of the query. Those defined with the CREATE MEMBER statement persist (on the local system) for the current system unless saved in a local CUBE. Although the current version of OLAP Services doesn't support the keyword CREATE GLOBAL MEMBER that allows for the sharing of member definitions beyond the scope of the client session, keep an eye out for it in the next version of OLAP Services. The CREATE MEMBER statement is handy when you're developing client-side applications, because you can add members without server access (see Figure 9.27).

MEMBER PROPERTIES RETURN STRINGS

Member properties always return values as strings. You can use the Val function to convert member property values to numbers when you use them in MDX expressions.

Using MDX

Although MDX is quite different from SQL, there's one thing they share—the fact that practice makes perfect. With that said, why don't you return to the MDX Sample Application (or re-run it).

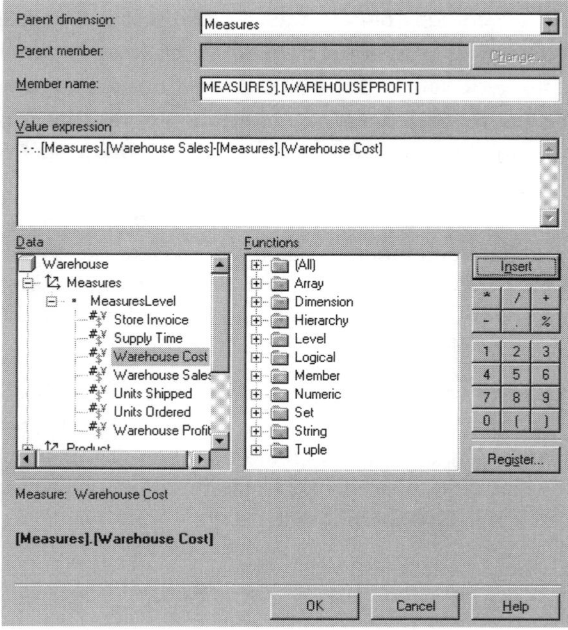

Figure 9.27 Defining a calculated member with OLAP Manager's Calculated Member Builder.

Now that we've done a whirlwind tour of MDX, the sample query shouldn't look so intimidating. Run it again and note that, in this case, we use a SQL SELECT statement. OLAP Services doesn't support the full SELECT syntax, but it does support the following syntax where <column_ref> must be a measure name, the <aggregate_func>, such as COUNT, MIN, MAX, or SUM must agree with the Aggregate Function property of the measure, and where <select_list> may only include levels or measures. If measures are specified, you must also specify <aggregate>.

```
SELECT [<options_clause>] <select_list> FROM <from_clause>
WHERE <where_clause>] [GROUP BY <groupby_clause>]
<options_clause> ::= <empty_clause> | DISTINCT
<select_list> ::= <scalar_exp_commalist> | ASTERISK
<scalar_exp_commalist> ::= <scalar_expression> [, <scalar_expression> [,
<scalar_expression> [...]]]
<scalar_expression> ::= <column_ref>
    | <aggregate>
    | (<column_ref>) AS IDENTIFIER
<aggregate> ::= <aggregate_func> (<column_ref>)
```

Try adding a WHERE ([store].[usa].[ca]) clause at the end to restrict the results to California promotions. Run the query again. Pretty cool, isn't it?

In fact, it turns out that the default sample query is just one of seven. Let's take a quick look at the others. Try running the second query (select it from the drop-down list to the right of Queries):

```
select
    { [Measures].[Units Shipped], [Measures].[Units Ordered] } on columns,
    NON EMPTY [Store].[Store Name].members on rows from Warehouse
```

To see the impact of NON EMPTY, delete it and re-run the query. Go back to the OLAP Manager and Browse Cube data to confirm what you're seeing in MDX. Are you beginning to understand the impact of default dimensions?

Now take a look at the third query. It's the first example that shows a calculated member, [Store Sales Last Period]. You know you're dealing with a calculated member because the "query" starts with WITH MEMBER, not SELECT.

```
WITH MEMBER [Measures].[Store Sales Last Period] AS '([Measures].[Store
Sales],
     Time.PrevMember)'
     SELECT
            {[Measures].[Store Sales Last Period]} ON COLUMNS,
     {TopCount([Product].[Product Department].members,5, [Measures].
     [Store Sales Last Period])} ON ROWS
     FROM Sales
     WHERE ([Time].[1998])
```

When you run it, you see a list of the five top-selling items in 1997. That's because, thanks to the WHERE clause, we have overridden the default current time dimension of 1997 and set it to 1998. That means that Time.PrevMember is, duh, guess what? 1997.

Not terribly useful except to illustrate one way to override a default dimension and how to use the PrevMember function.

Now try adding a format string just prior to the select (see Figure 9.28), then #.##, then #,#.00, then #,#.##.

```
, format = '$#.00'
```

If you run Query #4, you'll notice that it's similar to Query #3, except that it's restricted to fourth-quarter sales.

Query #5 shows how to calculate profit rate as a percentage. I imagine most "real" stores have neither such high-profit rates, nor profit rates that are so clustered. Do you see how a "real" manager, however, might want to see how promotions affected his profit rate? How he might want to integrate overhead expenses into the cube in order to calculate something closer to net rather than gross profit?

Query #6 shows the percentage of alcoholic beverage sales compared to total drink sales in Washington stores. Edmonds (Karen graduated from Edmonds High School a *long* time ago) and Sedro Wolley don't seem to be selling as much beer and wine as the other stores indicating the managers might consider a promotion or sale.

The last query shows how you can have a running total in your output.

Here's a more complicated one that shows the relative percentage contribution of food and drink sales:

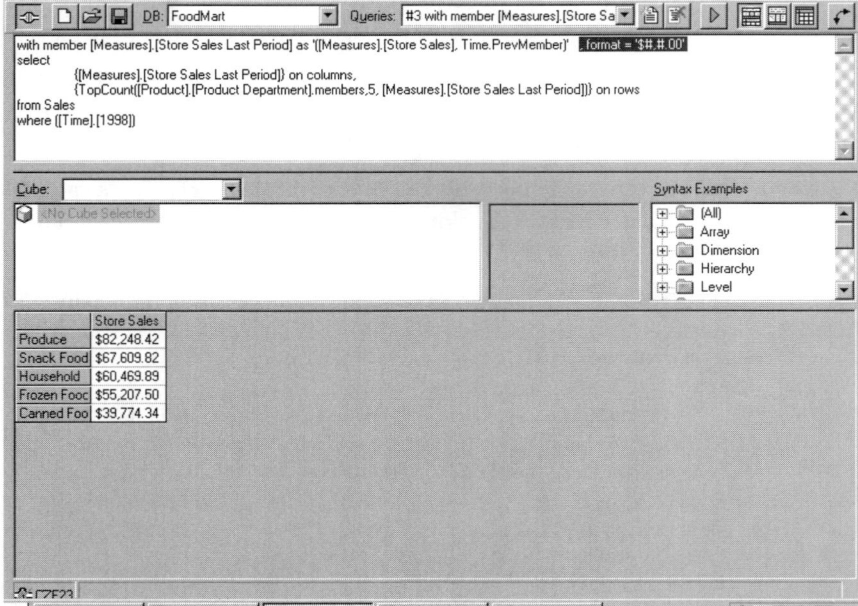

Figure 9.28 Applying some primitive formatting to the results. From a program, you can use the FormatString property of the Measure interface.

```
WITH member [Measures].[Store Sales Perc] AS
'iif(Product.CurrentMember.Level.Ordinal > 0, ((Product.CurrentMember,
[Store Sales]) / (Product.CurrentMember.Parent, [Store Sales])),
((Product.CurrentMember, [Store Sales]) / (Product.CurrentMember, [Store
Sales])))',
FORMAT = '#.00% '
SELECT { [Measures].[Store Sales Perc] } ON COLUMNS , { [Product].[All
Products],
[Product].[All Products].[Drink], [Product].[All Products].[Food]} ON
ROWS
from [sales]
```

This query introduces a new MDX function, IIF, to our calculated member expression. We use it to check whether the Product level is at the [All Products] level by checking the ordinal property. You know you're at the products root level—the [All Products] level—if Product.CurrentMember.Level.Ordinal = 0.

Before we leave the MDX Sample Applicatation, there are two things worth pointing out. First, the MDX Sample Application has its own help (see Figure 9.29) that can provide additional ideas for things to try. Notice also, that it contains help on the MDX functions without forcing you to jump back and forth and use the OLE DB for OLAP specification or OLAP Manager's Help. The second item is related. You can effectively use the Syntax Examples in the lower-right part of the MDX Sample by expanding the categories you're interested in and pasting the desired functions into a new (or existing) query.

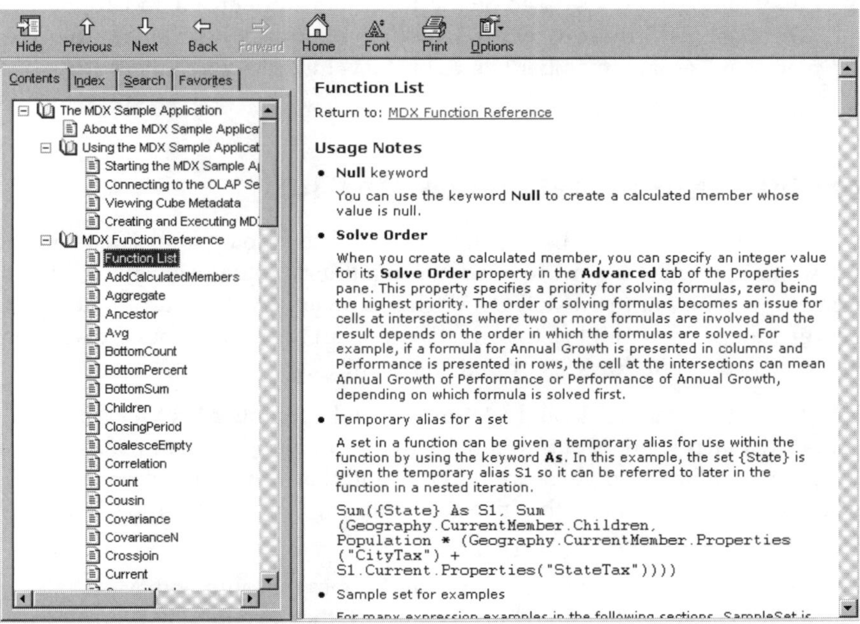

Figure 9.29 MDX Sample has its own help.

Exploring Cubes with Third-Party Tools

Earlier in this chapter, you saw how to use Excel 2000 as an OLAP client. As we said then, Excel is fairly rudimentary as far as OLAP clients go. Table 9.2 listed over a dozen third-party products—many of which are on the book CD in evaluation copy versions—and now is a great time to explore some of them. Here are some of the questions you might want to keep in mind as you look at them:

- Was the product written specifically for OLE DB for OLAP?
- Can the client be implemented in a browser? What are the differences in look-and-feel and functionality between the "fat client" and the Web client versions?
- Does the product provide any admin module to handle security—restricting users to seeing/selecting certain data?
- Does the GUI distinguish between calculated members and "real" members in the selection process? Does the GUI make it easy to move dimensions between axes? When there are multiple dimensions on an axis, how easy it is to specify the precedence for nesting?
- Can users create their own calculated members? If so, is this functionality restricted to measures or can it be done on all dimensions? How is the process handled?
- Are member properties supported in the client? Can users display values for them and filter queries on them?
- Can you do selections based on the TopCount, TopPercent and TopSum MDX functions? Can you sort by rows and/or columns, within levels (to preserve the hierarchy), and by member names or the values of a given measure?
- Can the user enter their own "raw" MDX queries?

Maximal Innovative Intelligence Max 1.0

Install Max 1.0 from the book's CD or download the latest version from www.maxsw.com. Be sure to read the readme.txt before installing either version. Remember that you can install OLAP clients on any PC that can connect to the OLAP Server—the server itself has to be installed on an NT system, but OLAP clients generally run on any Windows 9.x or higher system.

Run Max, and either click on the leftmost icon to get into Max View or select the View pull-down menu and de-select Initial View. From the View menu, make sure that both the Main and Panels toolbars are selected, and that you've also selected the Explorer's Structure option to make the hierarchy information visible. Tools | Options lets you change several defaults.

You may want to connect to the two sample cubes that ship with Max: Sales and Warehouse. Refreshingly, they aren't just FoodMart; they're cubes that can be created—on a daily or weekly basis, for example—for certain end users. Sales takes a look at trends in food sales in Washington stores, and Warehouse looks at warehouse performance. To load them, you'll have to use Files | Connect, and then specify a Cube File (Sales or Warehouse) in the ..\Maximal\Max subdirectory.

If you pick Sales, for example, and double-click on the Max cube icon, you'll see an attractive display as in Figure 9.30. Note that the icons alongside the charts provide basic functions such as sorting and drilling.

Experiment and take advantage of Max's online help that provides a basic tutorial. Your CD also contains the Max user manual (which purchasers get as hard copy) in PDF format.

Once you've explored the Sales and Warehouse cubes, try to connect to the Airline workspace—that's right, workspace, not cube. Most of the third-party tools have names for cube "views" that contain predefined axes, measures, and so on. In Excel, you selected the dimensions and measures. Maximal has provided a starter view for you and called it FLIGHT.MDV. (Maximal Innovative Intelligence actually supplied us with the FLIGHT.CUB sample airline cube and gave us permission to use it and its associated view/workspace file in the book.) Your screen should look like Figure 9.31.

Select Color Scale from the View menu and drill down into the West Europe and Far East regions to see how Max will color code losses. Use the Format option from the menu to toggle the display between bars and grid format. Use the right mouse context menus to see what Max can do. Explore...

Figure 9.30 The basic Max View in Max 1.0.

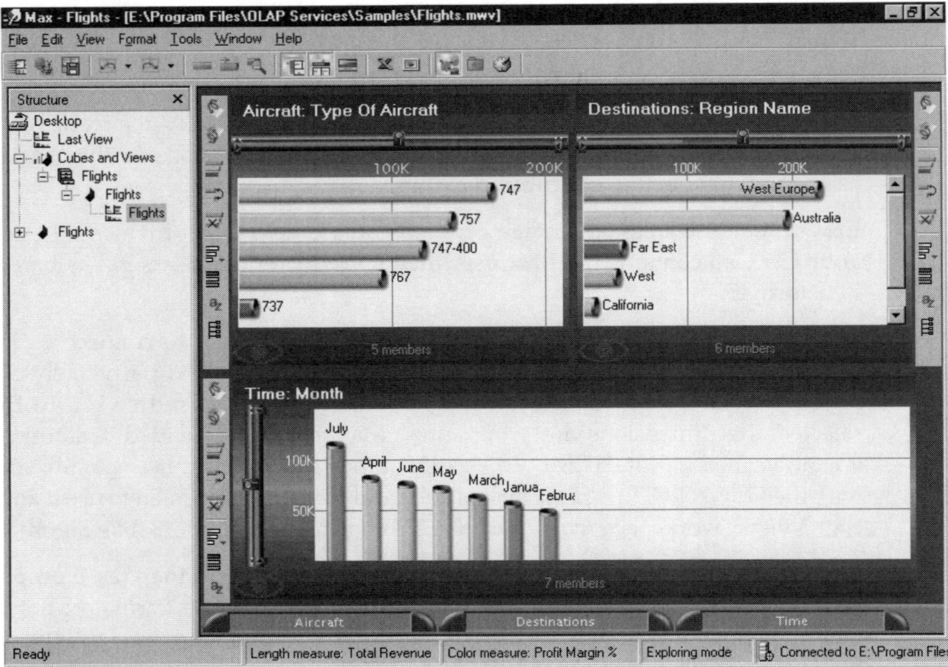

Figure 9.31 Maximal's FLIGHT.MDV file stores a predefined workspace view.

Cognos NovaView 2.0

Now install Cognos NovaView. This, remember is the OLAP client that Panorama Software, the original creators of OLAP Services, created and maintains. The default screen is a demo that lets you investigate the now familiar FoodMart database, along with some attractive views for financial analysts. Both the profitability and trends bars come with several pre-built charts. We encourage you to explore and, again, look at NovaView's online help. Once you're ready to look at the FLIGHTS data, exit the domain you're in (Finance, Sales, or Warehouses) from the File menu. Select Edit | Domains and add a new domain called Airline. You'll see a pretty bare screen.

Now select File | New and click on Cube file. Point to the FLIGHTS.CUB file that you copied to your hard disk for the Excel example, and view the result (see Figure 9.32).

Once again, explore the main menu's options under View, Chart, and Crosstabs. Take advantage of online help. NoveView, for example, lets you create special .PNC (for Panorama compressed) files from the File | Send to menu. Find out what you can do with the right mouse button context menus. Again, explore.

Each OLAP client has its own look and feel, and it behooves you to spend some time experimenting with them if you're going to work with OLAP Services—or build appli-

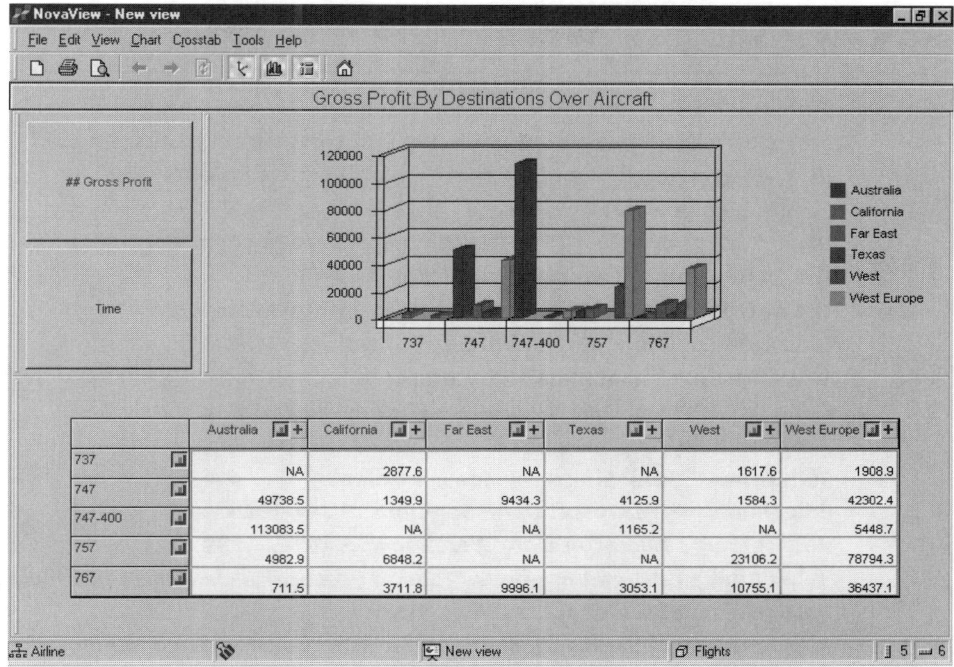

Figure 9.32 NovaView 2.0's default display of FLIGHTS cube data.

cations for people who will. Although it might grind you to have to pay $300-$500 per seat for an OLAP client package that lets you use Microsoft's "free" OLAP server, think about the time it would take you to duplicate the easy-to-use GUI that the third-party tools provide.

Take the time to load the other OLAP client evaluation software we've provided on the book's CD, and play with them. We can almost guarantee that each time you use another OLAP client, you'll learn something new about Microsoft's OLAP Services. And remember the context. You're comparing them with Excel 2000 and the MDX Sample Application.

Well, that wraps up our quick overview of the basics of both the server and client sides of OLAP. My recommendation to you is to experiment. The only way to learn how to build cubes is by trial and error. Go through the tutorial if you haven't already to see how to set up a database and then create cubes. Or try creating duplicate cubes such as Sales2 or Warehouse2. Use a sample dataset of your own, or download a statistical data set from your state or country's statistics site (census data lets you build some interesting cubes).

In other words, go forth and OLAP!

OLAP Resources

Microsoft's OLAP site: www.microsoft.com/sql/70/gen/olap.htm
Microsoft's OLAP newsgroup: msnews://Microsoft.public.sqlserver.olap
Usenet newsgroup: www.deja.com/ = liszt/dnquery.xp?query = ~g%20comp.databases.olap
OLAP Council and the APB-1 benchmark: www.olapcouncil.org
The OLAP Report, www.olapreport.com
The Data Warehousing Institute: www.dw-institute.com
Metadata Coalition and the MDIS specification: www.ne.net/~metadata/index.html
German OLAP and Data Warehouse Forum: www.winf.ruhr-uni-bochum.de/olap/index.htm
Seth Grimes' OLAP Site: altaplana.com/olap
Erik Thomsen's *Microsoft OLAP Solutions*, Wiley, 1999
Robert Craig's *Microsoft Data Warehousing*, Wiley, 1999
Ralph Kimball's *Data Warehouse Toolkit: Practical Techniques for Building Dimensional Warehouses*, Wiley, 1996
Alex Berson and Stephen J. Smith's *Data Warehousing, Data Mining, and OLAP*, McGraw-Hill, 1997
Rick Tanler's *Intranet Data Warehouse*, Wiley, 1997
OLAP Services Training: www.olaptrain.com

Summary

In this chapter, even though we've covered a tremendous amount of material, we've left a lot of doors unopened. Others we've just barely opened, providing you with a glimpse of what's inside. We hope you've had fun, but that you're also rarin' to go. Those of you who are programmers will want to explore the Web sample application (type in Web in the OLAP Manager's Help) in the ..\MSOLAP\Samples folder on the SQL Server CD-ROM and read the Help topic *Creating a Sample Program Using Decision Support Objects*. You may very well want to purchase Erik Thomsen's *Microsoft OLAP Solutions* that comes with its own data sets (in case you're tired of FoodMart!).

We're convinced that OLAP is going to be an increasing important part of many business solutions, so we encourage you to dig in and enjoy.

In the next chapter we leave data marts, warehousing, and OLAP behind and explore replication. Which reminds us if you've already installed the Add-ins, you can archive and restore cubes. Why don't you try it? Then, at the end of the replication chapter, you can test replicating a cube—just a thought.

CHAPTER 10

Project #7: Implementing Replication

Goal

There are two goals for this chapter. First, we want to ensure that you have a fundamental understanding of the replication technology available in SQL Server 7. Our second goal is to show you how to implement a particular replication strategy. We accomplish the first goal by covering the various components that make up the three replication models and tackle the second goal with hands-on learning in the Project Sections.

- ✔ Microsoft SQL Server 7 WorkOrd database on accompanying CD-ROM
- ✔ Microsoft Access 2000

Replication is generally considered one of the more difficult technologies to implement in SQL Server 7. Therefore, instead of just throwing you to the "wizards" we plan to cover the replication processes and components in detail so that you will have a solid understanding of this technology before you actually replicate any data.

Background

SQL Server 7 replication is a technology that facilitates the distribution of data from a source database to one or more target databases without requiring a continuous networked connection between the source and target servers. The target database can reside on the same server as the source database, or it can reside on a different server. In a multi-server scenario, the connections between servers are established via a LAN, WAN, or the Internet. SQL Server 7 replication not only supports replication to databases that reside in SQL Server 7 and 6.x, but also supports other databases such as Access and Oracle.

KB REPLICATION ARTICLES

SQL Server 7's replication has proved very reliable and remarkably bug free. As you can see from the list below, as of late 1999, there were only a handful of KB articles related to replication.

Q190690 INF: How to Set Up Replication on Tables with an Identity Column

Q190797 INF: Replication: How to Rebuild the Distribution Database

Q191384 PRB: Replication: Distribution Task Timeout Expired

Q191412 INF: Replication: Cleanup Task Takes a Long Time to Complete

Q195757 INF: Frequently Asked Questions - Replication

Q199217 BUG: Uninstall Does Not Remove All Replication Files

Q207809 INF: DTS/Replication Licensing for Desktop SQL Server 7.0

Q218149 FIX: Replication Log Reader Task Causes Memory Leak

Q239458 BUG: Replication Problems Mapping Chars to DB2 OLEDB Subscribers

Q240039 FIX: DBCC OPENTRAN Does Not Report Replication Information

Q240193 PRB: Upgrading Replication Settings May Fail When Inserting Rows

Q240290 FIX: Replication Error: 14262 Specified @job_id Not Found

Q240688 PRB: Replication Subscribers Unable to Synchronize w/ Pull Sub.

Q241149 INF: How to Automate Replication over a Dial-Up Connection

Q241678 FIX: Replication Merge JOIN Filters Not Completely Evaluated

You may also want to download Microsoft's basic white papers on replication. They're each just over 300K; the first one covers basic replication, and the second one replication over the Internet, i.e. using Proxy Server:

www.microsoft.com/sql/DeployAdmin/replication.htm

www.microsoft.com/sql/DeployAdmin/proxyreplication.htm

If you've heard horror stories about replication with SQL Server 6.x, you're not alone. Take it from us—that was definitely a "1.0" effort. It was essentially a one-way model that didn't particularly scale well. Not only is the replication in SQL Server 7 far more flexible, it's something that you can count on to work correctly. SQL Server 7 also ships with two new ActiveX controls—SQL distribution and SQL merge—that can be used to control replication from your own applications. Refer to the *Books Online* topics *Programming Replication ActiveX Controls* and *Using SQL Merge and SQL Distribution Controls in a Custom Application* if you're interested in learning more about these new controls.

SQL Server 7 builds on the original transactional replication model introduced in SQL Server 6.0 and introduces two new models: *snapshot* and *merge*. All models are based on the notions of a publisher, distributor, and subscriber. A *publisher* gathers and assimilates data into a publication, a *distributor* is responsible for delivering the publication, and the *subscriber* agrees to receive a publication via a subscription. In a similar manner, the SQL Server 7 replication model designates servers that have data that need to be distributed as a publisher, those that deliver the data as a distributor, and those that receive the data as a subscriber. The replication model can be further defined by the following:

- A publisher distributes data in the form of a publication.
- A publication consists of one or more articles.
- A subscriber receives a publication via a subscription.

In the SQL Server 7 model, a single published data set has only one publisher, but can have many distributors and subscribers. Each server that participates in replication can be both a publisher and subscriber, but only one server can be designated as the publisher for a single published data set. There are, of course, numerous details and nuances to replication technology, but keeping this model in mind will give you a good frame of reference. Figure 10.1 shows the general replication model.

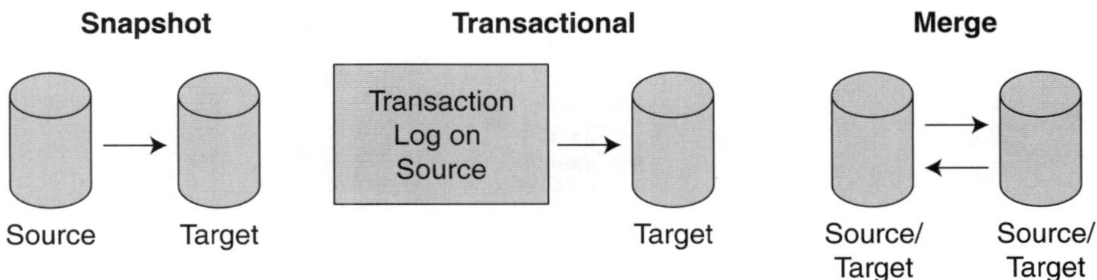

Figure 10.1 Replication model.

Distributed Data

The *distributed data* concept is concerned with the ability of disparate business sites/individuals to work from the same data. As the global economy becomes increasingly service-based, rather than manufacturing-based, and the dependence on data grows, so too does the desire to ensure that all business parties have the ability to access the same corporate data in a timely and efficient manner. This doesn't mean that all business parties must have up-to-the-minute access to corporate data, but rather that each party has the necessary access, to ensure that the actions they take, or the job functions they perform, are based on data that is correct for their particular purpose.

The following two scenarios may help you visualize how replication can be used to support the distributed data concept. Imagine a golf club manufacturer who has four manufacturing sites that are located in four different states. The corporate headquarters, which is also a manufacturing site, is located in Arizona and maintains the corporate inventory database for all parts that are used in the manufacturing process at each site. The other three sites depend on the corporate inventory database for scheduling production runs and estimating when they need to place orders to replenish their stock. There are several ways that the disparate sites can obtain the necessary information. They can receive daily or weekly hard-copy reports via mail, use dial-in access to read and analyze the data online, or establish WAN connections between all sites to provide access to the corporate database. The costs involved for each solution varies significantly. The hard-copy report distribution approach is the least expensive while establishing a WAN connection between all sites is the most costly. You should also be aware that the viability of the dial-in access and WAN solutions depends on the reliability of the communication links available in the specific areas. Figure 10.2 shows how the distributed sites might communicate.

In a second scenario, we have a laptop-dependent mobile sales force. The salespeople create all their sales orders on their laptops while at client sites and need a method for

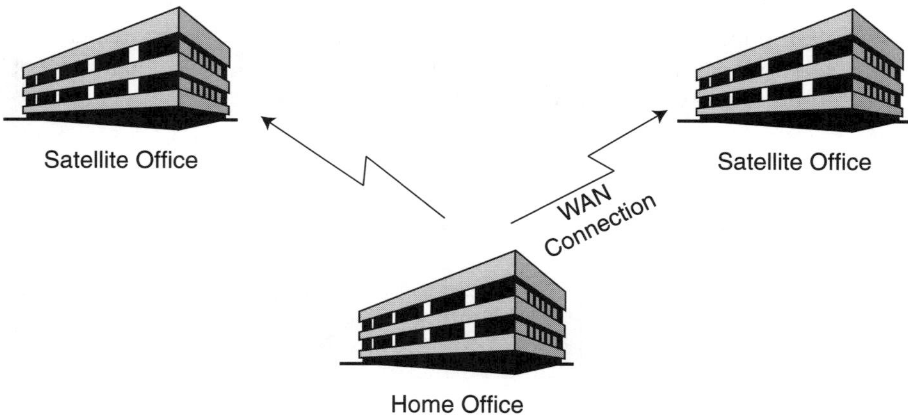

Figure 10.2 Distributed sites.

relaying this information to corporate headquarters on a daily basis. Possible solutions include printing each order and faxing it to headquarters, e-mailing a database of orders as an attachment, or dialing in and then re-entering the orders into another system.

As you can imagine, there are a multitude of other business scenarios that can use distributed data concepts. As we cover SQL Server's three replication models, you'll notice that it isn't always clear which model should be used for a given scenario. For many business needs, there's no clear solution—more than one replication model can be used, so you'll have to weigh the pros and cons for each.

Introduction to the Replication Process

SQL Server 7's replication technology facilitates the transfer of data from a source database to any number of target databases. Like many other computer-based technologies, there is not a single replication strategy that can be used to fulfill all business needs. SQL Server 7 uses three models to represent its replication technology and all three models are based on the publisher/distributor/subscriber analogy mentioned earlier. Before you can understand the logic for having three replication models, it's important to understand the goals that you hope to attain when choosing a distributed data strategy: *transactional consistency* and *site autonomy*. A particular business situation will dictate which goal is more important and thus which replication model is most appropriate.

Transactional Consistency

Transactional consistency refers to the ability to access and modify multiple copies of the same data as if there were only one copy. If you have three sites that are dependent on replicated data from a source site and transactional consistency is maintained, none of the dependent sites will ever know that the data they access was not created or modified locally.

Transactional consistency has the following classifications:

- Immediate guaranteed consistency
- Latent guaranteed consistency
- Convergence

Immediate guaranteed consistency ensures that all sites that access the same data have exactly the same data at exactly the same time. Data is accessed without regard to where it was created or last modified, because the two-phase commit (2PC) protocol is used to ensure that all copies are either modified simultaneously, or not modified at all. The 2PC protocol ensures that data modifications don't occur until all sites that use the data agree to the change. For example, if Site A and Site B have the same database at their sites and Site B wants to make a change, it must *ask* Site A if the change can be made without affecting Site A's operations. If Site A says it's OK with the change, then they both agree to commit the change and the modification is applied to both databases. SQL Server 7 uses Remote Procedure Call (RPC), Distributed Transaction Coordinator

(DTC), and a continuous, reliable network connection to implement this strategy. If you cannot guarantee a reliable network connection or users who can always be connected, this isn't a viable solution.

Latent guaranteed consistency ensures that all sites will eventually have access to the same data, and that when they eventually have access to this data it will appear as if all modifications occurred at one site. Latent refers to the time delay between when the initial data modification occurs and when the modification is distributed to all dependent sites. When Site A (publisher) makes a change, it is not immediately available at Site B (subscriber). There's a time delay (latency) between when the change is made at Site A and when Site B actually receives the change. When the change is eventually applied, it will be as if the change originated at Site B. In other words, the delay in applying the change at Site B will not affect the consistency of the data.

Convergence ensures that all sites will *eventually* end up with the same data. However, it does *not* guarantee that the data will be in the same state had all the data modifications occurred at one site. Convergence is applied to a scenario where data changes are merged from multiple sources and a conflict resolution strategy is used to determine which change is retained and which change is discarded. If Site B (subscriber) submits changes to Site A (publisher) that cause a conflict and the conflict resolution strategy is such that Site A always wins, then Site B's changes will be discarded. Subsequently, Site A will replicate its data to Site B and the original changes that Site B submitted will be replaced. The data has converged to a single state, but certainly not in the same manner as if all the changes occurred at one site.

Site Autonomy

Site autonomy is the degree of independence at which a site can operate without regard to another site's actions. For example, if site A can operate without being affected by site B's actions, its operations are completely autonomous. If Site A needs to be aware of some of the actions at Site B, it becomes less autonomous and somewhat dependent on Site B. When Site A needs to know every action that occurs at Site B in order to function, it has no autonomy and is completely dependent on Site B.

The degree of autonomy that is required will dictate which replication model is best suited to a particular business situation. A business situation that uses a database with few changes can be much more autonomous than one with frequent changes that must be communicated to all users.

Now that we covered transactional consistency and site autonomy, let's look at some general descriptions of the replication models and then explore replication components. Don't be concerned if the model's descriptions leave you wanting more. We are just trying to provide a frame-of-reference for the component descriptions that follow.

Model One: Snapshot

When *snapshot replication* is used, the schema and data from a publisher is output to text files and then transferred and loaded at the subscriber(s). This process is best illustrated with a simple example. Let's say that you have a database at Site A that consists of one table that is populated with 1000 records. You also have another site, Site B, that wants a complete copy of the table on a periodic basis. In order to accomplish this you must first re-create the table at Site B and then load the data into that table. So, when the snapshot process is started, a script is created that contains the T-SQL necessary to create the table at Site B and another file is created that contains the data. Once both files are transferred to Site B, the T-SQL file is executed (this creates the table) and then the data is loaded.

Snapshot replication has an extension to its base functionality called *immediate updating of subscribers*. This additional functionality allows a subscriber to make changes to its copy of the data and send these changes to the publisher for redistribution to other subscribers. Immediate subscriber updates require the 2PC protocol.

Model Two: Transactional

Transactional replication involves the capture of transactions generated by the publisher where they are then applied to the subscriber. The capture part is accomplished by monitoring the publisher's transaction log. Remember that all INSERT, UPDATE, or DELETE statements are recorded in the transaction log. So, when one of these statements is executed the log monitoring process captures the transaction log entry and forwards it to the subscriber. Once it has been received at the subscriber, it is applied to the target database. This process might seem a little confusing, but just think of it as executing the same data modification statements in both databases.

The transactional replication model, like snapshot replication, supports immediate subscriber updates.

Model Three: Merge

Merge replication is based on capturing data changes at both the publisher and subscriber and, using conflict resolution, converging the data into a uniform state. An example will help explain this model. Let's say that you have two sites—Site A and Site B—and each wants to maintain company contact information (customers' names and telephone numbers). The CEO, however, wants the primary source to be stored centrally at the company's headquarters (Site A). In order to facilitate both requests you set up merge replication between both sites.

The data changes at Site A move to Site B and vice versa. However, what happens if both sites update the same record? The next time Site B sends its' changes to Site A, a conflict occurs. There has to be a mechanism in place that decides who *wins* the conflict. You simply assign a priority (a numerical value) to each site participating in merge replication and the site with a higher priority wins. In this example, Site A is assigned the higher priority because it's the company's headquarters. Site B's change to the record is rejected by Site A and the value at Site B is subsequently overwritten by the value *coming* from Site A. Unlike the other models, merge replication does *not* support immediate subscriber updates.

PUSHING VERSUS PULLING

The replication data transfer process can be initiated by either the publisher or the subscriber. When the publisher initiates the process it is referred to as *pushing* the data and when the subscriber initiates the process it is referred to as *pulling* the data.

Replication Components

The components of replication are listed here:

Article. The fundamental unit of data to be replicated.

Publication. One or more articles.

Publisher. The server on which the publication is located.

Distributor/Distribution Database. The server that distributes replicated data via a distribution database.

Subscriber. A server that subscribes to a publication.

Subscription. The publication(s) the subscriber receives.

Snapshot Agent. The agent that prepares snapshots for initial synchronization or for snapshot replication.

Log Reader Agent. The agent responsible for monitoring the transaction log. The agent can be configured to read the log either periodically or on a continuous basis.

Merge Agent. The agent responsible for delivering the initial synchronizing snapshot when a merge publication is created and for merging updates—detecting any conflicts and calling the resolver if needed.

Distribution Agent. The agent that actually oversees data movement (copying data and schemas) according to the instructions stored in the distribution database.

Replication Monitor. A monitoring tool that is available in the Enterprise Manager when the server is enabled as a distributor. The Replication Monitor is only available for users who are members of the sysadmin fixed server role.

Replication Wizards. SQL Server's programs that walk you through implementing replication solutions.

Replication System Stored Procedures. System stored procedures that allow you to configure/manage replication.

A detailed description of the components is provided in the following sections.

Article

An *article* is a complete table, a partial table, or a stored procedure that has been designated for replication. An article is the fundamental unit of a publication and a publication is the fundamental unit of replication. In other words, a publication consists of one or more articles and a unit of replicated data is called a publication. An article is always associated with a publication and does not exist as a standalone object.

Articles that are based on tables can contain all the rows and columns of the underlying table, a partial number of columns, a partial number of rows, or a partial number of rows and columns. When a partial number of columns are designated for replication it is called *vertical partitioning*, and when a partial number of rows are designated for replication, it's called *horizontal partitioning*. In addition to partitioning, there's a strategy called *filtering* that limits the data that is replicated by enforcing a WHERE clause on the underlying article.

An article can also be based on a stored procedure. Stored procedures are replicated differently depending on the replication model that is used and the property settings that are applied to the article. If snapshot replication is used, the stored procedure's schema is replicated to the subscriber. If transactional replication is used, an article property setting and the context in which the stored procedure is executed determine what is replicated to the subscriber. A stored procedure article has a property setting called *type* that can be set to either *proc exec* or *serializable proc exec*. If it is set to proc exec, the execution of the stored procedure is sent to the subscriber without regard to the context of its execution. If it is set to serializable proc exec, the execution of the stored procedure is only replicated if its execution occurred within a serializable transaction. If its execution does not occur within a serializable transaction, the individual data-modification statements that are caused by the stored procedure are executed. The later setting ensures data consistency between the publisher and subscriber.

The main benefit of stored procedure replication is efficiency. An update example shows how replicating a stored procedure article is much more efficient when updating large amounts of data than a table-based article. In order to update 500 records with a table-based article, 500 individual UPDATE...WHERE PrimaryKeyField = PrimaryKey statements are replicated to and executed on the destination table. The same modification with a stored procedure-based article is much more efficient because the destination database simply receives the stored procedure execution and its parameters and executes an UPDATE...SET FieldName = Value.

STORED PROCEDURE REPLICATION

Stored procedure replication can only be used with native SQL Server subscribers. You cannot, however, use it with merge replication.

You can use the Create Publication Wizard (Tools, Replication, Create and Manage Publications) to create an article. The wizard steps you through the article creation process and is very easy to use.

Publication

A *publication* is the fundamental unit of replication. It is composed of one or more articles from the same database and is replicated as a single unit of data. For example, if publication_1 is created with Pubs..authors as an article, one publication composed of one article has been created. If publication_2 is created with Pubs..authors, Pubs..royalties, and the stored procedure Pubs..byroyalty, then one publication composed of two table-based articles and one stored procedure-based article has been created. Both publication_1 and publication_2 are replicated as a single unit of data. In general, a publication is composed of more than one article. You can also use the Create Publication Wizard (Tools, Replication, Create and Manage Publications) to create a publication.

PUBLISHER ACCESS LIST (PAL)

An additional feature of publications is the ability to limit access by login. When a server is configured as a publisher, a default publication access list (PAL) is created that allows its members to access all publications that don't have a custom PAL. A custom PAL allows access to be restricted to logins that were explicitly granted access. By default, the distributor_admin, sysadmin, and db_owner fixed roles are all members of the server's PAL. Custom PALS are created at the time a publication is created.

Publisher

A *publisher* is a server that has been configured to replicate data to other servers. Once a server has been configured as a publisher, its databases can be enabled for publication and articles can be created for the tables and stored procedures that reside in its databases. A publisher's responsibilities include storing information about all of its publications and monitoring data changes to these publications. You configure a server for replication by using one of the following:

- The Create and Manage Publications Wizard
- The Configure Publishing and Distribution Wizard

In order to execute either of these wizards, you must be a member of the sysadmin fixed server role.

DISTRIBUTORS FIRST

A distributor must be configured before a server can be configured as a publisher.

Distributor/Distribution Database

In general, a *distributor* is as a server that has been configured to store and forward replicated data via the distribution database. A distribution database is a database whose only function is to collect and distribute data. For example, let's say that you use the transactional model with production data on Server A, which you then want to replicate to two, non-production servers (Server B and Server C). If you want Servers B and C to remain autonomous (not connected via a network), you need a database that stores the replicated data until the non-production servers are ready to receive it. The distributor/distribution database will hold the replicated data until the recipients are ready to connect via a LAN, WAN, or the Internet and request the data.

The distributor can reside on its own server or the same server as the publisher. In environments with large amounts of replicated data, the distributor should reside on its own server.

A server is configured as a distributor with a distribution database by using one of the following:

- The Create and Manage Publications Wizard
- The Configure Publishing and Distribution Wizard

In order to execute one of these wizards, you must be a member of the sysadmin fixed server role.

Subscriber

A *subscriber* is a server that has been configured to receive replicated data. A server is configured as a subscriber by using one of the following:

- The Configure Publishing and Distribution Wizard
- The Create and Manage Publications Wizard

In order to execute one of these wizards, you must be a member of the sysadmin fixed server role.

Subscription

SQL Server 7 uses the word *subscription* for both pull and push subscriptions. Traditionally, subscription describes a situation in which one party asks for information from another party. SQL Server uses the traditional meaning to define a situation where a subscriber specifically requests information from a publisher and calls this a *pull subscription*. Microsoft adds to the traditional use of the word by describing a publication that has been defined to replicate information to a subscriber without specifically being asked as a *push subscription*. Given these two situations, a subscription is either a directive to send data to a subscriber or a request from a subscriber to receive replicated data.

In addition to push and pull, there's also an *anonymous subscription*, which allows subscribers that aren't registered with the publisher to retrieve replicated data. This type of subscription facilitates the distribution of data to numerous subscribers (especially over the Internet) and reduces operational overhead by not storing subscriber information at the publisher and replication statistical information at the distributor.

The type of subscription that a publication can participate in is determined by a property setting that is configured when the publication is created.

A subscription is created using one of the following:

- The Push Subscription Wizard
- The Pull Subscription Wizard

As we mentioned previously, you must be a member of the sysadmin fixed server role to run the wizards.

Snapshot Agent

The *Snapshot Agent* is responsible for creating the initial snapshot for a publication's schema and data, moving the snapshot files to the distributor, and updating synchronization information that is stored in the distribution database. The Snapshot Agent moves the physical schema and data files to the distributor, but does not apply them to the destination database. A Snapshot Agent is created:

- Automatically when the Create and Manage Publication Wizard is used
- With the Snapshot Agent Utility (SNAPSHOT.EXE)

The Snapshot Agent is always created on the distributor.

Log Reader Agent

The *Log Reader Agent* monitors the transaction log for a replication-enabled database and moves the transactions that are marked for replication to the distribution database. Only those data changes that occur to an article are marked for replication. A Log Reader Agent is created:

- Automatically when the Create and Manage Publication Wizard is used
- With the Log Reader Agent Utility (LOGREAD.EXE)

The Log Reader Agent is always created on the distributor.

Merge Agent

The *Merge Agent* applies initial snapshot schema and data files to the destination database, tracks changes that occur to merge articles, monitors changes that are sent to and received from other sites, and evaluates the conflict resolution strategy to decide which data element dominates in a conflict. A Merge Agent is created:

- Automatically when the Create and Manage Publication Wizard is used
- Using the Merge Reader Agent Utility (MERGE.EXE)

The two methods create the Merge Agent on the distributor.

Distribution Agent

The *Distribution Agent* applies snapshot schema and data files to the destination database, and also pushes or pulls replicated data from the distributor. A Distribution Agent is created:

- Automatically when the Create and Manage Publication Wizard is used
- By using the Distribution Agent Utility (DISTRIB.EXE)

If push subscriptions are used, the Distribution Agent runs on the distributor and pushes data to the subscribers. When pull subscriptions are used, the agent runs on the subscriber and pulls replicated data from the distributor.

Replication agents run under the account that is set up for the SQL Server Agent. You must ensure that this account has permissions for all needed servers, databases, and directories in order for the agents to work properly.

Replication Monitor

The *Replication Monitor* allows you to monitor all publishers, their associated publications, and the replication agents that run on a server. It's available as a server component in the Server Manager window of Enterprise Manager, is only visible when the user is a member of the sysadmin fixed server role, and the server is configured as a distributor. The Replication Monitor acts as a filter for the SQL Server Agent by displaying only those jobs that are related to replication.

SYSTEM STORED PROCEDURES

There are a number of system stored procedures whose purpose is to facilitate replication creation and maintenance. We will not, however, cover these in this chapter. Earlier versions of SQL Server did not have a GUI for creating and managing replication and this made replication a very complicated process. With version 7 Microsoft has gone through the trouble of creating a nice interface, we can now try to forget that the "old" method was ever available.

REPLICATION ROLES AND PERMISSIONS

Only sysadmins can do the following:

- **Configure distribution or publication**
- **Enable, modify, or drop a distributor, publisher, or subscriber**
- **Enable a database for replication**
- **Configure agent profiles**
- **Monitor replication agents**
- **Update the default publication access list**

Either sysadmins or db_owners can do the following tasks:

- **Create or drop a publication**
- **Create a push subscription**
- **Update a custom publication access list**
- **Enable snapshots for FTP downloading using the Internet**
- **Drop a subscription (creating a login that a pull subscription can also drop)**
- **Snapshot, Log Reader Agent logging into publisher or distributor**

Any login in the publication's publication access list (PAL) can create a pull subscription. A Merge Agent that logs into the publisher login must also be in the publication access list for the referenced publication.

Log Shipping

Microsoft added log shipping functionality to SQL Server 7.0 when it shipped the Microsoft BackOffice 4.5 Resource Kit (look for the files in the i386\sql\logshipping directory). Log shipping is a transaction log-based replication scheme that relies on a scheduled pattern of backup, copy, and restore of transaction logs to provide the foundation for building a custom "warm backup" solution. Transaction logs are backed up for the primary database, copied to a secondary location, and then restored onto a secondary database. The secondary database is maintained in a read-only state. To install Log Shipping, you need to perform the following:

1. Create the database on the primary server. (Both Truncate Log on Checkpoint and the Select into/Bulk Copy option must be set to false.)
2. Create the transaction log backup job.
3. Install the log shipping control tables, its stored procedures and the log shipping monitoring stored procedures (they all go into msdb).
4. Backup, copy, and restore the database to the secondary server.
5. Create the log shipping entities.

About the Projects

We recommend that you read the three projects used in this chapter in succession because they build upon one another. You should also know that the instructions and screen shots used are from a server that was newly-configured for replication. This doesn't mean that you cannot proceed if you don't plan on completing the projects in succession or have already configured your server for replication. We just wanted to let you know that, depending on what type of replication activities have occurred on your server, your screen shots or default values might be slightly different than ours.

Project 7A: Snapshot Replication

In this first project we cover snapshot replication. More specifically, we show the steps required to replicate data from a single table (tlkpRequestReason) in the WorkOrd database to a new database that we create for this project. If you are not already familiar with the WordOrd database, please see its E-R Diagram and brief description in Appendix C. Seeing how the WorkOrd database is designed should make the project a little easier to comprehend. The tlkpRequestReason table is very small (only four rows) and, as such, is perfect for snapshot replication. Why? Because it's a lookup table which, in theory at least, isn't likely to change very often. If it were a large table like tblRequest with numerous changes then it would *not* be a good candidate for snapshot replication. Transactional replication is better suited for a large table that's modified on a frequent basis.

The first thing you must do before you can set up the publication on tlkpRequestReason is to configure your server for replication. (We assume that your server has not already been configured for replication.) This entails configuring your server as a publisher

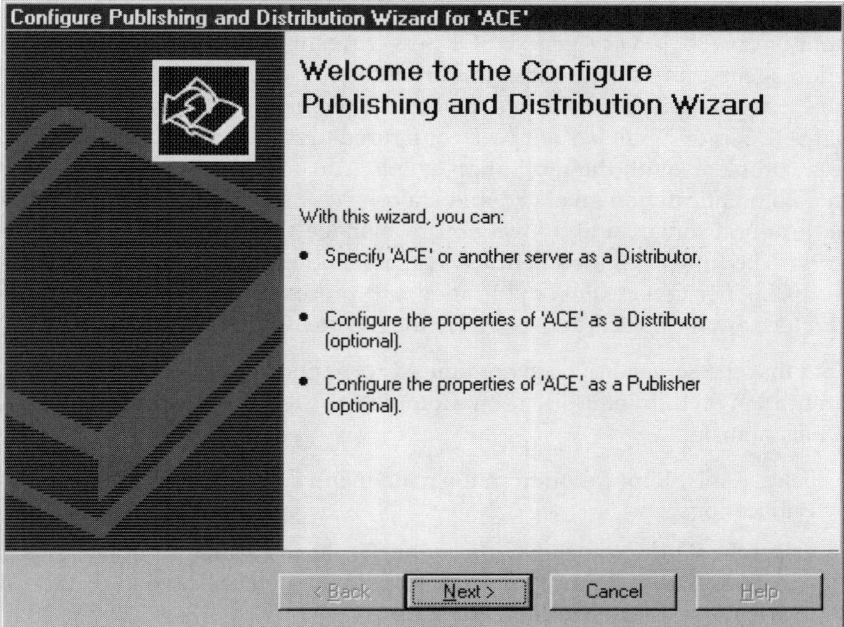

Figure 10.3 Configuring a server for replication.

and distributor and can be accomplished with a single wizard. From Enterprise Manager complete the following steps:

1. Expand a server group and highlight the server you want to configure for replication.
2. Select Tools/Replication from the main menu and choose Configure Publishing and Subscribers.... This invokes the Configure Publishing and Distribution Wizard as shown in Figure 10.3.
3. Click Next to proceed past the Welcome screen.
4. Accept the default Yes, use [your server name]... on the Choose Distributor dialog.
5. Accept the default value of No, use the... on the Use Default Configuration dialog.
6. Click Finish on the Completing screen. The wizard will then create the distribution database and enable the server's databases for replication. When the process is complete, you should see the message displayed in Figure 10.4.

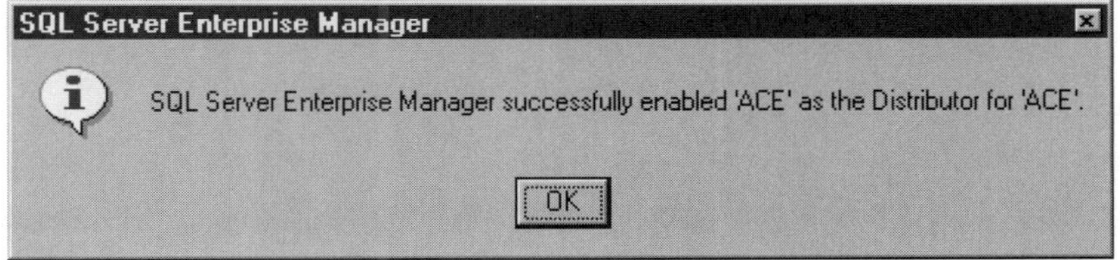

Figure 10.4 Replication configuration success.

Once you click OK, you'll see a screen that either displays information on Replication Monitor or SQL Server Agent. If SQL Server Agent (the service under which the replication agents run) is configured to start automatically, you will see a screen that indicates that a new item has been added to the server tree. Otherwise, you'll be notified that SQL Server Agent has not been configured to start automatically and that this may cause problems with the replication agents. You will have a choice to configure it to start automatically, so go ahead and choose, Yes. The new server tree item is labeled Replication Monitor and allows you to manage the replication components on the server. The fully expanded item list available in Replication Monitor is shown in Figure 10.5. After you create a publication and process a few replication sessions, you'll start to see some objects and events in the hierarchy.

Now that the server has been configured for replication, you can proceed to create a publication on tlkpRequestReason. Complete the following steps to create the desired publication:

1. Select Tools/Replication from the main menu and choose Create and Manage Publications.
2. Select the WorkOrd database from the Create and Manage Publications dialog and press Create Publication to invoke the Create Publication Wizard. Click Next to advance past the Welcome screen.
3. Accept the default of Snapshot Publication from the Choose Publication Type dialog.

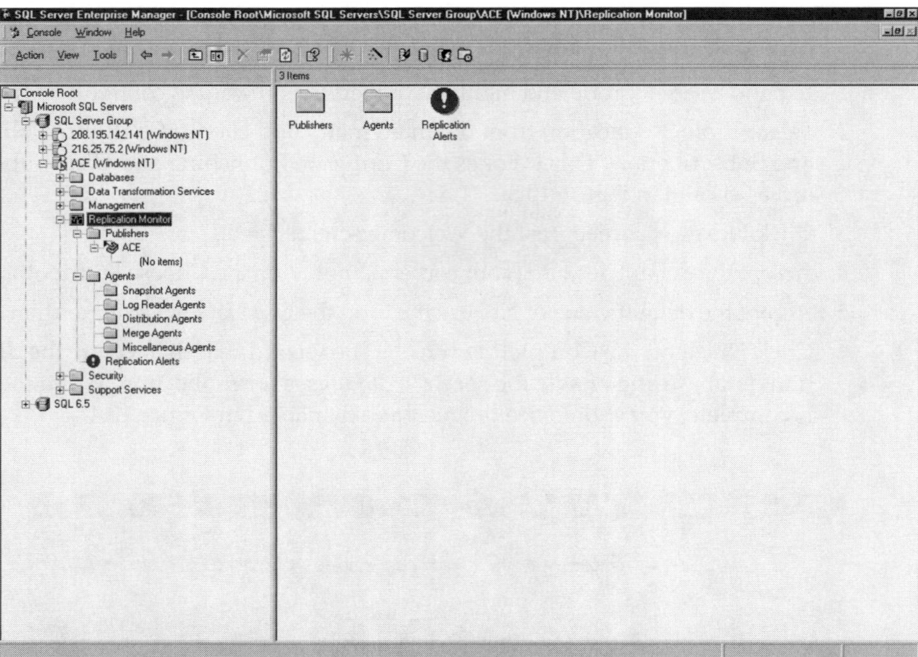

Figure 10.5 Replication Monitor.

EXISTING PUBLICATIONS

If you created a publication before starting this project you will not see the Choose Publication Type dialog. Instead, you'll see the Use Publication Template dialog. Simply accept the default of No, I will define the articles and properties and click Next.

4. Accept the default of No, do not allow… in the Allow Immediate-Updating Subscriptions dialog.
5. Accept the default of All subscribers will be. . . on the Specify Subscriber Types dialog.
6. You should see a listing with all of the tables in the WorkOrd database as displayed in Figure 10.6. Click the left-most column in the table listing for tlkpRequestReason and then click Next.
7. Input the following in the Choose Publication Name and Description dialog and click Next.
   - Publication Name: WorkOrd_Snapshot_tlkpRequestReason
   - Publication Description: Snapshot publication of WorkOrd..tlkpRequestReason
8. Select Yes, I will define… in the Use Default Properties of the Publication dialog and click Next.

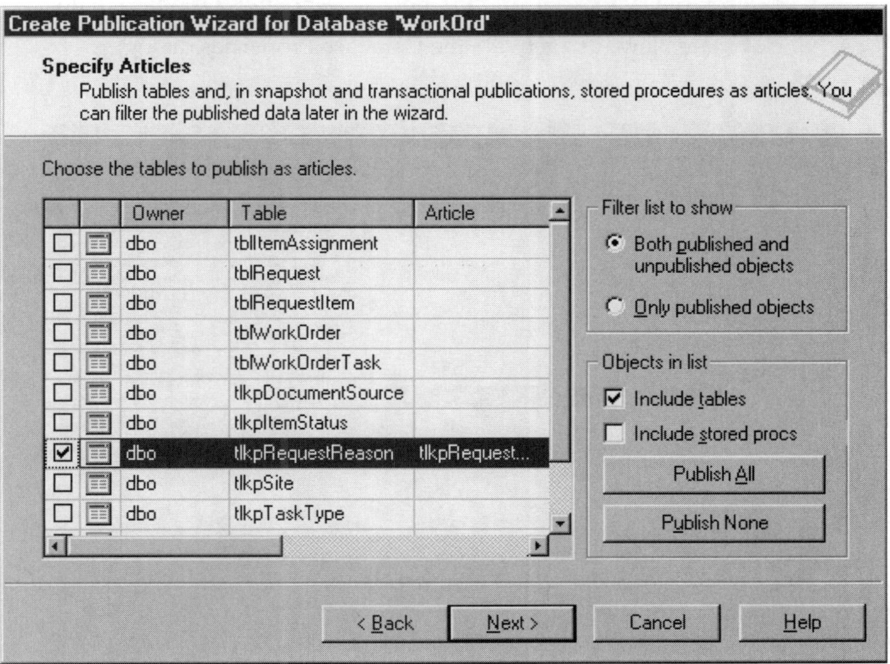

Figure 10.6 Specify Articles dialog.

9. Select No, I want to publish... in the Filter Data dialog and click Next.
10. Accept the default of No, only known… in the Allow Anonymous Subscribers dialog
11. Click the Change button on the Set Snapshot Agent Schedule dialog.
12. Make sure Occurs once at in the Daily frequency section is selected and specify a time that is 15 minutes ahead of the current time. Make a note of the time you scheduled the agent to execute. Click OK and then Next.
13. Click Finish to complete the wizard. Once the wizard has created all of the required database objects, a success message is displayed.
14. Click OK and the Create and Manage Publications dialog (shown in Figure 10.7) is displayed.

Now what? Well, at this point, all we've done is create a publication and configure the Snapshot Agent to run in roughly 15 minutes. If we stop now, the data in tlkp-RequestReason won't be replicated—the snapshot files will be created, but they will not be distributed. The next series of steps shows how to create the subscription that actually allows the data to be replicated.

1. Click Push New Subscription from the Create and Manage Publications dialog shown in Figure 10.7. To activate the Push Subscription Wizard, click Next to advance past the Welcome screen.
2. Select your local server in the Choose Subscribers dialog and click Next.
3. Click Browse Databases… in the Choose Destination Database dialog.
4. Click Create New… to activate the Database Properties dialog.

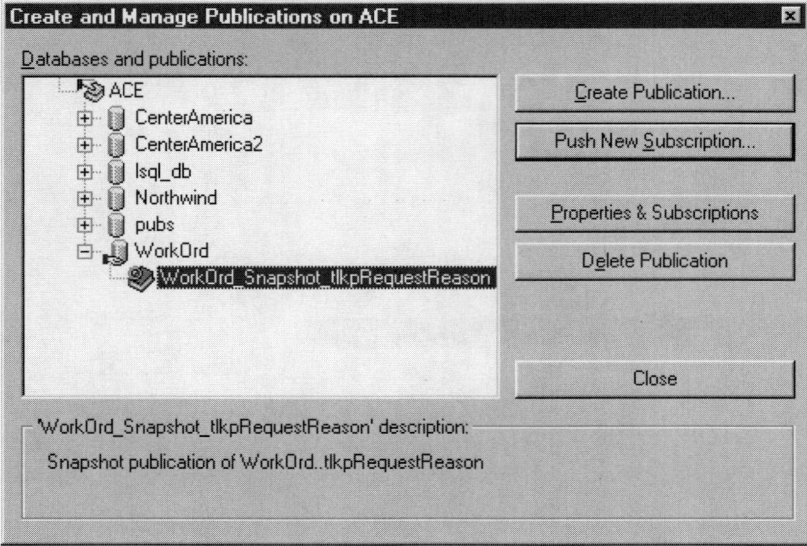

Figure 10.7 Create and Manage Publications dialog.

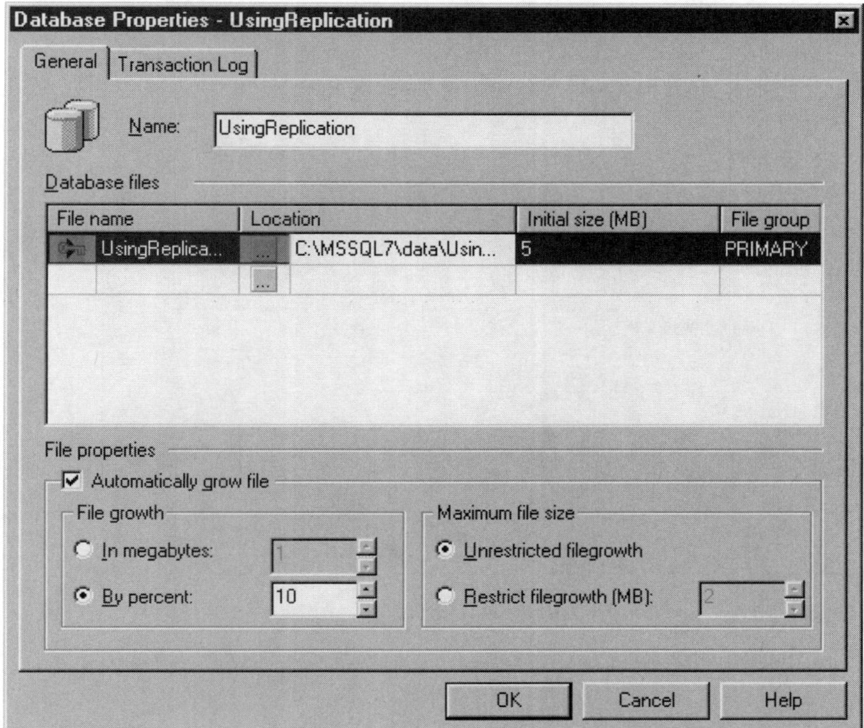

Figure 10.8 Creating a new database.

5. Specify UsingReplication as the new database's name and set the initial size to 5 MB as shown in Figure 10.8.
6. Click OK to create the database.
7. Verify that the new database is selected and click OK to specify it as the destination database.
8. Click Next to activate the Set Distribution Agent Schedule dialog and then click Change.
9. Select the Occurs Once At option in the Daily Frequency section and specify a time that's about 15 minutes ahead of your current time. Make a note of the time you scheduled the agent to execute. Click the End Date option to specify that the agent will only run today and click OK. Figure 10.9 displays the desired selections.
10. Click Next and then select Start the Snapshot Agent to Begin… in the Initialize Subscription dialog. Click Next to accept the default of Yes, initialize the schema and data at the subscriber.
11. If the SQL Server Agent shows a status of Stopped, select the left-most column in the Start Required Services dialog. Click Next to advance to the final screen.

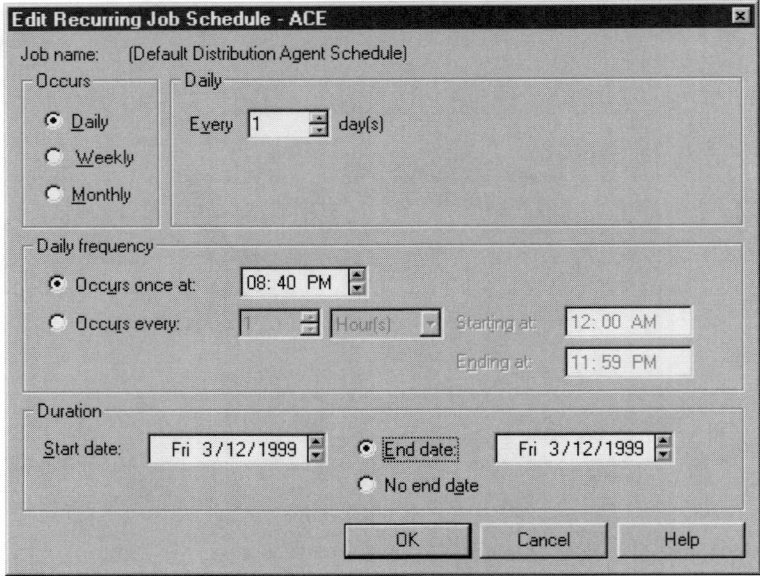

Figure 10.9 Setting the agent's schedule.

12. Review the information on the Completing screen and click Finish.
13. Click Finish to complete the wizard. Once the wizard creates and initializes the components required to support this model, a message (shown in Figure 10.10) that indicates that the publication was successfully created is displayed. Close the open dialog boxes to return to Enterprise Manager.

You should pay particular attention to the last sentence in Figure 10.10. It means *you* must monitor the Snapshot Agent in order to know when it has completed the schema and data files creation for the publication. Once it completes, *you* must manually start the Distribution Agent to ensure that the files are applied to the UsingReplication database. In order to tell when the Snapshot Agent has successfully created the needed files, complete the following:

1. Expand Replication Monitor and highlight Snapshot Agents under Agents. Notice the entry in the Details pane.

Once the Agent creates the files, the Status will show Succeeded as in Figure 10.11.

Now that you know the Snapshot Agent has created the needed files, you must manually start the Distribution Agent so that the table can be created in the UsingReplication database and the data is loaded into the table. To do this, complete the following:

1. Highlight Distribution Agents under Agents and notice that the entry in the Details pane has an entry of Never… in the Status field.

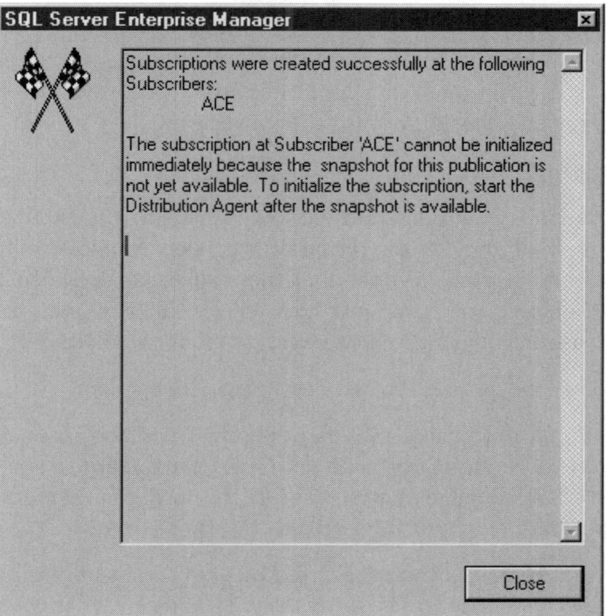

Figure 10.10 Completion message.

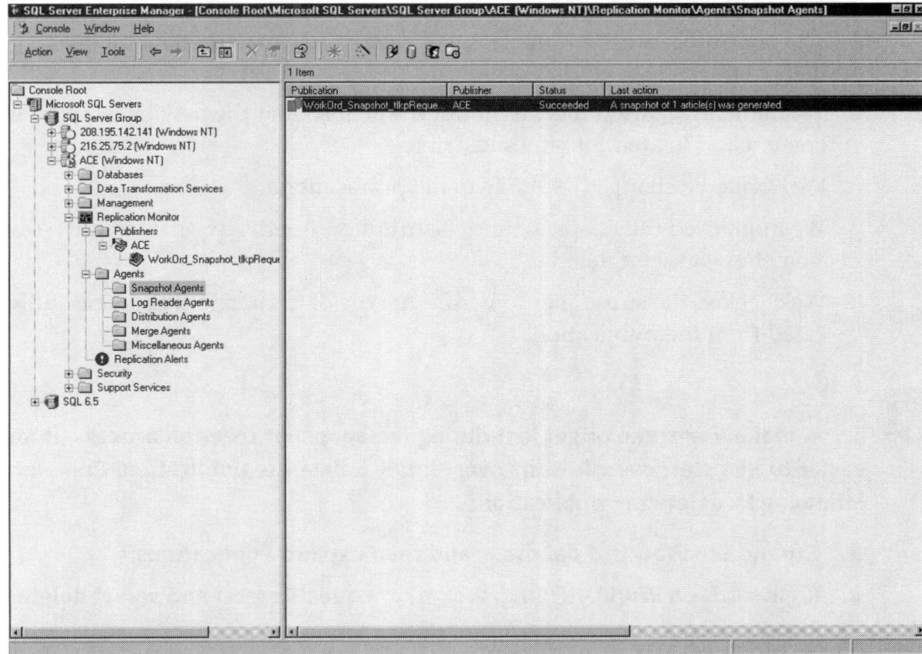

Figure 10.11 Verifying that the Snapshot Agent completes.

2. Right-click on the entry and select Start.

Once the Distribution Agent has completed, the Status field changes to Succeeded and the new table and data are now in the UsingReplication database. If you don't believe us, go into Query Analyzer and check for yourself by executing:

```
SELECT * FROM  UsingReplication..tlkpRequestReason.
```

We now know that the initial synchronization worked, but what about the scheduled processes? To make sure that they work properly we need to make a change to WorkOrd..tlkpRequestReason and then verify that the change is replicated to Using-Replication..tlkpRequestReason.after the agents have executed Let's add a record to WorkOrd..tlkpRequestReason via Query Analyzer with the following INSERT statement.

```
INSERT WorkOrd tlkpRequestReason VALUES (5, 'Snapshot Test')
```

You can use the Replication Monitor to verify that the scheduled Snapshot and Distribution Agents completed successfully and then use Query Analyzer to make sure that the record was transferred. Remember that you wrote down the scheduled times for each agent, so make sure that you check their status after those times.

This probably seems like a tedious process, but tedious isn't the same as hard. Basically, implementing snapshot replication is pretty easy. Let's recap what we did:

1. We enabled the server for replication.
2. We created a publication.
3. We created a subscription.
4. The Snapshot Agent automatically created a schema and data file for the published table.
5. We manually started the Distribution Agent so that the new table and data were created and loaded into the subscriber.
6. We applied a change (INSERT) to the publication.
7. We monitored the Snapshot and Distribution Agents to verify that the scheduled snapshot was completed.
8. We checked the subscriber to verify that the data change was successfully replicated from the publication.

RECOVERING FROM A MISTAKE

If you make a mistake or get lost during the snapshot creation process, it might be easier to just start over. To start over simply delete the publication. Complete the following to delete the publication:

1. **Expand the WorkOrd database and then expand Publications.**
2. **Right-click on WorkOrd_Snapshot_tlkpRequestReason and select delete from the pop-up menu.**

WHERE ARE THE SCHEMA AND DATA FILES?

The Snapshot Agent creates a schema, data, and an index file for each publication in order to synchronize the publisher and subscriber. These files are located in a folder under C:\Mssql7\Repldata\unc on the distributor. Each publication gets its own working folder that has the naming convention of *Servername_DatabaseName_ publicationName*. For our first project in this chapter, the folder is ACE_WorkOrd_ WorkOrd_Snapshot_tlkpRequestReason. When the Snapshot Agent executes, it creates the files in another time-specific working directory whose naming convention is YYYYMMDDHHMMSS.

Project 7B: Transactional Replication (Tables and Stored Procedures)

In the previous project we created a simple snapshot replication that consisted of an initial synchronization and a one-time execution. In this project we create a continuous replication scenario that applies the changes from the publisher to the subscriber on a near real-time basis. If you didn't complete the previous section, you need to become familiar with the WordOrd database and configure your server for replication before proceeding. If you need to do this, please refer to the first two paragraphs in Project 7A.

We'll use the tblRequest table in the WordOrd database for this project. WorkOrd..tblRequest is much larger (26,117 rows) than the five-row table we used in Project 7A and will be updated much more frequently. When you have a table of this size and you want changes replicated frequently, it's simply not feasible to use snapshot replication because of the resources required to transfer the data. A large table with frequent updates is a prime candidate for transactional replication and this is the model that we use for this project.

Before we proceed, we need to create a stored procedure that performs a simple UPDATE on WorkOrd..tblRequest. This stored procedure (see Chapter 12 for more on stored procedures) will allow us to see the differences in applying a change to the publication based on a stored procedure versus a row-by-row change from the transaction log. In short, if you make a change to thousands of rows in the publication and you do not use stored procedure replication, all of the individual changes that are recorded in the transaction log are applied to the target. If stored procedure replication is used, the stored procedure is executed at the subscriber and you avoid the unnecessary overhead involved in applying all of the individual statements. Execute the following in Query Analyzer.

```
USE WorkOrd
go
CREATE PROCEDURE ps_tblRequest_UPDATE
@RequesterOld nvarchar(50),
@RequesterNew nvarchar(50)
```

```
AS

UPDATE tblRequest
SET Requester = @RequesterNew
WHERE Requester = @RequesterOld
```

Now that we have all of the pieces in place, lets create the publication. To create a publication on tblRequest, complete the following:

1. Select Tools/Replication from the main menu and choose the Create and Manage Publications option.
2. Select the WorkOrd database and click Create Publication.
3. Click Next to advance past the Create Publication Welcome screen.
4. Accept the default value of No, I will define… in the Use Publication Template dialog.
5. Select Transactional Publication from the Choose Publication Type dialog and click Next.
6. Accept the default of No, do not allow. . . from the Allow Immediate-Updating Subscriptions dialog.
7. Accept the default of All subscribers will be. . . from the Specify Subscriber Types dialog.
8. Select the check box Include Stored Procs. A warning message will be displayed, so click Yes to close the screen.
9. Select tblRequest and ps_tblRequest_UPDATE from the Specify Articles dialog (as shown in Figure 10.12) and click Next.
10. Enter the following in the Choose Publication Name and Description dialog and click Next.
    - Publication Name: WorkOrd_Transactional_tblRequest
    - Publication Description: Transactional publication of WorkOrd..tblRequest
11. Accept the default of No, create a publication without… in the Use Default Properties of the Publication dialog.
12. Click Finish and, once the process completes, a message that indicates that the publication was successfully created is displayed.
13. Click OK to return to the Create and Manage Publications dialog. Your dialog, assuming you created Project 7A, will look like Figure 10.13.

We have created the publication, but need a subscription to complete the process. To create the subscription complete the following steps:

1. Click Push New Subscription on the Create and Manage Publications dialog to launch the Push Subscription Wizard. Click Next to advance past the Welcome screen.
2. Select your local server in the Choose Subscribers dialog and click Next.
3. Click Browse Databases in the Choose Destination Database dialog.
4. Select UsingReplication as the destination database and click OK.

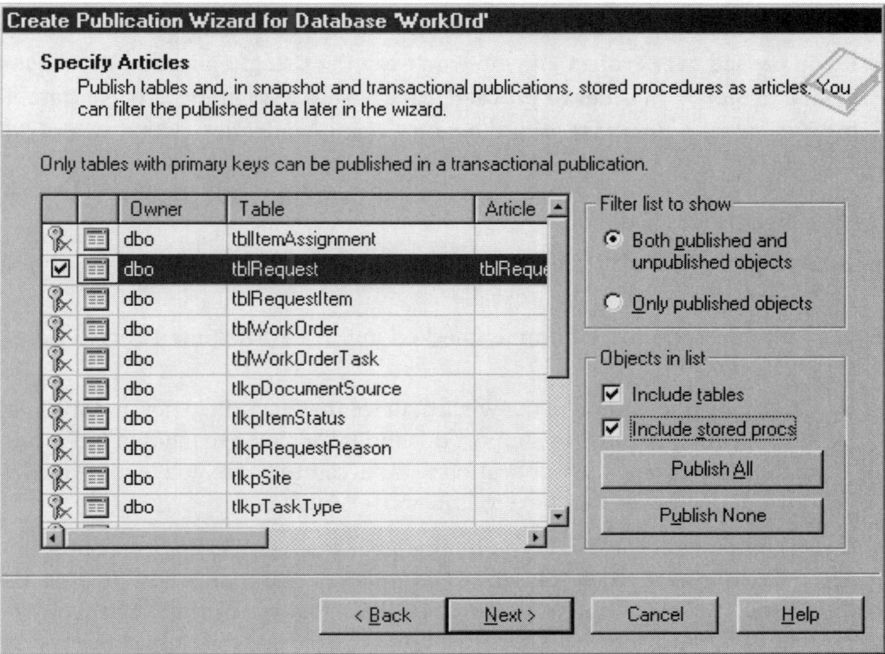

Figure 10.12 Select articles for publication.

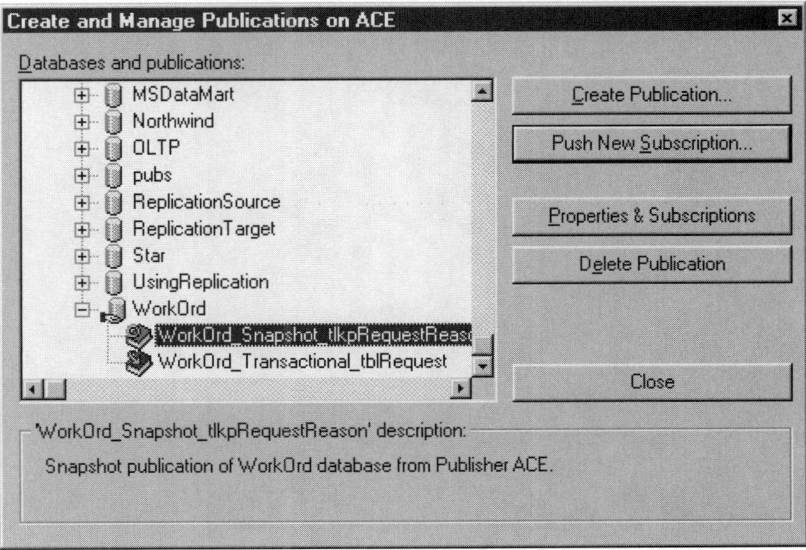

Figure 10.13 Create and Manage Publications dialog.

IF YOU SKIPPED (TSK TSK!) PROJECT 7A

If you passed over Project 7A, you won't see the UsingReplication database as suggested in Step 4. In order to proceed, click Create New in the Browse Databases dialog and create a database with the name, UsingReplication with a size of 5 MB.

5. Click Next and then accept the default of Continuously on the Set Distribution Agent Schedule dialog.
6. Accept the default of Yes, initialize the schema... in the Initialize Subscription dialog.
7. Verify the left-most column is checked in the Start Required Services dialog, and click Next.
8. Click Finish to complete the wizard. Once the wizard creates and initializes the components required to support this model, a message (shown in Figure 10.14) that indicates that the publication was successfully created is displayed. Close the open dialog boxes to return to Enterprise Manager.

If you completed Project 7A, you'll remember that we specified the Snapshot Agent to automatically start when the wizard completed its initialization process. Because we didn't specify that option in this project, the initial synchronization won't occur until we manually start the Snapshot Agent. In order to see the publication's current state, complete the following steps:

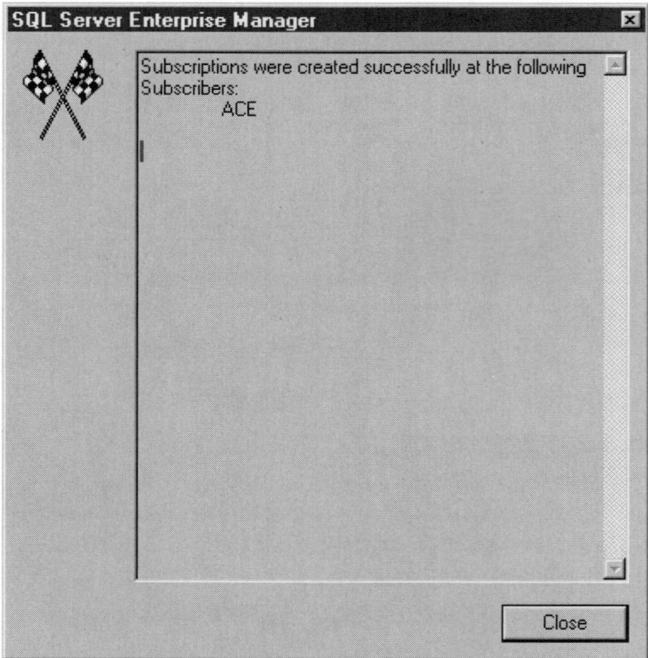

Figure 10.14 A successful subscription creation.

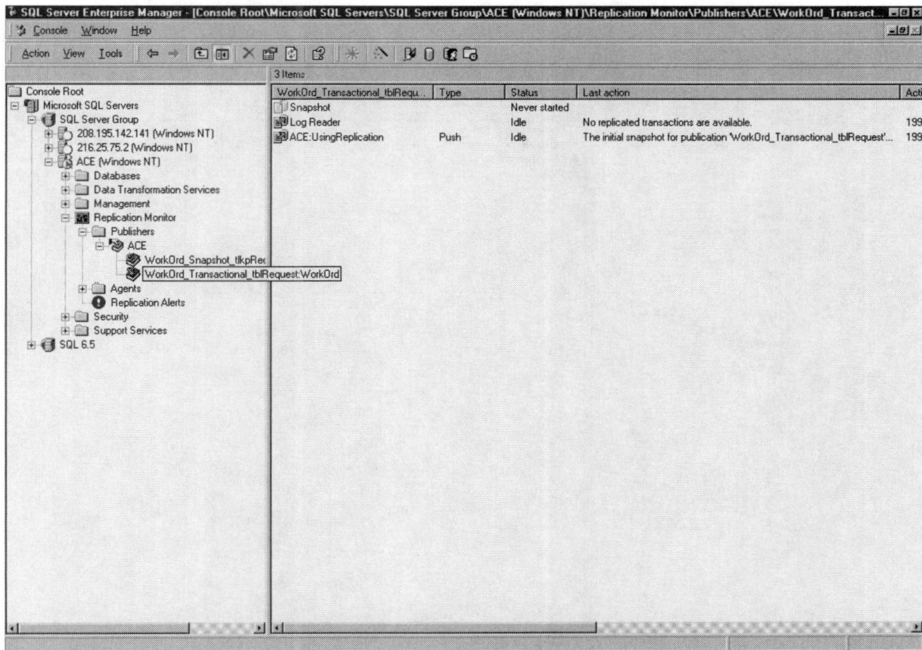

Figure 10.15 Examining the publication.

1. Expand Replication Monitor, and then Publishers.
2. Expand your server and then select WorkOrd_Transactional_tblRequest.
3. Review the contents of your Details pane. The contents of our Details pane is shown in Figure 10.15.

Notice that the Status for the Snapshot Agent is Never Started. In order to start the Snapshot Agent simply right-click on Snapshot in the Details Pane and select Start. After the Snapshot Agent completes you can see the files created by this process by viewing the folders under C:\MSSQL7\Repldata\unc. Figure 10.16 shows that the agent created two schema files—one for the table and one for the stored procedure, an index file, and a bcp file that contains the data in WorkOrd..tblRequest.

Now that the required files have been created, we need to start the Distribution Agent so that the files can be applied to the UsingReplication database. To start the Distribution Agent simply right-click on Ace: Using Replication in the Details pane and select Synchronize Now. When the Distribution Agent is finished you can use Query Analyzer to verify that both the table and stored procedure were created and that the data was transferred successfully. Execute the following in Query Analyzer to verify that the objects were created and the data transferred.

```
USE UsingReplication
go
sp_help ps_tblRequest_UPDATE
go
SELECT * FROM tblRequest
```

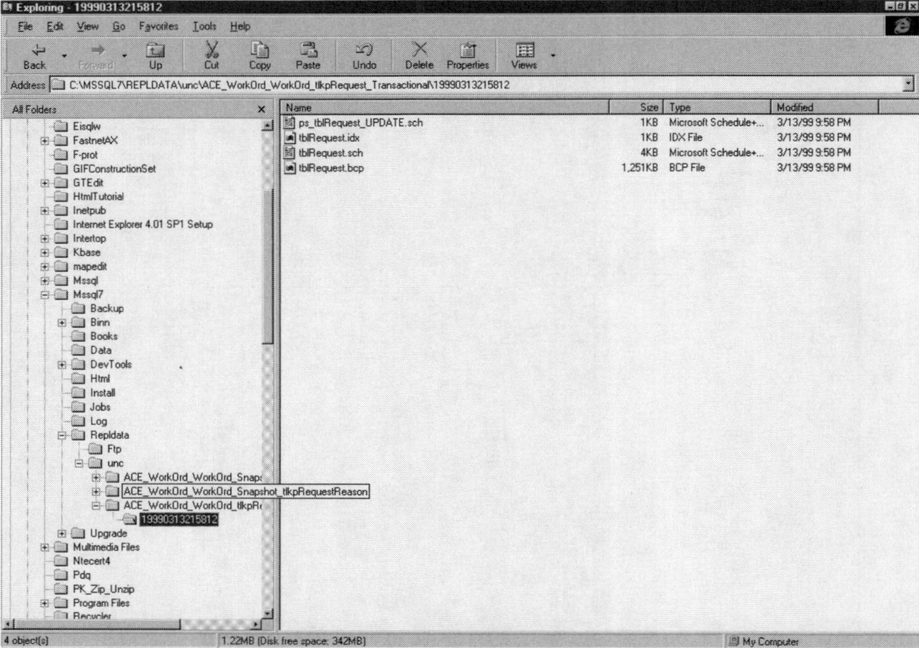

Figure 10.16 Snapshot files.

We don't know about you, but we've had enough of manually starting the Distribution Agent every time we want to move some data. Let's configure it so that it runs continuously. That will reduce our work and cause the data to be replicated to the target as soon as it's added to the distribution database. To configure the Distribution Agent to run continuously, complete the following steps:

1. Select Distribution Agents under the Agents option in Replication Monitor.
2. Right-click on the entry in the Details panel and select Agent Properties.
3. Select the Schedules tab and click Edit.
4. Select Start automatically when SQL Server agent starts and click OK.
5. Click OK to return to the Enterprise Manager main screen.
6. Right-click on the entry in the Details pane and select Start, as shown in Figure 10.17.

To this point, all we've done is synchronize the databases—no transactions have been replicated from WorkOrd to UsingReplicaton. Let's get started with this process by applying some transactions to WorkOrd..tblRequest. Execute the following in Query Analyzer so we can establish the state of the tables before the transactions are applied:

```
SELECT COUNT(*) FROM WorkOrd tblRequest WHERE Requester = 'N. Gale'
```

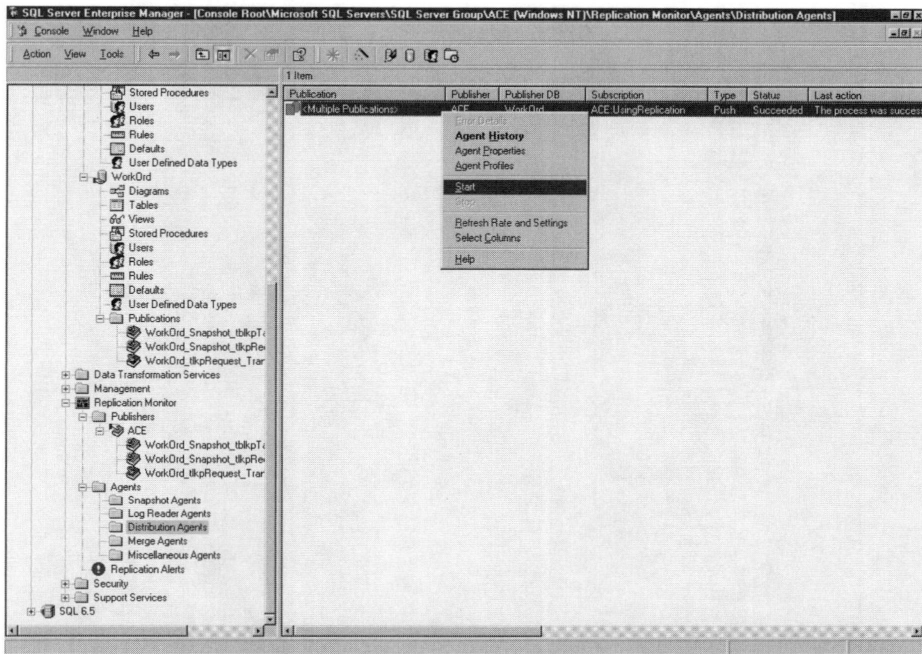

Figure 10.17 Starting the Distribution Agent.

```
SELECT COUNT(*) FROM UsingReplication tblRequest WHERE Requester
= 'N. Gale'
```

Both statements return a count of 1472 rows. Let's change all of the N. Gale requests with the following:

```
UPDATE WorkOrd tblRequest
SET Requester = 'Mark McGwire'
WHERE Requester = 'N. Gale'
```

After the UPDATE is applied, the Log Reader Agent goes to work and moves all of the transactions from the WorkOrd log file to the distribution database. Figure 10.18 shows the agent's recording of this action.

Once the distribution database is updated with the replication information, the Distribution Agent kicks in and applies the changes to UsingReplication. You can use the Replication Monitor to determine when the process is complete and then execute the following in Query Analyzer to ascertain if the process was successful:

```
SELECT COUNT(*) FROM UsingReplication tblRequest WHERE Requester
= 'Mark McGwire'
```

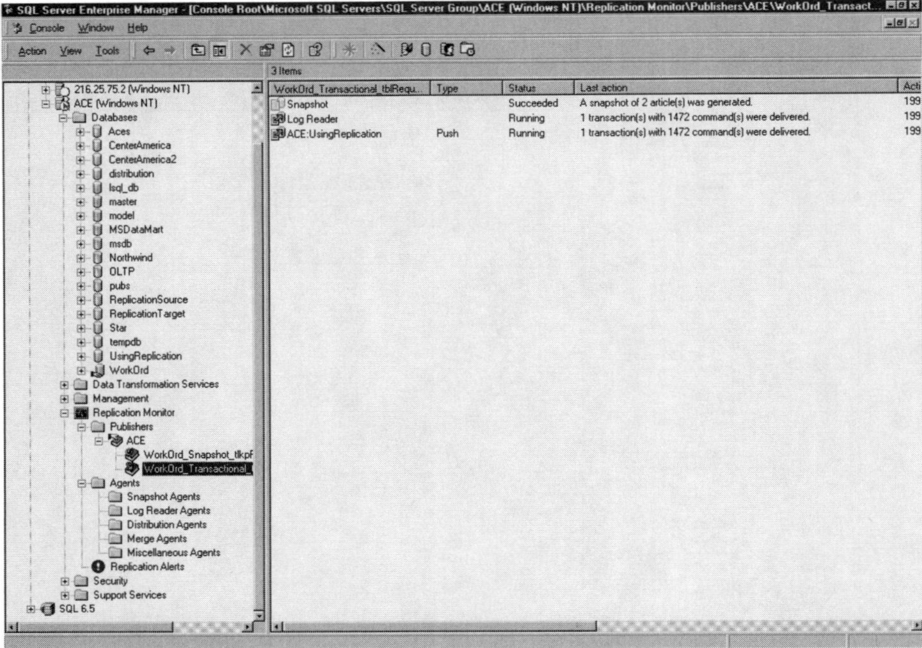

Figure 10.18 Log Reader results.

Well, what was your count? Our count was 1472, so we're convinced that the replication process was successful.

Now that we've had some success with transactional replication, let's compare the UPDATE statement approach with a stored procedure update and see if we can find any benefit to using one method over the other. Execute the following in Query Analyzer to reverse the Requester change we made with the UPDATE statement:

```
EXEC WorkOrd ps_tblRequest_UPDATE 'Mark McGwire','N. Gale'
```

The main difference in the stored procedure approach is the number of transactions recorded in the distribution database and applied at the subscriber. The UPDATE statement approach creates 1472 individual commands that are applied at the subscriber while the stored procedure approach only creates one. You can get the number recorded/applied by viewing the Last Action field in either the Log Reader or Distribution Agent items in the Replication Monitor (see Figure 10.18). Obviously, the time it takes to apply one command is less than 1472 commands, so not only does the stored procedure approach reduce the number of records recorded in the Distribution Database, you also reduce the time it takes to apply them.

WHAT HAPPENS TO THE SNAPSHOT/ SYNCHRONIZATION FILES?

The snapshot/synchronization files created under C:\MSQQL7\Repldata\unc\... don't stay there forever. If they did, and your publications were large, you would have a lot of disk space wasted on files that were only used one time. Instead of manually managing these files, SQL Server uses an agent to monitor when the files are used and deletes them accordingly.

PRIMARY KEYS AND TRANSACTIONAL REPLICATION

Take a quick look at Figure 10.12 and notice the Key/red X graphic next to all the tables except tblRequest. This graphic indicates that the tables do not have a primary key and thus cannot participate in transactional replication. A primary key is necessary so that the UPDATE and DELETE statements replicated to the subscriber can *find* the target records.

Project 7C: Heterogeneous Replication with Access 2000

We've had some success with replication "inside" SQL Server 7. Now, lets see how to go about configuring replication with a heterogeneous data store. As the project's title suggests, we use Access 2000 for our heterogeneous data store. The Access database that we use with this project is called SQL_To_Access.mdb and is located under the Chapter10 sub-directory on the CD-ROM that accompanies this book. We can't replicate to the CD, so create a directory on your server called Chapter10 and copy this file to that location. Just so you know, there is nothing special about the SQL_To_Access database—it's simply an empty database. We include it here to expedite the project-creation process and allow those that do not have Access to complete the project.

The first thing you need to know about replicating with a non-SQL Server data store is that all of the SQL Server features may not be supported by the subscribing data store. Therefore, you need to make sure that your SQL Server configuration options will not prevent successful replication. Luckily for us, there are only two crucial issues that we need to be aware of when replicating to Access 2000 (for a quick overview on Access 2000 replication, see the Sidebar, *Replication via Office 2000 Developer*):

1. Jet 4.0, the Access 2000 database engine, does not support case-sensitive sort orders, so servers with this configuration cannot participate in replication with Access 2000.
2. SQL Server does not support anonymous pull subscriptions from Jet 4.0, but does support pull subscriptions once the Jet engine has been registered as a linked server.

The only other issue that you need to be aware of before we proceed concerns how your server is configured for licensing. SQL Server has two licensing options:

1. Per Seat. A client computer with a client access license (CAL) can connect to any number of SQL Server servers. In addition, any given server in this configuration does not have an upper-limit on the number of connections it can support. This mode is generally used in organizations that have multiple SQL Server servers.
2. Per Server. The maximum number of connections to the server is limited to the number of CALs purchased for the server. In Per-Server mode, you configure SQL Server for the maximum number of simultaneous connections and when that limit is reached the next person who tries to access SQL Server receives an error message that indicates that there are no more licenses available. This mode is typically used when you require only one SQL Server and the number of simultaneous connections required can be reasonably determined.

In order to replicate with a non-SQL Server data store, your server must be configured in Per-Seat mode. You specify the licensing mode at install, but if you don't remember the option you selected it's easy to check. Simply open the Control Panel and double-click on the Licensing icon. Figure 10.19 shows one of our server's licensing configurations.

LICENSING CONCERNS

If you aren't already configured for Per-Seat mode, you have several options. You can simply select that option and click OK, but this may cause more problems than it's worth. If you're currently in Per-Server mode and switch to Per-Seat mode to complete the project and subsequently change back to Per-Server mode so that the server is configured for the proper number of CALs, you have technically violated the License Agreement because it only supports a one-time, one-way switch from Per-Server to Per-Seat mode.

We monitor the SQL Server newsgroups on a daily basis and have noticed that there are frequent questions about licensing. Because this issue is so important (there are legal ramifications for not having sufficient licenses), even the MVPs refer the posters to Microsoft. So, if you have questions about whether you own the proper number of licenses for a particular configuration, don't guess and put yourself in jeopardy of violating the License Agreement. Call Microsoft and explain your configuration and let the experts tell you what you need to do.

Now that we understand the limitations of this type of replication and how the server's licensing mode must be configured, we're ready to get started. If you haven't completed Projects 7A or 7B or haven't configured your server for replication, you'll need to do this before proceeding. Refer to the second paragraph in Project 7A for guidance.

We want to keep this project simple because we're interacting with another piece of software and any time you involve multiple pieces of software together you increase the likelihood that something will go wrong. With this in mind, we'll create a snapshot publication in SQL Server on WorkOrd..tlkpUrgency and have it replicated to an Access database once an hour. To create the publication, complete the following steps:

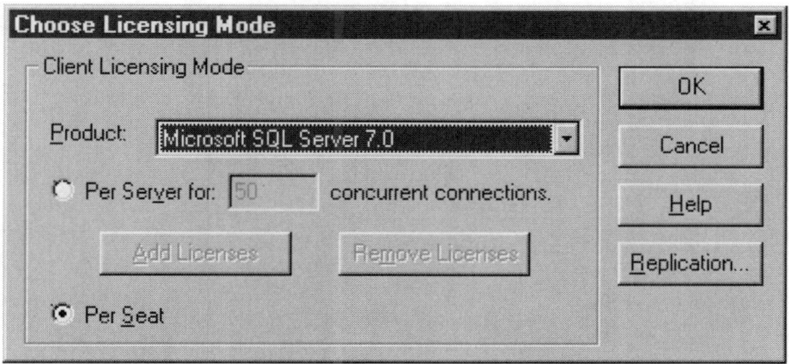

Figure 10.19 Licensing configuration.

1. Select Tools/Replication from the main menu in Enterprise Manager and choose Create and Manage Publications.
2. Select the WorkOrd database in the Create and Manage Publications dialog and click Create Publication. (Bet you're getting pretty good at this.)
3. Click Next to advance past the Create Publication Wizard's Welcome screen
4. Accept the default of No, I will define… in the Use Publication Template dialog.
5. Accept the default of Snapshot Publication in the Choose Publication Type dialog.
6. Accept the default of No, do not allow… in the Allow Immediate-Updating Subscriptions dialog.
7. Select One or more servers… in the Specify Subscribers Type dialog and click Next.
8. Select tlkpUrgency as the article for replication (as shown in Figure 10.20) and click Next.
9. Supply the following for the Choose Publication Name and Description dialog and click Next:
   - Name: WorkOrd_Snapshot_tlkpUrgency
   - Description: Snapshot publication of WorkOrd_Snapshot_tlkpUrgency to Access (Jet 4.0)
10. Accept the default of No, create a publication without… on the Use Default Properties of the Publication dialog.
11. Click Finish to complete the wizard. Once the wizard creates and initializes the components required to support this model, a message that indicates that the publication was successfully created will be displayed. Close the open dialog boxes to return to Enterprise Manager.

Now that we have a publication, we must create the subscription that actually allows the data to be transferred. Before we can do this, however, we must "tell" SQL Server about the Access database that we want to replicate to. Keep in mind that SQL Server is not "aware" of other data stores until its configured with their communication parameters. The term, *linked server* is used to describe an external data store that has been configured

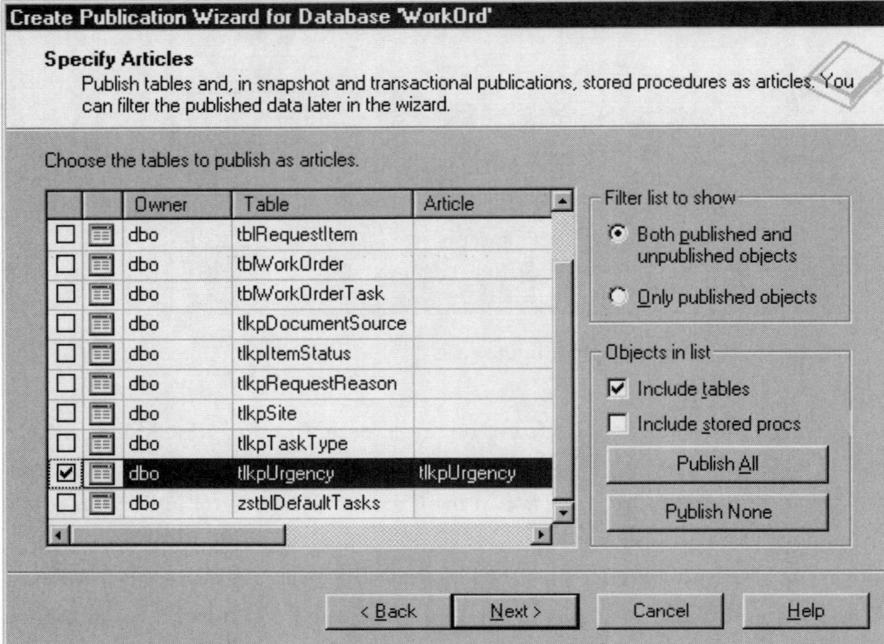

Figure 10.20 Specifying the article for replication.

for communications. A detailed discussion of linked servers is not germane to this project, but if you want more information please see the *Books Online* topic, *Configuring Linked Servers*. To configure Access as a linked server, complete the following steps:

1. Select Tools/Replication from the main menu in Enterprise Manager and choose Configure Publishing, Subscribers and Distribution....
2. Click the Subscribers tab and then click New Subscriber....
3. Select Microsoft Jet 4.0 database (Microsoft Access) as shown in Figure 10.21 and click OK.

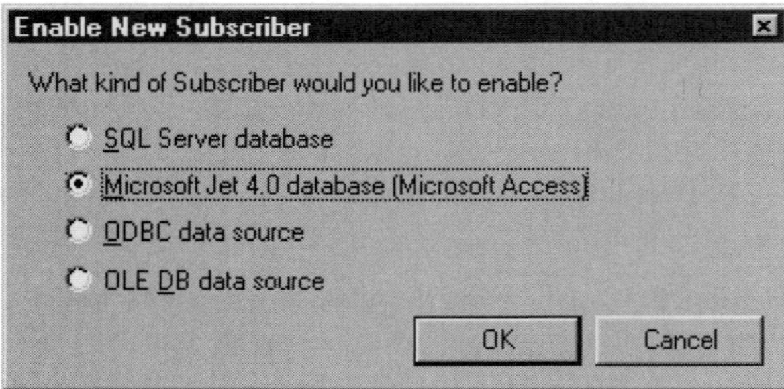

Figure 10.21 Specifying the new subscriber.

4. Click Add, supply the following values, and click OK until you return to the main screen in Enterprise Manager.
   - Linker Server Name: ACCESS_DB
   - Database Path and Filename: C:\Chapter10\SQL_To_Access.mdb
5. Close the dialogs until you return to the main screen in Enterprise Manager.
6. Expand the Security server tree option under your local server and notice that there is no "+" next to Linked Servers (assuming this is the first time you've added a linked server).
7. Press F5 to refresh the server tree and notice the "+" sign appears. Expand the option and it should look like Figure 10.22.

If you ever need to change the properties of a linked server, right-click on the server's name and select Properties. Go ahead and take a peek at the options available for our linked server just to see what's available.

Now that Access has been configured as a linked server, we can create the subscription. To create the subscription complete the following steps:

1. Select Tools/Replication from the main menu in Enterprise Manager and choose Push Subscriptions to Others....
2. Expand your local server and select WorkOrd_Snapshot_tlkpUrgency as shown in Figure 10.23.

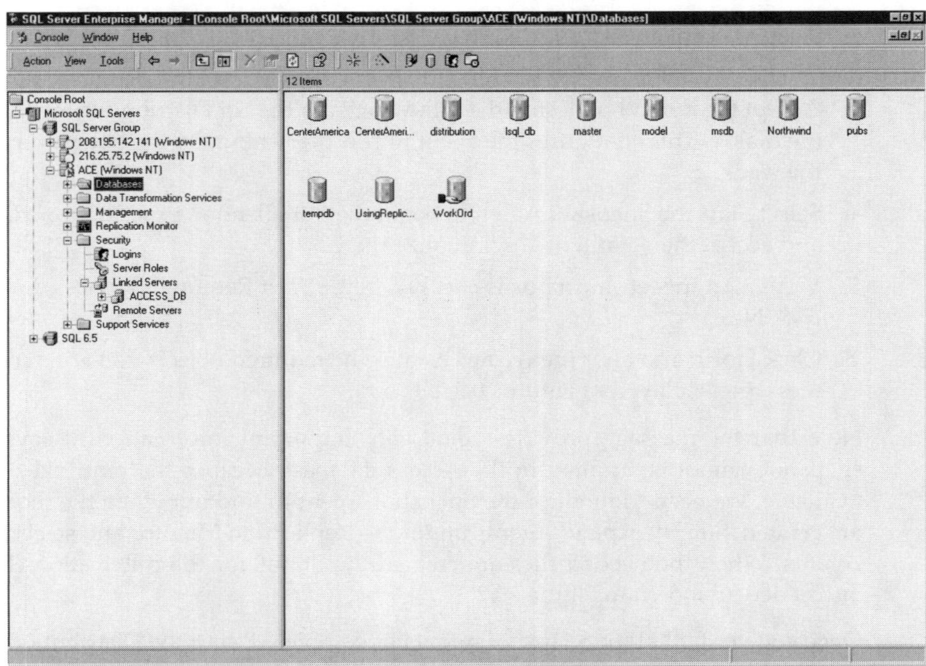

Figure 10.22 Viewing linked servers.

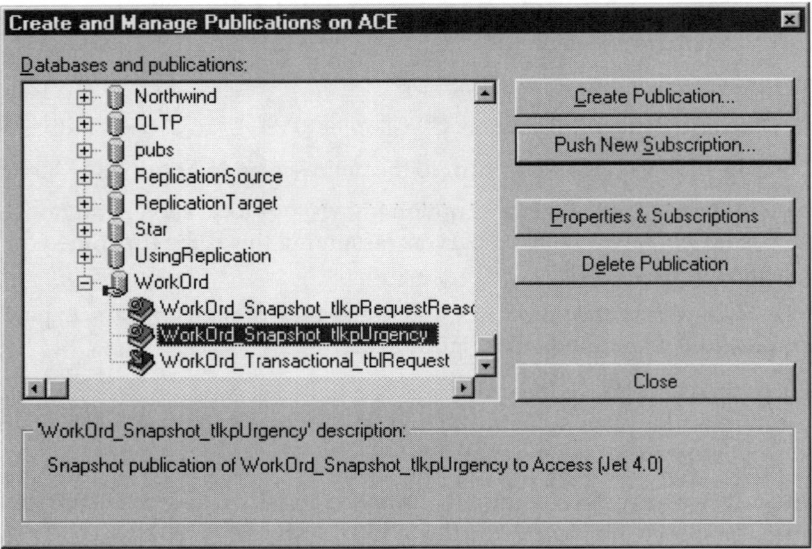

Figure 10.23 Selecting the publication.

3. Click Push New Subscription to invoke the Push Subscription Wizard. Click Next to advance past the Welcome screen.
4. Select our linked server, ACCESS_DB (Microsoft Jet 4.0), from the list in the Choose Subscribers dialog and click Next.
5. Accept the default of Using the following…on the Set Distribution Agent Schedule dialog. This configures the agent to run every hour, on the hour, every day of the week.
6. Select Start the Snapshot Agent to begin the initialization process immediately and accept the default of Yes, initialize the….
7. Verify that the left-most box is checked in the Start Required Services dialog and click Next.
8. Click Finish and after the wizard creates the required objects you will receive the message displayed in Figure 10.24.

Note that the message provides some very important information. It says that the snapshot cannot be applied in the Access database because the required files aren't available. We need to monitor the Snapshot Agent to find out when the required files are created. Simply expand Agents under the Replication Monitor and select Snapshot Agents. When the needed files are created the Status for the publication changes to Succeeded as shown in Figure 10.25.

Once you verify that the Snapshot Agent has completed, start the Distribution Agent so that the files are applied to SQL_To_Access.mdb. To start the Distribution Agent complete the following steps:

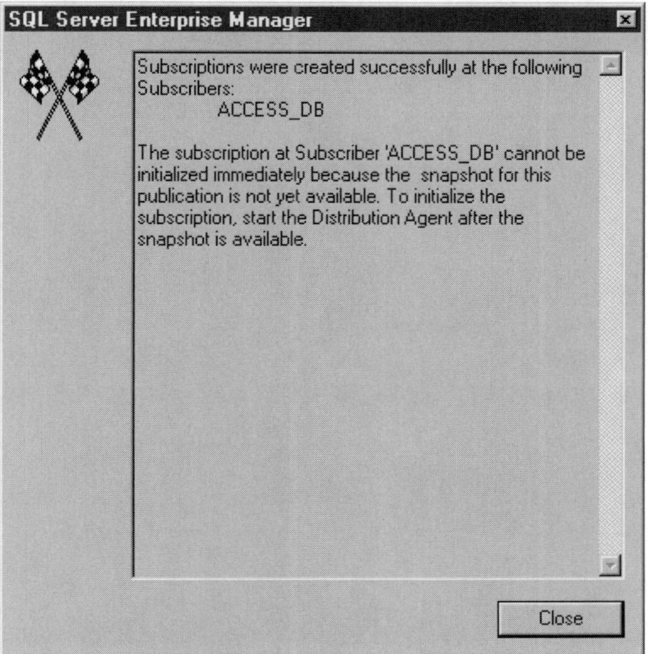

Figure 10.24 Message generated by the wizard.

1. Select Distribution Agents under Replication Monitor/Agents.
2. Right-click on the entry in the Details pane with the Subscription value of ACCESS_DB:DSN, and select Start.

Monitor the Distribution Agent in the same manner as the Snapshot Agent, and once you confirm it has finished, you can use Access to verify that the schema and data were transferred successfully.

At this point you can apply a change to tlkpUrgency and either wait until the top of the next hour to see what happens or modify your system clock to force the Distribution Agent to run more quickly. We will make the following modification to tlkpUrgency and adjust the system clock to a minute before the next hour in order to force the Distribution Agent to execute.

```
INSERT WorkOrd..tlkpUrgency VALUES (7,'replication Test',1)
```

If you do this and check the Access database (SQL_To_Acccess) after the Distribution Agent completes, you'll find that the modification was *not* applied to the target data store. Why? Well, the Distribution Agent can run all day long, but if it does not have anything to apply then the target will never change. Take a look at the Distribution Agent and you'll see that the Last Action entry is No replicated transactions are available as shown in Figure 10.26.

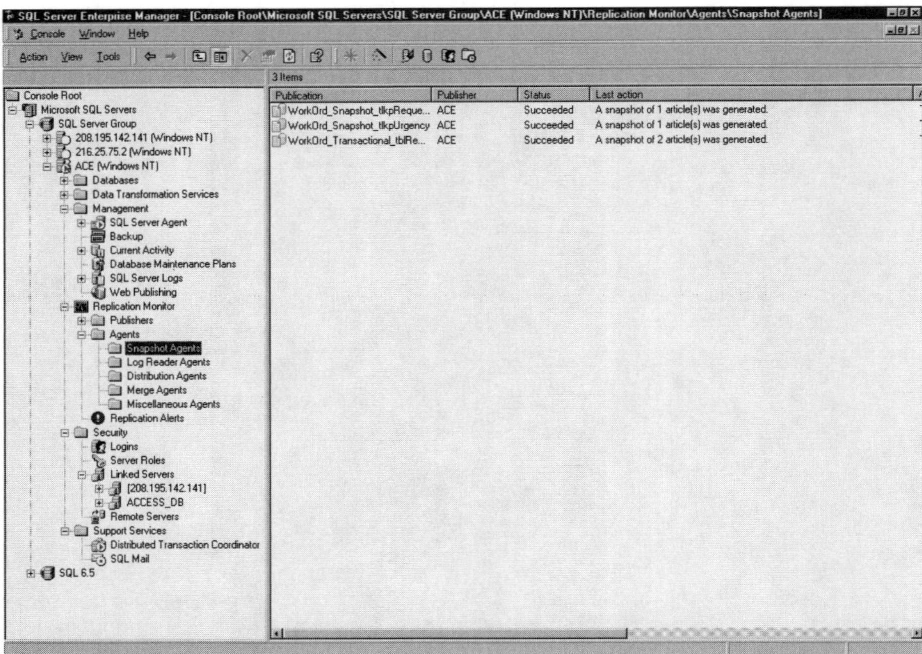

Figure 10.25 Verifying that the Snapshot Agent has completed.

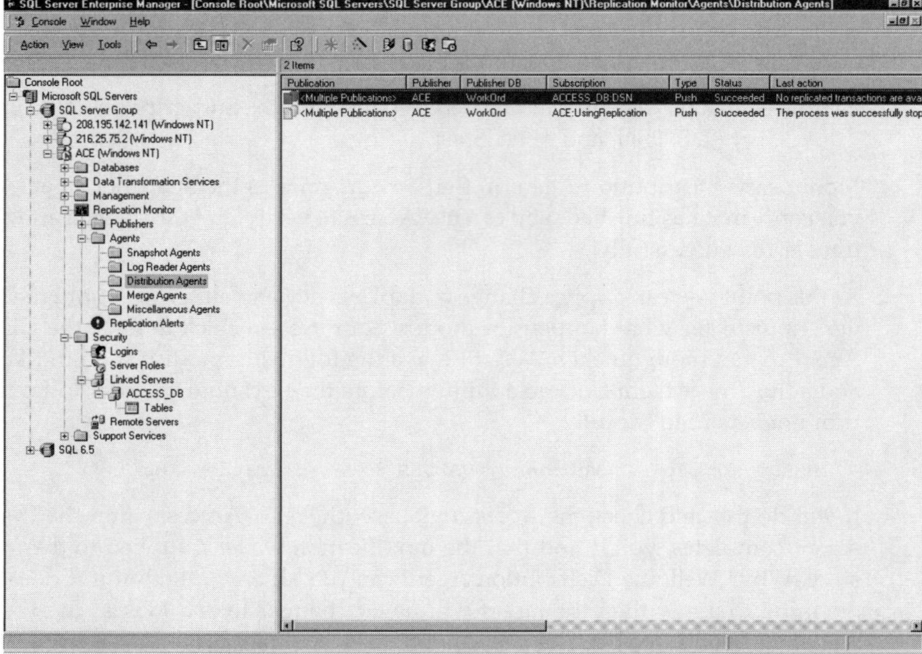

Figure 10.26 The Distribution Agent's last action.

What do we need to do in order to make sure that the Distribution Agent has something to distribute? We need to configure the Snapshot Agent so that it runs a few minutes before the Distribution Agent. That way, the table's latest "picture" is always available. This doesn't mean that the Distribution Agent will never show No replicated transactions... as the last action. If no changes occur in the publication, then there are none that need to be applied to the subscriber. To configure the Snapshot Agent to execute at five before the hour complete the following steps:

1. Expand Agents off the Replication Monitor and select Snapshot Agents.
2. Right-click on WorkOrd_Snapshot_tlkpUrgency and select Agent Properties.
3. Select the Schedules tab and click Edit. Change the options so that the agent will run five minutes before the hour as shown in Figure 10.27.

You now have an hourly feed from SQL Server to Access. When a change applies to the publication, it is replicated to Access at the top of each hour. One thing to keep in mind, though, is that the Access table should not be in use when the replication occurs. If it's in use, the Distribution Agent fails because it cannot place a lock on the table.

If you completed Project 7A, you may remember that we did not configure the Snapshot Agent in the same manner as we did here. In 7A, we opted to set the Snapshot Agent's schedule during the publication creation process, so it was ready to go as soon as we completed the wizard. We skipped this step in this project, so that the agent was configured to run on the daily default schedule at 11:30 P.M.

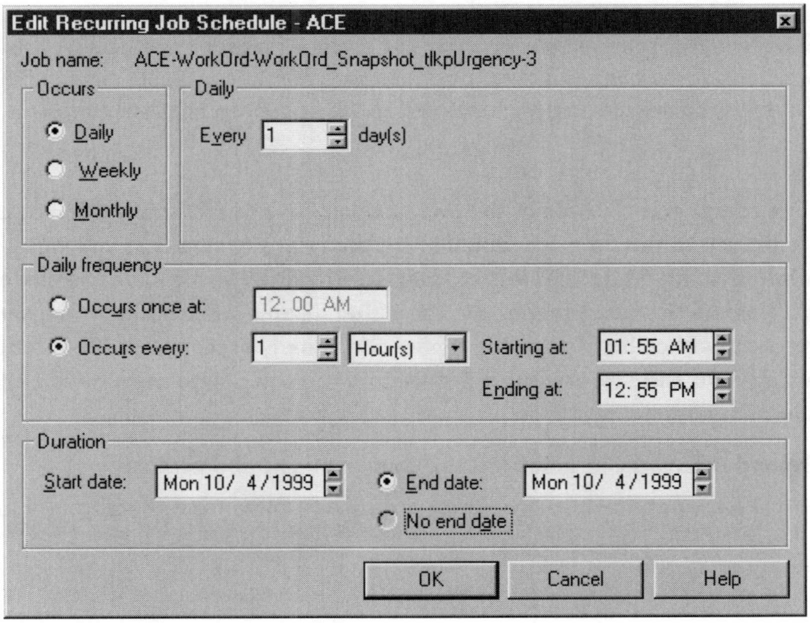

Figure 10.27 Snapshot Agent's schedule.

SQL SERVER TO ACCESS REPLICATION IN *BOOKS ONLINE*

Books Online **has several good topics with more information on using replication between SQL Server and Access databases, notably *About Access Subscribers, How to Enable a Jet 4.0 Database as a Subscriber, Implementing Merge Replication to Access Subscribers,* and *How to Add a Push Subscription to a Jet 4.0 Subscriber.***

Troubleshooting

Replication Monitor is one of the best places to start if you encounter problems with replication. The agents that handle replication indicate that a problem has occurred visually (a big, white X in a red circle) in the Enterprise Manager. Locate any errors and expand the console tree. You can select Publishers to view a list of all publications handled by this distributor; failing publications are marked with the error indicator.

You can also analyze replication problems by looking at the SQL Server Agent's log (which is different from the "main" SQL Server error log).

In addition to harnessing some of SQL Server 7's pre-configured event alerts to route replication-related problems to the appropriate people, you can also add your own. In Replication Monitor, right-click on Replication Alerts and select New Alert. Fill out the dialog box, specify the error number that you want the alert to react to, and specify the actions of the alert.

To handle conflicts that will almost inevitably occur in merge replication, you need to know how SQL Server's *resolver* works and consider creating your own customer conflict resolver. *Books Online*, as you might expect, has lots of good information on this topic along with advice on how to minimize the opportunities for conflicts.

CLEANING UP THE PROJECTS

If you've completed all three of the projects you have several replication agents that are configured to run on a scheduled basis. We're pretty sure that you won't need them for anything other than this chapter, so why don't you go ahead and delete them. To delete the components you can either disable replication on the server or delete each publication. To disable replication, simply access Tools/Replication off the main menu and select Disable Publishing. You can delete the individual publications with the following steps:

1. **Expand the WorkOrd database and then expand Publications.**
2. **Select each publication, right-click and select Delete from the pop-up menu.**

Summary

This chapter had quite a few steps, but if you completed all three of the projects, you should be pretty comfortable with both snapshot and transactional replication. Just remember, there are a few "moving parts" involved with implementing replication and all must work properly before you can be successful. The Snapshot Agent takes the initial picture, the Log Reader Agent monitors the database's transaction log, and the Distribution Agent transfers and applies the initial snapshot and subsequent changes to the subscriber. All three of these agents must be configured to execute on a schedule that ensures that the changes to the subscriber are applied in a timely manner.

Replication can also be used in conjunction with the Internet, and *Books Online* has over 50 topics that illustrate different aspects of Internet replication. Aside from the obvious configuration and security issues, Internet replication works pretty much the same way as with the other types of replication presented in this chapter's projects. Remember that you can use DTS packages as a source of replication, as well as SQL Server's ActiveX replication controls in your own applications. In the *Books Online* topic, *Advanced Replication* (which covers Internet replication and use of ActiveX controls), you'll also find sections on how to back up and restore replicated databases and how to replicate between different versions of SQL Server.

CHAPTER 11

Project #8: Getting Started with E-Commerce

Goal

The goal of this chapter is to show you how to create e-commerce Web sites that use a SQL Server 7 "back end." After you've completed these projects, you will have all of the knowledge necessary to successfully build a data-driven Web site that can process online credit card transactions.

- ✔ Microsoft SQL Server 7
- ✔ Windows NT Option Pack 44 for Internet Information Server (IIS)
- ✔ V-Nursery files found on the accompanying CD-ROM
- ✔ Microsoft Site Server 3.0 Commerce Edition

Recommended:

- ✔ Microsoft Site Server Commerce Edition SP2

Optional:

- ✔ VisualCommerce's VisualCommerce Constructor (evaluation copy found on the accompanying CD-ROM, requires Site Server Commerce Edition)

You don't have to be a genius to know that e-commerce is one of the hottest topics in business today. Companies are jumping on the e-commerce bandwagon at an incredible rate. *Online or the Bread Line* was the way *Forbes* magazine put it in an August 9, 1999, headline. It's easy to forget that there are two sides of e-commerce: business-to-consumer (B2C) and business-to-business (B2B). E-commerce goes far beyond just the business-to-consumer model that many of us are familiar with thanks to Amazon.com, eBay, and all the other "dot coms" out there. But whether you're interested in doing B2B or B2C, there are a couple of fundamentals that all e-commerce sites have to deal with—order and secure payment processing. Typically that involves the credit-card transaction model.

In this chapter, we'll make sure that you possess the knowledge to apply Web-specific technologies to create a site that supports e-commerce. We'll also cover the various hosting options that are available to help you decide whether to do it yourself or to use an ISP. As you complete the first project, you'll be amazed at how easy it is to create a data-driven, e-commerce-enabled Web site. For the second project, you'll need Microsoft's Site Server 3.0 Commerce Edition.

For both projects, you need to have a fundamental understanding of both HTML and ASP. You don't need to be an expert at HTML or ASP—just experienced enough to use ASP to extract data stored in SQL Server and then display it in HTML Forms. If you can do this and also have a good grasp of basic programming principles such as variables and control-of-flow, then you won't have any trouble with the code that's used as the foundation for the sample e-commerce Web site supplied on the CD-ROM. We do, however cover some not-so-basic aspects of ASP when building what is commonly referred to as a shopping cart application.

MORE THAN ONE KIND OF ASP

You may want to keep in mind that ASP can refer either to Microsoft's Active Server Page technology or the industry-wide term, *Application Service Providers*. The latter term defines firms that host applications, generally for a fixed monthly fee. Think of that kind of ASP as a special type of outsourcing service where you contract someone else to run your e-mail, ERP, or CRM applications, for example. Active Server Pages, however, are text files associated with server-side scripting and saved with the .ASP extension. They can contain HTML tags, VBScript, JavaScript, and ActiveX controls. The result is a series of instructions (a program or sequence of programs) that tell a server what to do.

The Components of E-Commerce

Regardless of their complexity, all e-commerce sites have the same base functionality—they allow people access to products that can be purchased over the Internet. That's very easy to say, but what's involved in the process? The following sections describe the components involved in e-commerce.

HTML and ASP

If you're not familiar with HTML or ASP, there are plenty of books, online resources, and newsgroups that are available to help you learn what you need to know to get started. A few helpful resources are shown here.

Web Sites:

www.htmlgoodies.com
msdn.microsoft.com/workshop/cframe.htm#workshop/author/default.asp
www.activeserverpages.com
www.15seconds.com
www.4Guysfromrolla.com
msdn.microsoft.com/scripting
devedge.netscape.com/tech/javascript/index.html

Newsgroups:

microsoft.public.inetserver.iis.activeserverpages
microsoft.public.inetserver.asp.db
microsoft.public.scripting.jscript
microsoft.public.inetsdk.programming.scripting.jscript

Domain Name

For many firms, the first step to setting up an e-commerce site is to establish a *domain name*. Although, strictly speaking, this isn't a requirement (Yahoo.com and other portals let users set up small e-commerce sites, for example). When we wrote this chapter, you had several options for obtaining a domain name: NetWork Solutions (www.network-solutions.com), ICANN (www.icann.com), or from your ISP. Registering a domain name in 1999 cost $70. This gives you exclusive use of the name for two years, and the option to renew your registration when the initial period nears expiration. Believe it or not, this may be one of the more challenging aspects in creating a site. Unless you or your company has already registered a domain name, you may have trouble finding one that is easy-to-remember and indicative of your business.

Site Location

This section's heading may seem pretty silly, but it's actually extremely relevant to those of you who want to implement a successful e-commerce site for the least amount of money. You may have just assumed that the most logical place to house your site is in your computer room with the rest of your servers. However, we advise you to explore your available options before you make this decision. For example, did you know that there are numerous ISPs that already have all of the hardware and software in place to host your site today? That's right, in a matter of hours (assuming you already have your domain name and your ISP provides good support) your ISP can create the accounts and access necessary for you to place your site online.

"Tell me more," you say. The following URL: www.hostreview.com/powersearch.html allows you to search for an ISP that will meet your hosting needs. You should be aware that not all ISPs have all of the necessary software/technology in place to allow you to establish an e-commerce site that is driven by a SQL Server 7 database. As a matter of fact, I (Garth) have a local ISP that provides great Internet access and service, but does not support the technology needed for me to implement a data-driven e-commerce site. Therefore, I had to search and find one that met all of my requirements—the toughest one being that they support SQL Server 7.

When you compare the pros and cons of local versus remote hosting you need to consider the following:

1. What are the costs associated with establishing a connection to handle the site's traffic?
2. What is the cost associated with purchasing the hardware and software (appropriate licenses included) necessary to implement the site?
3. Who controls server configuration and operation?

The cost to ensure that your site has the proper connectivity to the Internet can vary significantly. If your site will only have high traffic, you may need a fractional T1 line that can run $500/month. If all you need is a dedicated ISDN (128K) line the cost will be approximately $250/month. Of course, the nice thing about remote hosting is that your ISP is connected to the Internet at either T1 or T3 speeds with costs less than $100/month.

The cost for purchasing all of the necessary hardware and software licenses (we assume you already own NT 4.0 and SQL Server 7, so the license issue is the difference) to keep your site local can also vary significantly. If you plan to keep the site local and want to have fast response times and the best chance of keeping it online 24x7, you need to purchase a dual-processor machine with at least 256 MB of RAM and a RAID 5 hard drive configuration. In addition you will have to purchase the appropriate license for SQL Server in order to allow people to access your database via the Internet. The SQL Server 7 license option that allows Internet access is called the *SQL Server Internet Connector 7.0 License Pack Per Processor* and as the name suggests you must buy one license for each processor that the host computer has. At press time, the License Pak was approximately $2999, so for a dual-processor, you're looking at a cost of about $6000.

Another factor that must be considered is the control you need over the host computer's configuration. With local hosting you can obviously do what you want to the server, but this isn't always a good thing. What if you have plenty of experience configuring SQL Server 7, but lack experience configuring IIS? What's worse, configuring IIS incorrectly or going through the trouble of trying to convince your ISP to change a SQL Server configurable option? A realistic downside to remote hosting is the frequency of backup. Most ISPs only perform backups once a day. Therefore, if you think you need backups on a more frequent basis you need to either find an ISP that will accept your requirement or weigh the cost of losing data versus the increased cost of local hosting.

There is another flavor of remote hosting called *co-location*. When you co-locate, you store your server at your ISP. Co-location gives you the advantage of high-speed access and complete control over how the server is configured. So, if you want to experiment with SQL Server configuration options (in SQL Server 7, the need to do this decreases significantly) you don't have to try and convince your ISP to make the change. You also have more control over the frequency at which backups are created. Ideally you want to co-locate at an ISP in your area of operation. Costs for co-locating varies from $350-$500/month plus all of the applicable hardware and software costs. As you can see, from a cost perspective, there are numerous advantages to remote hosting.

BE SMART WHEN SELECTING AN ISP TO HOST YOUR SITE

When you research a potential host, ask for reference sites that have configurations similar to what you're considering. Then, go to the sites and make sure they operate as expected. E-mail the Webmasters at the reference sites and ask whether or not they would recommend the ISP. After all, when virtual hosting is involved, the relationship you have and the service you can expect from you ISP are crucial.

MANAGING YOUR SITE REMOTELY

One of the biggest concerns you may have when considering remote hosting is how to manage your site if it's not where you can get to it. Well, as long as it's on the Internet, you really have all of the access that you need. A common approach is to have a mirror site that you develop on locally and then transfer/ftp the "working" code to your live site. You may be thinking, "This is great for my HTML/ASP pages, but what about database access?" Good question, but easily solved. ***You can access your SQL Server 7 database as long as it is located on a computer with a fixed IP Address and connected to the Internet.*** **Simply register the server in Enterprise Manager just like any other SQL Server, but instead of specifying the computer's name you specify the IP Address or URL. Please note that certain firewall configurations may prohibit you from registering a remote server. Your ISP will provide you with all of the connection information you need. Your ISP will also create a login for you that is aliased as dbo so that you can create and manage your database objects as needed. Figure 11.1 shows the processes involved in remote management.**

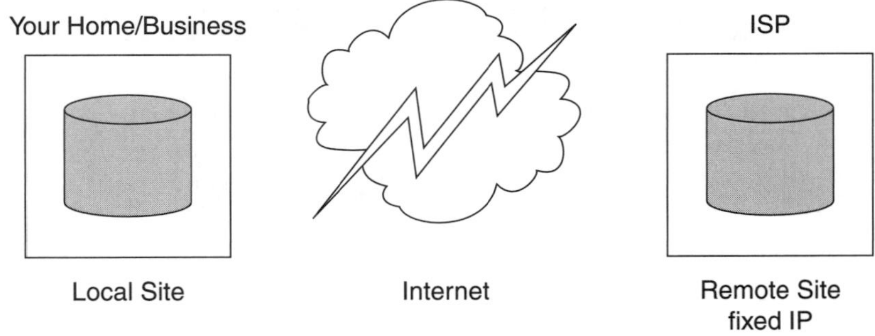

Figure 11.1 Managing your site remotely.

REGISTERING REMOTE SQL SERVERS

In order to register a remote SQL Server your local machine's SQL Server Client Network Utility must run the TCP/IP protocol. If you don't know what protocol is running simply access the Client Network Utility option in the Microsoft SQL Server 7 Program Group. Make sure the default network library is configured to TCP/IP as shown in Figure 11.2.

Security

One of the biggest concerns for Internet users is the assurance that their confidential, credit-card information can't be accessed by unauthorized parties. The main component to handling secure transactions is the Secure Sockets Layer (SSL) protocol—at least in North America (many international sites have opted for the SET, Secure Electronic Transactions, protocol). The details of SSL (and SET) are really beyond the scope of this chapter, but the main thing that you need to know is that in order for a secure transaction to transpire, both participating computers must have a SSL digital certificate.

A digital certificate provides a unique identifier for computers and allows encryption/decryption to occur. The good news is that you don't have to get a digital certificate if you use an Authorization Service (discussed in the next section) that provides a

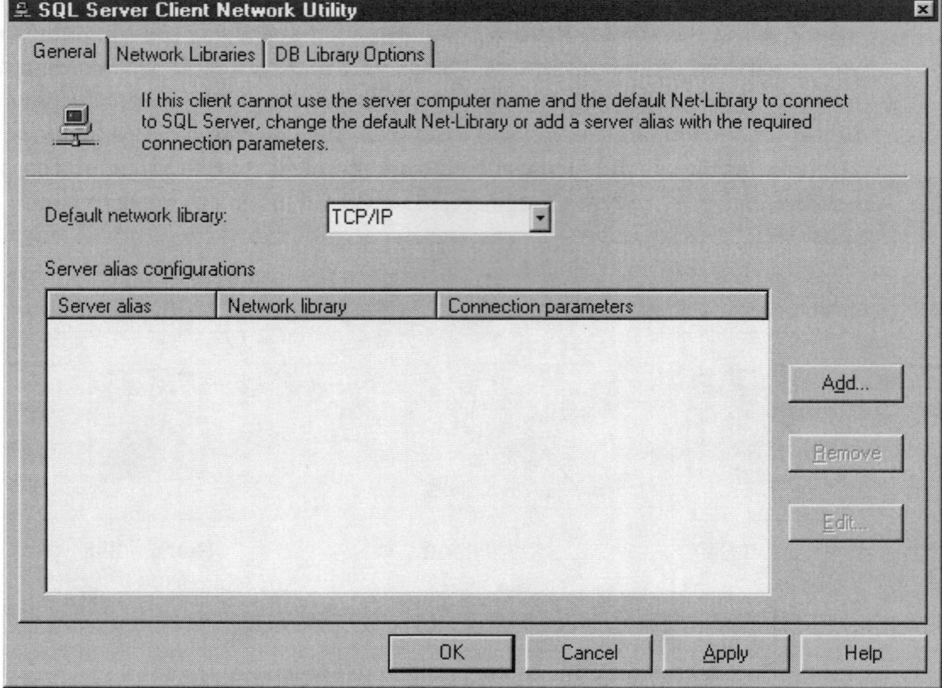

Figure 11.2 SQL Server Client Network Utility.

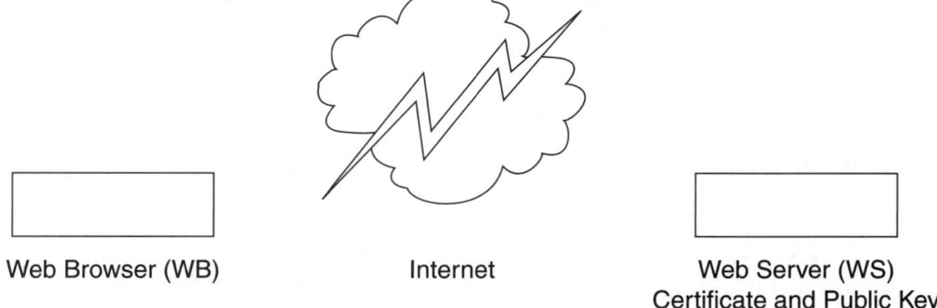

1. WB performs an action (e.g., activating credit card payment screen) that indicates it wants to communicate in a secure manner.
2. WS sends WB its certificate and public key.
3. The level of encryption (e.g., 40 bit) is negotiated and then the WB creates a session key, encrypts it with the public key, and sends it to the WS.
4. The WS uses its private key to decrypt the session key and establish a secure channel.
5. Once the secure channel is established, the session key is used to encrypt/decrypt communications.

Figure 11.3 Digital certificate and encryption/decryption.

secure server for your use. This may seem a little confusing, but right now we just want you to keep in mind that in order for a secure transaction to occur both computers (one does not necessarily have to be yours) must have their own digital certificate. After the next section we'll re-visit this topic. Figure 11.3 illustrates the process for encryption/decryption using digital certificates.

FYI PKI AND DIGITAL CERTIFICATES

***Public-key infrastructure (PKI)* and digital certificates are all the rage today. PKI is based on public-key cryptography that refers to technology in which a user has a pair of cryptographic keys: one that is kept secret (the private key) and one that's an associated public key. Any data encrypted by either one of the keys can only be decrypted by the other.**

There's also something called a *digital signature* which is created by running some data such as a file through a mathematical algorithm to get a large numerical value that's unique to the original data. The value is then encrypted (and referred to as "signed") in the private key of the sender. The signature is then sent along with a message. The receiver decrypts the digital signature using the sender's public key, and the resulting value is compared to the result that the receiver obtains after running the data through the same algorithm that the sender used.

To use either PKI or digital signatures, you need to have a reliable way to get public keys. Enter the digital certificate authorities, which are generally either commercial

firms or banks. Examples include VeriSign (www.verisign.com), Entrust Technologies (www.entrust.com), GTE (www.gte.com), and startups such as Valicert (www.valicert.com).

How to Obtain and Install a Digital Certificate

When we went to press, there were several major digital certificate authorities available that offered services that ranged from about $150 to almost $400/year. However, the market is still emerging. It behooves you to investigate your options, and, again, talk to customers with sites and expected sales volumes similar to yours. Once you decide which company is for you, the actual process of obtaining a digital certificate can be either easy or difficult depending on how well your company's ownership is documented. Digital certificate companies generally require the following information:

- Documentation that proves that you own the URL on which the certificate will be installed
- Documentation that proves that you have the right to conduct business under the provided business name
- A public key generated by IIS Key Manager

You'll need to visit the company's Web site that you choose in order to determine its specific documentation requirements. If you're going to use virtual hosting, you'll need to submit a request to your ISP for a public key. If you plan to host your site locally, you can generate a public key with the following steps:

1. Open Internet Service Manager.
2. Click the Key Manager icon (hand holding a key) on the toolbar.
3. Right-click on WWW and select Create New Key.
4. Respond to the prompts and when finished you will have a text file that contains your public key. The contents of the file look something like the following:

```
Webmaster: YourName@ISP.net
Phone: 123.555.1234
Server: Microsoft Key Manager for IIS Version 4.0
Common-name: CompanyName
Organization Unit: DepartmentName
Organization: OrganizationName
Locality: YourCity
State: YourState
Country: YourCountry
—--BEGIN NEW CERTIFICATE REQUEST—--
MIIBqzCCARQCAQAwazELMAkGA1UEBhMCVVMxCzAJBgNVBAgTAlRYMRAwDgYDVQQH
EwdIb3VzdG9uMRMwEQYDVQQKEwpHYXJ0aFdlbGxzMRMwEQYDVQQLEwpUZWNobm9s
b2d5MRMwEQYDVQQDEwpHYXJ0aFdlbGxzMIGfMA0GCSqGSIb3DQEBAQUAA4GNADCB
iQKBgQChT2B26+If8BPPYBqchIdQMcjNgHQnJ7v7nTP5pZDvHdYoEAaePzi9HcmC
bEVXOSprvHe9rDXwLAQlGQscNxyqsNxFdZVDv+pMvGyDOcwYhv5LsdQ78gnenrvx
```

```
t/W3PTWuQ5HARWpfHfjxuC/duGJWY6SvoVa3E6UKiO0n5QMIaQIDAQABoAAwDQYJ
KoZIhvcNAQEEBQADgYEARoyxZdQjaeZth7Um74Xwegfg7vBdpAdY7nrrgTWyJIve
CQqzcV5seThV55OjBRcuJwF7rU7EHhbn3v0r/rKG9wCCOhSGX0bsC/tjEQNL6HSY
ZA2zUqDKSHkavhIYR90TIIVH8UeNRwLEm45TRV3izJKMO9Fkai7qUQ+zN4m/BxQ=
—-END NEW CERTIFICATE REQUEST—-
```


Once you've completed all of the requirements and the certificate provider has verified your paperwork, you can expect to receive your certificate within a matter of hours or, at most, days. To install the certificate on the previously created key, you need to complete the following steps:

1. Open Internet Service Manager.
2. Click the Key Manager icon (hand holding a key) on the toolbar.
3. Right-click on New Key and select Install Key Certificate.
4. Specify the file that was provided and you will be prompted for the password you used when you created the public key.

Site Security Checklist for E-Commerce Sites

A good starting point is to have a reputable firm perform an independent security audit for you. If you're unwilling to pay for this, at least do a self-assessment. Identify what you're trying to protect, and put a price tag on its value if it were lost or temporarily unavailable. With management's support, create a security policy. Obvious areas of vulnerability include logs and employees who were terminated. Here are some more tangible suggestions for anyone building an e-commerce site:

- **Build a firewall.**
- **Keep public Web servers separate from internal Web and data servers. Make sure that the database servers are "hardened."**
- **Do your homework. Don't accept defaults that are well-documented "back doors" to hackers. Do it right the first time; you may not get a second chance.**
- **Test your site. Use freeware and commercial scanning tools that determine potential vulnerabilities.**
- **Read your logs and watch traffic like a hawk.**
- **Invest in digital certificates and a VPN if you're doing B2B commerce.**
- **Develop Web content offline.**

There are loads of sites and newsgroups that offer up-to-date security information, not the least of which is Microsoft's own security sites including www.microsoft.com/security/default.asp and www.microsoft.com/technet/security/. We also subscribe to the NT Security digest maintained by ISS (send a message subscribe nt-securitydigest to majordomo@iss.net. Take advantage of the resources that are out there to protect the "good guys."

DON'T FORGET YOUR PUBLIC KEY PASSWORD

When you create the public key you need to make sure that you write the password down and store it in a safe place. If you forget the password you'll have to start the process all over again—including payment.

Handling Online Transactions

To handle online credit-card transactions, you need to have the business relationships in place to ensure that the amount entered by your customers is within their credit limit and that the funds are transferred to an account that you can access. There are two relationships that you must establish before this can occur. The first is to form a relationship with a processing agent that verifies that your customer's credit card information is valid and that the amount they want to purchase is within their credit limit. Next, establish a relationship with a bank at which you establish a *merchant account*. A merchant account is just a commercial account that allows you to accept credit-card transactions. A handful of processing agents are listed here:

AuthorizeNet: www.authorize.net.com

CyberCash: www.cybercash.com

IC Verify: www.icverify.com

vPOSTM/Verifone: www.verifone.com

ICOMS: www.icoms.com

Segue Systems: www.seguesystems.com

CyberSource: www.cybersource.com

You can establish a merchant account with almost any bank. The only thing that you need to ensure is that the bank you choose has a working relationship with the transaction-processing agent you choose. Just remember that the companies that provide these services are all in competition with one another, so do your research before making a decision as to which one to use. A detailed transaction costs comparison can save you lots of money if your site sells a lot of goods. Figure 11.4 outlines the components involved in handling an online transaction.

ACTIVATING YOUR MERCHANT ACCOUNT

Each bank has a minimum set of requirements that your site must adhere to before they can activate your account. A good example of this is that your business name and contact information must be clearly displayed so that your customers can contact you if they have a problem with either their transaction or product. Once you feel your site is setup according to their guidelines, you need to contact a bank representative so that they can review your site and activate your account. Just remember, every time a customer has to contact the bank to resolve a transaction dispute the bank loses money, so they want as many customers as possible to resolve any disputes with you.

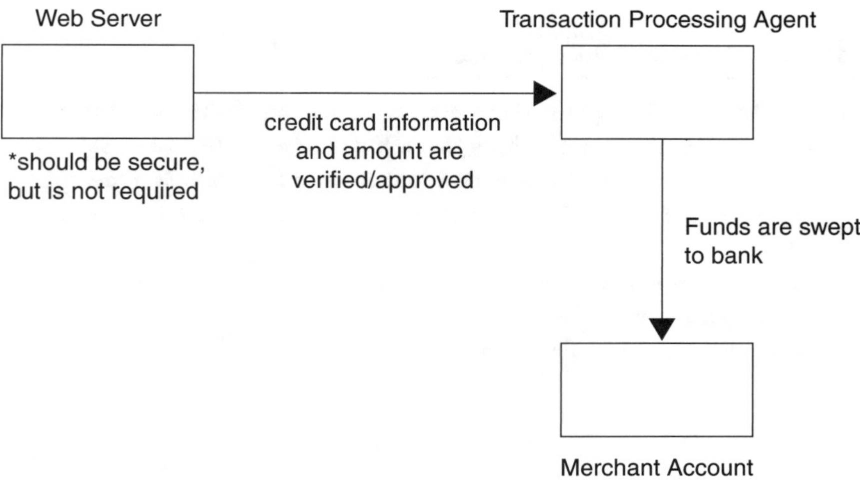

Figure 11.4 Online processing components.

Tips for Your E-Commerce Site

1. Plan your site vocabulary and graphics very carefully. Try to be sensitive to non-English speakers and other multi-cultural issues. Generally, it's not a bad idea to embrace the KISS (keep it simple, stupid) principle.
2. Consult an attorney, post a privacy policy, and abide by it.
3. Customer Relationship Management (CRM) is what e-commerce is all about, so use direct mailings to inform customers about special offers, new content, and any other important news. Give customers the option of opting in or out of direct mailings.
4. If you're using cookies to personalize a person's experiences on your Web site, try to set things up so that users can access their personalized settings from multiple machines.
5. Create "rules" so that users see only content that has been changed since their last time online if that's what they want.
6. Let users send e-mail to customer service, but have procedures set up to respond to the e-mail within 24 hours.
7. Keep an eye on your competition. Sign up for their mailing lists so that you'll know what they're up to.

Continues

Tips for Your E-Commerce Site *(Continued)*

8. **If you're not using spanned servers, create a membership directory and store your users' session information there. If you're using ADSI and SSL, you may want to refer to the KB article Q236050 *How to Bind to a Membership Directory with ADSI Using SSL* at support.microsoft.com/support/kb/articles/q236/0/50.asp.**
9. **Schedule automatic analysis reports for your site. Review them and make sure that they are sent to the appropriate parties, or post them in a secure folder where they can be easily viewed.**

Security Re-Visited

Now that we know about SSL digital certificates and the parties required to handle online transactions, let's look at why you may not need to obtain a digital certificate. If the transaction-processing agent allows you to use their secure server, you can simply "pass" your customers on to them to handle the credit-card transaction. They in turn send the approval/decline information back to you so that you can act accordingly. This can be done so that the "passing" process is transparent to your customer. This means that all of the customer's product browsing and selections occur on your server (no security needed here), but when it comes time to process the credit-card transaction, you send them to a secure server maintained by the processing agent. We cover the details of how to implement this in the section entitled *The Credit Card Processing Code.*

The Shopping Cart

The term *shopping cart* is sometimes used to refer to the software that allows you to operate an e-commerce site, but we're going to use it to refer to the specific code that allows the customer to select and accumulate products for purchasing. Once the customer selects all of the products that they want, they leave the shopping cart code and move into the credit-card processing code.

Do you need a shopping cart to have an e-commerce site? Probably, but that depends on whether or not you want to allow your customers to purchase more than one item at a time. What if your sole product was access to your site? Let's say that you are a financial investing specialist and feel that people will pay to read your investment analysis and advice, so you sell access to your site on a monthly or annual basis. You certainly don't need a shopping cart to handle this type of transaction. You simply allow the customer to select a subscription option and pass the product, price, and customer information to the Authorization Agent.

FYI PURCHASING A SHOPPING CART APPLICATION

Just like any other software application, shopping cart code can be purchased. As a matter of fact, when you're researching which Authorization Agent to use, you'll see references to companies that sell shopping cart applications with whom they already have a working relationship. This, of course, is key if you're going to buy an application. It doesn't matter if it's the best one on the market, if it doesn't work with your Authorization Agent.

The First Project

We thought long and hard about the best way to show you how to create an e-commerce site and decided that we should just create one and then show you the steps we took to put it in place. The URL for the sample site is www.sqlbook.com/vnursery.asp. The name of our business is 10 Project's V-Nursery and we carry four product lines that you would find in a typical brick-and-mortar nursery. When it's all said and done you will understand the components needed to create this site.

From a very high-level perspective the site consists of a small inventory stored in a SQL Server 7 database that anyone with a browser and Internet connectivity can access, review, and make purchases from. It may seem over-simplified, but this is e-commerce. If your site's activity is relatively small (less than 1000 hits per day) then the site described in this first project will work just fine. If you plan on creating an e-commerce site to rival Amazon.com, you can still use SQL Server 7 to manage your inventory, but you'll need to explore applications like Site Server Commerce Edition that allow you to implement a more scalable (and more complex) site that is based on a multi-tier architecture. We'll get you started building a Site Server-based site in the second project. Figure 11.5 shows the general layout for our V-Nursery.

Examining the V-Nursery Site

If you have access to the Internet, go ahead and take a look at the site before continuing. The code used to create the V-Nursery site is on the CD-ROM that accompanies this book in the Chapter11 sub-directory. One of the files is used to create the database and the rest of the files are pages that make up the site. A brief description of each file is shown here:

VNursery.sql. Contains the T-SQL statements that create the database and all of the database objects.

Global.asa. Creates the session identifier and deletes cart items associated with expired sessions.

Sql-Conn.inc. Creates database connections. We do not place the connection object in a session variable because this can introduce threading problems, which can limit

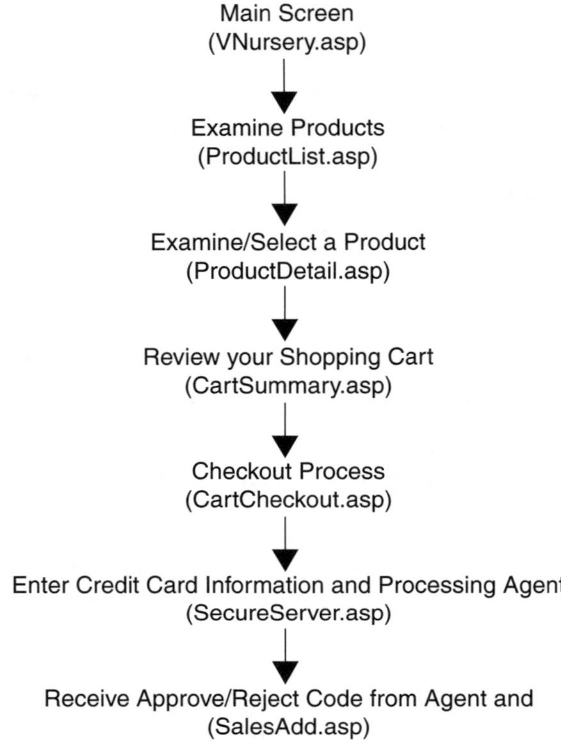

Figure 11.5 10 Projects V-Nursery layout.

your applications scalability. For more information, please see the Knowledge Base Article: Q176056.

NavBar.inc: Contains the code for the navigation bar that is used throughout the site.

Vnursery.asp: The main page.

ProductList.asp: Displays all the products for a given category.

ProductDetail.asp: Displays detailed information for a given product ID.

CartAdd.asp: Inserts an item into the temporary cart table.

CartSummary.asp: Displays all of the products that are selected during the session.

CartClear.asp: Deletes all of the products selected during the session.

CartCheckOut.asp: Displays the total sales amount and allows customers to enter information.

SecureServer.asp: Simulates a screen that you would see when accessing your processing agents secure server.

SecureServerRespond.asp: Simulates the response that you would see once the Authorization Agent successfully processes the credit-card information.

SalesAdd.asp: Accepts the values returned by the processing agent and, when an approval code is returned, inserts the sales data.

CookiesDisabled.asp: Displays a message that informs the user that they cannot use the cart portion of the site because their browser is configured to reject cookies.

The site uses stored procedures to perform all data manipulation and a table to temporarily store the products selected during a session. Some shopping cart applications use a session-level array to temporarily keep track of product selections, but we went with the table approach in order to reduce the memory requirements for IIS. If you use the session-level array approach and your site has thousands of simultaneous shoppers, then IIS will have to manage all of those variables. When the table approach is used, the resource requirements are reduced because IIS has less to manage. You can use any text editor to examine the files. You can create this Web site on a local machine in a matter of minutes—assuming that you already have IIS and SQL Server installed.

In order to create the V-Nursery site, complete the following steps:

1. Open the VNursery.SQL file (located in the Chapter11 sub-directory on the CD-ROM) in Query Analyzer. This script creates a database that is used for the site. The script will fail if you already have a database named VNursery. If you happen to have a database named VNursery, simply modify line 5 of the script with a new database name.
2. Create a new Web site in IIS and name it VNursery. If, for some strange reason, you already have a Web site with this name, choose another.
3. Copy all of the files, except Vnursery.sql, located in the Chapter11 sub-directory into your new Web site. Please note that if you create a virtual directory for the site global.asa, it must reside in the root directory. If you do not do this, the shopping cart will always be empty.
4. Modify the GLOBAL.ASA and sql-conn.inc files so that the database connection information is correct per your SQL Server. So, if your SQL Server is named SS1, lines 6 and 16 (in global.asa) should be modified to look like this (assuming you did not make any modifications to Step 1):

```
SQLConn.Open "Provider=SQLOLEDB;Server=SS1;Database=VNursery;
Uid=UserName;Pwd=Password"
```

Note that you must supply a valid UserName and Password for a successful connection. You should also note that we use OLE DB to connect to the database. If you use a hosting service that only supports ODBC connections you will have to modify both files accordingly. The sql-conn.inc file has examples of the three possible connection types, so if you cannot use OLE DB pick the one that applies to your setup and make the needed changes. There you have it. As long as you started the Web site you should be able to run the V-Nursery Web site on your local computer.

The Database

The database diagram for the database that supports the V-Nursery site is shown in Figure 11.6.

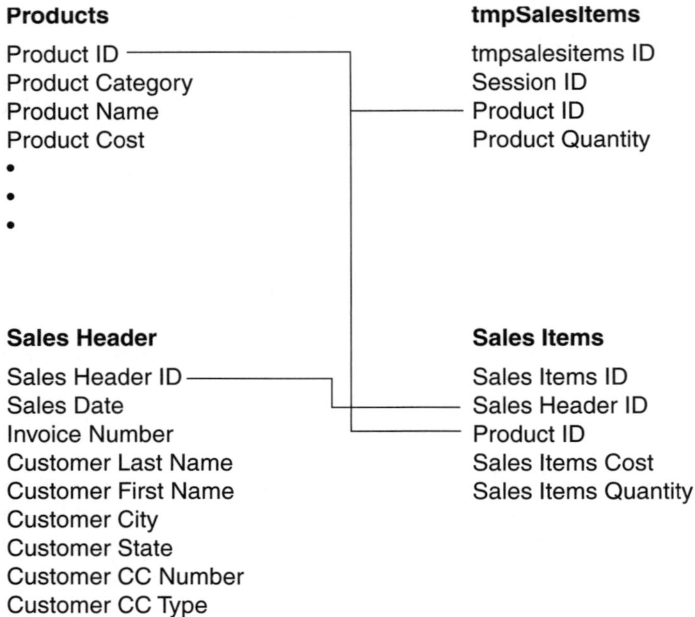

Figure 11.6 Database diagram.

As you can see, the design is extremely simple. We have a Products table that holds the inventory and SalesHeader and SalesItems tables to hold sales information. The tmpSalesItems table is used as a temporary holder for the items that a customer selects throughout their session. The design can be simple because we plan to manage the rest of the processes locally. The only thing that we want to track on our site is sales information.

As stated earlier, all data manipulation is completed with stored procedures. A brief description of the function performed by each stored procedure is shown here:

ps_Products_SELECT_ByCategory: Selects products by the supplied Category parameter.

ps_Products_SELECT_ByProductID: Selects detailed product information by supplied ProductID.

ps_tmpSalesItems_INSERT: Inserts a product selected by the user into tmpSalesItems. This acts as a temporary holder for selected items until the user decides to check out.

ps_tmpSalesItems_SELECT_BySessionID: Selects the products by supplied SessionID. This allows a user to review their cart.

ps_tmpSalesItems_SELECT_TotalBySessionID: Calculates the sales total for all products that are selected.

ps_tmpSalesItems_DELETE: Deletes all products that are selected. This allows the user to empty their cart.

ps_SalesHeader_INSERT: Inserts the sales information into the SalesHeader and SalesItems tables. It uses the products in tmpSalesItems to create the *final* SalesItems records. This is the most important stored procedure used on the site.

The Shopping Cart Code

The shopping cart aspect of the site is contained in three files: CartAdd.asp, CartSummary.asp, and CartClear.asp. The contents of the CartAdd.asp file is shown here:

```
<!— #include file="sql-conn.inc"—>
<%
 If Session("Session Check") = "" Then
    response.redirect "CookiesDisabled.asp"
 End If
 sSQL = "EXECUTE ps_tmpSalesItems_INSERT " & "'"
 sSQL = sSQL & Session("SessionCheck") & "',"
 sSQL = sSQL & request.form("ProductID") & ","
 sSQL = sSQL & request.form("Qty")
 SQLConn.Execute(sSQL)
 response.redirect "CartSummary.asp"
%>
```

This code is called when the user clicks the Add to Cart button on the ProductDetail screen. It simply requests the selected product information and inserts it into tmpSalesItems via the ps_tmpSalesItems_INSERT stored procedure. It then calls the CartSummary.asp file that shows the contents of the user's cart.

The contents of CartSummary.asp file is too long to show here, but if we take a look at the stored procedures that it uses we can see what's happening. The stored procedures are shown here:

```
CREATE PROCEDURE ps_tmpSalesItems_SELECT_BySessionID
@SessionID char(38)
AS
SELECT a.tmpSalesItemsID,
       b.ProductName,
       a.ProductQuantity,
       b.ProductCost,
       b.ProductCost*a.ProductQuantity AS ItemTotal
FROM tmpSalesItems a, Products b
WHERE a.SessionID = @SessionID AND
      a.ProductID = b.ProductID
CREATE PROCEDURE ps_tmpSalesItems_SELECT_TotalBySessionID
@SessionID char(38)
AS
SELECT SUM(b.ProductCost*a.ProductQuantity) AS SalesTotal
FROM tmpSalesItems a, Products b
WHERE a.SessionID = @SessionID AND
      a.ProductID = b.ProductID
```

The first stored procedure retrieves the products that the user has placed in their cart. The second stored procedure then calculates the total sales amount for all of the products that are selected. Nothing fancy here, we just put the values in recordset and display them on the page.

The contents of the CartDelete.asp file is shown here:

```
<!— #include file="sql-conn.inc"—>
<%
 sSQL = "EXECUTE ps_tmpSalesItems_DELETE '" & Session("SessionID") & "'"
 SQLConn.Execute(sSQL)
 response.redirect "CartSummary.asp"
%>
```

This code simply calls the ps_tmpSalesItems_DELETE stored procedure, which deletes all of the records associated with the supplied SessionID. It then calls the CartSummary.asp file to show that the cart has been emptied.

There are three other pages that relate to the cart code: CartCheckOut.asp, SalesAdd.asp, and Global.asa. CartCheckOut.asp simply shows the total for the pending purchase and allows the user to input name and address information. SalesAdd.asp adds the customer and sales-related information to the *final* tables. The stored procedure it uses takes the product information from tmpSalesItems and moves it into SalesItems. The related Global.asa code does some cleanup work for the site. The code specific to this process is shown here:

```
REM Delete temporary cart items for expired sessions
 Sub Session_OnEnd
  SET SQlConn = SERVER.CREATEOBJECT("ADODB.Connection")
  SQLConn.OPEN
"Provider=SQLOLEDB;Server=ServerName;Database=VNursery;Uid=UserName;Pwd
=Password"
  sSQL = "EXECUTE ps_tmpSalesItems_DELETE '" & Session("SessionID") &
"'"
  SQLConn.Execute(sSQL)
 End Sub
```

When a user's session expires (five minutes of inactivity on the sample site), this code is executed and deletes any products that the user might have placed in their cart. This is very handy because your bound to have many users who stop by your site, place a few items in a cart, and then decide not to finalize the purchase. If we didn't have this code in global.asa, tmpSalesItem could become very large and degrade the site's performance.

BROWSERS MUST ACCEPT COOKIES

A browser must be configured to accept cookies in order for session variables to work properly. We trap for browsers that don't accept cookies on our site and send them to a page that explains the need for cookies. The *trapping* code is shown on lines 3-5 of CartAdd.asp.

SESSION VARIABLES TIMEOUT

IIS' default setting is for session variables to timeout after 20 minutes of inactivity. So, if a customer adds items to their cart and leaves their computer for more than 20 minutes, he or she will have to start over when they return. The computer on which the sample site is hosted is configured for session variables to timeout after 5 minutes of inactivity.

The Credit-Card Processing Code

The credit-card processing code is simulated on our sample site because we are not connected to a processing agent. The simulated code is contained in SecureServer.asp and is shown here. This example assumes that we use the secure server provided by our transaction-processing agent.

```
<form name="CCProcess" method="post"_
_action="http://www.sqlbook.com/SecureServerRespond.asp"
onsubmit="return checkData()">
  <table align="center" width=400 cellpadding=0 cellspacing=0>
   <input type="hidden" name="LOGIN" value="VNursery">
   <input type="hidden" name="AMOUNT" value="<%=rs("SalesTotal")%>">
   <input type="hidden" name="CUSTID" value="<%=Session("SessionID")%>">
<input type="hidden" name="INVOICE" value="<%=Session("SessionID")%>">
 <input type="hidden" name="Approved" value="Y">
   <tr>
...
</form>
```

This code should look familiar to you as it is no different than any other <Form method="Post"> page that you've seen. The only unique aspect to this page is that the names for the <Input> fields are dictated by the processing agent. When you sign up with an agent, they will provide access to documentation that details how to connect to their servers—most provide sample code. In addition to providing *fixed* names for data elements like CUSTID, they will allow you to use custom fields that are named something like USER1…USER20. This will allow you to track up to 20 additional data elements that are not deemed necessary by the processing agent, but important to you.

After the customer completes the initial submission form (CartCheckOut.asp) on our site, they click the Submit button and all of the data elements that you want to track are then sent to the secure server (SecureServer.asp). The secure server displays the required information and then the customer supplies their credit-card information. The important thing here is that the customer does not supply any credit-card information before they get to the secure server. Once the credit-card information is input, the customer clicks the Submit button once more and the data is validated and an Accept or Decline code is sent back to the secure server (SecureServerRespond.asp). If an Accept code is sent back to the server, the customer is shown a Receipt screen that they can print for their records. If a Decline code is sent back, the customer is given another opportunity to submit a valid credit card. After the customer prints their receipt, they click a Continue button to return to your site. The transaction agent sends

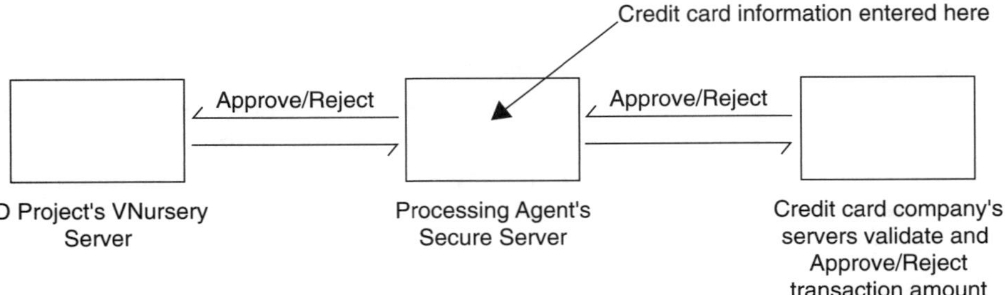

Figure 11.7 Credit card processing process.

all of the information that you sent to it back to you so that you can modify your database accordingly (SalesAdd.asp). Figure 11.7 shows what this process looks like, but the only real way to understand how it works is to look at and work with the code that we supply on the CD-ROM. This process is actually very simple, but since there's another company/server involved, it seems more complicated than it really is.

That's all there is to setting up a rudimentary e-commerce site based on IIS and SQL Server. Amazingly simple, isn't it?

In the next section, we show you how to build a more sophisticated site using Microsoft's Site Server Commerce Edition. This is not available on the book's CD and is not "free," though you may have access to it if you're an MSDN member or own Microsoft BackOffice.

Before we continue though, it's a good time for a break. We recommend that you read MSDN's *Duwamish* case study. It's the story of a fictitious Seattle-area bookstore that builds an e-commerce site. MSDN programmers actually developed the Duwamish site in stages over the course of almost two years—very "real world." You should be able to find it by searching the msdn.microsoft.com Web site. It's very good reading, with tons of code.

What Microsoft Site Server Brings to the Table

Now that you're familiar with the whole design and deployment principles that surround building an e-commerce Web site, it's time to expand on what you've learned to build a more complex site using Microsoft Site Server 3.0 Commerce Edition. But first, a quick overview of Site Server and Site Server Commerce Edition.

Site Server 3.0 (there really isn't a version 2.0, in case you're curious) comes in two flavors: the Standard Edition for small business sites and intranets and a Commerce Edition for large-scale retail sites. The Standard Edition is part of Windows NT BackOffice but can be purchased separately with 5 CALs for $1239 (SRP, Fall 1999). The Commerce Edition retails for $4609 with 25 CALs. Both require a Site Server Internet Connector license ($2999) if they're going to be accessed by external users.

FYI DISTINGUISHING AMONG IIS, SITE SERVER, AND MCIS

IIS is the Web Server in Windows NT Server and is a part of the Windows NT Server 4.0 Option Pack. Site Server runs on top of the combination of Windows NT Server and IIS Server. Site Server and Site Server 3.0, Commerce Edition take advantage of ASP and Microsoft Transaction Server (MTS) technology that ships with the Windows NT Option Pack. Site Server extends this platform to streamline the publishing, location, and delivery of targeted information throughout corporate intranets. Site Server Commerce Edition is a superset of Site Server that adds functionality for conducting online business.

The Microsoft Commercial Internet System (MCIS) 2.0 is a superset of Site Server Commerce Edition for Commercial Service Providers (CSPs) such as ISPs or telephone and cable network operators.

Component Object Model (COM) and COM+

Microsoft's Component Object Model (COM) is a technology for transparently transferring encapsulated data across boundaries. It doesn't matter whether or not the boundaries are separate modules, threads, or processes.

A very simple example of COM is sharing a DLL between two applications. Consider application A, which is a program that runs on the server. Application A extracts data from a variety of different Web sites and compiles a profile on a particular site. This profile is constantly updated. Application B is a program that runs on a desktop in the office that uses the server running Application A. Application B sends requests to application A to update the site profile object. Seconds after the site profile object is updated Application B displays the changes.

That doesn't sound too complicated, now does it? But that's not all. The key to COM is that the objects referenced by Application A can maintain *state*. For example, when you declare a variable in ASP, that variable has *scope* only on the current page. When you move off the current page, the variable goes out of scope and the data contained in that variable (or object) is lost. This is not so with a COM object.

As you move to the next page, you can reference the COM object and request the data posted to the object by the previous page.

How is COM different? COM objects are more complicated then their VB and C++ brethren and very different from SQL Server "objects" such as tables.

Continues

Component Object Model (COM) and COM+ *(Continued)*

Here are some COM basics:

- Standard objects always run in the same process space. COM objects can run across processes or across computers. To create a COM object, some executing entity (an EXE or a Service) has to perform remote memory allocation and object creation. This is a very complex task. By remote, we mean in or on another process. This is performed with a concept called a *COM server*. This other entity must maintain tight communication with the client.
- COM methods can be called across a network. Since your COM object won't necessarily be on the local machine, you need a good way to "point to" it, even though its memory is somewhere else. When data is passed between processes, threads, or over a network, it's called m*arshalling*. Standard object method names must be unique in a given process space.
- COM object names must be unique throughout the world. COM must guarantee that there will only be one object of a given name even though the number of objects available on a worldwide network is huge. This problem is solved by creating a *globally unique identifier (GUID)*.
- COM objects implement interfaces according to "the rules." At its simplest, an interface is nothing but a named collection of functions. One of COM's cardinal rules is that you can only access a COM object through an interface. The client program knows nothing about the COM object or a class that implements the COM object. All it can see is the interface. The interface is like a window into the COM object. The interface designer allows the client to see only those parts of the object that he or she wishes to expose.

A COM server is the program that implements COM interfaces and classes. COM servers come in four basic configurations:

- In-process or DLL servers
- Stand-alone EXE servers
- Windows NT-based services
- Surrogate servers (a program that lets an in-process server run remotely)

The important thing to remember is that COM objects are the same regardless of the type of server. COM interfaces don't care what type of server is used. To the client program, the type of server is almost entirely transparent.

So, What's COM+?

As you can probably guess, COM+ is COM on steroids—the next Big Thing for Windows 2000 and beyond. COM+ consists of runtime, extensible services including some provided by Microsoft such as transaction handling (COM+ basically sub-

sumes MTS), security, load balancing, and automatic memory management. Additional extensible services can and will be provided by third-party developers.

COM+ introduces the concept of attribute-based programming. The key points to attribute-based programming are that after coding your basic logic, you add "innovations," that is, set the attributes, rely on the runtime to provide basic services such as those listed in the previous paragraph, and then use "interceptors."

Interception and interceptors are key parts of COM+. *Interceptors* provide services based on attributes, which have been previously set on an object by a developer. These interceptors provide automatic behavior at runtime based on the attribute set. Different interceptors will provide different extensible services at runtime. Events such as instance creation, method call and return, field access, force fail, pre and post call, binding an instance to a reference, and dynamically redefining a method can all be intercepted.

Site Server Standard Edition

Site Server 3.0 is basically an intranet server optimized for publishing and locating information on an internal Web site (see Figure 11.8). It isn't a standalone product. You run it on an NT Server that's already running IIS. Site Server adds a collection of services, components, APIs, and sample "starter" applications that can automate the advanced management and targeted delivery of information. You can download the Site Server 3.0 SDK from Microsoft's Site Server Web site and virtually every Site Server service provides a COM object model to allow the site builder to extend the functionality of the underlying services. Site Server's object model is documented in the SDK. SDK Version 1.1 offers "starter" applications for:

- Directory monitoring coordination with Search
- Customizing the Commerce Server Order Processing Pipeline
- Integrating applications with Personalization and Membership Authentication
- Building a custom Active Channel Server Agent for dynamic and automatic refreshing of channel content
- Managing Content Deployment
- Extending the functionality of Microsoft Wallet
- Using Active Directory Service Interfaces—ADSI—Explorer

Publishing. Site Server Publishing provides the Web developer with core services and a series of ActiveX COM objects to assist with development.

Search. Site Server Search provides a service that indexes the contents and metadata (properties) of documents into catalogs. It also provides a COM object model that application developers can use to search these catalogs.

Figure 11.8 Site Server Administration page.

INDEX SERVER VERSUS SITE SERVER SEARCH

If you're familiar with Index Server, another Microsoft BackOffice product, you're probably thinking, "Hey, isn't that what Index Server does?" The short answer is yes. In fact, Site Server Search uses some of the underlying functionality of Index Server to do its catalog builds. The one thing that you get with Site Server Search that you don't get with Index Server is the ability to perform a remote catalog build (called a *crawl*) and to propagate the completed catalog to another server. This allows you to set up both a dedicated catalog build server and a dedicated search server for your entire Web farm. This obviously helps out your performance and scalability. This white paper provides great details: www.microsoft.com/siteserver/site/DeployAdmin/EnterpriseSearch.htm

SQL Server's Full-Text Indexing feature uses the same basic search engine, but only indexes database text fields. Moving forward, Microsoft promises to make the three more integrated. In the meantime, this white paper may help you integrate database indexing into Site Server's catalog: www.microsoft.com/siteserver/site/DeployAdmin/SearchDatabase.htm.

Microsoft has an excellent white paper on integrating Site Server Search with Microsoft Exchange. Although it may have been updated for Exchange Platinum by the time you read this, it contains a wealth of useful implementation hints: www.microsoft.com/siteserver/site/DeployAdmin/IntegrateExchange.htm.

Personalization and Membership. Site Server Personalization and Membership (P&M) allows you to manage user communities of virtually any size. P&M has services and components that handle almost every aspect of user management and personalization issues.

Push. Push automates the process of targeted information delivery to users. Push is based on Microsoft's Active Channel Technology, which was first introduced with IE4. Site Server Push has two main components: Active Channel Server and Active Channel Multicaster.

1. Active Channel Server is an NT service that builds and manages Channel Definition Format (CDF) files that are based on user preferences. Users can then subscribe to these channels, and have targeted information pushed to them whenever content is updated. Active Channel Servers utilize *Active Channel Agents*, which are scripts that retrieve the content from a specified source. Active Channel Agents can run automatically to update each channel's content items according to a refresh schedule. Site Server provides several Active Channel Agents to gather content from any file on the network, any ODBC database, Microsoft Index Server, Site Server Commerce Edition databases, Site Server Search catalogs, and Knowledge Manager shared knowledge briefs. You can also create your own custom agent scripts to gather content from other sources.
2. Active Channel Multicaster is an NT service that simultaneously delivers content to multiple users through a process called *multicasting*. Multicasting allows a server to send the same piece of data to multiple clients at the same time. In contrast, if you had a network that didn't use the Active Channel Multicaster, each client would separately pull the same channel content. This means the same content would go across the network N times. Where N is the number of clients that subscribe to a network.

Analysis. Analysis evaluates two things: how people use your site and how the content is structured. Tools allow you to perform both content and usage analysis. These tools include the Content Analyzer, Custom Import tool, Report Writer, and the Usage Import tool.

Knowledge Manager. Knowledge Manager is a customizable ASP application that brings together all of the previously explained services into a knowledge management application.

Many of Site Server's features are targeted towards what might be called document management, workflow, or knowledge management. In other words, Site Server is typically used to power corporate, intranet-based document management systems based on a strategy that helps integrate these systems into a smooth flow for managing the publishing, indexing, and searching of documents.

KNOWLEDGE MANAGER IS REALLY JUST A SAMPLE

Site Server's Knowledge Manager isn't a functional area of Site Server 3.0, though that will undoubtedly change in the future. It's simply an application included with Site Server that helps leverage the functional areas to provide services to your end users. It includes the ability to share information, search for content, and have that content delivered to you.

Site Server Commerce Edition

In the V-Nursery project, you saw that you can build a very simple e-commerce application by adding shopping cart and credit-card functionality to IIS. You've seen that "plain old" Site Server targets intranets, workflow, and document management. Site Server Commerce Edition is Microsoft's basic e-commerce server for conducting online business. Site Server Commerce Edition creates Web storefronts that are three-tier ASP applications hosted on a server that runs Windows NT Server and IIS (and, in some cases, MTS). What's a three-tier application? Three-tier applications are basically computer programs that are broken into three levels of interoperability.

The first level (or tier) is the user interface. That's where the application captures input from the user. This input data is then passed to the business logic or second tier—one that's independent from the data and user interfaces. Why? By avoiding hard coding and using "business objects," you end up with a more modular, easier-to-maintain application. The third tier is the back end database(s.)

Site Server Commerce Edition applications are generally written using VBScript, JavaScript, or any other scripting language that has an interpreter written to the Microsoft Active Scripting Interface standard. Site Server Commerce Edition applications can use any of the 50+ COM objects that ship with Site Server Commerce Edition. These COM objects each encapsulate a particular commerce-related business rule, such as credit-card validation, price adjustment, inventory control, and purchase-order generation and make use of a framework known as a *pipeline*. Site Server Commerce Edition's pipeline framework gives the e-commerce site builder an extensible, scaleable architecture, and an open API. We'll talk more about both COM/COM+ objects and pipelines later in the chapter.

Another key difference between Site Server Standard Edition and Site Server Commerce Edition is that Site Server Commerce Edition provides a variety of wizards to help with the building of your site. All you have to do is specify a few NT configuration options, input some specific site details and pow (!) the wizard generates the Web pages for both the starter and administration sites. It also creates the database schema files that it loads into SQL Server.

According to Microsoft's marketing wizards, the Site Server Commerce Edition development team had four major design goals in mind when they built Site Server Commerce Edition:

1. **Build.** Site Server Commerce Edition should let customers implement and create a fully functional e-commerce-enabled business application.
2. **Engage.** Site Server Commerce Edition should "engage" customers and partners by creating cost-effective business solutions and applications that through their marketing and advertising efforts can provide a customized and personal shopping experience.
3. **Transact.** Site Server Commerce Edition should include functionality that lets organizations built applications that support secure online order processing.
4. **Analyze.** Site Server Commerce Edition needs to be flexible enough to support "one-to-one" marketing ad personalization.

Installing Site Server Commerce Edition

Let's talk hardware. Why? Because you need a fairly, beefy server for Site Server. No wimps allowed. Whatever you do, do NOT skimp on your server's hardware. To start, we recommend:

1. A dedicated server (this is key as you will see later on in this chapter)
2. A server with AT LEAST 128 MB of RAM, which is what Microsoft recommends
3. Dual or quad processors if you can afford it

Again, remember that Site Server Commerce Edition doesn't play well with other resource-intensive Microsoft products such as Exchange Server, Proxy Server, or SQL Server.

Before we jump into the installation for Site Server Commerce Edition, we need to point out that Microsoft recommends that you do not install Site Server Commerce Edition and SQL Server 7 on the same computer, or on a server that runs Microsoft Proxy Server. SQL Server 7 installs the Microsoft Data Access Components version 2.1, which is not fully compatible with Active Directory Service Interface 2.0 included with Site Server 3.0. The Microsoft Data Access Components are automatically installed by Microsoft Visual Studio 6.0 Service Pack 3, Microsoft Internet Explorer 5.0, Microsoft SQL Server 7, Microsoft Office 2000, and Microsoft BackOffice 4.5. However, for the purposes of this example, we performed the install as suggested by Microsoft for when you have only one machine. This type of installation is extremely useful during the development phase or for "road shows" (yes, we have installed Site Server Commerce Edition on an NT laptop).

Pre-Installation Suggestions

Here are some suggestions to follow before you install Site Server:

- Assemble all of the CDs, including service packs that you'll need and read their ReadMe files.
- Check out www.siteserver.com, which contains the most up-to-date instructions for installing Site Server Commerce Edition that we've seen. You should read the instructions carefully and check for updates on the site before you install. This is very important. Do not attempt to install Site Server Commerce Edition without doing some

homework. You should inventory your computer system, and search for any known conflicts with other software packages before performing the installation.

- Do *not* install Site Server 3.0 on a computer that functions as a Windows NT Server Backup Domain Controller.
- Do *not* install Microsoft Exchange Server on a computer with Site Server installed. Both server products are resource intensive. Performance decreases greatly when these products are installed on the same computer.
- Do *not* install Site Server 3.0 on a computer that runs Microsoft Cluster Service (MSCS).
- Do *not* change any default settings in Microsoft Internet Information Server (IIS) before you install Site Server (on a new installation). In particular, do not disable NTLM support, change IP binding from "all unassigned," or change port "80" on the default Web site.
- If you installed Microsoft Proxy Server 2.0, some ISAPI filters are installed and the default Web site is modified. As a result, do not attempt to install Site Server Commerce Edition on a machine that runs Proxy Server 2.0 and do not attempt to install Microsoft Proxy Server on a machine that runs Site Server Commerce Edition.
- Do not install Commerce Server on a computer with Microsoft Commercial Internet System (MCIS) because the latter requires Internet Explorer 5.0.
- Keep in mind that not only does size matter (have a powerful server with gobs of hard disk space), order, that is the order in which items need to be installed, matters, too. If you don't, we guarantee many hours of frustration.

READ THE MANUALS

You're probably familiar with the rather crude saying, "read the @#$% manual," and we admit that we're not as good as we should be about reading manuals—or even the ReadMe files that are on most products' CDs today. Based on all of the horror stories that we heard and read about, however, we made an exception as we prepared to install Site Server Commerce Edition. One of the useful tidbits that we learned from the manual is that when you set up Windows NT 4, you shouldn't use more than a 10-character name for the NetBIOS. Site Server does not properly recognize a name of more than 10 characters and causes an LDAP error.

A related recommendation: before running the installation, review the documentation from the startup screen. On the installation setup screen (see Figure 11.9) select Setup Instructions then read them carefully (see Figure 11.10).

Site Server Installation Steps

Now we're ready (*finally*) to start the fun stuff—actually installing Site Server Commerce Edition. We'll start with a "clean" machine onto which we'll install Windows NT Server, so you may want to skip the first steps if you already have your NT server set up. Note that this installation worked as of Fall 1999, but as newer versions of various components become available, the order in which you need to install them may change. Please consult the Microsoft Site Server Commerce Edition site, the independent www.siteserver.com site, and the Microsoft newsgroups for tips and news about up-to-

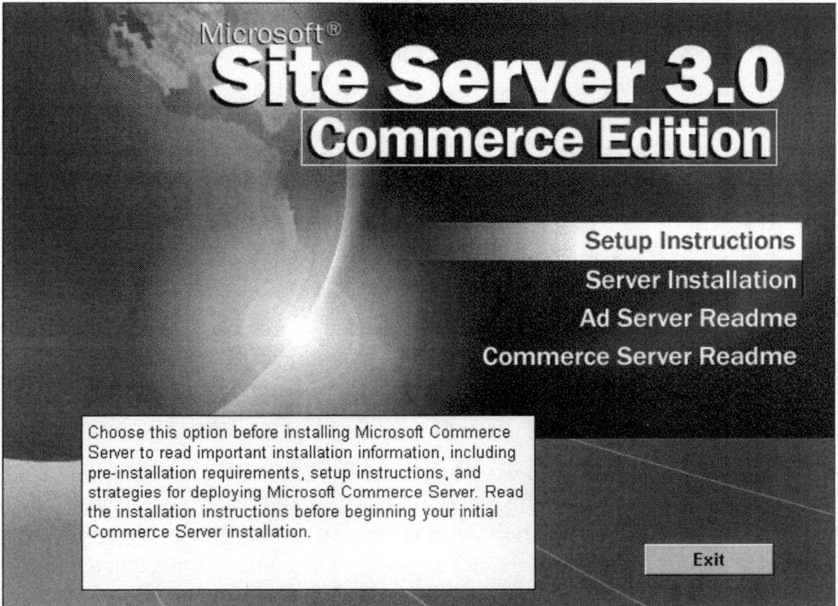

Figure 11.9 Site Server Commerce Edition setup screen.

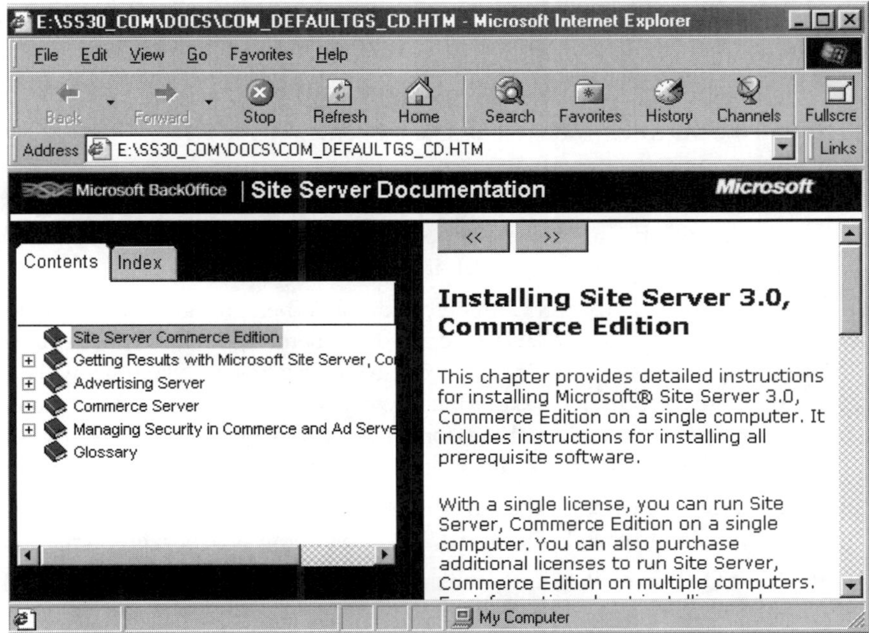

Figure 11.10 Site Server Commerce Edition documentation.

www.siteserver.com site, and the Microsoft newsgroups for tips and news about up-to-date installation information.

1. Install Microsoft Windows NT Server 4.0. Select Primary or Backup Domain Controller. If your version of Windows NT is pre-service Pack 3, you should install the service pack. Do not install Service Pack 4, or higher at this point. Do not install the NT 4.0 Option Pack.
2. Next, you should install Internet Explorer 4.01 with Service Pack 1 using the Standard Installation. The Standard Installation can be found on the NT Option Pack CD. Do not install IE 4.0 Service Pack 2 or IE 5.0 (yet).
3. Install NT 4.0 Option Pack. Select to Install Index Server, SMTP, and Windows Scripting Host, but do not install the Microsoft FrontPage Server Extensions—we'll install them later.
4. Configure Microsoft Transaction Server for local administration.
5. In you're a developer who wants a single system with everything on it for development purposes, this is the place to install Visual Studio 6.0. If you do, do *not* install the Visual Studio Analyzer component as it will *severely* impact scalability and performance. It's important to note that you should not install Microsoft Visual Studio 97 Service Pack 3 or Microsoft Visual Studio 6 Service Pack 3 on the same computer as Site Server 3.0 because both Visual Studio 97 Service Pack 3 and Visual Studio 6.0 Service Pack 3 install MDAC 2.1.
6. Now install the FrontPage 98 Server Extensions. You should not install the FrontPage 2000 Server Extensions because they do not work properly when installing Site Server Commerce Edition. (Aren't "dependencies" great?)
7. Change the default Net Library to TCP/IP on the Web server.
8. Configure the MSDTC service to start automatically.
9. Install the Microsoft Data Access Components version 2.1.
10. Configure the database connectivity. It is not necessary to create a database or DSN for Personalization and Membership. If you choose to create a SQL Sever-based membership instance after you install Site Server, create your database before setting up the membership instance.
11. Install Microsoft Site Server Commerce Edition. When prompted to overwrite the existing files, click No to all. Do *not* create new membership instances before installing Site Server 3.0, Commerce Edition, because the Trey Research Web site will not install or configure correctly. Please note that if you plan to install Ad Server or Commerce Server, create individual databases for Ad Server or Commerce Server, respectively. The databases may reside on different database servers or share the same server.
12. Create a System DSN for the Ad Server and/or Commerce Server databases. When you create each DSN for Ad Server or Commerce Server, do the following:
    - Use SQL Server standard authentication rather than Windows NT authentication.
    - Specify a SQL Server account with at least DBO rights.

- Do not use the default master database. Specify the corresponding database for each DSN.

13. Install Site Server 3.0. Please note that if you install Analysis, do not run the Analysis SQL Server Database Setup Wizard until Site Server 3.0 Service Pack 2 is installed. Only run this wizard if the SQL Server computer is dedicated for Analysis. The wizard will make global SQL Server configuration changes.
14. Install Windows NT 4.0 Service Pack 4.
15. Install Microsoft Data Access Components 2.0 Service Pack 2 Redistribution Typical Setup. Make sure to add the MaxBlock registry setting for MDAC.
16. Install the Site Server 3.0 Service Pack 2. Configure the Personalization and Membership database on the SQL Server computer for single-user mode.
17. Use the Site Server Microsoft Management Console (MMC) to access Commerce Host Administration. Remove ":80" from the Non-Secure Host Name field and ":443" from the Secure Host Name field for all sample stores. Repeat this procedure for all stores that you create.
18. Run the Mcis2upd.sql script against all pre-existing SQL Server databases that support LDAP. You do not need to run this script against SQL Server databases created after Site Server 3.0 Service Pack 2 is applied. Now, reconfigure the Personalization and Membership database on the SQL Server computer for multi-user mode.
19. Install Commerce Interchange Pipeline Manager (CIPM) for Site Server Commerce Edition.
20. Install Microsoft Windows NT 4 Service Pack 5.

Although Microsoft is touting IE 5, we suggest that you avoid installation of IE 5 on a computer with Site Server Commerce Edition. A complete list of the problems that can result from installing IE 5 on a computer with Site Server Commerce Edition is located on the Microsoft Web site, www.microsoft.com/siteserver/commerce.

Odds and Ends: Things to Remember

- **Read the documentation. It's there for a reason.**
- **Plan. Write out everything. Write down a complete execution plan, and then stick with it.**
- **Avoid installing Site Server into the system partition.**
- **Keep computer names short to avoid LDAP errors.**
- **Test everything. From your browser enter every URL you ever want to go to. If you don't see it in IE, neither can Site Server.**
- **Crawl internal Web servers using file crawls. This preserves any NTFS security that you have in place. Map the crawls to HTTP access.**
- **Use Site Indexes when you can. They provide better searches than default home pages.**

Lightweight Directory Access Protocol (LDAP)

Until recently the most generally accepted solution for Directory Service was X.500. This is a standard produced by ITU/ISO and defines the protocols and services at a level that is platform independent. X.500 provides a global distributed directory that contains hierarchically named objects. The model encompasses a set of servers called Directory System Agents (DSAs), where each holds a directory section in its Directory Information Base (DIB).

DSAs cooperate in such a way that applications can connect to any server to issue queries for a data resident anywhere in the global directory. The actual data location is transparent to the requesting application. X.500 defines how the information is structured and distributed in the directory.

Lightweight Directory Access Protocol (LDAP) is a simplified version of Directory Access Protocol, and provides a mechanism to query and manage an arbitrary hierarchical database of objects each containing attribute/value pairs. LDAP operates over TCP/IP and normally uses port 389 or 636 for secured sockets. However, it's important to remember that LDAP is only a protocol and does not specify the actual Directory Service model or how it should function.

Pipelines

What is a pipeline? In commerce the word *pipeline* is a generic term that describes a business-process model. Simply put, a pipeline is a channel through which goods flow from the manufacturer to the end consumer. For example, let's say that you go to a bookstore and looking for a few new books on computer programming. There are certain tasks that have to be performed by you, the consumer. For example:

1. You must search through the bookstore until you find the title (or titles) that you wish to purchase.
2. Once you have the book or books that you want to purchase, you might put them into a shopping cart, or basket for carrying until you are ready to purchase them.
3. If you decide you don't want a book, you simply take it out of the shopping cart and place it back on the shelf.
4. When you are through browsing you proceed to the checkout counter.
5. The cashier will then ring up your order and provide a total cost for your purchases.
6. You whip out your credit card and pay for your purchases.
7. Your bill is now paid and you leave the store with your purchases.

This is a pipeline process. Site Server Commerce Edition automates the process. How? By defining two generic COM object interfaces: IPipeline to represent a collection of tasks and IPipelineComponent to represent the tasks themselves.

Site Server 3.0 Commerce Edition provides three generic pipeline classes:

1. **MtsTxPipeline.** Holds an MTS transaction across all of its components. You should use this object to maintain transactional integrity across components. This allows you to commit or rollback an entire pipeline as a single unit.
2. **MtsPipeline.** Registered under MTS, but doesn't support transactions.
3. **OrderPipeline.** An older object that ships for backwards compatibility with prior versions of Site Server.

Pipelines execute their components in a sequence. Each pipeline component encapsulates code that enforces a rule on a business object. Site Server Commerce Edition typically uses two types of business objects in a pipeline: the *Commerce.OrderForm object* (more commonly known as the OrderForm object) for B2C transactions and the *Commerce.Dictionary object* (also known as the Transport Dictionary) for B2B transactions.

An OrderForm object stores information relevant to a customer's order, such as a customer's shipping address or credit-card information. The Transport Dictionary stores a collection of key-value pairs that associate transactional metadata (such as transaction ID and whether or not a key has been requested) with a business data object, such as the OrderForm object.

There are two different functional types of pipelines. Site Server Commerce Edition defines the *Order Processing Pipeline (OPP)* for B2C transactions and the *Commerce Interchange Pipeline (CIP)* for B2B transactions. The most common scenario for an OPP is a Web storefront, such as the V-Nursery site.

A Web storefront OPP generally has three component pipelines:

1. A product pipeline with components that compute the price and any discounts
2. A plan pipeline with components that handle the basic order itself
3. A purchase pipeline with components that perform credit-card validation and fund commitment, write the order to the store's database, and generate a receipt for the customer

The CIP has to be flexible enough to model the various fashions in which two (or more) companies can conduct business. The true beauty of CIP is that it automates a process and is based on a framework into which you can plug components that implement specific functionality such as EDI. A CIP has two distinct parts: the *transmit pipeline* and the *receive pipeline*. The transmit pipeline models the following processes:

Mapping. Takes information from an object (such as the OrderForm) and maps it to virtually any type of business document format, such as an EDI PO or an XML document. Site Server Commerce Edition comes with a MakePO component that allows you to generate text-based purchase orders in any format from a VBScript template.

Header data generation. Appends the transaction metadata (such as transaction ID) to the mapped document.

Digital Signing. Signs the document with a digital certificate to allow your trading partners to authenticate that this document came from you.

Encryption. Using a key, the document is encrypted to prevent prying eyes and unwanted third parties from viewing your document.

Transport. Sends the document.

Auditing. Verifies transaction reliability.

The CIP receive pipeline is basically the reverse of the transmit pipeline. A document is received, decrypted, verified by checking the digital signature, and then parsed so the appropriate database tables can be updated.

Pipeline information (both OPP and CIP) is stored in a *pipeline file*. A pipeline file is a binary file (generally with a .PCF extension) that provides persistent storage of the metadata. Pipeline metadata includes the component names, the order in which they should be executed, and any state information. Figure 11.11 shows how to use the Pipeline Editor to design a pipeline.

PIPELINE STAGES

Remove all of the empty pipeline stages for better performance.

As we've said, pipelines are where the action is, especially for programmers. You may still be able to hear Jon Nicponski's 44-minute Web seminar on building and adding custom components to the pipeline at www.microsoft.com/Seminar/1033/199812071-07Build&Add(JN)/seminar.htm.

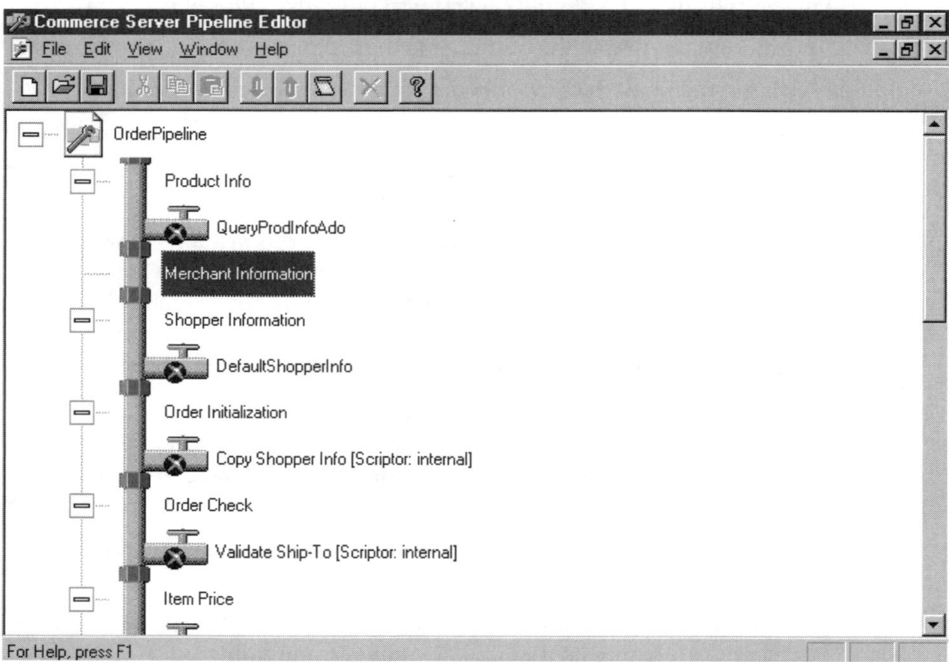

Figure 11.11 The Commerce Server Pipeline Editor.

XML

XML (Extensible Markup Language) is sometimes described as "doing for data what HTML does for text." However, XML really does more for data than HTML does for text.

How is XML better? In XML you can define an unlimited set of tags. While HTML tags can only be used to display a word in bold or italic, XML provides a framework for tagging structured data. An XML element can declare its associated data element to be any number of different things ranging from a book title to a picture, or any other desired data element.

As XML tags are adopted, it will become a lot easier to search for and manipulate data regardless of the applications within which it is found. Once data has been located, it can be delivered over the Internet or it can be handed off to other applications for further processing and viewing.

Structural Representation of Data

XML is a subset of Standard Generalized Markup Language (SGML) that has been optimized for delivery over the Web, and its syntax (standard) is controlled by the World Wide Web Consortium (www.w3c.org/XML).

XML's roots go back to the 1970s when Dr. C. F. Goldfarb and two of his colleagues proposed a method for describing text that was not specific to an application (or a device for that matter). The method had two different parts:

1. Markups should describe the document's structure and not its formatting style characteristics.
2. The markup's syntax should be strictly enforced so that the code could be clearly read by a software program or by a programmer.

The result of these suggestions was the Document Composite Facility Generalized Markup Language (or GML for short) which was developed for IBM. GML was the pre-cursor to Standard Generalized Markup Language (SGML) which was adopted as a standard by the International Organization for Standardization (ISO, www.iso.ch/welcome.html) back in 1986.

XML came about as a result of shortcomings with SGML. SMGL was (and is) an incredibly powerful and flexible language. Only one real problem—it's very difficult to work with. As a result of SGML's poor ease of use, XML was designed from the ground up to be extensible, simple, and flexible. It would seem that so far the attempt was successful.

This resulting interoperability has kick started a new generation of business and electronic-commerce Web applications. XML, which provides a data standard that can encode the content, semantics, and schema for a wide variety of cases ranging from simple to complex, can be used to mark up anything from standard .DOC files to ActiveX controls, database records, maps, and so on.

Continues

XML *(Continued)*

Once the data is on the client desktop, it can be manipulated, edited, and presented in multiple views, without return trips to the server. Servers now become more scalable, due to lower computational and bandwidth loads.

Another added benefit is that since data is exchanged in the XML format, it can be easily merged from different sources. No longer do you have to convert data from dissimilar databases to merge it together. In other words, the back end database becomes irrelevant. This provides new and easy access to legacy databases, which can then be delivered to Web clients in a simple and easy fashion, without re-tooling the back end. Applications can be built more quickly, more easily maintained, and can provide multiple views on the structured data.

The power of XML comes from the fact that it separates the user interface from the structured data. HTML specifies how to display data in a browser and XML defines the content.

For example, in HTML you use tags to tell the browser to display data as bold or italic, whereas in XML you use tags to describe data, such as name, dollar amount, or temperature. For example:

```
<name>Jane Doe</name>
```

The separation of the data from presentation enables the seamless integration of data from many sources. Customer Information, purchase orders, and other information can be converted to XML on the middle tier, allowing data to be exchanged online as easily as HTML pages display data today.

Data encoded in XML can then be delivered over the Web to the desktop. No retrofitting is necessary for legacy information stored in mainframe databases or documents. Why? Well, because HTTP is used to deliver XML over the wire.

XML documents are easy to create, and if you're familiar with HTML, it won't be hard to learn how to create an XML document. In this example, we use XML to describe a purchase order:

```
<purchase-order>
      <ponum>1234985</ponum>
      <date>June 28, 1999</date>
      <company>
           <name>Johnson Control</name>
           <contact>Mike Elliott</contact>
           <phone>(305) 975-5454</phone>
           <address>134 Jackson Street</address>
           <city>Orlando</city>
           <state>FL</state>
           <zip>33062</zip>
      </company>
```

Continues

```
        <items>
            <inventory>Programming</inventory>
            <descr>Custom Programming for Tracking System</descr>
            <units>40</units>
            <price>90</price>
        </items>
        <total_cost>3600</total_cost>
    </purchase-order>
```

Now, we can also use ASP that runs on an NT Server to access a database and extract and create an XML document. Here is where the real beauty of XML comes in. We access the data, then create a Purchase Order page, download that page to the browser, let the user modify the data, and then with a click, update the server. You can also display this data in many different ways, or hand it off to other applications for further processing.

Basic XML Rules

As with everything programmers have to do, XML also works best if you create your document using a few basic rules. The XML format is simpler than HTML, but that doesn't mean you should be sloppy.

Start tags and end tags must match.

XML, like HTML, contains tags (or elements) which can in turn contain text and other elements according to the exact rules for a specific document type given in its schema. However, elements must be strictly nested—each start tag must have a corresponding end tag.

Elements can't overlap.

If you have sub elements, their end tag must occur within the parent elements' start and end tags. The following example does not adhere to proper XML syntax:

```
<title>10 Projects You Can Do with Microsoft SQL Server 7<sub>Today
and in the New Millennium</title> by Karen Watterson et al</sub>
```

The following syntax corrects the overlap problem:

```
<title>10 Projects You Can Do with Microsoft SQL Server 7<sub>Today
and in the New Millennium</sub> <author>by Karen Watterson et
al</author>
</title>
```

XML tags are case-sensitive.

Just like Java and JavaScript, XML tags are case sensitive which means that the *case* of a tag must be observed when using an end tag. For example,

```
<Title><title><TITLE>
```

are considered three separate tags.

Continues

XML *(Continued)*

Reserved characters.

Several characters are part of the syntactic structure of XML and will not be interpreted as themselves if placed within an XML data source. You need to substitute a special character sequence (called an *entity* by XML). Once again, case matters (see Table 11.1).

Table 11.1 XML's Case-Sensitive Entities

SYMBOL	ENTITY
<	<
&	&
>	>
"	"
'	'

Each XML document must have a unique root element.

For instance, in the purchase order example, the element <purchase-order> denotes the unique root element of the XML document.

XML Data Islands

A *data island* is an XML document that exists within an HTML page. One advantage to using an XML document within a page is that you can run scripts against the document without having to load the document. Almost anything that can be in an XML document can also be inside a data island.

The XML element is used to create the data island, and the ID attribute combined with the <XML> tag identifies a name used to reference the data island—XML ID.

The XML for a data island can be either inline, like this:

```
<XML ID="XMLID">
  <customer>
    <name>Microsoft Corporation</name>
    <custID>7404</custID>
  </customer>
</XML>
```

or referenced through a SRC attribute on the XML tag like this:

```
<XML ID="XMLID" SRC="customer.xml"></XML>
```

Continues

And finally, just like VBScript or JavaScript, you can also use the script tag to create a data island:

```
<SCRIPT LANGUAGE="xml" ID="XMLID">
  <customer>
    <name>Microsoft Corporation</name>
    <custID>7404</custID>
  </customer>
</SCRIPT>
```

An XML *document object* is created when an XML data island is loaded and parsed. What is an XML document object? It's an object that contains properties and methods just like any VB or Java object. Using these properties or methods, you can access and manipulate an XML document.

Manipulating the Data Island

Here is a simple HTML page with a data island. The data island is contained within the XML tag element.

```
<html>
  <head>
    <title>A Simple XML Data Island Example </title>
  </head>
  <body>
    <p>Apartment Listing for Collin County</p>
    <XML ID="xml_apartment_listing">
      <apartment_buildings>
        <apartment>Hunters Hill</apartment>
        <apartment>AMLI of North Dallas</apartment>
     <apartment>Deerfield Run</apartment>
     <apartment>The Colony</apartment>
      </apartment_buildings>
    </XML>
  </body>
</html>
```

You can access the data island through the defined ID attribute, xml_apartment_listing, which becomes the name of the document object. Since the object is defined you can now use the properties and methods of this xml_apartment_listing to access the child nodes and return that node's. For example, the <apartment_buildings> tag defines the child nodes collection, and the <apartment> tag defines each sub element. So to return the name of the second apartment building (AMLI of North Dallas), we would use the following syntax:

```
' Retrieve the apartments
xml_apartment_listing.XMLDocument.documentElement.childNodes(1).Text
```

Continues

XML *(Continued)*

How Do I Create XML Files?

For Visual Basic or ASP developers, you can create an XML document programmatically using the following syntax:

```
Dim mDoc As DOMDocument

' Create the XML document
Set mDoc = CreateObject("Microsoft.XMLDOM")
```

For those ASP developers, just drop the type definition of mDoc. You must also add a reference to the Microsoft XML Version 2.0 object. In order to see this object, you need to have IE5 installed.

Where Does BizTalk Fit In?

While XML is an industry standard, BizTalk is a Microsoft-led initiative that defines a framework for developing specialized vertical market XML schemas. Part of the framework is a public repository of these specialized schemas. You can find out which industries have developed BizTalk schemas at www.biztalk.com.

There are a host of resources about XML. Some of our favorites include www.xml.org, www/icc/ie/xml, and msdn.microsoft.com/voices/xml.asp.

Project Two: Building a Web Storefront with Site Server Commerce Edition

For this sample application, we'll use the product data in the Adventure Works Microsoft Access database that ships with IIS. The first thing to do is to create an empty SQL Server database to store all of the data used by the storefront (see Chapter 2 for more information on this). This includes product data, customer data, order data, and promotional data. You don't need to worry about creating any tables or other objects for this database, as the Site Builder Wizard will generate a schema for you. In this example, we call the database Adventure*L*ine Virtual Store (A*L*VS).

After you create the database, you'll need to create a system DSN for it. To create a new system DSN:

1. Open the Control Panel.
2. Select ODBC32 (ODBC Data Sources if no 16 bit drivers are installed).
3. Click on the System tab.
4. Click Add.

5. Follow the Wizard to create a System DSN for SQL Server.
6. Name the DSN, ALVS_Store.

Figure 11.12 shows the ODBC Data Source Administrator configuring a new system DSN.

LESSONS LEARNED

- **Remember to test your store from a variety of browsers, including the two most-recent AOL browsers. There are a lot of AOL users out there.**
- **Avoid using Java on the client side if you need to support a variety of browsers.**
- **Some payment systems don't support rollback. Test, test, test.**

Creating and Configuring A Virtual Root

The next step is to create a Virtual Directory under IIS to host the e-commerce site. To make our lives just a little easier, Microsoft Site Server Commerce Edition provides a browser-based tool called the Site Foundation Wizard. To start the wizard, type:

```
Http://ServerName/SiteServer/Admin/Commerce
```

Next, click on the Server Administration link, which can be found in the left frame. This will start the Server Administration tool. Figure 11.13 shows the Server Administration page.

Click on the Create button and we're on our way. In the next window you'll be asked to select a currently installed Web site to host your new site. For this example, select the default Web site. Then click Next.

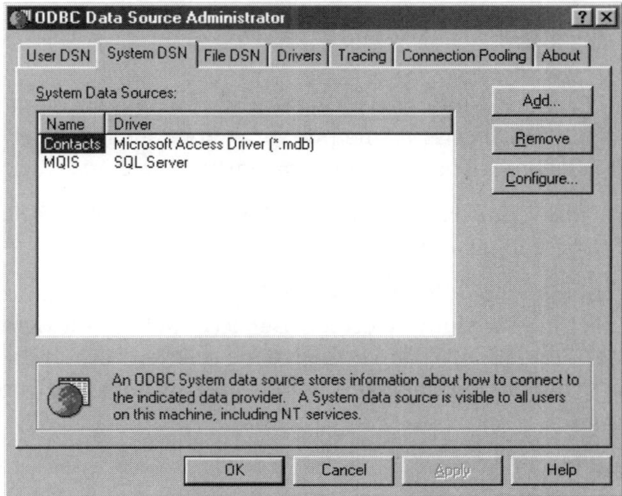

Figure 11.12 The ODBC Data Source Administrator.

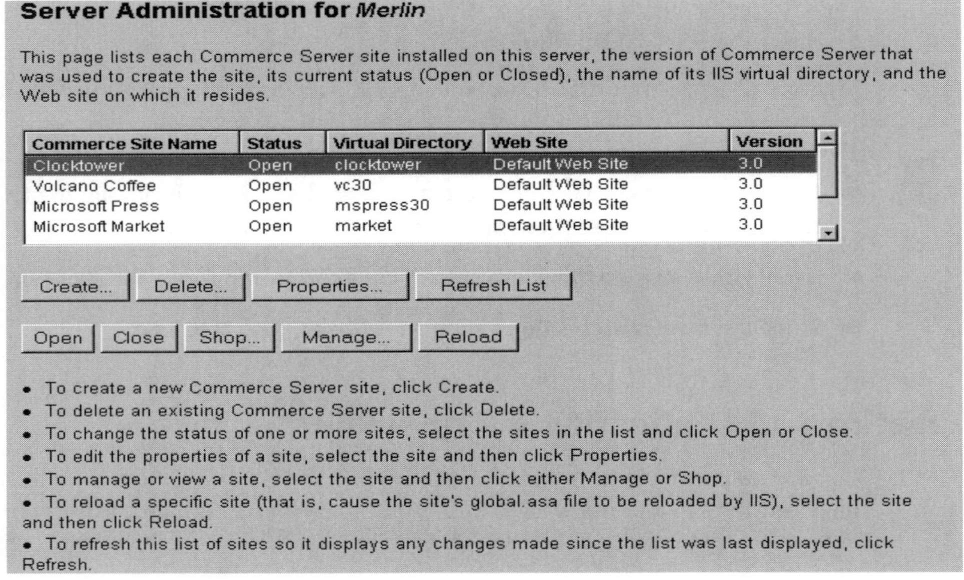

Figure 11.13 The Commerce Server administration page.

In the next frame, you'll be asked for both a short and long name for your storefront. The short name is used for naming the directories and database tables and therefore must be unique. Existing sites are displayed in a list on the right-hand side so you don't need to worry about remembering which names are taken. The long name is for descriptive purposes. Type in:

```
Short Name: ALVS_Store
Display Name: Adventure Line Virtual Store
```

Then click Next.

In the Select a Directory Location window, type in the physical path for the storefront's files. The default physical directory is c:\inetpub\wwwroot\alvs_store. This is the physical directory that will actually be mapped to the virtual directory. Click Next.

In the Formulate a Database Connection String window, select the ALVS_Store DSN, and then supply the database login and password. Click Next.

The last step is to determine who will administer this particular site. You do this by identifying a Windows NT user account. Select the user account from the displayed list and click Next. The Site Foundation Wizard will give the selected account the permissions to modify the site's content. Run the Store Manager application, and perform any other administrative tasks.

The way that the Site Foundation Wizard accomplishes this is to create a new group in the NT security. The group is named Commerce_sitename_1 (Commerce_ALVS_Store_1). The selected account is then added to this group and the group Access Control List (ACL) is modified to give this group full access to the site's directory.

Once you click the Finish button, the Site Foundation Wizard uses this information to create the IIS virtual root directory and to bring up a page with a hyperlink to the custom Site Manager application. From the Site Manager application, we can now run the Site Builder Wizard. Ready?

Using the Site Builder Wizard to Create the Adventure Line Virtual Store

The *Site Builder Wizard (SBW)*, shown in Figure 11.14 is a great tool from Microsoft—one that helps automate what could be a very complex and tedious process for creating an online store. However, like most code generators, the Site Builder Wizard should only be run once. If you generate a site more than once, you risk overwriting changes that you may have already made to the site. The Site Builder Wizard creates the following items:

- ASP scripts for both the storefront and the manager applications.
- Order processing pipeline files including the Plan pipeline, the Product pipeline, and the Purchase pipeline.
- A SQL Script to build the schema for your site's database.

In our example, we'll create a custom site. However, we do recommend that you spend some time looking over the sample sites that come with Site Server Commerce Edition. Start the Site Builder Wizard and select Create a Custom Site. Fill in the contact information and any other information that you may wish in the description field.

When you move to the next page you'll want to define a style for your site. You can specify the navigation bar type (horizontal or vertical), font, buttons styles, and colors. Check the Use Logo check box. This will put a placeholder logo on the site that you can

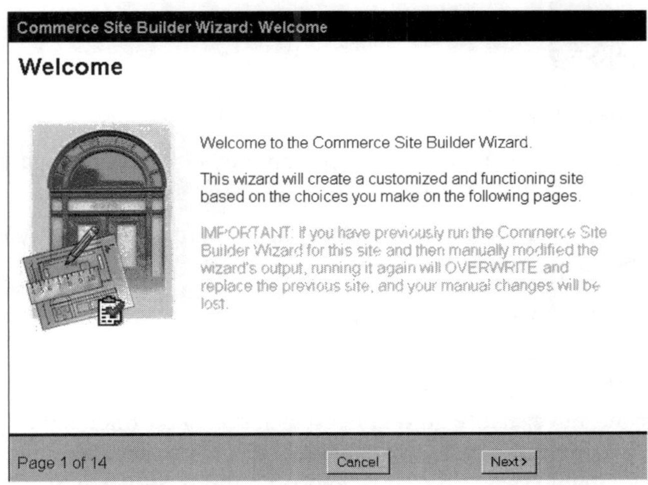

Figure 11.14 The Site Builder Wizard.

replace with your own later. In general, you can modify any, and all attributes set by SBW by simply opening the ASP scripts and changing them. Click Next.

In the next window, tell SBW whether or not you want promotions built into your storefront. There are two types of promotions: *price promotions* and *cross promotions*.

1. **Price Promotions.** A price promotion is a type of promotion that ties a discount for a product to the purchase of a certain quantity of another product. The classic example for this can be found in the supermarket. If you purchase two boxes of Oreos, you receive a dollar off a gallon of milk.
2. **Cross Promotion.** This promotion is a bit more complicated; it actually uses data-mining technology developed by Microsoft (see Chapter 14). The objective is to get the shopper to buy not just one item, but a series of other items that are related to the primary item. A prime example is buying a car. When you buy a car, you get a perfectly functional automobile. However, a cross promotion would try to get you to buy additional, related items such as chrome wheels, leather seats, a GPS receiver, and so on.

For the purposes of this example we'll skip using promotions, but you can find out more about them at msdn.microsoft.com/workshop/server/commerce/promotions101.asp. Click Next.

The next window provides options for shopper registration, department type, and product searching. Registration includes three types:

1. None. No shopper registration capabilities will be built into the site.
2. On Entry. Each time a new user enters the site they will be required to register. Then when they return they must log in.
3. When Ordering. A new user may enter and browse the site to their hearts content, but when they finally decide to buy something they must complete a profile or log on.

Select When Ordering

A *department type* defines a level for each product. There are two types of departments:

1. Simple. One level deep. This department type can only contain products and not other departments.
2. Variable Depth. Supports multiple levels. A department may have many items and may have other departments within it.

For this sample site, we only want to use Simple.

The final entry on this screen is *product searching*. The concept of product searching is key to any truly commercial site with a large number of products. Simple sites that contain only a few products and never really go that deep as far as departments may not need searching. However, even in those cases, we consider search functionality a requirement for today's Web sites. Enable searching via Microsoft's Index Server which "indexes" keywords about the products on your site, thereby allowing for searching against this "Indexed" database. Click Next.

The next screen asks you about *product attributes*. Product attributes are the features that define a product such as color and size. There are two basic types of attributes: *static* and *dynamic*. Static attributes are for sites that sell products that all have the same identifying characteristics such as an analyst report or a hardback book. A good example is a software company that sells only a few products. The product line is small and definitive and makes a good case for having a static set of attributes. However, in our example we'll be selling clothing with variable attributes such as color and size. Click Next.

If you selected dynamic (and you should have), you'll be presented with a page that requests the maximum number of multi-valued attributes per product. What's a *multi-valued attribute*? Something like color or size. For this example enter 5. Click Next.

The next page is where you enter any shipping and handling rules such as overnight shipping for $15.00. This shipping and handling rule is only applied to orders that did not use the standard shipping method, but instead chose rush delivery. Handling charges are charges incurred as a result of having to prepare a product in some manner. For this example, check Enabled on the first Shipping method, enter Overnight and add a cost of $15.00. Click Next.

The next page applies to tax rates for residents of various states. In most cases you are only required to charge tax to residents of the same state, or states, that you hold tax certificates. For example, Adventure Lines Virtual Store is located in Texas, so check Enabled, select TX, and then enter a rate of 8 percent. Click Next.

Now we get to the fun page, Payment Methods. We are greedy and we want to take every credit card. Select them all and click Next.

The next page presented is the Order History Page. Depending on how, and even if you wish to profile your customers you may or may not decide to retain order history and receipt information on your customers. (Most sites do retain the customer data in order to use it for CRM or data mining at some point in the future.) In almost all cases, we recommend that you keep order history. Check the Retain Order History option then click Next.

You are now at the final frame of the Site Builder Wizard. This page simply displays all of the tasks that are about to be performed by the wizard. The wizard will generate ASP scripts for the store and manager sites, pipeline files for order processing, and SQL Scripts for the database. Uncheck the Load Sample Data into Database option. We'll use the Adventure Works Access database and import it into our site. Click Finish, and let the fun begin! We have now completed generating the site. You can view your handiwork by pointing your browser to:

```
http://server_name/ALVS_Store
```

At this point, you still have to add the actual product data such as price, sizes, and graphics into the site's database. A script is available for you to automatically import sample data into Microsoft SQL Server. In the case of a production site, you would have to decide whether or not to use the company's "main" inventory database live, or just a copy of it.

Index Server

Microsoft Index Server 2.0 is a BackOffice product that allows you to integrate document-searching functionality into your Web sites. Index Server provides a means of indexing—compiling a list of keywords for documents and other files.

With Index Server, you can index HTML files, files created by the various Microsoft Office applications, Network News Transfer Protocol (NNTP) stores, and include an API that allows you to create custom filters to index other file types.

In addition to a file's content, Index Server will also index its metadata for Microsoft Office documents. Metadata is stored as OLE Structured Storage document properties, and for HTML documents, as META tags. What does this mean? This allows you to create search scripts that will perform content searches as well as metadata (or document property) searches.

Index Server performs a "near real-time" indexing of documents. In other words, Index Server will continuously monitor the file system for changes (similar to FindFast in Windows, only it's a lot less annoying). Once a change occurs, Index Server will update the index information about the document in its catalog.

An *Index Server catalog* is a collection of rather large files with cryptic file names stored in a directory called Catalog.wci. The exact location of this catalog depends on how you installed and configured Index Server, but it's usually located in the C:\INetPub directory.

The easiest and perhaps the most common way to create an Index Server search engine for your site is to write an IDQ script and companion HTX template. IDQ scripts are simple Index Server queries—ASCII text files that are saved with an .IDQ file extension and executed by an ISAPI filter called idq.dll.

When an IDQ script is executed, Index Server retrieves the search results and merges them with the HTX template that's then streamed back to the browser.

One of the disadvantages of IDQ scripts and HTX templates is that they're rather primitive in the amount of logic you can code into them. To get around this problem, Microsoft provides a COM object (ixsso.Query) that you can use within an ASP script or any other COM client. This allows you to write infinitely more sophisticated Index Server search scripts, and still retain the familiar IDQ syntax.

Although we're getting a little ahead of ourselves, you'll probably also want to figure out how to do banner ads. Read a good white paper at msdn.microsoft.com/workshop/server/comerce/promotions101.asp.

Secure Shopping with Microsoft Wallet and the Microsoft Passport Service

The Adventure Line Virtual Store is now ready for shopping. All sites created with the Site Builder Wizard integrate support for Microsoft Wallet. Configuring your site to accept payment and address information from Microsoft Wallet is one of the easiest ways to make shopping convenient and secure for your customers.

The Microsoft Wallet ships with IE 4.0 and is also available for free for Netscape Navigator 3.x and above and IE 3.02a and above. The Wallet simplifies the checkout and purchase process for each customer by storing the frequently used address information (e.g. Jon Kilburn, Vivd Software, and so on) and payment information (such as Visa, MasterCard, AMEX, and so on) and using this information during the purchase process. It's easy to enable any commerce site with the Wallet Webmaster Kit. This kit is free from Microsoft at www.passport.com/business/wallet services.asp.

The downside of Microsoft Wallet is that it takes a long time to download when a shopper initially installs it on his machine, especially the Netscape plug-in version, which does not use Authenticode technology for seamless installation within the browser environment. This might be a "point of friction" for an impatient shopper, especially if he is shopping your site via a dial-up analog modem connection.

Another spin on the Microsoft Wallet is a new service from Microsoft is called the Microsoft Passport Wallet Service. This service is simple and easy to use. Microsoft Passport simplifies consumers' online experience by allowing them to create a single "wallet," member name, and password, which can be used at participating Passport Web sites and services.

The Passport wallet service is easy to implement. It uses standard HTTP and SSL to "POST" form data to your site. Since it server-based, no special software is needed for your site or for your customers. Also, the wallet service supports the Electronic Commerce Modeling Language (ECML) industry standard e-commerce schema developed by Microsoft, Visa, American Express, MasterCard, and others. A consumer activates the service by clicking a wallet button or link on the merchant site, and then he or she selects a stored card and address and sends the selected information to the merchant.

Customer Security

Site Server Commerce Edition 3.0 provides a secure environment for customers who wish to purchase goods from the Internet. It's important to recognize that customers may be a bit hesitant about buying goods or services from the Web, and so Site Server Commerce Edition provides several strategies for the protection of customer information.

Secure Socket Layer (SSL). SSL is a method of data encryption that resides between the transport and the socket layer of the TCP/IP protocol stack, and is used to secure, that is encrypt, transactions between the client and the server. When a customer submits personal information such as a credit card number using a form or the Microsoft Wallet, the ASP page that retrieves the data should be secured using SSL. The client—the customer's browser—and server—your commerce site—communicate and share the data via an encryption key that is generated by the browser. This encryption key is transferred to the server using the server's public key.

The Microsoft Wallet for Securing Personal Information. Microsoft Wallet also provides an excellent security layer by encrypting the payment data stored on a customer's computer. The Microsoft Wallet requires a password for accessing the credit card information stored within the wallet. Address data is never sent without the customer's approval.

Microsoft Wallet and Secure Electronic Transactions (SET). When using a payment provider that is SET compliant (an industry standard secure payment specification), you can encrypt transactions between your Site Server Commerce Edition 3.0 site and the acquiring financial institution. Numerous payment software providers are developing SET-compliant components that work with Microsoft Wallet and Site Server Commerce Edition, but, as we mentioned earlier, SET is more popular abroad than it is in the US. You can find the most up-to-date listings on the Microsoft Site Server Partners Web site at www.microsoft.com/siteserver.

The Microsoft Wallet helps shoppers purchase items quickly, easily, and securely at their favorite online stores. In addition, merchants can benefit from an enhanced shopper experience through increased sales and shopper traffic at Web store sites. The Microsoft Wallet facilitates electronic transactions using Address Selector and Payment Selector. The *Address Selector* and *Payment Selector* are available as plug-ins for site visitors who use Netscape Navigator and as ActiveX controls for site visitors who use IE4 or IE5.

Address Selector

The Address Selector stores users' personal and business addresses securely on their computer. To add an address, a user completes a dialog box with business or personal address information that is stored according to a display name or nickname. Shoppers at merchant Web sites that support the Microsoft Wallet can select addresses from the Address Selector by their display name, without having to fill out a series of merchant HTML forms. Wallet ensures security by storing this information in an encrypted, pasword-protected file on the local file system. The Address information is only released to the merchant if the user clicks OK in an Address Security dialog box.

The Address Selector is fully integrated with the Windows Address Book (WAB), if the WAB is on the user's computer. Clicking the Address Book button of the Address Selector allows users to select from addresses in their Windows Address Book and add them to the Address Selector. The ten most recently selected addresses are displayed in a drop-down list in the Address Manager. Users can access any other addresses by clicking the "All" addresses button, which displays a dialog box that lists all other addresses in the Wallet storage.

USING WALLET ON AN E-COMMERCE SITE

When using Microsoft Wallet on an e-commerce site, you must *always* give your shoppers the option to provide registration information via a regular HTML form. Relying solely on Microsoft Wallet to collect shopper information will most likely result in lost sales for your Web storefront.

Payment Selector

Users can complete online transactions using the Payment Selector to choose a type of payment. The Payment Selector currently contains the VISA, MasterCard, JCB (only in Japan), American Express, and Discover (only in North America) payment types. Other third-party payment providers are developing payment types that extend the Microsoft Wallet payment platform. Third-party payment types range from a bank debit card to an electronic cash card. In addition, merchants who want to offer branded credit cards can easily write components to plug into the Payment Selector interface. The Payment Selector can store any number of credit card types.

The Payment Selector Add Wizard guides Wallet users through establishing a new credit card by entering credit-card information, providing a billing address, and assigning a password to the credit card. The credit-card information is encrypted and stored in the Wallet-protected storage on the client computer.

If a merchant site supports Microsoft Wallet, shoppers can quickly and easily select their preferred type of payment from the Payment Selector without having to complete HTML forms for billing and credit card information. The ten credit cards most recently used are displayed in a drop-down list. The remainder of credit cards in the Wallet are displayed by clicking the All payment types button. Payment information is stored securely on the client computer and released to the merchant only if the user enters the credit card password to approve the purchase amount.

SINGLE PAYMENT SELECTORS PROTECT YOUR CARDS

A single Payment Selector can store credit cards owned by different people because each credit card is protected from improper use by a password assigned by the card-holder.

The Wallet SDK provides the tools for third parties to extend the Microsoft payment platform with their payment types. The SDK contains the following sample code and documentation so that third-party payment providers can develop payment extensions:

- Sample code for credit-card components
- Sample code for third-party payment types
- Sample code for Credit Card Payment Builders
- Sample install .cab files for payment type distribution
- Interface technical references
- Complete documentation that describes how to build and distribute payment types to extend the Microsoft payment platform

These controls facilitate an electronic purchase at a merchant Web site. Aside from providing a convenient method of posting shopper information to a merchant site, the Microsoft Wallet provides the most secure environment for storing credit-card information.

A Payment Selector client payment component (CPC) object implements a payment method. A payment method is a credit card, or electronic cash debit cards, or even an electronic check. The Credit Card CPC that ships with the Microsoft Wallet contains several default payment types, such as Visa, MasterCard, and so on.

A Payment Selector client payment component (CPC) object implements a payment method. A payment method is a credit card, or electronic cash debit card, or even an electronic check. The Credit Card CPC that ships with the Microsoft Wallet contains several default payment types, such as Visa, MasterCard, and so on.

Using the Wallet SDK, you can create and support your own CPC payment methods. You can also create new payment types (such as a department store card like Sears or Dillards, or even your own Credit Card) that plug into the default Credit Card CPC. Shoppers can then add, delete, or edit instances of this new payment type in the same way they manage the default payment types. Because there are many varied types of credit cards, this payment type is referred to as the Other Card.

The Protected Store

Microsoft's *Protected Store*, which is a component of Internet Explorer, supports securely storing important, private information such as credit cards, electronic driver's licenses, ATM cards, and electronic cash. The Protected Store stores this information so that no one can access this information without the user's permission. In addition, the Protected Store allows this information to be securely transmitted to any computer and used with any application through the use of PFX technology.

Microsoft Wallet is designed so that if Internet Explorer is installed on a system, payment control data is automatically migrated to the Protected Store.

That wraps up our quick tour of Site Server Commerce Edition. Even if you were not able to follow along hands-on for this project, you're probably feeling pretty overwhelmed. Site Server and Site Server Commerce Edition are both extremely powerful applications—applications that keep evolving. However, there is one third-party product that we'd like to introduce because it makes setting up an e-commerce site even easier than SBW.

VisualCommerce Constructor

What is VisualCommerce Constructor? It's a wizard-based application that automatically generates fully-integrated Microsoft Site Server Commerce Edition/SQL Server based e-commerce sites. VisualCommerce Constructor (hereafter, Constructor) targets mid-sized firms and can save hundreds of hours of development time by generating the fundamental features required by most mid-sized businesses, that is firms with over 500 SKUs. Because of its open architecture, developers can customize and extend the base solution for future requirements. Additionally, Constructor delivers the following:

- Allows the user to set order status.
- Integrates with Commerce Server's pipelines.
- Builds and configures the SQL Server database.

- Builds a complete, robust store manager application.
- Generates attractive, customizable ASP storefronts.

The Interaction of an Online Purchase

Authorization, capture, and refund are the most common operations that your Web site must support in order to accept credit cards. It's important to note that merchants must pay transaction fees for each operation to the processor. Transaction fees vary according to volume and other factors.

Authorization. This operation takes place when you first process a customer's credit card. It involves the merchant, the software gateway, and the processor. The authorization does not transfer the funds to the merchant account at this point: It just places a hold on the customer's credit card for a specific amount with the merchant's ID. This hold usually lasts no longer than a week. During this period, the merchant must either fulfill the order and perform a capture or re-authorize the amount if the time expires before the order is shipped. Depending on the processor and the software vendor this re-authorization is performed automatically, but it may also mean another transaction charge for the merchant.

Capture. As soon as you confirm that the goods are being shipped, you can send a capture request to the processor. The capture operation involves the merchant, the software gateway, and the bank. The processor evaluates the authorization information and completes the transaction. For digital goods such as software, information access, and immediately-accessible online subscriptions, it is common to authorize and capture at the same time. However, for non-digital goods, the capture must take place only after the goods are shipped. There is a small caveat: if an order has several items and only some of them have been shipped, you can capture only the goods that have been shipped. This process is also known as a partial capture. It means that only part of the funds have been transferred. Depending on your processor, you may have to re-authorize the remaining amount due in order to capture the goods that have not yet been shipped.

Refund. This is the reverse of the capture process and involves the merchant, the software gateway, the processor, and the bank. There are several reasons that this operation may need to occur, including the return of items, order cancellation, and captured order adjustments. It usually requires that you provide the original authorization number and the refunded amount. The processor will then reverse the funds from the merchant to the client.

Depending on your choice of credit-card software, you may have other services provided for each operation. Most of these services have to do with fraud detection and credit-card address verification. These extra services are also based on service fees and on per-transaction usage.

Constructor, like Site Server, generates two applications: the e-commerce store and a store manager application. However, Constructor's store manager application is more targeted than Site Server's Administration site. The following features are included in stores built by Constructor:

- Customer registration
- Credit card processing
- Stock status
- Full order tracking detail, including order history, confirmation, back order status, and lookups
- Cross-sell and up-sell promotions that are more sophisticated than the ones included with Commerce Server 3.0
- Full invoicing section
- Full reporting

In our opinion, the Store Manager application is the major value add of Constructor, since it automates many routine management functions, eliminating the need to custom develop reports and entry forms. This contributes to reducing the overall development cycle even further. The developer can turn over data maintenance functions by giving store management personnel instantaneous access to their data.

Installing the Constructor Evaluation Version from the CD-ROM

In order to use Constructor, site builders must have a fully-configured server running the Microsoft Commerce Platform (Windows NT, IIS 4.0, MTS, SQL Server 7 or 6.5, and Site Server 3.0 Commerce Edition). Constructor must be installed on a machine with FrontPage 98. If you have trouble, you may want to check the VisualCommerce Knowledge Base located in the Support section of www.visualcommerce.com.

Included on the CD-ROM is the Evaluation version of VisualCommerce Constructor 1.5. Insert the CD into your CD drive and open Explorer. Next select the VisualCommerce Constructor directory. Click on the Setup icon. The rest of the setup is fairly standard, with a licensing screen, and so on.

After you agree to the license agreement, you'll see a User Information screen (shown in Figure 11.15). You must supply a user name, company name, and serial number to proceed to the next step in the installation. Enter Trial as the serial number (unless you have a real one). *Under no circumstances is the store built with the evaluation copy or Constructor code to be engaged for development or for commercial use: You must purchase a developer version and/or store license.*

The next screen is the Check Setup Information screen. The user can review the simple installation options selected. Clicking the Next button finishes the installation by copying the appropriate files to their correct places on the user's machine and registers any necessary files. You'll then be required to restart your PC.

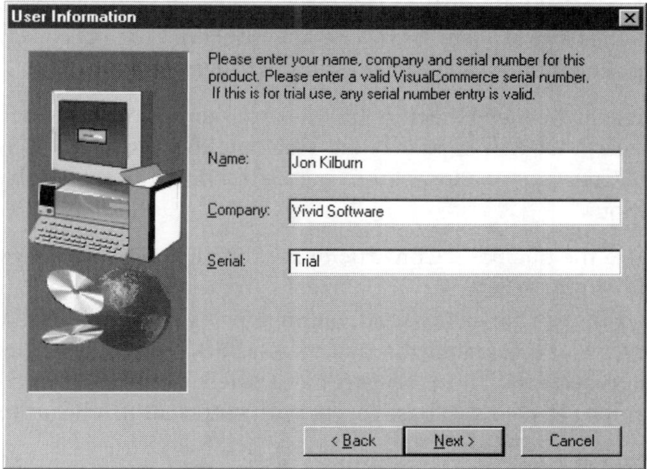

Figure 11.15 User Information screen.

Building an E-Commerce Site Using Constructor

Open Microsoft FrontPage 98. In FrontPage Explorer you should go to File, New, and FrontPage Web. If FrontPage is not running, Constructor will detect that it is not and start it for you. Then from the Getting Started dialog box, select Create New FrontPage Web and click OK. Figure 11.16 shows what FrontPage will then request of you:

1. Choose the kind of FrontPage Web to create. Select From Wizard or Template, and then choose VisualCommerce Constructor 1.5.

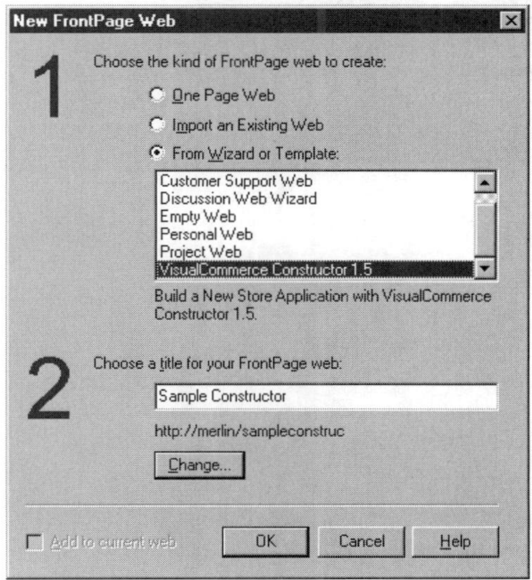

Figure 11.16 Creating a new VisualCommerce Constructor site using FrontPage.

2. Choose a title for your FrontPage Web. The chosen title will be the URL for the store. Limit the name to 15 alphanumeric characters. Do not use special characters, such as the pound symbol (#), percent symbol (%), and so on.

FrontPage will then create the Web Directory (in this case sampleconstruc on the server Merlin). The next screen that will appear is the Welcome to Constructor screen. The evaluator's version of Constructor allows for five store builds. After the five builds, the wizard will not function.

Now we need to create the database. Constructor will create a new SQL Server database and automatically find the SQL Server databases on the user's network. Select the drop-down arrow and choose the database server on which you want to build data for the new store. After you have created the database, select Login (see Figure 11.17). Enter the appropriate username and password, and select OK. Note that you must have a login name on the selected database server with sufficient privileges to create a new database.

You're now ready to begin to enter the data that will appear on your store. You'll be asked to enter information into the screens represented by three tabs: Store Application Display, Address Details, and Contact Details. The default tab is the Store Application Display tab. Fill in all of the appropriate fields, then move through each tab (see Figure 11.18).

Constructor 1.5 offers two templates—a simple one and an advanced one. Both templates generate B2C sites, and both feature the Store Manager application that comes with Constructor 1.5. The simple template features fewer graphics, a simpler layout, and caters to the HTML-experienced developer who seeks a foundation but will extensively customize the site. The advanced template has a much more sophisticated layout and is suitable for a developer who wants to quickly build a professional quality store without doing a lot of HTML work.

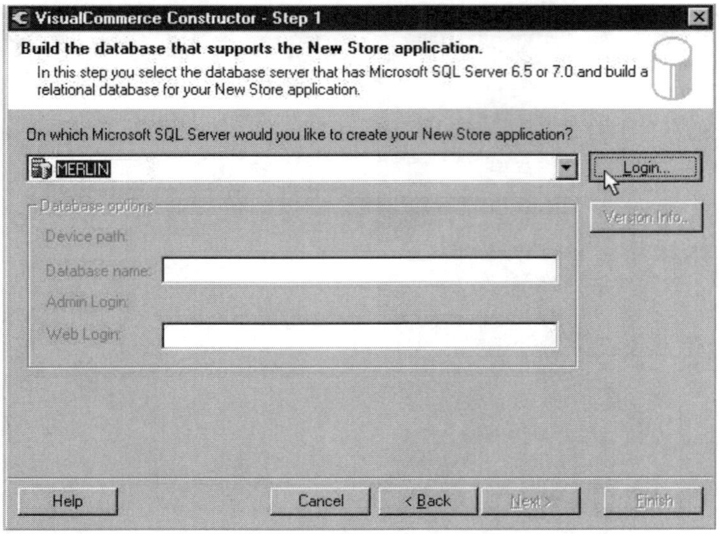

Figure 11.17 Select the SQL Server database.

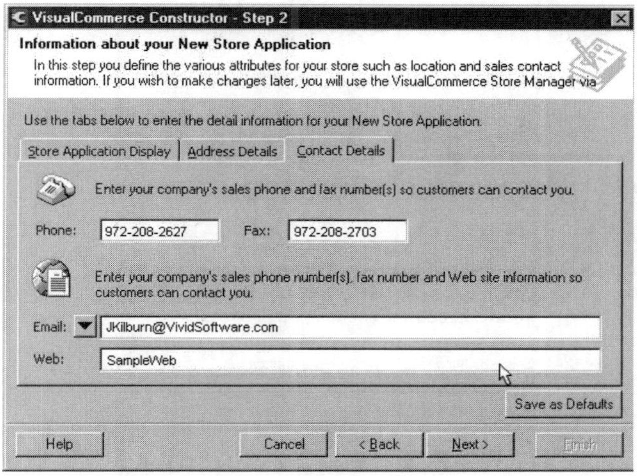

Figure 11.18 Information dialog.

Select the Advanced Template and then click Next. This will bring us to the Pipeline Configuration. The pipeline is one of the defining characteristics of Site Server and the Microsoft Site Server Commerce Edition platform. The advantage of an Order Processing Pipeline like Site Server's is that it separates the custom business requirements from the code of the store. This allows customization and editing of the business process behind the store without editing the code of the ASP pages.

In the dialog the site builder can choose the configuration that matches the requirements of his or her store. First, the site builder must decide if they want Canadian or US tax support. Then, they must decide if they want Simple or Integrated payment. The Integrated payment system includes the CyberCash component to validate credit cards. The Simple payment system checks the credit card number, but doesn't actually process the credit card. The site builder needs to use a third-party component or Microsoft Wallet to complete credit-card transactions. Choose Simple United States Commerce from the list of available options (Figure 11.19).

You're now ready to review the information that you've just entered for the database—store information, template choice, and pipeline configuration. You cannot edit information displayed on this screen. If this information is incorrect then use the Back button to change any choices, otherwise when you are satisfied with the information that you've entered, select Next. This will bring up the finished screen. Select Finish to generate the site.

Once the user clicks the Finish button, Constructor begins the process of building the store. The process takes a few minutes. Constructor builds the database and populates it with sample data (if requested), creates security accounts on the database and on the Web site, creates Web pages for the store, and builds the store manager.

Your store is now fully functional. Click View Summary.

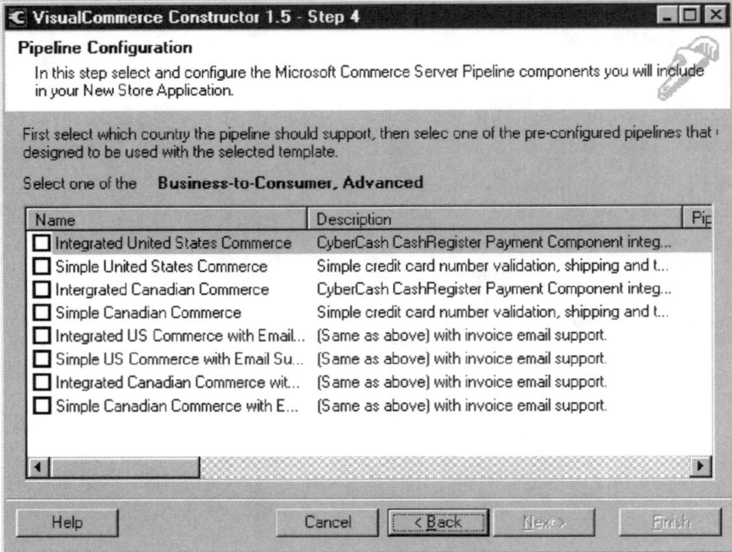

Figure 11.19 Selecting a pre-configured pipeline.

From the Summary screen, the site builder can view the new store application as shown in Figure 11.20. The URL for the store is hyperlinked. The site builder will register and provide name and address details online. Close the browser and return to the Summary screen. Click Done.

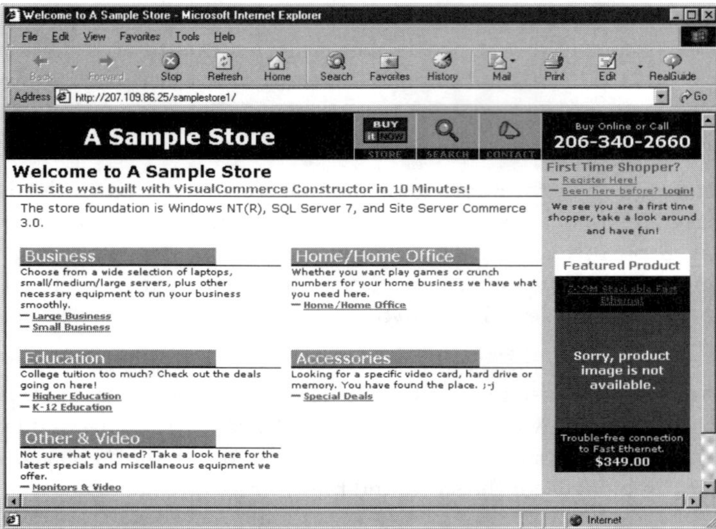

Figure 11.20 The finished sample store.

With Constructor you can create e-commerce stores that satisfy most of the feature requirements of mid-sized businesses, and then you can customize using tools like Visual InterDev. Install it and start playing with it. We think you'll be impressed.

Summary

The goal of this chapter was to explain the components and relationships that are involved in creating an e-commerce Web site that uses a SQL Server 7 backend. In addition, we wanted to reduce the time it takes to implement your own e-commerce site by giving you the code that we used to create the sample site used in this chapter. If you have read this chapter and examined the code on the CD, you should be prepared to embark on your first e-commerce Web site. Web development is a lot of fun and implementing a simple e-commerce site is not that difficult. So, why don't you start thinking about how you can make a little money and have some fun at the same time? As retired Intel CEO Andy Grove said on September 21, 1999, when addressing the Confederation of British Industry in London, "In some years time, there will be no such thing as Internet business—because all businesses will be using the Internet in their operations." That pretty much sums it up. Learn e-commerce. As the *Forbes* headline said, it's "online or the bread line."

CHAPTER 12

Project #9: Encapsulating Business Logic with Stored Procedures and Triggers

Goal

The goal of this chapter is to demonstrate how to use T-SQL to encapsulate business logic in stored procedures and triggers. In other words, we want to show you how to convert business logic that's derived from an end user's specifications into T-SQL that is contained in stored procedures and triggers.

YOU WILL NEED

- ✔ Microsoft SQL Server 7, including the Pubs and Northwind databases
- ✔ WorkOrd database found on the accompanying CD-ROM

Optional:

- ✔ Visual Basic 5 or later

One of our main objectives when designing or modifying a software application is to ensure that the different processes that the system performs occur on the right "part" of the system. The idea that a system has different "parts" may be foreign to those of you who have only been exposed to PC database systems like Access or FoxPro, but read on and you will quickly see the benefit of segmenting processes.

A common use for PC databases is to have a shared database on the network with a local copy of the application code on each PC that uses the system. The code is separate from the database so that the data manipulation occurs in the client application—the database simply acts as a container for that data. Therefore, when you look for a particular record within a table you can grab all of the records in that table (or open up a recordset on the table) and loop through the key fields until you locate the target record. This approach certainly works, but isn't very efficient. In addition, you really don't get to take advantage of the server's processing power, which should certainly have more power than the clients who access it.

What if you could pass the data manipulation code to the server, let the server process the data, and then return the results? With this scenario, the system's client portion only gathers or displays the data and does not perform any data manipulation. The data manipulation code resides within the database and the clients simply access the code as needed. What if the data manipulation code is independent of the client? Can you think of any advantages that this might add to your development efforts? If the data manipulation code is truly independent and written in a format that multiple development languages can access, then developing new applications based on existing code would be a breeze.

An example may help to show how this approach can reduce development efforts. Let's say that your company develops an application with Visual Basic and SQL Server that's for internal use only. All of the data access for the application is accomplished with either data-bound controls or SQL passthrough. After the application is implemented, the feedback from the end users is so positive that management decides to package the application and sell it to companies who perform similar business operations. For argument's sake, let's say that the one thing you must do before you can market the application is to convert the Visual Basic front-end to C++ and make the data accessible to Internet browsers like Internet Explorer and Navigator.

In order to meet these requirements you must convert all of the data manipulation code that resides in the VB client to a form that can be used by the new C++ client and Internet browsers. One solution is to simply cut-and-paste the SQL passthrough statements to both front-end applications, but this is terribly time consuming and inefficient. A better way to accomplish the task is to create database-side code that can be accessed by both interfaces. This can be done by taking the business logic/data manipulation code that resides in the VB client and then transferring it to stored procedures and triggers. Of course, the real benefit is that you have not only accomplished your short-term objective of C++ and browser access, but now have a system that can support any front-end that is developed in a language that can talk to stored procedures.

What Are Stored Procedures and Triggers?

A *stored procedure* is one or more T-SQL statements that are stored as a unit for server-side execution. Stored procedures allow you to encapsulate data manipulation and business logic into a single unit of work instead of retrieving a recordset and then applying business logic on the client-side of the system. A *trigger* is a special kind of stored procedure that is associated with a table. It contains similar functionality to a stored procedure, but is "attached" to an INSERT, UPDATE, or DELETE event. In other words, the only way to activate the code in a trigger is to perform an INSERT, UPDATE, or DELETE on the table.

Central Management of Code

One of the main benefits gained from stored procedures and triggers is the central management of programming logic. This is best demonstrated by comparing how client-side data manipulation code is modified compared to server-side modifications. Let's say that you have an ASP application that uses SQL passthrough to execute the programming logic that we've shown here. Let's also assume that the code is scattered across 10 different ASP pages.

```
UPDATE Authors
SET Au_Lname = @Name
WHERE Au_ID = @Au_ID
```

If you want to change the name that is updated from Au_Lname to Au_Fname, you need to first locate the 10 places where the code is used and then make the modification. When server-side code is used, you only have to make the change in one place—within the stored procedure.

Stored Procedures to Simplify Security

Another benefit of stored procedures is the reduced effort required to implement security. Let's say that you have the following SELECT statement embedded in a client-side application.

```
SELECT a.Au_Lname + ','  + a.Au_Fname AS Name,
       b.Au_Ord,
       c.Title,
       c.Type,
       c.Price,
       d.Qty
FROM Authors a, TitleAuthor b, Titles c, Sales d
WHERE a.Au_ID = b.Au_ID AND
      b.Title_ID = c.Title_ID AND
      c.Title_ID = d.Title_ID
```

SELECT SYNTAX

Please note that the fields retrieved in the previous example have been placed on separate lines to increase readability—not because this is the required syntax. SQL Server is flexible when it comes to formatting T-SQL, so you are free to make your code as pleasing to the eye as you want. A *line continuation character,* used in many other programming languages, is not necessary.

In order to allow an end user to execute this SELECT statement, they must have the SELECT permission on the following tables: Authors, TitleAuthor, Titles, and Sales. However, if the same SELECT statement was encapsulated in a stored procedure, then the end user would only need the EXECUTE permission on the stored procedure (assuming that the ownership chain was not broken—see *Books Online's*, *Ownership Chains* topic for more information on this).

System Stored Procedures

The stored procedures we talk about in this chapter are *user-defined stored procedures*—-where a user is responsible for their content and creation. SQL Server also has another type of stored procedure called *system stored procedures*. There are quite a few system stored procedures that come with the product and all were written by the SQL Server development team.

The bulk of the system stored procedures facilitate server management by providing useful information about database objects or allowing you to more easily implement admin-related features. Most are written in T-SQL, so if you want to see some advanced coding just open one up in Query Analyzer and take a look around. They're located in the *master*, *msdb*, and *distribution* databases. Expand the Stored Procedure option in one of these databases and double-click on any of the ones that begin with sp_. Note that you will only have a distribution database if you enabled your server as a distributor for replication.

There is a special type of system stored procedure called *general extended procedures* or *extended stored procedures*. Extended stored procedures are Dynamic Link Libraries (DLLs) that allow you to extend the functionality of SQL Server. If you run across a task that cannot be handled with the inherent functionality of SQL Server, you can use a development language to create a DLL and then reference the DLL as if it were a normal stored procedure. In order to reference the DLL as a stored procedure it must be registered with the server using the system stored procedure *sp_addextendedproc*. For a listing of extended stored procedures expand the Extended Stored Procedures option in the master database.

If you want to be a SQL Server guru you need to spend some time learning about the features and functionality available with system stored procedures. For more information on system stored procedures see the *Books Online* topic, *System Stored Procedures (T-SQL)*.

NAMING CONVENTIONS

We recommend that you start the name of your stored procedures with something other than sp_. By doing so you avoid the confusion of which stored procedures come with SQL Server and which ones are written by you or other developers. If you *really* want to prefix your procedures with sp, one solution is to use sp, but leave off the underscore. Another solution, and one that we use, is to switch the letters and use ps_ as the prefix. You can also prefix your stored procedure with a subject area abbreviation such as ap for Accounts Payable.

THE ORIGIN OF STORED PROCEDURES

Sybase, from which Microsoft SQL Server was spawned (see Chapter 1), seems to be the first RDBMS vendor to support stored procedures. Informix was another pioneer—Oracle and IBM were slower to buy into the idea. Sybase's impressive TPC-B benchmarks (www.tpc.org for the Transaction Processing Council's current benchmarks) "turbo-charged" with stored procedures clearly encouraged its competition to adopt them as well. As far as formal ANSI SQL standards, Len Gallagher was the first to bring the idea to the ANSI X3H2 committee, and Andrew Eisenberg was the main architect of the ANSI SQL/PSM that describes standards for stored procedures.

How to Create, Edit, and Delete Stored Procedures

Like most of the objects in SQL Server 7, stored procedures are created with either Enterprise Manager or by executing T-SQL in Query Analyzer. We show both methods because we realize that some of you may prefer the Enterprise-Manager approach, while others will want to use T-SQL.

Creating a Stored Procedure

Creating a stored procedure is quite simple and can be accomplished with any of the following three methods:

1. Stored Procedure Editor
2. Query Analyzer
3. Stored Procedure Wizard

The Stored Procedure Editor is the most basic of the three, so we'll start there and cover the other methods later. In order to access the Stored Procedure Editor complete the following steps:

1. Expand the Server Tree.
2. Expand Pubs under the Databases option.
3. Right-click on Stored Procedures and select New Stored Procedure.

The Stored Procedure Editor is shown in Figure 12.1.

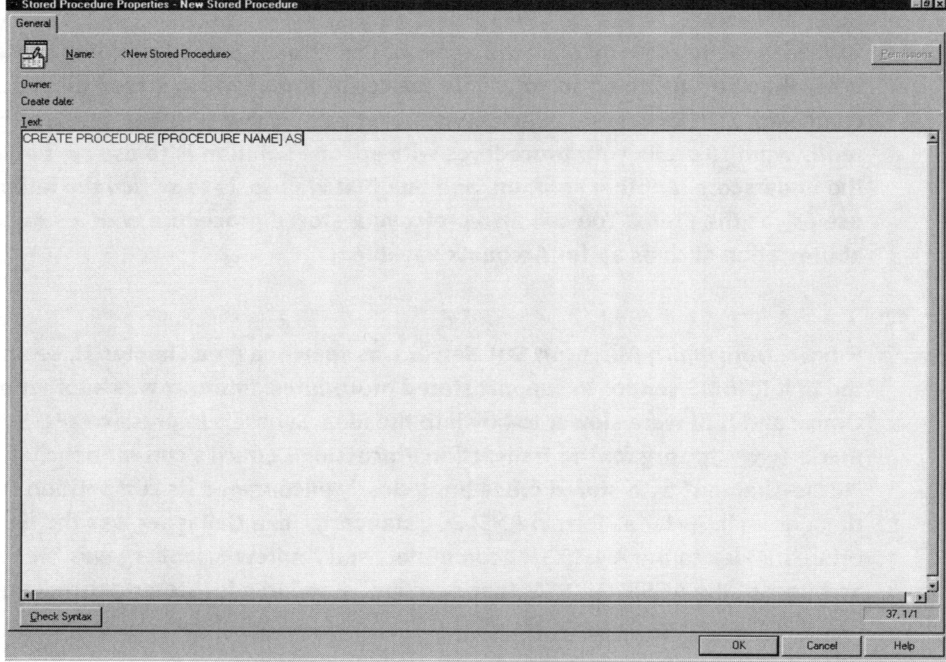

Figure 12.1 Stored Procedure Editor.

By default, the basics of the CREATE PROCEDURE command are listed in the editor. The complete syntax for creating a stored procedure is listed here:

```
CREATE PROC[EDURE] procedure_name [;number]
   [
      {@parameter data_type} [VARYING] [= default] [OUTPUT]
   ]
   [,...n]
[WITH
   {
    RECOMPILE |
    ENCRYPTION |
    RECOMPILE, ENCRYPTION
   }
]
[FOR REPLICATION]
AS
sql_statement [...n]
```

Instead of becoming bogged down in the various options, let's concentrate on the required portion of the command and cover the options later. The only parameters that you need to supply are shown in Table 12.1.

Table 12.1 Required CREATE PROCEDURE Arguments

ARGUMENT	FUNCTION
Procedure_name	128 characters using valid identifier characters
sql_statement	Any valid SQL statement(s)

The following example uses the required arguments to retrieve the system time:

```
CREATE PROCEDURE ps_Util_Select_SystemTime
AS
SELECT GETDATE()
```

The name of the stored procedure is given and the SELECT statement supplied. You should note that the syntax of the procedure name, ps_Util_Select_SystemTime, has no relevance other than that of an indicator that helps us remember the purpose of the stored procedure. We use the ps_ prefix to differentiate our stored procedures from that of other database objects; Util_ (short for utility) is used to indicate that the stored procedure does not act on a table; Select_ indicates that the main action (verb) that the stored procedure performs is a SELECT statement; and SystemTime is a comment to tell us what the stored procedure actually selects. The naming convention is completely arbitrary and can be modified to suit your needs. The naming convention for stored procedures created in this chapter will adhere to the following:

ps_TableName_ VerbIndicator_Comment

Table 12.2 provides a detailed description for each segment used in the naming convention.

It may seem like a little bit of overkill to have such detailed stored procedure names, but keep in mind that complex applications may require hundreds of stored procedures and an intuitive naming convention will allow you to better manage your server-side programming logic.

Table 12.2 Stored Procedure Naming Convention

SEGMENT	DESCRIPTION
TableName	The primary table on which the stored procedure operates. If the stored procedure does not act on a table, Util_ is used
VerbIndicator	Can be either: INSERT, UPDATE, DELETE, or SELECT. You may prefer other verbs such as get, add, remove, or edit.
Comment	Additional information that indicates the stored procedure's purpose.

CONVENTIONS

Unfortunately, we aren't likely to ever achieve universal agreement regarding naming conventions. Partly, it's a controversial issue reminiscent of the COBOL (wordy) versus C (terse) styles. Some DBAs and developers prefer shorter names because they're easier to remember and type while others appreciate content-rich names. Consistency is the important thing, and, if you work as part of a team, agree to a set of naming conventions and stick with it.

To create our SystemTime stored procedure complete the following steps:

1. Access the Stored Procedure Editor using the instructions described previously.
2. Type in the stored procedure name and the SELECT statement.
3. Click Check Syntax to verify that there are no typos.
4. Click the OK button.

The results are displayed in Figure 12.2. Once you click the OK button, you'll see the new procedure listed in the Details pane.

The easiest way to execute the ps_Util_Select_SystemTime stored procedure is from within Query Analyzer:

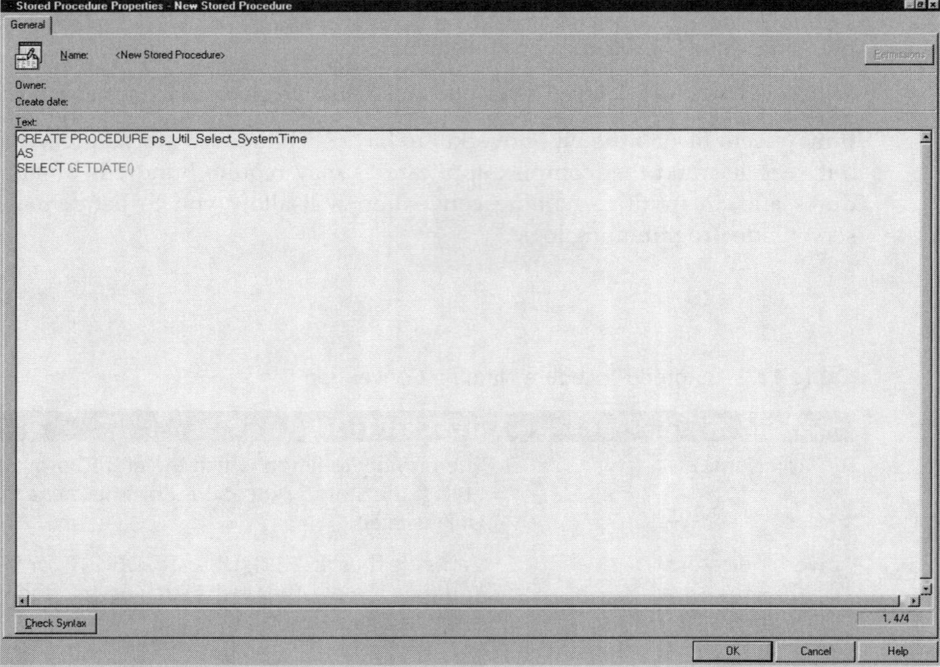

Figure 12.2 A simple stored procedure.

1. Invoke Query Analyzer (Tools/SQL Server Query Analyzer from the main menu in Enterprise Manager).
2. Select Pubs as the target database.
3. Type in ps_Util_Select_SystemTime.
4. Click the Execute Query button.

The executed stored procedure results are displayed in Figure 12.3.

Congratulations! You've just created a stored procedure. As you can see, creating and executing a stored procedure is very easy. The SQL statements that actually *do* the data manipulation can get pretty complex, but the creation/execution process will always remain as easy as it is in this example.

The next step is to create a stored procedure that retrieves information from a table. Use the instructions described previously to create the stored procedure listed here:

```
CREATE PROCEDURE ps_Authors_Select_AuIDName
AS
SELECT Au_ID,
  RTRIM(Au_Lname)+', '+ Au_Fname AS AuthorName
FROM Authors
```

Did you notice how, thanks to our naming convention, the name of the stored procedure indicates the table on which it acts (Authors) and the action that the stored procedure

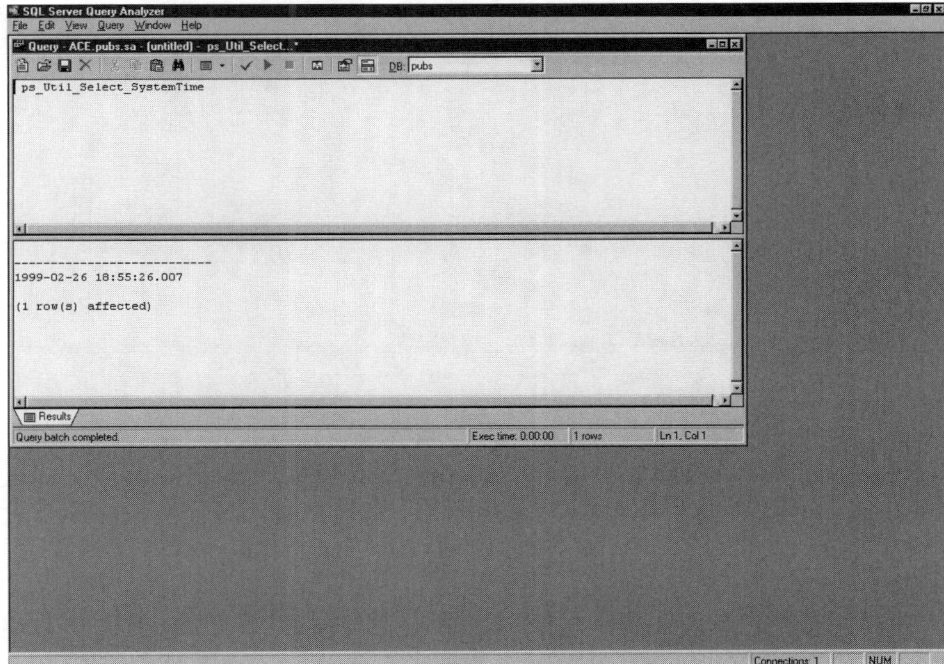

Figure 12.3 Executing a stored procedure.

executes (SELECT)? As a bonus, we even get a brief comment that tells us what is returned (AuIDName). Execute the ps_Authors_Select_AuIDName stored procedure in Query Analyzer and review the output. The output is shown in Figure 12.4.

You can also use the Create Stored Procedure Wizard to quickly create INSERT, UPDATE, and DELETE stored procedures. The wizard can be accessed under the Database option from the Tools/Wizards Main Menu option in Enterprise Manager.

PERMISSIONS

The CREATE PROCEDURE permission defaults to the database owner, but can be assigned to other users with the GRANT statement.

Editing a Stored Procedure

In this section you'll learn how to edit a stored procedure by modifying the ps_Authors_Select_AuIDName stored procedure that we created in the previous section. To edit our stored procedure, complete the following steps:

1. Expand the Server Tree.
2. Expand Pubs under the Databases option.
3. Highlight Stored Procedures.

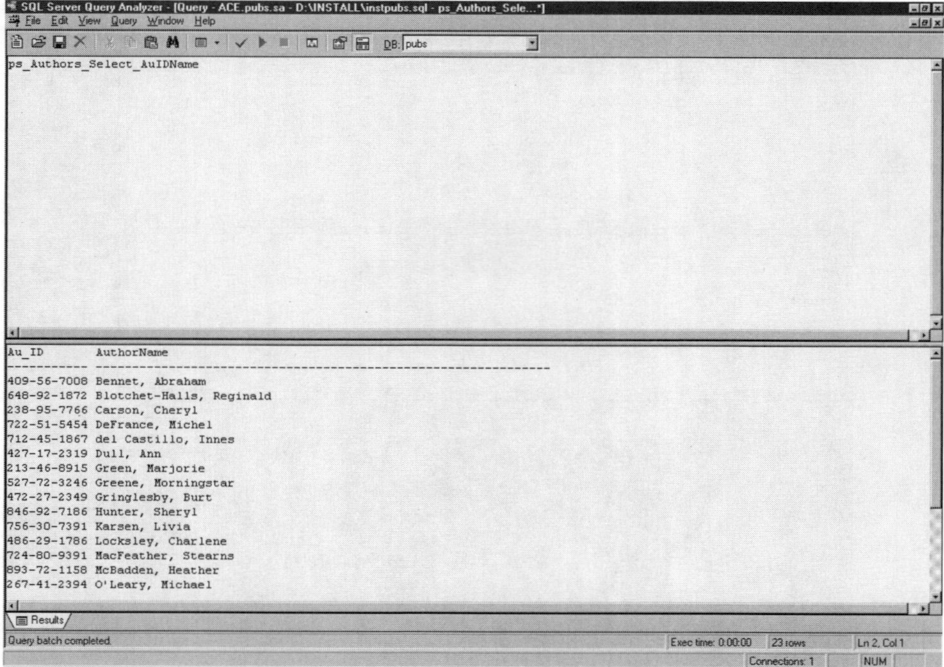

Figure 12.4 Executing the ps_Authors_Select_AuIDName stored procedure.

4. Double-click on ps_Authors_Select_AuIDName in the Details pane. This will invoke the Stored Procedure Editor and display the stored procedure's existing text.
5. Add the Address and Phone fields to the SELECT statement and click Check Syntax.

```
CREATE PROCEDURE ps_Authors_Select_AuIDName
AS
SELECT Au_ID,
       RTRIM(Au_Lname)+', '+ Au_Fname AS AuthorName,
       Address,
       Phone
FROM Authors
```

The stored procedure will return the additional information the next time it's executed.

You can also use two T-SQL methods to edit stored procedures. The first method requires that you explicitly drop the procedure before the modification is completed. To accomplish the same modification of the ps_Authors_Select_AuIDName stored procedure with a SQL statement, execute the following in Query Analyzer:

```
DROP PROCEDURE ps_Authors_Select_AuIDName
GO
CREATE PROCEDURE ps_Authors_Select_AuIDName
AS
SELECT Au_ID
       RTRIM(Au_Lname)+', '+ Au_Fname AS AuthorName,
       Address,
       Phone
FROM Authors
```

DROPPING A STORED PROCEDURE

When you execute DROP PROCEDURE, all information, including permissions, is lost. Losing the permissions associated with a stored procedure is a pain, and the main reason we recommend using the other two methods.

The second method, which is new with SQL Server 7, uses ALTER PROCEDURE. The benefit of using ALTER PROCEDURE over DROP PROCEDURE is that permissions are retained. In the previous example, once you DROP the store procedure all associated permissions are also dropped. The following code accomplishes the same modification as with the DROP PROCEDURE example except that it does not impact permissions.

```
ALTER PROCEDURE ps_Authors_Select_AuIDName
AS
SELECT Au_ID,
       RTRIM (Au_Lname)+', '+ Au_Fname AS AuthorName,
       Address,
       Phone
FROM Authors
```

Deleting a Stored Procedure

Deleting a stored procedure is very easy and can be accomplished with both Enterprise Manager and T-SQL. To delete a stored procedure in Enterprise Manager complete the following steps:

1. Expand the Server Tree.
2. Expand Pubs under the Databases option.
3. Highlight Stored Procedures.
4. Highlight the stored procedure you want to delete.
5. Right-click and select Delete.

To delete a stored procedure with T-SQL simply execute the DROP PROCEDURE statement in Query Analyzer as shown here:

```
DROP PROCEDURE StoredProcedureName
```

As with all other object deletions, the only way to recover a stored procedure after it's been deleted is to perform a restore from a database backup.

Debugging Stored Procedures

Stored procedures, like other programming endeavors, don't always work as expected when they are first created. When a stored procedure doesn't perform as expected, you must have a systematic way to determine where the problem lies. Unfortunately, SQL Server doesn't include a debugger. So, if you want to "break apart" the execution of a stored procedure the process is somewhat tedious.

The following stored procedure acts on the Urgency table in the WordOrd database (included on the CD). It doesn't really do much, but its simplicity should make the debugging process a little easier to learn.

```
CREATE PROCEDURE ps_tlkpUrgency_SELECT_Cursor
@Prefix varchar(10)

AS

DECLARE @Message varchar(100),
        @Urgency nvarchar(50)

DECLARE crsr_tlkpUrgency CURSOR
FOR
SELECT Urgency FROM tlkpUrgency

OPEN crsr_tlkpUrgency

FETCH NEXT FROM crsr_tlkpUrgency INTO @Urgency
```

```
   WHILE @@FETCH_STATUS = 0
      BEGIN
        SELECT @message = @Prefix+@Urgency
        FETCH NEXT FROM crsr_tlkpUrgency INTO @Urgency
      END

  CLOSE crsr_tlkpUrgency
  DEALLOCATE crsr_tlkpUrgency
```

This stored procedure accepts a parameter, creates a cursor on the Urgency field in tlkpUrgency, and loops through the cursor concatenating the parameter and the current value in the cursor. A cursor is nothing more than a temporary storage object that facilitates looping operations. For a detailed explanation of cursors please see the *Books Online* topic, *DECLARE CURSOR (T-SQL)*. If this stored procedure did not achieve the desired results, you would want to find out what the parameter values were through the looping process. In order to do this you must explicitly SELECT or PRINT the parameters in the code. The following code segment alters the procedure to display the values as they change and helps to determine where the problem occurs.

```
ALTER PROCEDURE ps_tlkpUrgency_SELECT_Cursor
@Prefix varchar(10)

AS

DECLARE @Message varchar(100),
        @Urgency nvarchar(50)

DECLARE crsr_tlkpUrgency CURSOR
FOR
SELECT Urgency FROM tlkpUrgency

OPEN crsr_tlkpUrgency

FETCH NEXT FROM crsr_tlkpUrgency INTO @Urgency

   WHILE @@FETCH_STATUS = 0
      BEGIN
        SELECT @Message
        SELECT @Message = @Prefix+@Urgency
        SELECT @Message
        FETCH NEXT FROM crsr_tlkpUrgency INTO @Urgency
        SELECT @Urgency
      END

  CLOSE crsr_tlkpUrgency
  DEALLOCATE crsr_tlkpUrgency
```

If you modify the stored procedure's original version with the previous code segment, you must return the stored procedure to its original state before you continue with this section.

As you can see, the debugging methods available with SQL Server are fairly crude. There are, however, stored procedure debuggers that come with both Visual Basic 5.0 and later and Visual C++ 6.0 Enterprise Edition and later. We've chosen to show how VB's debug tool works since it's so widely used. Before you can load the SQL Debugger Add In, you need to make sure the following prerequisites are met:

1. The MSSQLServer Service doesn't run under a System Account. You can verify this by selecting Settings/Control Panel/Services and double-clicking on the MSSQLServer Service. If it's configured to run under a System Account, change this to a Domain Account before you continue.
2. The Remote Procedure Call Service is running. You can determine this by selecting Settings/Control Panel/Services and verify that the Service has started.
3. A Data Source Name (DSN) has been created for the database in which the stored procedure is located. For our example, you need a DSN for the WorkOrd database. The WordOrd database comes on the CD that accompanies the book and is discussed in Appendix C. Use ODBC Data Sources in the Control Panel to configure the DSN.
4. The Sdi.dll file *must* be located in the C:\MSSQL7\BINN sub-directory. If this file is not located in the BINN sub-directory, you can obtain a copy from the SQL Server 7 CD in the x86\Other\SDI sub-directory. Installing SP1 does not affect the use of the sdi.dll file on the original CD.

Now that you've got the requirements in place, go ahead and launch Visual Basic. Do *not* choose any particular project template—just cancel the initial screen. Once VB has started, complete the following:

1. Select Add-Ins from the Main menu.
2. Select Add-In Manager from the drop-down menu.
3. Scroll down until you see the VB T-SQL debugger and then double-click on this entry. The Load Behavior column changes to Loaded as shown in Figure 12.5. Click OK to close the dialog.

NOT ALL T-SQL DEBUGGERS ARE CREATED EQUAL

Strange, but true. At VBits '99, Microsoft's Bill Vaughn, author and developer trainer in Microsoft's internal technical education group, told attendees that the SQL Debugger was a little different in VC++ 6.0, Visual InterDev, and VB6, and that the VB and VC++ versions were both sub-sets of the Visual InterDev version. He also admitted that future versions of the T-SQL Debugger would undoubtedly be less likely to crash.

Once the Add-In has been added, you can select it from the Add-Ins selection off the Main menu. In order to load a stored procedure for debugging complete the following steps:

1. Select Add-Ins/T-SQL Debugger…from the Main menu.
2. Select the WorkOrd DSN from the drop-down menu.

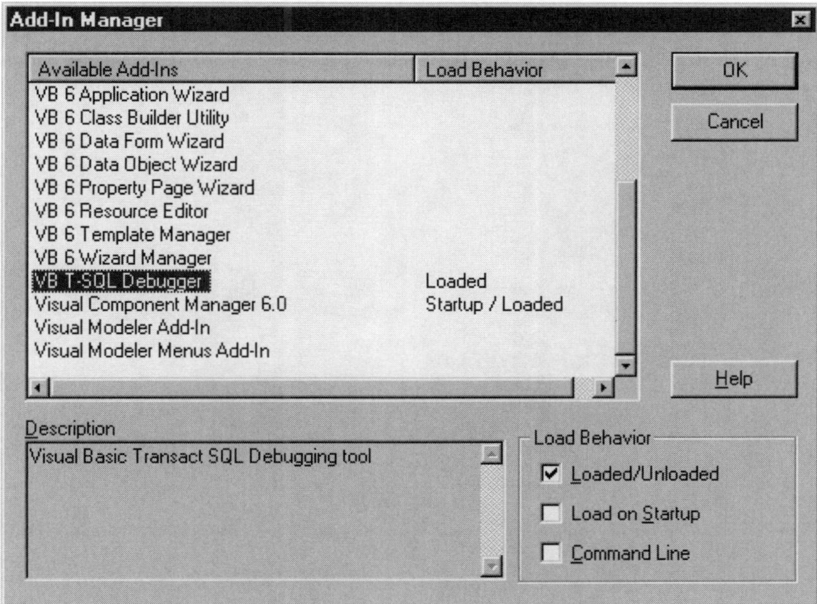

Figure 12.5 Activating the T-SQL Debugger Add-In.

3. Click the Stored Procedure tab.
4. Select the ps_tlkpUrgency_SELECT_Cursor stored procedure.
5. Type in pre --> (the arrow is two dashes and the greater-than sign)in the value field and click Execute.
6. Press the F8 key to start the step-through process and then notice how the Local Variables window changes—the @Prefix parameter now has a value.
7. Press F8 five times (stopping after each time to observe the changes to the Local Variables window) and the screen should look like Figure 12.6. Figure 12.6 shows that the local variable @Urgency has been loaded with the first value in the cursor and that @Message contains the concatenated value of pre --> +@Urgency.

As you continue to press F8 you will see how the cursor progresses through the values until the end of the cursor is reached. The VB T-SQL debugger can be useful for debugging stored procedures that contain cursors and many changing variables, but don't use it for run-of-the-mill, SELECT or UPDATE statement-based stored procedures.

RELOADING STORED PROCEDURES

If you modify a stored procedure during the debugging process, you must re-activate the T-SQL Debugger screen so that the client-side copy of the stored procedure is updated. If you create a stored procedure during the debugging process, you must disconnect/reconnect to the ODBC DSN so that the procedure name drop-down box is populated with the new procedure's name.

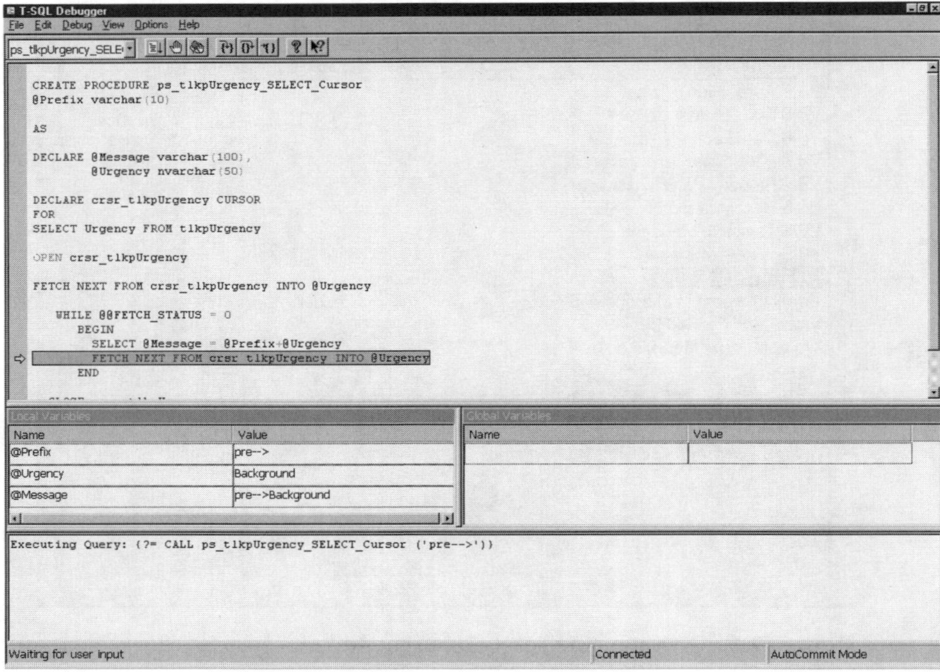

Figure 12.6 T-SQL Debugger.

USE CURSORS SPARINGLY

We used a cursor in the previous example because it helped to show the debugging process. In general, you should try to avoid cursors because they do not produce optimal SQL code. Cursors are procedural-oriented, but SQL is a set-based language. Implementing set-based versus procedural-oriented solutions will allow you to better utilize SQL Server 7's architecture.

Triggers

As mentioned earlier, a trigger is simply a stored procedure that is "attached" to a table. A trigger is associated with an INSERT, UPDATE, or DELETE statement and is executed when one of these actions occurs on the table. A simple example will help illustrate the benefit of triggers. Let's say that you want to implement a process that automatically deletes all child records that are associated with a parent record when the parent record is deleted. If SQL Server 7 did not support triggers, you would have to implement a somewhat cumbersome process that checks for and deletes child records before the parent record is deleted. With triggers, the child-record deletion code can be attached to the parent table and the process is made much easier.

Creating a Trigger

The following example will show how easy it is to create a trigger. Let's assume that we have two tables: Invoices and InvoiceItems. To establish a relationship between these two tables, Invoices has its primary key (InvoiceID) stored in InvoiceItems. We use the T-SQL code shown here to create a DELETE trigger on Invoices. So, when a record is deleted from Invoices, the trigger ensures that all associated records in InvoiceItems are also deleted.

```
CREATE TRIGGER trg_Invoices_Delete_InvoiceItems
ON Invoices
FOR DELETE
AS
DELETE InvoiceItems
FROM InvoiceItems, Deleted
WHERE InvoiceItems.InvoiceID = Deleted.InvoiceID
```

The interesting thing about this trigger is that it uses a server-created table called Deleted. When a DELETE statement is executed on Invoices, a temporary table named Deleted is automatically created by SQL Server. Deleted has the same structure as Invoices and contains the records that were affected in the DELETE statement. So, the child records that are deleted from InvoiceItems are specified by matching the InvoiceID in InvoiceItems with the InvoiceID in the Deleted table. SQL Server also creates a table called Inserted that contains the records that are inserted into a table using the INSERT statement. For more information on the special Deleted and Inserted tables, consult the *Books Online* topic, *Using the Special Inserted and Deleted Tables*.

TRIGGERS AND FOREIGN KEY CONSTRAINTS

Our previous trigger would fail if there were a foreign key constraint defined on the child table (InvoiceItems) that referenced the key of the parent table (Invoices). Why? Well, the record in the parent table is not deleted until the transaction is complete and the transaction is not complete until the trigger code is complete. So, when the trigger tries to delete the child record it fails because there is still a parent record in Invoices.

An additional trigger use is to "kick-off" another SQL Server process. The trigger shown here calls the sp_runwebtask system stored procedure whenever there's a record inserted into the Northwind Orders table. Remember how you used the Web Assistant Wizard back in Chapter 5 to publish HTML pages? Do you remember the option for creating new HTML pages whenever the data changed? Well, if you go back to the Web Assistant Wizard and create a "job" that outputs CompanyName, ContactName, and Phone from the Customers table whenever there's a new OrderID, SQL Server actually creates a trigger for you:

```
CREATE TRIGGER NewOrder_1
ON Orders
FOR INSERT AS
IF UPDATE(OrderID)
   BEGIN EXEC sp_runwebtask @procname =  'NewOrder'
END
```

How's that for cool? So, whenever data is inserted, the trigger fires the sp_runwebtask stored procedure to run our NewOrder stored procedure.

To view the trigger you have to select the Tables option in the Northwind database, right-click on the Orders table, point to All Tasks, and then click Manage Triggers. Find your trigger in the drop-down box. Depending on how you set your trigger up, it should look similar to the NewOrder code segment.

The full syntax of the CREATE TRIGGER statement is listed here. The argument descriptions are shown in Table 12.3.

```
CREATE TRIGGER trigger_name
ON table
[WITH ENCRYPTION]
{
{FOR { [DELETE] [,] [INSERT] [,] [UPDATE] }
[WITH APPEND]
[NOT FOR REPLICATION]
AS
sql_statement [...n]
}
|
{FOR { [INSERT] [,] [UPDATE] }
[WITH APPEND]
[NOT FOR REPLICATION]
AS
{ IF UPDATE (column)
[{AND | OR} UPDATE (column)]
[...n]
| IF (COLUMNS_UPDATED() {bitwise_operator} updated_bitmask)
{ comparison_operator} column_bitmask [...n]
}
sql_statement [ ...n]
}
}
```

Modifying a Trigger

To modify a trigger, use the ALTER TRIGGER statement. It's used in the same way as ALTER STORED PROCEDURE described earlier in this chapter.

If you want to modify our trg_Invoices_Delete_InvoiceItems trigger to add another WHERE criteria, use the following:

```
ALTER TRIGGER trg_Invoices_Delete_InvoiceItems
ON Invoices
FOR DELETE
AS
DELETE InvoiceItems
FROM InvoiceItems, Deleted
WHERE InvoiceItems.InvoiceID = Deleted.InvoiceID AND InvoiceItems.Active
= 'Y'
```

Table 12.3 CREATE TRIGGER Arguments

ARGUMENT	FUNCTION
Trigger_name	The name of the trigger.
table	The table to which the trigger is attached.
WITH ENCRYPTION	Specifies that the trigger's text will not be displayed in the syscomments system table.
{ [DELETE] [,] [INSERT] [,] [UPDATE] } | { [INSERT] [,] [UPDATE]}	Specifies the data modification action(s) that cause the trigger to execute. More than one data modification action can be associated with the trigger.
WITH APPEND	For backward compatibility. Specifies that an additional trigger is added to an existing data modification action or trigger. When the database is at a compatibility level 7.0 or higher, WITH APPEND is not needed.
NOT FOR REPLICATION	Specifies that the results of the trigger will not be replicated.
AS	Indicates that the actions that the trigger will perform will follow.
sql_statement	The actions that the trigger performs.
n	Additional T-SQL statements that are executed when the trigger fires.
IF UPDATE (column)	Specifies that the trigger is executed only when a column's value is INSERTed or DELETEd.
IF (COLUMNS_UPDATED())	Tests to see whether a specified column is modified. COLUMNS_UPATED() returns the name of the columns that were modified in the INSERT or UPDATE statement
Bitwise_operator	The bitwise operator used to determine if a column was updated.
Updated_bitmask	Integer bitmask of those columns actually updated or inserted.
Comparison_operator	Used to check whether all columns specified in updated_bitmask are actually updated
Column_bitmask	Integer bitmask of those columns to check whether they're updated or inserted.

This is a good example of how to use ALTER TRIGGER, but a bad example of database programming. Do you know why? This example can result in orphaned records—a child record without a corresponding parent record—and orphaned records are very frustrating. Let's say that you have an Invoice that has two InvoiceItems whose Active values are Y and N. If the Invoice is deleted, only one of the two associated InvoiceItems will be deleted and there will be no parent record for the remaining InvoiceItem.

An orphaned record is not only useless, but also very frustrating because it immediately tells you that some aspect of your design is very poor and needs to be fixed.

FYI DECLARATIVE REFERENTIAL INTEGRITY VERSUS TRIGGERS

Like naming conventions, approaches to enforcing referential integrity (RI)—a fancy way to say that you don't want orphaned records—can vary. Some DBAs prefer the so-called *declarative referential integrity approach* where you perform RI up front in your CREATE TABLE statements. Others prefer to enforce it via triggers. See the *Books Online* topic, *Triggers Compared to other Data Integrity Methods* for more insight on this important topic. The more up-front checks on data you provide, the less your chance of dirty data.

The full syntax for the ALTER TRIGGER statement is listed here.

```
ALTER TRIGGER trigger_name
ON table
[WITH ENCRYPTION]
{
{FOR { [DELETE] [,] [UPDATE] [,][INSERT] }
[NOT FOR REPLICATION]
AS
sql_statement [...n]
}
|
{FOR { [INSERT] [,] [UPDATE] }
[NOT FOR REPLICATION]
AS
{ IF UPDATE (column)
[{AND | OR} UPDATE (column)]
[...n]
| IF (COLUMNS_UPDATED() {bitwise_operator} updated_bitmask)
{ comparison_operator} column_bitmask [...n]
}
sql_statement [...n]
}
}
```

The arguments are the same as the CREATE TRIGGER statement listed in the previous section.

Deleting a Trigger

To delete a trigger use the DROP TRIGGER statement. The following code segment drops the trg_Invoices_Delete_InvoiceItems trigger.

```
DROP TRIGGER trg_Invoices_Delete_InvoiceItems
```

The Project: Encapsulating Business Logic with Stored Procedures and Triggers

This project is based on the WorkOrd database (included on the CD that accompanies this book). So far, we've focused on defining stored procedures and triggers, and how to create, update, and delete them. It's important to fully understand these topics in order to progress to the more interesting part of this chapter—how to use these objects to encapsulate business logic. So, now that we have covered the basics, let's simulate a real-world scenario where the goal is to add functionality to the WorkOrd database. We will introduce some basic specifications for the functionality that need to be added, derive the associated business logic, and then convert the business logic to T-SQL, which is captured (encapsulated) in stored procedures and triggers.

Specifications

The tables that we use in this project are shown in Figure 12.7.

As you can see, there are descriptions, dates, and individuals that are captured in the tables.

- Descriptions: tblRequestReason.ReasonDesc
- Dates: tblRequest.RequestDate
- Individuals: tblRequest.Requester

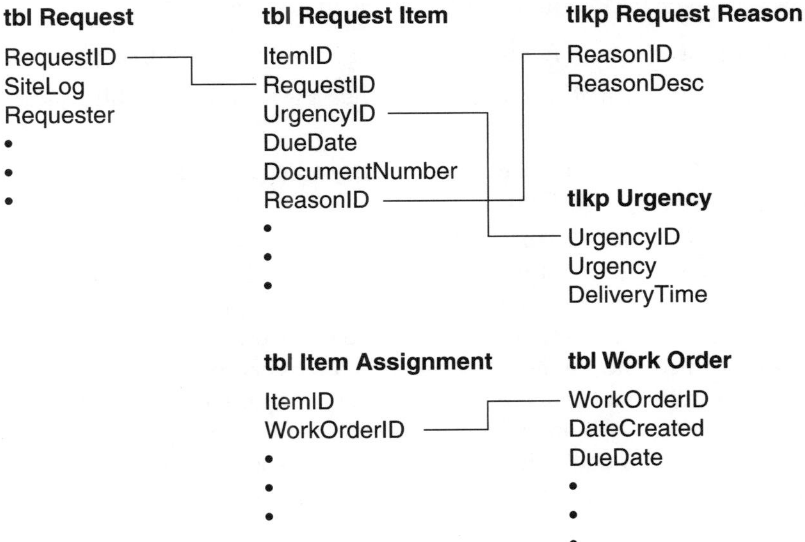

Figure 12.7 WorkOrd table relationships.

The end users want to add functionality by implementing the three requirements shown here:

1. Track all Open Requests. This allows end users to gauge how much work is in the queue.
2. Analyze completed Requests by Requester, Request Date, and Reason Description. Access to historical information is important so that they can note any trends that reveal a business process/manufacturing deficiency.
3. When a Request is entered whose Urgency Level is RUSH, send an e-mail to the database owner. This notification signals the database owner about "hot" requests.

Business Logic/Pseudocode

Requirement 1

The business logic for Requirement 1 is very simple.

A Request is considered open when the associated tblWorkOrder.Completed field = 0. Relating a Request to tblWorkOrder.Completed is accomplished through the tblRequestItem and tblItemAssignment tables shown in Figure 12.7.

The pseudocode for Requirement 1 looks something like the following:

```
Display all Requests where tblWorkOrder.Completed = 0.
```

Requirement 2

The business logic for Requirement 2 is a little more complex.

Closed Request. A Closed Request is one where tblWorkOrder.Completed = 1.

Requester. The individual who initiates a Request is stored in the tblRequest.Requester field.

Request Date (Search by Date Range). The day a Request is submitted is stored in the tblRequest.RequestDate field.

Reason Description. The Reason a request is submitted is stored in the tlkpRequestReason.ReasonDesc field. The unique identifier for a Reason is tlkpRequestReason.ReasonID. This value is stored as a foreign key in the tblRequest table as tblRequest.ReasonID. The search criteria are not independent. That is, one or more of the criteria can be specified and the resultset must be filtered accordingly. For example, if the end user wants to see all of the Closed Requests requested by N. Gale whose Request Date is between 1/1/98 and 8/1/98, where the Reason Description is Missing, then the code must accommodate the query. A browser-based GUI that accepts all of these parameters might look something like Figure 12.8.

The psuedocode for Requirement 2 is shown here. Please note that we only show the dependent scenarios. However, our code allows us to efficiently account for all of the different scenarios.

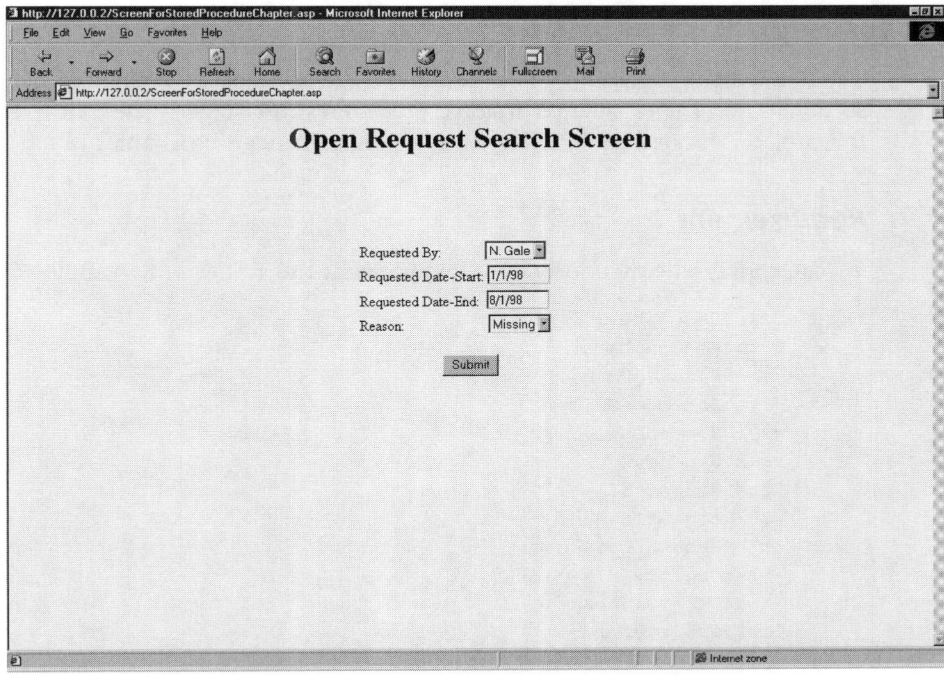

Figure 12.8 ASP GUI.

If the end user supplies a Requester, display all Requests where tblWorkOrder.Completed = 1 and tblRequester = the supplied value.

If the end user supplies a Requester and a StartDate, display all Closed Requests where tblWorkOrder. Completed = 1, tblRequester = the supplied value, and tblRequest.RequestDate > the supplied StartDate.

If the end user supplies a Requester, StartDate, and an EndDate display all Closed Requests where tblWorkOrder.Completed = 1, tblRequester = the supplied value, tblRequest.RequestDate > the supplied StartDate, and tblRequest.RequestDate < the supplied EndDate.

If the end user supplies a Requester, StartDate, EndDate, and a Reason, display all closed requests where tblWorkOrder.Completed = 1, tblRequester = the supplied value, tblRequest.RequestDate > the supplied StartDate, tblRequest.RequestDate < the supplied EndDate, and tlkpRequestReason.ReasonDesc = the supplied Reason.

Requirement 3

The business logic for Requirement 3 is listed here.

The urgency status of a request is stored in the tlkpUrgency.Urgency field. This value is related to a Request via the tblRequestItem table and is shown in Figure 12.7. When this value = RUSH, send an e-mail to the database owner.

The psuedocode for Requirement 3 is also straightforward and shown here.

If the end user creates a Request whose tlkpUrgency.Urgency = RUSH, an e-mail is sent to the database owner.

Converting the Pseudocode to SQL

The following sections show how to convert the pseudocode defined in the previous section to T-SQL encapsulated in stored procedures and triggers. The code referenced in this project is located on the CD in the file Ch12.sql, under the Chapter 12 sub-directory.

Requirement 1

We can convert the pseudocode for Requirement 1 to T-SQL with the following:

```
SELECT a.Requester,
       a.RequestDate,
       a.ReceiveDate,
       b.DocumentNumber,
       c.ReasonDesc,
       d.Urgency
FROM tblRequest a,
     tblRequestItem b,
     tlkpRequestReason c,
     tlkpurgency d,
     tblItemAssignment e,
     tblWorkOrder f
WHERE a.RequestID = b.RequestID AND
      b.ReasonID = c.ReasonID AND
      b.UrgencyID = d.UrgencyID AND
      b.ItemID = e.ItemID AND
      e.WorkOrderID = f.WorkOrderID AND
      f.Completed = 0
ORDER BY Requester, RequestDate
```

Note that we specified a minimum number of fields and included an ORDER BY clause to make the resultset easier to comprehend. To make this a stored procedure, simply add the required portions of the CREATE PROCEDURE statement as we've done here.

```
CREATE PROCEDURE ps_tblRequest_SELECT_OpenItems
AS
SELECT a.Requester,
       a.RequestDate,
       a.ReceiveDate,
       b.DocumentNumber,
       c.ReasonDesc,
       d.Urgency
FROM tblRequest a,
     tblRequestItem b,
     tlkpRequestReason c,
     tlkpurgency d,
     tblItemAssignment e,
     tblWorkOrder f
```

```
WHERE a.RequestID = b.RequestID AND
      b.ReasonID = c.ReasonID AND
      b.UrgencyID = d.UrgencyID AND
      b.ItemID = e.ItemID AND
      e.WorkOrderID = f.WorkOrderID AND
      f.Completed = 0
ORDER BY Requester, RequestDate
```

Requirement 2

The pseudocode for Requirement 2 can be converted using both static and dynamic SQL. *Static SQL* refers to statements that are always executed in the same manner, while *dynamic SQL* allows you to build statements based on supplied parameters. Dynamic SQL, in this particular example, helps us to build our query based on parameters supplied by the end user. Let's build this part one section at a time so we can better understand how to build complex SQL statements with variables.

The first requirement is that we allow the end user to query by Requester. We can do this in an error-prone manner by allowing the end user to type in the information or we can do it so that end-user error is eliminated by providing a drop-down box from which they can select a value. When given a choice, we will always choose to eliminate end-user error, so we use a drop-down box that contains the names of all the individuals who have entered a Closed Request. The SQL that's used to create a stored procedure to populate the Requester drop-down box is provided here.

```
CREATE PROCEDURE ps_Request_SELECT_Requesters
AS
SELECT DISTINCT Requester
FROM tblRequest a,
     tblRequestItem b,
     tblItemAssignment c,
     tblWorkOrder d
WHERE a.RequestID = b.ItemID AND
      b.ItemID = c.ItemID AND
      c.WorkOrderID = d.WorkOrderID AND
      d.Completed = 1
ORDER BY Requester
```

As you can see, the key part of the WHERE clause is to ensure that only Requesters with completed work orders are selected. Now that we have a mechanism for populating the drop-down box, let's take a look at a stored procedure that will accept the Requester value and return the appropriate closed work orders.

```
CREATE PROCEDURE ps_tblRequest_SELECT_ByRequester
@Requester nvarchar(50)
AS
SELECT a.Requester,
```

```
        a.RequestDate,
        a.ReceiveDate,
        b.DocumentNumber,
        c.ReasonDesc,
        d.Urgency
FROM tblRequest a,
     tblRequestItem b,
     tlkpRequestReason c,
     tlkpurgency d,
     tblItemAssignment e,
     tblWorkOrder f
WHERE a.Requester = @Requester AND
      a.RequestID = b.RequestID AND
      b.ReasonID = c.ReasonID AND
      b.UrgencyID = d.UrgencyID AND
      b.ItemID = e.ItemID AND
      e.WorkOrderID = f.WorkOrderID AND
      f.Completed = 0
ORDER BY RequestDate
```

This stored procedure accepts a parameter, @Requester, and then retrieves the desired data based upon the supplied value. The parameter can be named anything that qualifies as an object identifier, but we always choose to use the name of the field that the parameter is filtered against. This type of intuitive naming convention can come in real handy when your code does not execute as expected.

The second requirement is to allow the end user to specify a Start Date, End Date, or both.

We can do this using one of two ways: we can create a section that accounts for each combination of supplied values or we can use Dynamic SQL to build the query based upon the supplied parameters. Since we mentioned earlier in this section that we would use Dynamic SQL, it shouldn't be a surprise as to which method we use here. The following stored procedure accomplishes the goal:

```
CREATE PROCEDURE ps_tblRequest_SELECT_RequesterAndDateRange
@Requester varchar(50),
@RequestDateStart varchar(10),
@RequestDateEnd varchar(10)
AS
—*Create variables
DECLARE @SqlBase varchar(500),
        @SqlAnd varchar(5),
        @SqlRequester varchar(200),
        @SqlRequestDateStart varchar(200),
        @SqlRequestDateEnd varchar(200)

—*Base SQL
SELECT @SqlBase = "SELECT a.Requester, "
+ "a.RequestDate, "
```

```
+ "a.ReceiveDate, "
+ "b.DocumentNumber, "
+ "c.ReasonDesc, "
+ "d.Urgency "
+ "FROM tblRequest a, "
+ "tblRequestItem b, "
+ "tlkpRequestReason c, "
+ "tlkpurgency d, "
+ "tblItemAssignment e, "
+ "tblWorkOrder f "
+ "WHERE a.RequestID = b.RequestID AND "
+ "b.ReasonID = c.ReasonID AND "
+ "b.UrgencyID = d.UrgencyID AND "
+ "b.ItemID = e.ItemID AND "
+ "e.WorkOrderID = f.WorkOrderID AND "
+ "f.Completed = 0 "

—*And
IF @Requester <> "" OR @RequestDateStart <> "" OR @RequestDateEnd <> ""
   SELECT @SqlAnd = " AND "
ELSE
   SELECT @SqlAnd = ""

—*Requester
IF @Requester <> "" AND @RequestDateStart = "" AND @RequestDateEnd = ""
  SELECT @SQLRequester = " a.Requester = '" + @Requester + "'"
ELSE
  SELECT @SQLRequester = " a.Requester = '" + @Requester + "' AND "

IF @Requester = ""
   SELECT @SQLRequester = ""

—*RequestDateStart
IF @RequestDateStart <> "" AND @RequestDateEnd = ""
  SELECT @SQLRequestDateStart = " a.RequestDate >= '"+ @RequestDateStart
+ "'"
ELSE
  SELECT @SQLRequestDateStart = " a.RequestDate >= '"+ @RequestDateStart
+ "' AND "

IF @RequestDateStart = ""
  SELECT @SQLRequestDateStart = ""


—*RequestDateEnd
IF @RequestDateEnd <> ""
  SELECT @SQLRequestDateEnd = " a.RequestDate <= '" + @RequestDateEnd +
"'"
ELSE
```

```
    SELECT @SQLRequestDateEnd = ""

EXECUTE (@SQLBase+@SQLAnd+@SQLRequester+@SQLRequestDateStart+@SQLRe-
questDateEnd)
```

DEALING WITH LONG STRINGS

Whenever you build a statement with multiple code segments as we've done here, it's a good habit to always put spaces before and after the individual segments. Why? Because when the segments are modified throughout the development process, concatenation can potentially make one segment a part of the next one and complicate troubleshooting.

Don't be overwhelmed by this stored procedure; all we've done is build pieces of a query with variables, concatenate them together, and then use the EXECUTE statement to run the resultant string. Let's examine the first variable, @SQLBase. This part of the query is executed regardless of whether or not the end user selects 0 or more filter options, so there are no IF statements required to determine its content. The next variable, @SQLAnd is used to hold the AND part for the WHERE clause when the end user specifies 1 or more filter criteria. The @SQLRequester variable contains the Requester join condition when the value is supplied, or nothing when the end user wants all Requesters in the resultset. Notice that the IF statement for @Requester checks to see if the end user selected a RequestDate filter and adds an AND to the variable when one is supplied. The two @SQLRequestDate variables are populated in the same manner as @SQLRequester. Once the variables are populated, they are concatenated together, and then execute a single statement with EXECUTE.

Let's see if it actually works. Create this stored procedure, either by typing it in or by copying it from the file (Chapter12\WorkOrd.sql) on the CD, and then execute it with the following:

```
EXECUTE ps_tblRequest_SELECT_RequesterAndDateRange
 @Requester = "N. Gale",
 @RequestDateStart = "11/1/98",
 @RequestDateEnd = "12/1/98"
```

Notice that we prefixed the stored-procedure call with EXECUTE (you can also use EXEC). The prefix ensures that the query engine doesn't have to determine what kind of call it is while parsing the string. It is also helpful when you have two stored procedures called within the same batch. The second stored procedure will fail unless it is prefixed by EXECUTE. EXECUTE is also required when nesting stored procedures—stored procedures that call stored procedures. If a nested stored procedure call is not prefixed with EXECUTE the call will fail.

The next stored procedure that we need to create allows the end user to select a Reason Description from a drop-down box.

```
CREATE PROCEDURE ps_tlkpRequestReason
AS
```

```
SELECT DISTINCT a.ReasonDesc, a.ReasonID
FROM tlkpRequestReason a, tblRequestItem b
WHERE a.ReasonID = b.ReasonID
ORDER BY ReasonDesc
```

This stored procedure is used as the data source for the drop-down box. The ReasonDesc is displayed to the end user, but the ReasonID is dropped into the stored procedure.

Now we can modify ps_tblRequest_SELECT_RequesterAndDateRange to accept the new filter criteria.

```
CREATE PROCEDURE ps_tblRequest_SELECT_RequesterAndDateRangeAndReason
@Requester varchar(50),
@RequestDateStart varchar(10),
@RequestDateEnd varchar(10),
@ReasonID varchar(5)
AS
—*Create variables
DECLARE @SqlBase varchar(500),
        @SqlAnd varchar(5),
        @SqlRequester varchar(200),
        @SqlRequestDateStart varchar(200),
        @SqlRequestDateEnd varchar(200),
        @SqlReason varchar(200)

—*Base SQL
SELECT @SqlBase = "SELECT a.Requester, "
+ "a.RequestDate, "
+ "a.ReceiveDate, "
+ "b.DocumentNumber, "
+ "c.ReasonDesc, "
+ "d.Urgency "
+ "FROM tblRequest a, "
+ "tblRequestItem b, "
+ "tlkpRequestReason c, "
+ "tlkpurgency d, "
+ "tblItemAssignment e, "
+ "tblWorkOrder f "
+ "WHERE a.RequestID = b.RequestID AND "
+ "b.ReasonID = c.ReasonID AND "
+ "b.UrgencyID = d.UrgencyID AND "
+ "b.ItemID = e.ItemID AND "
+ "e.WorkOrderID = f.WorkOrderID AND "
+ "f.Completed = 0 "


—*And
IF @Requester <> "" OR @RequestDateStart <> "" OR @RequestDateEnd <> ""
   SELECT @SqlAnd = " AND "
ELSE
```

```
   SELECT @SqlAnd = ""


—*Requester
IF @Requester <> "" AND @RequestDateStart = "" AND @RequestDateEnd = ""
  SELECT @SQLRequester = " a.Requester = '" + @Requester + "'"
ELSE
  SELECT @SQLRequester = " a.Requester = '" + @Requester + "' AND "

IF @Requester = ""
   SELECT @SQLRequester = ""


—*RequestDateStart
IF @RequestDateStart <> "" AND @RequestDateEnd = ""
  SELECT @SQLRequestDateStart = " a.RequestDate >= '"+ @RequestDateStart + "'"
ELSE
  SELECT @SQLRequestDateStart = " a.RequestDate >= '"+ @RequestDateStart + "' AND "

IF @RequestDateStart = ""
  SELECT @SQLRequestDateStart = ""


—*RequestDateEnd
IF @RequestDateEnd <> "" AND @ReasonID = ""
  SELECT @SQLRequestDateEnd = " a.RequestDate <= '" + @RequestDateEnd + "'"
ELSE
  SELECT @SQLRequestDateEnd = " a.RequestDate <= '" + @RequestDateEnd + "' AND "

IF @RequestDateEnd = ""
  SELECT @SQLRequestDateEnd = ""

—*RequestReason
IF @ReasonID <> ""
  SELECT @SQLReason = " b.ReasonID = " + @ReasonID
ELSE
  SELECT @SQLReason = ""


EXECUTE (@SQLBase+@SQLAnd+@SQLRequester+@SQLRequestDateStart+@SQLRequestDateEnd+
    @SQLReason)
```

As you can see, we simply extend on the same logic used to create the previous stored procedure in order to add the new filter criteria. If you want to make sure that it works, execute the following in Query Analyzer.

```
—*Execute stored procedure
EXECUTE ps_tblRequest_SELECT_RequesterAndDateRangeAndReason @Requester =
"N. Gale",
@RequestDateStart = "11/1/98",
```

```
@RequestDateEnd = "12/1/98",
@ReasonID = "1"
```

TROUBLESHOOTING DYNAMIC SQL STATEMENTS

As you can probably imagine, it would be very easy to make a typing error when building stored procedures like the ones we used in this section. When you encounter a problem with this type of stored procedure, simply print the individual variables such as @SQLBase to screen, cut and paste them into Query Analyzer and then see if you can successfully execute the string. This will allow you to quickly determine if the problem is caused by faulty programming logic or, more likely, by a simple typo.

DYNAMIC SQL AND PERMISSIONS

If you recall from the beginning of this chapter, we said one of the main benefits of using stored procedures is that they reduce the burden associated with implementing database security. This is certainly true, but you do encounter some unexpected results with permissions when Dynamic SQL is used. When Dynamic SQL is used, the login under which the statement is executed must have the appropriate permissions on the underlying object(s).

A quick example will help illustrate this issue. Let's say that you create a login called SQLGuru and grant it Execute permission on the stored procedure: ps_thlRequest_SELECT_RequesterAndDateRange. Assume that SQLGuru has no other permissions in the entire database. The SQLGuru login cannot successfully execute the stored procedure because the dynamic part (the string inside EXECUTE(...)), runs outside the context of the stored procedure. SQLGuru can execute the stored procedure, but until it is granted the appropriate permissions on all of the objects that are accessed within the string, a permissions error will be generated when the Dynamic SQL is executed. In this example, all you need to do in order to allow SQLGuru to successfully execute the stored procedure is to grant SELECT permission on all of the tables accessed by the SELECT statement.

Requirement 3

To fulfill Requirement 3, we need to use a trigger and the xp_sendmail extended stored procedure (no, we didn't write it—xp_sendmail ships with SQL Server). The following trigger demonstrates how to create a notification e-mail based on the Urgency field for an entered tblRequestItem.

```
CREATE TRIGGER trg_tblRequestItem_Urgency
ON tblRequestItem
FOR INSERT
```

```
AS
IF (SELECT UrgencyID FROM Inserted) = 5
    EXEC master..xp_sendmail 'Joe','Rush item entered'
```

In the section, *Creating a Trigger*, we discussed two tables (Inserted and Deleted) that SQL Server automatically creates when an INSERT, UPDATE, or DELETE statement is executed on a table. The previous trigger uses the Inserted table to determine if the INSERT statement created a record whose UrgencyID corresponds to a RUSH Request. If the Request has an Urgency Level of RUSH, then an e-mail is sent to Joe, the database owner.

To use this trigger you must have SQL Mail configured. If you need help configuring SQL Mail, please refer to the *Books Online* topic, *Setting Up SQLAgentMail*. You'll also find several Microsoft Knowledge Base articles online at Microsoft's support site (support.microsoft.com/support). Search for *SQL Mail*.

Summary

The goal of this chapter was to show you how to encapsulate business logic in stored procedures and triggers. We started by learning the basics of both database objects, and then progressed by converting some business logic applicable to the WorkOrd database. As you have seen, the basics of both stored procedures and triggers are fairly straightforward. The real challenge is to become familiar enough with T-SQL to make sure that you can convert the business logic in an efficient manner. This is certainly not a skill you can master overnight, but one whose long-term benefit is worth the effort.

CHAPTER 13

Project #10: Using Visual Basic to Write SQL Applications

Goal

The goal of this chapter is to show you how to use each of Microsoft's data access methods from Visual Basic and to create a VB application using ADO (the current preferred method) that implements a dynamic SQL data window.

YOU WILL NEED

- ✔ Microsoft SQL Server 7 on Win9x, WinNT, or Windows 2000
- ✔ Visual Basic 6 Enterprise Edition, SP1 or higher or Visual Basic 5 Enterprise Edition, SP3
- ✔ The VBSQL application code found on the book's CD-ROM (VB5 Code or VB6 Code)
- ✔ The WorkOrd database available on the accompanying CD-ROM (\Shared\Data\Access2000\WorkOrd.MDB)
- ✔ ADO 2.1

Visual Basic (www.microsoft.com/vbasic) is arguably the most popular programming language on the planet with literally millions of developers using it or its derivatives—Visual Basic for Applications (VBA) and VBScript—every day. Part of the reason for its success is the widespread availability of so-called *controls*—pre-written chunks of code that accomplish a discrete task. Today's generation of 32-bit controls are referred to as both ActiveX controls and by their older name, OCXs (OLE—object linking and embedding custom controls).

Today you can buy or download thousands of freeware, shareware, and commercial ActiveX controls, and there are hundreds of other VB-related tools and supporting utilities. No one really knows how many programs have been written in VB, but there are a lot.

There are a variety of ways to get information to and from VB and SQL Server. These range from *low-level*, code-intensive methods that make direct calls to SQL Server's DB-Library API to *higher-level* approaches such as ADO (discussed in detail later in this chapter) that don't require as much coding.

In this chapter, we focus on the three most prevalent approaches—DAO, RDO, and ADO—and also speculate on how we expect things to evolve in the future. Shucks, we even promise to define, discuss, and de-mystify the entire mess of data access acronyms in the lead-up text to the book's final project.

DATA CONTROLS: THE NO-CODING APPROACH

VB includes a control that makes it fairly easy to interact with a database. The *Data Control* provides properties to select a database and the table within that database to use. This control returns a list of columns within the selected table, which can then be attached to the DataSource and DataField properties of data-bound controls, such as a text box. After establishing this direct linkage, and without entering a single line of SQL, you can then edit individual columns within the chosen table.

Data Controls *also* provide flexibility so you can enter more sophisticated SQL statements. This enabless you to join tables and/or reduce the number of columns worked with at run time.

See Data Controls under VB Help for more on this topic.

In the project presented in this chapter, you'll learn how to use ADO to access SQL Server, and you'll be able to experiment with any number of different SQL commands at runtime—without changing the application's source code.

Ancient History

Today's VB6 developers have an overabundance of data-aware controls to work with. However, in earlier versions, and especially prior to VB3, it was a very different world.

Those first versions of VB relied on traditional BASIC (Beginners' All Purpose Symbolic Instruction Code) commands like Open, Close, Write, and Print for file manipulation. If you wanted to access commercial relational databases you either wrote your own data-access routines or bought code from firms like Q + E Software (later acquired by Intersolv, which was then acquired by MicroFocus, and which has now renamed itself Merant!).

This left VB in the doghouse with many corporate developers who required that enterprise-caliber development tools provide drivers for popular relational databases. The lack of database integration made it easy for Powersoft's PowerBuilder to become the corporate development tool of choice for client/server team development. PowerBuilder, now part of Sybase, shipped with a half dozen pre-written, native (as opposed to ODBC—open database connectivity—which was originally fairly slow) database drivers.

Starting with version 3 of VB, Microsoft addressed these issues by including the so-called *Jet* engine in the box. Jet, which is basically Microsoft Access without the GUI, let VB programmers create, access, or maintain databases from within VB programs. Each successive version of Jet (Office 2000 includes Jet 4.0) has sported different, generally incompatible file formats and object models.

Where We Are Today

VB has progressed tremendously from its early "database-challenged" days, and you'll find it relatively easy to create SQL Server applications with VB or VBA. All of these changes has not only made VB competitive with the PowerBuilder-types of team development tools, but has also moved VB (through VB, VBA, VBScript, and close cousins, such as LotusScript) into a commanding lead among development tools.

E-I-E-I-O

Sometimes we can't help but be reminded of the refrain from *Old Macdonald Had a Farm* when you think about all of the data-access models and connectivity standards out there today. But whether or not you agree that running through the list of names makes you start humming, "with a quack quack here. . .," there really is a sort of natural progression to the different pieces of the puzzle.

We think it's useful to categorize the nine (according to our calculations, anyway) APIs and data-access models available to developers into two groups: low-level and high-level. The so-called low-level or API (Application Programming Interface) is recommended for applications where performance is important. If your inclination is to think that performance is always important—*so that it's better to use the API approach*—you may want to think again. Using APIs generally requires a good understanding of DLL calling conventions and often involves such intricacies as integrating C/C++-based DLLs with VB applications. For example, strings are treated differently in each language and you have to be careful how they are passed back and forth between VB and DLLs. However, for organizations (and often vendors) which need performance and low-level control, the API approach is the way to go. Remember though that while performance is always an issue, it is the *perceived* performance that's really important.

Sometimes ADO itself is fast enough for even mission-critical applications. You might want to include some time for basic performance testing in your projects to help to decide which level of data access is *fast enough* for your particular application.

On the other hand, the high-level approach is ideal for prototyping or building non-mission critical applications where performance is less important than simply accomplishing the task at hand. This is often referred to as the *wrapper approach* since it wraps an easier interface around the complexities of the underlying one. ODBC, originally introduced in 1993, was the first of a series of high-level approaches, and it remains the bedrock of many of today's data-access techniques.

There is a tradeoff, however. More wrappers or layers mean easier programming, but more "middle men" and handoffs between the layers, which can result in a less-than-optimal performance. Low-level programming generally delivers better performance, but is harder to write and maintain. We'll be honest. Most VB programmers use a high-level model. This approach places a layer over the API level to reduce the complexity of dealing with the lower-level calls. You may need to write six calls to DB-Library to accomplish the same task that ODBC can do in three and OLE DB in one. See Table 13.1 for a quick rundown of the methods involved.

For the History Buffs: How ODBC Came to Be

In early 1988, Microsoft's Applications Group realized it had a problem. Microsoft had a whole slew of applications they wanted to share data. Enter Kyle Geiger. Geiger, fresh from eight years experience at Wang Laboratories—primarily in PC databases recalls that he was given this sort of ill-defined problem and told to go "think about it for awhile." Geiger thought about it for awhile and restated the problem as one of delivering data "from anywhere" into Microsoft applications, producing a first specification by Spring of 1988.

By Spring of 1989, the emerging ODBC spec had gone through several drafts. Geiger and members of Microsoft's Applications and Systems Groups wrestled with how much reliance they should put on the just-inherited Sybase DB-Library API. Concurrently, Geiger heard about what was to become the SQL Access Group (SAG). Then came three grueling years of consensus building as a member of the SAG. The culmination of phase one was the March 92 ODBC Developers Conference where the ODBC 1.0 SDK was demonstrated and distributed.

The design goals of ODBC were to provide location, DBMS, and in particular ODBC driver transparency; to provide SQL as a language for universal data access, even to non-SQL data sources; to leverage existing and evolving standards; and to provide tools for easy ODBC setup and administration.

Although ODBC was designed as a Windows-specific API, because it was built on top of the SAG Call Level Interface (CLI) specification, the potential for cross-platform ODBC compliant APIs was always present. In fact, in 1994, ODBC links for both the UNIX and Macintosh worlds (via Apple Data Access Language, or DAL) began to appear.

Continues

Meanwhile, Microsoft revised the ODBC spec and introduced it as the ODBC 2.0 SDK. The main difference between ODBC 1.0 and ODBC 2.0 was new 32-bit support and enhanced functionality for the so-called "navigational" model. The latter essentially maps SQL functionality to non-SQL databases and data sources including xBASE and Paradox. (As of late 1999, ODBC 4.x drivers are shipping.)

ODBC Architecture

The ODBC architecture has four components:

1. *Application*: performs processing and calls ODBC functions to submit SQL statements and retrieve results.
2. *Driver Manager*: loads drivers on behalf of an application.
3. *Driver*: processes ODBC function calls, submits SQL requests to a specific data source, and returns results to the application. If necessary, the driver modifies an application's request so that the request conforms to syntax supported by the associated RDBMS.
4. *Data Source*: consists of the data that the user wants to access and its associated operating system, RDBMS, and network platform (if any) used to access the RDBMS.

The ODBC Process

To interact with a data source, an application:

- Connects to the data source. It specifies the data source name and any additional information needed to complete the connection.
- Processes one or more SQL statements.
  - The application places the SQL text string in a buffer. If the statement includes parameter markers, it sets the parameter values.
  - If the statement returns a result set, the application assigns a cursor name for the statement or allows the driver to do so.
  - The application submits the statement for prepared or immediate execution.
  - If the statement creates a result set, the application can inquire about the attributes of the result set, such as the number of columns and the name and type of a specific column. It assigns storage for each column in the result set and fetches the results.
  - If the statement causes an error, the application retrieves error information from the driver and takes appropriate action.
  - Ends each transaction by committing it or rolling it back.
- Terminates the connection when it has finished interacting with the data source.

Oh, and by the way, ODBC drivers aren't limited to Windows-only systems. You can get ODBC drivers to run under just about any operating system—UNIX, OS/400, Macintosh, even mini-computer and mainframe operating systems. Merant Software (www.merant.com) and International Software Group Ltd. (ISG, isgsoft.com) have especially good selections. Ken North's site (ourworld.compuserve.com/homepages/Ken_North) is another excellent resource, complete with links.

Table 13.1 An Overview of Data Access Methods circa 1999

ACCESS LAYER	DESCRIPTION	INTRODUCED	HIGH-LEVEL (ODBC) OR LOW-LEVEL (API)	WORKS UNDER 16-BIT WINDOWS	WORKS UNDER 32-BIT WINDOWS
DB-Library	Original programmatic access into SQL Server via C language API calls. Developed by Sybase.	1986	Low	√	√
Jet Engine	The "heart" of Microsoft Access. Essentially a set of DLLs that provide standardized database access methods. Contains its own SQL interpreter that provides SQL access to the data itself.	1993	Low	√	√
DAO (Data Access Objects)	Developed to provide easier access to ODBC.	1993	Hi	√	√
ODBC (Open Database Connectivity)	Generic layer designed to provide access to relational database engines via the Driver Manager. Early competitors included IDAPI (promoted largely by Inprise) and DRDA (IBM's API that's still used in some IBM shops.	1993	Medium	√	√
ODBC API	Higher performance method for using ODBC.	1993	Low	√	√

Table 13.1 *(Continued)*

ACCESS LAYER	DESCRIPTION	INTRODUCED	HIGH-LEVEL (ODBC) OR LOW-LEVEL (API)	WORKS UNDER 16-BIT WINDOWS	WORKS UNDER 32-BIT WINDOWS
ODBCDirect	An interim solution that provides ODBC access without going through Jet. Essentially wrapped a DAO shell around RDO2.	1997	Hi		√
RDO (Remote Data Objects)	Introduced to help with implementing remote server data access. Also preceded ODBCDirect as a way to get at ODBC directly.	1996	Hi		√
OLE DB (Object Linking and Embedding Data Base)	Flexible, next-generation engine that provides support for any data source such as e-mail. It can accept some query or command and respond with data that looks like a table. Microsoft's answer to the need for "extended" or object/relational DBMSs.	1997	Low		√
ADO (ActiveX Data Objects)	Provides access to OLE DB services from OLE automation clients like VB, VBA, and VBScript.	1997	Hi		√

The Big Three

Let's take a look at Figure 13.1 which provides an excellent overview of Microsoft's data access strategy of how all of the pieces stack up. Actually, it's not as hard to understand these pieces as it may seem and we'll show you how to use DAO, RDO, and ADO in a moment. The good news is that despite their different names and vintages, you'll notice a great deal of similarity between the different object models. After all, they all have to provide programmers with a means to connect to a database, open it, and then provide various ways for programmers (and ultimately their end users) to interact with the data, typically via tables, views, or result sets.

The Basics

Here's a quick overview of the high-level methods.

DAO came first. DAO was released with Access 1.0 and VB 3.0. DAO uses the Jet engine, which in turn uses the ODBC layer to access different data sources. DAO was primarily born to provide access to Microsoft Access data.

RDO, also built on top of the ODBC API, came next and was an access method particularly geared towards addressing remote databases (databases on servers other than the one you are on). RDO added a lot of functionality, but was more complex than DAO and just wasn't as easy to use. Further slowing RDO acceptance was the ongoing rumors of the arrival of the next, err, final access method … ADO.

ADO (the rumors were true!) is the latest, high-level product from Microsoft. It's an abstracted layer that isn't geared to any particular database—or even to databases in general. ADO is not built on top of ODBC, but rather on top of OLE DB.

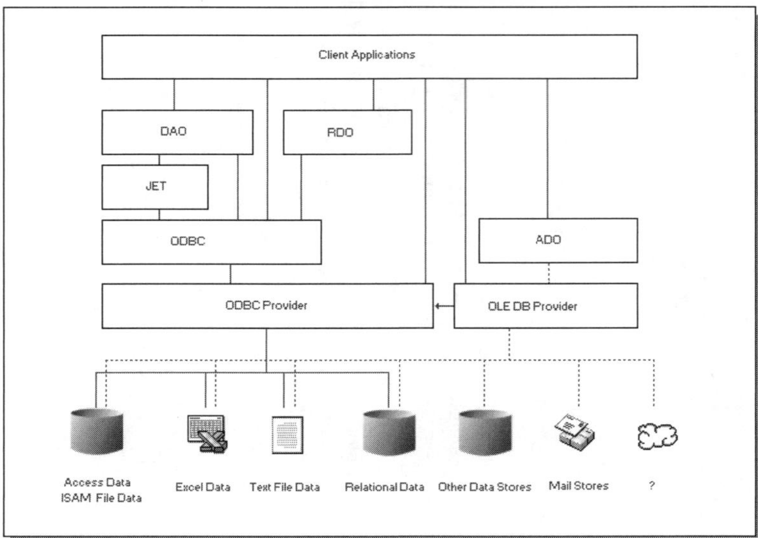

Figure 13.1 Pieces of the Microsoft data access puzzle.

UDA: THE HOTTEST BUZZWORD

***Universal Data Access (UDA)* is hopefully the last verse in our E-I-E-I-O refrain for a while. UDA is comprised of the following, current Microsoft data-access components: ADO, RDS (Remote Data Service) which used to be Advanced Database Connector (ADC), OLE DB, and ODBC. Smart developers will check out the www.microsoft.com/data site periodically for updates in UDA technology. Table 13.2 provides a taste of what we found on that page in late 1999.**

Table 13.2 Important Data Access-Related Information

1. UNIVERSAL DATA ACCESS PRODUCT INFORMATION
Universal Data Access Overview
■ Universal Data Access Architecture
■ Universal Data Access Articles
■ What is Universal Data Access?
■ What are the Microsoft Data Access Components?
Universal Data Access Strategy Whitepaper
Universal Data Access Fact Sheet
Manage Data from Myriad Sources with the Universal Data Access Interfaces
OLE DB/ADO: Making Universal Data Access a Reality
2. UNIVERSAL DATA ACCESS TECHNICAL MATERIALS
Universal Data Access Documentation
■ OLE DB Technical Materials
■ OLE DB Documentation
■ OLE DB White Papers
■ OLE DB Leveling: Choosing the Right Interfaces
■ Universal Data Access Through OLE DB
■ OLE DB for the ODBC Programmer
ADO Technical Materials
■ ADO Documentation
■ ADO Book Exerpts
■ ADO Overview
■ ADO White Papers
■ Migrating from DAO to ADO and Using ADO with the Jet Provider
■ Mapping ADO Methods to OLE DB Interfaces

Continues

Table 13.2 Important Data Access-Related Information *(Continued)*

2. UNIVERSAL DATA ACCESS TECHNICAL MATERIALS *(Continued)*
ADO/WFC vs. JDBC
■ Hands-On: ADO Programming
Implementing ADO with Various Development Languages: The ADO Rosetta Stone
■ ADO Workshop Archive
■ Overview of ADO
■ Output Parameters Wrong after ADO Command.Execute Call
RDS Technical Materials
■ RDS Documentation
■ RDS White Papers
■ Using the Customization Handler Feature in RDS 2.0
ODBC Technical Materials
■ ODBC Documentation
■ ODBC White Papers
■ Understanding ODBC Security Issues
■ Securing Windows NT to Prevent Tracing
3. DOCUMENTATION
UDA (Microsoft Data Access Components (MDAC) SDK)
ADO Documentation
OLE DB Documentation
OLE DB for OLAP Documentation
ODBC Documentation
4. DOWNLOADS
Three releases of MDAC are available here: one release for MDAC 2.0, and two releases for MDAC 2.1.
Component Checker
DAO 2.0 SP2
DAO SDK 2.0
DAO 2.1.2.4202.3
MDAC 2.1.2.4202.3
MDAC 2.1.1.3711.11
HOTFIX: Access ODBC Keyset Cursor Becomes Corrupt After a Delete
Data Access SDK 2.1
ISG's Custom Data Control for Visual Basic 5.0

Drilling Down into DAO

As we stated previously, DAO first shipped with VB3 and Office 97. We think that the combination of DAO and the built-in report writer (Crystal Reports) were the main factors (aside from the VBXs mentioned earlier) that propelled VB into such widespread use. Today, VB6 also ships with a so-called "banded" report writer called the *Data Report Designer* that allows you to create reports without using Crystal if you don't want to. (See the Sidebar, *Using VB6's Data Report Designer* later in this chapter.) At the time, most programmers didn't like database programming and didn't know that much about the relational model, so DAO was considered extremely helpful.

DAO and the other access methods in this chapter add a layer of abstraction between the underlying physical data storage and the coding level that most developers will hazard into. This layer provides an object model based on collections.

DAO's object model is relatively straightforward and easy to work with (see Figure 13.2). While easy to use, you will see that subsequent higher-level data models provide even more functionality and ease of use.

When you work with DAO, the first thing that is created is a DBEngine object. You don't need to explicitly create a DBEngine; this happens automatically if you create any of the objects contained within the DBEngine object. The DBEngine holds all of the DAO objects that are found in the DAO model. You can only have one DBEngine object per application.

DAO from VB

To create a new DAO VB project, open a new VB project. (If you don't want to create the files yourself, you can find both VB5 and VB6 versions on your CD-ROM.)

You'll also want to create a DSN for the WorkOrd SQL Server database. See the text file example that can be found on the accompanying CD-ROM.

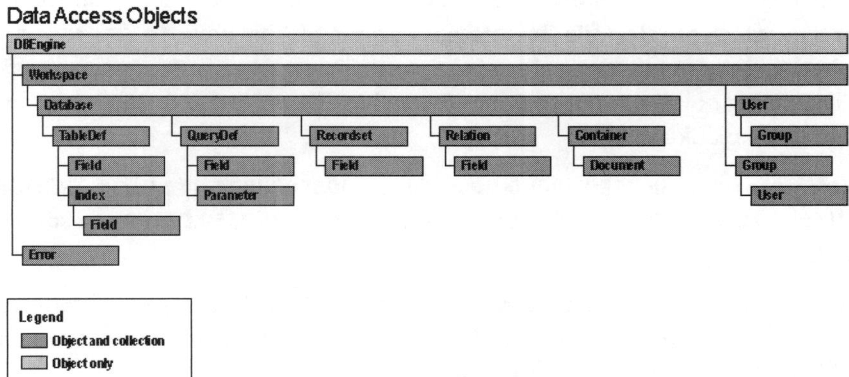

Figure 13.2 The DAO object model.

The first thing that you'll want to do when creating a new DAO VB project is to include a reference to the DAO libraries from within VB. Go to the Project, References… menu. You'll see references for Microsoft DAO 2.5 through 3.51. Select the Microsoft DAO 3.5 Object Library.

There are some basic properties associated with the DBEngine object, including the DAO version and the default user. By running the VB application for this chapter (see the Sidebar, *Running VBSQL*) and clicking on the DBEngine button, the properties associated to the DBEngine layer are displayed in the dialog box as shown in Figure 13.3.

Running VBSQL

The VBSQL application for this chapter can be found in both VB5 and VB6 formats on the companion CD-ROM.

To install the SQL Server WorkOrd database for this chapter, copy the file from the CD-ROM, which will be .MDF and .LDF into your SQL Server data directory (\MSSQL7\DATA by default). Then, within SQL Server's Query Analyzer tool, attach this database into your default SQL Server, by using the following stored procedure.

```
EXEC sp_attach_db @dbname='WorkOrd',
@filename1 = 'c:\mssql7\data\WorkOrd.mdf',
@filename2 = 'c:\mssql7\data\WorkOrd.ldf'
```

As a default, execute the copy under the sa login id.

If you only have the data component (MDF) of the two files for other databases you can use sp_attach_single_file_db to attach it.

THE .VBP FILE REFERENCES ARE USEFUL

Knowing where your control and DLL references are located is useful. You can see exactly which physical file the reference points to. This helps to diagnose problems when there are multiple copies of the same file on a user's PC. To see exactly what file is being pointed to, open your VBP project file in Notepad. An example reference line will look like this:

```
Reference=*\G{00025E01-0000-0000-C000-000000000046}#4.0#0#..\PROGRAM FILES\COMMON FILES\MICROSOFT SHARED\DAO\DAO350.DLL#Microsoft DAO 3.5 Object Library
```

This is especially useful in the cases where the VB project references window chops off a portion of your control/DLL filename at the end. Otherwise, you can only guess which actual file is in use at runtime.

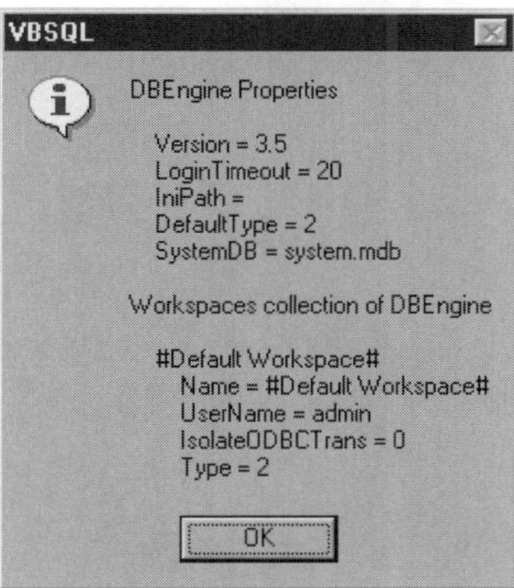

Figure 13.3 Properties of the DBEngine object.

Once we've added a reference to DAO, we then want to add some code to our project to open and look for records within the WorkOrd Access database.

To start with, let's create a Workspace in our code. A *Workspace* is an object (of which there can be more than one), that contains one or more open databases and the objects that are used to work with those databases. Each Workspace provides a unique user session. A major reason behind a Workspace is to control whether or not you're working with Jet or ODBCDirect. You can have multiple Workspaces open in the same application at the same time.

Let's open both a Workspace and a database to see how these pieces fit together. After that , we'll set up a routine with the tblRequest table in our WorkOrd database that returns the fields (columns) and their data types as stored within this table. If you want to play (err, that is, work) along with a pre-written project, you can load the VB project that contains our example from the accompanying CD-ROM. Open the VB project and look at the code under the DAO Workspaces button. Listing 13.1 shows the DAO_WorkSpaces routine that is called when you click on this button. Walking through this code together provides us with the framework that we use to discuss all of the following DAO examples.

NAMING CONVENTIONS

The VBSQL application that we discuss in this section contains code that works with DAO, RDO, and ADO. Notice that we add a DAO. or ADO. in front of objects that are common across the models. This allows VB to understand which of the libraries it should refer to. For example, each of the three access types includes a Recordset object. Using DAO.Recordset allows you to pinpoint which Recordset to actually use.

Running this routine pops up the dialog box shown in Figure 13.4, which shows the fields associated to a table, opened within a database in our Workspace.

```
Public Sub DAO_WorkSpaces()
    '=====================================
    ' Demonstrates DAO Workspace and
    ' Fields collections.
    '=====================================
    On Error GoTo DAO_WorkSpacesErr
    Dim ws As dao.Workspace
    Dim db As dao.Database
    Dim td As dao.TableDef
    Dim objTable As Object
    Dim objField As Object
    Set ws = dao.Workspaces(0)
    Dim strBuf$
    strBuf$ = "Table" & Chr$(9) & "Field" & Chr$(9) & _
        Chr$(9) & "Type" & Chr$(9) & "Size" & vbCrLf
    strBuf$ = strBuf$ & _
        "----------------------------------" & _
        "----------------------------------------" & vbCrLf

    Set db = ws.OpenDatabase(dbFile)
    For Each objTable In db.TableDefs
        If objTable.Name = "tblResult" Then
            strBuf = strBuf & objTable.Name & vbCrLf
            For Each objField In objTable.Fields
                strBuf = strBuf & Chr$(9) & objField.Name
                strBuf = strBuf & Chr$(9) & Chr$(9) & _
                    FieldType(objField.Type) & _
                     Chr$(9) & objField.Size & vbCrLf
            Next
        End If
    Next
    MsgBox strBuf$, vbInformation
    db.Close
    ws.Close
    Exit Sub
DAO_WorkSpacesErr:
    If errRoutine(Err, Error$(Err), "frmMain:DAO_WorkSpaces") Then
        Resume
    Else
        Resume Next
    End If
End Sub
```

Listing 13.1 The DAO_WorkSpaces routine that is called when you click on the application's button.

The first thing that we want to do in our routine is to set up three object variables—a Workspace (ws) object, a Database (db) object, and a Table Definition (td) object. We'll set these objects to point to their respective objects at runtime, within the DAO_WorkSpaces routine. Our db object will contain an object reference that allows us to work with a single database—which in this example is the Access 2000 database WorkOrd.MDB (\Shared\Data\Access2000\WorkOrd.MDB). Like the DBEngine and Workspace objects, a Database object contains properties and methods that allow you to work with the objects associated to a Database object in the DAO model. It's through the Database object that you'll open and work with the tables within the WorkOrd database. It's also through this same database reference that we'll open up and work with Table Definition objects. This allows us to inspect the structure of the tables themselves. Figure 13.4 shows that, through td, we can see what the column names are in a given table (or all of the tables), as well as the properties associated with these columns. For example, we can display the data type for each column as well as what the actual column size was set to.

The line Set ws = Workspaces(0) sets our ws object equal to the default Workspace object, which is the first (that is, the 0th) Workspace in the Workspaces collection. Similar to the DBEngine object, you don't have to explicitly issue this line of code. Working with a Database object first in your code will not only immediately create a DBEngine object for you; it will also automatically assign you to the default (0th) Workspace. For example, you don't have to dimension ws altogether. However, from the Database object on down to the DAO model, you'll need to enter explicit lines of code. As with all of the objects that we work with, at the end of the DAO_WorkSpaces routine, you'll see that we close the ws object, freeing its reference, with the ws.Close statement.

Once our Workspace is open, we can move along to opening the database itself. The line Set ds = ws.OpenDatabase (dbFile) is used to create our runtime database reference. OpenDatabase is a method associated with a Workspace, which takes one to four parameters, and returns a database reference. The first parameter, which is mandatory, is the name of the database to open. The optional parameters include Options, Read-Only—a Boolean value which locks a database against updates at its top-most level, and Connection information which holds user and password information for remote database connection.

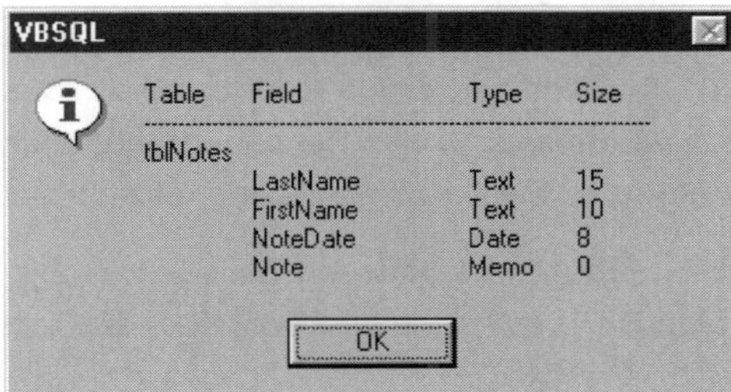

Figure 13.4 Digging into the Workspace.

DYNAMIC DATABASE NAMES IN VISUAL BASIC

In our example, we pass a value dbFile to the OpenDatabase call. The dbFile, which points to the database that we want to open, is a Property of the Base module in our VBSQL code. The dbFile property sets a private variable called mdbFile, which is loaded exactly once, at start up, with the actual name of the database to open. Setting up the database to open in this way allows us to use dbFile throughout our application code, while still being able to change the physical database location in exactly one place within our project. This works like a Const, except that it can be changed at runtime. For example, the database location can be changed via a user option screen, at runtime. Any subsequent code that works with dbFile picks up the new database location. To see how this is set up, click once on dbFile in the code and press Shift-F2 to go to the definition of this variable.

Once our database is open, we can inspect any of the DAO model database properties—or call any of the database methods within the model—using our db reference. The next layer *below* the database is accessed via object collections. Through our db object, we also gain access to the object collections shown in Table 13.3.

Our DAO_WorkSpaces example digs a bit more deeply into the TableDefs collection to allow us to look into the structure of an existing table.

CONFUSED ABOUT CLASSES, OBJECTS, AND COLLECTIONS?

At the top of the DAO hierarchy is the Microsoft Jet database engine itself, the DBEngine object. It's the only data-access object that is not "contained" in anything. It owns a collection called Workspaces (the name of a collection is always the plural of the objects it contains) which contains one or more Workspace objects. Each Workspace object has a Databases collection, which contains one or more Database objects. Each Database object has a TableDefs collection that contains one or more TableDef objects, and so on.

The elements in the DAO hierarchy are actually classes, not objects. They are the "blueprints" for the objects that you create to build your database application. A class is similar to a data type in that it describes what "kind" of object you're referring to. For example, when you declare Dim ws As dao.Workspace, you're stating that ws is a variable that stands for an object of the dao.Workspace class. Remember that a term like *Database object* actually means "an object of the Database class," not an *object* per se.

If you want more information about the differences between classes and objects, in Microsoft terms, see the VB help topics: Object Browser and search on the text "class."

A TableDef reference holds properties about a table's columns such as the columns' Names, Sizes, Types (data), and Default Values. The TableDef information is held within a Fields collection, associated with our TableDef reference. You can access the values stored within the Fields collection by any of the following ways:

Table 13.3 DAO Collections

COLLECTION	DESCRIPTION
TableDefs	A collection of TableDef (tables' stored definitions) objects
QueryDefs	A collection of stored Jet query definitions or temporary ODBCDirect Workspace query definitions
RecordSets	A collection of read-only or "updatable" objects used to manipulate data within your tables
Containers	A collection of documents and properties
Relations	A collection of objects to create or view existing relationships in your database

Fields(0)

Fields("name")

Fields![name]

With this information in hand, we can use a For Each loop, to look at every table within our database. The associated code for this is For Each objTable In db.TableDefs…Next. Within that loop, we can also loop through all of the Field objects within each TableDef. Listing 13.1 goes on to show how we print out the Name and Type of each field (column) within the tblRequest table. Remember that once you have access to a Field object, you can inspect any of the properties associated with it including whether or not the column is required, what its default value is, whether or not it can have a zero length, if it has any other validation rules, and so on. See the extensive VB help topic on DAO and drill into the model graphics (which are hypertext graphics) to find out more of what's available.

Sample Code for Accessing SQL Server with DAO

This time, instead of connecting to a local Access MDB let's take our simple code example shown in Listing 13.1 and connect to our SQL Server database. There are a number of ways to do this that involve setting parameters to control the flow of the connection to the server, but the two main approaches to consider are Data Source Name (DSN) connections or DSN-less connections. A DSN connection is one where you specify, through tools or code, a previously named data source that you want your program to connect to. *You* can create and name this source, which ends up as an ASCII parameter file, or it could have been previously created by another user or administrator. We'll connect to our SQL Server, by first setting up, and then using, a new DSN called WorkOrd.

Throughout the rest of this chapter, we use two separate PCs to illustrate remote server connections. The server, a WinNT PC named NTWebSrv, has the WorkOrd database loaded within SQL Server 7. A Win9x PC, called PCV-120-1 in our examples, runs the VB code against the SQL Server machine. You don't need two separate PCs to work through these examples, but you do need to be aware of what's happening on the "back end" (where SQL Server is) and the "front end" (the VB part). The VB project includes text boxes where you can define your own NT Server name, User ID, and

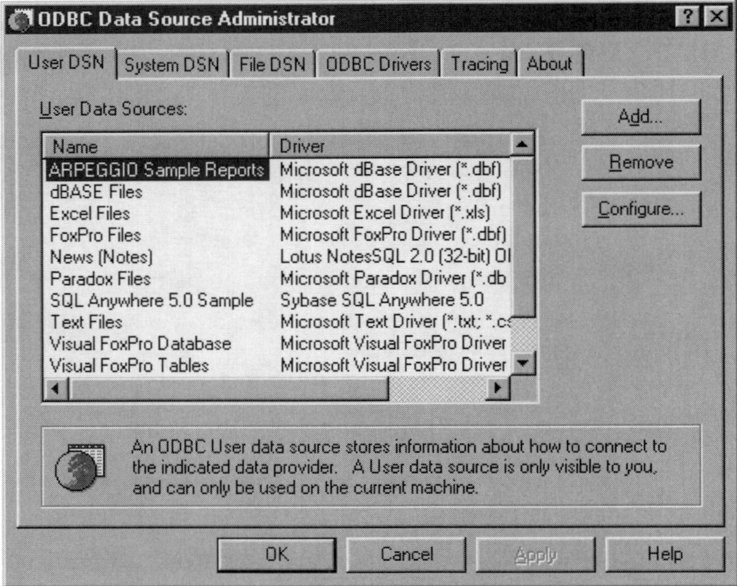

Figure 13.5 Setting up a data source name.

Passwords, which are picked up for DSN-less connections at runtime. Make sure to change them on the frmMain form so that you don't need to re-enter these again each time that the program is run.

To set up our WorkOrd DSN, go to your system control panel (Start, Settings, Control Panel) and click on the ODBC icon and study the dialog shown in Figure 13.5. This screen is where you set up data sources that can only be viewed and used by you (User DSN).

The two main types of data sources are File and System. *File data sources* point to specific files (or databases) that are shared by users (File DSN) on potentially different machines. A File DSN can be placed on a shared file system. *Drivers* list the data drivers that have already been set up on your PC. *System data sources* can be shared by other users on the same machine (via System DSN) and multiple File DSNs. With this information in hand, let's start to create a File DSN for our WorkOrd database.

We're going to set up a File DSN. Click on the File tab within the ODBC control panel applet and press Add.... This brings up a dialog where you can select what the data source for your DSN will be. Example choices include:

Lotus NotesSQL 2.0 (32-bit) ODBC Driver (*.nsf)

Microsoft Access Driver (*.mdb)

Microsoft dBase Driver (*.dbf)

Microsoft Excel Driver (*.xls)

Microsoft Text Driver (*.txt, *.csv)

SQL Server

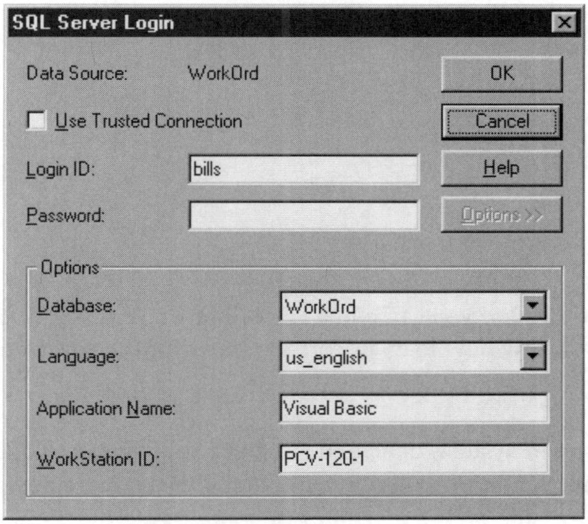

Figure 13.6 Providing server-specific information to ODBC.

Choose SQL Server and fill in the details for your server similar to what you see in Figure 13.6.

Clicking the Advanced button on this screen allows you to fill in more detail about which Server to use, the Database, the default USERID, or other DSN properties as illustrated in Figure 13.7.

By default, a file is created in your \Program Files\Common Files\ODBC\Data Sources folder with the same name as you specified within the DSN setup—WorkOrd

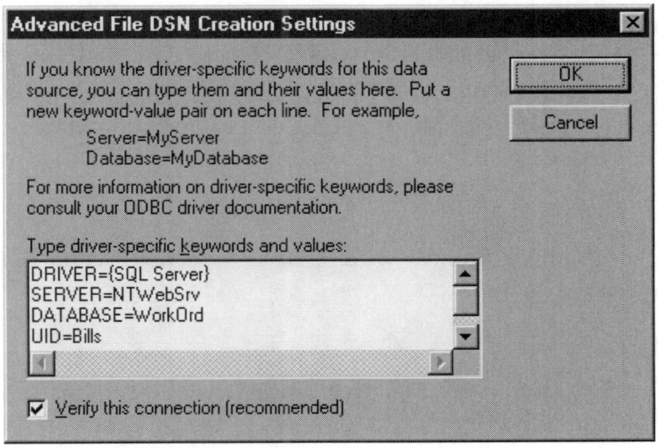

Figure 13.7 Adding additional DSN properties.

in our case. The WorkOrd.DSN file that we just created generates a small text file that contains the following lines:

```
[ODBC]
DRIVER=SQL Server
UID=sa
DATABASE=WorkOrd
WSID=PCV-120-1
APP=Microsoft® Windows® Operating System
SERVER=NTWebSrv
```

Since it's a text file, this means that you can edit a DSN file with Notepad or any other text editor—as long as you know how to enter correct values for the parameters.

THE SCOOP ON DSNS

What's the difference between System, User, and File Data Source Names (DSNs)? File DSNs keep their connection information in a file that you can store anywhere, but System and User DSNs reside on the machines that you create them on. As you might expect, a User DSN is associated with a single user, while a System DSN is associated with a system and can be used by several different users, that is who may share the system. Both User and System DSNs are faster than File DSNs. Of course, all DSN connections have the advantage relative to DSN-less connections that you don't have to recompile if you have to change the database location. The following examples illustrate DSN-less connections that use OLE DB and then ADO 2.0:

"Provider=SQLOLEDB;Data Source=Your_server_name;Initial

Catalog=the_database;UID=your_user_id:PWD=your_password:"

ConnectionString =

"PROVIDER=MSDASQL.1;UID=;PWD=;DATABASE=PURCHASING;SERVER=FOO;DRIVER={SQLSERVER};DSN=";"

Sample Code for Reading Data with DSN and DSN-Less Connections with DAO

Let's start by writing a VB application that displays the very last (logical) record that was added to the tblRequest table within our SQL Server WorkOrd database. We start with a DSN connection, but also show you how to implement the DSN-less approach.

DSN Connections

Our VB application has a simple interface with three main sections on it—one each for DAO, RDO, and ADO (see Figure 13.8).

Model-Specific Buttons

To make it easy to track through the code, each of the DAO, RDO, and ADO section buttons call their own individual routines, as is shown in the DAO button code shown in Listing 13.2. The buttons are set up as an array, with the button clicked on then passing an index to the click routine for handling.

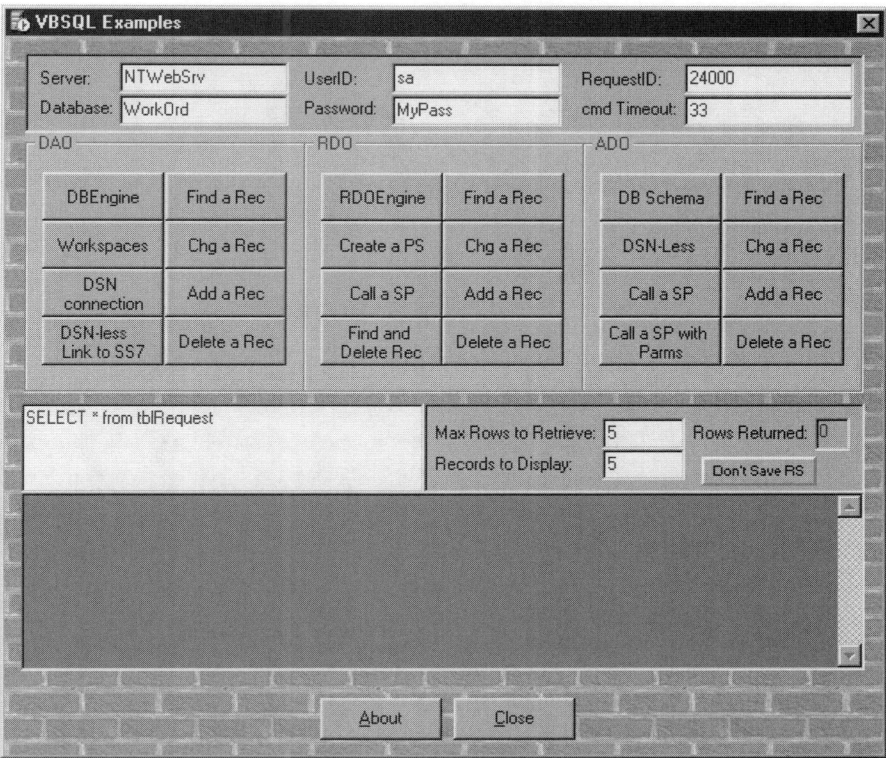

Figure 13.8 Our project's interface.

```
Private Sub cmdDAO_Click(Index As Integer)
    Dim strResult$
    RetrieveCurrentParms
    Select Case Index
        Case 0: Call DAO_DBEngine
        Case 1: Call DAO_WorkSpaces
        Case 2: Call DAO_DSN_Connection
        Case 3: Call DAO_SS7Link
        Case 4: MsgBox ("Found Requester: " & DAO_Maint("FND"))
        Case 5: MsgBox ("Requester Changed to: " & DAO_Maint("CHG"))
        Case 6: MsgBox (DAO_Maint("ADD"))
        Case 7: MsgBox (DAO_Maint("DEL"))
    End Select
End Sub
```

Listing 13.2 DAO button click control code in the VBSQL project.

The DSN button under the DAO section of the VBSQL application executes the code in Listing 13.3.

```
Public Sub DAO_DSN_Connection()
    On Error GoTo DAO_DSN_ConnectionErr
    Dim ws As Workspace
    Dim db As Database
    Dim rs As Recordset
    Dim td As TableDef
    Dim strMsg$
    Set ws = Workspaces(0)
    Set db = ws.OpenDatabase("WorkOrd", dbDriverComplete, _
           False, "DSN=WorkOrd")
    setHGOn
    Set rs = db.OpenRecordset("SELECT * from tblRequest " & _
           "Order by RequestDate DESC", dbOpenSnapshot)
    setHGOff
    strMsg$ = vbCrLf & "Requester: " & rs("Requester") & vbCrLf & _
            "Request Date: " & rs("RequestDate") & vbCrLf & _
            "Date Received: " & rs("ReceiveDate")
    MsgBox strMsg$, vbInformation, APP_NAME & _
    " - Last Record Entered"
    strMsg = ""
    ' List the names of the tables in the TableDef collection
    For Each td In db.TableDefs
        If UCase$(Mid$(td.Name, InStr(td.Name, "."), 4)) <> ".SYS"
           Then
                strMsg = strMsg & "Table Name (" & td.Name & ")" _
                & vbCrLf
        End If
    Next
    rs.Close
    db.Close
    ws.Close
    MsgBox strMsg, vbExclamation, APP_NAME
    Exit Sub
DAO_DSN_ConnectionErr:
    If errRoutine(Err, Error$(Err), "frmMain:DAO_DSN_Connection")
Then
        Resume
    Else
        Resume Next
    End If

End Sub
```

Listing 13.3 Reading a table with a DAO DSN connection.

The first parameter in the OpenDatabase call can contain either a name for an existing Jet database file such as XYZ.MDB, or a DSN. In our case, we're going directly against the Access version of our WorkOrd table. The second parameter, dbDriverComplete in our example, controls if and how the user is prompted for login information. You can choose to allow the user to enter their login id and password at runtime, and even to specify a different database than the one shown in the OpenDatabase call (see Figure 13.9). If you select dbDriverNoPrompt, ODBC uses the information in the first and fourth parameters to make the connection, and if the information is incorrect or incomplete, you will get a runtime error.

Using dbDriverPrompt ODBC always prompts the user for the parameters, as shown in Figure 13.9, but the information in the first and fourth parameters is used as default values within the prompt. The dbDriverComplete parameter opens the database without prompting the user, if the first and fourth parameters provide all of the information needed, otherwise it behaves like dbDriverPrompt.

Finally, dbDriverCompleteRequired behaves like dbDriverComplete except that ODBC doesn't allow the user to override any values that have been supplied in the first and fourth parameters.

TRUE OR FALSE

The list of data types that SQL Server supports may look pretty encouraging, but you may run into a few wrinkles. For example, in Access the actual value for the Boolean data type, True differs from that which is stored within SQL Server. In Access and the VB line (VB, VBA, VBScript), the constant True equals -1 and False equals 0. Of course, nearly every other programming language considers True to be a 1 and False to be a 0.

Make sure to check your data type mappings before making any assumptions.

SQL Server Login
Data Source:
Login ID: bills
Password: ******
OK
Cancel
Options >>
Options
Database: WorkOrd
Language:
Application Name: Visual Basic
WorkStation ID: PCV-120-1

Figure 13.9 SQL Server login dialog.

DSN-Less Connections

Building upon the code example shown in Listing 13.3, we'll now add code to open a recordset, display columns (fields) within a result set, and add some basic error handling. While we are in the database, we will also use the TableDef collection to dump out all of the table names within the WorkOrd database. This time we'll use a *DSN-less connection* to access SQL Server. That is, we will access SQL Server *without* using the DSN text file that we created in the previous example.

As before, the first thing that we need to do is to create a ws object to open our database table. From there, we can issue a ws.OpenDatabase call to open the WorkOrd database in SQL Server. Notice how we close the database and Workspace objects (in that order) to close out the connections when we're finished with them.

The first thing that you'll probably notice in the code from Listing 13.4 is that we've placed a DAO. in front of the data access objects that we plan to use. Since each of the DAO, RDO, and ADO access methods use objects such as Fields and Databases, an easy way to distinguish among them is to use a dao., rdo., or adodb. prefix. Secondly, you'll notice that we have parameterized the OpenDatabase call. Now parameters, such as Database (sDatabase) and User ID (sUserID) are obtained from variables, not from the DSN control file. These variables are loaded from the top set of text boxes in our VBSQL application, with a RetrieveCurrentParms routine. This routine is run when you click on the buttons within the application. This syntax allows you to play with differing User IDs or Databases (to some degree) without having to stop the program and change the code directly.

USE PREFIXES

If you have multiple references in the Project References dialog that define the same name (as in Fields or Databases), then VB uses the definition nearest the top of the list, unless you explicitly add a qualifier such as DAO. or RDO. in front of the name in the code. So, if you want to mix and match database-access methods, you had better make sure to qualify the declarations. This can be a problem even if you don't use DAO, RDO, and ADO all in the same project. Consider what would happen (been there, done that) if you used your favorite database-access method, with unqualified names and added a reporting package that also defined a "Fields" collection for example. This would result in the same issue as if you had several unqualified database methods in use.

Aside from these housekeeping types of additions, the major change in this routine is within the OpenDatabase call. This time we don't specify a DSN=DSN connection string. Instead, we add a Server= and point directly at the NTWebSrv SQL Server machine. Remember that you'll have to modify this to match your own NT Server name. We also select a type of driver to use to access this server—{SQL Server}. Note that the brackets are optional, in our case. By simply adding these Driver and Server properties, we can directly connect to the SQL Server with our OpenDatabase call.

HOW TO DECIDE WHEN TO USE DSN OR DSN-LESS

- **Use DSN connections when users are not comfortable with changing parameters to access SQL Server directly or there are multiple types of applications like Lotus Notes, Excel, VB, or Access, that all need to access the same data source easily. Also consider DSN connections if you can maintain remote .DSN files from a central LAN location.**
- **Use DSN-less connections when the users are more experienced or the parameters that go into your database connection change frequently.**

Doing this allows us to access SQL Server from any PC that can go against the server.

```
Dim ws As dao.Workspace
Dim db As dao.Database
Dim td As dao.TableDef
Dim fd As dao.Field
Dim fc As dao.Fields
Dim strMsg$
Set ws = Workspaces(0)
Set db = ws.OpenDatabase("", dbDriverPrompt, False, _
    "ODBC;Driver={SQL Server};SERVER=" & sServer & ";" & _
    "DATABASE=" & sDatabase & ";" & _
    "UID=" & sUserID & ";" & _
    "PWD=" & sPassword & ";")
For Each td In db.TableDefs
    If UCase$(Mid$(td.Name, InStr(td.Name, "."), 4)) <>  _
       ".SYS" Then
            strMsg = strMsg & "Table Name (" & td.Name & _
                   ")" & vbCrLf
    End If
Next
db.Close
ws.Close
Set db = Nothing
Set ws = Nothing
```

Listing 13.4 DSN-less code. Modify the parameters for your own system names.

PASSING DBUCK

While we show that we open and close a Database (ds) object within each of our code routines, this does take a long time to do, since the database schema must be returned to the called routine each time that the database is opened. Depending upon the application, you may wish to open the database once and then pass the ds object to different routines, each of which may open and work with the tables within the database. A final CloseData (ds as Database) routine could be set up to close the database connections once you have finished working with them.

Listing 13.5 (this code can be found within the DAO Find a Rec button in the VBSQL code) shows how to look for a specific record using DAO. As we did in Listing 13.4, we first open a workspace and then a database.

```
Public Function DAO_Maint(strAction As String) As String
    On Error GoTo DAO_MaintErr
    Dim ws As dao.Workspace
    Dim db As dao.Database
    Dim rs As dao.Recordset
    Dim strSQL$
    Dim strMsg$
    setHGOn
    Set ws = dao.Workspaces(0)
    Set db = ws.OpenDatabase("WorkOrd", dbDriverPrompt, _
        False, "Driver={SQL Server};" & _
        "Server=" & sServer & ";" & _
        "Database=" & sDatabase & ";" & _
        "UID=" & sUserID & ";" & _
        "PWD=" & sPassword & ";")
    Select Case strAction$
        Case "FND"
            ' N. Frankel is the initial value for this field.
            strSQL$ = "SELECT * from tblRequest " & _
                        "WHERE RequestID=" & sRequestID
            Set rs = db.OpenRecordset(strSQL, dbOpenSnapshot)
            If Not rs.EOF Then
                strMsg$ = vbCrLf & "Request ID: " & _
                    rs("RequestID") & vbCrLf & _
                    "Requester: " & rs("Requester") & vbCrLf & _
                    "Request Date: " & rs("RequestDate") & _
                    vbCrLf & "Date Received: " & rs("ReceiveDate")
                MsgBox strMsg$, vbInformation, APP_NAME
                DAO_Maint = rs("Requester")
            Else
                ' if the requested record was not found, then just
                ' return the highest RequestID in the database.
                rs.Close
                strSQL$ = "SELECT * FROM tblRequest " & _
                        "ORDER BY RequestID DESC"
                Set rs = db.OpenRecordset(strSQL, dbOpenSnapshot)
                If Not rs.EOF Then
                    rs.MoveFirst
                    strMsg$ = vbCrLf & "Request ID: " &
                            rs("RequestID") & vbCrLf & _
                    "Requester: " & rs("Requester") & vbCrLf & _
                    "Request Date: " & rs("RequestDate") & _
                    vbCrLf & "Date Received: " & rs("ReceiveDate")
                    MsgBox strMsg$, vbInformation, _
```

```
                    "Record not found, returning " & _
                    "highest RequestID # instead."
                DAO_Maint = rs("Requester")
            Else
                DAO_Maint = Format$(23079) & _
                    " Record not found!"
            End If
        End If
        rs.Close
    End Select
    db.Close
    ws.Close
    setHGOff
    Exit Function
DAO_MaintErr:
    setHGOff
    If Err = 3059 Then  ' operation cancelled by the user
        Exit Function
    End If
    Dim errObj As Error
    ' Enumerate Errors collection and display properties of
    ' each Error object.
    For Each errObj In DBEngine.Errors
        With errObj
            strMsg = _
                "Error #" & .Number & vbCrLf
            strMsg = strMsg & _
                "    " & .Description & vbCrLf
            strMsg = strMsg & _
                "    Error occurred in: " & .Source & vbCrLf
        End With
        MsgBox strMsg
    Next
    If errRoutine(Err, Error$(Err), "frmMain:DAO_Maint",
NO_ERROR_DISPLAY) Then
        Resume
    Else
        Resume Next
    End If
End Function
```

Listing 13.5 Finding information with DAO.

Sample Code to Add Data with DAO

In Listing 13.6, we show how to add a record with DAO. This code can also be found within the DAO Add a Rec button in the VBSQL code. We use the INSERT SQL statement

```
Case "ADD"
            Dim dtRequest As Date
            Dim dtReceive As Date
            dtRequest = Format(Now - 7, DATE_STRING)
            dtReceive = Format(Now, DATE_STRING)
            strSQL$ = "INSERT INTO tblRequest " & _
                "(RequestID,SiteLog, Requester, SiteID, " & _
                "RequestDate, ReceiveDate) " & _
                "VALUES " & _
                "(24000,'" & "PH-832" & "','" & "Shadish" & _
                    "'," & 100 & ",'" & dtRequest & _
                    "','" & dtReceive & "')"
            MsgBox strSQL, vbOKOnly + vbInformation, _
                "Example of runtime syntax"
            db.Execute strSQL$, dbSQLPassThrough
            DAO_Maint = "Added a 24000 'Shadish' record."
```

Listing 13.6 Adding records with DAO.

to add a new tblRequest row. The format of INSERT includes parameters for the table to add to, the columns to use, and the actual values to place into the record when created.

Rather than open an explicit recordset object as we did with the Find method, this time we'll use the Database object's *Execute method*. Execute is used whenever a returned resultset is not required. In this case, we just want to add the record and don't care to manipulate individual columns after doing so. Notice that we include a dbSQL-PassThrough parameter to the Execute call. This allows the SQL to pass directly through to SQL Server for processing and doesn't run through the local DAO Jet SQL interpreter first. The SQL is just sent along to SQL Server untouched. This allows you to use proprietary features (features not supported by ODBC) including T-SQL. A word of caution, you need to be aware of the differences between how the receiving database server handles data types and SQL when using dbSQLPassThrough. In this example, we rely on the SQL Server to accept the specified format for dates and that the dates are submitted in quotes. Other database back ends may require a different format for dates that would require you to change the code.

SQLPASSTHROUGH

All queries executed by the Jet query processor must be written using Jet SQL syntax. However, Jet's SQL syntax isn't always the same as the SQL syntax used on your server database. By default, the Jet query processor is invoked when any DAO query is executed. In other words, unless you use the dbSQLPassThrough option with the Execute or OpenRecordset methods or create a SQLPassThrough QueryDef object, the Jet query processor will parse and execute the query's SQL syntax. It then attempts to perform whatever operations are needed on the workstation and the remote server to carry out the request.

You can also attack adding records by opening a recordset and calling the recordset's method to add rows. For example, the following lines of code both open the tblResult table and call Recordset method calls to add a record. The AddNew method creates a new, empty record with any specified default data values set. Each field is loaded individually. The Update method actually saves the row to the database. This approach provides a bit more flexibility and control, as well as readability, than using INSERT, but it's slower to code and execute since you need to explicitly open a recordset. Note that you also don't *need* to format the dates in this case because DAO and ODBC convert them automatically for the target data source.

```
strSQL$ = "SELECT * from tblRequest WHERE 1=0"

Set rs = db.OpenRecordset(strSQL, dbOpenDynaset)
rs.AddNew
rs("RequestID") = 24000
rs("SiteLog") = "PH-832"
rs("Requester")= "Shadish"
rs("SiteID")= 100
rs("RequestDate") = dtRequest
rs("ReceiveDate") = dtReceive
rs.Update
```

The WHERE 1=0 on the previous SQL SELECT statement allows us to return the columns to perform our AddNew method with, but doesn't return any actual data rows. If you don't need them, be sure to let SQL Server know in the interest of performance.

Sample Code to Change and Delete Data with DAO

Changing data with DAO is very similar to Add. The direct-database-execute approach is performed with the UPDATE statement. To do the same thing with a recordset requires opening the recordset to be updateable and then using the Edit method to allow the actual changes. Edit opens the specified row and exposes the fields for change. In the following example, we use the ! (bang) syntax to pass a new value to the requester field. Again, Update is called to actually save the information to the database.

```
        Case "CHG"
            ' N. Frankel is the initial Requester field value.
            strSQL$ = "SELECT * from tblRequest " & _
                            "WHERE RequestID=23079"
            Set rs = db.OpenRecordset(strSQL, dbOpenDynaset)
            rs.Edit
            rs!Requester = "Henry"
            rs.Update
            DAO_Maint = rs!Requester
            rs.Close
        Case "DEL"
```

Continues

```
            strSQL$ = "DELETE from tblRequest " & _
                "WHERE requestid=Requester='Shadish'"
            db.Execute strSQL$, dbSQLPassThrough
            DAO_Maint = "All 'Shadish' records deleted"
'============================================='
'                 Or                           "
=============================================='
        strSQL$ = "SELECT * from tblRequest " & _
                "WHERE requestid=Requester='Shadish'"
            Set rs = db.OpenRecordset(strSQL, dbOpenDynaset)
            While Not rs.EOF
                rc = MsgBox("Are you sure that you want to " & _
                  " delete (" & rs!Requester & "), " & _
                  "request id# " & rs!RequestID, vbYesNo)
                If rc Then
                    rs.Delete
                End If
                rs.MoveNext
            Wend
            rs.Close
```

Listing 13.7 Changing and deleting data with DAO.

The DELETE example code removes ALL of the records for the specified requester from the database in one shot. You can also choose to open a recordset that contains just this requester's records and then move through them one at a time, perhaps deleting the records after prompting the user for confirmation to do so.

Moving Around a DAO Recordset

With an open DAO recordset, easy-to-use methods are available to move around the rows in the recordset. You've seen us use the rs.MoveNext method to progress to the next row in a recordset. In the same fashion, MovePrev, MoveFirst, and MoveLast provide additional ways to get around your data. There's also a Move method that allows you to jump "n" number of rows from where you are at, taking a position to start from as an optional parameter.

The FindFirst, FindPrev, FindLast, and FindNext DAO methods accept criteria parameters that allow you to search through the results within a recordset. A rs.AbsolutePosition method returns (or lets you set) your relative position within a recordset directly. Finally, the BookMark method allows you to deposit programmatic breadcrumbs along your path through the recordset data—allowing you, or your users, to easily return to a record of interest later on.

As you move through the other data-access methods described in this chapter, keep in mind that they also provide very similar methods to move through data. This removes some of the headaches that would otherwise result from having so many data methods in play at the same time.

FYI LINKED TABLES VERSUS OPENDATABASE CALLS

When you issue an OpenDatabase call, the database's schema (structure) is returned to the calling machine. Although this may only result in a slight performance degradation for local database calls, it can cause serious performance problems when you connect to a remote database. If you use LinkedTables, to link a local table to your remote server's data, the database's schema is copied and created locally, meaning that subsequent database reads operate much faster. The downside of using linked tables is that you can't issue DML and DDL statements against a locally-linked table, nor can you make T-SQL calls against a linked table that's under the control of Jet.

ADO? DAO? RDO? WHEN TO USE WHAT?

For a quick explanation of when to use which method, consider the following:

- **DAO. Use it if you're working on 16-bit platforms, maintaining (dare we say it) legacy Access applications, or must use Access databases as a core component of your solution.**
- **RDO. Use it if you want the added functionality of things like prepared statements *and* a performance boost over DAO, but are maintaining existing RDO code or cannot upgrade your operating systems to Win32 versions that support ADO 2.x yet.**
- **ADO. For anything other than the above and, for all new projects.**

Drilling Down into RDO

RDO emerged mainly to provide a better match to the underlying ODBC API set than was available with DAO. The RDO object model is shown in Figure 13.10. DAO, remember, had been created mainly for Microsoft Access and Jet. As developers came to require remote database support and full use of stored procedure calls, DAO just couldn't meet the needs. Enter RDO in 1996.

RDO was initially rolled out only in the top-of-the-line (read most expensive) Enterprise Edition of Visual Basic. The idea was that developers who only created desktop applications in the other versions of VB did not need *advanced* database features.

Figure 13.10 shows how similar the RDO model is to the DAO model. Some slight differences are immediately apparent—like the fact that RDO has ResultSets and not RecordSets (don't you love it when Microsoft does things like this to you?). Also, the Workspace concept gives way to an Environment collection.

Remember how you had to add a reference to the DAO libraries when you started the VB DAO project? Well, guess what? You have to do the same thing with RDO. So, the first thing that you want to do when creating a new VB project to work with RDO is to include a reference to the RDO libraries from within VB. Open the References dialog and add in Microsoft Remote Data Object 2.0.

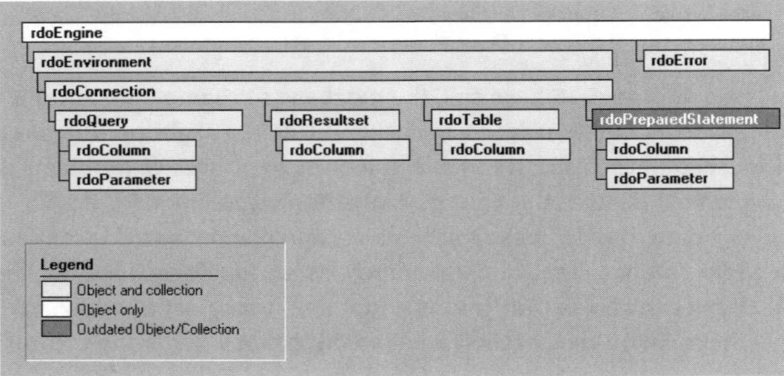

Figure 13.10 The RDO object model.

Sample Code to Access SQL Server with RDO

Our VBSQL example includes RDO code to read, update, add, and delete information from the WorkOrd table. As the code is largely the same between the different data-access models, we will run through only the read portion here, allowing you to browse the sample code for specifics on adding, updating, and deleting. The code shown in Listing 13.8 finds a record in the tblRequest table.

Again, you'll note many similarities with DAO. However, one of the most important differences is that now you can open a "connection" to the data. This connection takes the familiar rdDriverComplete and Connection strings that we used for DAO. When we open a RDO Resultset (aka dao.Recordset), we pass it a parameter to describe how to open the data in the second parameter position. This is rdOpenDynamic in Listing 13.8. Other possible values are shown in Table 13.4.

Table 13.4 Recordset Options

CONSTANT	VALUE	DESCRIPTION
rdOpenForwardOnly	0	(Default) Opens a forward-only-type rdoResultset object. You can change the record that you are on, but only move forward through the Resultset.
rdOpenKeyset	1	Opens a keyset-type rdoResultset object. Keys to access each row are cached locally. You can fully change the data and move forward or backward through the data.
rdOpenDynamic	2	Opens a dynamic-type rdoResultset object. Similar to a Keyset, except that changes to the Resultset made by other users while you have it open are automatically updated in your Resultset without having to explicitly refresh it.
rdOpenStatic	3	Opens a static-type rdoResultset object. You cannot add, change, or delete the data within the Resultset.

The find code in Listing 13.8 not only locates the specified records, but also prompts the user to see if they want to delete the record.

```
Public Function RDO_Maint() As String
   On Error GoTo RDO_MaintErr
    Dim en As rdoEnvironment
    Dim cn As rdoConnection
    Dim rs As rdoResultset
    Dim strSQL As String
    Dim rc As Variant
    setHGOn
    Set en = rdoEngine.rdoEnvironments(0)
    Set cn = en.OpenConnection("", rdDriverComplete, False,
"Driver={SQL Server};" & _
        "Server=" & sServer & ";" & _
        "Database=" & sDatabase & ";" & _
        "UID=" & sUserID & ";" & _
        "PWD=" & sPassword & ";")
    strSQL$ = "SELECT * from tblRequest WHERE
RequestID=24000"
    Set rs = cn.OpenResultset(strSQL$, rdOpenDynamic)
    While Not rs.EOF
        rc = MsgBox("Delete tblRequest " & vbCrLf & vbCrLf &
            "Record # " & rs!RequestID & vbCrLf & _
            "Name=" & rs!Requester & vbCrLf & _
            "Request Date=" & rs!RequestDate & vbCrLf & _
            "Receive Date=" & rs!ReceiveDate, vbYesNo +
vbExclamation, APP_NAME)
        If rc = vbYes The
            rs.Delete
        End If
        rs.MoveNext
    Wend
    rs.Close
    cn.Close
    setHGOff
    Exit Function
RDO_MaintErr:
    If errRoutine(Err, Error$(Err), "frmMain:RDO_Maint")
Then
        Resume
    Else
        Exit Function
    End If
End Function
```

Listing 13.8 Searching for data with RDO.

Stored Procedures and Prepared Statements

Once you've connected to SQL Server, it makes sense to take advantage of the power that it provides in a client/server system by pushing some of the work that needs to be done onto the server itself. If you read Chapter 12, you realize that we're referring to stored procedures. As discussed in that chapter, stored procedures are units of SQL code that reside within the SQL Server engine itself as pre-compiled code—almost as if they were extensions of the engine.

It won't take you long to appreciate the real power of RDO relative to DAO. Unlike DAO, RDO allows you to create prepared statements in a RDBMS. A *prepared statement* is one where you define a set of SQL syntax, along with any parameters that are required to use that SQL statement at runtime. You *prepare* your code by giving it to SQL Server ahead of time so that SQL Server can pre-compile it and pre-determine a runtime execution path.

Our RDO_CreatePS function prepares a somewhat detailed SQL statement that is used to insert data rows into the tblResult table. The ? syntax in the SQL text statement (strSQL$ = "INSERT into tblRequest Values (?, ?, ?, ?, ?, ?)") are placeholders for where the runtime data parameters are placed. The Set ps = cn.CreatePreparedStatement ("Insert", strSQL$) line uses a RDO prepared statement object to enter the Insert prepared statement into our server. Following this is the runtime code that loads the parameters and executes the SQL statement. You can easily parameterize a routine like this so that the Requester Name, RequestID, and any other fields can be changed by the user at runtime. (See Listing 13.9.)

```
Private Function RDO_CreatePS() As String
    On Error GoTo RDO_CreatePSErr
    Dim en As rdoEnvironment
    Dim cn As rdoConnection
    Dim ps As rdoPreparedStatement
    Dim strSQL As String
    setHGOn
    Set en = rdoEngine.rdoEnvironments(0)
    Set cn = en.OpenConnection(" ", rdDriverComplete, False,
        "DSN=WorkOrd;" & _
        "Driver={SQL Server};" & _
        "Server=" & sServer & ";" & _
        "Database=" & sDatabase & ";" & _
        "UID=" & sUserID & ";" & _
        "PWD=" & sPassword & ";")
    strSQL$ = "INSERT into tblRequest Values (?, ?, ?, ?, ?, ?)"
    Set ps = cn.CreateQuery("Insert", strSQL$)
    With cn.rdoPreparedStatements!Insert
        .rdoParameters(0).Value = 24000
        .rdoParameters(1).Value = "PH-832"
        .rdoParameters(2).Value = "Shadish"
        .rdoParameters(3).Value = 104
```

```
        .rdoParameters(4).Value = Format(Now - 2, DATE_STRING)
        .rdoParameters(5).Value = Format(Now, DATE_STRING)
    End With
    cn.rdoPreparedStatements!Insert.Execute
    ps.Close
```

Note: You probably won't want to close the prepared statement at this point since any work done to prepare will be lost. And you definitely wouldn't want to put the prepare inside a subroutine that does just one record and then call that subroutine in a loop. Be sure to keep the prepare statement outside the loop.

```
    cn.Close
    RDO_CreatePS = "Added (another) record key 24000 for '" & _
        "Shadish" & "'"
    setHGOff
    Set ps = Nothing
    Set cn = Nothing
    Set en = Nothing
    Exit Function
RDO_CreatePSErr:
    If errRoutine(Err, Error$(Err), "frmMain:RDO_CreatePS") Then
        Resume
    Else
        Resume Next
    End If
End Function
```

Listing 13.9 A RDO prepared statement.

Calling a Stored Procedure

The RDO code shown in Listing 13.10 demonstrates how to call a SQL Server stored procedure. We start by creating a stored procedure called ps_CountRequests, that is defined like the routine shown at the top of Listing 13.10. This stored procedure simply returns the number of rows that contain the Requester Name specified. You can display the contents of this stored procedure itself by issuing sp_HelpText ps_CountRequests in the WorkOrd database.

LISTING STORED PROCEDURE CODE

You can view stored procedures from the Enterprise Manager, but you can also use sp_stored_procedures to list out all of the stored procedure names in the current database (assuming you have access rights). You can run the sp_HelpText system stored procedure to display any stored procedure that you have the rights to see. See Chapter 12 for more information on stored procedures in general including how to use the Stored Procedure Editor.

```
ps_CountRequests
create proc ps_CountRequests (@rows integer output)
as
SELECT @rows = count(*)
from tblRequest WHERE requester= 'Shadish'

Private Sub RDO_CallSP()
    On Error GoTo RDO_CallSPErr
    Dim en As rdoEnvironment
    Dim cn As rdoConnection
    Dim ps As rdoPreparedStatement
    Dim strSQL As String
    setHGOn
    Set en = rdoEngine.rdoEnvironments(0)
    Set cn = en.OpenConnection(" ", rdDriverComplete, _
        False, "Driver={SQL Server};" & _
        "Server=" & sServer & ";" & _
        "Database=" & sDatabase & ";" & _
        "UID=" & sUserID & ";" & _
        "PWD=" & sPassword & ";")
    strSQL = "{ call ps_CountRequests(?) }"
    Set ps = cn.CreateQuery(" ", strSQL)' RDO 2.0
    ' Set ps = cn.CreatePreparedStatement (" ", strSQL) ' RDO 1.0
    ps.rdoParameters(0).Value = rdParamOutput
    ps.Execute
    MsgBox ps.rdoParameters(0).Value
    ps.Close
    cn.Close

    Set ps = Nothing
    Set cn = Nothing
    Set en = Nothing

    setHGOff
    Exit Sub
RDO_CallSPErr:
    If errRoutine(Err, Error$(Err), "frmMain:RDO_CallSP") Then
        Resume
    Else
        Resume Next
    End If
End Sub
```

Listing 13.10 Calling a stored procedure via RDO.

As before, we open a RDO environment and connection. Our SQL statement in this case is to call our stored procedure. This time we add a Prepared Statement (ps) object, into which we pass our sp call, using the connection's CreateQuery method. The CreateQuery method is the RDO 2.0 version of RDO 1.0's CreatePreparedStatement method.

The Prepared Statement object includes a parameters array, into which you can load variables to be used on parameterized stored procedures, similar to our previous RDO example. In this case, we want to designate the first parameter (0) as an output parameter (ps.rdoParameters(0).Value = rdParamOutput)—a place where the result from calling our sp is stored.

From there, we move on to run the sp, by calling the prepared statement Execute method. The results of our call are then retrieved from our output parameter at runtime.

BORK 4.5

Microsoft's BackOffice 4.5 Resource Kit (BORK 4.5), which is available from both Microsoft Press and as part of the Universal MSDN subscription, includes over a dozen useful utilities for SQL Server developers. One that we like is SQL Converter, a convenient tool that reformats strings of T-SQL for use in VB. For example, a T-SQL query such as:

```
select c.CompanyName, p.ProductName, sum(d.Quantity * d.UnitPrice)
from Customers c, Orders o, Order_Details d, Products p
where c.CustomerID = o.CustomerID
and o.OrderID = d.OrderID
and d.ProductID = p.ProductID
and p.ProductID in (5, 11, 12)
group by c.CompanyName, p.ProductName
go
```

must be formatted with quotes and line continuation characters for VB. SQL Converter will reformat the query to look something like this:

```
"select c.CompanyName, p.ProductName, sum(d.Quantity " _
& "* d.UnitPrice) from Customers c, Orders " _
& "o, Order_Details d, Products p where c.CustomerID " _
& "= o.CustomerID and o.OrderID = d.OrderID and " _
& "d.ProductID = p.ProductID and " _
& "p.ProductID in (5, 11, 12) group " _
& "by c.CompanyName, p.ProductName go"
```

SQL Converter can also be used to strip quotes and line continuations from VB code and turn it into T-SQL statements. This should be useful when developers want to use SQL Server Query Analyzer to debug a query embedded in a page of Visual Basic code.

Drilling Down into ADO

ADO is the high-level data access method promoted by Microsoft as the current standard. ADO now provides much of the functionality originally provided by DAO and RDO, but in an even easier-to-use format. ADO also adds a number of new features (see Table 13.5). As you can see from Table 13.5, ADO really is meant to provide access to any kind of structured or unstructured data.

ADO 1.0 (1996) was used to access data from Active Server (ASP pages) using VBScript code. To be honest, ADO 1.0 was weak and buggy. It provided less capability than DAO or RDO, but gave developers a vision for where Microsoft was heading. ADO 1.5 (1997) was rolled into the Microsoft Data Access (MDAC) kit and also distributed with IIS 4.0 and IE 4.0. MDAC included RDS and disconnected Recordsets, which allowed for retaining a Recordset between randomly attached connections—something that is frequently required for remote sales support applications. ADO 2.0 (1998) was included within MDAC 2.0 and was the first really reliable version of ADO. ADO 2.0, which is the version we primarily discuss in this book, provides all of the functionality of both DAO and RDO, but is easier and faster to use. ADO 2.5 (1999), adds OLAP recordsets, persistable recordsets, and bug fixes. ADO 2.5 is part of Win2000, with betas for WinNT 4.0 now available from Microsoft.

Learning from the difficulties that programmers had in moving from DAO to RDO, Microsoft spent some effort in making it easier for us to transition to ADO. ADO contains fewer objects than DAO, but is easier to use, since more can be controlled by properties rather than drilling down into objects. Just as RDO retained some of the best features of DAO, the ADO object model retains a number of familiar features as well. We still need to work with collections of objects, including Errors, Parameters and, yes, Recordsets too. Figure 13.11 shows the objects associated to the ADO model.

ADO 2.1 includes two new (oh, joy!) object models: ADOx for DDL operations and Jet Replication Objects (JRO) for replication operations. ADO 2.1 also adds better routines

Table 13.5 Features of ADO 2.0 and/or 2.1 Not Found in RDO/DAO

FEATURE	DESCRIPTION
Ability to use Native Providers	Allows you to directly call third-party OLE DB drivers.
OLAP Recordsets	Allows you to create data in a format suited for business intelligence applications like OLAP Services.
Recordset Persistence	Allows you to retain a Recordset after the connection to the database is broken—good for remote applications. You can also save and open a Recordset as a standalone file.
Createable Recordsets	Allows you to create temporary record sets on the fly.
Asynchronous Operations	ADO supports calling events upon the completion of some tasks. For example, this allows you to call an asynchronous Recordset. Open operation is notified by an execution complete event when the operation concludes.
Client Cursor Resyncs	Allows you to copy a result set to a client, manage the cursor (pointer into the data) locally, and maintain an overall reference to where the pointers point.

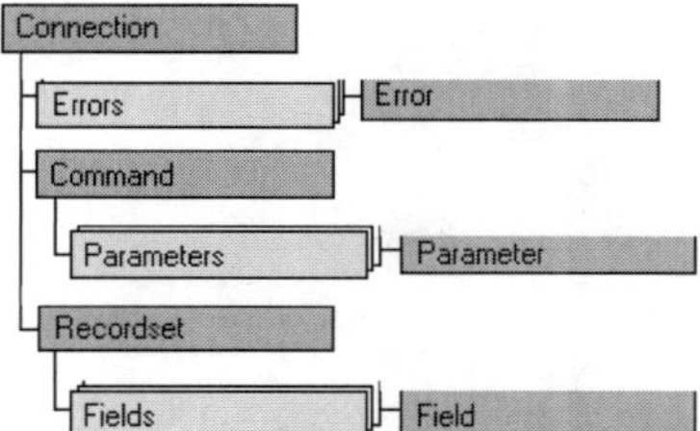

Figure 13.11 The ADO object model.

for seeking and indexing data, row updates on joined Recordsets, and data synchronization which facilitates replication.

Sample Code Examples for Accessing SQL Server with ADO

When you first create a new ADO VB project, you need to add a reference to the external Microsoft ADO library (DLL) files. Go to the Project, References...menu. Add in the reference for Microsoft ActiveX Data Objects 2.0 Library.

Sample Code for Reading Data with ADO

In the ADO_Maint function shown in Listing 13.11, we start off by retrieving data from our WorkOrd table. Unlike our RDO examples, we first create a Command object (cmd), which also includes the connection information. We can also start by creating the Connection object itself and then set up its Command object from that point. Next, we set our cmd object's activeConnection property with the now familiar looking DSN-less connection string. Notice again that the actual connection parameter values are pulled from the VBSQL screen at runtime. This allows you to change the connection parameter values in one place within the application rather quickly. The Command object contains very useful properties such as cmd.CommandTimeout and cmd.Properties (Maximum Rows) which are used to shut down a connection that doesn't respond in a timely manner (sTimeout) and also to restrict the number of rows that are returned. The CommandText property holds our actual SQL syntax and, with an Execute method call, away we go. Again, just as with DAO's Recordsets and RDO's Resultsets, the familiar column-value syntax, rs (Requester), is used to retrieve or set the actual data values.

```
Public Function ADO_Maint(strAction As String) As String
    On Error GoTo ADO_MaintErr
    Dim cn As New adodb.Connection
    Dim rs As New adodb.Recordset
    Dim cmd As adodb.Command
    Dim objData As Object
    Dim strSQL As String
```

Continues

```
Dim strMsg As String
Dim strOldName As String
Select Case strAction$
    Case "FND"
        setHGOn
        ' N. Frankel is the initial value for this field.
        Set cmd = New adodb.Command

        cmd.ActiveConnection = "Driver={SQL Server};" & _
            "Server=" & sServer & ";" & _
            "Database=" & sDatabase & ";" & _
            "Uid=" & sUserID & ";" & _
            "PWD=" & sPassword & ";"
        cmd.CommandText = "SELECT * from tblRequest " & _
            "WHERE RequestID=24000"      '23079"
        cmd.CommandTimeout = sTimeout
        cmd.Properties("Maximum Rows") = sMaximumRows
        Set rs = cmd.Execute
        If Not rs.EOF Then
            strMsg$ = vbCrLf & "Request ID: " & _
                rs("RequestID") & vbCrLf & _
                "Requester: " & rs("Requester") & vbCrLf & _
                "Request Date: " & rs("RequestDate") & _
                vbCrLf &"Date Received: " & _
                rs("ReceiveDate")
            MsgBox strMsg$, vbInformation, APP_NAME & _
            " - Record Found!"
                ADO_Maint = rs("Requester")
        Else
                ADO_Maint = "Record not found! " & _
                "Press the Add button."
        End If
        rs.Close

          Set rs = Nothing
          Set cn = Nothing
          setHGOff
```

Listing 13.11 Reading data with ADO.

Sample Code for Adding Data with ADO

You'll notice that the ADO add code looks pretty familiar. In ADO, as with RDO, we start by opening a Connection object. However, this time it's an *ADO* connection object. One of the Connection object's properties is Provider. We set it to the default of MSDASQL. Other possible options are shown in Table 13.6.

Yes, Virginia, there *are* differences between the providers. For example, MSDASQL and SQLOLEDDB use different connection properties that specify things like which database they want to use. MSDASQL uses Initial Catalog, while SQLOLEDB uses either Initial Catalog or Database. See the *MSDASQL* topic in *Books Online* for more information.

After opening the Connection object we want to create a Command object next. The Connection object is loaded into the Command object with the line Set cmd.ActiveConnection

Table 13.6 Provider Descriptions

PROVIDER OPTION	DESCRIPTION
.Provider = "MSDASQL"	The Default: maps OLE DB interfaces and methods to ODBC APIs
.Provider = "MSDAORA"	To access ODBC Oracle data sources
.Provider = "Microsoft.Jet.OLEDB.3.51"	To Access via Jet
.Provider = "SQLOLEDB"	To use the SQL Server OLEDB provider

= cn. This is a useful technique when you want to have one connection held open while executing multiple commands against that connection. Notice in particular the line of code cmd.CommandTimeout = cLng(sTimeout) that sets the amount of time that SQL Server will spend processing your SQL statement before automatically returning with a timeout error.

```
    Dim cn As New adodb.Connection
    Dim rs As New adodb.Recordset
    Dim cmd As adodb.Command
    Dim objData As Object
    Dim strSQL As String
    Dim strMsg As String
    Dim strOldName As String
       Case "ADD"
            Dim dtRequest As Date
            Dim dtReceive As Date
            dtRequest = Format(Now - 7, DATE_STRING)
            dtReceive = Format(Now, DATE_STRING)
            setHGOn
            With cn
                .Provider = "MSDASQL"
                .ConnectionString = "Driver={SQL Server};" & _
                    "Server=" & sServer & ";" & _
                    "Database=" & sDatabase & ";" & _
                    "Uid=" & sUserID & ";" & _
                    "PWD=" & sPassword & ";"
                .Open
            End With
            strSQL$ = "INSERT INTO tblRequest " & _
                "(RequestID,SiteLog, Requester, SiteID,
                       RequestDate, ReceiveDate) " & _
                "VALUES " & _
                "(24000,'" & "PH-832" & "','" & "Shadish" & _
                "'," & 100 & ",'" & dtRequest & _
                "','" & dtReceive & "')"
            Set cmd = New adodb.Command
            cmd.CommandTimeout = cLng(sTimeout)
```

Continues

```
Set cmd.ActiveConnection = cn
cmd.CommandText = strSQL$
cmd.Execute
ADO_Maint = "Shadish" ' return the name we set this to.
cn.Close

  Set cmd = Nothing
  Set cn = Nothing

setHGOff
Exit Function
```

Listing 13.12 Adding data the ADO way.

Sample Code for Updating and Deleting Data with ADO

By now, you should be able to follow the logic of the Change and Delete methods pretty easily. The Change routine uses an ADO Recordset rather than a command object to change the Requester's Name (rs.Open strSQL, cn, adOpenDynamic, adLock-Pessimistic). The third and fourth parameters allow you to change from the default Forward-Only Recordset type and to select when and where other users can access the data record that you're changing while *you* actually change it.

Our Change routine also has cn.BeginTrans and cn.CommitTrans connection statements wrapped around it. These statements allow you to roll back a complex update if a problem arises during the actual update itself. You can roll back (remove) a series of updates—all the way back to the last BeginTrans that was encountered in the code. You can see that the Change function opens a connection and then works with a Recordset object to change the Requester column, while the Delete function first opens a connection and then opens a Command object, to execute the desired SQL delete string.

Sample Code for Calling a Stored Procedure with ADO

The code in Listing 13.14 shows how to call a SQL Server stored procedure from ADO. We call the sp_Stored_Procedures proc that will return all of the stored procedures that our current login has the rights to run. Figure 13.12 shows what is returned as a result of our sp call.

Notice that we load the sp into the cmd object's CommandText property, and tell ADO that we want to call an sp by setting the CommandType property to adCmdStoredProc.

Locating ADO Drivers

There have been many different ways that Microsoft has distributed ADO since it was first released. ADO 1.0 and 1.1 were released as standalone .EXE files. After this, the MDAC toolkit was created, which came with IIS 4.0 and IE 4.0, or could be downloaded from Microsoft's Web site. MDAC 1.5 includes the ADO 1.5 drivers and the OLE-DB libraries. At the time of writing, MDAC 2.1 SP2 containing ADO 2.1 was the current release. (ADO 2.1 had originally shipped with IE5 and Office 2000.) You could also download a new—

```
        Case "CHG"
            ' N. Frankel is the initial value for this field.
         setHGOn
            cn.Open "Driver={SQL Server};" & _
                "Server=" & sServer & ";" & _
                "Database=" & sDatabase & ";" & _
                "Uid=" & sUserID & ";" & _
                "PWD=" & sPassword & ";"
            strSQL$ = "SELECT * from tblRequest " & _
                "WHERE RequestID=23079"
            rs.Open strSQL, cn, adOpenDynamic, adLockPessimistic
            cn.BeginTrans
            rs("Requester") = "Jerome Bettis"
            rs.Update
            ADO_Maint = rs("Requester")
            cn.CommitTrans
            cn.Close
            setHGOff
            Exit Function
        Case "DEL"
            setHGOn
            With cn
                .Provider = "MSDASQL"
                .ConnectionString = "Driver={SQL Server};" & _
                    "Server=" & sServer & ";" & _
                    "Database=" & sDatabase & ";" & _
                    "Uid=" & sUserID & ";" & _
                    "PWD=" & sPassword & ";"
                .Open
            End With
            strSQL$ = "DELETE from tblRequest " & _
                "WHERE RequestID=24000"
            ' Create command object.
            Set cmd = New adodb.Command
            cmd.CommandTimeout = sTimeout
            Set cmd.ActiveConnection = cn
            cmd.CommandText = strSQL$
            cmd.Execute
            ADO_Maint = "Shadish"
            cn.Close
            setHGOff
            Exit Function
```

Listing 13.13 Changing and deleting data with ADO.

and very helpful—Component Checker, which was designed to help you determine installed version information and diagnose MDAC installation issues. Microsoft had also posted an MDAC FAQ at www.microsoft.com/data/MDAC21info/ MDACinstQ.htm.

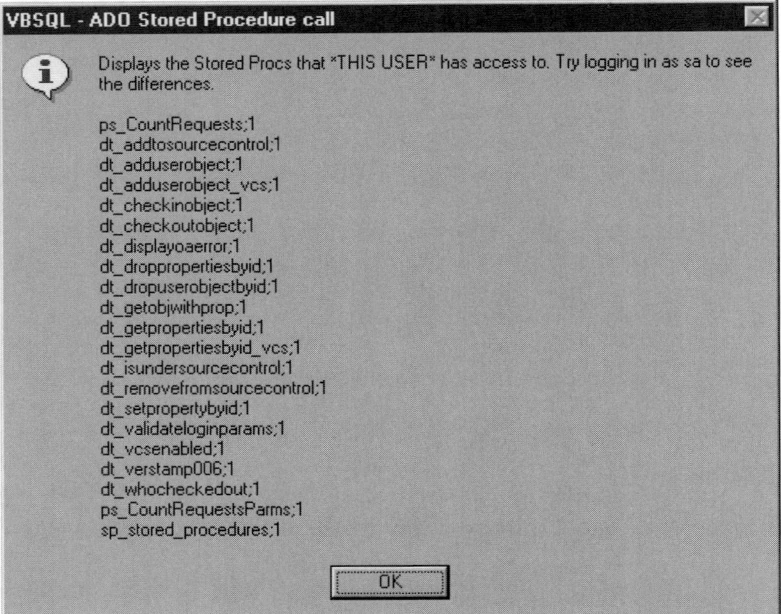

Figure 13.12 Calling a stored procedure with ADO.

Also, the MDAC 2.0 kit was released, which contains ADO 2.0. ADO 2.1 was available as part of IE 5.0 and Office 2000, and is now available as a series of drivers on Microsoft's Web site. Table 13.7 lists the Microsoft sites at the time (they really like to change their URL addresses) of this writing.

```
Public Sub ADO_DisplaySP()

    '==========================================
    ' Displays the stored procedures that
    ' THIS User has access to.
    '==========================================
    On Error GoTo ADO_DisplaySPErr
    Dim cmd As New ADODB.Command
    Dim rs As New ADODB.Recordset
    Dim strMsg As String

    cmd.ActiveConnection = "Driver={SQL Server};" & _
        "Server=" & sServer & ";" & _
```

```
            "Database=" & sDatabase & ";" & _
            "Uid=" & sUserID & ";" & _
            "PWD=" & sPassword & ";"
        cmd.CommandText = "sp_Stored_Procedures"
        cmd.CommandTimeout = 33
        cmd.CommandType = adCmdStoredProc
        setHGOn
        Set rs = cmd.Execute()
        Dim objField As ADODB.Field
        While Not rs.EOF
            For Each objField In rs.Fields
                If objField.Name = "PROCEDURE_NAME" Then
                    strMsg = strMsg & objField.Value & vbCrLf
                End If
            Next
            rs.MoveNext
        Wend
        setHGOff
        MsgBox "Displays the Stored Procs that *THIS USER* " & _
            "has access to. Try logging in as sa to see the " & _
            "differences." & _  vbCrLf & vbCrLf & _
          strMsg, vbInformation, APP_NAME & _
            " - ADO Stored Procedure call"
        rs.Close
        Set rs = Nothing
        Set cmd = Nothing

        Exit Sub
    ADO_DisplaySPErr:
        Dim rc
        rc = errRoutine(Err, Error$(Err), "frmMain:ADO_DisplaySP")
        Select Case rc
            Case True        ' resume
                Resume

            Case 0           ' resume next
                Resume Next

            Case Is > 0      ' exit function/routine
                If rc = 1 Then
                    Exit Sub
                Else
                    Call ShutDown
                End If
        End Select
    End Sub
```

Listing 13.14 Calling a stored procedure with ADO.

Cursors

Cursors are like row pointers. They're a SQL construct that emulates the kind of row processing that many programmers like to do and the list scrolling that end users prefer. Sounds great, right? Wrong. Cursors are notoriously slow and tend to be over used by VB programmers who think that all users want backward and forward scrolling.

Cursors have such a bad reputation with most DBAs that they're one of the first things DBAs look for when troubleshooting a performance problem.

One of the problems with cursors is that SQL Server simply has too many flavors. And they're not all "standard." SQL Server supports both the ANSI SQL-92 standard cursor syntax and its own curious menagerie of T-SQL cursors. Don't expect Oracle or DB2 DBAs to know what you're talking about if you bring up *keyset cursors*. As you might expect, you can't mix and match ANSI SQL and T-SQL cursor syntax.

```
SQL-92 Syntax
DECLARE cursor_name [INSENSITIVE] [SCROLL] CURSOR
FOR select_statement
[FOR {READ ONLY | UPDATE [OF column_name [,...n]]}]
Transact-SQL Extended Syntax
DECLARE cursor_name CURSOR
[LOCAL | GLOBAL]
[FORWARD_ONLY | SCROLL]
[STATIC | KEYSET | DYNAMIC | FAST_FORWARD]
[READ_ONLY | SCROLL_LOCKS | OPTIMISTIC]
[TYPE_WARNING]
FOR select_statement
[FOR UPDATE [OF column_name [,...n]]]
```

The colorful Bill Vaughn, author of the book, *Hitchhiker's Guide to Visual Basic and SQL Server* (a great book which we highly recommend), reminds VB programmers to distinguish between client-side (the worst offenders) and server-side cursors and to avoid dynamic cursors like the plague. He also recommends limiting rows to as few as possible ("*never* over 200") and to use Fetch More as needed.

That's not to say that you should dismiss cursors outright. One good use of cursors for DBAs is a stored procedure that executes DBCC against all of the tables in a database by walking through a cursor of table names.

Cursors are a powerful structure in any RDBMS, but they are easy to abuse. *Books Online* has over 300 topics related to cursors, but we recommend you start with the topics *Cursors* and *DECLARE CURSOR (T-SQL)*.

Table 13.7 Microsoft Data Access Sites

DATA ACCESS METHOD	INTERNET SITE
Universal Data Access	www.microsoft.com/data/
OLE DB	www.microsoft.com/data/oledb/
ADO	www.microsoft.com/data/ado/
ODBC	www.microsoft.com/data/odbc/
OLEDB for OLAP	www.microsoft.com/data/oledb/olap/

Error Handling

In the first DAO example for this chapter (see Listing 13.1), we briefly discussed our method for trapping errors in the client application—should a database error occur within a routine. Unfortunately, in the real world, error handling is never a "brief" portion of your coding effort. The better the error handling, the less time you'll spend on the phone with support calls and, most importantly, the happier your customers will be.

Be that as it may, it's not enough to just worry about trapping client-side errors—you need to handle remote server errors as well. And there's often more than one way to handle an error. You can display the error, log it to a database, write it out to an ASCII log file, or even do a bit more "modern" things such as sending an administrative e-mail if an error occurs, or alerting someone by pager when a problem occurs.

OLE ERROR SERVER

You might want to consider setting up a separate VB OLE Automation server to handle errors. This approach is not limited to WinNT's error handling scheme and is portable across the various Windows platforms. It can also be integrated with existing error handlers within a company, allowing them to work together. See www.fo.com/artvbd6.htm for an example error server and code.

ADO Error Handler

The following ADO-error-handler example takes as a parameter the open ADO connection at the time of the error. Of course, if you have bypassed creating an explicit connection by going right for a command object, you cannot access the connection's errors collection directly. (See Listing 13.15.)

The Dynamic SQL Project

Let's say that you want to allow a level of sophistication to your users' application where they can work with SQL statements against their own data at runtime. Or, perhaps

```
Private Function ADOErrorHandler(cn As adodb.Connection)
    Dim errObj As adodb.Error
    Dim strMsg As String
    For Each errObj In cn.Errors
        strMsg = strMsg & "Error Number: " & errObj.Number & _
       vbCrLf & _
                "  Description: " & errObj.Description & vbCrLf & _
                "  Source: " & errObj.Source & vbCrLf & _
                "  SQL State: " & errObj.SQLState & vbCrLf & _
                "  Native Error: " & errObj.NativeError & vbCrLf
    Next

    ADOErrorHandler = Format$(cn.Errors.Count) & __
        " errors occurred. " & vbCrLf & vbCrLf & strMsg
End Function
```

Listing 13.15 A sample ADO Error handler.

you've simply found it annoying to have to press the Go button, rather than simply pressing Enter in the Microsoft Query Analyzer to execute a SQL statement.

An interesting way to solve these problems is to create a Dynamic SQL processor within your application. Dynamic SQL is SQL that a user enters interactively at runtime. No, you won't (necessarily) be able to take advantage of things like pre-prepared statements (although see the rest of the discussion later in this section). But you can provide users with the ability to query whatever they want, or rather, whatever they have access to.

It's always been IT's fear that users would enter "runaway" queries like SELECT * FROM GeneralLedgerDetail and cause the dimming of computer lights and the ensuing man-hunt. A SQL query that returns a huge amount of data in this way can clog the network bandwidth, slowing everything down to a crawl. However, since ADO provides properties that allow you to control how many records are retrieved by a query (something you can also do at a database level, not just an application level, in SQL Server 7), dynamic SQL is no longer something that should be prevented out-of-hand.

If you really feel ambitious, you can watch the SQL that the user is about to execute and dis-allow such statements, issue a warning first, or require a password to execute it. This is a great feature for technical support people on the other end of the phone to use in diagnosing problems as well.

Project Specs

We'd like to create a text window where the user can enter a SQL statement. Pressing Enter anytime within this box executes the currently displayed SQL text. An ADO recordset is created as a result, and they are displayed in the dark gray text box under the actual names of the columns that were selected.

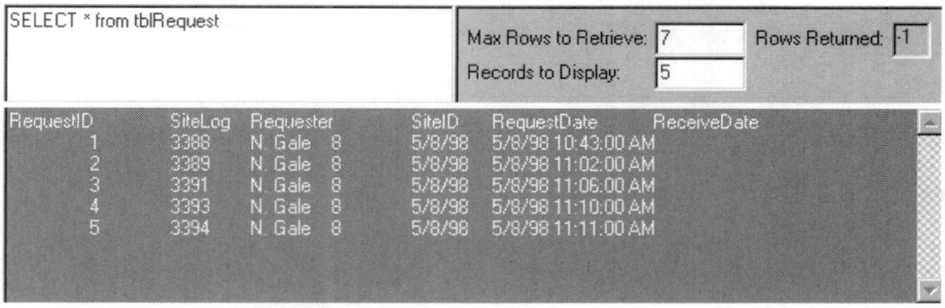

RequestID	SiteLog	Requester	SiteID	RequestDate	ReceiveDate
1	3388	N. Gale	8	5/8/98	5/8/98 10:43:00 AM
2	3389	N. Gale	8	5/8/98	5/8/98 11:02:00 AM
3	3391	N. Gale	8	5/8/98	5/8/98 11:06:00 AM
4	3393	N. Gale	8	5/8/98	5/8/98 11:10:00 AM
5	3394	N. Gale	8	5/8/98	5/8/98 11:11:00 AM

SELECT * from tblRequest
Max Rows to Retrieve: 7 Rows Returned: -1
Records to Display: 5

Figure 13.13 The VBSQL data window.

At the bottom of our VBSQL application screen, you'll see an output area that looks like Figure 13.13. There are two text box parameters shown on the right of the screen. The first text box parameter is used to control the maximum number of rows to retrieve at runtime. This depends on your organization and is something that you may want to wrap a profile-based restriction around, so that overworked users can't enter 12 million for the maximum to return as a result of not being allowed to take a break that day. The other parameter controls how many rows to actually display within the resulting text box at the bottom.

As you will discover, VBSQL is pretty easy to use. Listing 13.16 shows how to pull from the parameters on the screen to control the flow of the SQL statement execution. First, and most importantly, the SQL text itself is loaded with the cmd.CommandText = Trim$(txtDataWindow.Text) statement. This and the resulting Execute method are all that you *must* have to allow for runtime SQL entry and execution.

As we mentioned earlier, it's possible to allow the users to execute pre-prepared statements and stored procedures as well. Take a look at Figure 13.14 and you'll see our little data window used to create a system stored procedure. It also can be used to issue "straight-up" SQL such as SELECT * from tblRequest. The power of this little utility should make for some very interesting applications development.

To demonstrate the increased functionality of ADO 2.1, remember that you can save the data returned in a Recordset to a file and then open it later on locally, without having to connect to the back-end database. Notice the small button on the VBSQL interface that can be toggled as shown in Figure 13.15.

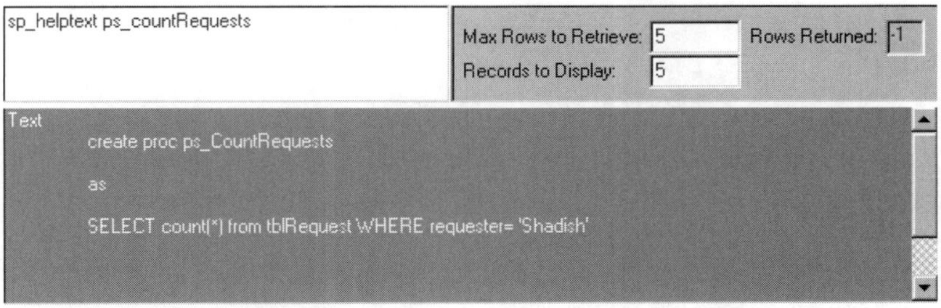

sp_helptext ps_countRequests
Max Rows to Retrieve: 5 Rows Returned: -1
Records to Display: 5

Text
create proc ps_CountRequests
as
SELECT count(*) from tblRequest WHERE requester= 'Shadish'

Figure 13.14 VBSQL lets you review and execute stored procedures.

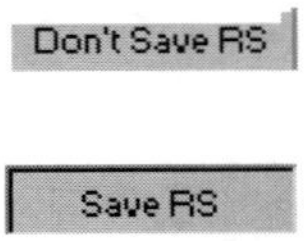

Don't Save RS

Save RS

Figure 13.15 VBSQL Toggle buttons.

```
Private Sub txtDataWindow_KeyPress(KeyAscii As Integer)
    If KeyAscii = vbKeyReturn Then
        Beep
        Call ProcessDataWindow
    End If
End Sub

Public Sub ProcessDataWindow()
    Dim cmd As adodb.Command
    Dim rs As adodb.Recordset
    Dim objField As adodb.Field
    Dim lMaxRowsToShow As Long
    Dim l As Long
    Dim strMsg As String
    RetrieveCurrentParms
    setHGOn
    Set cmd = New adodb.Command
    cmd.ActiveConnection = "Driver={SQL Server};" & _
        "Server=" & sServer & ";" & _
        "Database=" & sDatabase & ";" & _
        "Uid=" & sUserID & ";" & _
        "PWD=" & sPassword & ";"
    cmd.CommandText = Trim$(txtDataWindow.Text)
    cmd.CommandTimeout = sTimeout
    cmd.Properties("Maximum Rows") = sMaximumRows
    Set rs = cmd.Execute
    txtDataResults.Text = ""
    If Not rs.EOF Then
        For Each objField In rs.Fields
            strMsg = strMsg & Trim(objField.Name) & Chr(9)
        Next
        strMsg = strMsg & vbCrLf
        txtDataResults.Text = strMsg & vbCrLf
        If txtShowRows.Text <> "" Then
            lMaxRowsToShow = CLng(txtShowRows.Text)
        End If
        Do While Not rs.EOF
            l = l + 1
            If l > lMaxRowsToShow Then Exit Do
```

```
                strMsg = strMsg & Chr(9)
                For Each objField In rs.Fields
                    strMsg = strMsg & objField.Value & Chr(9)
                Next
                rs.MoveNext
                strMsg = strMsg & vbCrLf
            Loop
        Else
            strMsg = "No Records found!"
        End If
        lblRowsReturned.Caption = rs.RecordCount
        txtDataResults.Text = strMsg
        rs.Close
        cmd.ActiveConnection.Close
        setHGOff
        Exit Sub
ProcessDataWindowErr:
End Sub
```

Listing 13.16 The data window VB6 source code.

The default is *not* to save the Recordset. By turning it on you can dump a copy of your Recordset to disk as a binary file which we call disk_rs.bin in the sample code in Listing 13.17. Once there, we can disconnect from the central server (perhaps going offline in a remote dial-up scenario), but continue to work with the data within the binary file version of the recordset. This is accomplished with the ADO Recordset.SAVE method as set up and demonstrated in the following code listing. For demonstration purposes, we go on to immediately re-open this disk-based Recordset, using the line rsIO.Open strFile$, adOpenStatic, adLockBatchOptimistic, adCmdFile and then pop up a MsgBox that shows the columns that are found in this version of the Recordset.

Using this approach will allow you to do many things—most notably to reasonably address remote call-up data issues, such as remote sale staff support.

```
Public Sub ProcessDataWindow()
        ' some declarations omitted here to save space.
        ' find it on your CD
        If picButton(1).Visible Then
        ' the user wants the recordset saved too.
          Dim strFile$
          Dim rsIO As New ADODB.Recordset
          strFile = App.Path & "\disk_rs.bin"
          If DoesFileExist(strFile$) Then
              Kill strFile$
          End If
```

Continues

```
        rsIO.CursorLocation = adUseClient
        rsIO.Open Trim$(txtDataWindow.Text), cn, adOpenStatic,
            adLockBatchOptimistic
        rsIO.Save strFile, adPersistADTG
        rsIO.Close
        Set rsIO = Nothing
        ' show that we can get it back
        Set rsIO = New ADODB.Recordset
        rsIO.Open strFile$, , adOpenStatic, adLockBatchOptimistic,
            adCmdFile
        strMsg = ""
        If Not rsIO.EOF Then
            For Each objField In rsIO.Fields
                strMsg = strMsg & Trim(objField.Name) & Chr(9)
            Next
        Else
            strMsg = "Record Set Not Opened"
        End If
        MsgBox strMsg, vbOKOnly, "Objects from the DISK " & _
            "file version of our RS"
        rsIO.Close
        Set rsIO = Nothing
    Else
        rsIO.Close
        Set rsIO = Nothing
    End If
    cmd.ActiveConnection.Close
    setHGOff
    Exit Sub
```

Listing 13.17 Saving an ADO recordset into a disk file.

Remember, of course, that saving Recordsets to disk takes a good deal longer than working directly against the database itself, since not only is the I/O of going to disk for the entire Recordset involved, but schema information for the Recordset must be stored along with it as well.

The Web Survey Project: Creating A New Database in SQL Server

For the second VB project in this chapter we create a database, and some tables, which we later publish over the Web. For the purpose of this exercise we'll create a database that's used to store users' responses to a survey. We also create a few support tables to go along with it. If you did the Intranet project in Chapter 6 or the e-commerce project in Chapter 11, you'll recognize our colleague, Jon Kilburn's, hand.

Using VB6's Data Report Designer

One of the biggest complaints VB programmers voiced—until VB6—was that VB lacked a decent built-in report engine. Yes, you can use the slightly outdated Crystal Reports engine that had always been bundled with VB, but that still meant leaving VB to create any reports. Why couldn't Microsoft give VBers the same report interface that Access had? Well, VB6's new Data Report Designer pretty much does just that. The easiest way to use it is to start a data project, because a data automatically includes a form, a Data Environment Designer (DED), and a Data Report Designer. You can, however, add data designers to any VB project from the Project menu. Generally, you'll work first with the DED to supply SQL statements that create one or more database objects, and then the Data Report Designer, pointing to the objects which return ADO Recordsets.

The Data Report Designer interface uses a traditional banded report writer format, where each report part—headings, footers, and body/detail—appear in a separate band of the report. The detail band is generally where you specify the "meat" of the report—what you want printed from each "row" in the Recordset. In design mode, the Data Report Designer works a lot like a VB form—you drag the special Data Report controls onto the Data Report Designer for the report that you're working on. Size the window so that you can see the DED and Data Report Designer at the same time. To add label and textbox controls for each Recordset field that the data command returns, drag and drop the data command onto the detail area of the Data Report Designer. The default format will resemble a table. You can print the report directly by calling either the PrintReport or ExportReport methods.

We use the data structures shown in Tables 13.8–3.10.

Please note, that while a Gender table may seem a bit extreme, there are FDA regulations for Gender specifications that have to do not only with Gender, but Gender at birth, Current Gender, and Future Gender. Yes, sigh, that says "Future Gender."

The Programming Language table is designed to keep track of the programming languages site that the visitors use.

Now that we have our table definitions, we have only to create the database and the tables using the SQL Enterprise Manager. The first step is to create a new database. To do so, right-click on the Database node. From the popup menu (see Figure 13.16) select New Database.

Next you must supply the database name, location, and initial size as shown in Figure 13.17.

Select OK and your database is created. Now that the database is created we have two methods to create tables. The first method (and probably the easiest) is to open the database, select Survey and click on the Tables node. Then in the right panel, right-click to bring up the popup menu with the option to create a new table (see Figure 13.18).

Table 13.8 Table Name: Survey

COLUMN NAME	DATA TYPE	SIZE	DESCRIPTION
Survey_ID	Varchar	6	Primary Key – Generated
First_Name	Varchar	30	First Name
Last_Name	Varchar	30	Last Name
Date_of_Birth	Datetime		Date of Birth
EmailAddress	Varchar	200	Email Address
Gender_ID	Varchar	6	Link To Gender Table
Prog_ID	Varchar	6	Link To Programming Language
VisitType	Varchar	1	Type of Visit (C, P, S, A)
CommentOn	Varchar	1	Comment Type (W, P, C, S, E, O)
SubjectOther	Varchar	30	Other Subject if CommentOn = O
Reason	Varchar	200	Reason For Visit
Contact	Char	1	Contact? (Y,N) Bit and binary are alternative data types for this field.

Table 13.9 Table Name: Gender

COLUMN NAME	DATA TYPE	SIZE	DESCRIPTION
Gender_ID	Varchar	6	Primary Key – Generated
Description	Varchar	30	Gender Description

Table 13.10 Table Name: Prog_Lang

COLUMN NAME	DATA TYPE	SIZE	DESCRIPTION
Prog_ID	Varchar	6	Primary Key – Generated
Description	Varchar	30	Programming Language Description

Once you elect to create a new table you are prompted for the name of the table. Type in Survey. Next you're presented with the database design browse, which allows the user to enter the database column name, data type, length, precision, scale, allow nulls, default value, identity, identity seed, identity increment, and Is Row GUID. For our simple example the only columns we need to concern ourselves with are the column name, data type, column length, and allow nulls.

We also want to make a brief mention here of the *User Defined Data Types (UDT)*. What is a UDT? Instead of creating a column of say a varchar(30) each time we need a name we can create a user defined type T_NAME and specify the default data type and length of 30. The result is that the T_NAME type is now present in the drop-down combo for data type.

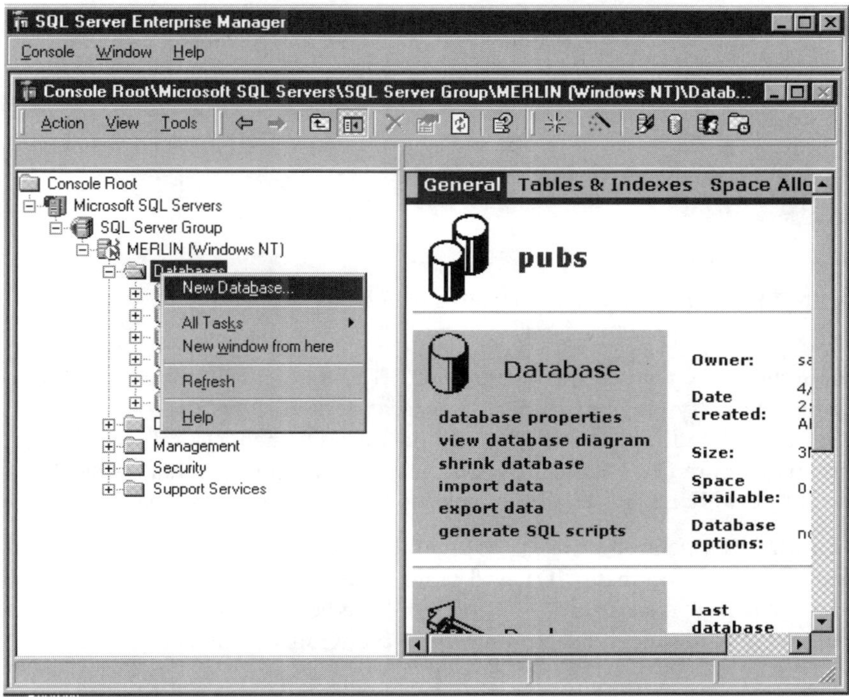

Figure 13.16 Creating a new database popup menu.

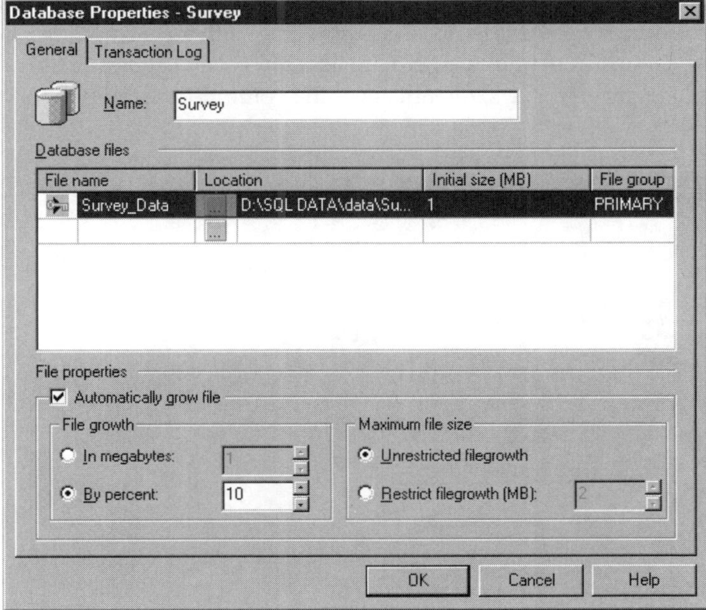

Figure 13.17 Creating a new database.

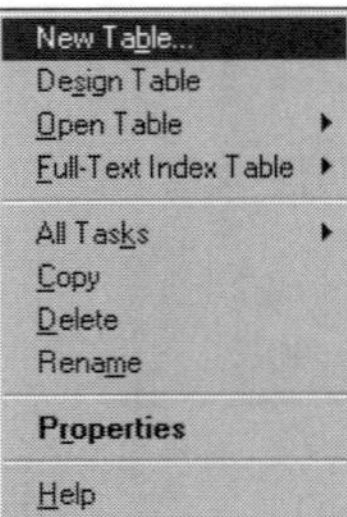

Figure 13.18 Popup menu to create a new table.

Again there are two ways to create a UDT. The first and simplest is to choose the User Defined Data Types node under databases, right-click and select New User Defined Data Type. You'll be presented with the User Defined Data Type Properties dialog shown in Figure 13.19. Enter T_NAME as the Type name, varchar as the Data type, then check Allow NULLs if you don't intend to let the survey participants enter a name.

Creating User Defined Data Types and tables can be time consuming. However, there is another way to create UDT and tables. We can devise and run a database script. What's a script? A *script* is a series of SQL-based commands (similar to a stored procedure) which are executed from the SQL Server Query Analyzer.

A simple database script for our exercise may look like Listing 13.18.

This script has several parts. The first part is the User Defined Data Type creation section. Logically before we can create a database table that uses an UDT we must create the UDT. The next section is the Table Creation section. Hear we simply use the "create table" command and define each of the table (field) elements along with any restrictions. Notice that we also created column constraints. There are actually several types of constraints that you can define here: primary keys, foreign keys, and column-level validation.

User-Defined Data Type Properties - MERLIN
General
Name: T_NAME
Data type: varchar
Length: 30
Allow NULLs
Rule: (none)
Default: (none)
Where Used...
OK Cancel Help

Figure 13.19 User Defined Data Type dialog.

```
/* ============================================   */
/*    Database name:        SURVEY               */
/*    DBMS name:            SQL Server 7x        */
/*    Created on:           5/12/99  11:45 AM    */
/*    by Jon Kilburn                            */
/* ============================================   */
if exists(select 1 from dbo.systypes where name ='T_NAME')
  execute sp_droptype T_NAME
go

execute sp_addtype T_NAME, 'varchar(30)', 'null'
go
/* ============================   */
/*    Table: GENDER               */
/* ============================    */
create table GENDER
(
    GENDER_ID       varchar(6)            not null,
    DESCRIPTION     varchar(30)           null,
constraint PK_PROG primary key (GENDER_ID)
)
go

/* ========================== */
/*    Table: PROG_LANG        */
/* ========================== */
create table PROG_LANG
(
    PROG_ID         varchar(6)             not null,
    DESCRIPTION     varchar(30)            null,
     constraint PK_PROG primary key (PROG_ID)
)
go

/* ============================   */
/*     Table: SURVEY              */
/* ============================   */
create table SURVEY
(

    SURVEY_ID                 varchar(6)           not null,
    FIRST_NAME                T_NAME               null,
    LAST_NAME                 T_NAME               null,
    DATE_OF_BIRTH             datetime             null,
    EMAILADDRESS              varchar(200)         null,
    GENDER_ID                 varchar(6)           not null,
    PROG_ID                   varchar(6)           not null,
    VISITTYPE                 varchar(1)           not null,
     constraint CHK_VISIT check(VISITTYPE IN('C', 'P', 'S', 'A')),
```

Continues

```
    COMMENTON                    varchar(1)           not null,
     constraint CHK_COMM check(COMMENTON IN('W', 'P', 'C', 'S',
'E', 'O')),
    SUBJECTOTHER,                varchar(30)          null,
    REASON                       varchar(200)          null,
    CONTACT                      char(1)              null,
     constraint CHK_CONTACT check(CONTACT IN('Y', 'N')),
      constraint PK_SURVEY primary key (SURVEY_ID)
)
go
```

Listing 13.18 CreSurv.bas script for generating Survey database tables and UDT.

In our example we have created a primary key on SURVEY_ID, and defined column-level constraints (which prevent invalid data entry into the database fields) on the Visit_Type and CommentOn columns.

To run the script we simply choose Tools, SQL Server Query Analyzer. The SQL Server 7 Query Analyzer is then launched. When the Query Analyzer first opens you *must* change the database from the default (which is master) to the database you wish to work with, in this case, Survey (see Figure 13.20).

To run the script, simply choose the File/Open menu option. A script file is generally saved with a .SQL extension. When the script is loaded you can either select the green arrow (Run) or you use the Query/Execute menu options. After the script is finished you can exit the SQL Query Analyzer. We are now ready to create the Web site that will interact with the Survey Database.

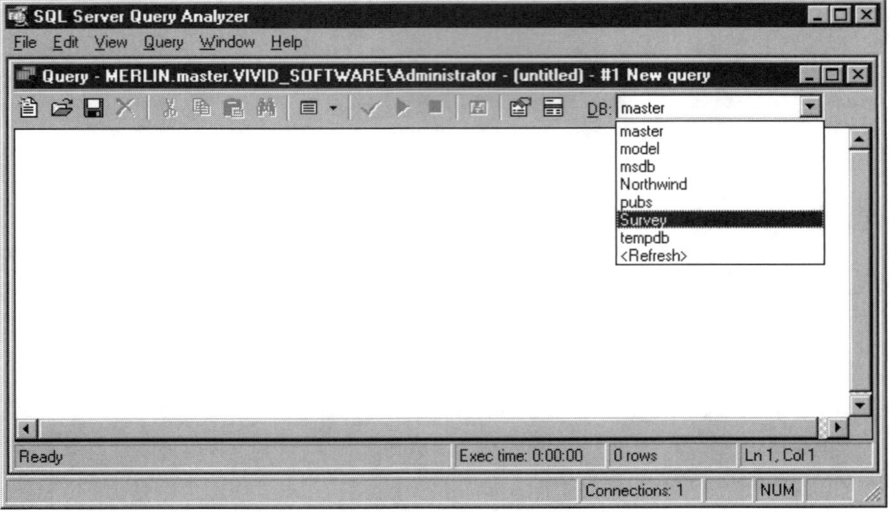

Figure 13.20 The SQL Query Analyzer.

HTML

HTML is the generally accepted language for creating Web pages. HTML documents really are just a series of beginning and ending tags. What is a tag? A *tag* is similar to the begin/end relationship in a programming language. Each tag has a specific and defined function as well as a number of parameters. HTML tags are enclosed within bracket "<>" symbols and each end tag sequence is prefaced with a forward slash, /. Here's an example:

```
Begin Tag: <html>
End Tag: </html>
```

Web browsers such as Internet Explorer and Navigator make use of HTML tags to display and represent document information. HTML is designed primarily for static representation. This means that it doesn't support looping, branching, or event trapping. A script language, such as VBScript (Active Server Pages) ASP or JavaScript generally provide these features. We'll discuss both in a moment. Tags are used for a variety of different functions such as headings, colors, tables, and much more.

While the HTML language is simple, it can often be confusing to a programmer who is looking at it for the first time. This is often due to the fact that many HTML programmers right justify all the begin/end tag sequences. The result is often a file, which looks something like this:

```
<html>
<head>
<META HTTP-EQUIV="Pragma" CONTENT="no-cache">
<title>Videoretailer.com Final Order Worksheet</title>
</head>
<body>
</body>
```

Everything that falls between <html> and </html> is executed as HTML code. Here are brief descriptions for each section within the HTML code.

Web Page Heading (<head>...</head>)

This is the heading used to have a formal structure that holds the formatting information about a page. Now it's become much more abbreviated and usually only holds the Web page title.

Web Page Title (<title>...</title>)

A Web page's title is quite important, even though many Web programmers don't realize it, and omit it, because the title is the text that appears in the title bar of the Web browser when your page is displayed. It's also the text that appears in your Web page directories like Yahoo, Lycos, and Alta Vista.

Continues

HTML *(Continued)*

Web Page Body (<body>...</body>)

This is the section where most of the action really takes place. The body can make use of several keywords, known as attributes, to control such things as the Web page's background color, the default color of the text, or the color of a hyperlink. This is the section where we create controls, display graphics, and even accept user input. The controls that are used within the body section are somewhat limited in that they are static and are not validated until such time as a submission occurs. Table 13.11 shows a list of control names.

Table 13.11 Data Entry Control Names

CONTROL NAME	DESCRIPTION
Text Box	A Standard Text Input
Text Area	Multi-Line Text Input
Radio Button	Radio Button
Check Box	Check Box
Push Button	Push Button

Some of the HTML controls share similar properties such as the <input> tag. The *<input> tag* identifies the type of control. For example:

```
<input type="text" size=10 name=FIRST_NAME>
```

This line of code within a body section creates a simple text edit named FIRST_NAME whose contents can be examined at a later time. Some quick notes on each of the controls.

Text Controls (Text and TextArea)

There are actually three types of HTML text controls: password, single line, and multi line. The password control is referenced as Password, the single-line text control is known as Text, and the multi-line text control is a TextArea control.

The major difference between a Text control and a TextArea control is that a TextArea control is its own tag and accepts two more parameters (rows and cols). For example:

```
<TextArea name="sample" rows=5 cols=6 value="This is just a sample multi
line text control">
</TextArea>
```

Whereas to create a Text or Password control you use an <input> tag and specify the input type.

```
<input type="Text" size=8 value="Jon">
```

Radio Button

Just like radio buttons used in Visual Basic, radio buttons used in HTML must also be placed within a group. To group a radio button you simply create each button with the same name.

Checkboxes

An HTML checkbox works just like in Visual Basic. Default values are assigned to the Checked property.

Push Buttons

The real oddity about a push button in HTML is that the Value property actually represents the button's caption. There are no height or width properties either. A push button's size depends on the width of the value (or caption). Push buttons can respond to a number of events such as OnClick, OnFocus, and OnSubmit.

Frames

Before we move ahead and create our first site we should examine another key piece of HTML—frames. What is a frame? A frame is one of the more recent innovations in HTML. It can divide an HTML page into a series of panels—each containing its own distinct URL. This allows for split-screen navigation. Often we open a Web site to discover navigation on the left and content on the right as shown in Figure 13.21.

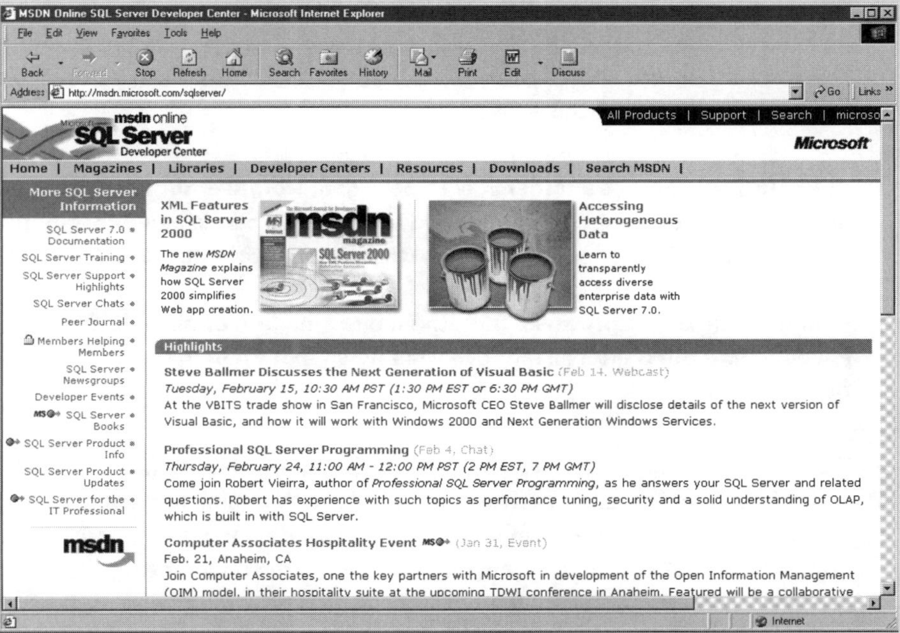

Figure 13.21 The Vivid Software Web site Navigation and Content page.

Continues

HTML *(Continued)*

Submission Methods

The following section explains more on how to move data, entered or changed by the user, back to the server. When a user submits (that is interacts with a Web page) either through a push button or hyperlink, the way a form passes information (or submits it) is determined by the form method attribute. Suppose you had a form with a couple of fields, say name and date of birth, and when the user selects a submit button you want to pass the information to the server.

```
<form name="sampleget" action="Respond.asp" method=get>
        Name : <input type="text" name=NAME_FIELD>
        Date of Birth : <input type="text" name=DOB>
        <input type=submit value="Submit">
</form>
```

When the page is submitted (via the Submit button) this information is passed to the Respond.asp page via the query string, appended to the URL, after a question mark. The complete URL is visible in the browser's Address field and looks like this:

```
merlin/respond.asp?name_field=Bob&dob=9/11/68
```

Limitations of Get

A query string is not always the best way to send information. Suppose we need a password, we certainly don't want the password to appear in the query string. There are other limitations as well—the amount of data that can be sent to the URL is limited to 1,000 characters.

Post

Don't despair. There is another way to pass data from the form section between pages. Instead of using the Get method attribute we can use the *Post method*. Post puts the information inside the HTTP header, rather than adding it to the query string.

In the case of our previous page, the name and date of birth fields are encoded into the request header, leaving no sign of them in the browser's Address box.

Scripts

We mentioned earlier that we would touch base on what a script language is. A *script language* is often a derivative of a full programming language such as Visual Basic. They generally share in syntax, but lack some of the more robust features of the programming language. Some of the script languages such as JavaScript are interpreted by the actual browser. Other languages such as VB Script and PERL require a server-side interpreter.

Some script languages are identified by a <script language> tag. JavaScript is one such language. For example:

```
<head>
<script language="JavaScript">

function rusure()
{

  var question;

  question = confirm ("Are you sure you want to cancel your order?
") clear your sheet.")

  if (question !="0") {
    return true;}
  else {
   return false;
 }
}
</script>
</head>
```

VBScript can also be placed within a <script> tag, but as you will soon learn it can be placed in the body section of an HTML document (only the document is now referred to as an Active Server Page) between which is held between <% and %> tags. A simple VBScript routine, InvalidResponse, follows.

```
<head>
<script language="VBScript">

Sub InvalidResponse
  MsgBox "You have entered an invalid response."
End Sub

</script>
</head>
```

Creating the Survey Web Site

Well, you've made it this far, so now we move on to the fun stuff. Creating and accessing our Survey Web site. For those of you new to HTML, we provide a brief lesson in HTML and submission methods. If you're already familiar with HTML, you can skip on to the Active Server Pages section.

Active Server Pages

So now that you have a grasp of what HTML is and what a script language is, we'll move ahead and focus on what an Active Server Page (ASP) document is. An HTML document is often referenced by its .htm extension. An Active Server Page document is referenced by its .asp extension. (Another common extension you may encounter is .cfm. They're created by Allaire's Cold Fusion.)

Active Server Pages is Microsoft's newest server-based technology to build dynamic and interactive Web sites. As with most new technologies, we're sure that you have a few questions. What can it do? How does it work? Can I use it to turn on the TV?

While we can't swear that you can use ASP to turn on your TV, we can answer a few of the simpler questions. ASP can do many things. It is, in fact, a useful (although not as robust as we'd like) script language. It allows developers and service providers to build dynamic and interactive pages.

Since it's a script language that runs server-side, it enables the development of more secure transactions—server-based applications—and ultimately better Web sites.

Dynamic Web Pages

So now that you've heard the hubbub, how about some practical examples? ASP is most useful in generating Dynamic Web Pages, and responding (or interacting) with those pages. Great, you say, but what's a Dynamic Web Page? A *Dynamic Web Page* is a Web page that is *generated* by the server. Meaning, that an initial *template* page (in this case an ASP document) is run by the server, and based upon the result a final *static* page is produced and uploaded to your browser.

Here is an example of what an ASP page can be used for. Consider the standard Login page of a Web site. You provide information, such as, a user name and a password. You then "submit" the information by pressing the Login button (or whatever the button is named). A welcome screen appears with your full name and welcomes you to the site. If you right-click in your browser and from the popup menu select View Source you

```
<html>

<head>
<title>MySite.Com Member Log In</title>
<meta HTTP-EQUIV="expires" CONTENT="Fri, March 26, 1999 GMT">
<meta HTTP-EQUIV="Pragma" CONTENT="no-cache">
</head>

<body bgcolor="#FFFFFF">
<div align="center"><center>

<table border="0" cellpadding="0" cellspacing="0" width="600">
  <tr>
```

```
    <td align="center" bgcolor="#FFFFCC"><font face="Arial,
         Helvetica" size="4"><b>MySite.com Member Login</b>
        <p>
        Please Type Your Username and Password, Then
        Click 'Log In':<br>
    <br>
    </font></td>
  </tr>
  <tr>
    <td align="center" bgcolor="#FFFFFF">
        <form method="POST" action="LoginValidation.asp">
        <div align="center"><center><table border="0"
        cellpadding="0" cellspacing="0" width="600"
        height="99">
        <tr>
          <td width="268" bgcolor="#FFFFCC" valign="top"
           align="right" height="25"><font face="Arial,
           Helvetica"><strong>Username:</strong></font></td>
          <td width="332" bgcolor="#FFFFCC" valign="top"
           align="left" height="25"><font face="Arial,
           Helvetica">
          <input type="text" name="USERNAME" size="20">
          </font></td>
        </tr>
        <tr>
          <td width="268" bgcolor="#FFFFCC" valign="top"
           align="right" height="25"><font face="Arial,
           Helvetica"><strong>Password:</strong></font></td>
          <td width="332" bgcolor="#FFFFCC" valign="top"
           align="left" height="25"><input
           type="password" name="PASSWORD" size="20"> </td>
        </tr>
        <tr>
          <td width="600" bgcolor="#FFFFCC" valign="top"
           align="center" colspan="2" height="49"><br>
          <font face="Arial, Helvetica">
          <input type="submit" value="Log In"></font></td>
        </tr>
      </table>
      </center></div>
    </form>
    </td>
  </tr>
</table>
</center></div>
</body>
</html>
```

Listing 13.19 Login.html.

will only see the final (or static) HTML. Now, let's unravel the mystery of how the welcome screen was built.

```
<!-- #include file="adovbs.inc" -->
<%
     Option Explicit

     Dim cSQL                 ' SQL statement
     Dim oConn                ' Connection Object
     Dim oRs                  ' Recordset
     Dim cUserName            ' UserName From Form
     Dim cPwd                 ' Password From Form
     Dim cFullName            ' Users Full Name

     ' Using the Request object get the user name
     cUserName = Request.Form("USERNAME")

     ' Using the Request object get the password
     cPwd = Request.Form("PASSWORD")

     ' Build the SQL Statement
     cSQL = "SELECT * FROM auth_users WHERE Ucase(username) = '" &
                    Ucase(cUserName) & "'"
     ' Open the Connection
    Set oConn = Server.CreateObject("ADODB.Connection")

     ' Make Native Connection Through ADO to SQL Server 7.0
    oConn.Open "Driver={SQL Server};Server=Merlin;UID=sa;" & _
            "WSID=;Language=us_english;DATABASE=Survey;" & _
            "PASSWORD=;"

     ' Open Recordset
     Set oRs = oConn.Execute(cSQL)

     ' No Records?
     If oRs.EOF then
             ' Not found!
             Response.Redirect "NotFound.Html"

     Else
             ' Validate Password
             If Trim(Ucase(oRs("password"))) <> Trim(Ucase(cPwd))
                     ' Not valid
                     Response.Redirect "NotValid.Html"
             Else
                     cFullName = Trim(oRs("firstname")) & " " &
```

```
                    Trim(oRs("lastname"))
               End If
        End If

        ' Close Recordset
        oRs.Close
        Set oRs = Nothing
        ' Close Connection

        oConn.Close
        Set oConn = Nothing

          ' The part that follows is the HTML for
          ' welcoming the user

%>

<html>

<head>
<title>New Page 1</title>
<meta name="GENERATOR" content="Microsoft FrontPage 3.0">
</head>

<body>

<form name="welcome" action="nextpage.html" method="post">
  <div align="center"><center><p><big><big>Welcome
<% Response.Write(cFullName) %> </big></big></p>

  </center></div><div align="center"><center><p>
       <input type="submit" value="Continue"
       name="Continue"></p>
  </center></div>
</form>
</body>
</html>
```

Listing 13.20 LoginValidation.Asp.

Let's first examine the simple login page (see Listing 13.19). Notice that the form method is POST and the action is to launch the file LoginValidation.asp. The LoginValidation.asp file attaches to a SQL Server database, validates the username and password, and generates a welcome screen using the user's First and Last names combined.

When the user clicks the Submit button the browser launches the file LoginValidation.asp. Let's look at the LoginValidation.asp page shown in Listing 13.20.

Notice that the top half of the page looks almost exactly like a Visual Basic application, with a few exceptions:

- Support for #include files.
- Variables cannot be typed.
- It contains HTML.

Combine the concepts and behold (!) a dynamic Web site. The interaction between the site and the user is now complete. Let's go back and look at the simple survey database we started out with.

Consider that we want to build a survey page. The page must interact with the user in the following ways.

- Accept field input.

```
<html>
<head>
<title>Survey</title>
</head>

<body>

<hr>

<p>Tell us what you think about our web site,
or anything else that comes to mind. We
welcome all of your comments and suggestions.</p>

<form method="POST" action="SaveResults.asp">
  <p><strong>Tell us how to get in touch with you:</strong><dl>
    <dd><pre>
    First Name            <input type="text" size="35"
        maxlength="256" name="FIRST_NAME">
    Last Name             <input type="text" size="35"
        maxlength="256" name="LAST_NAME">
    Date Of Birth         <input type="text" size="35"
        maxlength="256" name="DATE_OF_BIRTH">
    Email Address         <input type="text" size="35"
        maxlength="256" name="FAVORITE_LINKS">
    Gender                <select name="GENDER" size="1">
<option value="1">Female
<option value="2">Male
      </option>
      </select>
    Programming Languages <select name="PROG_LANG" size="1">
<option value="1">Visual Basic
```

```
<option value="2">Java / JavaScript
     </option>
     </select>

     </pre>
    </dd>
  </dl>
  <p><strong>What kind of comment would you like to
send?</strong><dl>
    <dd>
     <input type="radio" name="MessageType" value="C">Complaint
     <input type="radio" name="MessageType" value="P">Problem
     <input type="radio" checked name="MessageType"
        value="S">Suggestion
     <input type="radio" name="MessageType" value="A">Approval
     </dd>
  </dl>
  <p><strong>What about us do you want to comment on?</strong><dl>
    <dd><select name="SUBJECT" size="1">
        <option selected value="W">Web Site</option>
        <option value="C">Company</option>
        <option value="P">Products</option>
        <option value="S">Store</option>
        <option value="E">Employee</option>
        <option value="O">(Other)</option>
      </select> Other: <input type="text" size="26" maxlength="256"
name="SUBJECTOTHER"></dd>
  </dl>
  <p><strong>Reason for your visit:</strong><dl>
    <dd><textarea name="Comments" rows="5"
cols="42"></textarea></dd>
  </dl>
  <dl>
    <dd><input type="checkbox" name="CONTACTREQUESTED" value="Y">
Please send me
      more information.</dd>
  </dl>
  <p><input type="submit" value="Submit Comments"> <input
type="reset" value="Clear Form"></p>
</form>

<hr>

<h5>Vivid Software Inc.<br>
Copyright © 1999 Vivid Software. All rights reserved.<br></h5>
</body>
</html>
```

Listing 13.21 Survey.html source code.

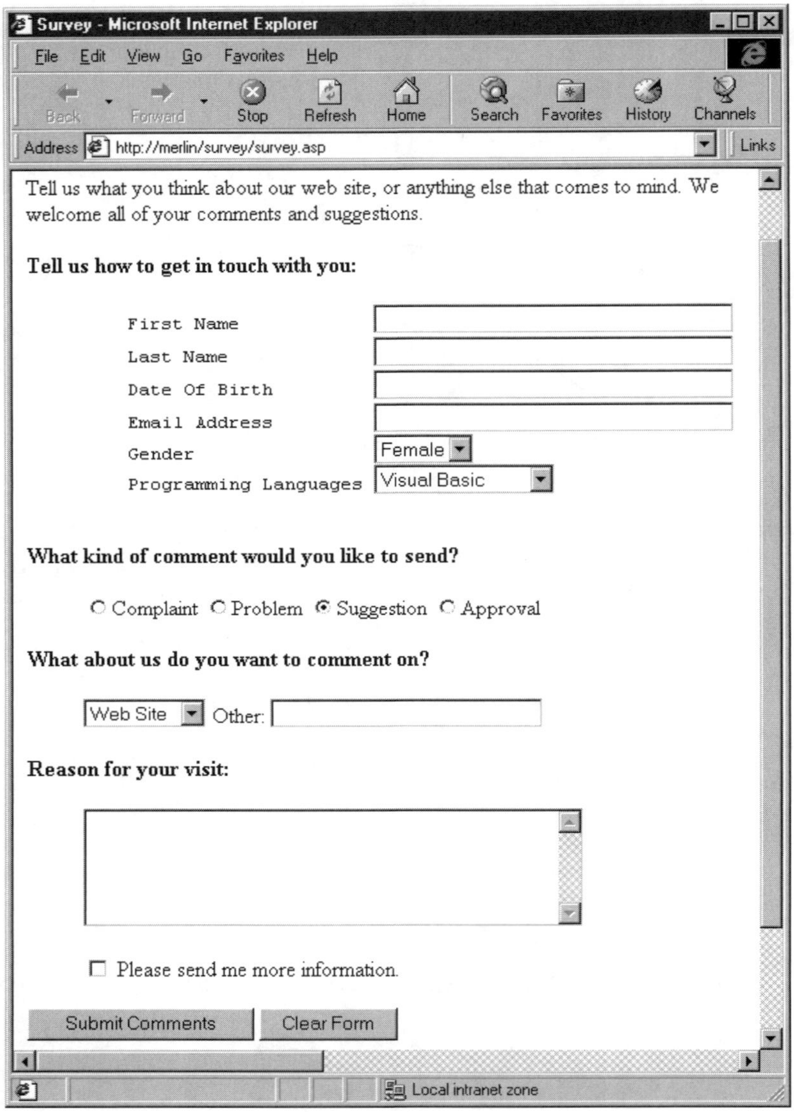

Figure 13.22 Survey page.

- Validate input.
- Write input to the database.
- Display confirmation of input.

Let's start by laying out (or designing) the Web page for the survey. Here is what the survey page's source code (see Listing 13.21) looks like (see Figure 13.22).

Notice that at this point the Web page is not dynamic in nature. It uses the POST form method to call the file SaveResults.Asp. If you run the page, Survey.asp, you'll notice that both the Gender and Programming Language combo boxes are filled with data. How did we do this?

ADO/OLE DB Database Access

First we must establish a connection to the SQL Server database, and we do this with ADO. To create and work with an ADO connection we must do two things. First, connect to the Server (SQL Server 7 in this case) and the database within the Server (Survey). Second, after the connection is established, we then choose the operation that we want to perform, such as SELECT, INSERT, DELETE, and so on.

You should, by now, be at least partially well versed in SELECT, INSERT, UPDATE and DELETE statements. If not, see Appendix A for our SQL Survival Guide. So, let's break down the parts of the ADO connection:

1. Driver—this is the portion that defines the data source type.
2. Server—this is the actual name of the Server—in our case, MERLIN.
3. User ID (UID)— this is defined at the Server level.
4. Language— what language?
5. Database— the database to open.
6. Password— the user's password.

The following code shows what the actual connection code looks like when attempting to connect using ADO to the SQL Server Merlin server and to open the Database Survey Web page.

```
Dim oConn   ' Connection Object

' Open the Connection
Set oConn = Server.CreateObject("ADODB.Connection")

' Make Native Connection Through ADO to SQL Server 7.0
oConn.Open "Driver={SQL Server};Server=Merlin;UID=sa;" & _
           "Language=us_english;DATABASE=Survey;" & _
           "PASSWORD=;"
```

Just like that, you have a connection that you can work with. We mentioned earlier that ASP supports the use of an Include file. *Include files* are files that contain any valid ASP definitions. Since ASP has no support for "Global" or module variables you should place all shared code in a central file (or set of files) which can then be "included" in your ASP pages.

```
' File --- SurvConn.Inc ---
'
'
' Open a Connection to The Server
'

Public Function OpenConnection()
'
' Function :  OpenConnection
' Params   :  None
'
' Author   :  Jon Kilburn
'             http://www.VividSoftware.Com
' Date     :  3/14/99
'
' Purpose  :  Consolidates the code to open a new database
'             Connection. This is essential since it will
'             allow for changes to be issolated to this file.
'
    Dim oConn    ' Connection Object

    ' Open the Connection
    Set oConn = Server.CreateObject("ADODB.Connection")

    ' Make Native Connection Through ADO to SQL Server 7.0
    oConn.Open "Driver={SQL Server};Server=Merlin;UID=sa;" & _
            "Language=us_english;DATABASE=Survey;" & _
            "PASSWORD=;"

    ' Return Connection
    Set OpenConnection = oConn
End Function

Public Sub CloseConnection(oConn)
'
' Function :  CloseConnection
' Params   :  None
'
' Author   :  Jon Kilburn
'             http://www.VividSoftware.Com
' Date     :  3/14/99
'
' Purpose  :  Consolidates the code to close an open database
'             Connection.
'
   oConn.Close

End Sub
```

Listing 13.22 SurvConn.Inc Include file.

In this case we've created a file that contains all of our connection information, and named it SurvConn.Inc. In this file we have the function to open a connection and close a connection. While this code can reside in an ASP file itself, by centralizing the functions in a single file, and then including the SurvConn file in all subsequent ASP pages, we only need to make a change in one place and all the ASP pages are instantly updated. Listing 13.22 holds the Include file that is added to the ASP page structure.

You saw in a previous example the use of an Include file. So in order to allow ASP to open the Survey database we need to copy the two Include files—one contains all of the defined constants for ADO (adovbs.inc) and the other contains our two functions to open and close connections. We simply place the following two lines of code at the top of the Survey.htm page, and now we have database accessibility.

```
<!-- #include file="adovbs.inc" -->
<!-- #include file="SurvConn.inc" -->
```

Next we must create the connection, then build a cursor for all of the different Genders, and then load the combo box. We simply repeat the process for each programming lan-

Section 1

```
<%
     Option Explicit

     Dim cSQL                  ' SQL statement
     Dim oConn                 ' Connection Object
     Dim oRs                   ' Recordset

     ' Create Connection
     Set    oConn = OpenConnection()

     ' Build SQL Statement
     cSQL = "SELECT * FROM gender"

     ' Retrieve Cursor
     Set oRs = oConn.Execute(cSQL)
%>
```

Section 2

```
<%
     ' Walk the Cursor Loading the Combo Box
     Do While Not oRs.EOF
%>
        <option value="<% = oRs("gender_id") %>"><% = oRs
            ("description") %>
```

Continues

```
<%
            oRs.MoveNext
     Loop
     ' Close Cursor
     oRs.Close
     Set oRs = Nothing

     cSQL = "SELECT * FROM prog_lang"
     Set oRs = oConn.Execute(cSQL)

%>
     </option>
     </select>
```

Section 3

```
Programming Languages <select name="PROG_LANG" size="1">
<%
     ' Walk the Cursor Loading the Combo Box
     Do While Not oRs.EOF
%>
        <option value="<% = oRs("prog_id") %>"><% = oRs
            ("description") %>
```

Section 4

```
<%
            oRs.MoveNext
     Loop
     ' Close Cursor
     oRs.Close
     Set oRs = Nothing

     ' Close Connection
     Call CloseConnection(oConn)
%>
     </option>
   </select>
```

Listing 13.23 Sections of ASP code to update gender and programming language combos.

guage. Note that Listing 13.23 is actually broken into four sections. The top section should appear at the very top of the Survey.htm document, the second and third sections appear right after the definitions for First Name, Last Name, Date Of Birth, and

```
<%@ language = "VBScript" %>
<% Option Explicit %>
<!-- #include file="adovbs.inc" -->
<!-- #include file="SurvConn.inc" -->
<%
     Dim cSQL                    ' SQL statement
     Dim oConn                   ' Connection Object
     Dim oRs                     ' Recordset

     ' Create Connection
     Set    oConn = OpenConnection

     ' Build SQL Statement
     cSQL = "SELECT * FROM gender"

     ' Retrieve Cursor
     Set oRs = oConn.Execute(cSQL)
%>

<html>
<head>
<title>Survey</title>
</head>

<body>

<hr>

<p>Tell us what you think about our web site,
or anything else that comes to mind. We
welcome all of your comments and suggestions.</p>

<form method="POST" action="SaveResults.asp">
  <p><strong>Tell us how to get in touch with you:</strong><dl>
    <dd><pre>
    First Name              <input type="text" size="35"
       maxlength="256" name="FIRST_NAME">
    Last Name               <input type="text" size="35"
       maxlength="256" name="LAST_NAME">
    Date Of Birth           <input type="text" size="35"
       maxlength="256" name="DATE_OF_BIRTH">
    Email Address           <input type="text" size="35"
       maxlength="256" name="FAVORITE_LINKS">
    Gender                  <select name="GENDER" size="1">
<%
```

Continues

```
      ' Walk the Cursor Loading the Combo Box
      Do While Not oRs.EOF
%>
         <option value="<% = oRs("gender_id") %>"><% =
oRs("description") %>
<%
             oRs.MoveNext
      Loop
      ' Close Cursor
      oRs.Close
      Set oRs = Nothing

      cSQL = "SELECT * FROM prog_lang"
      Set oRs = oConn.Execute(cSQL)

%>
      </option>
      </select>
     Programming Languages <select name="PROG_LANG" size="1">
<%
      ' Walk the Cursor Loading the Combo Box
      Do While Not oRs.EOF
%>
         <option value="<% = oRs("prog_id") %>"><% = oRs
             ("description") %>
<%
             oRs.MoveNext
      Loop
      ' Close Cursor
      oRs.Close
      Set oRs = Nothing

      ' Close Connection
      Call CloseConnection(oConn)
%>
      </option>
      </select>

      </pre>
     </dd>
   </dl>
   <p><strong>What kind of comment would you like to
         send?</strong><dl>
     <dd>
      <input type="radio" name="MessageType" value="C">Complaint
      <input type="radio" name="MessageType" value="P">Problem
      <input type="radio" checked name="MessageType"
             value="S">Suggestion
      <input type="radio" name="MessageType" value="A">Approval
```

```
      </dd>
    </dl>
    <p><strong>What about us do you want to comment
  on?</strong><dl>
      <dd><select name="SUBJECT" size="1">
          <option selected value="W">Web Site</option>
          <option value="C">Company</option>
          <option value="P">Products</option>
          <option value="S">Store</option>
          <option value="E">Employee</option>
          <option value="O">(Other)</option>
        </select> Other: <input type="text" size="26"
  maxlength="256" name="SUBJECTOTHER"></dd>
    </dl>
    <p><strong>Reason for your visit:</strong><dl>
      <dd><textarea name="Comments" rows="5"
         cols="42"></textarea></dd>
    </dl>
    <dl>
      <dd><input type="checkbox" name="CONTACTREQUESTED" value="Y">
         Please send me
       more information.</dd>
    </dl>
    <p><input type="submit" value="Submit Comments"> <input
  type="reset" value="Clear Form"></p>
  </form>

  <hr>

  <h5>Vivid Software Inc.<br>
  Copyright © 1999 Vivid Software. All rights reserved.<br></h5>
  </body>
  </html>
```

Listing 13.24 Final Survey.asp document.

Email Address Inputs, and the fourth section appears right after the end option tag (</option>) portion. They are broken out here so that you can see them more clearly than when they are actually embedded in the HTML document.

Also note that once the code is placed into the Survey.htm file you must re-save the file as an Active Server Pages document—.asp file—so that IIS can properly interact with the file. In addition, the files adovbs.inc and SurvConn.inc must be in the same directory.

Handling Input

Now that we have completed the survey setup, we need to respond to the action of the submitting the comments (Submit Comments button). Since the input type of the button is "submit" it will call the action defined by the form post method. The other button, defined as an input type of reset, will cause the form to reset itself, clearing any data entry that has occurred.

Notice that the form method defines SaveResults.asp as the file that's executed by the Post action. When the user presses the Submit Comments button the browser opens the SaveResults.asp page and processes the contents. There are several actions that we must do in order to make the update occur properly.

Create a New Row ID

First, we need to create a new row id. This is accomplished by using a special type of SELECT statement known as SELECT MAX. We pass the column name to the max function so that the statement reads SELECT MAX(survey_id) + 1 FROM survey. This generates a new column id.

We'll create another table such as a Next_Sequence table. The Next_Sequence table contains two columns: Name and Sequence_ID. The Name column is a varchar(30) and the Sequence_ID column is a numeric. We then create a function (either in ASP or VB) which fetches the next sequence number for the new column.

For example:

```
' Function Call
New_id  = GetNextSequence("survey_id")
```

The code for Get NextSequence Function is as follows:

```
Function GetNextSequence(cSequence)
                    Dim cSQL        ' Select Statement
                    Dim oConn       ' Connection
                    Dim oRs         ' Recordset Object
                    Dim nNext       ' Next Sequence

                    Set oConn = OpenConnection
                    CSQL = "SELECT * FROM next_sequence
                      WHERE Ucase(name) ='" & Ucase(cSequence) & "'"

                    Set oRs = oConn.Execute(cSQL)

                    ' Generate the Next ID
                    nNext = CLng(oRs("sequence_id")) + 1

                    ' Build the UPDATE SQL Statement
                    CSQL = "UPDATE next_sequence SET sequence_id = " & _
                            CLng(oRs("sequence_id")) + 1 & _
                            "WHERE Ucase(name) ='" & _
                            Ucase(cSequence) & "'"

                    ' Perform an Update
                    oConn.Execute(cSQL)
```

```
            ' Close Everything
            oRs.Close
            CloseConnection(oConn)

            ' Set Return Value
            GetNextSequence = nNext

End Function
```

```
<%@ language = "VBScript" %>
<% Option Explicit %>
<!-- #include file="Adovbs.inc" -->
<!-- #include file="SurvConn.inc" -->
<%
     Dim cSQL         ' Insert Statement
     Dim cContact     ' Contact ?
     Dim iNext        ' Next ID for Survey
     Dim oConn        ' Connection Object
     Dim oRs          ' Recordset Object

     Const Field_Count = 0

     ' Create a New Connection
     Set oConn = OpenConnection

     ' Get Next Id
     cSQL = "SELECT MAX(survey_id) + 1 FROM survey"
     Set oRs = oConn.Execute(cSQL)

     ' Store Next Id
     iNext = oRs(Field_Count)

     ' Check for first time entry
     If IsNull(iNext) Then
            iNext = 1
     End If

      ' Handle conversion of Check Box to a
      ' Y or N
     If Request.Form("CONTACTREQUESTED") = "Y" Then
            cContact = "Y"
     Else
            cContact = "N"
     End If

      ' Build the SQL Statement
      cSQL = "INSERT INTO survey " & _
      "(survey_id, first_name, last_name, gender_id, prog_id, " & _
```

Continues

```
        "date_of_birth, visittype, commenton, subjectother, " & _
        "reason, emailaddress, contact) VALUES (" & _
       iNext & ", '" & _
     Request.Form("FIRST_NAME") & "', '" & _
             Request.Form("LAST_NAME") & "', " & _
             Request.Form("GENDER") & ", " & _
             Request.Form("PROG_LANG") & ", '" & _
             Request.Form("DATE_OF_BIRTH") & "', '" & _
             Request.Form("MESSAGETYPE") & "', '" & _
             Request.Form("SUBJECT") & "', '" & _
             Request.Form("SUBJECTOTHER") & "', '" & _
             Request.Form("COMMENTS") & "', '" & _
             Request.Form("EMAILADDRESS") & "', '" & _
             cContact & "')"

     ' Execute this Insert
     oConn.Execute(cSQL)

     ' Done
     Call CloseConnection(oConn)
     Set oConn = Nothing
%>

<div align="center"><center>
<table border="0" cellpadding="0" cellspacing="0" width="600"
bgcolor="#FFFFFF">
  <tr>
    <td align="center" bgcolor="#FFFFCC">
       <font face="Arial, Helvetica">Survey Information
       has been properly updated.</font></td>
    </td>
  </tr>
</table>
</div>

<table>
   <tr>
      <td><center><font face="arial" size="2"><p><br>
        <a href="javascript:history.go(-1)">< Back </a>
      | <a href="default.htm">Return To Homepage</a>
      </center>
     </td>
   </tr>
</table>

</body>

</html>
```

Listing 13.25 SaveResults.asp.

Build the Insert Statement

Our next step is to build an Insert statement. To do this, we need to retrieve the values from the Survey page so that we can insert them into the Survey database. How do we retrieve the fields? Since the form method is Post we can expect the values to be passed in the header. We use the Request.Form(<field name>) method to retrieve the value of the field. Please note, if the field is empty it will always return an empty string, since VBScript is not strong typed.

Execute the Insert

The code in Listing 13.2 shows how to execute the actual Insert statement from VBScript.

Inform the User of Success

As developers, we usually spare "none of the Rod" when the user makes a mistake; and are quick to provide them with feedback so that they can correct the errors of their ways. However, it is ALSO good practice to somehow let the user know when they've done something good. This section shows a variety of ways to let the user know that they've succeeded in their data entry exploits.

Direct the User to the New page/ Previous Page

Listing 13.25 shows how you can contol the flow of screens that the user is presented with after submitting their data changes. You can prompt them along to a new page to work with, or return them from the page that they were on when they started the data submission process.

Final Setup Steps

Now we need to place all of the files in a directory on the server so that we can access them using Internet Explorer. IIS creates a directory named InetPub on the server. Under InetPub you will find the root directory for all www activity. It is named www-root. In order to keep the files in there own sub-directory, create a Survey directory underneath wwwroot. So the fully qualified path is InetPub\wwwroot\Survey on the server Merlin. The following four files should be present:

1. Survey.asp—the ASP Survey document.
2. SaveResults.asp—the ASP document that updates the database.
3. Adovbs.inc—the ADO Include file.
4. SurvConn.inc—the Survey Include file.

To access the survey, bring up Internet Explorer and type the http://server name (since the server name is Merlin, if you type Merlin it maps to the InetPub\wwwroot directories) followed by the Survey directory and Survey page.

```
http://merlin/survey/survey.asp
```

The survey should now pop up in your browser. Once you have entered the data, click Submit and the page will update the Survey database.

Creating Server Components with Visual Basic

By now you should be familiar with how components are used in ASP. The components that we've worked with thus far have already been written and provided by Microsoft. So, what if we need a special behavior that we don't have available in ASP? We can attempt to write the behavior in VBScript or JavaScript, but depending on the complexity of such an operation it might not be the best approach.

This brings us to the next level—creating our own server components using Visual Basic 6.0. Server components are nothing more than ActiveX controls that can interact with ASP. ActiveX controls can run on a variety of different host platforms such as Visual Basic, Visual C++, Internet Explorer, or as a server component under IIS.

Any programming language that is used to create an ActiveX control can be used to create a server component. Until the release of Visual Basic 5, that usually meant using C++, CA-Visual Objects, or Delphi (just to name a few).

Server Components

One of the most important reasons to create and use a server component written in Visual Basic is *speed*. A server component can be used for a number of different tasks. Much of what we code in a component can be done in VBScript, but since VB is a strong-typed language with a native code compiler, the performance is often much better.

When we create a server component that encapsulates some of our site functionality we can often improve our application architecture in a number of ways:

Improved code reuse. Since the code is contained in a single binary entity (DLL) the code isn't replicated in a number places (either in Include files or ASP pages).

Source code protection. A DLL is a binary file, and as such the code written is translated to machine language. This means that unlike an ASP page the user cannot view the source code, thus protecting proprietary information.

Maintenance. Updating and maintaining the application is easier, since we only have to recompile the component rather than modify large amounts of source code.

Flexibility. Visual Basic provides us with quite a few more features than VB Script and allows us to perform actions and operations, which might otherwise be difficult.

Visual Basic is one of the easiest languages to create an ActiveX component in. It provides a rich code set while shielding the programmer from the more tedious programming tasks. This is both good and bad. Good, because we can create powerful components in a short amount of time. Bad, in that we are somewhat limited in a few other areas, such as the low-level memory twiddling that one can do with languages like C++.

For our example let's start with something very simple. Let's validate a user name and password. This gives us a chance to re-work the Login source code from a previous example. We begin by creating a new Visual Basic 6 Project, and select which type of ActiveX component we wish to create. There are two types: ActiveX DLL and ActiveX EXE.

We'll begin with the ActiveX DLL. An ActiveX DLL is referred to as an in-process server, which means that the code is executed in the same process (or memory) space as the calling application. In the case of a server component, the calling application is actually IIS.

The second type is the ActiveX EXE. An ActiveX EXE is referred to as an out-of-process server, which means that the code is executed in its own process (or memory) space. This difference can cause a serious performance issue when dealing with an application like IIS. This relates primarily to the way in which an ActiveX EXE must pass information to the calling application.

For the purposes of this example we'll use the ActiveX DLL. On the Visual Basic New Project dialog select ActiveX DLL (see Figure 13.23).

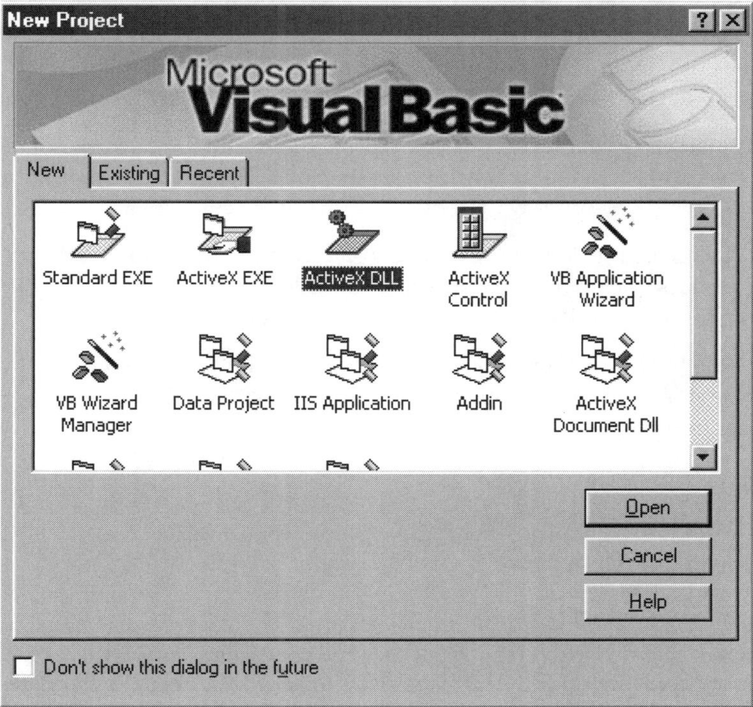

Figure 13.23 Creating a new ActiveX DLL project.

Visual Basic creates a new project named Project1, with a default class of Class1. Before we can compile this component we must change a few things. First, we must name the project.

Using the Project menu select Project1 Properties. First double check that the Project Type is set to ActiveX DLL, then change the name of the project to LoginCheck. Click OK and notice that the change in the Project window (if you don't have the Project window open select View/Project explorer or press Ctrl + R). The project has been changed to reflect the new name.

With the project properly named, we now determine the name of the class and change it as well. If the Code window for Class1 is not already open, open the Property explorer and expand the LoginCheck project until you see Class1. Select Class1 and in the Properties window (if the Properties window isn't open select View/Properties window or press F4), type the name ValidateUser.

We want to point out, that if you plan to do a more sophisticated DLL and need access to the information on a Web page, you should use the ScriptingContext object.

The ScriptingContext Object

Active Server Pages implement an object that allows access to the very core structure of ASP. There are several core objects: Application, Request, Response, Server, and Session. The ScriptingContext object contains methods, which return a reference to any of the primary core objects. This allows for better interaction than we might achieve by using instance variables or parameters.

We can use instance variables, and if you plan to distribute the ActiveX component for use with other servers that may not support the ScriptingContext, we recommend that you do so.

Before we can access the ScriptingContext object we must first add it to the Visual Basic Project References. We do this by selecting Project/References, followed by the Browse button. Locate the file ASP.DLL and then add it as a reference.

ASP allows us to use the ScriptingContext object in the OnStartPage method within our component. All server components that interact with ASP should save a reference to this object for later use:

```
Dim mScriptObj As ScriptingContext

Public Sub OnStartPage(objScript As ScriptingContext)
   mScriptObj = objScript
End Sub
```

Now let's use our sample ASP page from earlier (LoginValidation.Asp). Instead of doing the validation from within the ASP page itself let's call the method Validate from our new LoginCheck.DLL. First we must add the references for ADO to the Visual Basic project. Select Project/References and locate the two references as shown in Figure 13.24.

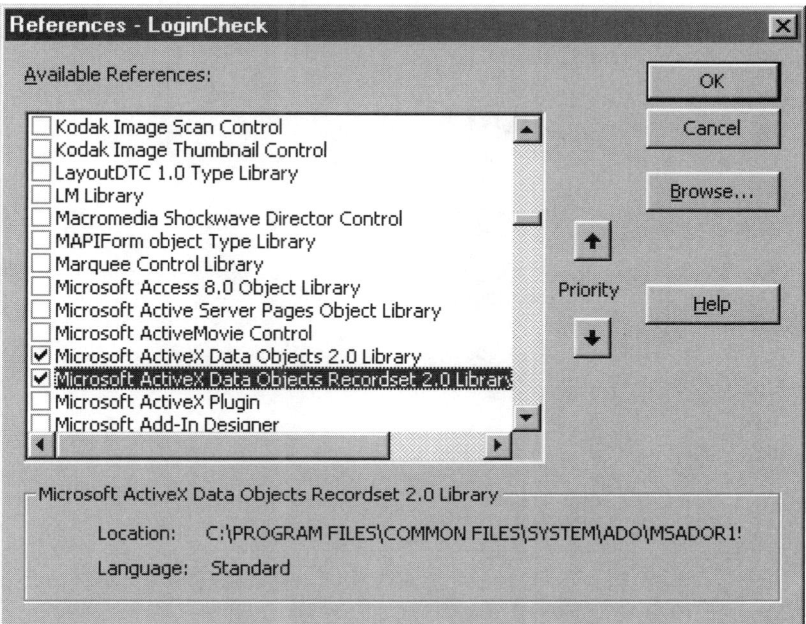

Figure 13.24 Adding the ADO references.

```
Public Function Validate() As Boolean
   Dim oRequest As Request
   Dim oConn    As ADODB.Connection
   Dim oRs      As ADODB.RecordSet
   Dim cSQL     As String
   Dim cUser    As String
   Dim cPwd     As String

   ' Get a reference to the Request Object
   Set oRequest = mScriptObj.Request

   ' Access the User_Name and Password fields
   ' on the Login Page.
   cUser = UCase(oRequest.Form("USER_NAME"))
   cPwd = UCase(oRequest.Form("PASSWORD"))

   ' Build the SQL Statement
    cSQL = "SELECT * FROM auth_users WHERE Ucase(username) =
```

Continues

```
'" & _
                        Ucase(cUser) & "'"

   ' Open the Connection
    Set oConn = Server.CreateObject("ADODB.Connection")

   ' Make Native Connection Through ADO to SQL Server 7.0
    oConn.Open "Driver={SQL Server};Server=Merlin;UID=sa;" &
            "WSID=;Language=us_english;DATABASE=Survey;" & _
            "PASSWORD=;"

   ' Open Recordset
   Set oRs = oConn.Execute(cSQL)

   ' No Records?
   If oRs.EOF then
      ' Not found!
      Validate = False
   Else
      ' Found, but is it a valid password?
      If Trim(Ucase(oRs("password"))) <> Trim(Ucase(cPwd))
         ' Not valid
         Validate = False
      Else
         Validate = True
      End If
   End If

     ' Close Recordset
     oRs.Close
     Set oRs = Nothing
     ' Close Connection

     oConn.Close
     Set oConn = Nothing

End Function
```

Listing 13.26 Validation Logic.

Next, we must create the Validate method of the ValidateUser Class (see Listing 13.26). We combine the use of ADO and the ScriptingContext object to interact with the calling ASP page LoginValidation.

Finally, we must change the LoginValidation Page to handle the new DLL. To open an ActiveX DLL from within an ASP page we must use a method of the Server, CreateObject.

The CreateObject method accepts as a parameter the ActiveX Server Name (iLoginCheck) followed by the Class to initialize (ValidateUser). So the source code to instantiate a new instance is:

```
oLogin = Server.CreateObject("LoginCheck.ValidateUser")
```

Now that we have the instance of the LoginCheck object we can validate the user name and password. In the Validate method of the LoginCheck Object the ScriptingContext object allows us to interrogate the page that has created the instance. To validate a user in ASP you only need to invoke the Validate method like so:

```
If oLogin.Validate Then
    ' Valid User
    ' Do something
Else
    ' Invalid User
    Response.Write("Invalid Username or Password!
Please Try Again.")
    Response.Write("<a href="javascript:history.go(-1)">
   < Back </a>")
End If
```

Installing the Server Components

Now that we have compiled the Server Component, we are ready to install the component on the NT Server. Once the component is copied to the Server it is registered so that it's accessible.

Generally, when you install an ActiveX component, registration is part of the installation routine, but since we've developed this component we must register it manually. To register an ActiveX component we use the Windows utility RegSvr32.Exe. Select The Start Menu Run option, and in the edit type:

```
RegSvr32  <Path>\LoginValidation.DLL
```

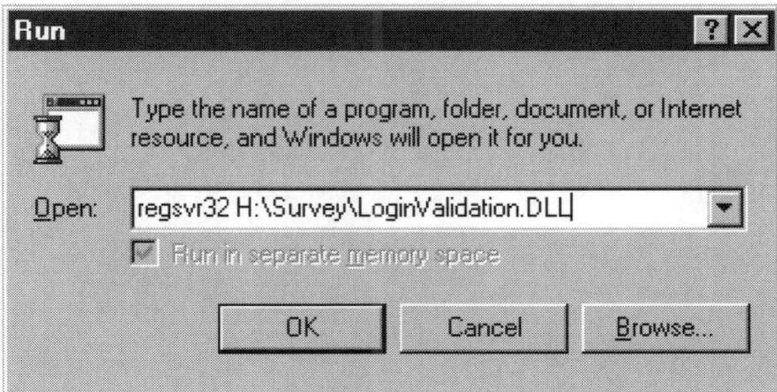

Figure 13.25 Running DLL registration.

Upon success the Server presents the user with a dialog box that confirms the registration. Replace the <Path> variable with the actual directory (see Figure 13.25).

Upgrading Your DLL Component

Finally, when you upgrade the ActiveX DLL you must do a few things to properly insure that the DLL is updated on the Server. If you attempt to copy a new DLL over top of the old one you will receive the message, "Unable to overwrite file. File is currently in use." This happens because once a call has been made to the DLL, IIS doesn't release the file.

To upgrade the LoginValidation.DLL file we must first stop IIS. To stop IIS open the Control Panel and select Services. From the Services dialog locate the IIS Admin Service and select Stop. You will be presented with the Stop Services dialog as shown in Figure 13.26.

Once the services have been stopped, don't close the Services dialog, since we need to restart IIS in a moment. Now you need to un-register the DLL, once again using the RegSvr.Exe Utility. Only now use the –u parameter.

```
RegSvr32 -u <Path>\LoginValidation.DLL
```

That should successfully un-register the DLL. Now you can delete or overwrite it. Next, restart the IIS Admin Service. However, restarting the service doesn't reset IIS. To do that you must open the Internet Information Server Manager and select each service—Default FTP, Default Web Site, and Administration Web Site in turn and start it by using the Action Start menu.

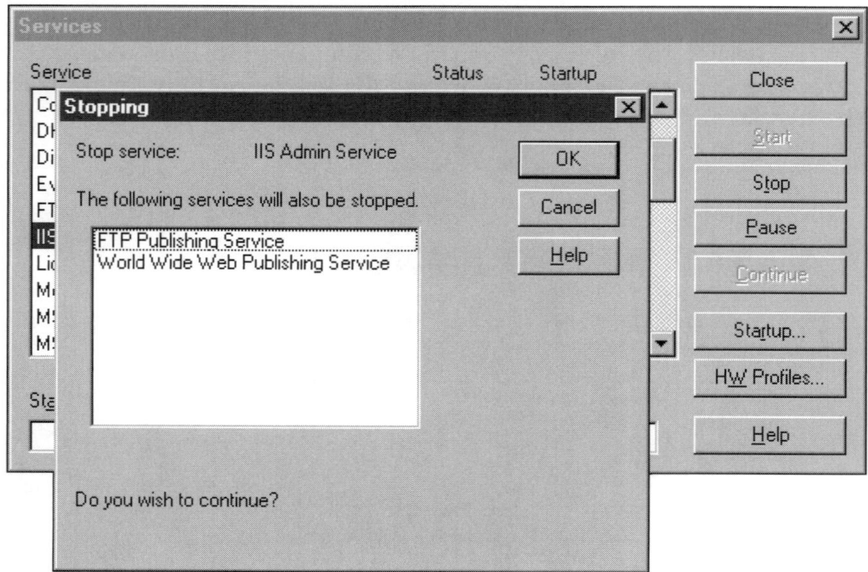

Figure 13.26 Stopping the IIS Admin Services.

Summary

As you can imagine, we've only scratched the surface of the types of things that you can do by pairing VB and SQL Server. Although other authors have written entire books on the topic, we hope we've given you the practice and background to use any of Microsoft's current "big three" data models in writing VB applications against SQL Server data, without having to invest in more books. The sky's the limit, folks.

CHAPTER 14

More Project Ideas

The projects found in this book illustrate how databases like SQL Server are the foundation for many applications ranging from transaction processing to decision support to even e-commerce. In selecting projects for this book, we tried to select the ones that we thought most of you would want to do, but it was very hard to limit ourselves to just 10. Each of us had ideas about other *really cool* projects that we should include. The solution we came up with was to include a chapter where we talked about some of those other projects and then provided not only some tangible ways to get started, but also links to resources we think can give you a jump start.

We decided not to talk about commercial off-the-shelf (COTS) accounting and enterprise relationship planning (ERP) packages that use SQL Server *under the hood*, but rather to focus on projects you'd probably be more likely to do by yourself such as:

- Knowledge management (KM) and full-text indexing
- Data mining
- Natural language processing (using English Query)
- Data synchronization applications with Windows CE devices
- Mapping applications using geographical information systems (GIS) engines

Ready?

Knowledge Management: Beyond the Hype

Knowledge management, or KM, is one of those slippery terms that can mean just about anything. Basically we think of it as a giant collection of information that's organized in some fashion. A more formal definition may read: *the preservation and exploitation of an organization's core intelligence.*

To get your head around KM, we think it's useful to see how the pioneers use it. As you might expect, most of the early adopters are either firms who are in the business of selling content or firms who need a better method for sharing information in order to stay competitive. Many systems integrator and services firms are in the business of selling expertise (read experience), often encapsulated into some sort of formal or informal knowledge base of *best practices*. The knowledge base usually starts life as an in-house effort, but sometimes parts of it are productized, as in the case of Arthur Andersen's KnowledgeSpace (see www.arthurandersen.com or www.knowlegespace.com).

Systems integrators, "Big Five" firms, brokerages, and so-called "analyst" firms almost all have strong KM efforts in house—whether they call them KM or not. Not only can employees tap into the corporate knowledge base; they're expected to contribute to it. Systems integrators typically write up detailed reports about their engagements, not only profiling the customer site (hardware, software, people, politics, budget, and so on), but also detailing the technical issues. A good KM system is integrated with an organization's customer relationship management system (CRM) so that the sales force, for example, can quickly scan any recent interaction between their firm and the customer.

Basically, chances are that any organization that has a lot of intellectual capital to track is doing KM. They may even have someone designated as Chief Information Officer or Chief Knowledge Officer. (For a very funny editorial on titles, see Russell Kay's "What's my line? Think of it as evolution in action" in the May 3, 1999, issue of *Computerworld*. Ultimately, observed Kay, the CKO may morph into a Wisdom Processing Officer, Cognitive Implementation Coordinator, or, yes, even a Philosopher King.) Irreverence aside, pharmaceuticals, aerospace firms, banks, and other financial institutions have been early adopters of KM projects.

One reason KM is hard to nail down is that it typically evolves from an existing application such as workflow/messaging, document management, data warehousing, customer service and/or the often-related e-commerce, ERP (a la SAP which, by the way, has just shipped its own Knowledge Warehouse 4.0, originally known as InfoDB), information retrieval/search, and perhaps even knowledge engineering/artificial intelligence (AI). As you might expect, KM implementations have different *feels* depending on their origins. Some KM efforts are database-centric, but the trend seems to be towards building them around a messaging infrastructure such as an email server.

ACCORDING TO *FAST COMPANY'S* ALAN WEBBER...

Alan Webber, founding editor of *Fast Company* magazine was interviewed in the January 1999 issue of *Lotus Conversations with Industry Innovators*. In the online article (www.lotus.com/home.nsf/welcome/interviews/), Webber defines knowledge management as something you can't just buy off the shelf—perhaps to the consternation of the Lotus interviewer! When he said, "This is not something where you take the off-the-shelf solution and slap it in and say 'Here is your ready-made kit to create knowledge management.'"

KM and Microsoft's Digital Nervous System

Back in Chapter 1, we talked about Microsoft's vision of the digital nervous system, a vision described in Bill Gates book, *Business at the Speed of Thought*, Warner Books, 1999. The gist is that to survive in today's competitive and ever-changing world, it's essential that organizations—and their (knowledge) workers—be prepared for technological advances and the evolution to a digital economy. As companies move to a digital work style, they need to figure out better ways to share information and knowledge across the enterprise. Enter KM.

As Gates observes, the most successful companies will be those with fast access to information and the ability to process that information and develop strategies to adapt quickly to change, planned and unplanned. The digital nervous system is Microsoft's vision for enabling technology. To underscore the linkage, find Microsoft's KM site at www.microsoft.com/dns/km. At press time, Microsoft had posted a white paper, *Building Knowledge Management Solutions Using BackOffice with Office 2000* at www.microsoft.com/BACKOFFICESERVER/bizsol/offboguide.htm. Included is a sample exercise that you can use to build a business workflow application. The Microsoft Office 2000 Developer (MOD) site should also have some good KM/workflow templates that you can use.

On September 13, 1999, just prior to its annual DevDays event held simultaneously at scores of locations around the world, Microsoft updated its KM strategy by demonstrating a variety of "digital dashboards," reinforcing its Exchange/Outlook-centric view of KM. In Microsoft parlance, a digital dashboard is a personalized and dynamic Web page that runs within the Outlook 2000 messaging and collaboration client. It's not hard to create your own customized digital dashboard by using FrontPage 2000.

Also announced at that time was the Digital Dashboard Starter Kit, an SDK for both end users and programmers. The Kit—available at http://www.microsoft.com/dns/km—contains six customizable digital dashboards (Your First Digital Dashboard, plus samples for health care professional, salespeople, and other professionals who work in manufacturing, insurance, or finance) along with white papers and sample code.

Overhead and Power Struggles

It generally isn't a smart idea to play the role of white knight, championing a new KM effort at your organization. Logical as such a project may seem to *you*, KM projects need a compelling business-driven *raison d'être*. Here are some examples:

- The CEO has noticed how much it costs to acquire and train new employees and wants to, as a first step, at least minimize the cost and time spent on breaking in new employees. Eventually, he thinks, it might be possible to capture information from employees about what they like, and don't like, about working for the firm.
- Team members in one division have noticed how much time is spent on "coordination" and wonder why their organization doesn't have a good corporate intranet portal that lets them locate and use shared project information.
- Too many employees have quit—taking corporate history with them.

- The board tells the CEO he doesn't have a good enough grip on his competition and suggests he implement a competitive intelligence effort.

You don't have to be a genius to see some of the problems with KM efforts. First, there's the temptation (a la enterprise data warehouse) to want to do the Whole Big Thing and Do It Right. Current wisdom indicates it's a lot smarter to go for targeted high-visibility, high-payoff projects first—the proverbial low-hanging fruit. Then, with one success implementation under your belt, KM can evolve incrementally.

Another problem is that KM is often perceived as more busy work—another chore that has no observable payoff to the folks in the trenches that are supposed to populate the knowledge base with their wisdom. Speaking of knowledge bases, we consider the Microsoft Developer Network (MSDN) Knowledge Base one of the best examples of KM on the planet. You can search by keyword, for recent articles, for a specific Knowledge Base article (Qxxxxxx), or even using natural language (more on this later in the chapter).

Another challenge KM projects face is overcoming the perception that "knowledge is power" and that your value is a function of your own private knowledge base. Sharing your wisdom with others, it would seem, will dilute your value. That's a very real and very tough issue, and there's no easy answer.

And that's not all. When KM projects are launched as problem solvers, this can cast an unflattering spotlight on the division with the problem. And KM projects aren't simply "load-and-go" type affairs. They have to be kept up to date. That means someone has to commit to financing them and supplying resources for their ongoing maintenance.

Microsoft's Approach to KM

Microsoft's KM strategy is still evolving, and is likely to be officially launched when Exchange 6.0 (Platinum) ships in late 1999. But Exchange is just part of Microsoft's KM strategy. To see both how serious Microsoft is about KM and to get an indication of how it's approaching KM, look at the Microsoft Research site at research.microsoft.com/areas/. The Interactivity and Intelligence Group hosts many teams, including one for KM. As of summer 1999, the KM team had seven major focuses:

1. Adaptive Systems and Interaction
2. Collaborative and Multimedia Systems
3. Data Mining and Exploration (DMX)
4. Information Retrieval and Analysis
5. Machine Learning and Applied Statistics
6. Natural Language Processing
7. User Interfaces

According to Microsoft's Senior VP Bob Muglia, in a keynote speech at TechEd 99 (www.teched99.com), Microsoft's Exchange group is driving the KM effort. Key features of the KM vision include a digital dashboard that provides customized views of information ranging from email to product sales to Web sites. The KM vision also includes Web Store that provides access to information from Web, file and collaborative servers, and transactional systems; and a new Team Productivity Application (TPA) for BackOffice 4.5. TPA promises to be Microsoft's first serious foray into the message-based collaboration and knowledge management markets (look out, Lotus Notes!) It will ship with several out-of-the-box applications including Team Documents using Office 2000 Server Extensions, several collaborative applications such as team calendar, contacts, discussions, and FAQs based on Exchange Server, and a SQL Server-based issues-tracking template.

For document-oriented KM projects, Microsoft hopes Office 2000 will serve as the foundation. Office 2000's Tools menu features an Online Collaboration sub-menu with options to "meet now", schedule meetings, or participate in Web discussions. Part of Microsoft's promotional material for Office 2000 says, "Office 2000 users should be knowledge-management empowered with the data features provided in each Office application or custom solution. They should be able to locate data from any source (including large data stores in an SQL-based data warehouse) and then create knowledge by synthesizing this data into professionally published content."

Elsewhere, Microsoft promotes Office not only as the "entry point to the Digital Nervous System," but also the crossroads of the digital nervous system, where knowledge workers transform data into information.

Office and Exchange aren't the only foundations Microsoft proposes for a KM system. Some initiatives might best be tackled using the SQL Server-based Site Server, for example. Site Server, you will recall, includes a full-text indexing capability that goes beyond SQL Server full-text indexing. Most KM efforts have powerful search functionality built into them. And Site Server has been the focal point for one Microsoft KM endeavor code-named Tahoe.

Another approach is to combine Site Server and Exchange. While Site Server provides the necessary features for full-text indexing, and search and knowledge delivery, Exchange Server provides the collaborative infrastructure and functionality that makes creating Internet newsgroups, threaded discussions, customer contact databases, and custom collaborative applications easy.

In other words, Microsoft doesn't seem to have a single KM strategy, and while this may be disconcerting, we think it also reflects the real world and the different directions from which people approach KM. Back in October 1998, at Microsoft's first "BizApps" conference, Sangita Gulati, Microsoft's KM Technical Evangelist, presented two graphics that help to illuminate Microsoft's KM framework (see Figures 14.1 and 14.2).

Figure 14.2 is a slightly updated version of Sangita's original slide.

So Where Does SQL Server Fit In?

Frankly, it doesn't look like SQL Server will have a starring role in Microsoft's KM efforts. It will, however, continue to be part of Microsoft's KM infrastructure and is likely to have a more visible role in many ISVs' KM solutions. In June 1999, for example,

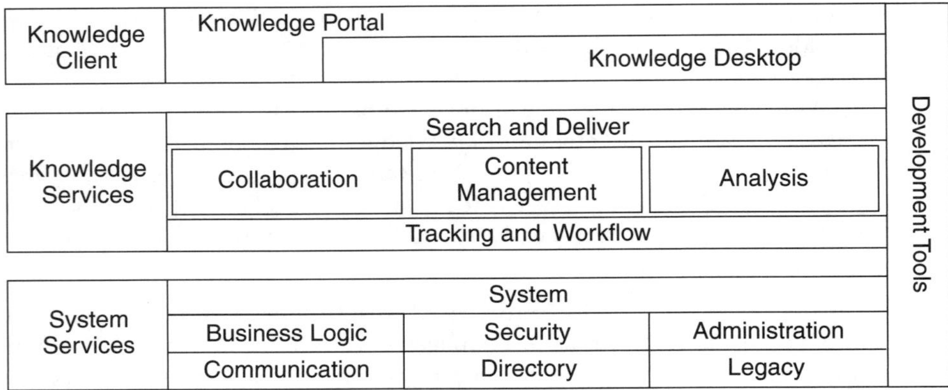

Figure 14.1 Microsoft's Framework for KM applications as presented by Sangita Gulati at Microsoft's BizApps conference.
Source: Microsoft Corporation © 1998

Siebel Systems, then a $390 million maker of CRM software, announced it would begin bundling Microsoft's SQL Server 7 database as an option with its front-office application suite. Although Siebel's software is called CRM, it can certainly be used for KM.

That said, there's nothing stopping you from building your own KM solution. I've seen several divisional KM projects—notably in HR and training—built from scratch using SQL Server. Think back on your last orientation at a new job. Chances are there was plenty of room for improvement—improvement a KM system could provide. Video

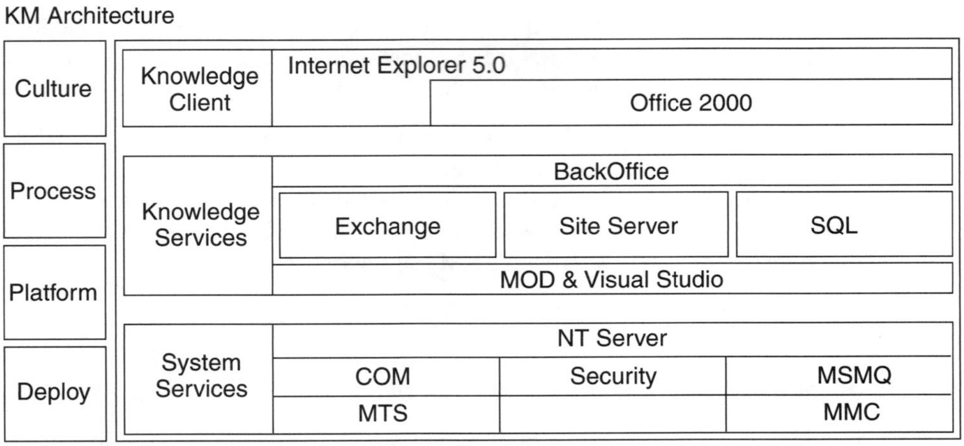

Figure 14.2 Mapping products onto the framework.
Source: Microsoft Corporation © 1999

clips of common tasks. An organization chart. Easy-to-follow interactive instructions on submitting expense reports, scheduling vacation or travel, and so on. Food for thought.

And don't forget SQL Server's full-text indexing engine.

FULL-TEXT INDEXING TECHNOLOGY

Although full-text indexing is a new feature in SQL Server 7, it's not exactly as though it's a 1.0 release. The Microsoft information retrieval technologies have been around for some time and are included with Indexing Services version 2.0 (the Index Server that is part of Windows NT 4.0 Option Pack) and Microsoft Site Server version 3.0. The SQL Server team combined various components from these applications, including the parser component of the OLE DB Provider for Indexing Services 2.0 that accepts the special SQL extensions FREETEXT and CONTAINS.

Working with Full-Text Indexing

SQL Server 7 is the first release of SQL Server to include a full-text indexing engine. So what's full-text indexing and how is it different from "normal" SQL Server clustered and non-clustered indexing?

Normal indexes only allow rapidly finding rows where the initial characters of specific columns are known. Of course, full-table scans are possible using T-SQL's powerful string functions, but full-table scans are notoriously slow.

SQL Server's full-text engine (MSSEARCH) individually indexes all of the significant words in one or more character-based column(s) of a table, and includes proximity information so that it can quickly determine if words or phrases are near each other within the text. The "near" feature you may be familiar with in some Internet search engines.

MSSEARCH also comes with built-in English language knowledge, so that multiple forms of words can satisfy a single query. In other words, MSSEARCH knows that it should look for drove and driving as well as drive or for mice when a query for mouse is submitted. Better still, having a full-text indexed table lets you use T-SQL predicates CONTAINS (see Figure 14.3) and FREETEXT and the related rowset-valued functions CONTAINSTABLE and FREETEXTTABLE. FREETEXT is a predicate used to search columns that contain character-based data types for values that match the *meaning* and not the exact wording of the words in the search condition. When FREETEXT is used, the full-text query engine internally word-breaks the freetext_string into a number of search terms and assigns each term a weight and then finds the matches. In Figure 14.3, prefix_term lets you use a "stem" such as hous for housing, housed, and so on. Proximity_term lets you use the NEAR which is defined by a complex algorithm. In other words, you don't have to supply an integer, MSSEARCH figures out what makes sense. A generation_term is similar to a prefix_term and allows so-called inflectional variations. Weighted_term can be useful for complex searches where you want to assign probabilistic weighting.

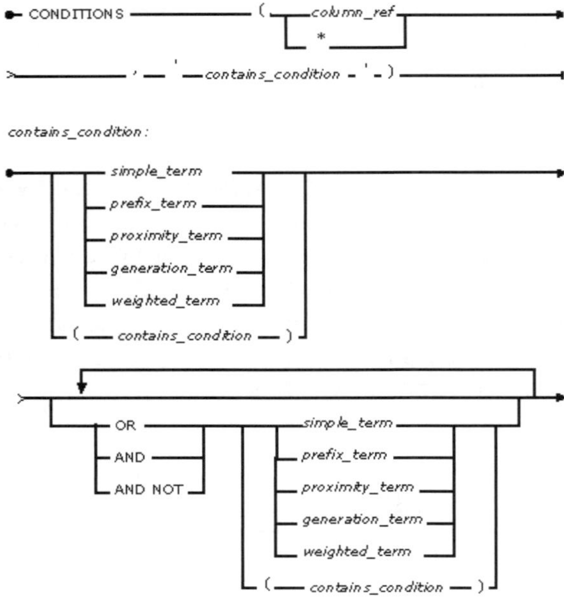

Figure 14.3 Syntax for the powerful CONTAINS predicate.

FYI PLAN AHEAD

If you issue a SQL statement that contains full-text predicates against a table that hasn't been full-text indexed, the following error occurs:

Server: Msg 7601, Level 16, State 2 Cannot use a CONTAINS or FREETEXT predicate on table 'titles' because it isn't full-text indexed.

Though powerful, the full-text isn't perfect. For example, while you can index multiple columns, all of the words to be used in a given query must be in the same row. In other words, there's no cross-index querying—at least not in the first version.

The indexes themselves are stored in external *catalog* files.

SQL Server maintains some information about these catalogs in the sysfulltextcatalogs table, but the NT-based Microsoft Search Service handles catalog management.

Table 14.1 summarizes the main differences between regular SQL indexes and full-text indexes. Figure 14.4 illustrates the overall architecture of SQL Server with full-text indexing. Figure 14.5 provides more detail.

Table 14.1 Comparing "Normal" SQL Server Indexes with Full-Text Engine Indexes

REGULAR SQL INDEXES	FULL-TEXT INDEXES
Stored under the control of the database in which they are defined	Stored in the file system, but administered through the database
Several regular indexes per table allowed. Only one full-text index per table allowed	Automatically updated when the data upon which they are based is inserted, updated, or deleted. Addition of data to full-text indexes, called population, must be requested through either a schedule or a specific request
Not grouped	Grouped within the same database into a full-text catalog
Created and dropped using T-SQL statements	Created, managed, and dropped using stored procedures or the Enterprise Manager including its full-text wizard
Automatically maintained by SQL Server	Not automatically maintained. Indexes must be explicitly re-populated

Installing Full-Text Indexing

Full-text indexing isn't installed by default and can only be installed on a Windows NT Server (but not an Enterprise Edition clustered one).

Once you do install full-text indexing, you have to do a bit of planning. Both the database itself and any tables you want to full-text index must be enabled for full-text support. At that time, metadata, such as the name of the table and its full-text catalog (a full-text catalog contains full-text indexes in a database and must reside on a local hard drive associated with the machine on which SQL Server is running) is created for the full-text index associated with the table. Once the table is enabled, you can populate it with the data in columns enabled for full-text support. If the full-text definition for a

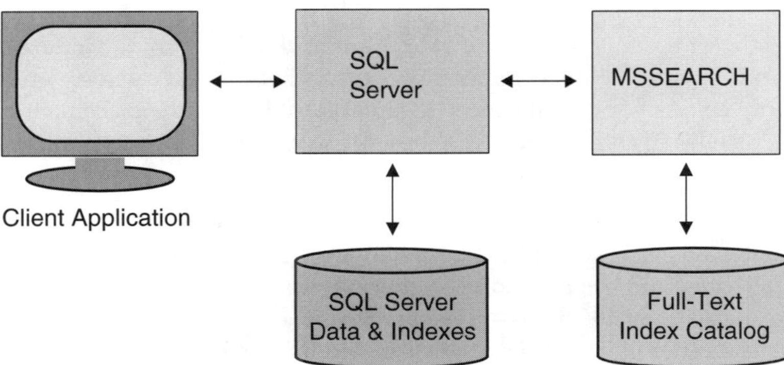

Figure 14.4 How SQL Server and MSSEARCH work together.

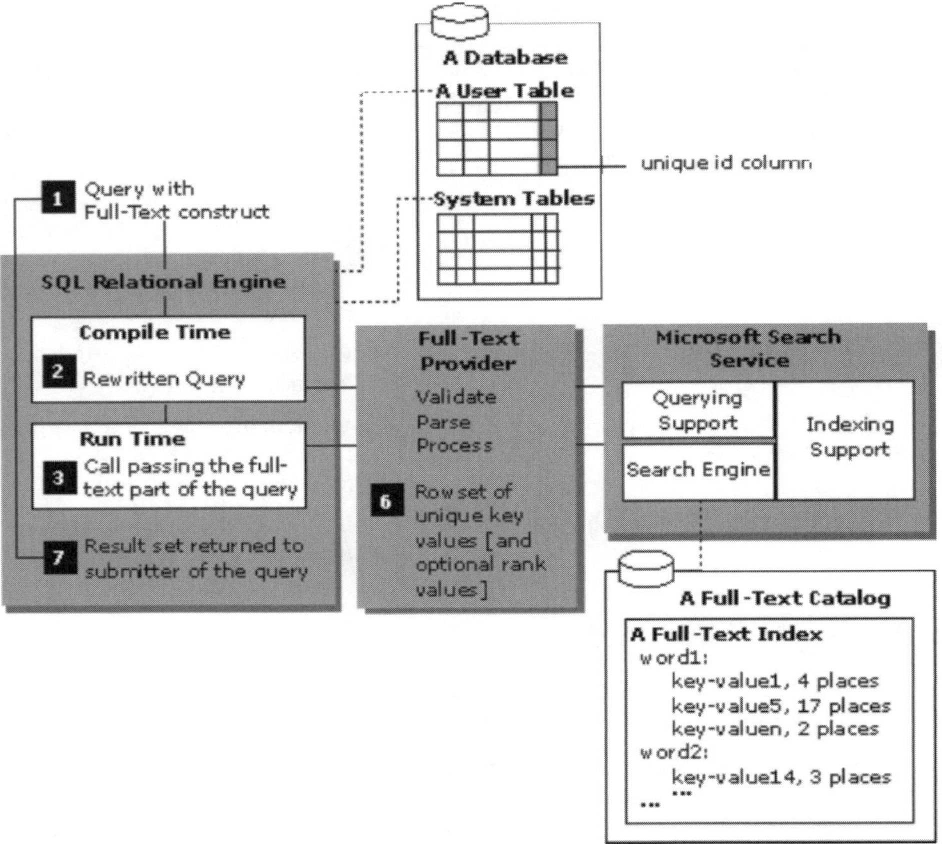

Figure 14.5 How the full-text search engine works.
Source: Microsoft SQL Server 7.0 Resource Guide

table is changed (for example, by including a new column that will also be indexed for a full-text search), the associated full-text catalog must be re-populated to synchronize the full-text index with the new full-text definition.

You can only set up an index on nullable columns that have unique indexes assigned to them. And, in order to do incremental population of full text catalog, you must have a timestamp col. As you might expect, it's important to plan the placement of full-text indexes for tables in full-text catalogs. When you assign a table to a full-text catalog, consider the following guidelines:

- Always select the smallest unique index available for your full-text unique key (a four-byte, integer-based index is optimal). Doing so significantly reduces the resources required by Microsoft Search service in the file system. If the primary key is large— over 100 bytes—consider choosing a unique index in the table or creating another unique index as the full-text unique key. Otherwise, if the full-text unique key size approaches the maximum size allowed (450 bytes) full-text population may not be able to proceed.

- If you're indexing a table that has millions of rows, assign the table to its own full-text catalog.
- Consider the amount of change that occurs in the tables that are full-text indexed, as well as the number of table rows. If the total number of rows being changed, together with the numbers of rows in the table present during the last full-text population, represents millions of rows, assign the table to its own full-text catalog.

Implementing Full-Text Indexing

There are several ways to set up and administer full-text features: using the full-text wizard, via SQL Server Enterprise Manager, and through a set of stored procedures and scalar functions. Figures 14.6 through 14.10 provide a feel for the wizard approach.

Using Enterprise Manager, expand the hierarchy, right-click on the database you want to index such as pubs, and you should see an option for Full-Text Catalogs which will be blank by default. Right-clicking on this option will give you additional selection, including one to set up scheduling (see Figure 14.11) and a New Full-Text Catalog (see Figure 14.12).

You can also do full-text indexing via code—T-SQL and SQL-DMO. Here's an example for enabling your database for full-text indexing via T-SQL:

```
USE mydb
EXEC sp_fulltext_database 'enable'
```

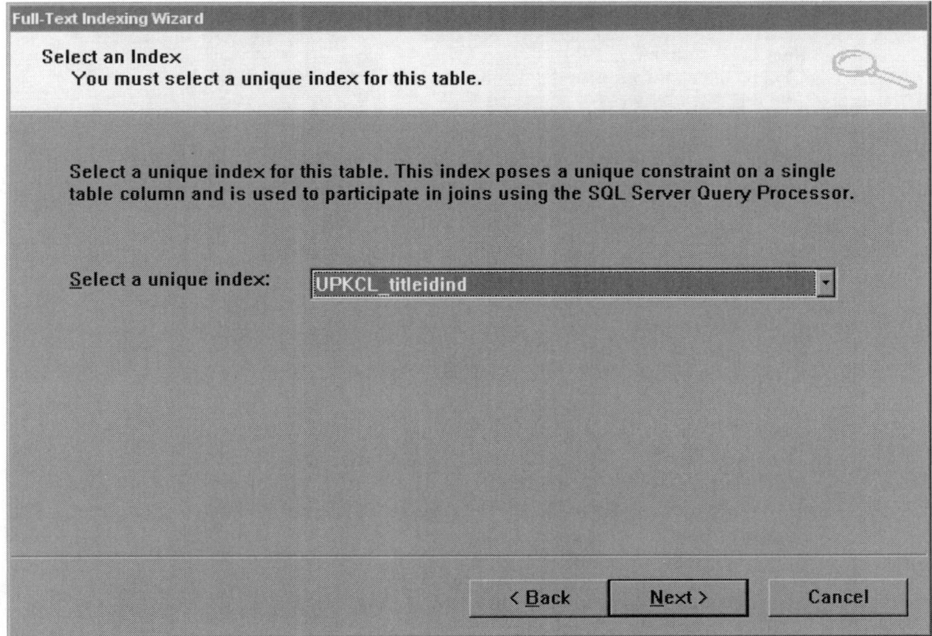

Figure 14.6 Selecting an index name of the table for full-text indexing.

```
Create a catalog
USE mydb
EXEC sp_fulltext_catalog  'mycatalog', 'create', 'D:\FullText'
```

Here's sample code to enable a table for full-text indexing:

```
USE mydb
EXEC sp_fulltext_table 'mytable', 'create', 'mycatalog', 'myindex' EXEC
sp_fulltext_table 'mytable', 'activate'
```

This is how you can add column(s) to the full-text index:

```
USE mydb
EXEC sp_fulltext_column 'mytable', 'mycolumn', 'add' EXEC
sp_fulltext_column 'mytable',      'mysecondcolumn', 'add'
```

And this is the type of code you need to populate the catalog initially, and then re-populate it:

```
USE mydb
EXEC sp_fulltext_catalog mycatalog', 'start_full'
—repopulate
EXEC sp_fulltext_catalog 'mycatalog', 'start_incremental'
—start_incremental requires that the table have a timestamp column
```

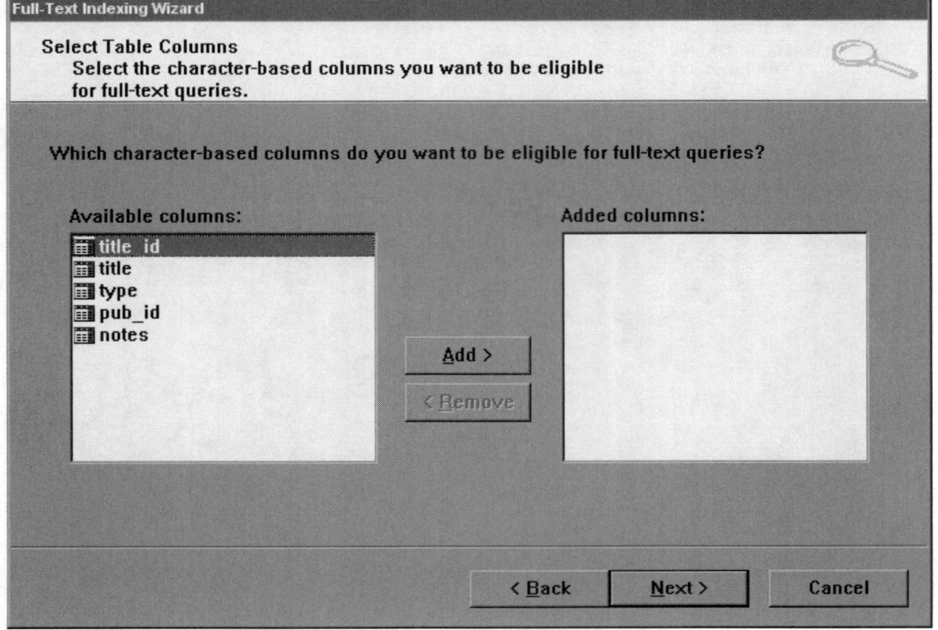

Figure 14.7 Selecting the columns for indexing.

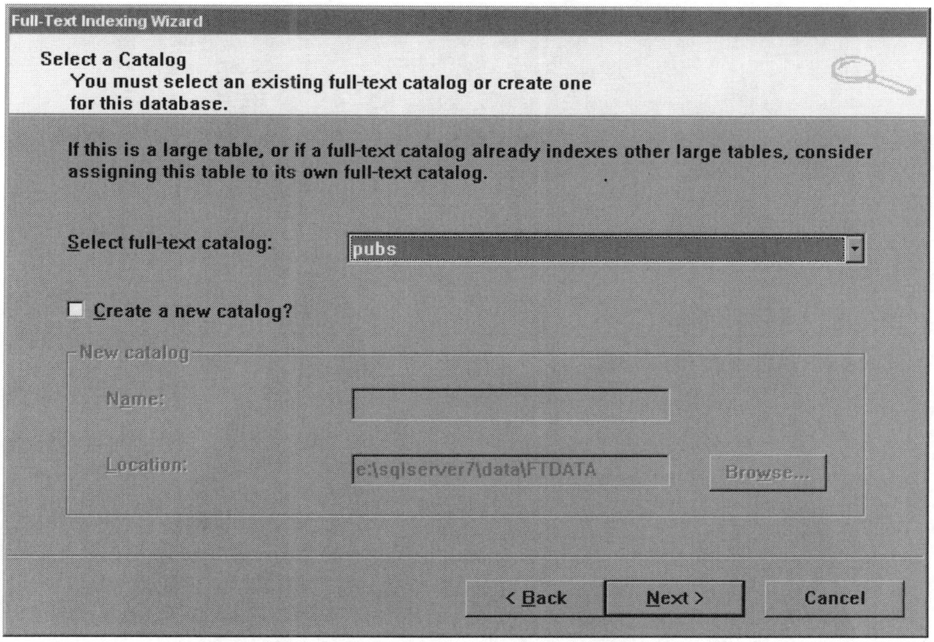

Figure 14.8 Adding the index to a catalog.

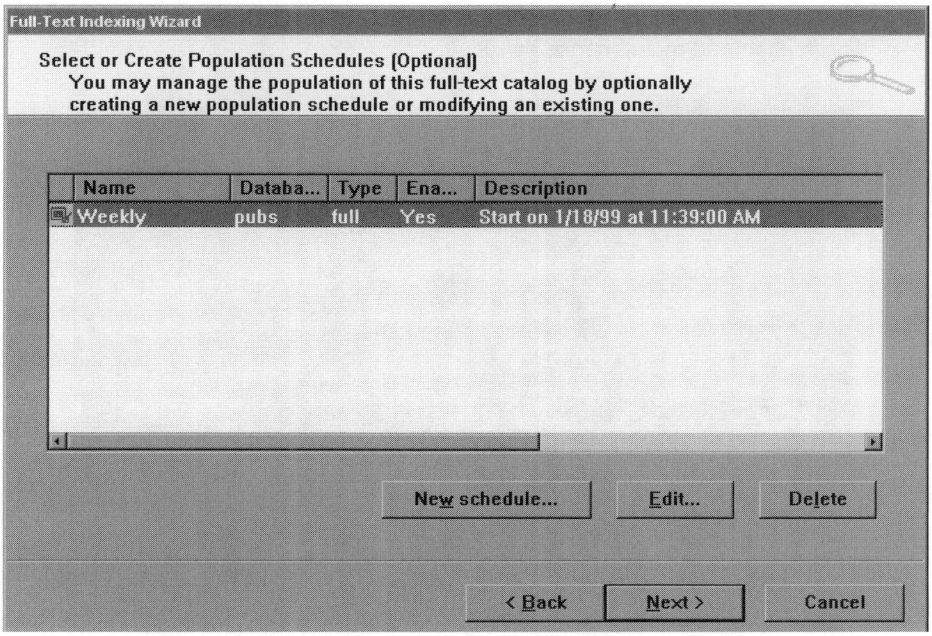

Figure 14.9 Setting up scheduled index maintenance via the wizard.

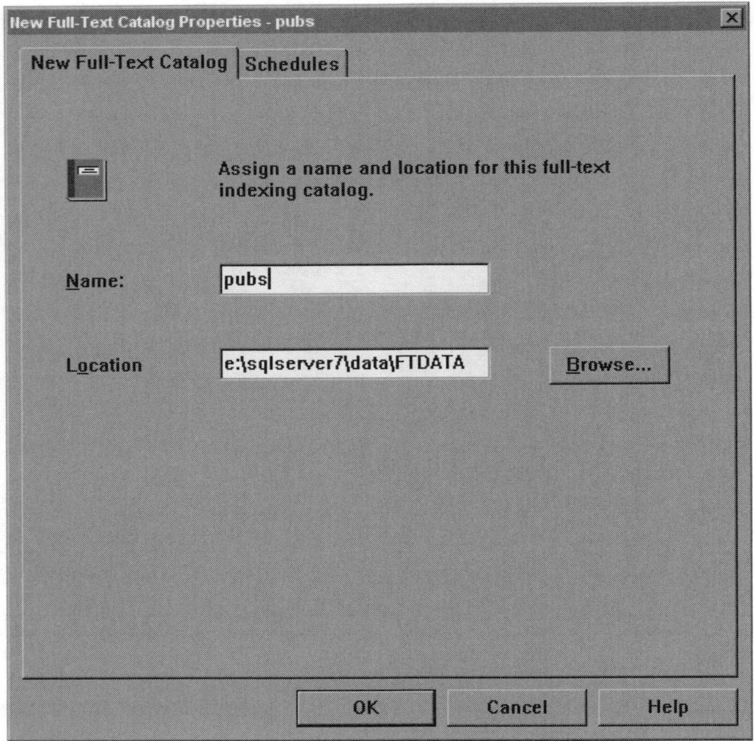

Figure 14.10 Choosing a name and location for your index, along with a schedule for its creation and maintenance.

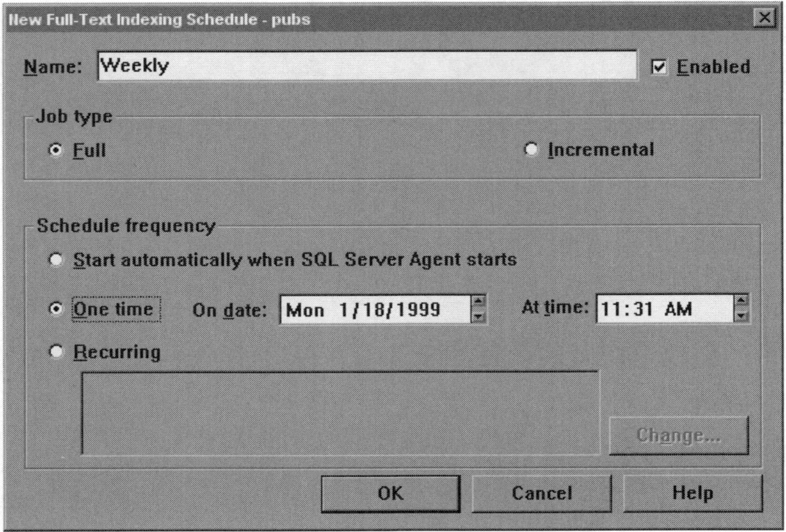

Figure 14.11 The schedule tab of this dialog, where you have a good deal of control over when the index will be refreshed.

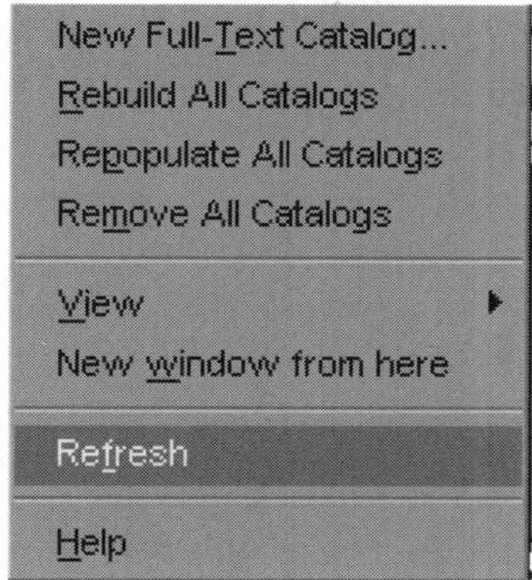

Figure 14.12 After creating the catalog, you'll find more options available on the right-clicking of the pubs catalog.

THE PERFORMANCE THING

The slowest part of using full-text indexing in your application is handling data in the resultset. One useful technique is to set up a user temp table containing the resultset—and then set up a cursor for the temp table.

You should set up SQL Agent jobs to automate these tasks. If you delve into the full-text world, you'll want to become familiar with sp_help_fulltext_catalogs that allow you to obtain a list of all the full-text catalogs in a given database. Other relevant stored procedures include sp_help_fulltext_tables that returns the names of the tables that have been enabled and sp_help_fulltext_columns.

NOISE WORDS

If you issue a SQL statement using FTS, that searches for a word that the indexer chooses to opt out of the index (for example, "who"), the following message occurs, with no results returned.

select * from titles where contains (title,'"who"')

Server: Msg 7619, Level 16, State 1

The query contained only ignored words. You can override this behavior by modifying the full-text engine's configuration file located in \Mssql\Ftdata\Sqlserver\Config —something you'd have to do if you were indexing music CDs, for example—assuming you wanted to include the rock group "Who". The configuration file is a simple ASCII file, and you can add or delete entries as needed. Actually, there are several versions of the config file depending on the language the server has been set up for.

Full-text indexing can obviously be a key component of a KM implementation, and SQL Server provides the basics for text indexing.

RESTORE DOESN'T

If you need to perform a RESTORE, you'll have to re-index from scratch. Backup doesn't back up the catalog files.

Here are some of our favorite resources for KM:

Knowledge Management Magazine, www.kmmag.com

KM World, www.kmworld.com

Knowledge Management Consortium, www.kmc.org

Institute for Knowledge Management (IBM and Lotus-sponsored at http://www.vistacompass.com/ikm_public/index.htm)

Tom Davenport's book, *Information Ecology: Mastering the Information and Knowledge Environment*, Oxford University Press, 1997

Ovum's report, *Knowledge Management: Applications, Markets, and Technologies*, www.ovum.com

We'll close this section on KM by citing one of our heroes, Peter Drucker.

> The source of (corporate) wealth is something specifically human: knowledge. If we apply knowledge to tasks we already know how to do, we call it productivity. If we apply knowledge to tasks that are new and different, we call it innovation.

We suppose that our advice to many of you is to think outside the box—as Drucker has done so often over the years—and to think about how better information flows at your workplace can be implemented to solve inefficiencies, annoyances, and other bottom-line sapping problems.

Data Mining

Knowledge management wasn't the only new strategic initiative Microsoft announced in 1999; it also officially *discovered* data mining in mid-year when it first announced its OLE DB Extensions for Data Mining specification at TechEd '99.

The kind of data mining Microsoft's talking about here isn't just fancy querying—it's high end stuff that tends to be fraught with statistics, predictive (classification) and dependency (density estimation) modeling, algorithms for clustering (segmentation) and deviation detection, and fairly compute-intensive summarization and visualization. And if that isn't bad enough, the truth is that it's often harder to get the data *ready* for the algorithms than to actually do the data mining. No wonder end-user data mining tools have met with lackluster success. Even Microsoft avoids suggesting that OLE DB for DM will magically bring data mining to the masses.

In fact, Microsoft Research's (MSR) Data Mining & Exploration (DMX) group, led by Usama Fayyad, has been instrumental in developing OLE DB for DM specification. According to Usama, Microsoft has used industry input to modify the initial OLE DB for data mining specification that only had a programmatic interface. Now, thanks to an SQL-like language similar to MDX, data miners will also have a command-line interface. The specification, according to Usama, has to accomplish a half dozen tasks: provide a mechanism for defining and shaping the data to be mined, provide a mechanism for accepting model metadata, support defining, building, populating (similar to SQL's CREATE and INSERT), and persisting the model, select mining methods to apply to the model, and provide the ability to browse and refine the model.

Although the specification and SDK should be available at www.microsoft.com/data, we recommend that you also read about data mining at research.microsoft.com. Fayyad's DMX team consists of about a half dozen very bright folks who focus on issues of "scaling data mining, reduction, and analysis algorithms so they can be used on large data sets". Their areas of emphasis include classification, clustering, sequential data modeling, detecting frequent events, and fast data reduction techniques. They collaborate with MSR's database group on "implications and requirements that data mining imposes on the database engine" and also work with the Commerce Server and SQL Server product groups.

Actually, data mining has been present in Microsoft's Site Server Commerce Edition beginning with Release 3.0 in the form of an intelligent cross-sell based on historical sales baskets in stores, the contents of the current shopper basket, and the browsing behavior of the shopper. Site Server ranks products that are likely to be most interesting to the shopper. If this sounds like amazon.com, which offers customers recommended books based on our past purchases and browsing behavior, you've got the gist of it. And according to Usama, Release 4.0 will add new data mining functionality: segmentation-based reporting and targeting based on clustering usage and purchase data.

To put things in perspective, there were over 40 sessions at TechEd '99 related to Exchange, but only one (5-203, *Introduction to Data Mining Technologies*, presented by Data Mining team lead David Marshall and viewable at www.teched99.com related to data mining. Given Microsoft's 1.5 year timeline for taking OLE DB for OLAP from spec to ship, along with Gartner Group's assessment of where data mining lies on the so-called "hype cycle" curve (see Figure 14.13) we think it's safe to say that data mining is still bleeding-edge stuff for Microsoft. Look to firms such as IBM (Intelligent Miner family), SPSS (Clementine), SAS (Intelligent Miner), NCR (Teradata's TeraMiner), and Oracle (thanks to its spring acquisition of Thinking Machines Corp.'s Darwin product family) to pick up the slack in the meantime.

What the Microsoft OLE DB for DM endeavor means is that we can expect to see data mining products that support the OLE DB for DM spec sometime in 2000. That doesn't mean you can't do data mining against SQL Server (or any other database) today.

There are dozens of data mining vendors. And that's part of the problem. There's no clear market leader and most of the products are expensive and complex to use. They were typically developed for the Unix workstation market for mathematicians or statisticians, not especially for database folks. In our opinion, Herb Edelstein's market analysis of data mining tools (*Data Mining '99: Technology Report* available at www.twocrows.com) is the single source of information about the 1999 data mining market. Edelstein provides analyses of the following vendors and tools:

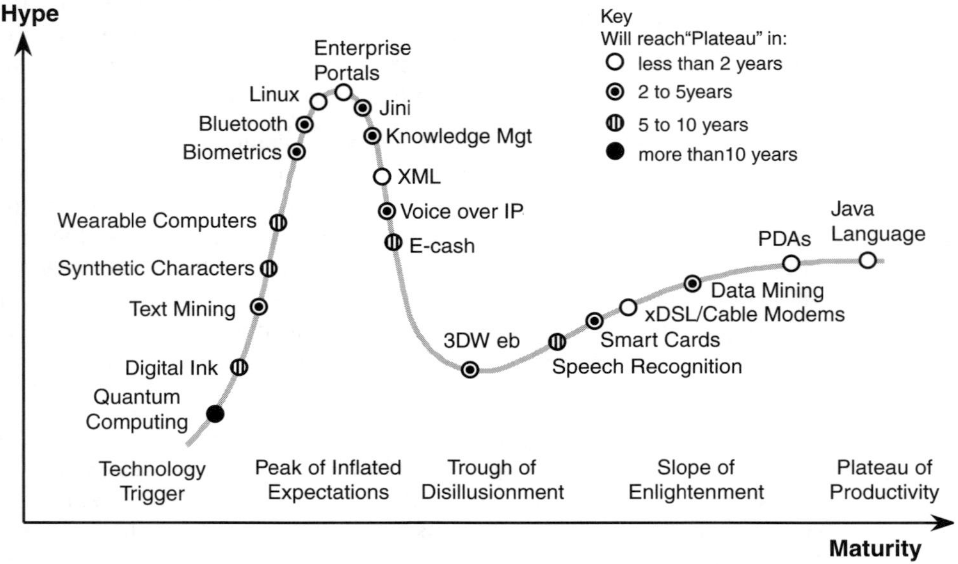

Figure 14.13 In late July 1999, Gartner Group's Jackie Fenn seems to have established what has become an annual event: publication of the latest GartnerGroup "hype cycle" curve.
Source: Gartner Group © 1999

AbTech Software (ModelQuest MarketMiner)

*Angoss Software (KnowledgeSEEKER, KnowledgeSTUDIO)

Attar Software (XpertRule Miner)

Business Objects (BusinessMiner)

Cognos Software (4Thought, Scenario)

Group 1 Corporation (Model 1)

HNC Software Inc. (DataBase Mining Marksman)

Integral Solutions (Clementine, acquired by SPSS in 1999)

IBM (Intelligent Miner)

Magnify (PATTERN)

MathSoft (S-Plus)

NCR (TeraMiner)

NeoVista Software (Decision Series)

Quadstone (Decisionhouse)

Salford Systems (CART, MARS)

*SAS Institute (Enterprise Miner)

*Silicon Graphics, Inc. (MineSet)

*SPSS (Base, AnswerTree, Neural Connection)

Tandem Division of Compaq

Thinking Machines Corp. (Darwin product acquired by Oracle in 1999)

Torrent Systems (Orchestrate Analytics)

Trajecta (dbProphet)

Unica Technologies (PRW)

Urban Science Applications Inc. (GainSmarts)

We have used an asterisk to indicate vendors who participated with Microsoft in creating the OLE DB for DM spec. In addition to Angoss, SAS, SGI, and SPSS, two other vendors, E.piphany and Datasage, also helped draft the initial spec.

ANOTHER DATA MINING MOTHER LODE

Herb Edelstein's book is great, but it's not exactly free. For free information, we recommend you subscribe to Gregory Piatetsky-Shapiro's KDNuggets at www.kdnuggets.com/subscribe.html. The KDNuggets website, www.kdnuggets.com, has back issues, a catalog of data mining tools, links to data mining companies, information about meetings, and so on.

Data Mining Techniques

You saw that there were several ways to approach KM. The same is true with data mining. Data mining was arguably invented by IBM well over a decade ago to help its mainframe customers perform "knowledge discovery", sometimes referred to as KD or KDD for knowledge discovery in databases. KDD and data mining basically refer to the algorithms and processes associated with the finding of relationships and patterns in data. KDD and data mining, as you have probably guessed from the work done by Microsoft Research, overlaps with fields such as statistics, AI, data visualization, machine learning, expert systems, and neural networks.

One way to help grasp the breadth of the field is to categorize data mining into six families of techniques (see Table 14.2).

There are dozens of books on data mining, often quite academic, where you can learn about clustering or segmentation algorithms, K-nearest neighbor, neural networks, and so on. What they often don't do very well is explain that data preparation is generally the hardest part of the data mining process.

Data mining has been widely used by companies involved in database marketing by telecommunications companies who want to reduce customer churn; by retail firms who want to do better at identifying profitable customers, performing sales promotions; and campaign management; and by credit card and insurance companies who want to reduce fraud.

Table 14.2 Techniques Used in Data Mining

DATA MINING TECHNIQUE	BEST USE
Statistics	Good at identifying instances where one variable causes or influences others. Good for trends, confirming hunches.
Induction techniques	Good for generating a literal explanation of results, for generating a hypothesis.
Neural networks	Good for sifting through large amounts of data to find unexpected patterns.
Visualization techniques	They say that a picture's worth a thousand words. Enables you to display analytical results in a fashion that's understandable to non-technical people.
OLAP	Flexible, slice-and-dice techniques are best suited for confirming a hypothesis.
Query languages like SQL	Good for answering specific questions. Purists usually don't consider this true data mining.

The Privacy Thing

Privacy has emerged as such a concern that you may want to rethink your database marketing and CRM efforts as they intersect with data mining.

Examples of Data Mining

To get a feeling for what's involved in data mining, imagine that you're a bank and that you want to identify your most profitable customers. In most cases, that's buried inside reams of transaction data that's probably spread out over multiple divisions (loans, savings, asset management, and so on) Let's assume the bank already has a data warehouse in place. The first step is to see if the data warehouse contains all the data that you need. You might want to add external demographic data. Assuming the data warehouse contained everything you wanted (not likely), you would then identify the data you wanted to extract and examine it for data quality and completeness. At this time, you're probably a little shocked and have to make major decisions about the value of spending more time and money to clean it up or simply eliminate it from the modeling process.

Next you'd figure out the best algorithms and methods to use. You'd buy (or obtain and evaluation copy of) potential tools and use them to develop predictive models. After many "runs" you would probably uncover some trends and patterns that could be used to forecast profitable customers, perhaps GartnerGroup-style (0.8 probability). Next, you would refine the predictive model, and run it to generate a list of profitable customers. Sales or marketing would do their campaign, and, if the system worked, you'd have a high return rate at reduced marketing costs.

Firms like Fingerhut, the $2 billion firm known for its catalog, direct marketing, and telemarketing ventures, reportedly has an active mailing list of some 12 million customers. According to an article in the July 5, 1999, *Data Mining News* (www.idagroup.com). Fingerhut has a 7 terabyte data warehouse that contains two years worth of aggregated weekly buying summaries on each of those 12 million customers. Fingerhut has 25 data miners who use SAS, SPSS, Angoss' KnowledgeSEEKER, and Unica's Model 1 and Project WorkBench.

The marketing analytics group maintains several hundred "generic" models that are used to build targeted segmentation models that suggest who to mail catalogues to. Typically, the data mining team combines four models: a response model (will the customer respond?), a purchase model (how much will he buy?), a return model (is the customer likely to return merchandise?), and a payment model (is the customer a credit risk?).

Fingerhut maintains over 1400 (!) variables for each customer and typically generates 200 discrete customer segments.

You can perform data mining against SQL Server and other data today, but it's likely to become much easier and more widespread once products that support OLE DB for DM hit the market.

Natural Language Processing

The first time I (Karen) experimented with natural language queries was almost 15 years ago when the now defunct Microrim released its Clout for R:Base System V. Touted as a natural language interface that let managers type things like "Gimme dem turkeys" to get a list of under performing sales reps, it was obviously way ahead of its time. One reason it never caught on was that there was so much tedious work involved to set up the dictionary. Other natural language programs including Natural Language Inc., once a Berkeley-based firm whose assets were purchased by Microsoft and are the basis for Microsoft's English Query, have been similarly criticized.

The idea of natural language programs for databases is to let people pose "natural language" (read, English) questions instead of having to learn SQL. Today, you can see a natural language interface in MSDN's Developer Search site (support.microsft.com/servicedesks/msdn, see Figure 14.14).

Microsoft Word 2000 and the other Microsoft Office 2000 programs also have a rudimentary form of natural language processing via the largely unloved "Assistants" as shown in Figure 14.15.

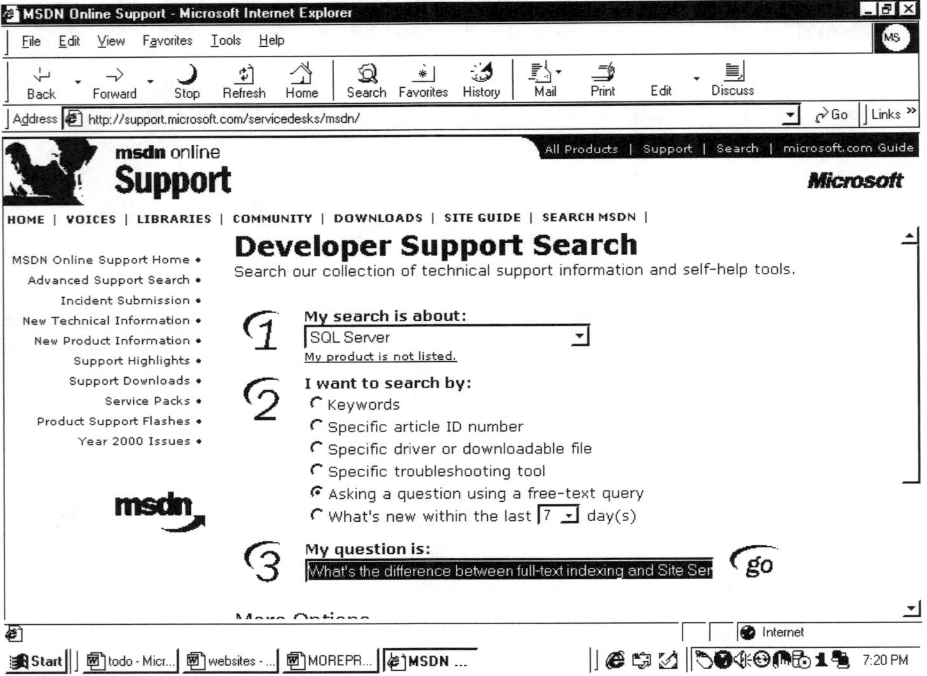

Figure 14.14 Unfortunately, cross product queries (like cross table queries under the current version of full-text indexing) don't work in the current natural language interface for MSDN Developer Support. Posing the question about the difference between full-text indexing for SQL Server and Site Server's indexing gave mutually exclusive answer sets depending on the product chosen.

Figure 14.15 The Office Assistants in Microsoft Office 2000 perform natural language processing.

WELL, THERE'S NATURAL LANGUAGE PROCESSING AND THEN THERE'S NATURAL LANGUAGE PROCESSING

According to Adam Blum, English Query's evangelist, the MSDN Support Online natural language support "most likely uses Office's Answer Wizard stuff… This does light syntactic parsing to try to find keywords and then generates full-text searches. It is qualitatively different from the deep semantic processing done in EQ."

The notion of having a natural language, spoken interface to one's computer is as old as science fiction. Indeed the HAL in *2001: A Space Odyssey* and the omniscient "computer" in Star Trek have done much to popularize the vision. More recently, Bill Gates has been promoting the idea, again, as part of his vision of a digital nervous system. Each year brings affordable and useful natural language processing a bit closer to reality, and the investments Microsoft is making in speech and natural language processing at Microsoft Research bode well for the future. There are over 20 researchers assigned to the natural language group. See research.microsoft.com for more information about both NL and Microsoft's voice recognition and speech research.

Other vendors who are poised to marry speech technology, linguistic analysis, and natural language processing include Dragon Systems (www.dragonsys.com), Lernout and Hauspie (www.lhs.com), and IBM (www.software.ibm.com/speech). More limited PC-oriented SQL database packages are available from Elfsoft (www.elfsoft.com) and Linguistic Technology (www.englishwizard.com).

All natural language programs have "starter" dictionary and lots of English language smarts including a built-in spell checker that go a long way towards automating the task and minimizing the grunt work associated with customizing the dictionary for given databases. To go back to the "gimme dem turkeys" example, someone had to tell Clout that "turkeys" were the same as "under performing salesmen," "bad salespeople," "losers," "scumbags," and so on. In addition those synonyms would have had to be mapped to a SQL statement that showed sales that were 50 percent below quota or 20 percent below the average, for example. This can be very time-consuming and isn't what we consider fun.

English Query

English Query, as we said previously, evolved out of a product from the now defunct, Berkeley-based Natural Language Inc. By the way, the version of English Query that shipped with SQL Server 7 was called Version 7 in order to match SQL Server, but was really a second Microsoft release, the first one having shipped with Visual Basic 5.0.

Microsoft released a beta version of English Query 7.5 at TechEd '99, and it should be available by the time you read this. EQ 7.5 will include support for OLAP cubes, tight integration with the Visual Studio family, support for SQL Server's full-text indexing—use of FREETEXT and CONTAINS, support for other back-end databases including Access and Oracle, and maybe even support for the Microsoft thesaurus.

English Query's home page is at www.microsoft.com/sql/70/gen/eqmain.htm, and you can find the English Query newsgroup via the msnews.Microsoft.com news server at microsoft.public.sqlserver.mseq. If, by chance, EQ 7.5 still isn't available, many of its new component pieces should still be available from the BackOffice downloads site where you can obtain sample ASP, VB, and VC++ sample programs as well as the updated schema modeling tool.

WHEN STEVE BALLMER ASKS...

Microsoft's Adam Blum, Team Lead for English Query/SQL Server, told a story at TechEd '99 about getting a call from Steve Ballmer's office in May asking him about putting together a cool natural language demo he could use in a presentation to financial analysts in NYC five days hence. "Well, sure," Adam must have answered. Sure enough, five 30-hour days later (just kidding), Adam delivered the EQ app to a delighted CEO Ballmer who reportedly wowed his audience with his "plain English" queries against a 200MB database of financial data. Speaking of financial data, Cognos, www.cognos.com, has invested a lot of time and effort in educating the marketplace about decision support and OLAP software and periodically posts a new interactive database—usually financial—for Web site visitors to play with. In July 1999, for example, it posted PowerPlay SE, Mutual Funds Edition that consists of almost 10,000 mutual funds.

Although Microsoft sometimes describes it as a tool for end users (due to its support for ASP development), English Query is basically a package for VB or VC++ programmers. Actually, it supports any development environment that is COM-compliant. EQ has two parts: the server and the authoring tool called the Domain Editor. The goal of EQ is to produce a natural language application that typically consists of six steps (see Figure 14.16):

1. The user submits a plain English question.
2. The question is submitted to the EQ engine.
3. The EQ engine sends the equivalent SQL to the EQ response object.

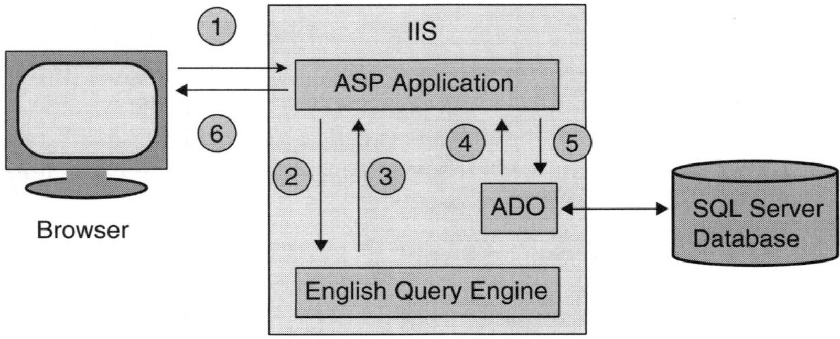

Figure 14.16 The flow of a typical EQ application.

4. SQL is submitted to the server via ADO.
5. The answer is returned from the server as an ADO recordset.
6. The answer is displayed to the user in an HTML table.

The Domain Editor

Most of your time is spent in the Domain Editor creating so-called *domain knowledge*. Think of domain knowledge as the information about your particular database and special jargon that the end users might employ. More technically, domain knowledge is information about the database schema (table names, column names, and so on) and the semantics (English phrases) that are used to identify schema objects.

In EQ 7, you had to do a lot of the modeling by hand, duplicating work already done in SQL Server itself. Fortunately, EQ 7.5 is smart enough to import the schema and figure out the basic entities and relationships itself. But that's only the beginning.

A *domain* is a collection of information about the database objects and semantic objects in an EQ application. Initially EQ only knows about English and how to generate SQL. Once you've imported the schema, it knows something about the tables and relationships, but you still have to provide it with additional information about *traits* (the minor entities that elaborate information about major entities) and relationship phrasings such as that authors have addresses and write books. You'll want to leverage primary and foreign key relationships by providing phrasings. You'll also want to provide as many synonyms as possible for both tables and columns.

Fleshing out the domain is the real work behind an EQ application and it tends to be iterative. You add some traits and phrasings and test the domain using sample queries (EQ ships with a runtime engine, so you don't have to exit the Domain Editor to test your application). You go back to the drawing board. You run some more sample questions. Yes, it pays to create some question files, and yes, you can submit them via EQ's Regression Test tool. The end result is a pair of files with .EQP and .EQM files—one with project information, one with the model information. You won't get a deployable .EQD domain file until you actually build the application.

TESTING IS KEY

One thing about natural language applications is that people tend to have high expectations, and if their first experience with a program that's supposed to understand "plain English" is lousy, not only are they likely to remember it ("dumb computers"), they'll probably also tell all their friends.

In other words, keep the image of an easily disenchanted novice fresh in your mind's eye, especially when you get tired of iterative work on the domain model and its semantics. Imagine Larry Ellison's mother. (Oracle's CEO often invokes her as a typical non-technical end user.)

As of summer 1999, there were three good interactive demos that you can run from the EQ main site, and we strongly recommend that you try those to get a flavor of what EQ

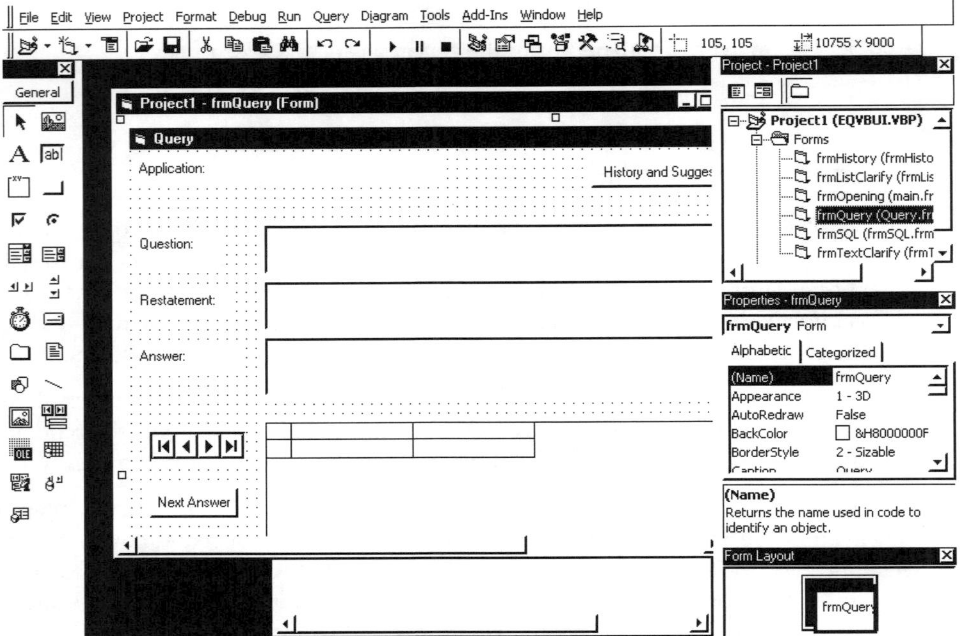

Figure 14.17 One of the sample EQ applications for VB developers.

can do for you. If you're interested, install EQ and go through the HLP file's tutorial. Run the samples in your preferred development language (see Figure 14.17). Study the code. Try to build some small "toy" apps using your own data. Scope out the questions and answers in the MSEQ newsgroup. And have fun!

At the Windows CE Developers Conference held in Denver in June 1999, Microsoft's Senior VP, Bob Muglia wowed most SQL Server fans in the audience with his announcement that a SQL Server "lite" version was scheduled for early 2000 and then demonstrating how an alpha version of "lite" can accept a plain-English question and receive an answer—no SQL required. At least not from the end user's perspective. What actually happened was that a slightly-modified version of ADOCE created by Odyssey Software (www.odysseysoftware.com) passed the English question to a remote EQ server (WinCE devices aren't likely to be powerful enough to run the EQ server themselves for some time) which then translated the English into T-SQL and passed the query to SQL Server for resolution. Pretty nifty. Which brings us to the role of Windows CE devices in your SQL Server world.

The Evolving World of Windows CE and Its Devices

Microsoft's Windows CE for Visual Basic Toolkit (VBCE) was out for over a year before there was a book on it (Larry Roof's *Professional Visual Basic Windows CE Programming*, Wrox Press, 1999). Java had only been out six months before there were almost a hundred books on it. In other words, VBCE hasn't really taken the world by storm. Even the preferred (at least initially) development platform for WinCE development, the Windows CE for Visual C++ Toolkit doesn't seem to be used by that many developers. As of summer 1999, there were about a dozen books on Windows CE programming.

FYI

VBCE SHIP DATES

Although Windows CE for Visual Basic had been available free in beta for most of 1997, the first version of it officially shipped in January 1998. Windows CE for Visual Basic 6.0, the version that was available when this book was written, shipped in March 1999.

We think there are several reasons why WinCE is taking a long time to catch on. First, WinCE devices are still fairly expensive, and there are too many different incompatible types. Second, WinCE is seen as a moving target. Windows CE 3.0 should be available by the time you read this, but like EQ, it's in a transition period as we write this chapter. Third, Palm Pilots have satisfied part of the market that WinCE has targeted. And fourth, WinCE devices aren't that easy to use or develop for.

What's Windows CE?

Windows CE, is a general purpose, 32-bit operating system that Microsoft built from the ground up to support a broad range of communication, entertainment (read games), and mobile computing devices. It includes about 2000 of the 10,000 or so Win32 APIs and is *ROMable*. In other words, it's built into Read Only Memory chips inside the device. It's also modular, so that GUI-less versions of it can occupy as little as 300KB. Microsoft provides both standard platform SDKs for the major *form factors* (classes of WinCE devices such as Handheld PCs, Handheld PC Pros, and Palm PCs) and also platform builders (both for VC++ and VB development) that let you define your own custom WinCE and generate your own SDK.

Palm PCs (P/PCs) are similar to Palm Pilots and are typically optimized for data access, not data entry. They're manipulated with a stylus and/or touch screen, the latter including a soft keyboard. They have built-in voice record and playback and can run MP3 software. Unlike the first generation P/PCs, today's P/PCs usually are color devices, have Visual Basic runtimes built into ROM, and ship with Pocket Access as well as other "pocket" applications. We highly recommend that you read Microsoft's six-page June 1999 white paper (it may have been updated or moved from msdn.microsoft.com/library/techart/pspcappvb.htm) entitled *Developing Applications for the Palm-Size PC with the Microsoft Windows CE Toolkit for Visual Basic 6.0*. As they say, "just the facts, ma'am."

Handheld PCs (H/PCs) include a normal keyboard, but typically also support both stylus and touch screen input. There's a similar June 1999 white paper, *Developing Applications for a Handheld PC* available from the Microsoft Web site.

The third family of devices are the so-called Handheld PC Pros (H/PC Pros) that are optimized for data entry, available in both compact and large displays, and include a reasonably rich suite of software (Plus! for Windows CE even includes Pocket Paint!) Microsoft licensed HP's Java VM, so Pocket Internet Explorer, for example, supports JScript, and a third Toolkit, Windows CE for Visual Java Toolkit, is in the pipeline.

The fourth form factor, the Auto PC (A/PC), has been designed to be mainly controlled by voice commands. At a minimum, A/PC devices will serve as high-end stereo and CD players, but GPS, mapping, and email applications are also available.

Of course, the best thing about all the WinCE devices is "instant on." You don't have to endure the delay of a boot process. However, none of the WinCE devices have hard disks or CD-ROMs. Most support so-called Compact Flash cards—not all of which are compatible—that can be used to store (and quickly load) programs. Loading your WinCE device with programs other than the pocket applications that it comes with, though, is something you generally have to do either by serial cable, modem, or infrared port-to-port communication. In order to do that, you need to install Windows CE Services on the host computer.

COMPACT FLASH CARDS

It's easy to get frustrated when using Compact Flash cards. For example, let's say you have some MP3 files on your Compact Flash card. You won't be able to "see" them from your P/PC device. The reason is that the standard File Open dialog built into Windows CE only shows files in the Compact Flash storage card if they're inside a folder called 'My Documents'. The simple solution is to create a folder called 'My Documents' on your storage card with the Windows CE Services remote file browser.

CE Services

Whenever you buy a WinCE device, you get a copy (hopefully the latest version) of Windows CE Services, which includes ActiveSync. ActiveSync versions 1.x and 2.x, though usually functional, didn't always offer what we would call "bulletproof" installation and/or performance. Rather than offer any number of war stories about less than stellar encounters with ActiveSync, we want to assure you that Windows CE Services 3.0 and the new ActiveSync 3.0 seem to solve the synchronization problems. We have successfully synched using four different CE devices with the newest version of CE Services.

Figures 14.18 through 14.20 give you an idea of how easy it is.

Let's say you have a WinCE device and have connected it to a host computer via a serial cable. You put the WinCE Services CD in the host computer, and install the software. A reboot is probably required. Assuming the installation was successful, you should see the wizard shown in Figure 14.18 automatically. If you don't you may have to click on the ActiveSync icon or run it from the Start | Programs menu. The decision you need to make is whether or not you want a "Partnership" between the host computer and your WinCE device. If the host is your main work computer, but you plan to use your WinCE device on the road, you'll probably want to synchronize them. However, for

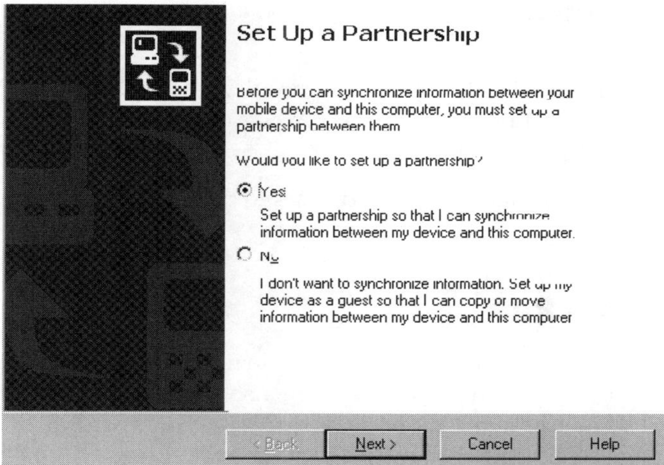

Figure 14.18 The Windows CE Services 3.0's first screen queries you about the nature of the partnership.

occasional file transfers, a "guest" account (see Figure 14.19) is also available which lets you manipulate WinCE files from the host computer.

If you choose the partnership option, the next screen asks you if this is to be an exclusive arrangement or not. In other words, you have the option of sync'ing your WinCE device with more than one host computers such as the one at work, and the one at home. By the way, it's easy to remove and recreate partnerships, so experimentation is

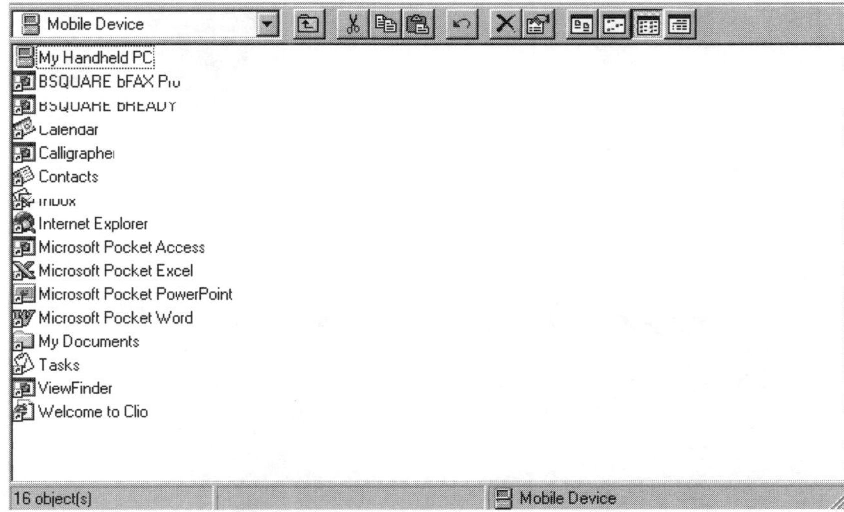

Figure 14.19 If you choose to connect to the host PC as a guest, the host PC can "browse" the WinCE device, and manipulate files.

something we encourage you to do. This seems to be a case where you don't wreak havoc with the Registry.

The third screen is where you decide what to synchronize (see Figure 14.20). For most database applications, you'll either choose Pocket Access (WinCE → Access on the host → SQL Server) or files (ASCII text files for import by bcp or DTS).

Windows CE Services 3.0 also allows WinCE devices to be mobile Windows Terminal Server clients.

Getting Your Ducks in a Row

If you want to write an application that lets WinCE devices interact with SQL Server data, you need more than just WinCE Services. You also need a Windows CE Toolkit (VC++, VB, or VJ++). We used the Windows CE for Visual Basic 6.0 Toolkit. You can install VBCE on either a Win9x or Windows NT system, but you need NT 4.0 or higher to run the WinCE emulator. You can use an emulator if you don't have any WinCE devices at all or to test your programs on the form factors that you don't own. The Toolkits aren't free; They're commercial programs.

OBJECTSTORE

If you develop for WinCE, sooner or later you'll run into references to *Object Store*, and you may wonder what the heck it is, especially since it sounds suspiciously like an object-oriented database—which is really what it is. Basically it's persistent storage available to WinCE apps (max 16MB). It's Windows CE's internal, built-in, heap-style database, but it's only accessible to VC++ programmers.

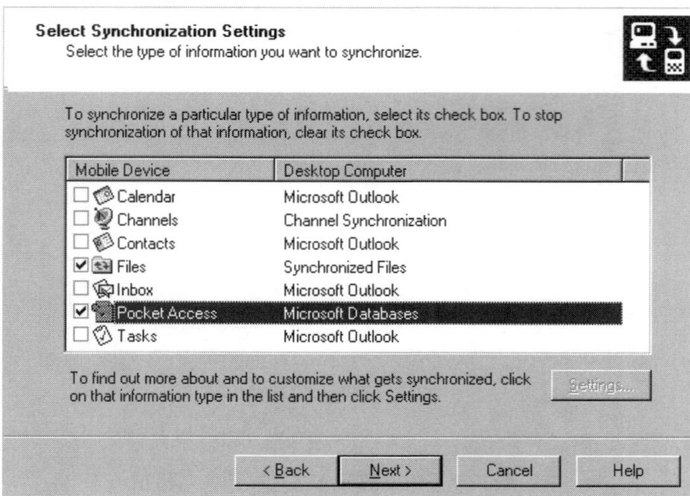

Figure 14.20 Windows CE allows you to select the kinds of information to keep synchronized.

That's two (but who's counting, right?) out of three: Windows CE Services and a WinCE toolkit. You also need the SDK (which *is* free) for the form factor you develop for. If you're targeting more than one form factor such as P/PCs and H/PC Pros, you'll need to install two SDKs.

Oh, how could we forget? You shouldn't just install them in any old order. Here's the recommended order for Windows NT 4.0 as of summer 1999 when CE Services 3.0 wasn't officially available. Basically, every time you install CE Services 2.2 or earlier, you need to reinstall any NT SPs.

1. Windows NT 4.0
2. Windows NT Service Pack 3
3. CE Services 2.2
4. Windows NT Service Pack 4
5. Visual Basic 6.0
6. Windows CE Toolkit for Visual Basic 6.0

For Windows 2000, it's the same as NT 4.0:

1. Win2K
2. CE Services 2.2
3. Visual Studio
4. CE Tools

For Windows 9x, this is the order:

1. Windows 98 (or 95, or 98 SE)
2. CE Services 2.2
3. Visual Studio products (VB6 or VC6)
4. CE Toolkits

If you're beginning to sense our frustration, you're right. We can almost guarantee that getting things installed is a lot harder than writing your first program.

Working with VBCE

The Windows CE for Visual Basic 6.0 Toolkit (typically abbreviated VBCE) is an add-in to VB. It adds special forms designers, supports a reasonable assortment of ActiveX controls (TabStrip, ListView, TreeView, Grid—not data-aware, FileSystem, WinSock, Comm, ImageList, Image, PictureBox, CommonDialog, and CommandBar), and includes a debugger that runs separate from the VB IDE.

As you can imagine VBCE was designed with size in mind—in fact it was designed to be ROMable, like Windows CE itself. Many WinCE devices will have the VB runtime (about 650KB) built into them.

WINCE PROCESSORS

Most retail Windows CE devices use one of five processors: SH3, MIPS, StrongARM, PPC, or x86.

As we said, once you have everything correctly installed, writing VBCE programs isn't that different from writing "normal" VB programs. Many of the standard VB6 controls are available, but, unfortunately, none of the data bound controls are included. Those controls are obviously high on the priority list of needed enhancements, so we expect third-party ISVs to fill in the gap until Microsoft ships its own.

What's Different

Here's a quick rundown of the major differences between "normal" VB development and VBCE development:

- All variables are Variants.
- You have fewer intrinsic controls.
- You have more granular control via References (see Figure 14.21) over the controls you use.
- Error handling is limited and isn't built into the VBIDE.
- You can't unload forms!
- You can't use MDI forms.
- You have to adapt to different file I/O.
- There's a different method for exiting applications.
- You can't use ADOCE to directly manipulate SQL Server data that runs on a network.

;oft CE ADO Control (ADOCE) 2.0
;oft CE Comm Control 6.0
;oft CE Common Dialog Control 6.0
;oft CE File System Control 6.0
;oft CE Grid Control 6.0
;oft CE Image Control 6.0
;oft CE ImageList Control 6.0
;oft CE ListView Control 6.0
;oft CE PictureBox Control 6.0
;oft CE TabStrip Control 6.0
;oft CE TreeView Control 6.0
;oft CE WinSock Control 6.0

Figure 14.21 VBCE won't include unneeded controls in your runtime. You'll have to explicitly add support for each control via the Project|References menu.

RESOURCES

Microsoft's main Windows CE site is www.microsoft.com/windowsce, and Microsoft's news server has newsgroups both for VC++ and VB programmers. However, an independent site, www.vbce.com, seems to be the most active for VBCE programmers. Here are some other sites that we can recommend:

www.winceonline.com
www.craigtech.co.uk/pie and hpc
www.wincecity.com
www.wincebiz.com
www.handheldmed.com
www.wincwosceresourceguide.net
www.thaddeus.com
members.aol.com/pdc.chrisd/wce/wce.htm
www.c/net.com
www.cecentral.com
www.cecity.com
www.ceglobe.com
www.celair.com
www.cemonster.com
www.cesoft.co.uk
www.ceware.com
www.hpc.net
www.mobileplanet.com
www.pdadash.com
www.wincearch.com
www.winceonline.com
www.winfiles.com/apps/ce
www.wincecity.com
www.nsbasic.com
www.conduits.com/ce
www.proxinet.com/prox/web/wince.html

Fast Ethernet connection: www.microsoft.com/windowsce/products/tips/using/com-981015.asp

Pocket IE versions: KB Q158479

You'll notice some new CE Toolkit for VB utilities on your Start menu (see Figure 14.22), but the main thing you'll notice when you fire up VB6 is that there are new designers as shown in Figure 14.23).

As we mentioned previously, there's no direct support for accessing SQL Server directly from WinCE devices. However, you can write VBCE applications for the WinCE device that work indirectly with any OLE DB database using ADO (and

Figure 14.22 VBCE includes some special utilities for developers. These options are also available from the VB IDE WinCE menu. Zoom, for example, lets you capture a .BMP screenshot of your WinCE device from a connected desktop PC.

ADOCE). You can also opt to move data via ASCII files, email messages, or Pocket Access. The one you select will be based on what the application is supposed to do, data volumes, security needed, and so on.

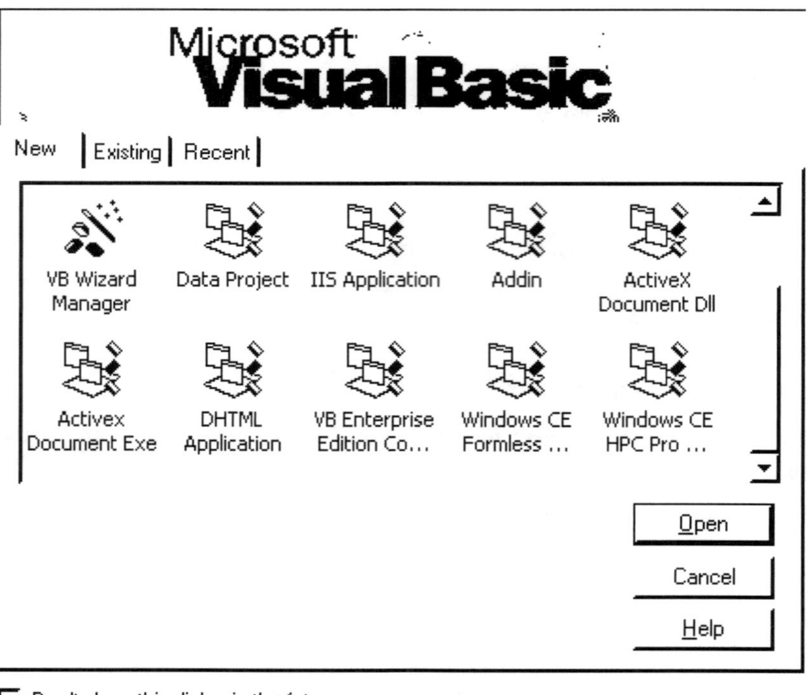

Figure 14.23 We installed H/PC Pro support, but can also design a formless application.

Most of you will want to use ADOCE. Here's a code fragment that illustrates how to set up the recordset and populate a listbox with a sorted list:

```
Dim rs
Set rs = CreateObject("ADOCE.RecordSet")
rs.open "create index i1 on mytable (firstfield desc)"
rs.open "select * from mytable order by firstfield desc", "",
adOpenKeyset, adLockOptimistic
If rs.RecordCount > 0 Then
  Do While Not rs.EOF
    ' assumes you have a control called List1
    List1.Additem rs.Fields("firstfield").Value
    rs.MoveNext
  Loop
End If
rs.Close
set rs = Nothing
```

As you know, ADO is Microsoft's strategic, high-level interface to any kind of structured or unstructured data. ADOCE (bet you can't guess!) is a subset of ADO for Windows CE that supports the Recordset and Field objects. This means that you can do things like set up cursors, obtain a RecordCount, and access the Field collection's Count property to find out how many fields are in a record. ADOCE, in conjunction with ActiveSync, makes two-way synchronization with the desktop host possible. There are a handful of good samples in on your VB CD in the \VisualStudio\VB98\VBCE\Samples sub-directory, but you'll probably want to look at more up-to-date samples at the online sites listed later in this chapter. Data is actually stored on the WinCE device in ADOCE tables that work with the fast native database engine built into Windows CE. So what happens when you've written your VB program (see Figure 14.24) and you press the F5 key? Well, if you're working on an NT system with the emulator involved, there will be a bit of a delay while your computer sets things up, but finally, you'll see what amounts to a fake WinCE GUI, and you'll be able to interact with the program from your development platform.

If, on the other hand, you have a WinCE device attached, you'll see the program automatically run on your device where you'll be able to interact with it (see Figure 14.25).

What has happened is that any needed runtimes are downloaded, along with the app.vb file (see Figure 14.26).

The VBCE Toolkits come with the normal installation wizards which are flexible enough to either transfer the VB runtimes or not depending on whether they're needed (most new devices have them and/or MFC built in).

Unlike the balkanized data mining and KM communities and the nascent NL community, there are thousands of WinCE and VBCE developers out there. There's a growing

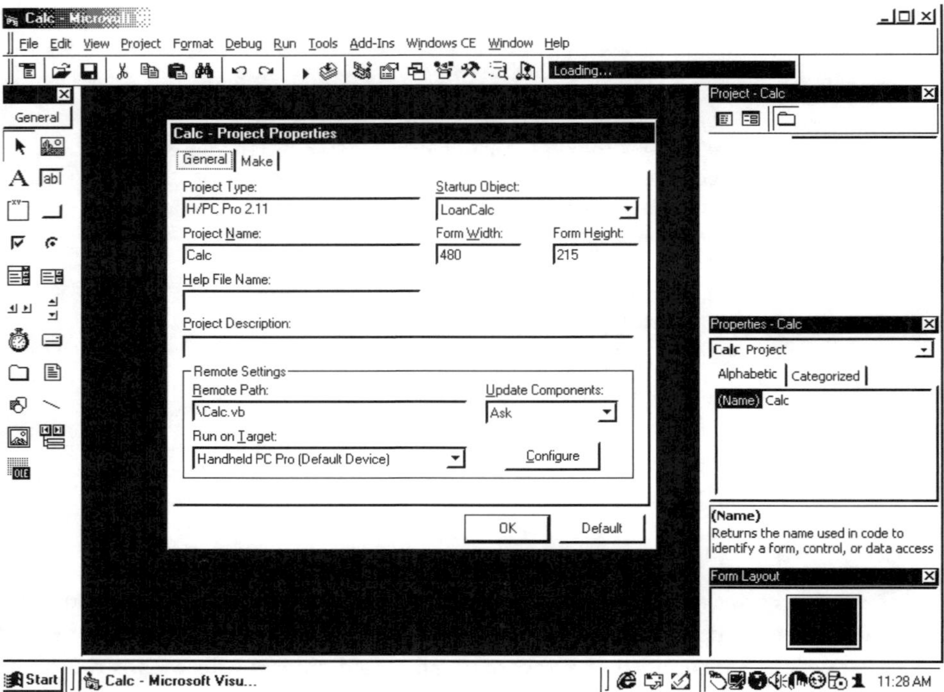

Figure 14.24 Creating a WinCE program in VB6 with the Windows CE for Visual Basic Toolkit installed.

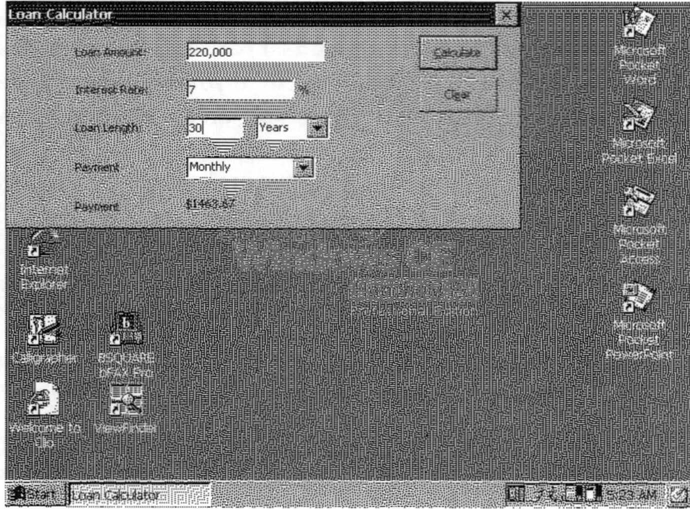

Figure 14.25 Running your app directly on the target device from VB's design time environment.

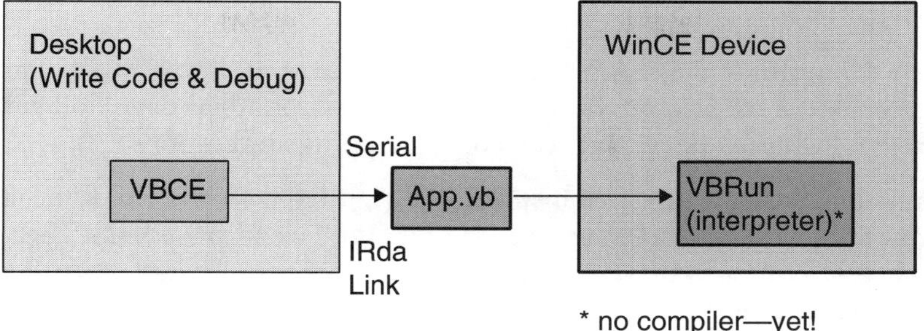

Figure 14.26 VBCE's runtime characteristics.

body of shareware, magazines, and, most importantly, demand for WinCE applications. Even now, prior to the shipment of any SQL Server "lite", the sky's the limit as far as WinCE/SQL Server applications go. Use your imagination, experiment, and, again, have fun!

Mapping Applications

Sometimes it's hard for a SQL Server DBA or developer to realize that not everyone needs a traditional analytical "business intelligence" or charting interfaces into their data.

Consider a municipal water department hotline operator or engineer who has just been told there's a broken water pipe at location x. Given today's technology, they should be able to locate the address on a map, click on the location, and fetch up any amount of data about the water main in that location such as how old it is, when it was last maintained, what its diameter is, perhaps even an image or video clip of its interior from its last maintenance. You could probably also quickly fetch up a payment history for the customers on that street and all sorts of other water-related information—assuming the municipality has a good data warehouse!

Or imagine the fire department has just received a call. Not only should their in-truck computer be able to give them directions to the reported fire, they should also be able to call up details about the property, especially if it's a large commercial property for which blueprints and fire extinguishing system data are available.

Or imagine a geochemist that wants to compare the data from drilling logs at two locations. By clicking on a drill site... well, you get the idea. These three examples are all "read only" applications. But it's not hard to imagine scenarios when you'd want to update the underlying data from the map interface.

In a map-centric application, data tends to be the popup stuff. Of course, there are exceptions, Microsoft's mega-terabyte Terraserver (www.terraserver.com) database is an example where the maps make up the database.

Mapping Engines

There are a handful of major GIS vendors, and as far as we know, all of them support SQL Server, and most also provide ActiveX controls from their development environment so that PC-based developers can create mapping applications.

Environmental Systems Research Institute, Inc. (ESRI, www.esri.com) is the largest GIS vendor in the world. If you haven't heard of it, don't be surprised. ESRI is a privately held company with a stellar reputation that speaks for itself. Its annual user conferences are attended by almost 10,000 people from nearly 100 different countries.

MapInfo (www.mapinfo.com) is arguably ESRI's biggest competitor, but other vendors such as MapQuest (www.mapquest.com), best known for its free maps with driving instructions and Microsoft with its new MapPoint 2000 (microsoft.com/office/mappoint/default.asp) are also used to develop applications with maps. The free online *Directions Magazine* (www.directionsmag.com), the best GIS site we've run into, has what seems to be a comprehensive list of GIS vendors, but we're going to focus on ESRI because it's the market leader.

ESRI has a host of products that run on multiple platforms. The most important ones are ESRI's flagship product ArcInfo, ESRI's Internet map server ArcIMS, ArcView, a projection utility for end users, ArcSDE, ESRI's spatial database engine that links ESRI client tools to back-end databases, and MapObjects, a popular COM-compliant development platform for programmers.

The key products for most applications built using SQL Server data, are ArcSDE (Spatial Database Engine) and MapObjects.

ArcSDE 8 is a software suite for storing and managing spatial data (vector, imagery, and CAD) within a commercial database management system such as Oracle or SQL Server. ArcSDE includes a library of spatial query functions that enable rapid query and retrieval of data based on spatial, topological, and attribute constraints. It's integrated with ESRI's family of client applications and leading CAD products like AutoCAD. SDE knows about mapping, so it lets you perform spatial and geometric analysis with 14 different topological searches, and it supports features like buffering, overlays and intersections, dissolve and clip, and topological data cleaning.

ArcSDE 8 consists of the SDE data server, administrative tools and data loaders, a loader viewer which lets you preview shape and coverage files before you load them to SDE, the C API, the MapObjects development kit (SDE software's OLE/COM API), and a copy of ArcView GIS for Windows. If you buy ArcInfo 8, you'll automatically get a copy of ArcSDE which includes support for Oracle 8 and 8i, SQL Server 7, Informix Dynamic Server, DB2 UDB, Sybase, *coverages*, and a copy of Personal ArcSDE which basically supports Jet (no, not MSDE) as the supported relational database.

Coverages basically refers to the original ArcInfo data file format—or a related PC version stored in dBASE file format—that describes spatial data—lines, points, and polygons. Coverages are one of the most popular and widely available spatial data formats found in digital mapping and GIS applications. SDE layers are similar to ArcInfo coverages, but the SDE engine in conjunction with the RDBMS stores them. ESRI has a third file format called shapefiles, which are ArcView's native file format, and also supports the major third-party file formats such as AutoDesk's AutoCAD.

MapObjects

So what's MapObjects? It's an ActiveX Control (OCX) with more than 45 programmable ActiveX Automation objects that can be plugged into a COM-compliant development environment like VB. MapObjects comes with tools that let you display, query, and analyze dynamic map data. You can leverage its geocoding to do complex address matching, for example, as well as perform on-the-fly projection to combine data from any projection into a common projection for viewing and analysis. MapObjects has methods for working with GPS applications that track points, lines, and/or polygons. MapObjects support recordsets with both spatial and attribute filters, and developers can also access the SDE API directly from MapObjects applications.

As you'd expect, you can invoke any number of geometric functions and can also do feature rendering using thematic methods such as value maps, class breaks, graduated symbols, dot density maps, and pie and bar charts. We're big fans of good sample apps, and MapObjects really excels in this domain, shipping with almost two dozen samples (each) for VB, VC++, Delphi, and PowerBuilder There are additional VB sample apps you can download from www.esri.com. Plus, you can sign up for free classes from ESRI's online virtual campus (http://campus.esri.com).

ESRI's online library (www.esri.com/library/index.html) also includes presentation notes from recent conferences.

But back to MapObjects, which, by the way, includes VBA, making it easy to customize ArcInfo 8 applications. With ESRI's permission, we've included diagrams of the MapObjects object model in PDF file format on the book's CD.

MapObjects lets you create client applications that can browse, view, and query SDE data. You can also create a MapLayer based on a coverage in SDE for Coverages. You can perform advanced queries and spatial operations on SDE layers and can also create custom transactional applications for editing the attributes and geometry of SDE spatial columns.

SDE stores your spatial data in a relational database in a collection of tables, some of which may contain spatial data and others that do not. Spatial data is stored in a spatial column of a table in the same way that numeric data is stored in a numeric column. Each table with a spatial column represents one SDE layer, which can be added to a Map control as a MapLayer. Using MapObjects, you can list the layers available in an SDE instance by reading the DataConnection object's GeoDatasets collection. The collection contains only the names of those tables that have spatial columns, and only the tables for which the specified User has permission.

Here's a generic strategy for accessing data and relating it to spatial features:

1. Create a variable for a Table object:

   Dim MyTable As New MapObjects2.Table

2. Assign a value to the Database property of the Table:

   MyTable.Database = "C:\ACCESS\DATA\SALES.MDB"

3. Assign a value to the Name property of the Table:

   MyTable.Name = "QTR3"

4. Relate the table associated with a MapLayer to the database table:

   Map1.Layers(0).AddRelate("RecName", MyTable, "ExtName")

A MapObjects application uses the DataConnection object to connect to your SDE Instance according to the parameters given here:

```
Server:     <server name>
Database:   <instance name>[:<database name>]
User:       <user name>
Password:   <password>
```

and then to find a GeoDataset within SDE which may be added as a MapLayer.

Here's a sample VB code snippet that connects to the SQLNJ database on the SDE server

MySDE:

```
Private Sub Form_Load()
  Dim dCon As New MapObjects2.DataConnection
  With dCon
    .Server = "MySDE"
    .Database = "esri_sde:NJ"
    .User = "myName"
    .Password = "myPassword"
  End With
```

The following VB code, which assumes that a database connection has already been made, gives an example of how you might perform a "relate" on a MapLayer based on an SDE layer:

```
Private Sub DoRelate()
  Dim lyr As New MapObjects2.MapLayer
  Dim relTable As New MapObjects2.Table
  Dim toField As String
  Dim fromField As String
'Set the MapLayer details to relate TO
Set lyr = Map1.Layers.Item("WORLD.CNTRY94.FEATURE.Polygons")
toField = "WORLD.CNTRY94.FIPS_CODE"
'Set a Table to relate FROM
With relTable
   .Server = "MySDE"
   .Database = "esri_sde:NJ"
```

```
    .User = "myName"
    .Password = "myPassword"
    .Name = "WORLD.DEMOG"
End With
fromField = "WORLD.DEMOG.FIPS_CODE"
If Not lyr.AddRelate(toField, relTable, fromField) Then
    MsgBox "SDE AddRelate failed"
    End If
End Sub
```

Let's assume you've downloaded an evaluation copy of the latest version of MapObjects 2 (MO2) from the ESRI Web site and installed it. Because it's an OCX, there's no "Map Objects" program on your start menu—just some HLP files and so on.

In other words, to use MapObjects, you need a COM-compliant development tool like VB or VC++. We used VB6, started a new project, and then added the ESRI MapObjects control (see Figure 14.27).

Then we launched the Object Browser (View | Object Browser) to see what we had, paying particular attention to AddRelate, since the AddRelate method is of interest to database developers (see Figure 14.28).

To create a bare-minimum map project, all you have to do is add the Map control to your new project's default form (resizing it to fill the form), and then add a map. To do

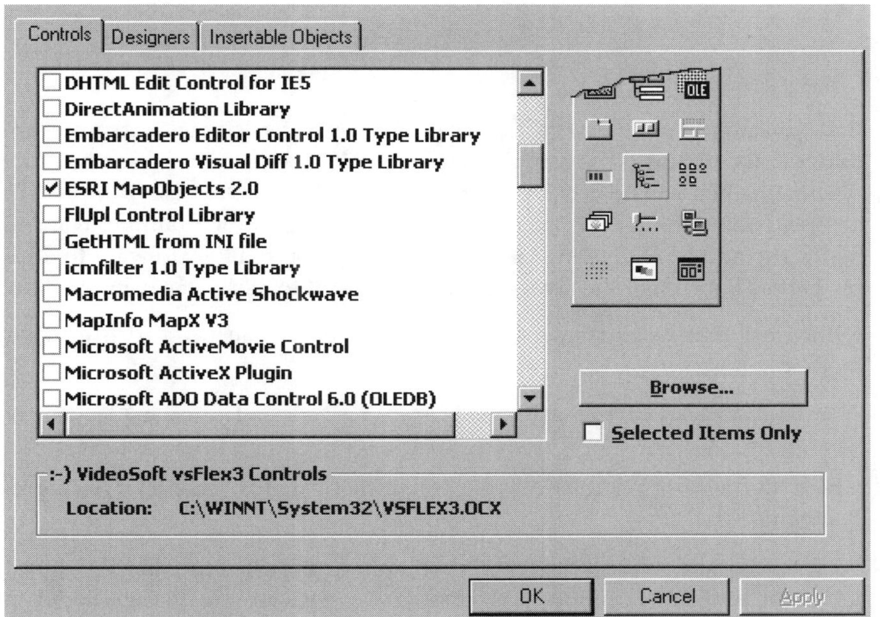

Figure 14.27 You can add a control from the Project|Components menu.

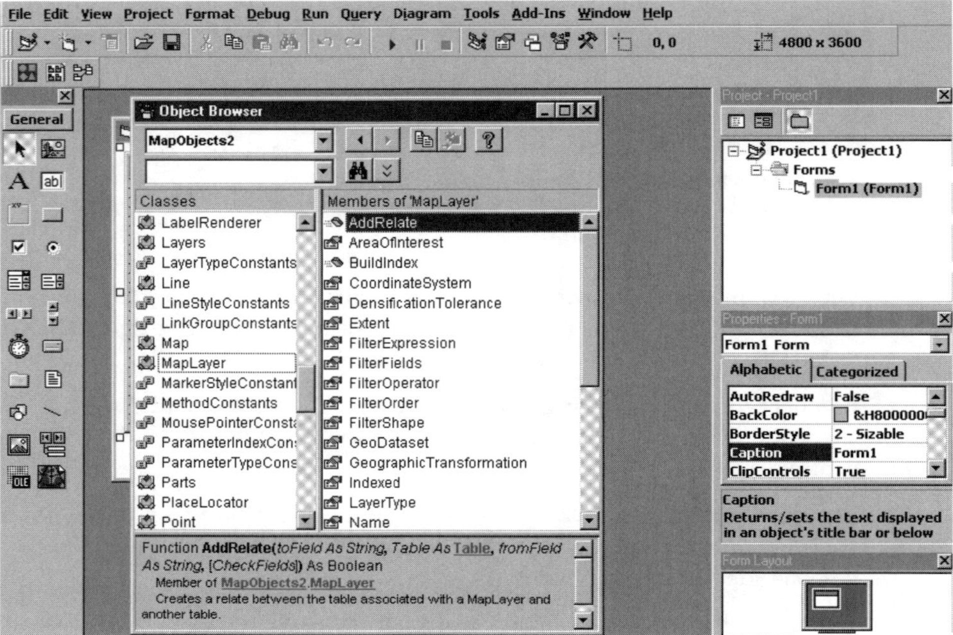

Figure 14.28 Examining the MapObjects control in VB's Object Browser.

that, you simply use the MapObject's property sheet, click the Add button and locate a folder that contains some sample map data. MO2 ships with a good selection of sample data, which will be in c:\Program Files\ ESRI\MapObjects2\Samples\Data if you accepted the defaults during installation. You might, for example, want to add the States.shp and USHigh.shp files. The next thing you're likely to want to do is set basic properties for each of the layers. Then you'll want to add some command buttons.

Remember that to add layers from database data, you need to use the AddRelate method whose syntax is:

```
object.AddRelate(toField, sourceTable, fromField,[checkFields as
Boolean])
```

where the supported relate types are numeric fields, character/string fields and Boolean fields.

Well, we've run out of steam (and time), but I'm pretty sure that if you're a VB programmer, and you're interested in maps, we've given you enough to get you going. Save this sample project if you like, but, better, yet, try some of the sample projects that are included in MO2, or open the tutorial DOC file and work through that example.

Conclusion

In this chapter, we've given you a taste of some other projects you can do with SQL Server. Naturally, we hope you've enjoyed it and that it's given you some ideas for your own projects.

This chapter also ends the book. We hope you've learned what you wanted to. You may want to skim the appendixes to see what they contain. We think there's some pretty good stuff in them.

Each of us invites your comments, and you may also want to stop by the Wiley Web site now and then for updates. In the meantime, go forth and do awesome things with SQL Server.

PART THREE

Appendices

APPENDIX A

SQL Survival Guide

As you read in Chapter 1, SQL was born in the 1970s as a way to provide an easy-to-use layer between a developer and the underlying data storage system. (See Table A.1 for a SQL timeline and more SQL and RDBMS milestones.) Pronounced as either "ess-cue-ell" or "sequel," SQL is a language to access the design and data of a database. Prior to SQL, developers had to understand, and code, very sophisticated file-retrieval (or, shudder, tape-retrieval in those days) routines within each program that they wrote. These routines determined the specific track and sector on a hard disk (or again, tape) where data was stored. This included calculating the number of bytes into the file where your data was stored, while being careful not to overwrite adjoining sections of data as you made your own updates. In other words, in order to retrieve your data, you had to know a good deal about the hardware and how it interacted with your computer.

Early versions of desktop databases such as dBase even forced application programmers to handle tasks such as lock management, transaction support, and so on via code.

Table A.1 SQL Timeline

YEAR	TECHNOLOGY
1970	Dr. E.F. Codd's seminal work, *A Relational Model of Data for Large Shared Data Banks* is published in the *Communications of the ACM* journal.
1973	IBM Research establishes the System R project to build a RDBMS based on Codd's ideas.
1974	IBM Research's Don Chamberlin and Ray Boyce publish a paper, *SEQUEL: A Structured English Query Language* in the *Communications of the ACM* journal.

Continues

Table A.1 *(Continued)*

YEAR	TECHNOLOGY
1979	Oracle ships its first commercial SQL database (Oracle 2.0).
1981	Relational Technology ships Ingres (subsequently acquired by ASK—now owned by Computer Associates).
1982	IBM ships SQL/DS.
1982	ANSI forms SQL standards committee.
1983	IBM ships DB2.
1984	Oracle ships first PC SQL database (Oracle 4.0).
1986	ANSI ratifies first SQL standard, ANSI X3.135-1986.
1986	Oracle ships first relational database with row-level locking (Oracle 5.0).
1986	Sybase ships SQL Server.
1987	First PC SQL database server (Oracle 5.0).
1989	Ashton-Tate and Microsoft ship SQL Server 1.0 for OS/2.
1989	First TPC benchmark (TPC-A) published for OLTP.
1990	TPC-B benchmark published, also for OLTP.
1991	IBM publishes its vision of data warehousing in a seminal paper, *Information Warehouse Architecture*.
1992	Microsoft ships Microsoft SQL Server 4.2.
1992	Oracle becomes first relational vendor to provide support for spatial data (Spatial Data Option).
1992	Microsoft publishes the ODBC specification.
1992	TPC-C benchmark published.
1992	ANSI adopts the SQL-92 standard.
1993	IBM ships DB2 for OS/2 and AIX.
1994	Oracle offers full text searching (ConText option).
1994	The TPC-D benchmark, geared for OLAP, is published.
1995	Oracle ships Oracle Video Server.
1995	Microsoft ships SQL Server 6.0.
1996	Microsoft ships SQL Server 6.5.
1997	IBM ships unified (across UNIX and NT platforms) IBM DB2 UDB with data extenders for text, image, audio, and video.
1998	Microsoft ships SQL Server 7.0.
1999	Oracle ships Oracle 8i.

E.F. Codd, a brilliant mathematician and IBM fellow, developed the relational model, and an IBM team developed tools, notably SQLR, to reduce some of the complexity of interacting with the relational model. As it evolved, the "database system" became responsible for knowing precisely where data was stored and how to retrieve it. Furthermore, the database system could present the data to the user as views of data, which could actually be made up of data from several physical underlying tables or even a portion of one table. You no longer had to worry as much about the order that the data was stored in—you could simply select the row that you were interested in, make your updates, and save it. SQL and the underlying database system—in conjunction with the operating system—took care of all of the "low-level" details associated with physical storage.

What Can SQL Do?

There are two major things that SQL can do for you:

1. Create, retrieve, and maintain the actual data within the tables. This portion of SQL is called *Data Manipulation Language (DML)*. This is the portion of the data that application developers work with most often.
2. Create and maintain the structure of your database, tables, and fields (columns) within those tables. This aspect of SQL is called *Data Definition Language (DDL)*. DDL is discussed at the end of this appendix.

DML Statements

We'll start by reviewing the key DML statements found in SQL. The most frequently used statements allow you to retrieve data, while variations allow you to add, change, and delete data.

Using the SELECT Statement to Locate Information

A great deal of SQL is wrapped up in the SELECT statement. This SQL command allows you to retrieve data from a database table and to create and populate (SELECT...INTO...) tables...) as well. Table A.2 shows the SELECT statement basics. We'll go into additional features later in this appendix.

Table A.2 The Basics of the Select Statement

SQL SYNTAX	ACCOMPLISHES
SELECT <field-list>	Picks what columns (fields) that you want to see.
FROM <table-list>	Picks what tables these fields come from. You can also use views, derived tables, and rowset functions here.
WHERE <selection criteria>	Allows you to add selection criteria to see less than everything.
ORDER BY <sorting criteria>	Allows you to sort the data that comes back.

THE EASIEST WAY TO GET STARTED WITH SQL

We recommend that you experiment in either SQL Server or Access by using those system tools to design SQL queries graphically, and then view the resulting SQL. You'll probably want to use a small database that you're familiar with so that you can invoke common sense when evaluating the rows that were returned—that is, were they the rows that you expected?

In SQL Server's Enterprise Manager, expand the hierarchy until you see the Tables and Views icons under your database. Navigate down to Views and right-click on it. Select New View, and you'll see the Visual Query Builder shown in Figure A.1. This is basically the Access query builder. You can drag and drop fields for retrieval and see the resulting SQL code in the pane located in the middle of the screen. Press F5 or click on the Run a Query icon when you're ready to run the query.

Let's use the following table from our WorkOrd database to experiment with the SELECT statement.

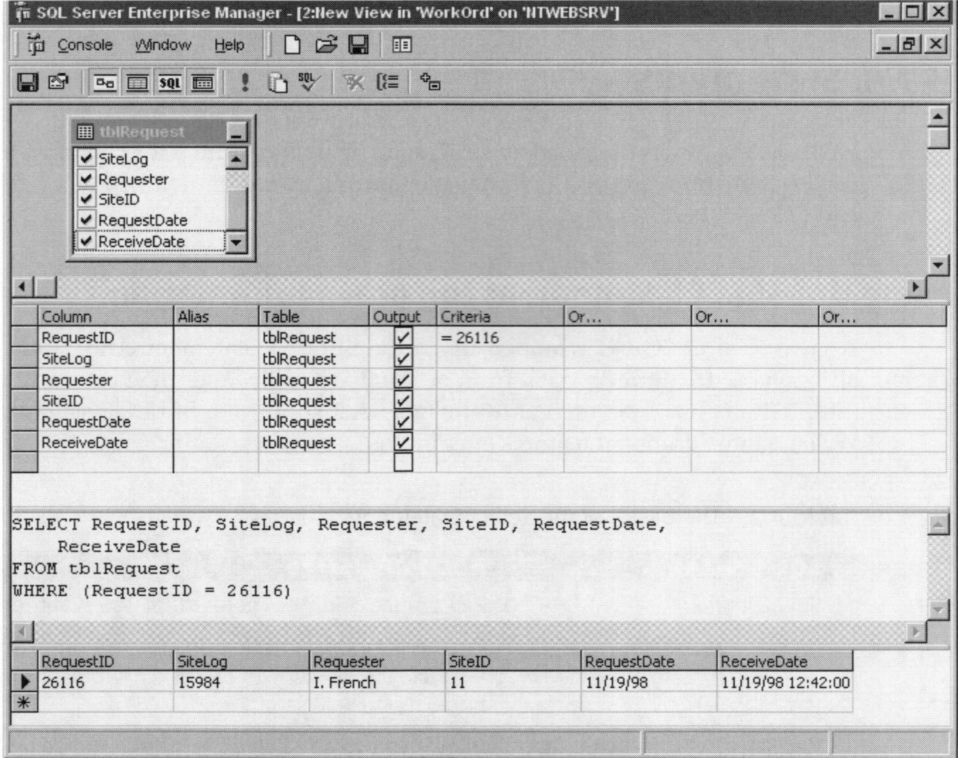

Figure A.1 The Enterprise Manager's visual query builder.

Table A.3 shows all of the columns from the "top" of the tblRequest table. (We only show the first few rows in Table A.3). Remember, with a RDBMS, you don't have any control over the physical storage of the data, nor the default order in which it's displayed. This is because SQL is *set-oriented,* not *row-oriented.* Let's explain our terminology in a little more detail. A row of data, sometimes called a *record* or a *tuple,* is all of the information from a table for one person, or one order, and so on. In our case, a row represents a request. Figure A.2 explains which elements from our results are columns and which ones are rows.

Columns represent the unique entities of data within the table. Columns are also called fields or attributes—especially when you get down into the ADO, RDO, and DAO object models. A column contains the actual data itself and knows characteristics about that data such as its data type or maximum size allowed. Visual Basic programmers may find the code in Chapter 13 helpful in understanding table structures and to see how the ADO, RDO, and DAO properties are set up.

Getting Selective with SELECT

The SQL command that we used to retrieve the data rows shown in Table A.3 was:

```
SELECT * FROM tblRequest
```

You can consider SQL to be a bit like chess. It doesn't take all that long to understand where to move the pieces to, or even to make a number of good moves from time to time. However, it does take time and practice to become a master.

The SELECT statement is certainly an illustration of this chess analogy. An example of this in the SQL command, SELECT * FROM tblRequest, where the * tells the SQL

Table A.3 Part of the WorkOrd tblRequest Table's Data

REQUESTID	SITELOG	REQUESTER	SITEID	REQUESTDATE	RECEIVEDATE
1	3388	N. Gale	8	08-May-98	08-May-98
2	3389	N. Gale	8	08-May-98	08-May-98
3	3391	N. Gale	8	08-May-98	08-May-98
4	3393	N. Gale	8	08-May-98	08-May-98
5	3394	N. Gale	8	08-May-98	08-May-98
6	78	N. Gale	8	25-May-98	25-May-98
7	79	N. Gale	8	25-May-98	25-May-98
8	80	N. Gale	8	25-May-98	25-May-98
9	81	N. Gale	8	25-May-98	25-May-98
10	82	N. Gale	8	25-May-98	25-May-98
11	83	N. Gale	8	25-May-98	25-May-98
12	84	N. Gale	8	25-May-98	25-May-98

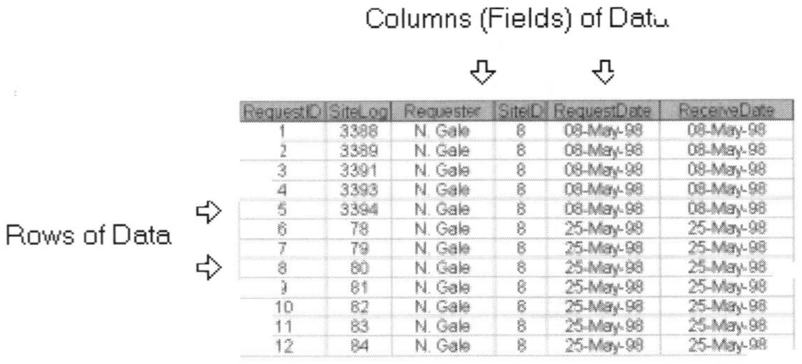

Columns (Fields) of Data

Rows of Data

RequestID	SiteLog	Requester	SiteID	RequestDate	ReceiveDate
1	3388	N. Gale	8	08-May-98	08-May-98
2	3389	N. Gale	8	08-May-98	08-May-98
3	3391	N. Gale	8	08-May-98	08-May-98
4	3393	N. Gale	8	08-May-98	08-May-98
5	3394	N. Gale	8	08-May-98	08-May-98
6	78	N. Gale	8	25-May-98	25-May-98
7	79	N. Gale	8	25-May-98	25-May-98
8	80	N. Gale	8	25-May-98	25-May-98
9	81	N. Gale	8	25-May-98	25-May-98
10	82	N. Gale	8	25-May-98	25-May-98
11	83	N. Gale	8	25-May-98	25-May-98
12	84	N. Gale	8	25-May-98	25-May-98

Figure A.2 Rows and columns.

parser to return all of the columns of data from our chosen table. This is straight and simple. However, you don't need to get back ALL of the columns each time. You can alternatively opt to ask for a few of the columns, such as RequestID, Requester, and RequestDate, instead of all of the columns for each of the rows. In this case, the SQL statement would look like this:

```
SELECT RequestID, Requester, RequestDate FROM tblRequest
```

Running this SQL statement results in a data selection similar to that shown in Table A.4. The exception is that your resultset (there's that "set" word again) will contain every row of information in the tblRequest table rather than just the eight rows shown in Table A.4.

Using the FROM and WHERE Clauses

The next SQL statement to understand is the FROM clause. FROM allows you to pick information from one or more tables or views. *Views*, sometimes called virtual tables, are SQL statements that you or someone else have created and saved. Our example pulls data only from the tblRequest table, but don't worry—we'll show you how to retrieve information from multiple tables later in the appendix.

Table A.4 The Rows and Columns That Make Up the tblRequest Table

REQUESTID	REQUESTER	REQUESTDATE
1	N. Gale	5/8/98
2	N. Gale	5/8/98
3	N. Gale	5/8/98
4	N. Gale	5/8/98
5	N. Gale	5/8/98
6	N. Gale	5/25/98
7	N. Gale	5/25/98
8	N. Gale	5/25/98

There are two primary methods to increase the performance of a SQL SELECT statement. You can reduce the number of rows (records) returned or you can choose to reduce the number of columns (fields) returned on each individual row.

For the first method, you can reduce the number of rows returned to you with the WHERE clause. It's faster to bring back only a few rows rather than bringing back many. This is especially important if you're operating over a slow connection such as a dial-up phone link to a remote server. For example, if you wanted to return only the rows that contain the value 3388 for the SiteLog column, the following SQL syntax accomplishes that goal:

```
SELECT RequestID, SiteLog, Requester, SiteID,
RequestDate, ReceiveDate
FROM tblRequest
WHERE SiteLog="3388";
```

Issuing the previous SQL statement returns the rows shown within Table A.5.

Since SiteLog is a text field, we enter our selection criteria of 3388 within quotes—single or double (see the Tip, *Quotes Can Be Your Undoing*). If SiteLog was a numeric value, this same sections would read WHERE Sitelog=3388. The WHERE clause accepts Boolean operators, so changing our SQL statement to the code shown here and our previous three-row result would look like this:

```
SELECT RequestID, SiteLog, Requester, RequestDate
FROM tblRequest
WHERE SiteLog="3388" AND Requester="N. Gale";
```

QUOTES CAN BE YOUR UNDOING

SQL Server's character data and character constants must be enclosed in single quotation marks (') or double quotation marks ("). Enclosing character data in single quotation marks is *always* allowed and is the recommended practice. Enclosing character data in double quotation marks can lead to ambiguous results because double quotes will always be interpreted as referencing an object—you'll *have* to use single quotes to delimit strings or date data.

If the character data includes a single quote, use an extra quotation mark as in 'O''Malley'.

SQL Server's datetime values also need to be enclosed in quotation marks.

We hate to say it, but plan to make mistakes with quotation marks. We all do. Chess masters aren't made overnight.

Table A.5 tblRequest Rows Where the SiteLog Column Equals 3388

REQUESTID	SITELOG	REQUESTER	REQUESTDATE
1	3388	N. Gale	5/8/98
21	3388	N. Gale	6/12/98
10399	3388	H. Brink	9/15/98

Relational Operators and LIKE

To return all rows with a RequestID between 3380 and 3389 inclusively, you can issue the following SQL statement:

```
SELECT RequestID, SiteLog, Requester, SiteID, RequestDate, ReceiveDate
FROM tblRequest
WHERE (RequestID>=3380 AND requestid <= 3389);
```

The relational operators shown in Table A.6 can be used to provide greater control over your WHERE selections.

SQL provides a more powerful keyword, called LIKE, that makes this type of query a bit easier and provides more flexibility. For example, the following SQL statements (for SQL Server and Access respectively) return the same set of information as the previous one did.

```
/* SQL Server */
SELECT RequestID, SiteLog, Requester, SiteID, RequestDate, ReceiveDate
FROM tblRequest
WHERE RequestID like '338_';

' Access SQL
SELECT RequestID, SiteLog, Requester, SiteID, RequestDate, ReceiveDate
FROM tblRequest
WHERE RequestID like '338?';
```

Notice the underscore ("_") wildcard ("?" in Access). This tells the SQL parser to replace the _ with any row that has four characters for RequestID, starting with a 338. You can also use a percentage symbol (% in SQL Server, * in Access). This tells SQL to return any rows with a RequestID starting with 338 regardless of how many characters follow those three numbers. You can use the wildcard character *in front of* the hard-coded value of 338. This way any rows with 338 at the end of their RequestID columns are returned. In the same way, %338% can be used to return any rows with RequestIDs that contain the three characters 338 anywhere within the value.

Table A.6 Relational Operators and Their Functions

RELATIONAL OPERATORS	FUNCTION
=	Equal To
<> -or- !=	Not Equal
<	Less Than
>	Greater Than
<=	Less Than or Equal To
>=	Greater Than or Equal To

BETWEEN and IN

As one further way of selecting our data, we can use BETWEEN. The following code example returns all rows where the RequestID field is between or including the numbers supplied to the BETWEEN logical operator.

```
SELECT RequestID, SiteLog, Requester, SiteID, RequestDate, ReceiveDate
FROM tblRequest
WHERE RequestID BETWEEN 3379 AND 3390;
```

And for a final way of selecting data, we can use the IN keyword. What this does is allow you to list a *set* of values, with any rows that contain those values in the WHERE column returned. The advantage to IN is that you can select rows of data, using values for the selection field that are *not* sequential in nature. They can be any valid values that you desire and represent an alternative to writing a series of OR conditions.

```
SELECT RequestID, SiteLog, Requester, SiteID, RequestDate, ReceiveDate
FROM tblRequest
WHERE Requester IN ('Shadish', 'N. Gale');
```

Sorting the Result with ORDER BY

There are many cases where you may wish to sort the resultset into a particular order. For example, let's say that you want to look through the tblResults data for possible bad data. It's difficult to come up with an exact WHERE clause for this, because if you absolutely know what the bad data is, you probably would have already corrected it by this point. This concept is sort of like the idea of the teacher asking anyone who isn't present to raise their hand. To explain this further, it so happens that there *are* some RequestDate data problems in tblRequest. We can pull these out by adding the ORDER BY clause. In the following SQL code, we order (sort) the data by the RequestDate column, sorted into ASCending order. You replace ASC with DESC, to sort the data into descending order.

```
SELECT RequestID, SiteLog, Requester, SiteID,
    RequestDate, ReceiveDate
FROM tblRequest
ORDER BY RequestDate ASC;
```

Table A.7 shows the results from this SQL statement.

If G. Imbored was really waiting from 1931 to 1998, he was either incredibly patient or, perhaps it is more likely that the RequestDate field in the first row contains bad data. Using queries to sort data into a logical order like this allows you to do spot checks of data, as well as produce repeating reports so that the users can validate the data on an ongoing basis.

QUERY BOOKS ONLINE

Here are some of the best help topics available from *Books Online*: *Query Fundamentals, SELECT (T-SQL) and the SELECT Clause.*

Table A.7 The tblRequest Data Sorted by RequestDate

REQUESTID	SITELOG	REQUESTER	SITEID	REQUEST DATE	RECEIVEDATE
15878	7761	G. Imbored	6	9/1/31	9/1/98 9:31:00 AM
12772	4358	G. Imbored	6	1/1/45	5/1/98 8:49:00 AM
9276	445-3211	J. Ester	12	12/1/47	12/4/98 12:50:00 PM
23346	11080	R. Leman	5	3/2/97	3/2/98 1:35:00 PM
23510	11326	I. French	11	3/5/97	3/5/98 1:02:00 PM
11504	3001	G. Imbored	6	3/18/97	3/19/98 9:52:00 AM
11500	2997	G. Imbored	6	3/18/97	3/19/98 9:44:00 AM
11507	3004	G. Imbored	6	3/18/97	3/19/98 9:57:00 AM

Aggregate Functions

SQL provides a number of function keywords that collect and provide information about rows. For example the COUNT function retrieves the number of rows that are returned by a SQL statement. Executing the following SQL statement simply returns the number 12.

```
SELECT COUNT (*)
FROM tblRequest
WHERE RequestID BETWEEN 3379 AND 3390;
```

Other aggregate functions include SUM and AVG (see Table A.8 for a list of T-SQL aggregate functions), which act on a particular column of data. You can use these functions together, to gain a better understanding of the data that you're working on, or just to measure how your data has grown. For example, to retrieve the results shown in Table A.9, enter the SQL code shown here. Notice that we can "name" the columns, using the *as* keyword to do so.

Adding, Changing, and Deleting Data

SQL provides ways to maintain your data as well as how to search for it. In addition to the SELECT keyword, INSERT, UPDATE, and DELETE are available to add, change,

Table A.8 T-SQL Aggregate Functions

AGGREGATE FUNCTION	WHAT IT DOES
AVG	Values average for the given column.
COUNT	Row count for rows returned.
GROUPING	Used on Grouping SQL statements, this function causes an additional column to be returned with your results, showing a 1 if the row was added as a result of the CUBE or ROLLUP operator.
MAX	Maximum value for the given column.
MIN	Minimum value for the given column.
STDEV	Statistical standard deviation.
STDEVP	Statistical standard deviation for the population.
SUM	Value sum for the given column.
VAR	Statistical variance.
VARP	Statistical variance for the population.

Table A.9 Requests Count within tblRequest Table

COUNT OF REQUESTIDS	MINIMUM REQUESTID	MAXIMUM REQUESTID
26122	1	27000

and remove rows within your tables. Much of the SQL syntax that you learned when selecting data, such as WHERE and FROM applies when maintaining your data as well.

```
SELECT       Count(*) as [Count of RequestIDs],
     Min(RequestID) as [Minimum RequestID],
     Max(RequestID) as [Maximum RequestID]
FROM tblRequest;
```

Using INSERT to Add Records

The INSERT statement allows you to create a new row in the tblRequest table. The format shows the fields (columns) that you want to add data into followed by their actual data values. It's up to you to make sure that the values entered are correct and of the required type. Note that the system error checking can be light at this level. For example, if you entered 3-18-99, 4-19-99 rather than "3-18-99","4-19-99" it results in the corresponding incorrect data values 9/7/1899, 9/7/1899 as stored. When working with INSERT like this, as Ronald Reagan once said, you will want to "Trust, but Verify." An immediate SELECT * FROM tblRequest WHERE RequestID=27000 goes a long way towards improving your sleep at night.

```
INSERT into tblRequest
(
```

```
 RequestID,
..
)
VALUES
(
 270000,
...
)
```

Using UPDATE to Change Records

UPDATE allows you to change the values within your data, using SQL. You can change the values of one or more of the columns in a given (or more than one at a time) row. This ability to change more than one row at a time, shared with the DELETE statement, makes using SQL for mass changes extremely powerful…and dangerous. In the next set of SQL statements, we change the SiteID and SiteLog columns for any requester with the given name.

```
UPDATE tblRequest
SET SiteId=300,
    SiteLog="PH-832"
WHERE ((tblRequest.Requester)="shadish");
```

Using DELETE to Delete Records

Perhaps the easiest to use, but most dangerous of the SQL statement is DELETE. The following example shows you how to delete all rows (records) associated with the Shadish requester.

```
DELETE FROM tblRequest WHERE requester='Shadish'
```

The line DELETE FROM tblRequest will delete ALL records from the tblRequest table. SQL doesn't bother to ask before deleting the records: It just does. It helps you to appreciate the value of a tested backup and restore plan doesn't it?

EVEN MORE *BOOKS ONLINE* TOPICS

Here are some more *Books Online* topics worth skimming: *Aggregate Functions (T-SQL), Adding Rows with INSERT, UPDATE (Searched), and DELETE (SEARCHED).*

Multi-Table Queries

The power of SQL really begins to show when you use it to draw from several tables (potentially drawn from different databases). See *Linked Tables* and *Distributed Queries and Distributed Transactions* in *Books Online* for more information.

For example, given our tblRequest data, perhaps we want to pull the data from a different table such as tblRequestItem, to see what the DueDate of a given request is. Table A.10 shows the first few rows of tblRequestItem to give you an idea of the data within this table.

Table A.10 Sample of the WorkOrd tblRequestItem Data

ITEMID	REQUESTID	URGENCYID	DUEDATE	DOCUMENT-NUMBER	SOURCEID	ASSIGNEDTO
1	1	1	6/5/98 10:44:00 AM	L2W7262003	2	1
2	1	1	6/5/98 10:44:00 AM	U2G4230428	2	1
3	1	1	6/5/98 10:44:00 AM	P7Y3506491	2	1
4	1	1	6/5/98 10:44:00 AM	Y6J1429103	2	1
5	1	1	6/5/98 10:44:00 AM	O9N4886793	2	1
6	1	1	6/5/98 10:44:00 AM	M4S1458545	2	1
7	1	1	6/5/98 10:44:00 AM	F6M6833215	2	1
8	1	1	6/5/98 10:44:00 AM	F5J8416767	1	2
9	1	1	6/5/98 10:44:00 AM	E8F9007341	1	2
10	1	1	6/5/98 10:44:00 AM	D1B7552477	1	2
11	1	1	6/5/98 10:44:00 AM	K9T0670442	1	2
12	1	1	6/5/98 10:44:00 AM	Z8S4723491	1	2
13	1	1	6/5/98 10:44:00 AM	Q3C1049549	1	2

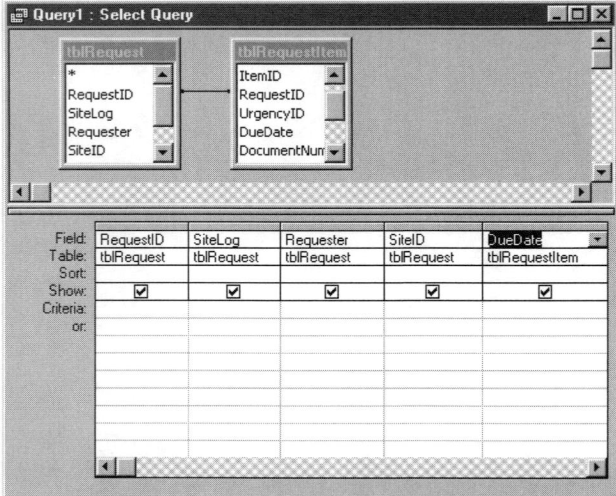

Figure A.3 Building a multi-table query.

Figure A.3 shows what the visual representation of our desired query looks like.

Let's say that we want to draw information from two different places and combine the result. Perhaps we want to pull all of the tblRequest data, and the DueDate of those requested from the related tblRequestItem table. Using the SELECT statement shown next, we can retrieve rows of information that draw from *both* the tblRequest and tblRequestItem tables. That way, we'll end up with one row for each tblRequest—with the corresponding DueDate from the tblRequestItem table appended to the end of the row. This SQL feature is one of the most powerful. It allows you to construct logical rows that hold all of the fields that you need to work with, and then saves these as queries (or views) that can be reused later. The following code demonstrates how to pull values from two different tables.

```
SELECT tblRequest.RequestID, tblRequest.SiteLog, tblRequest.Requester,
tblRequest.SiteID, tblRequest.RequestDate, tblRequest.ReceiveDate,
tblRequestItem.DueDate
FROM tblRequest, tblRequestItem
WHERE tblRequest.RequestID = tblRequestItem.RequestID
```

The key to this statement is the WHERE tblRequest.RequestID = tblRequestItem.-RequestID portion. To break this down, we ask for the specified columns from the tblRequest table—*join*ed to the tblRequestItem table where the two respective RequestID key values match. This is called an EQUIJOIN, because we ask for information where a set of columns is equal.

Keys

Tables are generally set up with unique keys assigned to each row of data. These keys are used not only to speed access to the data (SQL Server creates indexes on key columns), but also to relate data in different tables together. For example, RequestID is the common (key) field that relates the (main or master) tblRequest table and tblRequestItem table that contains the work order details. The tblRequest row is created first, with a key of RequestID. There is 0 to many tblRequestItem rows associated to each tblRequest row. They're "associated" by placing the tblRequest.RequestID value into each corresponding tblRequestItem row.

Notice how table names are pre-pended to the field names this time. Until now, we have worked with single tables within the WorkOrd database. By default, SQL Server supplies the current server, database, and database owner (loginID of the current connection) as you supply T-SQL statements to work with the tables. If you need to retrieve data from a different database, or a different server, you can add the fully-qualified name to the desired table object in order to do so. For example,

```
SELECT * FROM tblRequest WHERE requester='N. Gale'
```

may become

```
SELECT  *  FROM  ntwebsrv.workord.dbo.tblRequest  WHERE  requester='N.
Gale'
```

There's nothing to keep you from using fully-qualified names *all* of the time to avoid ambiguity. However, that means a lot of typing. If you'd prefer to reduce the number of keystrokes, you may want to use aliases. And if you venture into the world of "self-joins." you have to learn aliases to help SQL Server keep things straight.

Aliases

Sometimes, you just want to get long table names (or complex ones that contain spaces) into an easier-to-use format with fewer characters. You may want to do this to make it easier to work with the resulting columns or to more easily display your results. To do this, create a table alias. In the following SQL command, we refer to our fully-qualified database table as t. This makes it easier to specify fully-qualified columns to return as well.

```
SELECT t.RequestID, t.Requester, '      ', t.ReceiveDate from NtWeb-
Srv.WorkOrd.dbo.tblRequest as t
```

TIP

Note that although we used a single-letter alias here, we recommend using three- or four-letter aliases for readability.

INNER JOIN

An INNER JOIN is essentially the same as an EQUIJOIN (a join based on equity only). INNER JOINs use a comparison operator (=, >, <) to match rows from two tables, returning results depending upon values in common columns from those tables. For example, retrieving all rows where the student identification number is the same in both the students and courses tables. Notice that the following statement adds the INNER JOIN syntax.

```
SELECT tblRequest.RequestID, tblRequest.SiteLog, tblRequest.Requester,
tblRequest.SiteID, tblRequest.RequestDate, tblRequest.ReceiveDate,
tblRequestItem.DueDate
FROM tblRequest INNER JOIN tblRequestItem ON tblRequest.RequestID =
tblRequestItem.RequestID;
```

LEFT JOIN

LEFT and RIGHT JOINs (sometimes referred to as OUTER JOINs) work in a similar way—returning all of the first table's rows, along with any matching rows from the JOINed to table. These are called OUTER JOINs. In the following code example, all rows from tblRequest are returned along with any tblRequestItem data from rows where the RequestID is equal in each table.

```
SELECT tblRequest.RequestID, tblRequest.SiteLog, tblRequest.Requester,
tblRequest.SiteID, tblRequest.RequestDate, tblRequest.ReceiveDate,
tblRequestItem.DueDate
FROM tblRequest LEFT JOIN tblRequestItem ON tblRequest.RequestID =
tblRequestItem.RequestID;
```

The previous code returns ALL of the tblRequest rows, and the DueDate column from only those tblRequestItem rows where the keys match as shown in Table A.11. If no tblRequestItem match is found for a given tblRequest row, then a NULL value is returned for that row's DueDate column.

RIGHT JOIN

You can also choose to use a RIGHT JOIN. A RIGHT JOIN brings back all tblRequestItem rows, but only those tblRequest rows where the keys match. This is essentially the reverse of our LEFT JOIN example. This is something that you can use if you're looking

Table A.11 The Result of LEFT JOINing tblRequest and tblRequestItem

REQUESTID	SITELOG	REQUESTER	SITEID	REQUEST-DATE	RECEIVE-DATE	DUEDATE
1	3388	N. Gale	8	5/8/98	5/8/98 10:43:00 AM	6/5/98 10:44:00 AM
1	3388	N. Gale	8	5/8/98	5/8/98 10:43:00 AM	6/5/98 10:44:00 AM
1	3388	N. Gale	8	5/8/98	5/8/98 10:43:00 AM	6/5/98 10:44:00 AM
1	3388	N. Gale	8	5/8/98	5/8/98 10:43:00 AM	6/5/98 10:44:00 AM

for errors within your data—perhaps to seek out tblRequest rows that are missing, but that you expect to find, by using existing tblRequestItem rows as the keys.

AVOID "RUNAWAY" QUERIES

With 26,119 tblRequest records and 164,656 tblRequestItem records, issuing the following SQL statement returns a one-to-one match for each row to the other, or roughly 4,300,650,064 rows of information. You (or your users) may be appreciably older by the time the results are returned to you from a query like this. Be careful when using more than one table to join the tables on one or more fields, so that your can make sure that you only receive the mix of information that you expect.

```
SELECT tblRequest.RequestID, tblRequest.SiteLog, tblRequest.Requester,
tblRequest.SiteID, tblRequest.RequestDate, tblRequest.ReceiveDate, tblRe-
questItem.DueDate

FROM tblRequest, tblRequestItem;
```

Setting the Query Analyzer's SQL Timeout property with the sp_configure system stored procedure and the Resource Timeout option protects you (and your users) from making mistakes like this. If nothing else, at least the system's control is returned to you before natural graying sets in. For more information on SP_configure, see *Books Online* topic, *sp_configure (T-SQL).*

Another handy tool is the Query Governor, which can be used to determine which SQL statements are run based on their anticipated "cost"—in terms of system resources.

Note that Enterprise Manager provides SQL Server parameters for everything from the amount of memory to use, to the number of database locks to allow open and to the amount of time to wait for a query to execute. This allows the administrator to control the way that SQL Server is used centrally, and to prevent users from consuming too many resources which can impact other users. The Query Governor for a server is available in Enterprise Manager by right-clicking on a Server, selecting Properties and then selecting Server Settings.

FULL JOIN or FULL OUTER JOIN

In addition to left and right (outer) joins, there's also a full outer join. A full outer join returns all rows in both the left and right tables. Any time a row has no match in the other table, the select list columns from the other table contain null values. When there's a match between the tables, the entire result set row contains data values from the base tables.

CROSS JOIN

Another JOIN option is the CROSS JOIN, which returns all of the first table's rows matched to *each and every* row from the second table for *each* of the first table's rows.

This is called the Cartesian product of the tables, and returns the total number of rows in the first table times the number of rows in the second table.

```
SELECT tblRequest.RequestID, tblRequest.SiteLog, tblRequest.Requester,
tblRequest.SiteID, tblRequest.RequestDate, tblRequest.ReceiveDate,
tblRequestItem.DueDate
FROM tblRequest CROSS JOIN tblRequestItem
ORDER BY tblRequest.Requester;
```

CROSS JOINs can be dangerous, in that they can return *very large* results and, are often submitted by a user who simply has incorrectly set up their SQL statement to select a smaller number of rows to deal with. Do not use CROSS JOINs on a system with a lot of users without parental guidance. Some recommended *Books Online* topics for more information are *Join Fundamentals* and *Using Joins.*

Advanced SELECT Syntax

Now let's take a look at what else is available with SQL's SELECT statement. Notice the new keywords DISTINCT, INTO, GROUP BY, WITH, and HAVING that are shown in Table A.12.

DISTINCT

The DISTINCT keyword is used to return only unique row values from a query. For example, if we query tblRequestItem for all of the RequestID values (as in, SELECT tblRequestItem.RequestID FROM tblRequestItem), we receive 164,656 rows in our result, since

Table A.12 Advanced SELECT Keywords

SQL SYNTAX	ACCOMPLISHES
SELECT <field-list> DISTINCT	If the result contains field-list duplicates, you will only get one instance of each, if you add the DISTINCT keyword.
INTO <new Table>	You can create a temporary or permanent table using INTO to copy the data that you retrieve.
FROM <table-list>	Specifies what tables to draw your results from.
WHERE <selection criteria>	Specifies criteria to limit the result with.
ORDER BY <sorting criteria>	Sorts your result into this field-list order.
GROUP BY <group by criteria>	Groups your result into the specified column groups.
WITH { CUBE | ROLLUP }	Used with GROUP BY to create multi-dimensional cubes used in business intelligence applications.
HAVING <selection criteria>	Selection criteria for a GROUP BY SQL statement.

there are many RequestID=1 rows, RequestID=2 rows and so on. Adding DISTINCT, as in the following code returns only 25,977 rows, although a good bit slower, since the SQL engine needs to weed out duplicates in the result set before presenting the results to you.

```
SELECT DISTINCT tblRequestItem.RequestID FROM tblRequestItem
```

INTO

INTO is used to create a new table, based upon a resultset that is returned from a SQL statement. This is very useful when you want to create a temporary local copy of data, perhaps to work against VB or another high-level tool. Rather than querying the SQL Server each time you need to read the data, you can go against your local copy instead. This greatly decreases your overall processing time. Note that permission to "SELECT INTO" must be given by DBA for the database.

GROUP BY

The GROUP BY syntax allows you to perform aggregate functions against groups within the resultset that are returned by your SQL statement. For example, to group by Requester and count the number of requests that each Requester has and then return the resultset sorted on the number of requests for each person that is returned, we'd issue the following command. Table A.13 is the result.

```
SELECT Count(*) AS Requests, tblRequest.Requester
FROM tblRequest
GROUP BY tblRequest.Requester
ORDER BY Count(*) DESC;
```

Table A.13 Request Counts Grouped by Their Requester

REQUESTS	REQUESTER
7014	G. Imbored
3611	N. Frankel
3042	H. Brink
2489	J. Ester
1825	R. Leman
1777	I. French
1591	A. Sellar
1472	N. Gale
1241	O. Sinclair
1031	B. Gateway
958	F. Night
63	M. Antwerp

HAVING

HAVING is essentially a WHERE clause that works with GROUP BY to filter records. You would use HAVING to select a subset of information to retrieve when grouping your results. To achieve the same results as the previous example, but only where the Requesters' names start with A through S, enter the following SQL statement:

```
SELECT Count(*) AS Requests, tblRequest.Requester
FROM tblRequest
GROUP BY tblRequest.Requester
HAVING requester between "a*" and "s*"
ORDER BY count(*) DESC
```

WITH

You can CREATE VIEWs with SQL Server that format data from one or more table columns, in a way that is best suited to each user. The WITH clause works with CREATE VIEW to allow you to control the way that the View is used. Options for the WITH command include ENCRYPTION, CHECK OPTION, GRANT, RECOVERY, STANDBY, RECOMPILE, and more.

See the *Books Online* topic *CREATE VIEW (T-SQL)* for more on Views and the WITH clause.

Subqueries

We can expand upon the SELECT statements, IN keyword discussed previously. In addition to using hard-coded values to drive the IN selection with, you can also use the result of a query to determine the set of data to match to. In the following example, we only want to report the request information for managers.

```
SELECT RequestID, SiteLog, Requester, SiteID,
       RequestDate, ReceiveDate
FROM tblRequest
WHERE Requester IN (SELECT EmpName from tblManagers);
```

The inner query looks up all of the employee names from the Managers' table. Using that resultset, the outer query selects tblRequest rows where the Requester name is among those employees pulled from the Managers' table.

Some recommended *Books Online* topics for more information: *Eliminating Duplicates with DISTINCT, Group By Clause, Having Clause, Into Clause, Subquery Fundamentals, Subquery Types.*

DDL Statements

DDL (Data Definition Language) is the series of SQL statements—notably CREATE, ALTER, and DROP—which are used to create, change or remove tables and fields within a relational database. DDL can be done directly by entering the appropriate SQL statements into the Query Analyzer SQL window, or by right-clicking your way to this via the Enterprise Manager. Let's take a look at the steps to create a new table.

CREATE

You can create a new table with the CREATE statement. The ALTER statement is used to change a table once you have created it. The syntax for CREATE is:

CREATE TABLE <tablename> (<columnname> <data type> <(size)> <constraints>)

For example, to create an Employees table, enter:

```
/* SQL Server */
Create table tblEmployees
(
 empKey  Numeric Identity Not Null,
 empNo Numeric Not Null,
 empName varchar (25) Not Null,
 empAddress varchar (50) Not Null,
)


' Access
Create table tblEmployees
(
 empKey counter Not Null,
 empNo Numeric Not Null,
 empName text (25) Not Null,
 empAddress text (50) NOT NULL
)
```

The Not Null syntax *forces* data to be entered into the respective column when the row is created.

TABLE CREATION DATA TYPES

The SQL Server system stored procedure sp_datatype_info returns to you the data types that are available to use when defining columns. You can create your own user-defined datatypes in SQL Server, using sp_addtype. See *Books Online* topic, *sp_addtype (T-SQL)*, for more information.

ALTER

ALTER TABLE allows you to *add* a column to a table, *change* the characteristics of a table's columns, or *delete* a column within a table. This is a very powerful (and popular!) command that's newly revised in SQL Server 7. In earlier versions of SQL Server, you had to unload your data, create a new table, and then reload the data in order to make any changes in a table's structure. An example that shows how to add a Title to tblEmployees table looks like this:

```
ALTER TABLE tblEmployees ADD Title VARCHAR(50) NULL
```

CHECK YOUR WORK

The SQL Server system stored procedure, sp_columns (as in EXEC sp_columns tblRequest) returns the columns' current settings within the specified database table. The returned values include TABLE_QUALIFIER, TABLE_OWNER, TABLE_NAME, COLUMN_NAME, DATA_TYPE, TYPE_NAME PRECISION, LENGTH, SCALE RADIX NULLABLE, REMARKS, COLUMN_DEF, SQL_DATA_TYPE, SQL_DATETIME_SUB, CHAR_OCTET_LENGTH, ORDINAL_POSITION IS_NULLABLE, and SS_DATA_TYPE.

DROP Is Fast and Can Be Dangerous

To remove the Employees' table—removing *all* of the data in the table as well—enter:

```
DROP TABLE Employees
```

You can also do this by right-clicking on a table within the Enterprise Manager and selecting Delete. When you DROP a table, it's gone. Along with all of the data that was stored within the table. You need to take special care to make sure that this is what the client desires before doing so. And, as always, a good backup before "dropping" may help with your ongoing employment status.

We recommend these *Books Online* topics for related information: *Create Table, Alter Table, Drop Table, Create Index.*

SQL Gotchas

There are some tricks in working with any vendor's version of SQL and Microsoft's SQL Server is no exception. We've included a few things that you will want to be aware of, before you start to create tables. Some of these items will need to be cleared with your clients themselves, such as whether to allow Null values within table values or not. Some of these items will need to be discussed with the developers working on the applications, such as how to handle quotes.

NULLs

Contrary to the ANSI standard, SQL Server creates columns by default that does not accept NULL values unless explicity declared in CREAT TABLE or ALTER TABLE commands. Curiously, both ODBC and OLE DB override this default setting, which can lead to confusion and frustration. In fact, there are a variety of settings related to NULLS that let you fine-tune how NULLs work. At the database level, you can select between ANSI-standard NULLs or backward compatible SQL Server NULLs via sp_dboption. You can, also, however, control the kind of NULLs you want by adjusting session settings, one connection at a time, using the T-SQL SET ANSI_NULL_DFLT_ON {ON | OFF}. Use the GETANSINULL() function to determine the default nullability for the current session.

You may also want to refer to these two *Knowledge Base* articles for additional insight into NULLs:

"Q170318 BUG: Error When Inserting NULL into Timestamp with ANSI_NULLS"

"Q214601 PRB: ANSI_NULLS OFF Behavior in SQL Server 6.x and 7.0"

Bottom line: we strongly encourage you to explicity declare NULL or NOT NULL whenever you create or alter a column—and obviously, to document your schema by saving your CREATE TABLE and ALTER TABLE scripts.

When NULL ≠ NULL

As you may know, when a field contains a NULL it means the value for that field is undefined. ANSI standard SQL-92 mandates that when comparison operations between NULLs and any other value (including other NULLs) occurs, the result must be false. So, the following operations will evaluate to false.

```
NULL = NULL
NULL = 'DataDrivenWebSites.com'
```

SQL Server 7 gives you the ability to control this behavior with a database setting called ANSI_NULLS. It is set to OFF by default so you would expect NULL comparisons to evaluate to true when perfoming queries in Query Analyzer, but this is not the case. Execute the following in Query Analyzer so you can see what happens.

```
CREATE TABLE TestNULL
(
 Field1 int NOT NULL,
 Field2 int NULL
)
GO
INSERT TestNULL (Field1) VALUES (1)
SELECT * FROM TestNULL WHERE Field2 = NULL
```

If you execute this script you will see that no records are returned. This doesn't really make much sense, does it? Well, the trick here is that Query Analyzer communicates with SQL Server via the ODBC Driver for SQL Server and every time a connection is established via the ODBC Driver SET ANSI_NULLS ON is executed. So the default behavior is overrode and we have SQL-92 compliance. ANSI_NULLS is also set to ON when the OLE DB Provider for SQL Server connects to SQL Server. When applications that use DB-Library (e.g., isql) connect to SQL Server the default value is not changed so NULL comparisons evaluate to true.

If you want to find records that have fields with NULL values you need to use IS NULL. Use the following to filter on NULLs in Field2 in the preceding table.

```
SELECT * FROM TestNULL Where Field2 IS NULL
COLUMN PROPERTY: NULL v. NOT NULL
```

The code shown here is a simple CREATE TABLE statement.

```
CREATE TABLE TableName
(
 Field1 int NOT NULL,
 Field2 int NULL
)
```

The thing you should notice is that we explicity listed the nullability for each field. Field1 can't contain NULL values while Field2 can. This is the proper way to specify nullability for a column, but sometimes even the best of us can forget to include it, so you need to understand SQL Server's default behavior when nullability is not specified.

The default behavior is to set nullability to NOT NULL. So, the following code:

```
CREATE TABLE TableName
(
 Field1 int,
 Field2 int
)
```

will result in both columns being set to NOT NULL. This default behavior can be altered by setting the database option: 'Ansi nulls default' to true or issuing the following command at the start of a session:

```
SET ANSI_NULL_DFLT_ON ON
```

This is certainly a very easy concept to understand, but there's a confusing aspect to the default behavior. When you use a tool that uses either ODBC or OLE DB to "talk" to SQL Server the default behavior is changed. So, before the tool (e.g., Query Analyzyer) passes a DML or DDL command to the server it issues the following:

```
SET ANSI_NULL_DFLT_ON ON
```

which changes the behavior so that when nullability is not specified, NULL is used.

You can see this for youself by executing the previous CREATE TABLE statement in both Query Analyzer and the command-line utility isql. Query Analyzer uses ODBC to communicate with SQL Server, so the columns will accept nulls. isql, on the other hand, uses DB-Library so the columns are set to NOT NULL.

Quotes

SQL Server allows you to use single quotes, or single and double quotes to enclose string and date variables. Double quotes and brackets [ ] are used to enclose delimited identifiers such as table names that include blank spaces between the words in the name. This also varies between differing database systems and is something that you will need to look at while porting code from one database to another. The SQL-92 standards (obtained by setting QUOTED_IDENTIFIER ON with T-SQL) indicate to use double quotes to enclose identifiers (like table names) and single quotes to enclose values (like 'B. Shadish'). See the *Books Online* topic *Using Identifiers, Delimited Identifiers, and SET QUOTED_IDENTIFIER* for more information.

Dates

As with Quotes and NULLs, different database systems and different countries handle dates in a variety of ways. SQL Server does handle SQL date constants of alphabetical types (May 1, 1999), numeric types (5/1/1999), and string types ('19990501') for you. '19990501' will cause the least trouble.

One thing to remember is that if you are doing a straight, native passthrough SQL against a database engine, then you will *need* to specify dates in the way that the DBMS expects. However, if you use ODBC, it attempts to handle the date conversions expected by the target database automatically for you.

See the *Books Online* topics, *Writing International Transact-SQL Statements* and *CAST and CONVERT (T-SQL)* for more on dates.

SQL: 1999—The Next Big Thing

The SQL-92 standard is obviously getting long in the tooth, but SQL: 1999—originally referred to as SQL3—is expected this year.

SQL: 1999 will include new relational features such as new data types. For example, there's a new UNKNOWN Boolean data type (in addition to TRUE and FALSE), plus a host of new large object data types like character large object (CLOB), national character large object (NCLOB), and binary large object (BLOB). SQL: 1999 also adds two type constructors (ROW and ARRAY) to extend its pre-defined data types, improved pattern matching via SIMILAR, more powerful triggers, recursive queries, and distinct types. SQL: 1999 also includes a host of new object-oriented features including structured types, single inheritance, typed tables, and a REF data type that can be defined for any structured data type.

Where to Go for More Information

You can find a lot of information about SQL on the Internet as we've indicated in Table A.14. We also recommend any of Joe Celko's books on SQL such as *Instant SQL Programming* (Wrox Press, 1995). Joe, who has helped forge the ANSI SQL standards and is known is some circles as "Mr. SQL," is known for his playful (yet deadly accurate) approach to SQL. We can also recommend Jim Melton's articles and books including *Understanding the New SQL* (Morgan Kaufmann, 1993). Jim, like Joe, serves on the ANSI SQL standards committee. One last book recommendation weighs in at almost 1000 pages, but it's comprehensive and does a good job covering product-specific SQL from the leading RDBMSs. In fact, James Groff's book, *SQL: The Complete Reference*

Table A.14 SQL-Related Information Web Sites

SQL-RELATED SITE	URL
ANSI standards	web.ansi.org/default.htm
ISO standards	www.iso.ch/welcome.html
Interactive online SQL tutorial	torresoft.netmegs.com
SQL standard syntax site	www.cs.cmu.edu/afs/andrew.cmu.edu/usr/shadow/www/sql.html#syntax
More standards syntax	epoch.cs.berkeley.edu:8000/sequoia/dba/montage/FAQ/SQL_TOC.html
SQL reference page	www.ida.his.se/ida/~bjorn/referenserMSc/refs-MSc-SQL-9697.chtml
The SQL standards process	www.jcc.com/sql_stnd.html
Introduction to Structured Query Language	w3.one.net/~jhoffman/sqltut.htm

(McGraw-Hill, 1999) comes with evaluation copies of not only SQL Server 7 (as this book does), but also of Oracle 8 Personal Edition, IBM DB2 Universal Database Personal Edition 5.2, Sybase Adaptive Server Anywhere 6.0, and Informix Dynamic Server 7.2.2 Personal Edition software.

More Information

Goal

This appendix includes all of the SQL-related Web sites covered in the book, plus more.

Contents at a Glance

Supplies

The only thing that you will need for this chapter is an Internet connection to browse to these sites, and Access 97 if you want to use the tool in this chapter to work with the web sites mentioned.

SiteView Overview

We have provided a listing of all of the web sites in this book, plus a large number of sites not specifically listed, both within the table at the end of this appendix, as well as in Microsoft Access 97 form.

SiteView

The Access application, called SiteView, can be found on the CD in the folder \Code\Additional-Sites\SiteView.MDB. Loading this application will present you with the screen shown in Figure 1. You can sort on the descriptions, the URLs and even the Chapters columns, by clicking on the respective column headings across the top of the screen. If you want to search for a specific piece of text, you can use the search selection criteria fields at the bottom of the screen; pressing the "Search" button when you are ready to see your results. The actual SQL statement that is used to search the database with is displayed in the Current Selection label at the bottom of the form, so that you can see how SQL is being used to retrieve your results.

Site Listings

Table B.1 lists useful Web sites, their URLs, and chapter references.

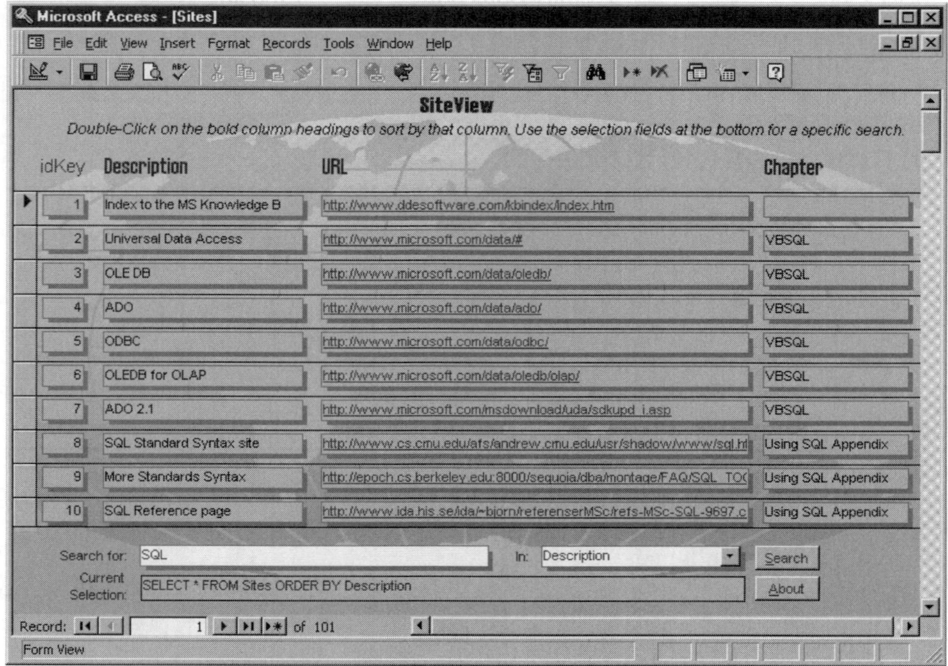

Figure B.1 SiteView—Dynamic URL listings.

Table B.1 Site Listings

DESCRIPTION	URL	CHAPTER
15Seconds Site	www.15seconds.com	11: Getting Started with E-Commerce
4 Guys from Rolla	www.4guysfromrolla.com	11: Getting Started with E-Commerce
Access 97 upsizing wizard	www.microsoft.com/ AccessDev/ProdInfo/ exe/wzcs97.exe	4: Upsizing Your Desktop Database
Access Developers Page	www.microsoft.com/ accessdev/a-a&sa.htm msdn.microsoft.com/officedev/	Appendix A: SQL Survival Guide
Aditi Updown (Upsizes Access 2.0 databases to SQL Server)	www.netsales.net/pk.wcgi/ csica/prod/1120405-1	4: Upsizing Your Desktop Database
ADO	www.microsoft.com/data/ ado/	13: Using Visual Basic to Write SQL Applications
ADO	www.microsoft.com/data/ download2.htm	13: Using Visual Basic to Write SQL Applications
ADO 2.0 SDK	www.microsoft.com/ msdownload/uda/ mdac_typ.asp	13: Using Visual Basic to Write SQL Applications
ADO 2.1	www.microsoft.com/ msdownload/uda/ sdkupd_i.asp	13: Using Visual Basic to Write SQL Applications
Advanced ADO for the VBA programmer	www.microsoft.com/ accessdev/articles /lavs305.htm	13: Using Visual Basic to Write SQL Applications
Angoss Software	www.angoss.com/	Appendix A: SQL Survival Guide
ANSI (American National Standards Institute)	www.ansi.org and web.ansi.org/default.htm	1: Introduction to SQL Server
Appsource's Wired for OLAP	www.appsource.com/ or www.hyperion.com	9: Working with OLAP Services
Bill Wunder's SQL Site	www.nyx.net/~bwunder	Appendix A: SQL Survival Guide
Bill Vaughn's BetaV site (Bill is author of *Hitchiker's Guide to Visual Basic and SQL Server*)	www.betav.com	Appendix A: SQL Survival Guide
Bluecurve Dynameasure	www.bluecurve.com/	Appendix A: SQL Survival Guide
Brio Technology	www.brio.com	9: Working with OLAP Services
Business Objects	www.businessobjects.com/	9: Working with OLAP Services
CAST Software	www.castsoftware.com/	Appendix C: What's on the CD-ROM

Continues

Table B.1 Site Listings *(Continued)*

DESCRIPTION	URL	CHAPTER
Charles Carroll's ASP site	activeserverpages.com and www.learnasp.com	11: Getting Started with E-Commerce
Codd white paper	warehouse.chime-net.org/ software/datastore/ dataware/coddc0.html	7: Create a Single-Source Data Mart
Cognos' NovaView and PowerPlay and Impromptu	www.cognos.com	9: Working with OLAP Services
Compaq's Active Answers	www.compaq.com/ activeanswers/about/lobby.html	2: Installing SQL Server
Compuserve SQL Server Forum	MSSQL Forum (Lib1 has FAQs)	2: Installing SQL Server
Computer Associates' database products	www.cai.com/products/ roadmaps/enterprise_ performance	4: Upsizing Your Desktop Database
Computer News and Review	www.newsrev.com	Appendix A: SQL Survival Guide
Comshare	www.comshare.com	9: Working with OLAP Services
Data Dynamics	www.datadynamics.com	9: Working with OLAP Services
Data Warehousing Institute	www.dw-institute.com	9: Working with OLAP Services
Data Warehousing supersite	www.datawarehousing.com/	7: Create a Single-Source Data Mart
Database Scanner	www.iss.net/prod/dbs.php3	Appendix A: SQL Survival Guide
DB-Examiner	www.dbesoftware.com/	Appendix C: What's on the CD-ROM
Dell's SQL Server site	www.dell.com/sql	2: Installing SQL Server
Embarcadero Software	www.embarcadero.com/	4: Upsizing Your Desktop Database
EMS Active Architect OLAP SDK	www.euroman.co.uk/	Appendix C: What's on the CD-ROM
Entrust Technologies	www.entrust.com	11: Getting Started with E-Commerce
Fundamental Objects, Inc	www.fo.com	Appendix A: SQL Survival Guide
GSQL Information	www.ncsa.uiuc.edu/SDG/ People/jason/pub/gsql/ starthere.html	Appendix A: SQL Survival Guide
GTE	www.gte.com	11: Getting Started with E-Commerce
HTML	htmlgoodies.com	11: Getting Started with E-Commerce

Table B.1 *(Continued)*

DESCRIPTION	URL	CHAPTER
Hummingbird Software's BI/Suite and Genio	www.hummingbird.com/	9: Working with OLAP Services
IBM's Intelligent Miner for Data	www.software.ibm.com/data/iminer	Appendix A: SQL Survival Guide
Inprise (now Corel was Borland) Visigenic ODBC, OLE DB, and JDBC Drivers	www.inprise.com/visibroker/	Appendix A: SQL Survival Guide
InterNetivity	www.internetivity.com	9: Working with OLAP Services
Introduction to Structured Query Language	w3.one.net/~jhoffman/sqltut.htm	Appendix A: SQL Survival Guide
ISG DataControl OLE DB/ADO ActiveX control	www.isgsoft.com/	Appendix A: SQL Survival Guide
ISO standards	www.iso.ch/welcome.html	1: Introduction to SQL Server and Appendix A: SQL Survival Guide
Javascript info	msdn.microsoft.com/scripting/jscript/default.htm devedge.netscape.com/tech/javascript/index.html	11: Getting Started with E-Commerce
Jim Gray's Microsoft Research site	research.microsoft.com/%7Egray	Appendix A: SQL Survival Guide
John Hindmarsh's SQL Server and T-SQL Standards	www.sql7dba.com/	Appendix A: SQL Survival Guide
Kalen Delaney's InsideSQLServer site	www.insidesqlserver.com/	Appendix A: SQL Survival Guide
KD Nuggets	www.kdnuggets.com/	Appendix A: SQL Survival Guide
Knosys ProClarity	www.knosysinc.com	9: Working with OLAP Services
Mappings of OLEDB interface calls to ADO 2.1	www.microsoft.com/data/ado/adotechinfo/ado2oledb.htm	13: Using Visual Basic to Write SQL Applications
Maximal Innovative Intelligence	www.maxsw.com	9: Working with OLAP Services
mb Cizer	www.cizer.com	9: Working with OLAP Services
MDAC 1.5c	www.microsoft.com/data/downloads.htm	13: Using Visual Basic to Write SQL Applications
Merant (was Intersolv) ODBC, OLE DB, etc. drivers	www.merant.com/datadirect	13: Using Visual Basic to Write SQL Applications

Continues

Table B.1 Site Listings *(Continued)*

DESCRIPTION	URL	CHAPTER
Metadata Institute	www.ne.net/~metadata/ index.html	9: Working with OLAP Services
Microsoft Access Site	www.microsoft.com/access	1: Introduction to SQL Server
Microsoft BackOffice SQL Server	www.microsoft.com/ backoffice/sql/default.htm	Appendix A: SQL Survival Guide
Microsoft Certified Hardware list	www.microsoft.com/ntserver/ info/hwcompatibility.htm	2: Installing SQL Server
Microsoft Chats on SQL Server 7	msdn.microsoft.com/chats/ Default.asp	Appendix A: SQL Survival Guide
Microsoft Data Components	www.microsoft.com/data	13: Using Visual Basic to Write SQL Applications
Microsoft Data Warehousing	www.microsoft.com/ backoffice/sql/70/gen/ dw.htm	Appendix A: SQL Survival Guide
Microsoft Foxpro Site	msdn.microsoft.com/vfoxpro	1: Introduction to SQL Server
Microsoft on COM, DCOM, COM+, and MTS	www.microsoft.com/com	Appendix A: SQL Survival Guide
Microsoft Repository	msdn.microsoft.com/ repository	Appendix A: SQL Survival Guide
Microsoft Scripting Central	msdn.microsoft.com/scripting	11: Getting Started with E-Commerce
Microsoft SQL Site	www.microsoft.com/sql	1: Introduction to SQL Server
Microsoft's BackOffice Home Page	backoffice.microsoft.com/	Appendix A: SQL Survival Guide
Microsoft's Data Access Home Page	www.microsoft.com/data	6: Building a Corporate Intranet with IIS and 9: Working with OLAP Services
Microsoft's DNA	www.microsoft.com/dna	1: Introduction to SQL Server
Microsoft's Knowledge Base	support.microsoft.com/ support/search/c.asp?FR=0	Appendix A: SQL Survival Guide
Microsoft's Mailing List Archives	microsoft.ease.lsoft.com/ archives/index.html	Appendix A: SQL Survival Guide
Microsoft's Migration white papers	www.microsoft.com/ backoffice/sql/70/gen/ migrateover.htm	4: Upsizing Your Desktop Database
Microsoft's MSDE site	msdn.microsoft.com/ vstudio/msde	Appendix A: SQL Survival Guide
Microsoft's NT Option Pack	backoffice.microsoft.com/ downtrial/optionpack.asp	5: Publishing SQL Server Data to HTML

Table B.1 *(Continued)*

DESCRIPTION	URL	CHAPTER
Microsoft's NT Server Home Page	www.microsoft.com/ ntserver	Appendix A: SQL Survival Guide
Microsoft's OLAP site	www.microsoft.com/sql/70/ gen/olap.htm.	9: Working with OLAP Services
Microsoft's security sites	www.microsoft.com/security/ default.asp www.microsoft.com/technet/ security	Appendix A: SQL Survival Guide
Microsoft's SQL Insider Web site	www.microsoft.com/sql/ productinfo/news/insider.htm	Appendix A: SQL Survival Guide
Microsoft's SQL Server and related newsgroups	news://microsoft.public .sqlserver.clients news://microsoft.public .sqlserver.connect news://microsoft .public.sqlserver.odbc news://microsoft.public .sqlserver.programming news://microsoft.public .sqlserver.replication news://microsoft.public .sqlserver.olap news://microsoft.public .inetserver.iis.active serverpages news://microsoft.public .inetserver.asp.db news://microsoft.public .scripting.jscript;etc. news://microsoft.public .sqlserver.xml	2: Installing SQL Server, 9: Working with OLAP Services 11: Getting Started with E-Commerce and Appendix A: SQL Survival Guide
Microsoft's SQL Server FAQs	support.microsoft.com/ support/sql/content/faq/ default.asp	2: Installing SQL Server
Microsoft's SQL Server Home Page	www.microsoft.com/sql	Appendix A: SQL Survival Guide
Microsoft's Upsizing whitepapers	support.microsoft.com/ support/access/content/ 97downloads.asp#97Whitepaper support.microsoft.com/support/ access/content/97downloads .asp#97Wiz	4: Upsizing Your Desktop Database

Continues

Table B.1 Site Listings *(Continued)*

DESCRIPTION	URL	CHAPTER
Microsoft's Upsizing whitepapers *(Continued)*	www.asia.microsoft.com/ accessdev/articles/autwp.htm technet.microsoft.com/cdonline/ content/complete/Desk/ Access/technote/Ofc404.exe microsoft.com/library/techart/ acc2sql_8.htm support.microsoft.com/support/ Kb/articles/Q237/9/80.asp support.microsoft.com/support/ SQL/content/inprodhlp/_ole_ db_provider_issues.asp	
Microsoft's Upsizing Database Wizards for Access to SQL Server	www.microsoft.com/Access Dev/Articles/Exe/Upsize95 .exewww.microsoft.com/products/ developer/officedeveloper/ Access/prodinfo/exe/wzcs97.exe support.microsoft.com/download/ support/mslfiles/AUT97.EXE	4: Upsizing Your Desktop Database
Microsoft's white papers on migration	www.microsoft.com/sql/ interopmigrate/migrate.htm	4: Upsizing Your Desktop Database
Mike Hotek's SQL Server site	www.mssqlserver.com	Appendix A: SQL Survival Guide
MSDN SQL Server Developer Portal	msdn.microsoft.com/ sqlserver	Appendix A: SQL Survival Guide
MSDN SQL Server Developer site	msdn.microsoft.com/ sqlserver	Appendix A: SQL Survival Guide
Neil Pike's SQL Server FAQs	www.ntfaq.com/sql.html and www.ntfaq.com	Appendix A: SQL Survival Guide
Newsgroup info	www.tile.net/ and www.liszt.com	Appendix A: SQL Survival Guide
ODBC	www.microsoft.com/data/ odbc/	13: Using Visual Basic to Write SQL Applications
ODBC vs. SQL API benchmarks	ourworld.compuserve.com/ homepages/Ken_North/ APIBENCH.HTM	13: Using Visual Basic to Write SQL Applications
OLAP Council	www.olapcouncil.org	9: Working with OLAP Services
OLAP@Work	www.olapatwork.com/	Appendix C: What's on the CD-ROM
OLE DB	www.microsoft.com/data/ oledb/	13: Using Visual Basic to Write SQL Applications

Table B.1 *(Continued)*

DESCRIPTION	URL	CHAPTER
OLEDB for OLAP	www.microsoft.com/data/oledb/olap/	13: Using Visual Basic to Write SQL Applications
OpenLink ODBC and JDBC drivers	www.openlinksw.com/	Appendix A: SQL Survival Guide
Pacific Northwest SQL Server User Group	www.pnwssug.org/	Appendix A: SQL Survival Guide
PASS User Group	www.sqlpass.org/	Appendix A: SQL Survival Guide
Portola Systems	www.portolasystems.com	9: Working with OLAP Services
Q articles (Microsoft's Knowledge Base)	support.microsoft.com/support/search/c.asp?FR=0	Appendix A: SQL Survival Guide
RAID info	www.acnc.com/raid.html	2: Installing SQL Server
Red Matrix Technologies' SQL Audit	www.redmatrix.com	Appendix A: SQL Survival Guide
Seagate Software	www.seagatesoftware.com	9: Working with OLAP Services
Seth Grimes' OLAP site	altaplana.com/olap	9: Working with OLAP Services
SFI Software	www.sfi-software.com/	Appendix C: What's on the CD-ROM
Shaku Atre's 12 Steps to Data Warehousing	www.atre.com/navigator	7: Create a Single-Source Data Mart
Software Technologies' Database site	www.swtech.com/db/	Appendix A: SQL Survival Guide
SQL Auditor	www.sqlauditor.com	Appendix A: SQL Survival Guide
SQL Server 7.0 Replication white paper	www.microsoft.com/sql/70/whpprs/repwp.htm	10: Implementing Replication
SQL Server Books Online (BOL) download	support.microsoft.com/download/support/mslfiles/sqlbol.exe	Appendix A: SQL Survival Guide
SQL Server I/O Stress utility	support.microsoft.com/support/downloads/LNP220.asp	2: Installing SQL Server
SQL Server Service Packs	support.microsoft.com/support/sql/content/spack.asp	Appendix A: SQL Survival Guide
SQL Standard Syntax site	www.cs.cmu.edu/afs/andrew.cmu.edu/usr/shadow/www/sql.html#syntax	Appendix A: SQL Survival Guide
SQL Standards Process	www.jcc.com/sql_stnd.html	Appendix A: SQL Survival Guide

Continues

Table B.1 Site Listings *(Continued)*

DESCRIPTION	URL	CHAPTER
SQL Tutorial (interactive)	torresoft.netmegs.com/	Appendix A: SQL Survival Guide
SQLExperts	www.sqlexperts.com/	Appendix A: SQL Survival Guide
Steve Genusa's site	www.serverobjects.com	Appendix A: SQL Survival Guide
Subquery Innovations	www.sqlprobe.com/	Appendix C: What's on the CD-ROM
Swynk SQL Server FAQs	www.swynk.com/faq/sql/ sqlserverfaq.asp	Appendix A: SQL Survival Guide
Sybase	www.sybase.com and www.sybase.com/sdn	1: Introduction to SQL Server
Systems Internals (NT utilities)	www.sysinternals.com/	Appendix A: SQL Survival Guide
The OLAP Report	www.olapreport.com/	Appendix A: SQL Survival Guide
The Open Group	www.opengroup.org	1: Introduction to SQL Server
Tony Rogerson's SQL Server site	www.sql-server.co.uk/	Appendix A: SQL Survival Guide
Transaction Processing Council	www.tpc.org/	Appendix A: SQL Survival Guide
Universal Data Access (UDA): OLE DB, ADO, ODBC, OLE DB	www.microsoft.com/data/#	13: Using Visual Basic to Write SQL Applications
USASoft's BCPump	www.usasoft.com/ bcmpump.htm	4: Upsizing Your Desktop Database
Usenet OLAP newsgroup	www.deja.com/=liszt/ dnquery.xp?query=~g% 20comp.databases.olap	9: Working with OLAP Services
Using the Remote Data Object	msdn.microsoft.com/library/ techart/msdn_intrordo.htm	13: Using Visual Basic to Write SQL Applications
ValiCert	www.valicert.com	11: Getting Started with E-Commerce
VeriSign	www.verisign.com	11: Getting Started with E-Commerce
Visual Basic	www.microsoft.com/vbasic	13: Using Visual Basic to Write SQL Applications
Visual Studio 6 SQL info	www.vigallery.com/vs6/	Appendix A: SQL Survival Guide
Washington State Wine Commission	www.washingtonwine.org	4: Upsizing Your Desktop Database
Weir Performance Oracle/SQL Upsizer	www.weirperf.com/ upsize.htm	4: Upsizing Your Desktop Database
Wiley Publishing	www.wiley.com/	Appendix B: More Information

Where To Go for More

The best thing to do, once you've consumed all of the information in the sites listed in Table B.1, is to check back periodically looking for new links from these sites to others. Not only will you pick up newly added information on the existing sites, but you'll also be able to leverage from the collective updates of new site information made by all of the site authors above.

Things do change, like Web sites' addresses—even their very existence.

APPENDIX C

What's on the CD-ROM

There are two CD-ROMs of software that accompany this book.

The first CD-ROM is an evaluation copy of Microsoft SQL Server 7.0 120-Day Evaluation Edition.

The second CD-ROM contains source code to accompany the chapters in the book, example applications, links to related Web sites (an Access application, called SiteView, can be found on the CD-ROM in the folder \Code\ Additional-Sites\SiteView.MDB. This database contains a large number of useful, related Web links to provide further growth paths for your ongoing study) and the data that is required for the book. CD-ROM 2 also contains the following software:

CAST Workbench 3.74 SR1 for SQL Server. This version includes a comprehensive work environment for SQL Server DBAs and programmers (www.castsoftware.com).

Data Dynamics DynamiCube™ 2.5.1.2. Data Dynamics' ActiveX cube control that Visual Basic and Visual C++ programmers can use to embed OLAP into their applications (www.datadynamics.com).

DB-Examiner Trial Version 4.1 Build 4.25. Evaluation version of a DBA utility that reports on your database's design (www.dbesoftware.com)

Db Maint 2.0. An alternative to Enterprise Manager (www.dbmaint.com).

Embarcadero DBArtisan Evaluation Copy. Evaluation version of a popular DBA utility that is an alternative to Enterprise Manager (www.embarcadero.com).

Embarcadero ER/Studio Evaluation Copy. Evaluation version of a database modeling utility (www.embarcadero.com).

EMS ActiveArchitect. An SDK/VB add-in that provides a programming environment for developing OLAP Services applications (www.euroman.co.uk).

Hummingbird BI/Suite Evaluation Software. Evaluation version of a multi-platform business intelligence suite (www.hummingbird.com).

Knosys ProClarity 2.0 Evaluation. Evaluation version of an OLAP client (www.knosysinc.com).

Maximal Innovative Intelligence Max 1.0. An OLAP client (www.maxsw.com).

MySQL for Linux. This is a SQL database server (www.mysql.com).

OLAP@Work 1.5. Another OLAP client (www.olapatwork.com).

Portola Systems Coronado 1.61. Evaluation version of an OLAP client (www.portolasystems.com).

Seagate Analysis. Freeware version of an OLAP and reporting client (www.seagatesoftware.com).

Subquery Innovations SQL Probe Version 7.0. A DBA utility (www.sqlprobe.com).

Sylvain Faust International SQL-Programmer IX Expert Edition Complete. A popular alternative to Enterprise Manager (www.sfi-software.com).

Verstand SQLServNT Version 6.5.5. Free 2-server version of a DBA utility (www.sqlservant.com).

Visual Commerce Constructor. A development environment to be used with Microsoft's IIS and Site Server Commerce Edition (www.visualcommerce.com).

What Is Freeware / Shareware?

Freeware is software that is distributed by disk, through BBS systems and the Internet free. There is no charge for using it, and can be distributed freely as long as the use it is put to follows the license agreement included with it.

Shareware (also known as user supported software) is a revolutionary means of distributing software created by individuals or companies too small to make inroads into the more conventional retail distribution networks. The authors of Shareware retain all rights to the software under the copyright laws while still allowing free distribution. This gives the user the chance to freely obtain and try out software to see if it fits his needs. Shareware should not be confused with Public Domain software even though they are often obtained from the same sources.

If you continue to use Shareware after trying it out, you are expected to register your use with the author and pay a registration fee. What you get in return depends on the author, but may include a printed manual, free updates, telephone support, and so on.

Hardware Requirements

To use this CD-ROM, your system must meet the following requirements:

Platform/Processor/Operating System. Pentium 300 MHz + running Windows 95 or or higher, or Windows NT 4 or higher.

RAM. At LEAST 64mbs of RAM for SQL Server

Peripherals. CD-ROM drive, Web browser for navigating software, Access MDB to use Site View (optional)

Installing the Software

To install any of the third party applications or source code from the CDs, please follow these simple steps.

1. Start Windows 9x or WinNT 4+ on your computer.
2. Place the CD-ROM into your CD-ROM drive. The CD contains an autorun feature that will automatically present you with the following screen (see Figure C.1).

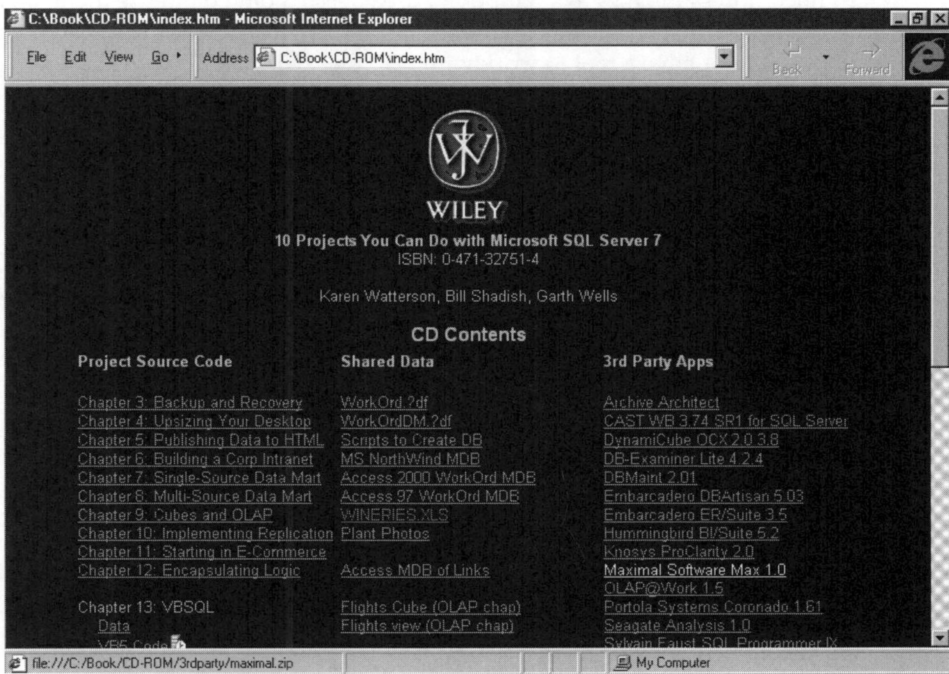

Figure C.1 The software screen.

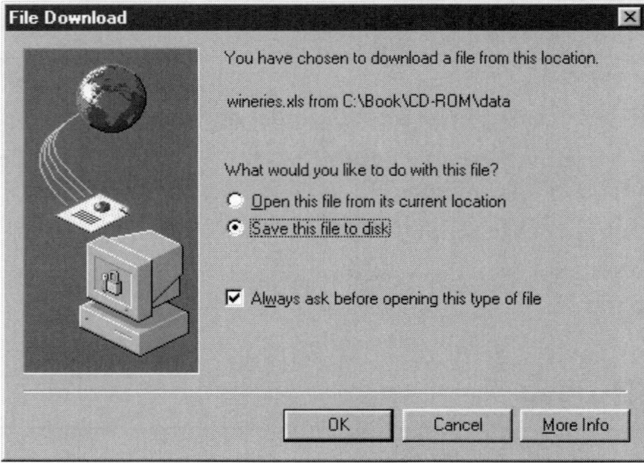

Figure C.2 Saving files locally.

3. From this screen, just double click on any of the pieces that you would like to use. You will be shown the following window (see Figure C.2), asking you to save the software locally on your hard drive.
4. The software on the CD is compressed using the ZIP file format. You will need to uncompress the files to a temporary area before going on to use them, or, in the case of third party tool evaluations, to run their corresponding install program. If you **do not** have a tool to work with .ZIP files, you can download a trial version from **www.winzip.com**.
5. Choose (or create) an appropriate directory and save the file there. Double click on the file to load your Zip utility and extract all of the files. Run the associated install program if necessary.
6. Follow the screen prompts to complete the installation.

User Assistance and Information

Unsupported ongoing updates to the CD-ROM software, or any large errata notes, will be maintained at **www.fo.com/ss7proj.htm**

The software accompanying this book is being provided as is without warranty or support of any kind. Should you require basic installation assistance, or if your media is defective, please call our product support number at (212) 850-6194 weekdays between 9 A.M. and 4 A.M. Eastern Standard Time. Or, we can be reached via e-mail at: **wprtusw@wiley.com**.

To place additional orders or to request information about other Wiley products, please call (800) 879-4539.

E

F

Q

R

T

U

X

Y

CUSTOMER NOTE: IF THIS BOOK IS ACCOMPANIED BY SOFTWARE, PLEASE READ THE FOLLOWING BEFORE OPENING THE PACKAGE.

To use this CD-ROM, your system must meet the following requirements:

Platform/Processor/Operating System. Pentium (300MHz+ recommended) running Windows 95 or higher, or Windows NT 4.0 or higher.

RAM. At least 64MB of RAM for SQL Server.

Hard Drive Space. For the book's companion code and data files, approximately 150MB is needed to store the files on a local drive. For all third party software, consult the individual software documentation for hard drive space requirements. In most cases, the amount of space required is displayed during the setup process, prior to any installation files being copied to the hard drive. You may, however, need up to 200MB of free space to temporarily store and extract compressed files from the evaluation software.

Peripherals. CD-ROM drive, Web browser for navigating software, Microsoft Access to use Site View (optional) and shared data files, WinZip or similar decompression application.